Ford Taurus & Five Hundred
Mercury Montego & Sable
Automotive Repair Manual

**by Jeff Killingsworth
and John H Haynes**

Member of the Guild of Motoring Writers

Models covered:

Ford Taurus - 2008 through 2014
Ford Five Hundred - 2005 through 2007
Mercury Montego - 2005 through 2007
Mercury Sable - 2008 through 2009

Does not include information specific to 3.5L twin turbo or police models

Haynes Group Limited (36076-10X2)
Sparkford Nr Yeovil
Somerset BA22 7JJ England
ABCDE
FGHIJ
KL

Haynes North America, Inc.
2801 Townsgate Road, Suite 340
Thousand Oaks, CA 91361 USA

www.haynes.com

Acknowledgements

Technical writers who contributed to this project include Demian Hurst, Trip Aiken, Dennis Gibb, Jay Hayes, Tracy Martin and Scott "Gonzo" Weaver.

© **Haynes North America, Inc. 2014**

With permission from Haynes Group Limited

A book in the Haynes Automotive Repair Manual Series

Printed in India

ISBN-13: 978-1-62092-116-6
ISBN-10: 1-62092-116-2

Library of Congress Control Number: 2014954966

Contents

Haynes mechanic and photographer with a 2013 Ford Taurus

About this manual

Its purpose

The purpose of this manual is to help you get the best value from your vehicle. It can do so in several ways. It can help you decide what work must be done, even if you choose to have it done by a dealer service department or a repair shop; it provides information and procedures for routine maintenance and servicing; and it offers diagnostic and repair procedures to follow when trouble occurs.

We hope you use the manual to tackle the work yourself. For many simpler jobs, doing it yourself may be quicker than arranging an appointment to get the vehicle into a shop and making the trips to leave it and pick it up. More importantly, a lot of money can be saved by avoiding the expense the shop must pass on to you to cover its labor and overhead costs. An added benefit is the sense of satisfaction and accomplishment that you feel after doing the job yourself.

Using the manual

The manual is divided into Chapters. Each Chapter is divided into numbered Sections, which are headed in bold type between horizontal lines. Each Section consists of consecutively numbered paragraphs.

The reference numbers used in illustration captions pinpoint the pertinent Section and the Step within that Section. That is, illustration 3.2 means the illustration refers to Section 3 and Step (or paragraph) 2 within that Section.

Procedures, once described in the text, are not normally repeated. When it's necessary to refer to another Chapter, the reference will be given as Chapter and Section number. Cross references given without use of the word "Chapter" apply to Sections and/or paragraphs in the same Chapter. For example, "see Section 8" means in the same Chapter.

References to the left or right side of the vehicle assume you are sitting in the driver's seat, facing forward.

Even though we have prepared this manual with extreme care, neither the publisher nor the author can accept responsibility for any errors in, or omissions from, the information given.

NOTE

A **Note** provides information necessary to properly complete a procedure or information which will make the procedure easier to understand.

CAUTION

A **Caution** provides a special procedure or special steps which must be taken while completing the procedure where the Caution is found. Not heeding a Caution can result in damage to the assembly being worked on.

WARNING

A **Warning** provides a special procedure or special steps which must be taken while completing the procedure where the Warning is found. Not heeding a Warning can result in personal injury.

Introduction

This manual covers the Ford Five Hundred (2005 - 2007), Ford Taurus (2008 - 2014, Mercury Montego (2005 - 2007) and the Mercury Sable (2008 - 2009). The available engines are: 2.0L turbocharged in-line four-cylinder, 3.0L V6 or 3.5L V6. This manual does not cover 3.5L twin turbo or police models.

The engine drives the front wheels through a six-speed automatic transaxle via independent driveaxles. On All-Wheel Drive (AWD) models, the rear wheels are also propelled via a driveshaft, rear differential, and two rear driveaxles.

Suspension is independent at all four wheels. The front suspension uses strut/coil spring assemblies with lower control arms.

The rear uses a multi-link design with shock absorbers and coil springs. The rack-and-pinion steering unit is mounted on the suspension crossmember. Some later models are equipped with electronic power assist steering.

The brakes are disc at the front and rear, with power assist standard. An Anti-lock Brake System (ABS) is standard equipment.

Vehicle identification numbers

1   Modifications are a continuing and unpublicized process in vehicle manufacturing. Since spare parts manuals and lists are compiled on a numerical basis, the individual vehicle numbers are essential to correctly identify the component required.

Vehicle Identification Number (VIN)

2   This very important identification number is stamped on a plate attached to the dashboard inside the windshield on the driver's side of the vehicle (see illustration). The VIN also appears on the Vehicle Certificate of Title and Registration. It contains information such as where and when the vehicle was manufactured, the model year and the body style.

Manufacturer's Certification Regulation label

3   The Manufacturer's Certification Regulation label is attached to the driver's side door opening (see illustration). The label contains the name of the manufacturer, the month and year of production, the Gross Vehicle Weight Rating (GVWR), the Gross Axle Weight Rating (GAWR) and the certification statement.

VIN engine code

4   Counting from the left, the engine code letter designation is the 8th character. On all models covered by this manual the engine codes are:

```
9 ........2.0L four-cylinder engine
```

```
1 ........3.0L V6 engine
W .......3.5L V6 engine (2012 and earlier)
8 ........3.5L V6 engine (2013 and later)
```

VIN model year code

5   Counting from the left, the model year code letter designation is the 10th character. On all models covered by this manual the model year codes are:

```
5 .................... 2005
6 .................... 2006
7 .................... 2007
8 .................... 2008
9 .................... 2009
A .................... 2010
B .................... 2011
C .................... 2012
D .................... 2013
E .................... 2014
```

Engine number

6   The engine identification numbers are on a sticker attached to the front side of the valve cover (see illustration).

Transaxle identification

7   The transaxle identification code is listed at the bottom of the Manufacturer's Certification Regulation label, under the heading "TR."
8   The codes are as follows:

```
6   6-speed automatic transaxle
J   6-speed automatic transaxle
```

3.2 The Vehicle Identification Number (VIN) is visible through the driver's side of the windshield

3.3 The Manufacturer's Certification Regulation label is located on the driver's door opening

3.6 Location of the engine identification number - four-cylinder engine shown, other engines similar

Recall information

Vehicle recalls are carried out by the manufacturer in the rare event of a possible safety-related defect. The vehicle's registered owner is contacted at the address on file at the Department of Motor Vehicles and given the details of the recall. Remedial work is carried out free of charge at a dealer service department.

If you are the new owner of a used vehicle which was subject to a recall and you want to be sure that the work has been carried out, it's best to contact a dealer service department and ask about your individual vehicle - you'll need to furnish them your Vehicle Identification Number (VIN).

The table below is based on information provided by the National Highway Traffic Safety Administration (NHTSA), the body which oversees vehicle recalls in the United States. The recall database is updated constantly. For the latest information on vehicle recalls, check the NHTSA website at www. nhtsa.gov, www.safercar.gov, or call the NHTSA hotline at 1-888-327-4236.

Recall date	Recall campaign number	Model(s) affected	Concern
NOV 09, 2005	05V51500	2005 Five Hundred	On some models, the straps that secure the fuel tank to the vehicle body may break, causing the fuel tank heat shield to drop on the driveshaft (on all wheel drive models) or exhaust system (front wheel drive models). If this happens, drivers may notice a noise or a fuel leak. Fuel leakage, in the presence of an ignition source, could result in a fire.
OCT 05, 2006	06V383000	2005 Five Hundred	On certain models currently registered in the following states: Alaska, Colorado, Connecticut, Delaware, Idaho, Illinois, Indiana, Iowa, Kansas, Kentucky, Maine, Maryland, Massachusetts, Michigan, Minnesota, Missouri, Montana, Nebraska, New Hampshire, New Jersey, New York, North Dakota, Ohio, Pennsylvania, Rhode Island, South Dakota, Utah, Vermont, West Virginia, Wisconsin, and Wyoming. The side door latch mechanisms may experience water intrusion allowing the latch mechanism to freeze in cold weather. As a result, the door latch pawl may not return to the latch position when the door is closed and the door could open while the vehicle is moving.
JULY 13, 2011	11V355000	2007 Ford Five Hundred and Mercury Montego	The manufacturer is recalling certain model year 2007 Ford Five Hundred and Mercury Montego vehicles manufactured from September 5, 2006, through September 11, 2006. The fuel tanks may not have consistent welds between the fuel tank and fuel filler neck spud which can affect the strength of the joint. Some fuel tank spud welds may not provide the expected strength in the event of a severe rear impact to the vehicle. An improper weld can result in a crack in the joint which could illuminate the emissions malfunction indicator light, cause a fuel odor, or allow fuel to leak out. Fuel leakage, in the presence of an ignition source, could result in a fire.

Recall date	Recall campaign number	Model(s) affected	Concern
MAR 27, 2013	13V109000	2012 Ford Taurus	On some models manufactured July 19, 2011, through March 15, 2012, the fuel tanks may have a marginally sealed seam in the side of the tank. As a result, the fuel tanks may not provide the expected strength in the event of an impact. The tanks may also leak. A fuel leak in the presence of an ignition source may result in a vehicle fire.
MAY 31, 2013	13V227000	2013 Ford Taurus	On some models, the fuel delivery module may develop a crack, allowing fuel to leak. A fuel leak in the presence of an ignition source may result in a vehicle fire.
JUNE 26, 2013	13V270000	2013 Ford Taurus	On some models manufactured November 29, 2012, through December 12, 2012, with sufficient door openings and closings, the child safety locks may change from an activated position to a deactivated position without notice. If the child lock is deactivated, the door could be unlocked and opened from the inside which could lead to personal injury to an unrestrained child.
MAY 29, 2014	14V285000	2010 through 2014 Ford Taurus	The manufacturer is recalling certain model year 2010-2014 Taurus vehicles manufactured November 24, 2008, through February 28, 2014, originally sold in, or currently registered in, Connecticut, Delaware, Illinois, Indiana, Iowa, Maine, Maryland, Massachusetts, Michigan, Minnesota, Missouri, New Hampshire, New Jersey, New York, Ohio, Pennsylvania, Rhode Island, Vermont, West Virginia, Wisconsin and the District of Columbia. When used in areas that use road salt, the license plate lamp assembly may experience an electro-chemical reaction and corrosion as a result of water intrusion. This corrosion may result in a short circuit, increasing the risk of a fire.

Buying parts

Replacement parts are available from many sources, which generally fall into one of two categories - authorized dealer parts departments and independent retail auto parts stores. Our advice concerning these parts is as follows:

Retail auto parts stores: Good auto parts stores will stock frequently needed components which wear out relatively fast, such as clutch components, exhaust systems, brake parts, tune-up parts, etc. These stores often supply new or reconditioned parts on an exchange basis, which can save a considerable amount of money. Discount auto parts stores are often very good places to buy materials and parts needed for general vehicle maintenance such as oil, grease, filters, spark plugs, belts, touch-up paint, bulbs, etc. They also usually sell tools and general accessories, have convenient hours, charge lower prices and can often be found not far from home.

Authorized dealer parts department: This is the best source for parts which are unique to the vehicle and not generally available elsewhere (such as major engine parts, transmission parts, trim pieces, etc.).

Warranty information: If the vehicle is still covered under warranty, be sure that any replacement parts purchased - regardless of the source - do not invalidate the warranty!

To be sure of obtaining the correct parts, have engine and chassis numbers available and, if possible, take the old parts along for positive identification.

Maintenance techniques, tools and working facilities

Maintenance techniques

There are a number of techniques involved in maintenance and repair that will be referred to throughout this manual. Application of these techniques will enable the home mechanic to be more efficient, better organized and capable of performing the various tasks properly, which will ensure that the repair job is thorough and complete.

Fasteners

Fasteners are nuts, bolts, studs and screws used to hold two or more parts together. There are a few things to keep in mind when working with fasteners. Almost all of them use a locking device of some type, either a lockwasher, locknut, locking tab or thread adhesive. All threaded fasteners should be clean and straight, with undamaged threads and undamaged corners on the hex head where the wrench fits. Develop the habit of replacing all damaged nuts and bolts with new ones. Special locknuts with nylon or fiber inserts can only be used once. If they are removed, they lose their locking ability and must be replaced with new ones.

Rusted nuts and bolts should be treated with a penetrating fluid to ease removal and prevent breakage. Some mechanics use turpentine in a spout-type oil can, which works quite well. After applying the rust penetrant, let it work for a few minutes before trying to loosen the nut or bolt. Badly rusted fasteners may have to be chiseled or sawed off or removed with a special nut breaker, available at tool stores.

If a bolt or stud breaks off in an assembly, it can be drilled and removed with a special tool commonly available for this purpose. Most automotive machine shops can perform this task, as well as other repair procedures, such as the repair of threaded holes that have been stripped out.

Flat washers and lockwashers, when removed from an assembly, should always be replaced exactly as removed. Replace any damaged washers with new ones. Never use a lockwasher on any soft metal surface (such as aluminum), thin sheet metal or plastic.

Fastener sizes

For a number of reasons, automobile manufacturers are making wider and wider use of metric fasteners. Therefore, it is important to be able to tell the difference between standard (sometimes called U.S. or SAE) and metric hardware, since they cannot be interchanged.

All bolts, whether standard or metric, are sized according to diameter, thread pitch and length. For example, a standard 1/2 - 13 x 1 bolt is 1/2 inch in diameter, has 13 threads per inch and is 1 inch long. An M12 - 1.75 x 25 metric bolt is 12 mm in diameter, has a thread pitch of 1.75 mm (the distance between threads) and is 25 mm long. The two bolts are nearly identical, and easily confused, but they are not interchangeable.

In addition to the differences in diameter, thread pitch and length, metric and standard bolts can also be distinguished by examining the bolt heads. To begin with, the distance across the flats on a standard bolt head is measured in inches, while the same dimension on a metric bolt is sized in millimeters (the same is true for nuts). As a result, a standard wrench should not be used on a metric bolt and a metric wrench should not be used on a standard bolt. Also, most standard bolts have slashes radiating out from the center of the head to denote the grade or strength of the bolt, which is an indication of the amount of torque that can be applied to it. The greater the number of slashes, the greater the strength of the bolt. Grades 0 through 5 are commonly used on automobiles. Metric bolts have a property class (grade) number, rather than a slash, molded into their heads to indicate bolt strength. In this case, the higher the number, the stronger the bolt. Property class numbers 8.8, 9.8 and 10.9 are commonly used on automobiles.

Strength markings can also be used to distinguish standard hex nuts from metric hex nuts. Many standard nuts have dots stamped into one side, while metric nuts are marked with a number. The greater the number of

dots, or the higher the number, the greater the strength of the nut.

Metric studs are also marked on their ends according to property class (grade). Larger studs are numbered (the same as metric bolts), while smaller studs carry a geometric code to denote grade.

It should be noted that many fasteners, especially Grades 0 through 2, have no distinguishing marks on them. When such is the case, the only way to determine whether it is standard or metric is to measure the thread pitch or compare it to a known fastener of the same size.

Standard fasteners are often referred to as SAE, as opposed to metric. However, it should be noted that SAE technically refers to a non-metric fine thread fastener only. Coarse thread non-metric fasteners are referred to as USS sizes.

Since fasteners of the same size (both standard and metric) may have different

strength ratings, be sure to reinstall any bolts, studs or nuts removed from your vehicle in their original locations. Also, when replacing a fastener with a new one, make sure that the new one has a strength rating equal to or greater than the original.

Tightening sequences and procedures

Most threaded fasteners should be tightened to a specific torque value (torque is the twisting force applied to a threaded component such as a nut or bolt). Overtightening the fastener can weaken it and cause it to break, while undertightening can cause it to eventually come loose. Bolts, screws and studs, depending on the material they are made of and their thread diameters, have specific torque values, many of which are noted in the Specifications at the beginning of each Chapter. Be sure to follow the torque recommendations closely. For fasteners not assigned a

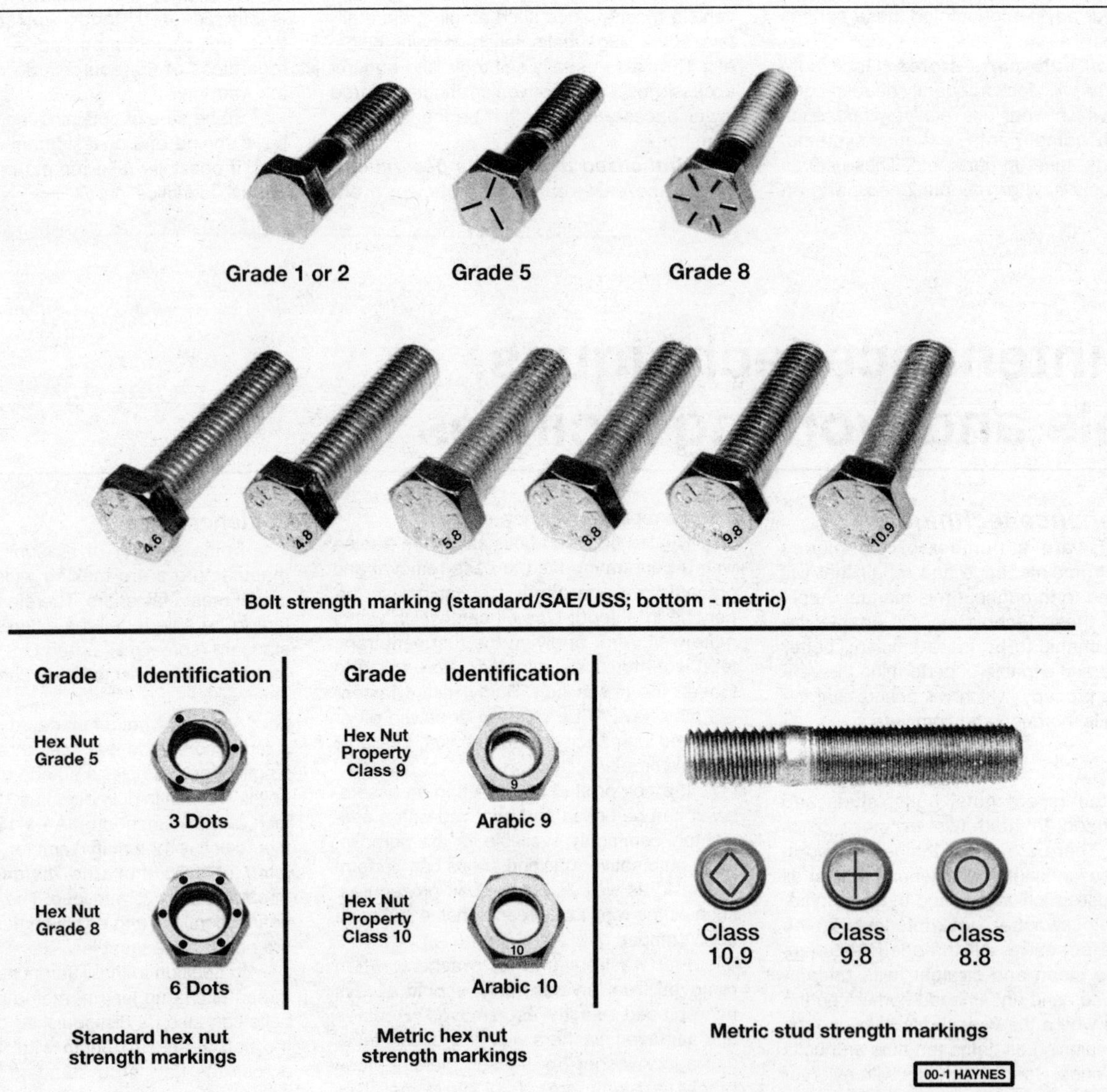

Bolt strength marking (standard/SAE/USS; bottom - metric)

Standard hex nut strength markings

Metric hex nut strength markings

Metric stud strength markings

specific torque, a general torque value chart is presented here as a guide. These torque values are for dry (unlubricated) fasteners threaded into steel or cast iron (not aluminum). As was previously mentioned, the size and grade of a fastener determine the amount of torque that can safely be applied to it. The figures listed here are approximate for Grade 2 and Grade 3 fasteners. Higher grades can tolerate higher torque values.

Fasteners laid out in a pattern, such as cylinder head bolts, oil pan bolts, differential cover bolts, etc., must be loosened or tightened in sequence to avoid warping the component. This sequence will normally be shown in the appropriate Chapter. If a specific pattern is not given, the following procedures can be used to prevent warping.

Initially, the bolts or nuts should be assembled finger-tight only. Next, they should be tightened one full turn each, in a criss-cross or diagonal pattern. After each one has been tightened one full turn, return to the first one and tighten them all one-half turn, following the same pattern. Finally, tighten each of them one-quarter turn at a time until each fastener has been tightened to the proper torque. To loosen and remove the fasteners, the procedure would be reversed.

Component disassembly

Component disassembly should be done with care and purpose to help ensure that

Metric thread sizes

Metric thread sizes	Ft-lbs	Nm
M-6	6 to 9	9 to 12
M-8	14 to 21	19 to 28
M-10	28 to 40	38 to 54
M-12	50 to 71	68 to 96
M-14	80 to 140	109 to 154

Pipe thread sizes

Pipe thread sizes		
1/8	5 to 8	7 to 10
1/4	12 to 18	17 to 24
3/8	22 to 33	30 to 44
1/2	25 to 35	34 to 47

U.S. thread sizes

U.S. thread sizes		
1/4 - 20	6 to 9	9 to 12
5/16 - 18	12 to 18	17 to 24
5/16 - 24	14 to 20	19 to 27
3/8 - 16	22 to 32	30 to 43
3/8 - 24	27 to 38	37 to 51
7/16 - 14	40 to 55	55 to 74
7/16 - 20	40 to 60	55 to 81
1/2 - 13	55 to 80	75 to 108

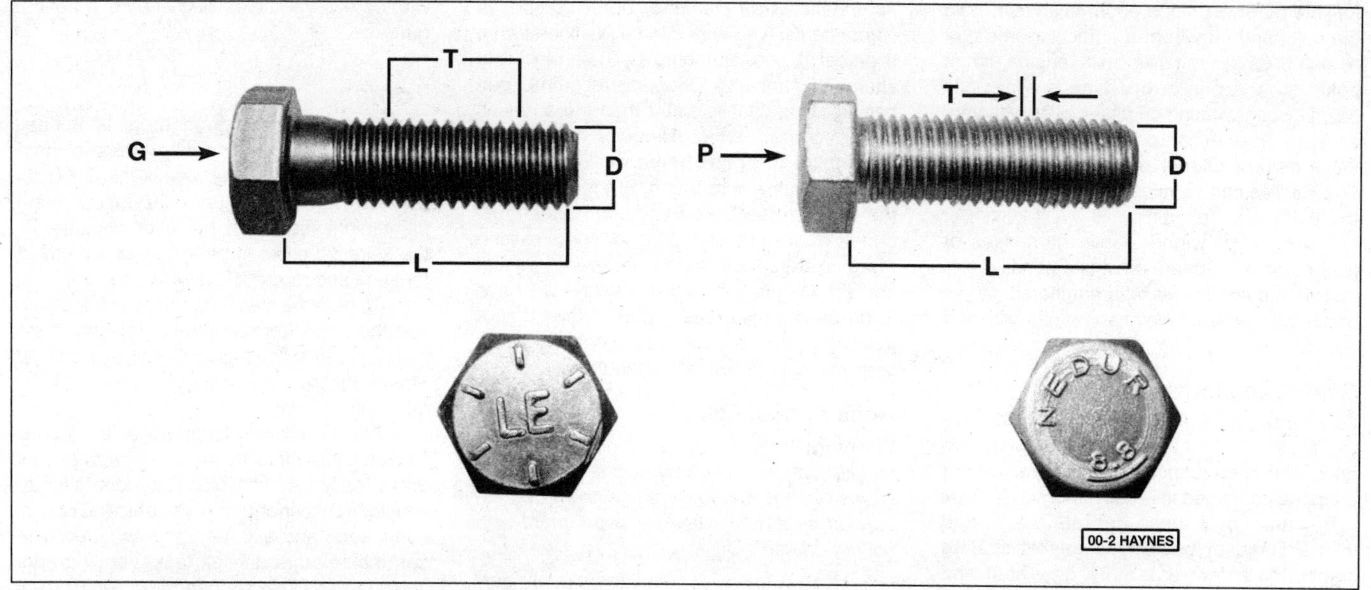

Standard (SAE and USS) bolt dimensions/grade marks

G   Grade marks (bolt strength)
L   Length (in inches)
T   Thread pitch (number of threads per inch)
D   Nominal diameter (in inches)

Metric bolt dimensions/grade marks

P   Property class (bolt strength)
L   Length (in millimeters)
T   Thread pitch (distance between threads in millimeters)
D   Diameter

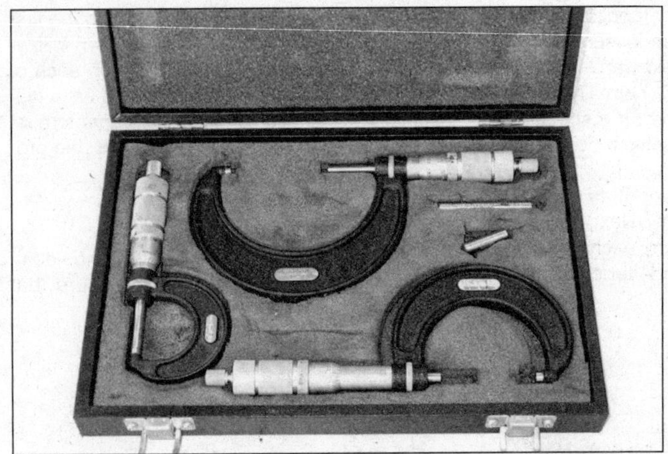

Micrometer set

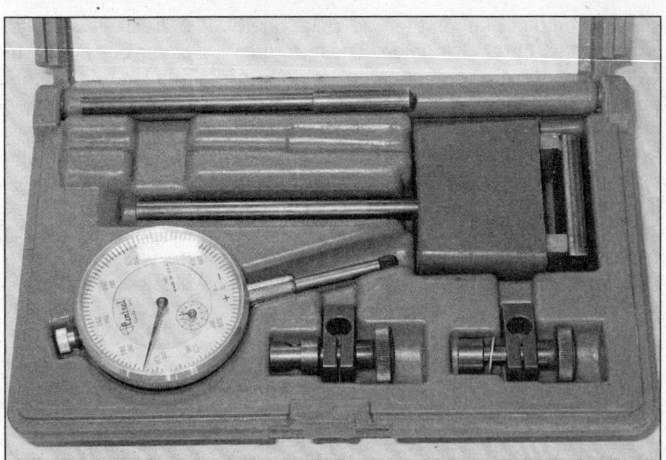

Dial indicator set

the parts go back together properly. Always keep track of the sequence in which parts are removed. Make note of special characteristics or marks on parts that can be installed more than one way, such as a grooved thrust washer on a shaft. It is a good idea to lay the disassembled parts out on a clean surface in the order that they were removed. It may also be helpful to make sketches or take instant photos of components before removal.

When removing fasteners from a component, keep track of their locations. Sometimes threading a bolt back in a part, or putting the washers and nut back on a stud, can prevent mix-ups later. If nuts and bolts cannot be returned to their original locations, they should be kept in a compartmented box or a series of small boxes. A cupcake or muffin tin is ideal for this purpose, since each cavity can hold the bolts and nuts from a particular area (i.e. oil pan bolts, valve cover bolts, engine mount bolts, etc.). A pan of this type is especially helpful when working on assemblies with very small parts, such as the carburetor, alternator, valve train or interior dash and trim pieces. The cavities can be marked with paint or tape to identify the contents.

Whenever wiring looms, harnesses or connectors are separated, it is a good idea to identify the two halves with numbered pieces of masking tape so they can be easily reconnected.

Gasket sealing surfaces

Throughout any vehicle, gaskets are used to seal the mating surfaces between two parts and keep lubricants, fluids, vacuum or pressure contained in an assembly.

Many times these gaskets are coated with a liquid or paste-type gasket sealing compound before assembly. Age, heat and pressure can sometimes cause the two parts to stick together so tightly that they are very difficult to separate. Often, the assembly can be loosened by striking it with a soft-face hammer near the mating surfaces. A regular hammer can be used if a block of wood is placed between the hammer and the part. Do

not hammer on cast parts or parts that could be easily damaged. With any particularly stubborn part, always recheck to make sure that every fastener has been removed.

Avoid using a screwdriver or bar to pry apart an assembly, as they can easily mar the gasket sealing surfaces of the parts, which must remain smooth. If prying is absolutely necessary, use an old broom handle, but keep in mind that extra clean up will be necessary if the wood splinters.

After the parts are separated, the old gasket must be carefully scraped off and the gasket surfaces cleaned. Stubborn gasket material can be soaked with rust penetrant or treated with a special chemical to soften it so it can be easily scraped off. **Caution:** *Never use gasket removal solutions or caustic chemicals on plastic or other composite components.* A scraper can be fashioned from a piece of copper tubing by flattening and sharpening one end. Copper is recommended because it is usually softer than the surfaces to be scraped, which reduces the chance of gouging the part. Some gaskets can be removed with a wire brush, but regardless of the method used, the mating surfaces must be left clean and smooth. If for some reason the gasket surface is gouged, then a gasket sealer thick enough to fill scratches will have to be used during reassembly of the components. For most applications, a non-drying (or semi-drying) gasket sealer should be used.

Hose removal tips

Warning: *If the vehicle is equipped with air conditioning, do not disconnect any of the A/C hoses without first having the system depressurized by a dealer service department or a service station.*

Hose removal precautions closely parallel gasket removal precautions. Avoid scratching or gouging the surface that the hose mates against or the connection may leak. This is especially true for radiator hoses. Because of various chemical reactions, the rubber in hoses can bond itself to the metal spigot that the hose fits over. To remove

a hose, first loosen the hose clamps that secure it to the spigot. Then, with slip-joint pliers, grab the hose at the clamp and rotate it around the spigot. Work it back and forth until it is completely free, then pull it off. Silicone or other lubricants will ease removal if they can be applied between the hose and the outside of the spigot. Apply the same lubricant to the inside of the hose and the outside of the spigot to simplify installation.

As a last resort (and if the hose is to be replaced with a new one anyway), the rubber can be slit with a knife and the hose peeled from the spigot. If this must be done, be careful that the metal connection is not damaged.

If a hose clamp is broken or damaged, do not reuse it. Wire-type clamps usually weaken with age, so it is a good idea to replace them with screw-type clamps whenever a hose is removed.

Tools

A selection of good tools is a basic requirement for anyone who plans to maintain and repair his or her own vehicle. For the owner who has few tools, the initial investment might seem high, but when compared to the spiraling costs of professional auto maintenance and repair, it is a wise one.

To help the owner decide which tools are needed to perform the tasks detailed in this manual, the following tool lists are offered: *Maintenance and minor repair, Repair/overhaul* and *Special.*

The newcomer to practical mechanics should start off with the *maintenance and minor repair* tool kit, which is adequate for the simpler jobs performed on a vehicle. Then, as confidence and experience grow, the owner can tackle more difficult tasks, buying additional tools as they are needed. Eventually the basic kit will be expanded into the *repair and overhaul* tool set. Over a period of time, the experienced do-it-yourselfer will assemble a tool set complete enough for most repair and overhaul procedures and will add tools from the special category when it is felt that the expense is justified by the frequency of use.

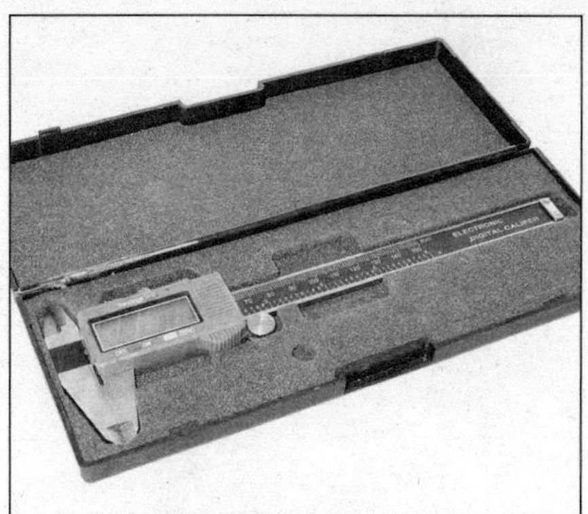

Dial caliper

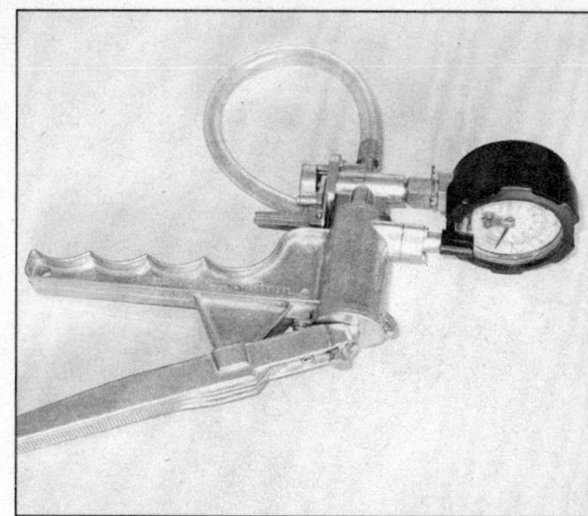

Hand-operated vacuum pump

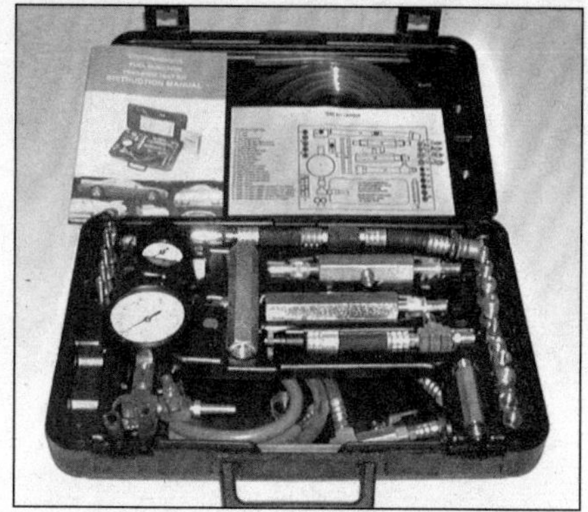

Fuel pressure gauge set

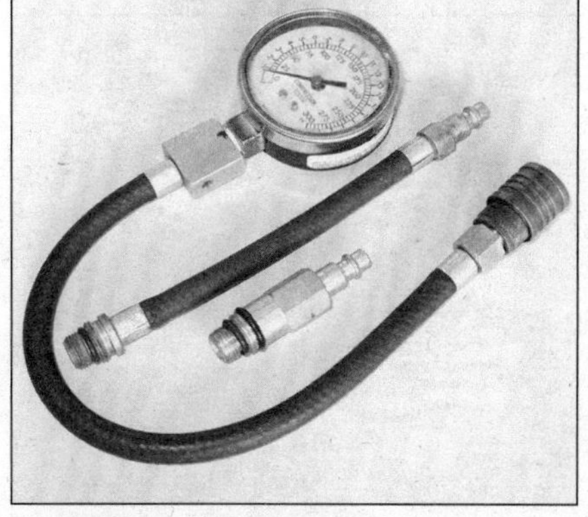

Compression gauge with spark plug hole adapter

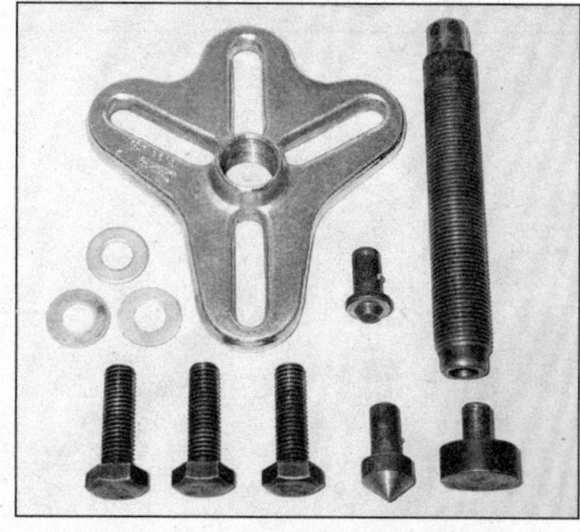

Damper/steering wheel puller

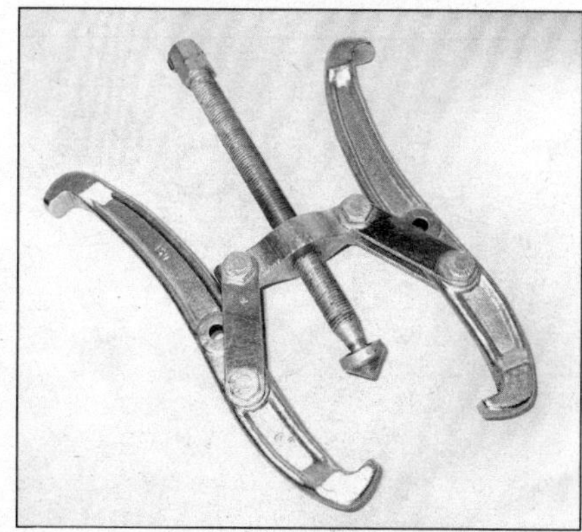

General purpose puller

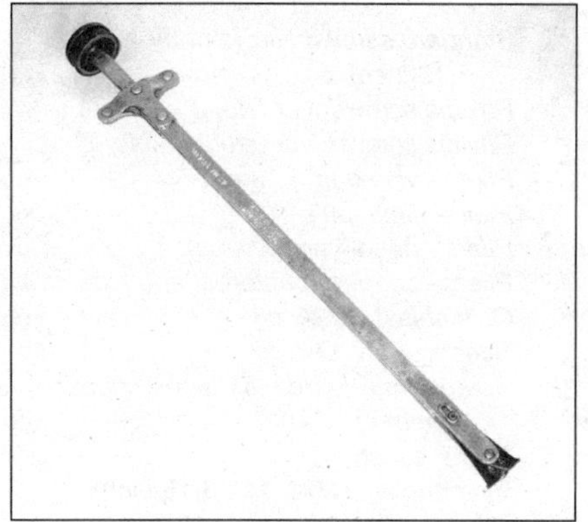

Hydraulic lifter removal tool

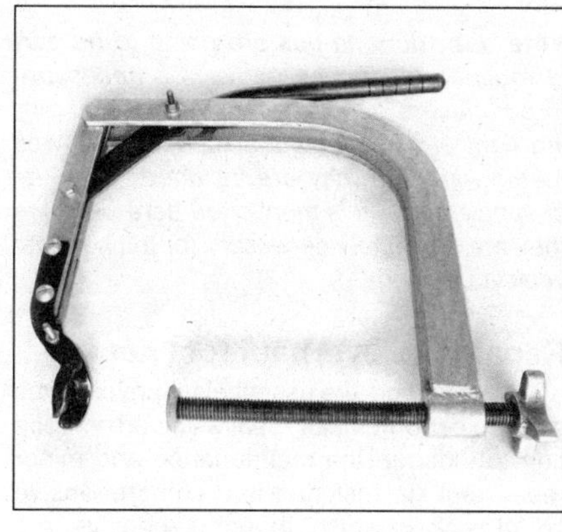

Valve spring compressor

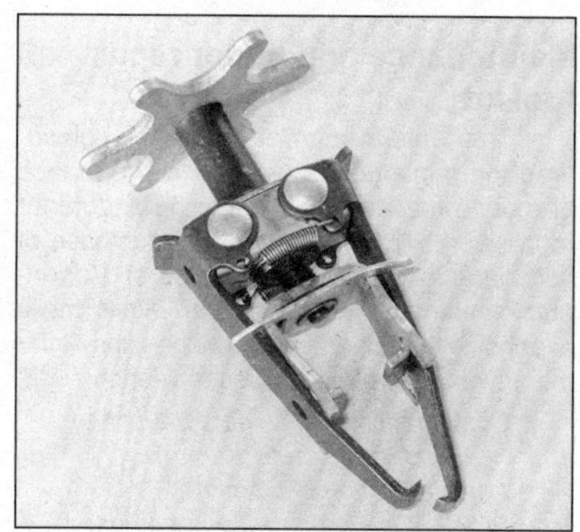

Valve spring compressor

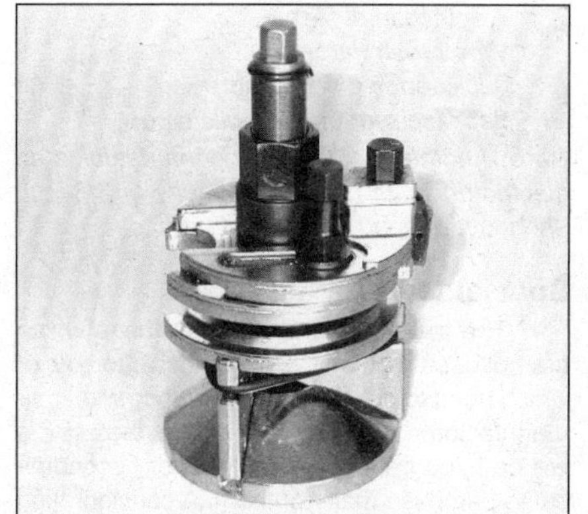

Ridge reamer

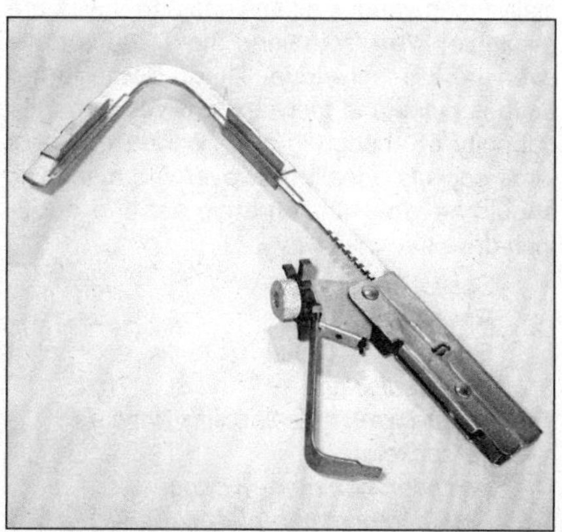

Piston ring groove cleaning tool

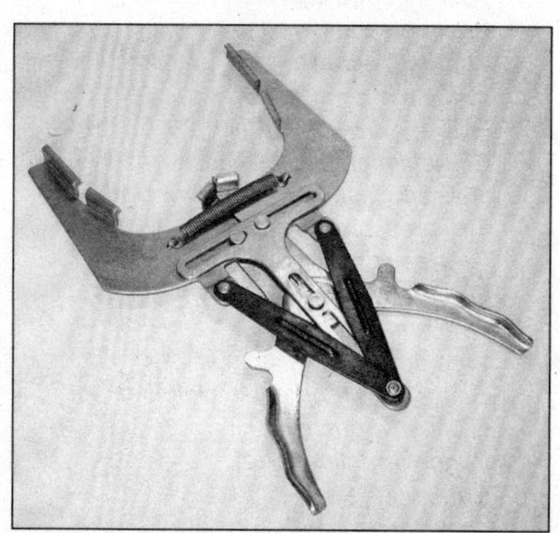

Ring removal/installation tool

Ring compressor

Cylinder hone

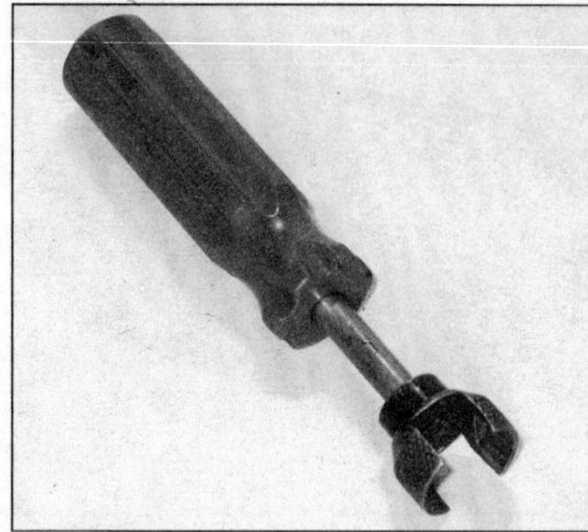

Brake hold-down spring tool

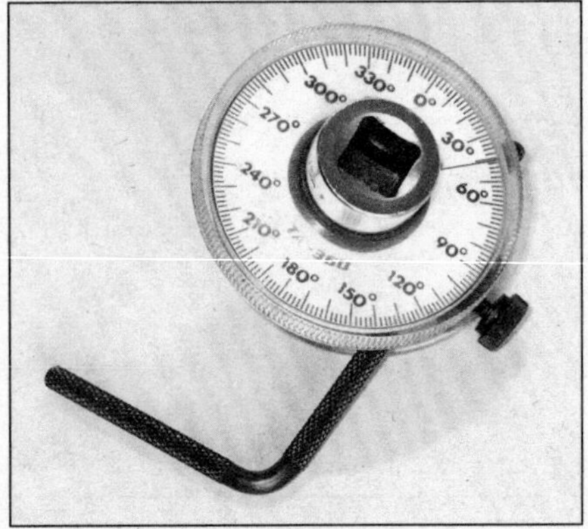

Torque angle gauge

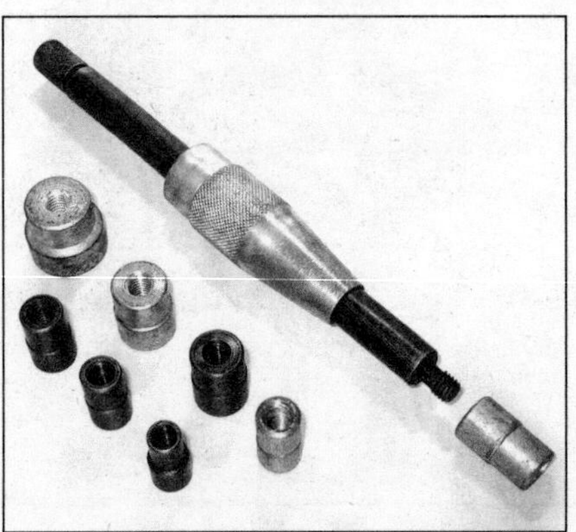

Clutch plate alignment tool

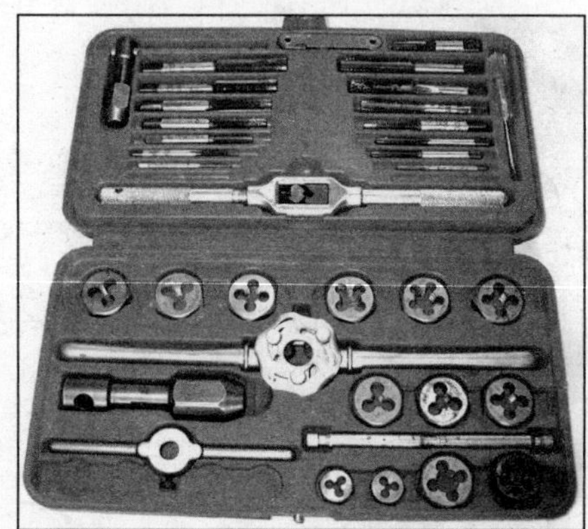

Tap and die set

Maintenance and minor repair tool kit

The tools in this list should be considered the minimum required for performance of routine maintenance, servicing and minor repair work. We recommend the purchase of combination wrenches (box-end and open-end combined in one wrench). While more expensive than open end wrenches, they offer the advantages of both types of wrench.

Combination wrench set (1/4-inch to 1 inch or 6 mm to 19 mm)
Adjustable wrench, 8 inch
Spark plug wrench with rubber insert
Spark plug gap adjusting tool
Feeler gauge set
Brake bleeder wrench
Standard screwdriver (5/16-inch x 6 inch)
Phillips screwdriver (No. 2 x 6 inch)
Combination pliers - 6 inch
Hacksaw and assortment of blades
Tire pressure gauge
Grease gun
Oil can
Fine emery cloth
Wire brush
Battery post and cable cleaning tool
Oil filter wrench
Funnel (medium size)
Safety goggles
Jackstands (2)
Drain pan

Note: *If basic tune-ups are going to be part of routine maintenance, it will be necessary to purchase a good quality stroboscopic timing light and combination tachometer/dwell meter. Although they are included in the list of special tools, it is mentioned here because they are absolutely necessary for tuning most vehicles properly.*

Repair and overhaul tool set

These tools are essential for anyone who plans to perform major repairs and are in addition to those in the maintenance and minor repair tool kit. Included is a comprehensive set of sockets which, though expensive, are invaluable because of their versatility, especially when various extensions and drives are available. We recommend the 1/2-inch drive over the 3/8-inch drive. Although the larger drive is bulky and more expensive, it has the capacity of accepting a very wide range of large sockets. Ideally, however, the mechanic should have a 3/8-inch drive set and a 1/2-inch drive set.

Socket set(s)
Reversible ratchet
Extension - 10 inch
Universal joint
Torque wrench (same size drive as sockets)
Ball peen hammer - 8 ounce
Soft-face hammer (plastic/rubber)
Standard screwdriver (1/4-inch x 6 inch)

Standard screwdriver (stubby - 5/16-inch)
Phillips screwdriver (No. 3 x 8 inch)
Phillips screwdriver (stubby - No. 2)
Pliers - vise grip
Pliers - lineman's
Pliers - needle nose
Pliers - snap-ring (internal and external)
Cold chisel - 1/2-inch
Scribe
Scraper (made from flattened copper tubing)
Centerpunch
Pin punches (1/16, 1/8, 3/16-inch)
Steel rule/straightedge - 12 inch
Allen wrench set (1/8 to 3/8-inch or 4 mm to 10 mm)
A selection of files
Wire brush (large)
Jackstands (second set)
Jack (scissor or hydraulic type)

Note: *Another tool which is often useful is an electric drill with a chuck capacity of 3/8-inch and a set of good quality drill bits.*

Special tools

The tools in this list include those which are not used regularly, are expensive to buy, or which need to be used in accordance with their manufacturer's instructions. Unless these tools will be used frequently, it is not very economical to purchase many of them. A consideration would be to split the cost and use between yourself and a friend or friends. In addition, most of these tools can be obtained from a tool rental shop on a temporary basis.

This list primarily contains only those tools and instruments widely available to the public, and not those special tools produced by the vehicle manufacturer for distribution to dealer service departments. Occasionally, references to the manufacturer's special tools are included in the text of this manual. Generally, an alternative method of doing the job without the special tool is offered. However, sometimes there is no alternative to their use. Where this is the case, and the tool cannot be purchased or borrowed, the work should be turned over to the dealer service department or an automotive repair shop.

Valve spring compressor
Piston ring groove cleaning tool
Piston ring compressor
Piston ring installation tool
Cylinder compression gauge
Cylinder ridge reamer
Cylinder surfacing hone
Cylinder bore gauge
Micrometers and/or dial calipers
Hydraulic lifter removal tool
Balljoint separator
Universal-type puller
Impact screwdriver
Dial indicator set
*Stroboscopic timing light (inductive
    pick-up)*
Hand operated vacuum/pressure pump
Tachometer/dwell meter
Universal electrical multimeter
Cable hoist
*Brake spring removal and installation
    tools*
Floor jack

Buying tools

For the do-it-yourselfer who is just starting to get involved in vehicle maintenance and repair, there are a number of options available when purchasing tools. If maintenance and minor repair is the extent of the work to be done, the purchase of individual tools is satisfactory. If, on the other hand, extensive work is planned, it would be a good idea to purchase a modest tool set from one of the large retail chain stores. A set can usually be bought at a substantial savings over the individual tool prices, and they often come with a tool box. As additional tools are needed, add-on sets, individual tools and a larger tool box can be purchased to expand the tool selection. Building a tool set gradually allows the cost of the tools to be spread over a longer period of time and gives the mechanic the freedom to choose only those tools that will actually be used.

Tool stores will often be the only source of some of the special tools that are needed,

but regardless of where tools are bought, try to avoid cheap ones, especially when buying screwdrivers and sockets, because they won't last very long. The expense involved in replacing cheap tools will eventually be greater than the initial cost of quality tools.

Care and maintenance of tools

Good tools are expensive, so it makes sense to treat them with respect. Keep them clean and in usable condition and store them properly when not in use. Always wipe off any dirt, grease or metal chips before putting them away. Never leave tools lying around in the work area. Upon completion of a job, always check closely under the hood for tools that may have been left there so they won't get lost during a test drive.

Some tools, such as screwdrivers, pliers, wrenches and sockets, can be hung on a panel mounted on the garage or workshop wall, while others should be kept in a tool box or tray. Measuring instruments, gauges, meters, etc. must be carefully stored where they cannot be damaged by weather or impact from other tools.

When tools are used with care and stored properly, they will last a very long time. Even with the best of care, though, tools will wear out if used frequently. When a tool is damaged or worn out, replace it. Subsequent jobs will be safer and more enjoyable if you do.

How to repair damaged threads

Sometimes, the internal threads of a nut or bolt hole can become stripped, usually from overtightening. Stripping threads is an all-too-common occurrence, especially when working with aluminum parts, because aluminum is so soft that it easily strips out.

Usually, external or internal threads are only partially stripped. After they've been cleaned up with a tap or die, they'll still work. Sometimes, however, threads are badly damaged. When this happens, you've got three choices:

1) *Drill and tap the hole to the next suitable oversize and install a larger diameter bolt, screw or stud.*
2) *Drill and tap the hole to accept a threaded plug, then drill and tap the plug to the original screw size. You can also buy a plug already threaded to the original size. Then you simply drill a hole to the specified size, then run the threaded plug into the hole with a bolt and jam nut. Once the plug is fully seated, remove the jam nut and bolt.*
3) *The third method uses a patented thread repair kit like Heli-Coil or Slimsert. These easy-to-use kits are designed to repair*

damaged threads in straight-through holes and blind holes. Both are available as kits which can handle a variety of sizes and thread patterns. Drill the hole, then tap it with the special included tap. Install the Heli-Coil and the hole is back to its original diameter and thread pitch.

Regardless of which method you use, be sure to proceed calmly and carefully. A little impatience or carelessness during one of these relatively simple procedures can ruin your whole day's work and cost you a bundle if you wreck an expensive part.

Working facilities

Not to be overlooked when discussing tools is the workshop. If anything more than routine maintenance is to be carried out, some sort of suitable work area is essential.

It is understood, and appreciated, that many home mechanics do not have a good workshop or garage available, and end up removing an engine or doing major repairs outside. It is recommended, however, that the overhaul or repair be completed under the cover of a roof.

A clean, flat workbench or table of comfortable working height is an absolute necessity. The workbench should be equipped with a vise that has a jaw opening of at least four inches.

As mentioned previously, some clean, dry storage space is also required for tools, as well as the lubricants, fluids, cleaning solvents, etc. which soon become necessary.

Sometimes waste oil and fluids, drained from the engine or cooling system during normal maintenance or repairs, present a disposal problem. To avoid pouring them on the ground or into a sewage system, pour the used fluids into large containers, seal them with caps and take them to an authorized disposal site or recycling center. Plastic jugs, such as old antifreeze containers, are ideal for this purpose.

Always keep a supply of old newspapers and clean rags available. Old towels are excellent for mopping up spills. Many mechanics use rolls of paper towels for most work because they are readily available and disposable. To help keep the area under the vehicle clean, a large cardboard box can be cut open and flattened to protect the garage or shop floor.

Whenever working over a painted surface, such as when leaning over a fender to service something under the hood, always cover it with an old blanket or bedspread to protect the finish. Vinyl covered pads, made especially for this purpose, are available at auto parts stores.

Jacking and towing

Jacking

Warning:The *jack supplied with the vehicle should only be used for changing a tire or placing jackstands under the frame. Never work under the vehicle or start the engine while this jack is being used as the only means of support.*

The vehicle should be on level ground. Place the shift lever in Park. Block the wheel diagonally opposite the wheel being changed. Set the parking brake.

Remove the spare tire and jack from stowage. Remove the wheel cover and trim ring (if so equipped) with the tapered end of the lug nut wrench by inserting and twisting the handle, then prying against the back of the wheel cover. Loosen, but do not remove, the lug nuts (one-half turn is sufficient).

Place the scissors-type jack under the vehicle and adjust the jack height until it engages with the proper jacking point. There is a front and rear jacking point on each side of the vehicle **(see illustration)**.

Turn the jack handle clockwise until the tire clears the ground. Remove the lug nuts and pull the wheel off, then install the spare.

Install the lug nuts with the beveled edges facing in. Tighten them snugly. Don't attempt to tighten them completely until the vehicle is lowered or it could slip off the jack. Turn the jack handle counterclockwise to lower the vehicle. Remove the jack and tighten the lug nuts in a diagonal pattern.

Stow the tire, jack and wrench. Unblock the wheels.

Towing

Two-wheel drive models can be towed from the front with the front wheels off the ground, using a wheel lift type tow truck. If towed from the rear, the front wheels must be placed on a dolly. All-wheel drive models must be towed with all four wheels off the ground. A sling-type tow truck cannot be used, as body damage will result. The best way to tow the vehicle is with a flat-bed car carrier.

In an emergency the vehicle can be towed a short distance with a cable or chain attached to one of the towing eyelets located under the front or rear bumpers. The driver must remain in the vehicle to operate the steering and brakes (remember that power steering and power brakes will not work with the engine off).

Booster battery (jump) starting

Observe these precautions when using a booster battery to start a vehicle:

a) *Before connecting the booster battery, make sure the ignition switch is in the Off position.*
b) *Turn off the lights, heater and other electrical loads.*
c) *Your eyes should be shielded. Safety goggles are a good idea.*
d) *Make sure the booster battery is the same voltage as the dead one in the vehicle.*
e) *The two vehicles MUST NOT TOUCH each other!*
f) *Make sure the transaxle is in Neutral (manual) or Park (automatic).*
g) *If the booster battery is not a maintenance-free type, remove the vent caps and lay a cloth over the vent holes.*

Connect the red jumper cable to the positive (+) terminals of each battery **(see illustration)**.

Connect one end of the black jumper cable to the negative (-) terminal of the booster battery. The other end of this cable should be connected to a good ground on the vehicle to be started, such as a bolt or bracket on the body.

Start the engine using the booster battery, then, with the engine running at idle speed, disconnect the jumper cables in the reverse order of connection.

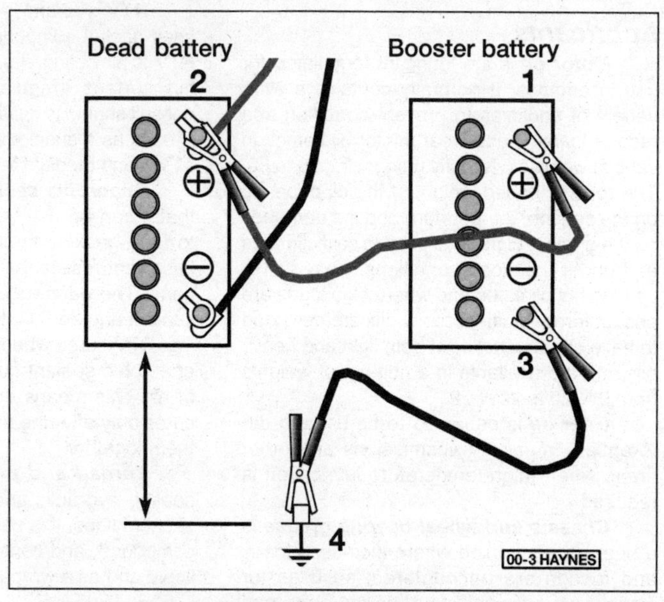

Make the booster battery cable connections in the numerical order shown (note that the negative cable of the booster battery is NOT attached to the negative terminal of the dead battery)

Automotive chemicals and lubricants

A number of automotive chemicals and lubricants are available for use during vehicle maintenance and repair. They include a wide variety of products ranging from cleaning solvents and degreasers to lubricants and protective sprays for rubber, plastic and vinyl.

Cleaners

Carburetor cleaner and choke cleaner is a strong solvent for gum, varnish and carbon. Most carburetor cleaners leave a dry-type lubricant film which will not harden or gum up. Because of this film it is not recommended for use on electrical components.

Brake system cleaner is used to remove brake dust, grease and brake fluid from the brake system, where clean surfaces are absolutely necessary. It leaves no residue and often eliminates brake squeal caused by contaminants.

Electrical cleaner removes oxidation, corrosion and carbon deposits from electrical contacts, restoring full current flow. It can also be used to clean spark plugs, carburetor jets, voltage regulators and other parts where an oil-free surface is desired.

Demoisturants remove water and moisture from electrical components such as alternators, voltage regulators, electrical connectors and fuse blocks. They are non-conductive and non-corrosive.

Degreasers are heavy-duty solvents used to remove grease from the outside of the engine and from chassis components. They can be sprayed or brushed on and, depending on the type, are rinsed off either with water or solvent.

Lubricants

Motor oil is the lubricant formulated for use in engines. It normally contains a wide variety of additives to prevent corrosion and reduce foaming and wear. Motor oil comes in various weights (viscosity ratings) from 0 to 50. The recommended weight of the oil depends on the season, temperature and the demands on the engine. Light oil is used in cold climates and under light load conditions. Heavy oil is used in hot climates and where high loads are encountered. Multi-viscosity oils are designed to have characteristics of both light and heavy oils and are available in a number of weights from 0W-20 to 20W-50.

Gear oil is designed to be used in differentials, manual transmissions and other areas where high-temperature lubrication is required.

Chassis and wheel bearing grease is a heavy grease used where increased loads and friction are encountered, such as for wheel bearings, balljoints, tie-rod ends and universal joints.

High-temperature wheel bearing grease is designed to withstand the extreme temperatures encountered by wheel bearings in disc brake equipped vehicles. It usually contains molybdenum disulfide (moly), which is a dry-type lubricant.

White grease is a heavy grease for metal-to-metal applications where water is a problem. White grease stays soft under both low and high temperatures (usually from -100 to +190-degrees F), and will not wash off or dilute in the presence of water.

Assembly lube is a special extreme pressure lubricant, usually containing moly, used to lubricate high-load parts (such as main and rod bearings and cam lobes) for initial start-up of a new engine. The assembly lube lubricates the parts without being squeezed out or washed away until the engine oiling system begins to function.

Silicone lubricants are used to protect rubber, plastic, vinyl and nylon parts.

Graphite lubricants are used where oils cannot be used due to contamination problems, such as in locks. The dry graphite will lubricate metal parts while remaining uncontaminated by dirt, water, oil or acids. It is electrically conductive and will not foul electrical contacts in locks such as the ignition switch.

Moly penetrants loosen and lubricate frozen, rusted and corroded fasteners and prevent future rusting or freezing.

Heat-sink grease is a special electrically non-conductive grease that is used for mounting electronic ignition modules where it is essential that heat is transferred away from the module.

Sealants

RTV sealant is one of the most widely used gasket compounds. Made from silicone, RTV is air curing, it seals, bonds, waterproofs, fills surface irregularities, remains flexible, doesn't shrink, is relatively easy to remove, and is used as a supplementary sealer with almost all low and medium temperature gaskets.

Anaerobic sealant is much like RTV in that it can be used either to seal gaskets or to form gaskets by itself. It remains flexible, is solvent resistant and fills surface imperfections. The difference between an anaerobic sealant and an RTV-type sealant is in the curing. RTV cures when exposed to air, while an anaerobic sealant cures only in the absence of air. This means that an anaerobic sealant cures only after the assembly of parts, sealing them together.

Thread and pipe sealant is used for sealing hydraulic and pneumatic fittings and vacuum lines. It is usually made from a Teflon compound, and comes in a spray, a paint-on liquid and as a wrap-around tape.

Chemicals

Anti-seize compound prevents seizing, galling, cold welding, rust and corrosion in fasteners. High-temperature anti-seize, usually made with copper and graphite lubricants, is used for exhaust system and exhaust manifold bolts.

Anaerobic locking compounds are used to keep fasteners from vibrating or working loose and cure only after installation, in the absence of air. Medium strength locking compound is used for small nuts, bolts and screws that may be removed later. High-strength locking compound is for large nuts, bolts and studs which aren't removed on a regular basis.

Oil additives range from viscosity index improvers to chemical treatments that claim to reduce internal engine friction. It should be noted that most oil manufacturers caution against using additives with their oils.

Gas additives perform several functions, depending on their chemical makeup. They usually contain solvents that help dissolve gum and varnish that build up on carburetor, fuel injection and intake parts. They also serve to break down carbon deposits that form on the inside surfaces of the combustion chambers. Some additives contain upper cylinder lubricants for valves and piston rings, and others contain chemicals to remove condensation from the gas tank.

Miscellaneous

Brake fluid is specially formulated hydraulic fluid that can withstand the heat and pressure encountered in brake systems. Care must be taken so this fluid does not come in contact with painted surfaces or plastics. An opened container should always be resealed to prevent contamination by water or dirt.

Weatherstrip adhesive is used to bond weatherstripping around doors, windows and trunk lids. It is sometimes used to attach trim pieces.

Undercoating is a petroleum-based, tar-like substance that is designed to protect metal surfaces on the underside of the vehicle from corrosion. It also acts as a sound-deadening agent by insulating the bottom of the vehicle.

Waxes and polishes are used to help protect painted and plated surfaces from the weather. Different types of paint may require the use of different types of wax and polish. Some polishes utilize a chemical or abrasive cleaner to help remove the top layer of oxidized (dull) paint on older vehicles. In recent years many non-wax polishes that contain a wide variety of chemicals such as polymers and silicones have been introduced. These non-wax polishes are usually easier to apply and last longer than conventional waxes and polishes.

Conversion factors

Length (distance)
Inches (in)	X 25.4	= Millimeters (mm)	X 0.0394	= Inches (in)
Feet (ft)	X 0.305	= Meters (m)	X 3.281	= Feet (ft)
Miles	X 1.609	= Kilometers (km)	X 0.621	= Miles

Volume (capacity)
Cubic inches (cu in; in^3)	X 16.387	= Cubic centimeters (cc; cm^3)	X 0.061	= Cubic inches (cu in; in^3)
Imperial pints (Imp pt)	X 0.568	= Liters (l)	X 1.76	= Imperial pints (Imp pt)
Imperial quarts (Imp qt)	X 1.137	= Liters (l)	X 0.88	= Imperial quarts (Imp qt)
Imperial quarts (Imp qt)	X 1.201	= US quarts (US qt)	X 0.833	= Imperial quarts (Imp qt)
US quarts (US qt)	X 0.946	= Liters (l)	X 1.057	= US quarts (US qt)
Imperial gallons (Imp gal)	X 4.546	= Liters (l)	X 0.22	= Imperial gallons (Imp gal)
Imperial gallons (Imp gal)	X 1.201	= US gallons (US gal)	X 0.833	= Imperial gallons (Imp gal)
US gallons (US gal)	X 3.785	= Liters (l)	X 0.264	= US gallons (US gal)

Mass (weight)
Ounces (oz)	X 28.35	= Grams (g)	X 0.035	= Ounces (oz)
Pounds (lb)	X 0.454	= Kilograms (kg)	X 2.205	= Pounds (lb)

Force
Ounces-force (ozf; oz)	X 0.278	= Newtons (N)	X 3.6	= Ounces-force (ozf; oz)
Pounds-force (lbf; lb)	X 4.448	= Newtons (N)	X 0.225	= Pounds-force (lbf; lb)
Newtons (N)	X 0.1	= Kilograms-force (kgf; kg)	X 9.81	= Newtons (N)

Pressure
Pounds-force per square inch (psi; lbf/in^2; lb/in^2)	X 0.070	= Kilograms-force per square centimeter (kgf/cm^2; kg/cm^2)	X 14.223	= Pounds-force per square inch (psi; lbf/in^2; lb/in^2)
Pounds-force per square inch (psi; lbf/in^2; lb/in^2)	X 0.068	= Atmospheres (atm)	X 14.696	= Pounds-force per square inch (psi; lbf/in^2; lb/in^2)
Pounds-force per square inch (psi; lbf/in^2; lb/in^2)	X 0.069	= Bars	X 14.5	= Pounds-force per square inch (psi; lbf/in^2; lb/in^2)
Pounds-force per square inch (psi; lbf/in^2; lb/in^2)	X 6.895	= Kilopascals (kPa)	X 0.145	= Pounds-force per square inch (psi; lbf/in^2; lb/in^2)
Kilopascals (kPa)	X 0.01	= Kilograms-force per square centimeter (kgf/cm^2; kg/cm^2)	X 98.1	= Kilopascals (kPa)

Torque (moment of force)
Pounds-force inches (lbf in; lb in)	X 1.152	= Kilograms-force centimeter (kgf cm; kg cm)	X 0.868	= Pounds-force inches (lbf in; lb in)
Pounds-force inches (lbf in; lb in)	X 0.113	= Newton meters (Nm)	X 8.85	= Pounds-force inches (lbf in; lb in)
Pounds-force inches (lbf in; lb in)	X 0.083	= Pounds-force feet (lbf ft; lb ft)	X 12	= Pounds-force inches (lbf in; lb in)
Pounds-force feet (lbf ft; lb ft)	X 0.138	= Kilograms-force meters (kgf m; kg m)	X 7.233	= Pounds-force feet (lbf ft; lb ft)
Pounds-force feet (lbf ft; lb ft)	X 1.356	= Newton meters (Nm)	X 0.738	= Pounds-force feet (lbf ft; lb ft)
Newton meters (Nm)	X 0.102	= Kilograms-force meters (kgf m; kg m)	X 9.804	= Newton meters (Nm)

Vacuum
Inches mercury (in. Hg)	X 3.377	= Kilopascals (kPa)	X 0.2961	= Inches mercury
Inches mercury (in. Hg)	X 25.4	= Millimeters mercury (mm Hg)	X 0.0394	= Inches mercury

Power
Horsepower (hp)	X 745.7	= Watts (W)	X 0.0013	= Horsepower (hp)

Velocity (speed)
Miles per hour (miles/hr; mph)	X 1.609	= Kilometers per hour (km/hr; kph)	X 0.621	= Miles per hour (miles/hr; mph)

Fuel consumption*
Miles per gallon, Imperial (mpg)	X 0.354	= Kilometers per liter (km/l)	X 2.825	= Miles per gallon, Imperial (mpg)
Miles per gallon, US (mpg)	X 0.425	= Kilometers per liter (km/l)	X 2.352	= Miles per gallon, US (mpg)

Temperature
Degrees Fahrenheit = (°C x 1.8) + 32

Degrees Celsius (Degrees Centigrade; °C) = (°F - 32) x 0.56

It is common practice to convert from miles per gallon (mpg) to liters/100 kilometers (l/100km), where mpg (Imperial) x l/100 km = 282 and mpg (US) x l/100 km = 235

DECIMALS to MILLIMETERS

Decimal	mm	Decimal	mm
0.001	0.0254	0.500	12.7000
0.002	0.0508	0.510	12.9540
0.003	0.0762	0.520	13.2080
0.004	0.1016	0.530	13.4620
0.005	0.1270	0.540	13.7160
0.006	0.1524	0.550	13.9700
0.007	0.1778	0.560	14.2240
0.008	0.2032	0.570	14.4780
0.009	0.2286	0.580	14.7320
		0.590	14.9860
0.010	0.2540		
0.020	0.5080		
0.030	0.7620		
0.040	1.0160	0.600	15.2400
0.050	1.2700	0.610	15.4940
0.060	1.5240	0.620	15.7480
0.070	1.7780	0.630	16.0020
0.080	2.0320	0.640	16.2560
0.090	2.2860	0.650	16.5100
		0.660	16.7640
0.100	2.5400	0.670	17.0180
0.110	2.7940	0.680	17.2720
0.120	3.0480	0.690	17.5260
0.130	3.3020		
0.140	3.5560		
0.150	3.8100		
0.160	4.0640	0.700	17.7800
0.170	4.3180	0.710	18.0340
0.180	4.5720	0.720	18.2880
0.190	4.8260	0.730	18.5420
		0.740	18.7960
0.200	5.0800	0.750	19.0500
0.210	5.3340	0.760	19.3040
0.220	5.5880	0.770	19.5580
0.230	5.8420	0.780	19.8120
0.240	6.0960	0.790	20.0660
0.250	6.3500		
0.260	6.6040		
0.270	6.8580	0.800	20.3200
0.280	7.1120	0.810	20.5740
0.290	7.3660	0.820	21.8280
		0.830	21.0820
0.300	7.6200	0.840	21.3360
0.310	7.8740	0.850	21.5900
0.320	8.1280	0.860	21.8440
0.330	8.3820	0.870	22.0980
0.340	8.6360	0.880	22.3520
0.350	8.8900	0.890	22.6060
0.360	9.1440		
0.370	9.3980		
0.380	9.6520		
0.390	9.9060		
		0.900	22.8600
0.400	10.1600	0.910	23.1140
0.410	10.4140	0.920	23.3680
0.420	10.6680	0.930	23.6220
0.430	10.9220	0.940	23.8760
0.440	11.1760	0.950	24.1300
0.450	11.4300	0.960	24.3840
0.460	11.6840	0.970	24.6380
0.470	11.9380	0.980	24.8920
0.480	12.1920	0.990	25.1460
0.490	12.4460	1.000	25.4000

FRACTIONS to DECIMALS to MILLIMETERS

Fraction	Decimal	mm	Fraction	Decimal	mm
1/64	0.0156	0.3969	33/64	0.5156	13.0969
1/32	0.0312	0.7938	17/32	0.5312	13.4938
3/64	0.0469	1.1906	35/64	0.5469	13.8906
1/16	0.0625	1.5875	9/16	0.5625	14.2875
5/64	0.0781	1.9844	37/64	0.5781	14.6844
3/32	0.0938	2.3812	19/32	0.5938	15.0812
7/64	0.1094	2.7781	39/64	0.6094	15.4781
1/8	0.1250	3.1750	5/8	0.6250	15.8750
9/64	0.1406	3.5719	41/64	0.6406	16.2719
5/32	0.1562	3.9688	21/32	0.6562	16.6688
11/64	0.1719	4.3656	43/64	0.6719	17.0656
3/16	0.1875	4.7625	11/16	0.6875	17.4625
13/64	0.2031	5.1594	45/64	0.7031	17.8594
7/32	0.2188	5.5562	23/32	0.7188	18.2562
15/64	0.2344	5.9531	47/64	0.7344	18.6531
1/4	0.2500	6.3500	3/4	0.7500	19.0500
17/64	0.2656	6.7469	49/64	0.7656	19.4469
9/32	0.2812	7.1438	25/32	0.7812	19.8438
19/64	0.2969	7.5406	51/64	0.7969	20.2406
5/16	0.3125	7.9375	13/16	0.8125	20.6375
21/64	0.3281	8.3344	53/64	0.8281	21.0344
11/32	0.3438	8.7312	27/32	0.8438	21.4312
23/64	0.3594	9.1281	55/64	0.8594	21.8281
3/8	0.3750	9.5250	7/8	0.8750	22.2250
25/64	0.3906	9.9219	57/64	0.8906	22.6219
13/32	0.4062	10.3188	29/32	0.9062	23.0188
27/64	0.4219	10.7156	59/64	0.9219	23.4156
7/16	0.4375	11.1125	15/16	0.9375	23.8125
29/64	0.4531	11.5094	61/64	0.9531	24.2094
15/32	0.4688	11.9062	31/32	0.9688	24.6062
31/64	0.4844	12.3031	63/64	0.9844	25.0031
1/2	0.5000	12.7000	1	1.0000	25.4000

Safety first!

Regardless of how enthusiastic you may be about getting on with the job at hand, take the time to ensure that your safety is not jeopardized. A moment's lack of attention can result in an accident, as can failure to observe certain simple safety precautions. The possibility of an accident will always exist, and the following points should not be considered a comprehensive list of all dangers. Rather, they are intended to make you aware of the risks and to encourage a safety conscious approach to all work you carry out on your vehicle.

Essential DOs and DON'Ts

DON'T rely on a jack when working under the vehicle. Always use approved jackstands to support the weight of the vehicle and place them under the recommended lift or support points.

DON'T attempt to loosen extremely tight fasteners (i.e. wheel lug nuts) while the vehicle is on a jack - it may fall.

DON'T start the engine without first making sure that the transmission is in Neutral (or Park where applicable) and the parking brake is set.

DON'T remove the radiator cap from a hot cooling system - let it cool or cover it with a cloth and release the pressure gradually.

DON'T attempt to drain the engine oil until you are sure it has cooled to the point that it will not burn you.

DON'T touch any part of the engine or exhaust system until it has cooled sufficiently to avoid burns.

DON'T siphon toxic liquids such as gasoline, antifreeze and brake fluid by mouth, or allow them to remain on your skin.

DON'T inhale brake lining dust - it is potentially hazardous (see *Asbestos* below).

DON'T allow spilled oil or grease to remain on the floor - wipe it up before someone slips on it.

DON'T use loose fitting wrenches or other tools which may slip and cause injury.

DON'T push on wrenches when loosening or tightening nuts or bolts. Always try to pull the wrench toward you. If the situation calls for pushing the wrench away, push with an open hand to avoid scraped knuckles if the wrench should slip.

DON'T attempt to lift a heavy component alone - get someone to help you.

DON'T *rush or take unsafe shortcuts to finish a job.*

DON'T allow children or animals in or around the vehicle while you are working on it.

DO wear eye protection when using power tools such as a drill, sander, bench grinder, etc. and when working under a vehicle.

DO keep loose clothing and long hair well out of the way of moving parts.

DO make sure that any hoist used has a safe working load rating adequate for the job.

DO get someone to check on you periodically when working alone on a vehicle.

DO carry out work in a logical sequence and make sure that everything is correctly assembled and tightened.

DO keep chemicals and fluids tightly capped and out of the reach of children and pets.

DO remember that your vehicle's safety affects that of yourself and others. If in doubt on any point, get professional advice.

Steering, suspension and brakes

These systems are essential to driving safety, so make sure you have a qualified shop or individual check your work. Also, compressed suspension springs can cause injury if released suddenly - be sure to use a spring compressor.

Airbags

Airbags are explosive devices that can **CAUSE** injury if they deploy while you're working on the vehicle. Follow the manufacturer's instructions to disable the airbag whenever you're working in the vicinity of airbag components.

Asbestos

Certain friction, insulating, sealing, and other products - such as brake linings, brake bands, clutch linings, torque converters, gaskets, etc. - may contain asbestos or other hazardous friction material. Extreme care must be taken to avoid inhalation of dust from such products, since it is hazardous to health. If in doubt, assume that they do contain asbestos.

Fire

Remember at all times that gasoline is highly flammable. Never smoke or have any kind of open flame around when working on a vehicle. But the risk does not end there. A spark caused by an electrical short circuit, by two metal surfaces contacting each other, or even by static electricity built up in your body under certain conditions, can ignite gasoline vapors, which in a confined space are highly explosive. Do not, under any circumstances, use gasoline for cleaning parts. Use an approved safety solvent.

Always disconnect the battery ground (-) cable at the battery before working on any part of the fuel system or electrical system. Never risk spilling fuel on a hot engine or exhaust component. It is strongly recommended that a fire extinguisher suitable for use on fuel and electrical fires be kept handy in the garage or workshop at all times. Never try to extinguish a fuel or electrical fire with water.

Fumes

Certain fumes are highly toxic and can quickly cause unconsciousness and even death if inhaled to any extent. Gasoline vapor falls into this category, as do the vapors from some cleaning solvents. Any draining or pouring of such volatile fluids should be done in a well ventilated area.

When using cleaning fluids and solvents, read the instructions on the container carefully. Never use materials from unmarked containers.

Never run the engine in an enclosed space, such as a garage. Exhaust fumes contain carbon monoxide, which is extremely poisonous. If you need to run the engine, always do so in the open air, or at least have the rear of the vehicle outside the work area.

The battery

Never create a spark or allow a bare light bulb near a battery. They normally give off a certain amount of hydrogen gas, which is highly explosive.

Always disconnect the battery ground (-) cable at the battery before working on the fuel or electrical systems.

If possible, loosen the filler caps or cover when charging the battery from an external source (this does not apply to sealed or maintenance-free batteries). Do not charge at an excessive rate or the battery may burst.

Take care when adding water to a non maintenance-free battery and when carrying a battery. The electrolyte, even when diluted, is very corrosive and should not be allowed to contact clothing or skin.

Always wear eye protection when cleaning the battery to prevent the caustic deposits from entering your eyes.

Household current

When using an electric power tool, inspection light, etc., which operates on household current, always make sure that the tool is correctly connected to its plug and that, where necessary, it is properly grounded. Do not use such items in damp conditions and, again, do not create a spark or apply excessive heat in the vicinity of fuel or fuel vapor.

Secondary ignition system voltage

A severe electric shock can result from touching certain parts of the ignition system (such as the spark plug wires) when the engine is running or being cranked, particularly if components are damp or the insulation is defective. In the case of an electronic ignition system, the secondary system voltage is much higher and could prove fatal.

Hydrofluoric acid

This extremely corrosive acid is formed when certain types of synthetic rubber, found in some O-rings, oil seals, fuel hoses, etc. are exposed to temperatures above 750-degrees F (400-degrees C). The rubber changes into a charred or sticky substance containing the acid. *Once formed, the acid remains dangerous for years. If it gets onto the skin, it may be necessary to amputate the limb concerned.*

When dealing with a vehicle which has suffered a fire, or with components salvaged from such a vehicle, wear protective gloves and discard them after use.

Troubleshooting

Contents

1   This section provides an easy reference guide to the more common problems which may occur during the operation of your vehicle. These problems and their possible causes are grouped under headings denoting various components or systems, such as Engine, Cooling system, etc. They also refer you to the chapter and/or section which deals with the problem.

2   Remember that successful troubleshooting is not a mysterious black art practiced only by professional mechanics. It is simply the result of the right knowledge combined with an intelligent, systematic approach to the problem. Always work by a process of elimination, starting with the simplest solution and working through to the most complex - and never overlook the obvious. Anyone can run the gas tank dry or leave the lights on overnight, so don't assume that you are exempt from such oversights.

3   Finally, always establish a clear idea of why a problem has occurred and take steps to ensure that it doesn't happen again. If the electrical system fails because of a poor connection, check the other connections in the system to make sure that they don't fail as well. If a particular fuse continues to blow, find out why - don't just replace one fuse after another. Remember, failure of a small component can often be indicative of potential failure or incorrect functioning of a more important component or system.

Engine

1   Engine will not rotate when attempting to start

1   Battery terminal connections loose or corroded (Chapter 1).
2   Battery discharged or faulty (Chapters 1 and 5).
3   Automatic transaxle not completely engaged in Park (Chapter 7A).
4   Broken, loose or disconnected wiring in the starting circuit (Chapters 5 and 12).
5   Starter motor pinion jammed in flywheel ring gear (Chapter 5).
6   Starter solenoid faulty (Chapter 5).
7   Starter motor faulty (Chapter 5).
8   Ignition switch faulty (Chapter 12).
9   Starter pinion or flywheel teeth worn or broken (Chapter 5).

2   Engine rotates but will not start

1   Fuel tank empty.
2   Battery discharged (engine rotates slowly) (Chapter 5).
3   Battery terminal connections loose or corroded (Chapter 1).
4   Leaking fuel injector(s), faulty fuel pump, pressure regulator, etc. (Chapter 4).
5   Broken timing chain (Chapter 2A or 2B).

6   Ignition components damp or damaged (Chapter 5).
7   Worn, faulty or incorrectly-gapped spark plugs (Chapter 1).
8   Broken, loose or disconnected wiring in the starting circuit (Chapter 5).
9   Broken, loose or disconnected wires at the ignition coil or faulty coil (Chapter 5).
10   Defective crankshaft or camshaft sensor (Chapter 6).

3   Engine hard to start when cold

1   Battery discharged or low (Chapter 1).
2   Malfunctioning fuel system (Chapter 4).
3   Faulty coolant temperature sensor or intake air temperature sensor (Chapter 6).
4   Faulty ignition system (Chapter 5).

4   Engine hard to start when hot

1   Air filter clogged (Chapter 1).
2   Fuel not reaching the fuel injection system (Chapter 4).
3   Corroded battery connections (Chapter 1).
4   Faulty coolant temperature sensor or intake air temperature sensor (Chapter 6).

5   Starter motor noisy or excessively rough in engagement

1   Pinion or flywheel gear teeth worn or broken (Chapter 5).
2   Starter motor mounting bolts loose or missing (Chapter 5).

6   Engine starts but stops immediately

1   Insufficient fuel reaching the fuel injector(s) (Chapters 1 and 4).
2   Vacuum leak at the gasket between the intake manifold/plenum and throttle body (Chapter 4).

7   Oil puddle under engine

1   Oil pan gasket and/or oil pan drain bolt washer leaking (Chapter 2A or 2B).
2   Oil pressure sending unit leaking (Chapter 2A or 2B).
3   Valve cover leaking (Chapter 2A or 2B).
4   Engine oil seals leaking (Chapter 2A or 2B).
5   Oil pump housing leaking (Chapter 2A or 2B).

8   Engine lopes while idling or idles erratically

1   Vacuum leakage (Chapters 2C and 4).

2   Leaking EGR valve (Chapter 6).
3   Air filter clogged (Chapter 1).
4   Malfunction in the fuel injection or engine control system (Chapters 4 and 6).
5   Leaking head gasket (Chapter 2A or 2B).
6   Timing chain and/or sprockets worn (Chapter 2A or 2B).
7   Camshaft lobes worn (Chapter 2A or 2B).

9   Engine misses at idle speed

1   Spark plugs worn or not gapped properly (Chapter 1).
2   Faulty coil(s) (Chapter 1).
3   Vacuum leaks (Chapter 2C).
4   Uneven or low compression (Chapter 2C).
5   Problem with the fuel injection system (Chapter 4).

10   Engine misses throughout driving speed range

1   Fuel filter clogged and/or impurities in the fuel system (Chapters 1 and 4).
2   Low fuel pressure (Chapter 4).
3   Faulty or incorrectly gapped spark plugs (Chapter 1).
4   Faulty emission system components (Chapter 6).
5   Low or uneven cylinder compression pressures (Chapter 2C).
6   Weak or faulty ignition system (Chapter 5).
7   Vacuum leak in fuel injection system, intake manifold, air control valve or vacuum hoses (Chapters 4 and 6).

11   Engine stumbles on acceleration

1   Spark plugs fouled (Chapter 1).
2   Problem with fuel injection or engine control system (Chapters 4 and 6).
3   Fuel filter clogged (Chapters 1 and 4).
4   Intake manifold air leak (Chapters 2A or 2B and 4).
5   Problem with the emissions control system (Chapter 6).

12   Engine surges while holding accelerator steady

1   Intake air leak (Chapter 4).
2   Fuel pump or fuel pressure regulator faulty (Chapter 4).
3   Problem with the fuel injection system (Chapter 4).
4   Problem with the emissions control system (Chapter 6).

13 Engine stalls

1   Idle speed incorrect (Chapter 1).
2   Fuel filter clogged and/or water and impurities in the fuel system (Chapters 1 and 4).
3   Faulty emissions system components (Chapter 6).
4   Faulty or incorrectly-gapped spark plugs (Chapter 1).
5   Vacuum leak in the fuel injection system, intake manifold or vacuum hoses (Chapters 2C and 4).

14 Engine lacks power

1   Obstructed exhaust system (Chapter 4).
2   Faulty or incorrectly-gapped spark plugs (Chapter 1).
3   Problem with the fuel injection system (Chapter 4).
4   Dirty air filter (Chapter 1).
5   Brakes binding (Chapter 9).
6   Automatic transaxle fluid level incorrect (Chapter 1).
7   Clutch slipping (Chapter 8).
8   Fuel filter clogged and/or impurities in the fuel system (Chapters 1 and 4).
9   Emission control system not functioning properly (Chapter 6).
10   Low or uneven cylinder compression pressures (Chapter 2A).

15 Engine backfires

1   Emission control system not functioning properly (Chapter 6).
2   Problem with the fuel injection system (Chapter 4).
3   Vacuum leak at fuel injector(s), intake manifold or vacuum hoses (Chapters 2C and 4).
4   Valve clearances incorrectly set (four-cylinder engines) and/or valves sticking (Chapter 2A or 2B).

16 Pinging or knocking engine sounds during acceleration or uphill

1   Incorrect grade of fuel.
2   Fuel injection system faulty (Chapter 4).
3   Improper or damaged spark plugs or wires (Chapter 1).
4   Knock sensor defective (Chapter 6).
5   EGR valve not functioning (Chapter 6).
6   Vacuum leak (Chapters 2C and 4).

17 Engine runs with oil pressure light on

1   Low oil level (Chapter 1).
2   Idle rpm below specification (Chapter 1).
3   Short in wiring circuit (Chapter 12).

4   Faulty oil pressure sender (Chapter 2C).
5   Worn engine bearings and/or oil pump (Chapter 2A or 2B).

18 Engine continues to run after switching off

Defective ignition switch (Chapter 12).

Engine electrical systems

19 Battery will not hold a charge

1   Drivebelt or tensioner defective (Chapter 1).
2   Battery electrolyte level low (Chapter 1).
3   Battery terminals loose or corroded (Chapter 1).
4   Alternator not charging properly (Chapter 5).
5   Loose, broken or faulty wiring in the charging circuit (Chapter 5).
6   Short in vehicle wiring (Chapter 12).
7   Internally defective battery (Chapters 1 and 5).

20 Alternator light fails to go out

1   Faulty alternator or charging circuit (Chapter 5).
2   Drivebelt or tensioner defective (Chapter 1).

21 Alternator light fails to come on when key is turned on

1   Instrument cluster defective (Chapter 12).
2   Fault in the Smart Junction Box or wiring harness (Chapter 12).

Fuel system

22 Excessive fuel consumption

1   Dirty air filter element (Chapter 1).
2   Emissions system not functioning properly (Chapter 6).
3   Fuel injection system not functioning properly (Chapter 4).
4   Low tire pressure or incorrect tire size (Chapter 1).

23 Fuel leakage and/or fuel odor

1   Leaking fuel line (Chapters 1 and 4).
2   Tank overfilled.
3   Evaporative emissions control system

problem (Chapters 1 and 6).
4   Problem with the fuel injection system (Chapter 4).

Cooling system

24 Overheating

1   Insufficient coolant in system (Chapter 1).
2   Water pump drivebelt defective or out of adjustment (Chapter 1).
3   Radiator core blocked or grille restricted (Chapter 3).
4   Thermostat faulty (Chapter 3).
5   Electric coolant fan inoperative or blades broken (Chapter 3).
6   Expansion tank cap not maintaining proper pressure (Chapter 3).

25 Overcooling

1   Faulty thermostat (Chapter 3).
2   Inaccurate temperature gauge sending unit (Chapter 3).

26 External coolant leakage

1   Deteriorated/damaged hoses; loose clamps (Chapters 1 and 3).
2   Water pump defective (Chapter 3).
3   Leakage from radiator core or coolant reservoir (Chapter 3).
4   Engine drain or water jacket core plugs leaking (Chapter 2A or 2B).

27 Internal coolant leakage

1   Leaking cylinder head gasket (Chapter 2A or 2B).
2   Cracked cylinder bore or cylinder head (Chapter 2A or 2B).

28 Coolant loss

1   Too much coolant in reservoir (Chapter 1).
2   Coolant boiling away because of overheating (Chapter 3).
3   Internal or external leakage (Chapter 3).
4   Faulty radiator cap (Chapter 3).

29 Poor coolant circulation

1   Inoperative water pump (Chapter 3).
2   Restriction in cooling system (Chapters 1 and 3).
3   Drivebelt or tensioner defective (Chapter 1).
4   Thermostat sticking (Chapter 3).

Automatic transaxle

30 Fluid leakage

1   Automatic transaxle fluid is a deep red color. Fluid leaks should not be confused with engine oil, which can easily be blown onto the transaxle by air flow.

2   To pinpoint a leak, first remove all built-up dirt and grime from the transaxle housing with degreasing agents and/or steam cleaning. Then drive the vehicle at low speeds so air flow will not blow the leak far from its source. Raise the vehicle and determine where the leak is coming from. Common areas of leakage are:

- *Dipstick tube (Chapters 1 and 7A)*
- *Transaxle oil lines (Chapter 7A)*
- *Speed sensor (Chapter 6)*
- *Driveaxle oil seals (Chapter 7A)*

31 Transaxle fluid brown or has a burned smell

Transaxle fluid overheated (Chapter 1).

32 General shift mechanism problems

1   Chapter 7A deals with checking and adjusting the shift cable on automatic transaxles. Common problems which may be attributed to poorly adjusted linkage are:
Engine starting in gears other than Park or Neutral.Indicator on shifter pointing to a gear other than the one actually being used.Vehicle moves when in Park.

2   Refer to Chapter 7A for the shift cable adjustment procedure.

33 Transaxle slips, shifts roughly, is noisy or has no drive in forward or reverse gears

There are many probable causes for the above problems, but the home mechanic should be concerned with only one possibility - fluid level. Before taking the vehicle to a repair shop, check the level and condition of the fluid as described in Chapter 1. Correct the fluid level as necessary or change the fluid and filter if needed. If the problem persists, have a professional diagnose the cause.

Driveaxles

34 Clicking noise in turns

Worn or damaged outboard CV joint (Chapter 8).

35 Shudder or vibration during acceleration

1   Excessive toe-in (Chapter 10).
2   Worn or damaged inboard or outboard CV joints (Chapter 8).
3   Sticking inboard CV joint assembly (Chapter 8).

36 Vibration at highway speeds

1   Out-of-balance front wheels and/or tires (Chapters 1 and 10).
2   Out-of-round front tires (Chapters 1 and 10).
3   Worn CV joint(s) (Chapter 8).

Brakes

37 Vehicle pulls to one side during braking

1   Incorrect tire pressures (Chapter 1).
2   Front end out of alignment (have the front end aligned).
3   Front, or rear, tire sizes not matched to one another.
4   Restricted brake lines or hoses (Chapter 9).
5   Malfunctioning caliper assembly (Chapter 9).
6   Loose suspension parts (Chapter 10).
7   Excessive wear of pad material or disc on one side (Chapter 9).
8   Contamination (grease or brake fluid) of brake pad material or disc on one side (Chapter 9).

38 Noise (high-pitched squeal when the brakes are applied)

Brake pads worn out. Replace pads with new ones immediately (Chapter 9).

39 Brake roughness or chatter (pedal pulsates)

1   Excessive lateral runout (Chapter 9).
2   Uneven pad wear (Chapter 9).
3   Defective disc (Chapter 9).

40 Excessive brake pedal effort required to stop vehicle

1   Malfunctioning power brake booster (Chapter 9).
2   Partial system failure (Chapter 9).

3   Excessively worn pads (Chapter 9).
4   Piston in caliper stuck or sluggish (Chapter 9).
5   Brake pads contaminated with oil or grease (Chapter 9).
6   Brake disc grooved and/or glazed (Chapter 9).

41 Excessive brake pedal travel

1   Partial brake system failure (Chapter 9).
2   Insufficient fluid in master cylinder (Chapters 1 and 9).
3   Air trapped in system (Chapter 9).

42 Dragging brakes

1   Incorrect adjustment of brake light switch (Chapter 9).
2   Master cylinder pistons not returning correctly (Chapter 9).
3   Caliper piston stuck (Chapter 9).
4   Restricted brakes lines or hoses (Chapter 9).
5   Incorrect parking brake adjustment (Chapter 9).

43 Grabbing or uneven braking action

1   Malfunction of proportioning valve (Chapter 9).
2   Binding brake pedal mechanism (Chapter 9).
3   Contaminated brake linings (Chapter 9).

44 Brake pedal feels spongy when depressed

1   Air in hydraulic lines (Chapter 9).
2   Master cylinder mounting bolts loose (Chapter 9).
3   Master cylinder defective (Chapter 9).

45 Brake pedal travels to the floor with little resistance

1   Little or no fluid in the master cylinder reservoir caused by leaking caliper piston(s) (Chapter 9).
2   Loose, damaged or disconnected brake lines (Chapter 9).

46 Parking brake does not hold

Parking brake improperly adjusted (Chapter 9).

Suspension and steering systems

47 Vehicle pulls to one side

1   Mismatched or uneven tires (Chapter 10).
2   Broken or sagging springs (Chapter 10).
3   Wheel alignment incorrect. Have the wheels professionally aligned.
4   Front brake dragging (Chapter 9).

48 Abnormal or excessive tire wear

1   Wheel alignment out-of-specification. Have the wheels professionally aligned.
2   Sagging or broken springs (Chapter 10).
3   Tire out-of-balance (Chapter 10).
4   Worn strut damper (Chapter 10).
5   Overloaded vehicle.
6   Tires not rotated regularly.

49 Wheel makes a thumping noise

1   Blister or bump on tire (Chapter 10).
2   Improper strut damper action (Chapter 10).

50 Shimmy, shake or vibration

1   Tire or wheel out-of-balance or out-of-round (Chapter 10).
2   Loose or worn wheel bearings (Chapter 10).
3   Worn tie-rod ends (Chapter 10).
4   Worn balljoints (Chapters 1 and 10).
5   Excessive wheel runout (Chapter 10).
6   Blister or bump on tire (Chapter 10).

51 Hard steering

1   Lack of lubrication at balljoints and/or tie-rod ends (Chapter 10).
2   Wheel alignment out-of-specifications. Have the wheels professionally aligned.
3   Low tire pressure(s) (Chapter 1).
4   Worn steering gear (Chapter 10).

52 Poor returnability of steering to center

1   Worn balljoints or tie-rod ends (Chapter 10).

2   Worn steering gear assembly (Chapter 10).
3   Wheel alignment out-of-specifications. Have the wheels professionally aligned.

53 Abnormal noise at the front end

1   Worn balljoints or tie-rod ends (Chapter 10).
2   Damaged shock absorber mounting (Chapter 10).
3   Worn control arm bushings or tie-rod ends (Chapter 10).
4   Loose stabilizer bar (Chapter 10).
5   Loose wheel nuts (Chapter 1).
6   Loose suspension bolts (Chapter 10).

54 Wander or poor steering stability

1   Mismatched or uneven tires (Chapter 10).
2   Lack of lubrication at balljoints and tie-rod ends (Chapters 1 and 10).
3   Worn shock absorber assemblies (Chapter 10).
4   Loose stabilizer bar (Chapter 10).
5   Broken or sagging springs (Chapter 10).
6   Wheels out of alignment. Have the wheels professionally aligned.

55 Erratic steering when braking

1   Wheel bearings worn (Chapter 10).
2   Broken or sagging springs (Chapter 10).
3   Leaking wheel cylinder or caliper (Chapter 10).
4   Excessive brake disc runout (Chapter 9).

56 Excessive pitching and/or rolling around corners or during braking

1   Loose stabilizer bar (Chapter 10).
2   Worn strut dampers or mountings (Chapter 10).
3   Broken or sagging springs (Chapter 10).
4   Overloaded vehicle.

57 Suspension bottoms

1   Overloaded vehicle.
2   Sagging springs (Chapter 10).

58 Cupped tires

1   Front wheel or rear wheel alignment out-of-specifications. Have the wheels professionally aligned.
2   Worn shock absorbers (Chapter 10).
3   Wheel bearings worn (Chapter 10).
4   Excessive tire or wheel runout (Chapter 10).
5   Worn balljoints (Chapter 10).

59 Excessive tire wear on outside edge

1   Inflation pressures incorrect (Chapter 1).
2   Excessive speed in turns.
3   Wheel alignment incorrect (excessive toe-in). Have professionally aligned.
4   Suspension arm bent or twisted (Chapter 10).

60 Excessive tire wear on inside edge

1   Inflation pressures incorrect (Chapter 1).
2   Wheel alignment incorrect (toe-out). Have professionally aligned.
3   Loose or damaged steering components (Chapter 10).

61 Tire tread worn in one place

1   Tires out-of-balance.
2   Damaged or buckled wheel. Inspect and replace if necessary.
3   Defective tire (Chapter 1).

62 Excessive play or looseness in steering system

1   Wheel bearing(s) worn (Chapter 10).
2   Tie-rod end loose (Chapter 10).
3   Steering gear loose (Chapter 10).
4   Worn or loose steering intermediate shaft U-joint (Chapter 10).

63 Rattling or clicking noise in steering gear

1   Steering gear loose (Chapter 10).
2   Steering gear defective.

Chapter 1
Tune-up and routine maintenance

Contents

Specifications

Recommended lubricants and fluids

Note: *Listed here are manufacturer recommendations at the time this manual was written. Manufacturers occasionally upgrade their fluid and lubricant specifications, so check with your local auto parts store for current recommendations.*

Engine oil	
Type	API "certified for gasoline engines"
Viscosity	
Four-cylinder engine	SAE 5W-30
V6 engines	SAE 5W-20
Fuel	Unleaded gasoline, 87 octane
Automatic transaxle fluid	
2005 through 2007 models	
Taurus	Mercon V automatic transmission fluid
Ford Five Hundred/Mercury Montego	
Aisin AW21	XT-8-QAW (USA), CXT-8-LAW12 (Canada) automatic transmission fluid
CVT	XT-7-QCFT (USA), CXT-7-LCF12 (Canada) continuously variable chain transmission fluid
2008 models	Mercon V automatic transmission fluid
2009 models	
Early build	MERCON V Automatic Transmission Fluid
Late build	MERCON LV Automatic Transmission Fluid
2010 and later models	MERCON LV Automatic Transmission Fluid

Caution: *Do not mix MERCON V and MERCON LV fluids. Transaxle damage could occur.*

Recommended lubricants and fluids (continued)

Note: *Listed here are manufacturer recommendations at the time this manual was written. Manufacturers occasionally upgrade their fluid and lubricant specifications, so check with your local auto parts store for current recommendations.*

Transfer case (AWD models)	MERCON LV Automatic Transmission Fluid
Rear differential lubricant (AWD models)	SAE 80W-90 Premium Rear Axle Lubricant
Brake fluid	DOT 3 brake fluid

Engine coolant

2007 and earlier models	50/50 mixture of Motorcraft premium engine coolant (yellow colored) with blistering agent and distilled water
2008 through 2012 models	50/50 mixture of Motorcraft premium engine coolant (green colored) and distilled water
2013 and later models	50/50 mixture of Motorcraft premium engine coolant (orange colored) and distilled water

Caution: *Do not mix coolants of different colors. Doing so might damage the cooling system and/or the engine. The manufacturer specifies either a green colored coolant or an orange colored coolant to be used in these systems, depending on what was originally installed in the vehicle.*

Power steering system	MERCON V automatic transmission fluid

Capacities*

Engine oil (including filter)

Four-cylinder engine	5.7 quarts	5.4 liters
V6 engines	6.0 quarts	5.7 liters

Coolant

2007 and earlier models		
Without auxiliary heater	Up to 10.6 quarts	Up to 10.0 liters
With auxiliary heater	Up to 12.7 quarts	Up to 12.0 liters
2008 through 2012 models		
Without auxiliary heater	Up to 11.9 quarts	Up to 10.5 liters
With auxiliary heater	Up to 13.2 quarts	Up to 12.5 liters
2013 and later models	Up to 11.1 quarts	Up to 10.3 liters

Automatic transaxle (dry fill)

Ford Five Hundred/Mercury Montego		
Aisin AW21	Up to 7.4 quarts	7.0 liters
CVT	10 quarts	9.6 liters
Taurus		
Four-cylinder models (6F35)	Up to 9 quarts	Up to 8.5 liters
V6 models		
6F50	Up to 10.9 quarts	Up to 10.3 liters
6F55	Up to 11.6 quarts	Up to 11.0 liters

Note: *Since this is a dry-fill specification, the amount required during a routine fluid change will be substantially less. The best way to determine the amount of fluid to add during a routine fluid change is to measure the amount drained. Begin the refill procedure by initially adding 1/3 of the amount drained. Then, with the engine running, add 1/2-pint at a time (cycling the shifter through each gear position between additions) until the level is correct on the dipstick. It is important to not overfill the transaxle. You will, however, need to purchase a few extra quarts, since the fluid replacement procedure involves flushing the torque converter (see Section 23).*

Transfer case (AWD models)	Up to 18 ounces	Up to 0.53 liter
Rear differential (AWD models)	Up to 2.43 pints	Up to 1.15 liters

** All capacities approximate. Add as necessary to bring up to appropriate level.*

Ignition system

Spark plug type and gap

Type		
Four-cylinder engine	Motorcraft 12405 or equivalent	
3.0L engine		
Early production	Motorcraft AGSF-32WM or equivalent	
Later production	Motorcraft AGSF-32N or equivalent	
3.5L engine	Motorcraft 12405 or equivalent	
Gap		
Four-cylinder engine	0.031 inch	0.8 mm
3.0L V6 engine	0.052 to 0.056 inch	1.32 to 1.42 mm
3.5L engine		
2013 and earlier models	0.051 to 0.057 inch	1.29 to 1.45 mm
2014 models	0.051 inch	1.295 mm

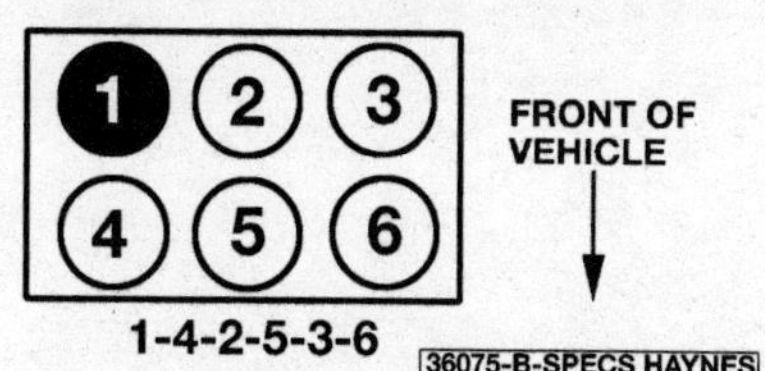

Engine firing order
   Four-cylinder engine 1-3-4-2
   V6 engines 1-4-2-5-3-6

Brakes
Disc brake pad lining thickness (minimum) .... 1/8 inch   3 mm

Torque specifications

Note: *One foot-pound (ft-lb) of torque is equivalent to 12 inch-pounds (in-lbs) of torque. Torque values below approximately 15 ft-lbs are expressed in inch-pounds, because most foot-pound torque wrenches are not accurate at these smaller values.*

	Ft-lbs (unless otherwise indicated)	Nm
Engine oil drain plug	20	27
Automatic transaxle drain plug		
Aisin AW2	35	47
CVT	18	25
6F35 (4-cylinder models)	106 in-lbs	12
6F50/6F55 (V6 models)	80 in-lbs	9
Automatic transaxle fill plug		
Aisin AW21	29	39
CVT	26	35
CVT transaxle pressure filter bolts	89 in-lbs	10
CVT fluid cooler tube flange bolt	132 in-lbs	15
CVT fluid pan bolts	108 in-lbs	12
Automatic transaxle oil leveling plug (four-cylinder models - 6F35)	71 in-lbs	8
Rear differential cover bolts (AWD)	17	23
Rear differential check/fill plug (AWD)	21	29
Transfer case check/fill plug	177 in-lbs	20
Spark plugs		
Four-cylinder engine	106 in-lbs	12
V6 engines	133 in-lbs	15
Drivebelt tensioner bolts	18	25
Wheel lug nuts	100	135

Typical engine compartment components (3.5L V6 engine)

1	*Automatic transaxle fluid filler tube*	*5*	*Air filter housing*	*8*	*Windshield washer fluid reservoir*
2	*Brake fluid reservoir*	*6*	*Radiator hose*	*9*	*Engine oil filler cap*
3	*Battery*	*7*	*Engine oil dipstick*	*10*	*Coolant expansion tank*
4	*Fuse/relay block*				

Typical engine compartment underside components (3.5L V6 engine)

1 Engine oil filter
2 Driveaxle boot
3 Front disc brake caliper
4 Engine oil drain plug
5 Automatic transaxle drain plug
6 Exhaust system
7 Drivebelt

Typical rear underside components (2WD)

1 Rear disc brake caliper
2 Muffler
3 Coil springs
4 Stabilizer bar
5 Exhaust system hanger
6 Shock absorbers
7 Parking brake cables
8 Fuel tank

1 Maintenance schedule

The maintenance intervals in this manual are provided with the assumption that you, not the dealer, will be doing the work. These are the minimum maintenance intervals recommended by the factory for vehicles that are driven daily. If you wish to keep your vehicle in peak condition at all times, you may wish to perform some of these procedures even more often. Because frequent maintenance enhances the efficiency, performance and resale value of your car, we encourage you to do so. If you drive in dusty areas, tow a trailer, idle or drive at low speeds for extended periods or drive for short distances (less than four miles) in below freezing temperatures, shorter intervals are also recommended.

When your vehicle is new, it should be serviced by a factory authorized dealer service department to protect the factory warranty. In many cases, the initial maintenance check is done at no cost to the owner.

Every 250 miles (400 km) or weekly, whichever comes first

Check the engine oil level (Section 4)
Check the engine coolant level (Section 4)
Check the brake fluid level (Section 4)
Check the windshield washer fluid level (Section 4)
Check the power steering fluid level (Section 4)
Check the tires and tire pressures (Section 5)

Every 3000 miles (4800 km) or 3 months, whichever comes first

All items listed above plus:
Change the engine oil and oil filter (Section 6)

Every 7500 miles (12,000 km) or 6 months, whichever comes first

All items listed above plus:
10 Inspect (and replace, if necessary) the windshield wiper blades (Section 7)
Check and service the battery (Section 8)
Check the cooling system (Section 9)
Rotate the tires (Section 10)
Check the seat belts (Section 11)

Every 15,000 miles (24,000 km) or 12 months, whichever comes first

All items listed above plus:
Check the automatic transaxle fluid level (Section 4)
Check all underhood hoses (Section 12)
Inspect the brake system (Section 13)*
Inspect the suspension, steering and driveaxle boots (Section 14)*
Check the fuel system (Section 15)
Check the transfer case lubricant level (AWD models) (Section 16)
Check (and replace, if necessary) the air filter (Section 17)*
Replace the cabin air filter (Section 18)

Every 30,000 miles (48,000 km) or 24 months, whichever comes first

All items listed above plus:
Check the exhaust system (Section 19)
Service the cooling system (drain, flush and refill) (Section 20)
Change the brake fluid (Section 21)
Check/adjust the engine drivebelts (Section 22)

Every 60,000 miles (72,420 km) or 48 months, whichever comes first

Replace the automatic transaxle fluid (Section 23)**
Replace the rear differential lubricant (AWD) (Section 24)**
Check (and replace, if necessary) the spark plugs (conventional, non-platinum or iridium type) (Section 26)

Every 100,000 miles (160,000 km)

Replace the spark plugs (iridium or platinum-tipped type) (Section 26)

* This item is affected by "severe" operating conditions as described below. If your vehicle is operated under "severe" conditions, perform all maintenance indicated with an asterisk (*) at 3000 mile/3 month intervals. Severe conditions are indicated if you mainly operate your vehicle under one or more of the following conditions:
Operating in dusty areas
Towing a trailer
Idling for extended periods and/or low speed operation
Operating when outside temperatures remain below freezing and when most trips are less than 4 miles

**If operated under one or more of the following conditions, change the automatic transaxle fluid and differential lubricant every 30,000 miles:
Operating in dusty areas
In heavy city traffic where the outside temperature regularly reaches 90-degrees F (32-degrees C) or higher
In hilly or mountainous terrain
On flex-fuel models, using E85 fuel more than 50% of the time

2 Introduction

1   This Chapter is designed to help the home mechanic maintain the Ford Five Hundred, Ford Taurus, Mercury Montego or Mercury Sable with the goals of maximum performance, economy, safety and reliability in mind.

2   Included is a master maintenance schedule, followed by procedures dealing specifically with each item on the schedule. Visual checks, adjustments, component replacement and other helpful items are included. Refer to the accompanying illustrations of the engine compartment and the underside of the vehicle for the locations of various components.

3   Servicing the vehicle in accordance with the mileage/time maintenance schedule and the step-by-step procedures will result in a planned maintenance program that should produce a long and reliable service life. Keep in mind that it is a comprehensive plan, so maintaining some items but not others at the specified intervals will not produce the same results.

4   As you service the vehicle, you will discover that many of the procedures can - and should - be grouped together because of the nature of the particular procedure you're performing or because of the close proximity of two otherwise unrelated components to one another.

5   For example, if the vehicle is raised for chassis lubrication, you should inspect the exhaust, suspension, steering and fuel systems while you're under the vehicle. When you're rotating the tires, it makes good sense to check the brakes since the wheels are already removed. Finally, let's suppose you have to borrow or rent a torque wrench. Even if you only need it to tighten the spark plugs, you might as well check the torque of as many critical fasteners as time allows.

6   The first step in this maintenance program is to prepare yourself before the actual work begins. Read through all the procedures you're planning to do, then gather up all the parts and tools needed. If it looks like you might run into problems during a particular job, seek advice from a mechanic or an experienced do-it-yourselfer.

Owner's Manual and VECI label information

7   Your vehicle owner's manual was written for your year and model and contains very specific information on component locations, specifications, fuse ratings, part numbers, etc. The Owner's Manual is an important resource for the do-it-yourselfer to have; if one was not supplied with your vehicle, it can generally be ordered from a dealer parts department.

8   Among other important information, the Vehicle Emissions Control Information (VECI) label contains specifications and procedures for applicable tune-up adjustments and, in some instances, spark plugs (see Chapter 6 for more information on the VECI label). The information on this label is the exact maintenance data recommended by the manufac-turer. This data often varies by intended operating altitude, local emissions regulations, month of manufacture, etc.

9   This Chapter contains procedural details, safety information and more ambitious maintenance intervals than you might find in manufacturer's literature. However, you may also find procedures or specifications in your Owner's Manual or VECI label that differ with what's printed here. In these cases, the Owner's Manual or VECI label can be considered correct, since it is specific to your particular vehicle.

3 Tune-up general information

1   The term tune-up is used in this manual to represent a combination of individual operations rather than one specific procedure.

2   If, from the time the vehicle is new, the routine maintenance schedule is followed closely and frequent checks are made of fluid levels and high wear items, as suggested throughout this manual, the engine will be kept in relatively good running condition and the need for additional work will be minimized.

3   More likely than not, however, there will be times when the engine is running poorly due to lack of regular maintenance. This is even more likely if a used vehicle, which has not received regular and frequent maintenance checks, is purchased. In such cases, an engine tune-up will be needed outside of the regular routine maintenance intervals.

4   The first step in any tune-up or diagnostic procedure to help correct a poor running engine is a cylinder compression check. A compression check (see Chapter 2C) will help determine the condition of internal engine components and should be used as a guide for tune-up and repair procedures. If, for instance, a compression check indicates serious internal engine wear, a conventional tune-up will not improve the performance of the engine and would be a waste of time and money. Because of its importance, the compression check should be done by someone with the proper equipment and the knowledge to use it properly.

5   The following procedures are those most often needed to bring a generally poor running engine back into a proper state of tune.

Minor tune-up

Check all engine related fluids (Section 4)
Clean, inspect and test the battery
  (Section 8)
Check the cooling system (Section 9)
Check all underhood hoses (Section 12)
Check the fuel system (Section 15)
Check the air filter (Section 17)
Check the drivebelt (Section 22)

Major tune-up

Note: *All items listed under Minor tune-up, plus . . .*
  Replace the air filter (Section 17)
  Replace the PCV valve (See Chapter 6)
  Replace the spark plugs (Section 26)

4 Fluid level checks (every 250 miles or weekly)

1   Fluids are an essential part of the lubrication, cooling, brake and windshield washer systems. Because the fluids gradually become depleted and/or contaminated during normal operation of the vehicle, they must be periodically replenished. See "Recommended lubricants and fluids" in this Chapter's Specifications before adding fluid to any of the following components.
Note: *The vehicle must be on level ground when fluid levels are checked.*

Engine oil

2   The oil level is checked with a dipstick, which is attached to the engine block (**see illustration**). The dipstick extends through a metal tube down into the oil pan.

3   The oil level should be checked before the vehicle has been driven, or about 5 minutes after the engine has been shut off. If the oil is checked immediately after driving the vehicle, some of the oil will remain in the upper part of the engine, resulting in an inaccurate reading on the dipstick.

4   Pull the dipstick out of the tube and wipe all the oil from the end with a clean rag or paper towel. Insert the clean dipstick all the way back into the tube and pull it out again. Note the oil at the end of the dipstick. At its highest point, the level should be between the MIN and MAX marks on the dipstick (**see illustration**).

5   It takes one quart of oil to raise the level from the MIN mark to the MAX mark on the dipstick. Do not allow the level to drop below the MIN mark or oil starvation may cause engine damage. Conversely, overfilling the engine (adding oil above the MAX mark) may cause oil fouled spark plugs, oil leaks or oil seal failures. Maintaining the oil level above the MAX mark can cause excessive oil consumption.

6   To add oil, remove the filler cap from the valve cover (**see illustration 4.2**). After adding oil, wait a few minutes to allow the level to stabilize, then pull out the dipstick and check the level again. Add more oil if required. Install the filler cap and tighten it by hand only.

7   Checking the oil level is an important preventive maintenance step. A consistently low oil level indicates oil leakage through damaged seals, defective gaskets or past worn rings or valve guides. If the oil looks milky in color or has water droplets in it, the cylinder head gasket(s) may be blown or the head(s) or block may be cracked. The engine should be checked immediately. The condition of the oil should also be checked. Whenever you check the oil level, slide your thumb and index finger up the dipstick before wiping off the oil. If you see small dirt or metal particles clinging to the dipstick, the oil should be changed (see Section 6).

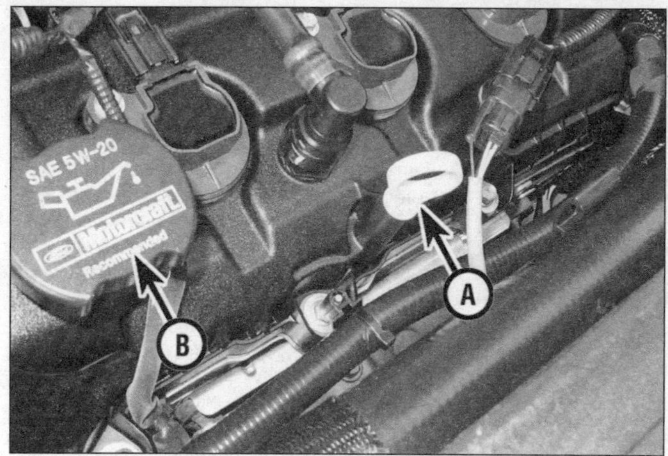

4.2 Engine oil dipstick (A) and oil filler cap (B) locations - 3.5L engine

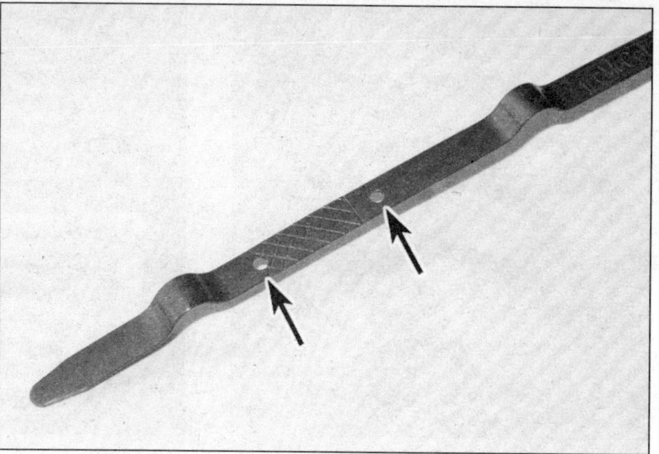

4.4 The oil level should be in the safe range - if it's below the MIN or ADD mark, add enough oil to bring it up to or near the MAX or FULL mark

4.8 The cooling system expansion tank is located at the right side of the engine compartment

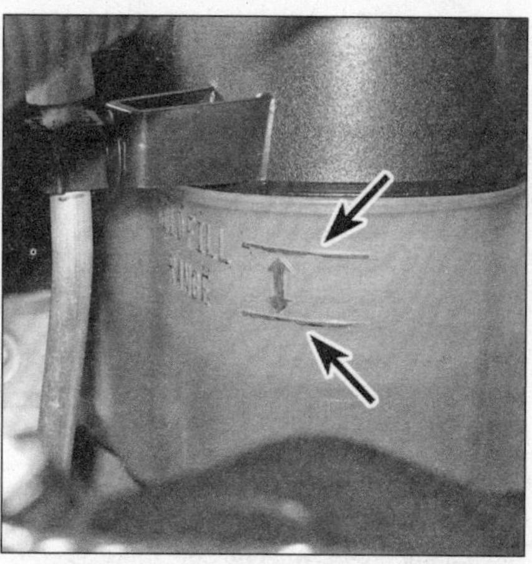

4.10 When the engine is cold, the coolant level should be in the COLD FILL range

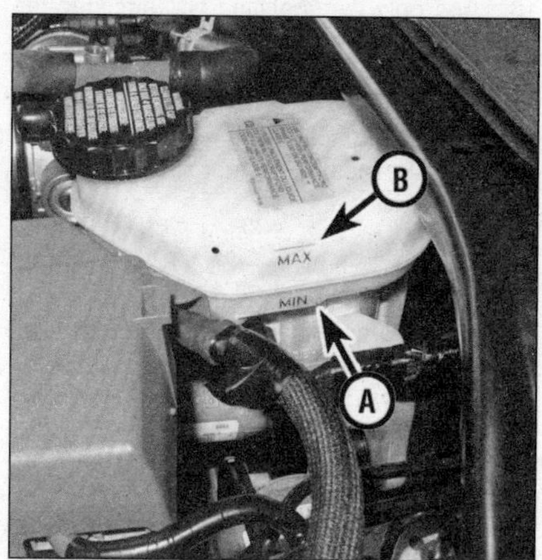

4.16 The brake fluid level should be kept between the MIN (A) and MAX (B) marks on the translucent plastic reservoir

Engine coolant

Warning: *Do not allow antifreeze to come in contact with your skin or painted surfaces of the vehicle. Flush contaminated areas immediately with plenty of water. Don't store new coolant or leave old coolant lying around where it's accessible to children or pets - they're attracted by its sweet smell. Ingestion of even a small amount of coolant can be fatal! Wipe up garage floor and drip pan spills immediately. Keep antifreeze containers covered and repair cooling system leaks as soon as they're noticed.*

8   All vehicles covered by this manual are equipped with a pressurized coolant recovery system. A plastic expansion tank located at the right front corner of the engine compartment is connected by hoses to the cooling system **(see illustration)**. As the engine heats up during operation, the expanding coolant fills the tank.

9   The coolant level in the tank should be checked regularly.

Warning: *Do not remove the expansion tank cap to check the coolant level when the engine is warm!*

10   The level in the tank varies with the temperature of the engine. When the engine is cold, the coolant level should be at the COLD FULL mark on the reservoir. If it isn't, remove the cap from the tank and add a 50/50 mixture of ethylene glycol-based antifreeze and water **(see illustration)**.

11   Drive the vehicle, let the engine cool completely then recheck the coolant level. Don't use rust inhibitors or additives. If only a small amount of coolant is required to bring the system up to the proper level, water can be used. However, repeated additions of water will dilute the antifreeze and water solution. In order to maintain the proper ratio of antifreeze and water, always top up the coolant level with the correct mixture. An empty plastic milk jug or bleach bottle makes an excellent container for mixing coolant.

12   If the coolant level drops consistently, there may be a leak in the system. Inspect the radiator, hoses, filler cap, drain plugs and water pump (see Section 9). If no leaks are noted, have the expansion tank cap pressure tested by a service station.

13   If you have to remove the expansion tank cap wait until the engine has cooled completely, then wrap a thick cloth around the cap and unscrew it slowly, stopping if you hear a hissing noise. If coolant or steam escapes, let the engine cool down longer, then remove the cap.

14   Check the condition of the coolant as well. If it's brown or rust colored, the system should be drained, flushed and refilled. Even if the coolant appears to be normal, the corrosion inhibitors wear out, so it must be replaced at the specified intervals.

Brake fluid

15   The brake master cylinder is mounted on the front of the power booster unit in the engine compartment.

16   To check the fluid level, simply look at the MAX and MIN marks on the brake fluid reservoir **(see illustration)**.

17   If the level is low, wipe the top of the reservoir cover with a clean rag to prevent contamination of the brake system before lifting the cover.

4.23 The windshield/rear window washer fluid reservoir is located in the right front corner of the engine compartment

4.29 At normal operating temperature, the power steering fluid level should be between the MAX (A) and MIN (B) marks

18   Add only the specified brake fluid to the reservoir (refer to "Recommended lubricants and fluids" in this Chapter's Specifications, or to your owner's manual). Mixing different types of brake fluid can damage the system. Fill the brake master cylinder reservoir only to the MAX line.

Warning: *Use caution when filling the reservoir - brake fluid can harm your eyes and damage painted surfaces. Do not use brake fluid that is more than one year old or has been left open. Brake fluid absorbs moisture from the air. Excess moisture can cause a dangerous loss of braking.*

19   While the reservoir cap is removed, inspect the master cylinder reservoir for contamination. If deposits, dirt particles or water droplets are present, the system should be drained and refilled.

20   After filling the reservoir to the proper level, make sure the lid is properly seated to prevent fluid leakage.

21   The fluid in the brake master cylinder will drop slightly as the brake pads at each wheel wear down during normal operation. If the master cylinder requires repeated replenishing to keep it at the proper level, this is an indication of leakage in the brake system, which should be corrected immediately. If the brake system shows an indication of leakage check all brake lines and connections, along with the calipers and booster (see Section 13 for more information).

22   If, upon checking the brake master cylinder fluid level, you discover the reservoir empty or nearly empty, the systems should be bled (see Chapter 9).

Windshield washer fluid

23   Fluid for the windshield washer system is stored in a plastic reservoir located at the right front of the engine compartment **(see illustration)**.

24   In milder climates, plain water can be used in the reservoir, but it should be kept no more than 2/3 full to allow for expansion if the water freezes. In colder climates, use windshield washer system antifreeze, available at any auto parts store, to lower the freezing point of the fluid. Mix the antifreeze with water in accordance with the manufacturer's directions on the container.

Caution: *Do not use cooling system antifreeze - it will damage the vehicle's paint.*

Power steering fluid

Note: *Some later models are equipped with electronic power assist and do not use power steering fluid.*

25   Check the power steering fluid level periodically to avoid steering system problems, such as damage to the pump.

Caution: *DO NOT hold the steering wheel against either stop (extreme left or right turn) for more than five seconds. If you do, the power steering pump could be damaged.*

26   The power steering reservoir, located at the right side of the engine compartment, has MIN and MAX fluid level marks on the side. The fluid level can be seen without removing the reservoir cap.

27   Park the vehicle on level ground and apply the parking brake.

28   Run the engine until it has reached normal operating temperature. With the engine at idle, turn the steering wheel back and forth about 10 times to get any air out of the steering system. Shut the engine off with the wheels in the straight-ahead position.

29   Note the fluid level on the side of the reservoir. It should be between the two marks **(see illustration)**.

30   Add small amounts of fluid until the level is correct.

Caution: *Do not overfill the reservoir. If too much fluid is added, remove the excess with a clean syringe or suction pump.*

31   Check the power steering hoses and connections for leaks and wear.

Automatic transaxle fluid

Note: *It isn't necessary to check the transaxle fluid weekly; every 15,000 miles or 12 months is adequate (unless fluid leakage is suspected).*

32   The level of the automatic transaxle fluid should be carefully maintained. Low fluid level can lead to slipping or loss of drive, while overfilling can cause foaming, loss of fluid and transaxle damage.

33   The transaxle fluid level should only be checked when the transaxle is hot (at its normal operating temperature). If the vehicle has just been driven over 10 miles (15 miles in a frigid climate), and the fluid temperature is 160 to 175-degrees F, the transaxle is hot.

Caution: *If the vehicle has just been driven for a long time at high speed or in city traffic in hot weather, or if it has been pulling a trailer, an accurate fluid level reading cannot be obtained. Allow the fluid to cool down for about 30 minutes.*

34   If the vehicle has not just been driven, park the vehicle on level ground, set the parking brake and start the engine. While the engine is idling, depress the brake pedal and move the selector lever through all the gear ranges, beginning and ending in Park.

Taurus models

V6 models (6F50/6F55 transaxles)

35   With the engine still idling, remove the dipstick from its tube. Check the level of the fluid on the dipstick and note its condition.

36   Wipe the fluid from the dipstick with a clean rag and reinsert it back into the filler tube until the cap seats.

37   Pull the dipstick out again and note the fluid level. The fluid level should be in the operating temperature range. If the level is at the low side of either range, remove the filler tube cap and add the specified automatic transmission fluid through the filler tube with a funnel.

Note: *To access the filler tube, the air filter housing must be removed (see Chapter 4).*

38   Add just enough of the recommended fluid to fill the transaxle to the proper level. It takes about one pint to raise the level from the low mark to the high mark when the fluid is hot, so add the fluid a little at a time and keep checking the level until it is correct.

39   The condition of the fluid should also be checked along with the level. If the fluid at the end of the dipstick is black or a dark reddish brown color, or if it emits a burned smell, the fluid should be changed (see Section 23). If you are in doubt about the condition of the fluid, purchase some new fluid and compare the two for color and smell.

Four-cylinder models (6F35 transaxle)

40   Remove the engine splash shield fasteners and shield.

41   Raise the vehicle on a hoist, keeping the vehicle in a level position, and place a drain pan under the transaxle.

42   With the engine still idling and in the park position, remove the oil leveling plug on the side of the transaxle **(see illustration)**. Check the level of the fluid - it should be even with the bottom of the plug hole.

43   If the level is low, remove the filler tube cap **(see illustration)** and add the specified automatic transmission fluid through the filler tube with a funnel until the fluid starts to drip out of the oil leveling plug.

Note: *Allow all excess fluid to drip out of the plug hole.*

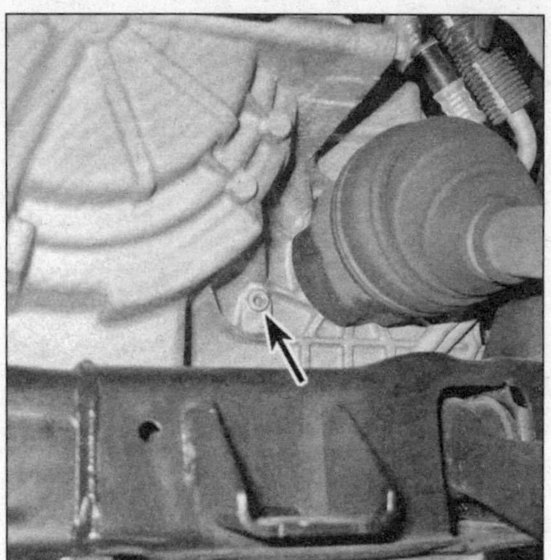

4.42 Location of the transaxle fluid leveling plug

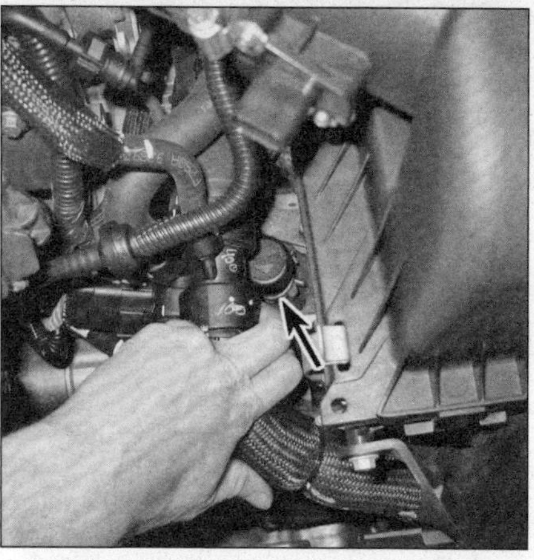

4.43 Remove the cap from the transaxle fill tube to add transaxle fluid

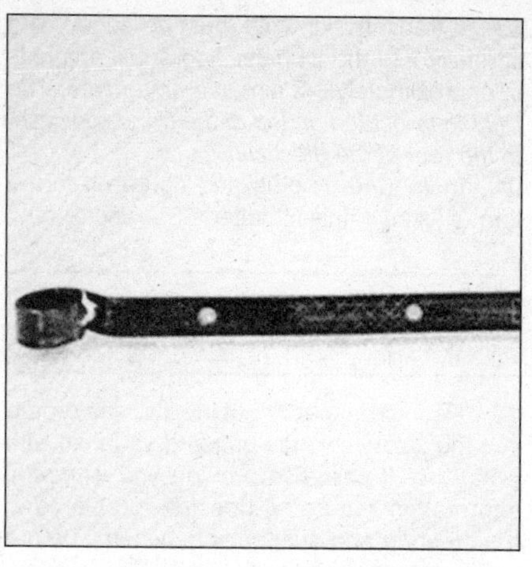

4.49 At operating temperature, the fluid level should be in the cross-hatched area of the dipstick

44 Once the fluid is even with the oil leveling plug hole, install the plug and tighten the plug to the torque listed in this Chapter's Specifications.

45 The condition of the fluid should also be checked along with the level. If the fluid is black or a dark reddish brown color, or if it emits a burned smell, the fluid should be changed (see Section 23). If you are in doubt about the condition of the fluid, purchase some new fluid and compare the two for color and smell.

Ford Five Hundred/Mercury Montego models

Aisin AW21 transaxle

Refer to illustration 4.49

47 Set the parking brake and with the engine idling, move the transmission shift lever through all the gear positions, finally placing the shift lever into PARK.

48 Wipe the fluid from the dipstick with a clean rag and reinsert it back into the filler tube until the cap seats.

49 Pull the dipstick out again and note the fluid level. With the transmission fluid temperature between 158 to 176 degrees F (70 to 80 degrees C), the fluid level should be in the operating temperature range **(see illustration)**. If the level is at the low side of either range, remove the filler tube cap and add the specified automatic transmission fluid through the filler tube with a funnel. **Note:** *The transmission fluid temperature must be checked using a scan tool for accuracy. Use an infrared laser temperature tool to check the fluid temperature if a scan tool is not available.* **Note:** *To access the filler tube, the air filter housing must be removed (see Chapter 4).*

50 Add just enough of the recommended fluid to fill the transaxle to the proper level. It takes about one pint to raise the level from the low mark to the high mark when the fluid is hot, so add the fluid a little at a time and keep checking the level until it is correct.

51 The condition of the fluid should also be checked along with the level. If the fluid at the end of the dipstick is black or a dark reddish brown color, or if it emits a burned smell, the fluid should be changed (see Section 23). If you are in doubt about the condition of the fluid, purchase some new fluid and compare the two for color and smell.

CVT transaxle

Checking the transmission fluid level

Note: *This procedure applies ONLY to vehicles that have recently been driving on the road with the transmission fluid in the normal operating range of 190 to 198 degrees F (88 to 92 degrees C). Do not add transmission fluid to the CVT transaxle at this temperature. The CVT transaxle fluid expansion characteristics are much different than other transmission fluids. Follow the procedure for adding transmission fluid to the CVT transaxle (Steps 58 through 64).*

52 Position the vehicle on a level surface.

53 Using a scan tool, check to make sure the transmission fluid temperature is in the normal driving range of 190 to 198 degrees F (88 to 92 degrees C). **Note:** *An infrared laser temperature tool can be used to check the transmission fluid for an approximate temperature reading also.*

54 Set the parking brake and with the engine idling, move the transmission shift lever through all the gear positions, finally placing the shift lever into PARK.

55 Remove the transmission fluid level dipstick and wipe it clean with a rag. Install the dipstick back into the tube and verify that it is completely seated at the bottom.

56 Remove the dipstick and check the level of the fluid. The fluid level should be indicated in the crosshatch area of the dipstick but not below or above **(see illustration 4.62)**. Double-check the temperature of the fluid.

57 If transmission fluid must be added, turn the engine OFF and allow the CVT transmission fluid to cool back down to 109 to 117 degrees F (43 to 47 degrees C). Follow Steps 58 to 64 to add transmission fluid.

Setting the transmission fluid level and adding CVT transmission fluid

Refer to illustration 4.62

58 Position the vehicle on a level surface.

59 Using a scan tool, check to make sure the transmission fluid temperature is in the fluid level setting range of 109 to 117 degrees F (43 to 47 degrees C). **Note:** *An infrared laser temperature tool can be used to check the fluid pan or body of the CVT transaxle to gain an approximate temperature reading also.*

60 Set the parking brake and with the engine idling, run the engine for 5 minutes, if necessary to bring the fluid temperature into range.

61 Double check that the transmission fluid temperature is in the correct range of 109 to 117 degrees F (43 to 47 degrees C) and move the transmission shift lever through all the gear positions, finally placing the shift lever into PARK.

62 Remove the dipstick, wipe it clean and check the level of the fluid. The fluid level should be at the bottom of the crosshatch area of the dipstick but not above **(see illustration)**.

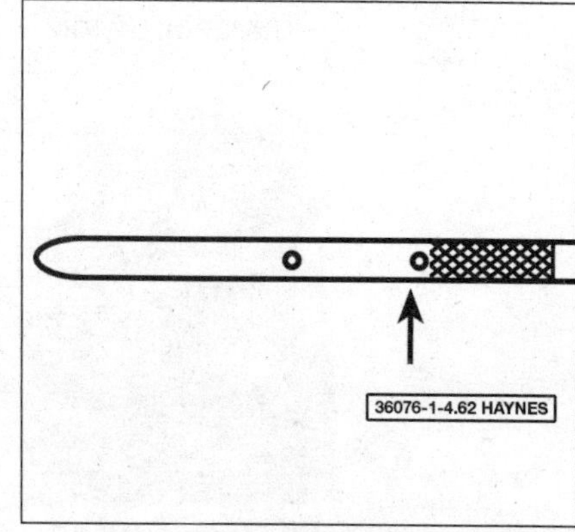

4.62 With the transaxle fluid temperature between 109 and 117-degrees F (43 to 47-degrees C), the fluid level should be at the bottom of the cross-hatched area, not above

63   If transmission fluid must be added, add carefully into the fill hole. Add small amounts of approximately 1/2 pint at a time. **Note:** *The fill hole is located on top of the transaxle case, to the rear of the dipstick.*

64   Install the fill plug and tighten it to the torque listed in this Chapter's Specifications.

5   Tire and tire pressure checks (every 250 miles or weekly)

1   Periodic inspection of the tires may spare you the inconvenience of being stranded with a flat tire. It can also provide you with vital information regarding possible problems in the steering and suspension systems before major damage occurs.

2   The original tires on this vehicle are equipped with 1/2-inch wide bands that will appear when tread depth reaches 1/16-inch, at which point they can be considered worn out. Tread wear can be monitored with a simple, inexpensive device known as a tread depth indicator **(see illustration)**.

3   Note any abnormal tread wear **(see illustration)**. Tread pattern irregularities such as cupping, flat spots and more wear on one side than the other are indications of front end alignment and/or balance problems. If any of these conditions are noted, take the vehicle to a tire shop or service station to correct the problem.

4   Look closely for cuts, punctures and embedded nails or tacks. Sometimes a tire will hold air pressure for a short time or leak down very slowly after a nail has embedded itself in the tread. If a slow leak persists, check the valve stem core to make sure it is tight **(see illustration)**. Examine the tread for an object that may have embedded itself in the tire or for a plug that may have begun to leak (radial tire punctures are repaired with a plug that is installed in a puncture). If a puncture is suspected, it can be easily verified by spraying a solution of soapy water onto the puncture area **(see illustration)**. The soapy solution will bubble if there is a leak. Unless the puncture is unusually large, a tire shop or service station can usually repair the tire.

5   Carefully inspect the inner sidewall of each tire for evidence of brake fluid leakage. If you see any, inspect the brakes immediately.

6   Correct air pressure adds miles to the life span of the tires, improves mileage and enhances overall ride quality. Tire pressure cannot be accurately estimated by looking at a tire, especially if it's a radial. A tire pressure gauge is essential. Keep an accurate gauge in the glove compartment. The pressure gauges attached to the nozzles of air hoses at gas stations are often inaccurate.

7   Always check tire pressure when the tires are cold. Cold, in this case, means the vehicle has not been driven over a mile in the three hours preceding a tire pressure check. A pressure rise of four to eight pounds is not uncommon once the tires are warm.

8   Unscrew the valve cap protruding from the wheel or hubcap and push the gauge

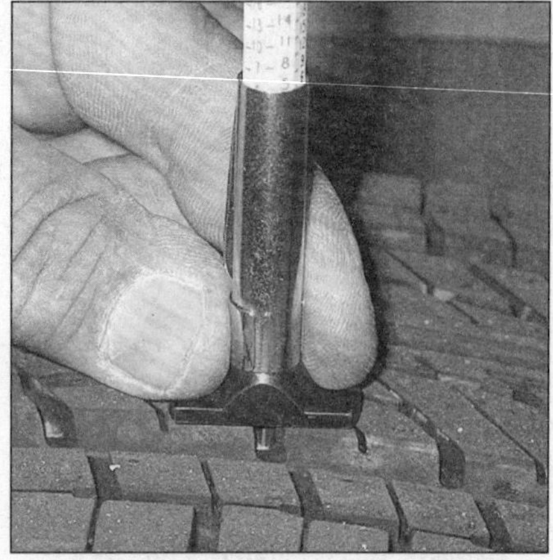

5.2 A tire tread depth indicator should be used to monitor tire wear - they are available at auto parts stores and service stations and cost very little

firmly onto the valve stem **(see illustration)**. Note the reading on the gauge and compare the figure to the recommended tire pressure shown on the tire placard on the driver's side door. Be sure to reinstall the valve cap to keep dirt and moisture out of the valve stem mechanism. Check all four tires and, if necessary, add enough air to bring them up to the recommended pressure.

9   Don't forget to keep the spare tire inflated to the specified pressure (refer to the pressure molded into the tire sidewall).

UNDERINFLATION

INCORRECT TOE-IN OR EXTREME CAMBER

CUPPING

Cupping may be caused by:
- Underinflation and/or mechanical irregularities such as out-of-balance condition of wheel and/or tire, and bent or damaged wheel.
- Loose or worn steering tie-rod or steering idler arm.
- Loose, damaged or worn front suspension parts.

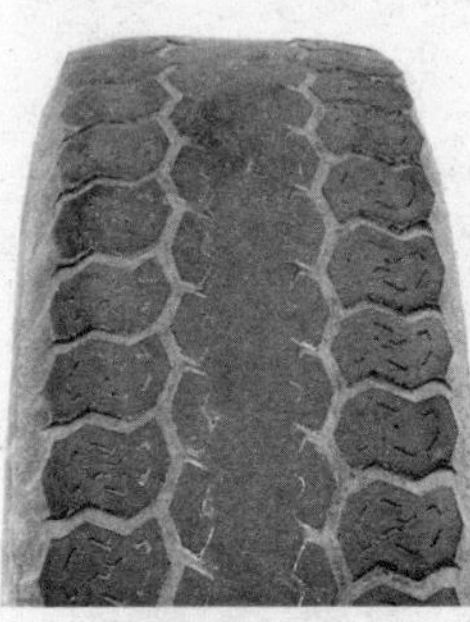

OVERINFLATION

FEATHERING DUE TO MISALIGNMENT

5.3 This chart will help you determine the condition of your tires, the probable cause(s) of abnormal wear and the corrective action necessary

5.4a If a tire loses air on a steady basis, check the valve core first to make sure it's snug (special inexpensive wrenches are commonly available at auto parts stores)

5.4b If the valve core is tight, raise the corner of the vehicle with the low tire and spray a soapy water solution onto the tread as the tire is turned slowly - slow leaks will cause small bubbles to appear

5.8 To extend the life of your tires, check the air pressure at least once a week with an accurate gauge (don't forget the spare!)

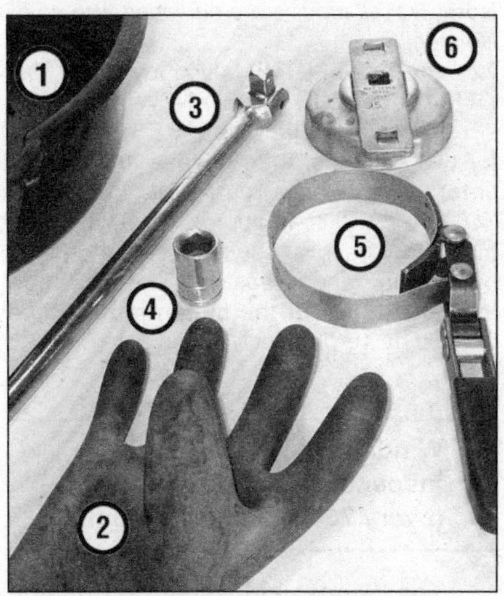

6.2 These tools are required when changing the engine oil and filter

1 **Drain pan** - *It should be fairly shallow in depth, but wide to prevent spills*
2 **Rubber gloves** - *When removing the drain plug and filter, you will get oil on your hands (the gloves will prevent burns)*
3 **Breaker bar** - *Sometimes the oil drain plug is tight, and a long breaker bar is needed to loosen it*
4 **Socket** – *To be used with the breaker bar or a ratchet (must be the correct size to fit the drain plug - six-point preferred)*
5 **Filter wrench** - *This is a metal band-type wrench, which requires clearance around the filter to be effective*
6 **Filter wrench** - *This type fits on the bottom of the filter and can be turned with a ratchet or breaker bar (different-size wrenches are available for different types of filters)*

6 Engine oil and filter change (every 3000 miles or 3 months)

Note: *Some models are equipped with an oil life indicator system that illuminates a light or message on the instrument panel when the system deems it necessary to change the oil. A number of factors are taken into consideration to determine when the oil should be considered worn out. Generally, this system will allow the vehicle to accumulate more miles between oil changes than the traditional 3000-mile interval, but we believe that frequent oil changes are cheap insurance and will prolong engine life. If you do decide not to change your oil every 3000 miles and rely on the oil life indicator instead, make sure you don't exceed 7,500 miles before the oil is changed, regardless of what the oil life indicator shows.*

1 Frequent oil changes are the most important preventive maintenance procedures that

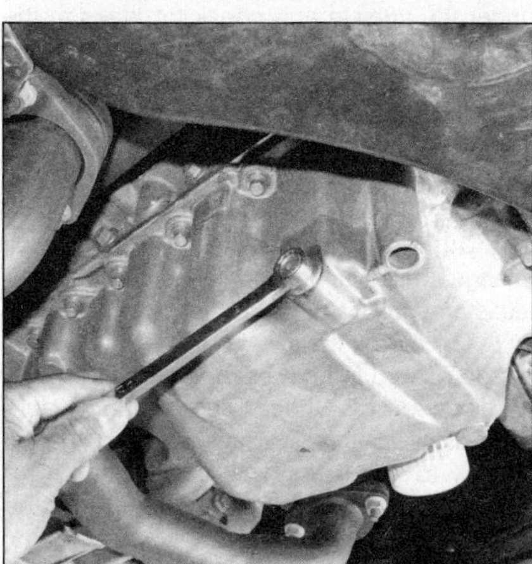

6.7 Use a proper size box-end wrench or socket to remove the oil drain plug and avoid rounding it off

can be done by the home mechanic. As engine oil ages, it becomes diluted and contaminated, which leads to premature engine wear.

2 Make sure that you have all the necessary tools before you begin this procedure **(see illustration)**. You should also have plenty of rags or newspapers handy for mopping up oil spills.

3 Access to the oil drain plug and filter will be improved if the vehicle can be lifted on a hoist, driven onto ramps or supported by jackstands.

Warning: *Do not work under a vehicle supported only by a jack - always use jackstands!*

4 If you haven't changed the oil on this vehicle before, get under it and locate the oil drain plug and the oil filter. The exhaust components will be warm as you work, so note how they are routed to avoid touching them when you are under the vehicle.

5 Start the engine and allow it to reach normal operating temperature - oil and sludge will flow out more easily when warm. If new oil, a filter or tools are needed, use the vehicle to go get them and warm up the engine/oil at the same time. Park on a level surface and shut off the engine when it's warmed up. Remove the oil filler cap from the valve cover.

6 Raise the vehicle and support it on jackstands. Make sure it is safely supported!

7 Being careful not to touch the hot exhaust components, position a drain pan under the plug in the bottom of the engine, then remove the plug **(see illustration)**. It's a good idea to wear a rubber glove while unscrewing the plug the final few turns to avoid being scalded by hot oil.

8 It may be necessary to move the drain pan slightly as oil flow slows to a trickle. Inspect the old oil for the presence of metal particles.

9 After all the oil has drained, wipe off the drain plug with a clean rag. Any small metal particles clinging to the plug would immediately contaminate the new oil.

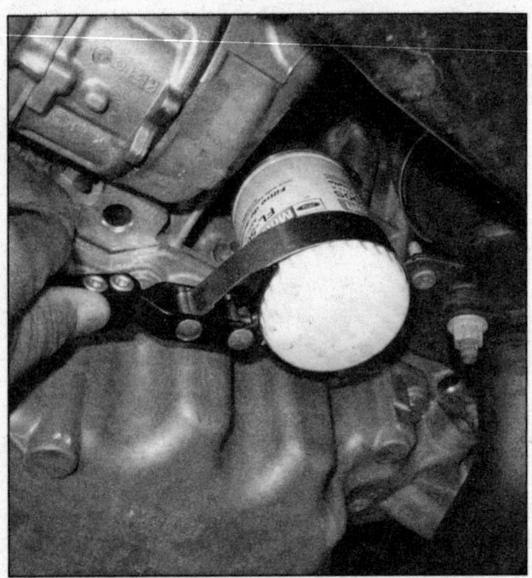

6.12 Use an oil filter wrench to remove the filter (four-cylinder engine shown)

6.15 Lubricate the oil filter gasket with clean engine oil before installing the filter on the engine

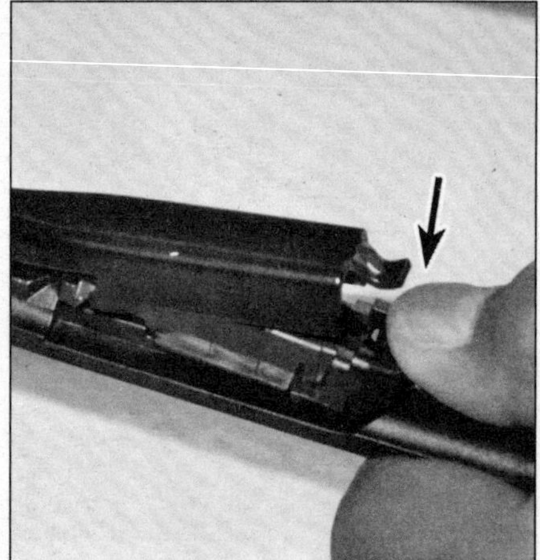

7.5a To release the blade holder, depress the locking tab downwards . . .

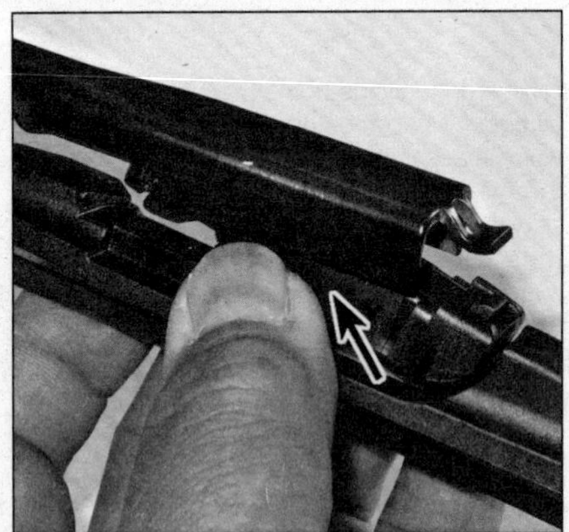

7.5b . . . then push the locking tabs inwards on each side and pull the wiper blade away from the arm

10   Clean the area around the drain plug opening, reinstall the plug and tighten it to the torque listed in this Chapter's Specifications.

11   Move the drain pan into position under the oil filter.

12   Loosen the oil filter by turning it counter-clockwise with a filter wrench **(see illustration)**. Any standard filter wrench will work. Some engines are equipped with a cartridge type oil filter. On these types, remove the oil filter cover and element.

13   Once the filter is loose, use your hands to unscrew it from the block. Just as the filter is detached from the block, immediately tilt the open end up to prevent the oil inside the filter from spilling out.

14   Using a clean rag, wipe off the mounting surface on the block. Also, make sure that none of the old gasket remains stuck to the mounting surface. It can be removed with a scraper if necessary.

15   Compare the old filter with the new one to make sure they are the same type. Smear some engine oil on the rubber gasket or O-ring seal of the new filter and screw it into place **(see illustration)**. On typical filters, overtightening the filter will damage the gasket, so don't use a filter wrench. Most filter manufacturers recommend tightening the filter by hand only. Normally they should be tightened 3/4-turn after the gasket contacts the block, but be sure to follow the directions on the filter or container. On cartridge type filters, install the new oil filter element and use the oil filter wrench to tighten the filter cover securely. Do not overtighten the oil filter cover.

16   Remove all tools and materials from under the vehicle, being careful not to spill the oil in the drain pan, then lower the vehicle.

17   Add new oil to the engine through the oil filler cap. Use a funnel to prevent oil from spilling onto the top of the engine. Pour four quarts of fresh oil into the engine. Wait a few minutes to allow the oil to drain into the pan, then check the level on the dipstick (see Section 4 if necessary). If the oil level is in the OK range, install the filler cap.

18   Start the engine and run it for about a minute. While the engine is running, look under the vehicle and check for leaks at the oil pan drain plug and around the oil filter. If either one is leaking, stop the engine and tighten the plug or filter slightly.

19   Wait a few minutes, then recheck the level on the dipstick. Add oil as necessary to bring the level into the OK range.

20   During the first few trips after an oil change, make it a point to check frequently for leaks and proper oil level.

21   The old oil drained from the engine cannot be reused in its present state and should be disposed of. Check with your local auto parts store, disposal facility or environmental agency to see if they will accept the oil for recycling. After the oil has cooled it can be drained into a container (capped plastic jugs, topped bottles, milk cartons, etc.) for transport to one of these disposal sites. Don't dispose of the oil by pouring it on the ground or down a drain!

Oil life monitor resetting

Note: *Not all models are equipped with an oil life monitor.*

22   Press the SETUP button to display "OIL LIFE XXX% HOLD RESET=NEW."

23   Press and hold the RESET button for two seconds, then release it. The indicator should now read "OIL LIFE SET TO 100%," which is approximately a 7,500-mile interval. This interval can be shortened by pressing and releasing the RESET button; each push of the button reduces the interval by 10-percent.

---

7   Windshield wiper blade inspection and replacement (every 7500 miles or 6 months)

1   The windshield wiper and blade assembly should be inspected periodically for damage, loose components and cracked or worn blade elements.

2   Road film can build up on the wiper blades and affect their efficiency, so they should be washed regularly with a mild detergent solution.

3   If the wiper blade elements are cracked, worn or warped, or no longer clean adequately, they should be replaced with new ones.

4   On 2007 and earlier models, lift the arm assembly away from the glass for clearance, rotate the wiper blade 90-degrees and slide the blade off of the arm.

5   On 2008 and later models, lift the arm assembly away from the glass for clearance, press locking tabs inwards, then slide the wiper blade assembly out of the hook in the end of the arm **(see illustrations)**.

6   Attach the new wiper to the arm. Connection can be confirmed by an audible click.

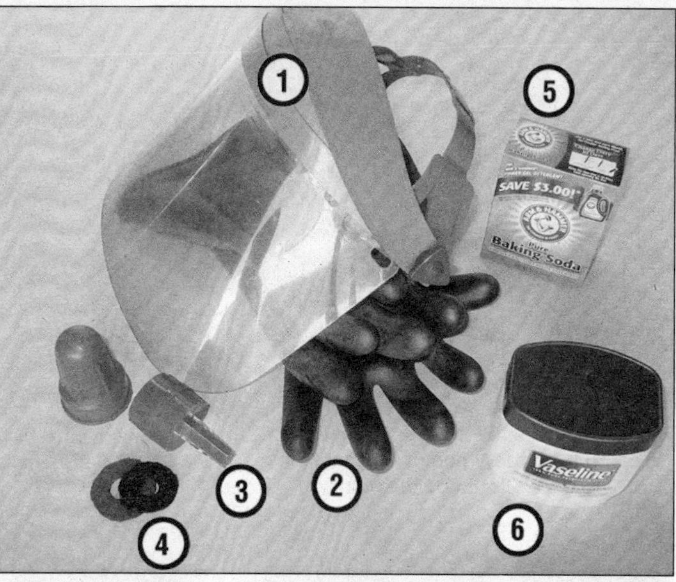

8.1 Tools and materials required for battery maintenance

1   ***Face shield/safety goggles*** *- When removing corrosion with a brush, the acidic particles can easily fly up into your eyes*

2   ***Rubber gloves*** *- Another safety item to consider when servicing the battery; remember that's acid inside the battery!*

3   ***Battery terminal/ cable cleaner*** *- This wire brush cleaning tool will remove all traces of corrosion from the battery and cable*

4   ***Treated felt washers*** *- Placing one of these on each terminal, directly under the cable end, will help prevent corrosion (be sure to get the correct type for side terminal batteries)*

5   ***Baking soda*** *- A solution of baking soda and water can be used to neutralize corrosion*

6   ***Petroleum jelly*** *- A layer of this on the battery terminal bolts will help prevent corrosion*

8.6a Battery terminal corrosion usually appears as light, fluffy powder

8.6b Removing a cable from the battery post with a wrench - sometimes a pair of special battery pliers are required for this procedure if corrosion has caused deterioration of the nut hex. Always remove the ground (-) cable first and hook it up last!

8.7a When cleaning the cable clamps, all corrosion must be removed (the inside of the clamp is tapered to match the taper on the post, so don't remove too much material)

---

8   Battery check, maintenance and charging (every 7500 miles or 6 months)

Warning: *Certain precautions must be followed when checking and servicing the battery. Hydrogen gas, which is highly flammable, is always present in the battery cells, so keep lighted tobacco and all other open flames and sparks away from the battery. The electrolyte inside the battery is actually diluted sulfuric acid, which will cause injury if splashed on your skin or in your eyes. It will also ruin clothes and painted surfaces. When removing the battery cables, always detach the negative cable first and hook it up last!*

1   A routine preventive maintenance program for the battery in your vehicle is the only way to ensure quick and reliable starts. But before performing any battery maintenance, make sure that you have the proper equipment necessary to work safely around the battery **(see illustration)**.

2   There are also several precautions that should be taken whenever battery maintenance is performed. Before servicing the battery, always turn the engine and all accessories off and disconnect the cables from the negative terminal of the battery (see Chapter 5).

3   The battery produces hydrogen gas, which is both flammable and explosive. Never create a spark, smoke or light a match around the battery. Always charge the battery in a ventilated area.

4   Electrolyte contains poisonous and corrosive sulfuric acid. Do not allow it to get in your eyes, on your skin on your clothes. Never ingest it. Wear protective safety glasses when working near the battery. Keep children away from the battery.

5   Note the external condition of the battery. If the positive terminal and cable clamp on your vehicle's battery is equipped with a rubber protector, make sure that it's not torn or damaged. It should completely cover the terminal. Look for any corroded or loose connections, cracks in the case or cover or loose hold-down clamps. Also check the entire length of each cable for cracks and frayed conductors.

6   If corrosion, which looks like white, fluffy deposits **(see illustration)** is evident, particularly around the terminals, the battery should be removed for cleaning. Loosen the cable clamp bolts with a wrench, being careful to remove the ground cable first, and slide them off the terminals **(see illustration)**. Then disconnect the hold-down clamp bolt and nut, remove the clamp and lift the battery from the engine compartment.

7   Clean the cable clamps thoroughly with a battery brush or a terminal cleaner and a solution of warm water and baking soda **(see illustration)**. Wash the terminals and the top of the battery case with the same solution but make sure that the solution doesn't get into

8.7b Regardless of the type of tool used to clean the battery posts, a clean, shiny surface should be the result

8.8 Make sure the battery hold-down fasteners are tight

Check for a chafed area that could fail prematurely.

Check for a soft area indicating the hose has deteriorated inside.

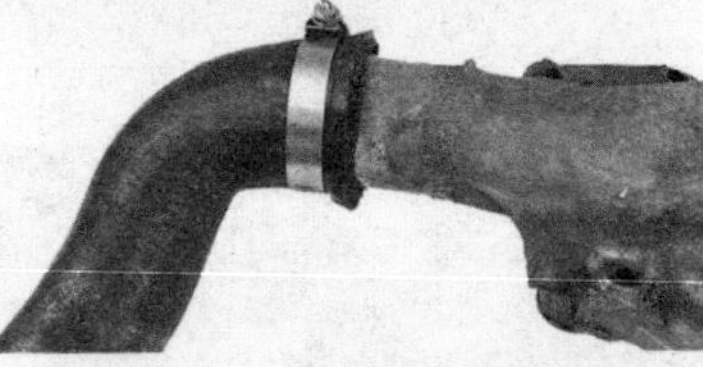

Overtightening the clamp on a hardened hose will damage the hose and cause a leak.

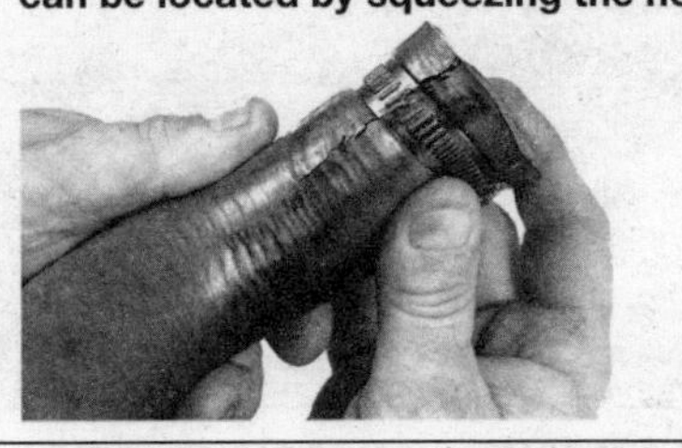

Check each hose for swelling and oil-soaked ends. Cracks and breaks can be located by squeezing the hose.

9.4 Hoses, like drivebelts, have a habit of failing at the worst possible time - to prevent the inconvenience of a blown radiator or heater hose, inspect them carefully as shown here

the battery. When cleaning the cables, terminals and battery top, wear safety goggles and rubber gloves to prevent any solution from coming in contact with your eyes or hands. Wear old clothes too - even diluted, sulfuric acid splashed onto clothes will burn holes in them. If the terminals have been extensively corroded, clean them up with a terminal cleaner **(see illustration)**. Thoroughly wash all cleaned areas with plain water.

8　Make sure that the battery tray is in good condition and the hold-down clamp fasteners are tight **(see illustration)**. If the battery is removed from the tray, make sure no parts remain in the bottom of the tray when the battery is reinstalled. When reinstalling the hold-down clamp bolts, do not overtighten them.

9　Information on removing and installing the battery can be found in Chapter 5. If you disconnected the cable(s) from the negative and/or positive battery terminals, the powertrain control module (PCM) must relearn its idle and fuel trim strategy for optimum driveability and performance (see Chapter 5 for this procedure). Information on jump starting can be found at the front of this manual. For more detailed battery checking procedures, refer to the *Haynes Automotive Electrical Manual*.

Cleaning

10　Corrosion on the hold-down components, battery case and surrounding areas can be removed with a solution of water and baking soda. Thoroughly rinse all cleaned areas with plain water.

11　Any metal parts of the vehicle damaged by corrosion should be covered with a zinc-based primer, then painted.

Charging

Warning: *When batteries are being charged, hydrogen gas, which is very explosive and flammable, is produced. Do not smoke or allow open flames near a charging or a recently charged battery. Wear eye protection when near the battery during charging. Also, make sure the charger is unplugged before connecting or disconnecting the battery from the charger.*

12　Slow-rate charging is the best way to restore a battery that's discharged to the point where it will not start the engine. It's also a good way to maintain the battery charge in a vehicle that's only driven a few miles between starts. Maintaining the battery charge is particularly important in the winter when the battery must work harder to start the engine and electrical accessories that drain the battery are in greater use.

13　It's best to use a one or two-amp battery charger (sometimes called a trickle charger). They are the safest and put the least strain on the battery. They are also the least expensive. For a faster charge, you can use a higher amperage charger, but don't use one rated more than 1/10th the amp/hour rating of the battery. Rapid boost charges that claim to restore the power of the battery in one to two hours are hardest on the battery and can damage batteries not in good condition. This type of charging should only be used in emergency situations.

14　The average time necessary to charge a battery should be listed in the instructions that come with the charger. As a general rule, a trickle charger will charge a battery in 12 to 16 hours.

9　Cooling system check (every 7,500 miles or 6 months)

1　Many major engine failures can be caused by a faulty cooling system.

2　The engine must be cold for the cooling system check, so perform the following procedure before the vehicle is driven for the day or after it has been shut off for at least three hours.

3　Remove the pressure-relief cap from the expansion tank at the right side of the engine compartment. Clean the cap thoroughly, inside and out, with clean water. The presence of rust or corrosion in the expansion tank means the coolant should be changed (see Section 20). The coolant inside the expansion tank should be relatively clean and transparent. If it's rust colored, drain the system and refill it with new coolant.

4　Carefully check the radiator hoses and the smaller diameter heater hoses (see illustrations in Chapter 3). Inspect each coolant hose along its entire length, replacing any hose which is cracked, swollen or deteriorated **(see illustration)**. Cracks will show up better if the hose is squeezed. Pay close attention to hose clamps that secure the hoses to cooling system components. Hose clamps can pinch and puncture hoses, resulting in coolant leaks.

5　Make sure that all hose connections are tight. A leak in the cooling system will usually show up as white or rust colored deposits on the area adjoining the leak. If wire-type clamps are used on the hoses, it may be a good idea to replace them with screw-type clamps.

6   Clean the front of the radiator and air conditioning condenser with compressed air, if available, or a soft brush. Remove all bugs, leaves, etc. embedded in the radiator fins. Be extremely careful not to damage the cooling fins or cut your fingers on them.

7   If the coolant level has been dropping consistently and no leaks are detectable, have the expansion tank cap and cooling system pressure checked at a service station.

10   Tire rotation
(every 7,500 miles or 6 months)

1   The tires should be rotated at the specified intervals and whenever uneven wear is noticed. Since the vehicle will be raised and the tires removed anyway, check the brakes also (see Section 13).

2   Radial tires must be rotated in a specific pattern **(see illustration)**. Don't include the spare tire in the rotation pattern.

3   Refer to the information in *Jacking and towing* at the front of this manual for the proper procedure to follow when raising the vehicle and changing a tire. If the brakes must be checked, don't apply the parking brake as stated.

4   The vehicle must be raised on a hoist or supported on jackstands to get all four wheels off the ground. Make sure the vehicle is safely supported!

5   After the rotation procedure is finished, check and adjust the tire pressures as necessary and be sure to check the lug nut tightness.

11   Seat belt check
(every 7,500 miles or 6 months)

1   Check seat belts, buckles, latch plates and guide loops for obvious damage and signs of wear.

2   See if the seat belt reminder light comes on when the key is turned to the Run or Start position. A chime should also sound.

3   The seat belts are designed to lock up during a sudden stop or impact, yet allow free movement during normal driving. Make sure the retractors return the belt against your chest while driving and rewind the belt fully when the buckle is unlatched.

4   If any of the above checks reveal problems with the seat belt system, replace parts as necessary.

12   Underhood hose check and
replacement (every 15,000 miles or 12 months)

Warning: *Replacement of air conditioning hoses must be left to a dealer service department or air conditioning shop that has the equipment to depressurize the system safely. Never remove air conditioning components or hoses until the system has been depressurized.*

General

1   High temperatures under the hood can cause deterioration of the rubber and plastic hoses used for engine, accessory and emission systems operation. Periodic inspection should be made for cracks, loose clamps, material hardening and leaks.

2   Information specific to the cooling system hoses can be found in Section 9.

3   Most (but not all) hoses are secured to the fittings with clamps. Where clamps are used, check to be sure they haven't lost their tension, allowing the hose to leak. If clamps aren't used, make sure the hose has not expanded and/or hardened where it slips over the fitting, allowing it to leak.

PCV system hose

4   To reduce hydrocarbon emissions, crankcase blow-by gas is vented through the PCV valve in the valve cover to the intake manifold via a rubber hose on most models. The blow-by gases mix with incoming air in the intake manifold before being burned in the combustion chambers.

5   Check the PCV hose for cracks, leaks and other damage. Remove the intake manifold (see Chapter 2A or 2B) and disconnect it from the valve cover then check the inside for obstructions. If it's clogged, clean it out with solvent.

Vacuum hoses

6   It's quite common for vacuum hoses, especially those in the emissions system, to be color coded or identified by colored stripes molded into them. Various systems require hoses with different wall thickness, collapse resistance and temperature resistance. When replacing hoses, be sure the new ones are made of the same material.

7   Often the only effective way to check a hose is to remove it completely from the vehicle. If more than one hose is removed, be sure to label the hoses and fittings to ensure correct installation.

8   When checking vacuum hoses, be sure to include any plastic T-fittings in the check. Inspect the fittings for cracks and the hose where it fits over each fitting for distortion, which could cause leakage.

9   A small piece of vacuum hose (1/4-inch inside diameter) can be used as a stethoscope to detect vacuum leaks. Hold one end of the hose to your ear and probe around vacuum hoses and fittings, listening for the hissing sound characteristic of a vacuum leak.
Warning: *When probing with the vacuum hose stethoscope, be careful not to come into contact with moving engine components such as drivebelts, the cooling fan, etc.*

Fuel hose

Warning: *Gasoline is flammable, so take extra precautions when you work on any part of the fuel system. Don't smoke or allow open flames or bare light bulbs near the*

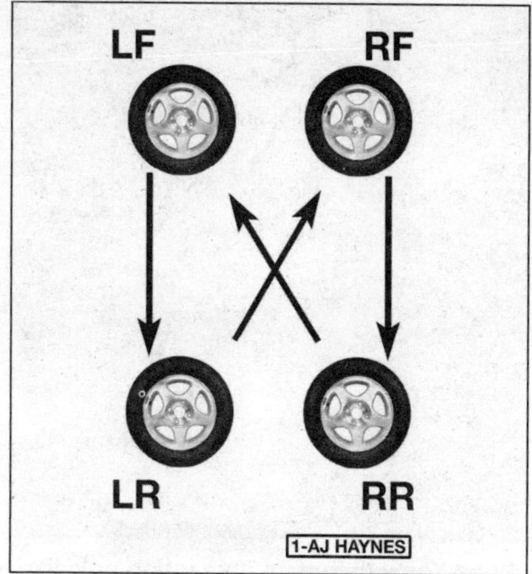

10.2 The recommended tire rotation pattern for these vehicles (FWD and AWD)

work area, and don't work in a garage where a gas-type appliance (such as a water heater or clothes dryer) is present. Since fuel is carcinogenic, wear fuel-resistant gloves when there's a possibility of being exposed to fuel, and, if you spill any fuel on your skin, rinse it off immediately with soap and water. Mop up any spills immediately and do not store fuel-soaked rags where they could ignite. The fuel system is under constant pressure, so, if any fuel lines are to be disconnected, the fuel pressure in the system must be relieved first (see Chapter 4 for more information). When you perform any kind of work on the fuel system, wear safety glasses and have a Class B type fire extinguisher on hand.

10   The fuel lines are usually under pressure, so if any fuel lines are to be disconnected be prepared to catch spilled fuel.
Warning: *Your vehicle is equipped with fuel injection and you must relieve the fuel system pressure before servicing the fuel lines. Refer to Chapter 4 for the fuel system pressure relief procedure.*

11   Check all flexible fuel lines for deterioration and chafing. Check especially for cracks in areas where the hose bends and just before fittings, such as where the fuel line attaches to the fuel rail.

12   When replacing a hose, use only hose that is specifically designed for your fuel injection system.

13   Some fuel lines use quick-connect fittings, which require a special tool to disconnect. See Chapter 4 for more information on these types of fittings.

Metal lines

14   Sections of metal line are often used for fuel line that runs underneath the vehicle. Check carefully to make sure the line isn't bent, crimped or cracked.

15   If a section of metal fuel line must be replaced, use seamless steel tubing only, since copper and aluminum tubing do not have the strength necessary to withstand vibration caused by the engine.

13.5a You will find an inspection hole like this in each caliper through which you can view the thickness of remaining friction material for the inner pad

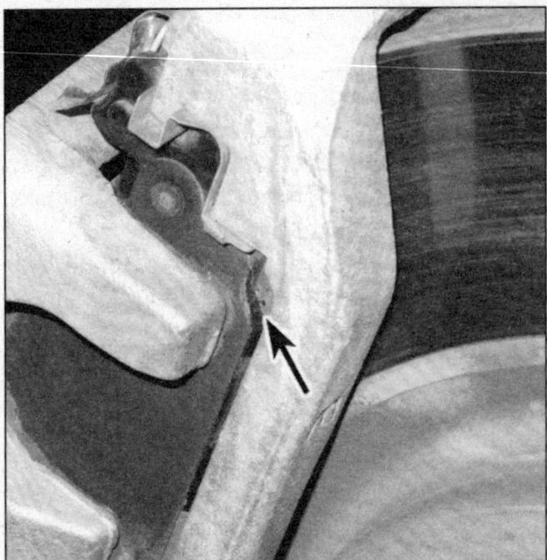

13.5b Check the thickness of the outer pad material, too

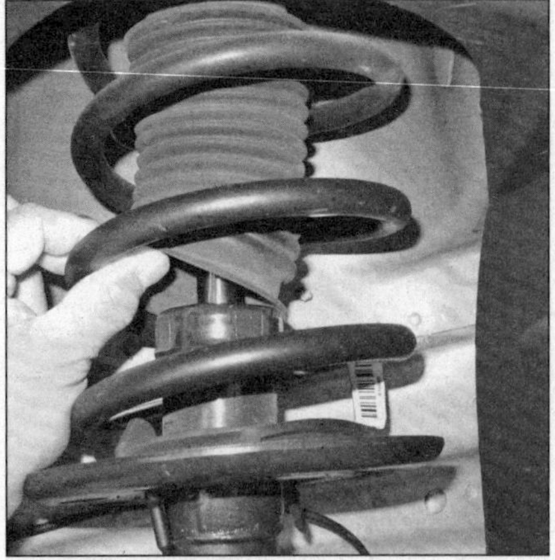

14.6 Check the shocks for leakage at the indicated area

16   Check the metal brake lines where they enter the master cylinder and brake proportioning unit (if used) for cracks in the lines and loose fittings. Any sign of brake fluid leakage calls for an immediate thorough inspection of the brake system.

13   Brake check (every 15,000 miles or 12 months)

Warning: *Dust created by the brake system is harmful to your health. Never blow it out with compressed air and don't inhale any of it. An approved filtering mask should be worn when working on brakes. Do not, under any circumstances, use petroleum-based solvents to clean brake parts. Use brake system cleaner only!*

1   The brakes should be inspected every time the wheels are removed or whenever a defect is suspected. Indications of a potential brake system problem include the vehicle pulling to one side when the brake pedal is depressed, noises coming from the brakes when they are applied, excessive brake pedal travel, a pulsating pedal and leakage of fluid, usually seen on the inside of the tire or wheel.

Note: *It is normal for a vehicle equipped with an Anti-lock Brake System (ABS) to exhibit brake pedal pulsations during severe braking conditions.*

Disc brakes

2   Disc brakes can be visually checked without removing any parts except the wheels. Remove the hub caps (if applicable) and loosen the wheel lug nuts a quarter turn each.

3   Raise the vehicle and place it securely on jackstands.

Warning: *Never work under a vehicle that is supported only by a jack!*

4   Remove the wheels. Now visible is the disc brake caliper which contains the pads. There is an outer brake pad and an inner pad.

Both must be checked for wear.

Note: *Usually the inner pad wears faster than the outer pad.*

5   Measure the thickness of the outer pad at each end of the caliper and the inner pad through the inspection hole in the caliper body **(see illustrations)**. Compare the measurement with the limit given in this Chapter's Specifications; if any brake pad thickness is less than specified, then all brake pads must be replaced (see Chapter 9).

6   If you're in doubt as to the exact pad thickness or quality, remove them for measurement and further inspection (see Chapter 9).

7   Check the disc for score marks, wear and burned spots. If any of these conditions exist, the disc should be removed for servicing or replacement (see Chapter 9).

8   Before installing the wheels, check all the brake lines and hoses for damage, wear, deformation, cracks, corrosion, leakage, bends and twists, particularly in the vicinity of the rubber hoses and calipers.

9   Install the wheels, lower the vehicle and tighten the wheel lug nuts to the torque given in this Chapter's Specifications.

Parking brake

10   Park the vehicle on a steep hill with the engine running (so you can apply the brakes if necessary) with the parking brake set and the transaxle in Neutral. If the parking brake cannot prevent the vehicle from rolling, it needs adjustment (see Chapter 9).

14   Steering, suspension and driveaxle boot check (every 15,000 miles or 12 months)

Note: *For detailed illustrations of the steering and suspension components, refer to Chapter 10.*

Shock absorber check

1   Park the vehicle on level ground, turn the engine off and set the parking brake. Check the tire pressures.

2   Push down at one corner of the vehicle, then release it while noting the movement of the body. It should stop moving and come to rest in a level position within one or two bounces.

3   If the vehicle continues to move up-and-down or if it fails to return to its original position, a worn or weak shock absorber is probably the reason.

4   Repeat the above check at each of the three remaining corners of the vehicle.

5   Raise the vehicle and support it securely on jackstands.

6   Check the shock absorbers for evidence of fluid leakage **(see illustration)**. A light film of fluid is no cause for concern. Make sure that any fluid noted is from the shocks and not from some other source. If leakage is noted, replace the shocks as a set.

7   Check the shocks to be sure that they are securely mounted and undamaged. Check the upper mounts for damage and wear. If damage or wear is noted, replace the shocks as a set (front or rear).

8   If the shocks must be replaced, refer to Chapter 10 for the procedure.

Steering and suspension check

9   Check the tires for irregular wear patterns and proper inflation. See Section 5 for information regarding tire wear and Chapter 10 for information on wheel bearing replacement.

10   Inspect the universal joint between the steering shaft and the steering gear housing. Check the steering gear housing for lubricant leakage. Make sure that the dust boots are not damaged and that the boot clamps are not loose. Check the tie-rod ends for excessive play. Look for loose bolts, broken or disconnected parts and deteriorated rubber bushings on all suspension and steering components. While an assistant turns the steering wheel from side to side, check the steering components for free movement, chafing and binding. If the steering components do not seem to be reacting with the movement of

14.11 To check a balljoint for wear, try to pry the control arm up and down to make sure there is no play in the balljoint (if there is, replace it)

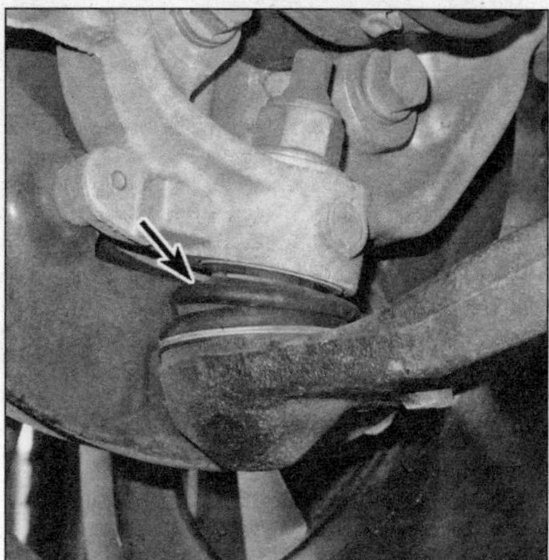

14.12 Check the balljoint boots for damage

14.15 Flex the driveaxle boots by hand to check for cracks and/or leaking grease

the steering wheel, try to determine where the slack is located.

11   Check the balljoints for wear by trying to move each control arm up and down with a prybar **(see illustration)** to ensure that its balljoint has no play. If any balljoint does have play, it's worn out. See Chapter 10 for the control arm replacement procedure (the balljoints aren't replaceable separately).

12   Inspect the balljoint boots for damage and leaking grease **(see illustration)**.

13   At the rear of the vehicle, inspect the suspension arm bushings for deterioration. Additional information on suspension components can be found in Chapter 10.

Driveaxle boot check

14   The driveaxle boots are very important because they prevent dirt, water and foreign material from entering and damaging the constant velocity (CV) joints. Oil and grease can cause the boot material to deteriorate prematurely, so it's a good idea to wash the boots with soap and water. Because it constantly pivots back and forth following the steering action of the front hub, the outer CV boot wears out sooner and should be inspected regularly.

15   Inspect the boots for tears and cracks as well as loose clamps **(see illustration)**. If there is any evidence of cracks or leaking lubricant, they must be replaced (see Chapter 8).

15   Fuel system check (every 15,000 miles or 12 months)

Warning: *Gasoline is flammable, so take extra precautions when you work on any part of the fuel system. Don't smoke or allow open flames or bare light bulbs near the work area, and don't work in a garage where a gas-type appliance (such as a water heater or clothes dryer) is present. Since fuel is carcinogenic, wear fuel-resistant gloves when there's a possibility of being exposed to fuel, and, if you spill any fuel on your skin, rinse it off immediately with soap and water. Mop up any spills immediately and do not store fuel-soaked rags where they could ignite. When you perform any kind of work on the fuel system, wear safety glasses and have a Class B type fire extinguisher on hand. The fuel system is under constant pressure, so, before any lines are disconnected, the fuel system pressure must be relieved (see Chapter 4).*

1   If you smell gasoline while driving or after the vehicle has been sitting in the sun, inspect the fuel system immediately.

2   Remove the fuel filler cap and inspect if for damage and corrosion. The gasket should have an unbroken sealing imprint. If the gasket is damaged or corroded, install a new cap.

3   Inspect the fuel feed line for cracks. Make sure that the connections between the fuel lines and the fuel injection system, and between the fuel lines and the fuel tank (inspect from below) are tight and dry. **Warning:** *Your vehicle is fuel injected, so you must relieve the fuel system pressure before servicing fuel system components. The fuel system pressure relief procedure is outlined in Chapter 4.*

4   Since some components of the fuel system - the fuel tank and part of the fuel feed line, for example - are underneath the vehicle, they can be inspected more easily with the vehicle raised on a hoist. If that's not possible, raise the vehicle and support it on jackstands.

5   With the vehicle raised and safely supported, inspect the gas tank and filler neck for punctures, cracks and other damage. The connection between the filler neck and the tank is particularly critical. Sometimes a rubber filler neck will leak because of loose clamps or deteriorated rubber. Inspect all fuel tank mounting brackets and straps to be sure that the tank is securely attached to the vehicle. **Warning:** *Do not, under any circumstances, try to repair a fuel tank (except rubber components). A welding torch or any open flame can easily cause fuel vapors inside the tank to explode.*

6   Carefully check all rubber hoses and metal lines leading away from the fuel tank. Check for loose connections, deteriorated hoses, crimped lines and other damage. Repair or replace damaged sections as necessary (see Chapter 4).

16   Transfer case lubricant level check (AWD models)

Note: *Do not service the transfer case fluid unless the vehicle is used in extreme off-road conditions or in sand.*

1   Raise the vehicle and support it securely on jackstands.

2   Using a ratchet or breaker bar, unscrew the check/fill plug from the transfer case. **Note:** *On some models, it may be necessary to remove the right side catalytic converter to access the plug.*

3   Using your little finger, reach inside the housing to feel the lubricant level. The level should be at or near the bottom of the plug hole. If it isn't, add the recommended lubricant through the plug hole with a syringe or squeeze bottle.

4   Install and tighten the plug. Check for leaks after the first few miles of driving. **Note:** *The manufacturer states that if the transfer case is ever submerged in water, the entire unit must be replaced (see Chapter 7B). However, it may be worth trying to gain more service life from the unit by draining the lubricant and refilling the unit with fresh lubricant (see Section 25).*

17.1a Unlatch these clips . . .

17.1b . . . pull the cover out of the way and lift out the element

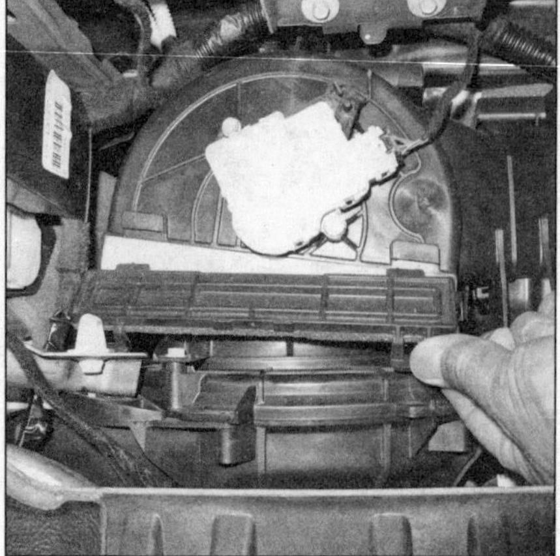

18.2a Depress the latch and swing the access panel open . . .

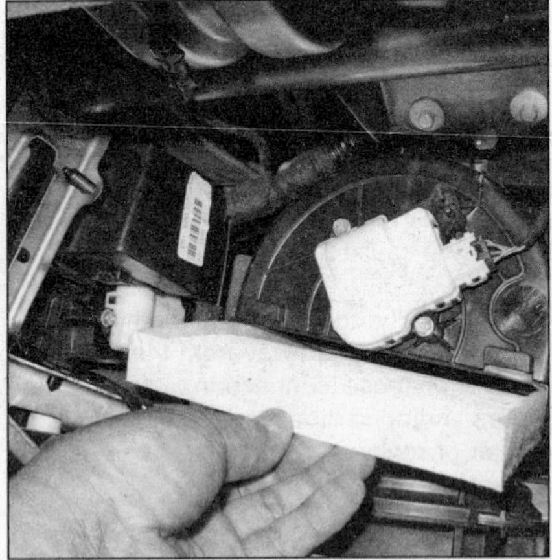

18.2b . . . then remove the filter from the housing. When installing, make sure the pleated side is facing up

19.2 Check each exhaust system rubber hanger for damage

17 Air filter check and replacement (every 15,000 miles or 12 months)

1   The air filter is located inside a housing at the left (driver's) side of the engine compartment. To remove the air filter, release the clamps that secure the two halves of the air filter housing together, then separate the cover halves and remove the air filter element **(see illustrations)**.

2   Inspect the outer surface of the filter element. If it is dirty, replace it. If it is only moderately dusty, it can be reused by blowing it clean from the back to the front surface with compressed air. Because it is a pleated paper type filter, it cannot be washed or oiled. If it cannot be cleaned satisfactorily with compressed air, discard and replace it. While the cover is off, be careful not to drop anything down into the housing.

Caution: *Never drive the vehicle with the air filter removed. Excessive engine wear could result and backfiring could even cause a fire under the hood.*

3   Wipe out the inside of the air filter housing.

4   Place the new filter into the filter housing, making sure it seats properly.

5   Make sure the top half of the housing is seated properly, then secure it with the clamps.

18 Cabin air filter replacement (every 15,000 miles or 12 months)

Note: *Not all models were equipped from the factory with a cabin air filter. If a filter was not installed, a screen was installed in its place. Check with your local auto parts store or dealer parts department for a retrofit filter available for these models.*

1   Unlatch the glove box door stop from the top, and lower the door.

2   Depress the tab on the left side of the filter door and pull the filter from the housing **(see illustrations)**.

3   Installation is the reverse of removal.

19 Exhaust system check (every 30,000 miles or 24 months)

1   With the engine cold (at least three hours after the vehicle has been driven), check the complete exhaust system from the engine to the end of the tailpipe. Ideally, the inspection should be done with the vehicle on a hoist to permit unrestricted access. If a hoist isn't available, raise the vehicle and support it securely on jackstands.

2   Check the exhaust pipes and connections for evidence of leaks, severe corrosion and damage. Make sure that all brackets and hangers are in good condition and tight **(see illustration)**.

3   At the same time, inspect the underside of the body for holes, corrosion, open seams, etc. which may allow exhaust gases to enter the passenger compartment. Seal all body openings with silicone or body putty.

4   Rattles and other noises can often be traced to the exhaust system, especially the mounts and hangers. Try to move the pipes, muffler and catalytic converter. If the components can come in contact with the body or suspension parts, secure the exhaust system with new mounts.

5   Check the running condition of the engine by inspecting inside the end of the tailpipe. The exhaust deposits here are an indication of engine state-of-tune. If the pipe is black and sooty or coated with white deposits, the engine may need a tune-up, including a thorough fuel system inspection and adjustment.

20 Cooling system servicing (draining, flushing and refilling) (every 30,000 miles or 24 months)

Warning: *Do not allow antifreeze to come in contact with your skin or painted surfaces of the vehicle. Rinse off spills immediately with*

20.4 Location of the cooling system bleed screw (four-cylinder models)

20.5 The radiator drain fitting is located at the lower left corner of the radiator - before opening the valve, push a short length of rubber hose onto the plastic fitting to prevent the coolant from splashing

plenty of water. Antifreeze is highly toxic if ingested. Never leave antifreeze lying around in an open container or in puddles on the floor; children and pets are attracted by its sweet smell and may drink it. Check with local authorities about disposing of used antifreeze. Many communities have collection centers which will see that antifreeze is disposed of safely. Never dump used antifreeze on the ground or pour it into drains.
Caution: *Do not mix coolants of different colors. Doing so might damage the cooling system and/or the engine. Refer to this Chapter's Specifications and read the warning label in the engine compartment for additional information.*
Note: *Non-toxic antifreeze is now manufactured and available at local auto parts stores, but even this type must be disposed of properly.*
1   Periodically, the cooling system should be drained, flushed and refilled to replenish the antifreeze mixture and prevent formation of rust and corrosion, which can impair the performance of the cooling system and cause engine damage. When the cooling system is serviced, all hoses and the expansion tank cap should be checked and replaced if necessary.

Draining

2   Apply the parking brake and block the wheels. If the vehicle has just been driven, wait several hours to allow the engine to cool down before beginning this procedure.
3   Once the engine is completely cool, remove the expansion tank cap.
4   On four-cylinder engines, loosen the cooling system bleed screw, located in a small hose attached to the water outlet at the left end (driver's side) of the cylinder head **(see illustration)**.
Note: *On models with a plastic bleed screw,*

it's only necessary to turn the screw counter-clockwise about 1/4-turn.
5   Move a large container under the radiator drain to catch the coolant. Attach a length of hose to the drain fitting to direct the coolant into the container, then open the drain fitting (a pair of pliers may be required to turn it) **(see illustration)**.
6   While the coolant is draining, check the condition of the radiator hoses, heater hoses and clamps (refer to Section 9 if necessary). Replace any damaged clamps or hoses.

Flushing

7   Fill the cooling system with clean water, following the "Refilling" procedure (see Step 13).
8   Start the engine and allow it to reach normal operating temperature, then rev up the engine a few times.
9   Turn the engine off and allow it to cool completely, then drain the system as described earlier.
10   Repeat Steps 7 through 9 until the water being drained is free of contaminants.
11   In severe cases of contamination or clogging of the radiator, remove the radiator (see Chapter 3) and have a radiator repair facility clean and repair it if necessary.
12   Many deposits can be removed by the chemical action of a cleaner available at auto parts stores. Follow the procedure outlined in the manufacturer's instructions.
Note: *When the coolant is regularly drained and the system refilled with the correct antifreeze/water mixture, there should be no need to use chemical cleaners or descalers.*

Refilling

13   Close and tighten the radiator drain.
14   Place the heater temperature control in the maximum heat position.

15   On a four-cylinder engines, slowly add new coolant (a 50/50 mixture of water and antifreeze) until coolant flows from the bleed screw, then tighten the bleed screw and continue to fill the expansion tank to the MAX fill mark. On V6 engines, add coolant to the expansion tank until the level is at the MAX fill mark on the expansion tank.
16   Install the expansion tank cap and run the engine at 2500 rpm for ten minutes.
Caution: *If at any time the engine begins to overheat, or the coolant level falls below the MIN fill line on the expansion tank, turn off the engine, allow it to cool completely, then add coolant to the expansion tank to the MAX fill line.*
17   Turn the engine off and let it cool. Add more coolant mixture to bring the level to the MAX fill mark on the expansion tank.
18   Repeat Steps 16 and 17 if necessary.
19   Start the engine, allow it to reach normal operating temperature and check for leaks. Also, set the heater and blower controls to the maximum setting and check to see that the heater output from the air ducts is warm. This is a good indication that all air has been purged from the cooling system.

21   Brake fluid change (every 30,000 miles or 24 months)

Warning: *Brake fluid can harm your eyes and damage painted surfaces, so use extreme caution when handling or pouring it. Do not use brake fluid that has been standing open or is more than one year old. Brake fluid absorbs moisture from the air. Excess moisture can cause a dangerous loss of braking effectiveness.*
1   At the specified intervals, the brake fluid should be drained and replaced. Since the brake fluid may drip or splash when pouring it, place plenty of rags around the master cylinder to protect any surrounding painted surfaces.
2   Before beginning work, purchase the specified brake fluid (see "Recommended lubricants and fluids" in this Chapter's Specifications).
3   Remove the cap from the master cylinder reservoir.
4   Using a hand suction pump or similar device, withdraw the fluid from the master cylinder reservoir.
5   Add new fluid to the master cylinder until it rises to the base of the filler neck.
6   Bleed the brake system (see Chapter 9) at all four brakes until new and uncontaminated fluid is expelled from the bleeder screw. Be sure to maintain the fluid level in the master cylinder as you perform the bleeding process. If you allow the master cylinder to run dry, air will enter the system.
7   Refill the master cylinder with fluid and check the operation of the brakes. The pedal should feel solid when depressed, with no sponginess.
Warning: *Do not operate the vehicle if you are in doubt about the effectiveness of the brake system.*

22.2 Remove the fasteners from the front area of the inner fender liner (A) then remove the remaining fasteners (arrows) and pull it back for access

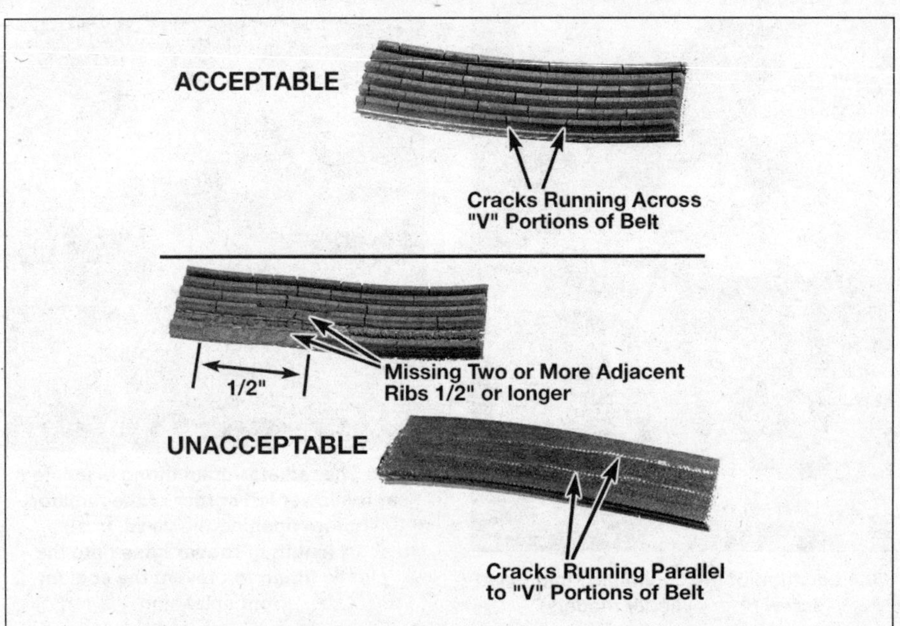

22.4 Small cracks in the underside of a V-ribbed belt are acceptable - lengthwise cracks, or missing pieces that cause the belt to make noise, are cause for replacement

22   Drivebelt check and replacement (every 30,000 miles or 24 months)

Accessory drivebelt

1   A single serpentine drivebelt is located at the front of the engine and plays an important role in the overall operation of the engine and its components. Due to its function and material make up, the belt is prone to wear and should be periodically inspected. On four-cylinder models, the serpentine belt drives the alternator, power steering pump, water pump and air conditioning compressor. On V6 models, the serpentine belt drives the alternator and air conditioning compressor; a second belt is used to drive the power steering pump. Although the belt should be inspected at the recommended intervals, replacement may not be necessary for more than 100,000 miles.

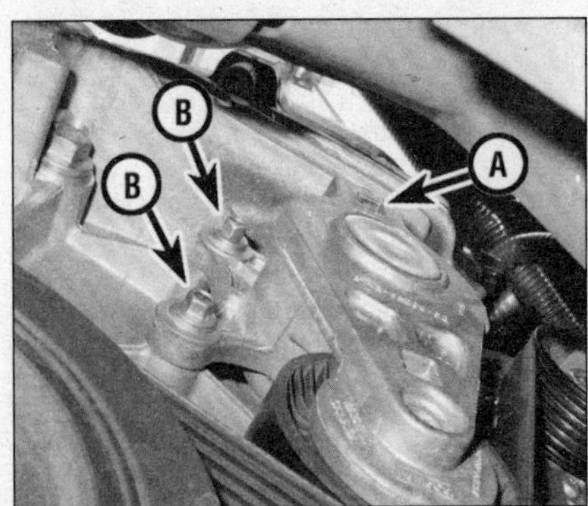

22.6 Insert a 3/8-inch drive ratchet or breaker bar into the square hole (A) and rotate the tensioner arm to relieve belt tension. (B) indicates the tensioner mounting bolts (two of three bolts shown)

Check

2   Since the drivebelt is located very close to the right-hand side of the engine compartment, it is possible to gain better access by raising the front of the vehicle and removing the right-hand wheel, then removing the splash shield in the right fenderwell **(see illustration)**. Be sure to support the front of the vehicle securely on jackstands.

3   With the engine stopped, inspect the full length of the drivebelt for cracks and separation of the belt plies. It will be necessary to turn the engine (using a wrench or socket and bar on the crankshaft pulley bolt, working clockwise only) in order to move the belt from the pulleys so that the belt can be inspected thoroughly. Twist the belt between the pulleys so that both sides can be viewed. Also check for fraying, and glazing which gives the belt a shiny appearance. Check the pulleys for nicks, cracks, distortion and corrosion.

4   Note that it is not unusual for a ribbed belt to exhibit small cracks in the edges of the belt ribs, and unless these are extensive or very deep, belt replacement is not essential **(see illustration)**.

Replacement

5   Disconnect the cable from the negative terminal of the battery (see Chapter 5). Loosen the right front wheel lug nuts, then raise the front of the vehicle and support it securely on jackstands. Remove the right front wheel and the splash shield **(see illustration 22.2)**.

6   Note how the drivebelt is routed, then remove the belt from the pulleys. Insert a 3/8-inch drive ratchet or breaker bar into the tensioner hole from above and pull the handle to release the drivebelt tension **(see illustration)**. Once tension has been released, remove the belt from the pulleys.

7   Install the new drivebelt onto the crankshaft, alternator, power steering pump, and air conditioning compressor pulleys, then turn the tensioner back and locate the drivebelt on the pulley. Make sure that the drivebelt is correctly seated in all of the pulley grooves, then release the tensioner.

8   Install the splash shield and wheel, then lower the vehicle. Tighten the lug nuts to the torque listed in this Chapter's Specifications.

Power steering pump drivebelt (V6 engines)

9   The power steering drivebelt is located at the lower right rear of the engine. The belt is of a unique design, called a stretchy belt, which provides tension without the use of a mechanical tensioner.

10   Disconnect the cable from the negative terminal of the battery (see Chapter 5). Loosen the right front wheel lug nuts. Raise the vehicle and support it securely on jackstands, then remove the wheel and the right inner fender splash shield (see Chapter 11). Insert a length of flexible material such as a leather or plastic strap under the belt at the pulley at the end of the camshaft. Rotate the engine (clockwise) with a socket and breaker bar on the crankshaft pulley bolt, while you feed the remover strap between the belt and the pulley **(see illustration)**. Pull the strap quickly to force the belt from the pulley on the camshaft.

Warning: *While performing this step, rotate the engine by hand only (do not use the starter)*

Caution: *Do not use hard plastic or metal tools to pry the belt off; it can be easily damaged.*

Note: *If the belt is not going to be re-used, you can simply cut it off.*

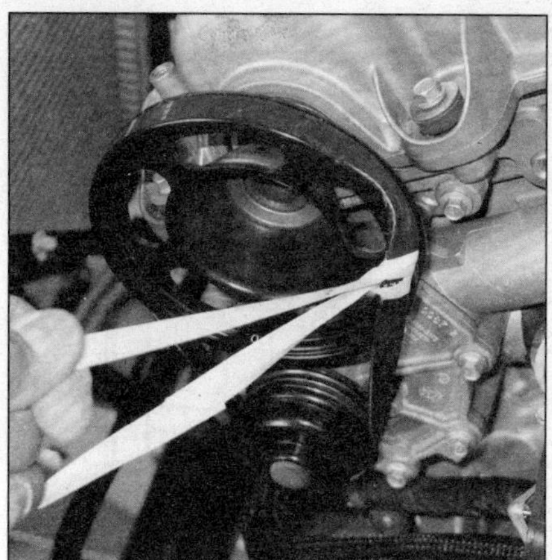

22.10 Typical stretchy belt removal (shown on a different model for illustrative purposes)

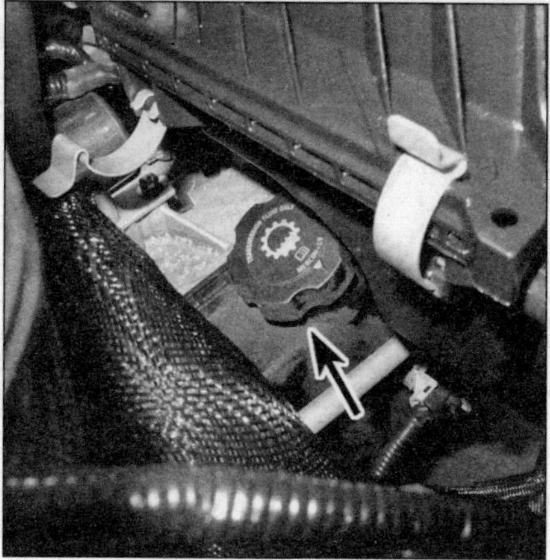

23.7 The dipstick/cap is on top of the transaxle, below the air filter housing

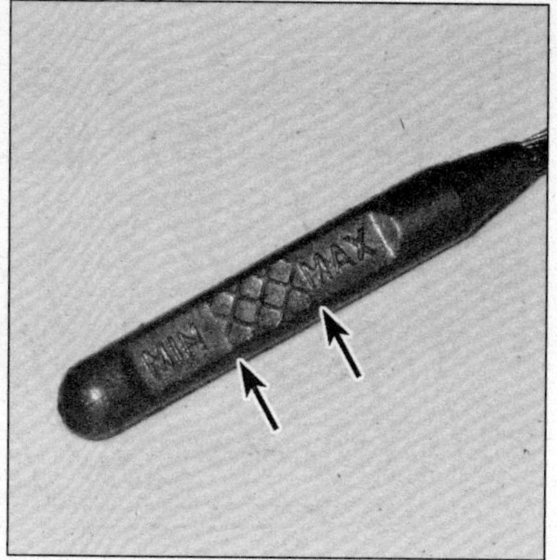

23.9 Fill the transaxle unitl the level is up to the COLD notch (the lowest notch) and not past the highest notch on the dipstick

11   Route the new belt under the drive pulley, then over the power steering pump pulley and rotate the engine again; the belt should pop over the pulley on the pump. Make sure the belt is positioned properly on both pulleys.

Accessory drivebelt tensioner

12   On four-cylinder models, remove the two bolts securing the tensioner to the engine block **(see illustration 22.6)** and remove the tensioner.

13   On V6 models, remove the three bolts securing the tensioner to the timing chain cover, then detach the tensioner from the cover.

14   Installation is the reverse of removal. Tighten the tensioner bolt(s) to the torque listed in this Chapter's Specifications.

---

23   Automatic transaxle fluid change (every 60,000 miles or 48 months)

Note: *For transaxle identification, refer to "Vehicle identification numbers" at the front of this manual.*

1   The automatic transaxle fluid should be changed at the recommended intervals.

2   Before beginning work, purchase the specified transmission fluid (see "Recommended lubricants and fluids" in this Chapter's Specifications).

3   Other tools necessary for this job include jackstands to support the vehicle in a raised position, wrenches, a drain pan, newspapers and clean rags.

4   The fluid should be drained immediately after the vehicle has been driven. Hot fluid is more effective than cold fluid at removing built-up sediment.

Warning: *Fluid temperature can exceed 350-degrees F in a hot transaxle. Wear protective gloves.*

5   After the vehicle has been driven to warm up the fluid, raise the front of the vehicle and support it securely on jackstands.

23.12 Location of the transaxle drain plug (6F35 transaxle)

Warning: *Never work under a vehicle that is supported only by a jack!*

Ford Taurus
V6 models (6F50/6F55 transaxle)

6   Place the drain pan under the drain plug in the transaxle and remove the drain plug. Once the fluid has drained, reinstall the drain plug and tighten it to the torque listed in this Chapter's Specifications.

7   Lower the vehicle and unscrew dipstick/cap from the fill tube on the top of the transaxle **(see illustration)**.

Note: *On 2010 and later models, the dipstick/cap is mounted directly to the top of the transaxle fluid pan.*

8   Add five quarts of new fluid to the transaxle through the fill plug hole (see "Recommended lubricants and fluids" for the recommended fluid type), then install the fill plug and tighten it to the torque listed in this Chapter's Specifications.

9   Start the engine and, while depressing the brake pedal, cycle the shifter through each gear position and return it to Park. With

the engine running, add fluid through the dipstick tube, 1/2-pint at a time as necessary (cycling the shifter through each gear position between additions) until the level is up to the COLD notch (the lowest notch) on the dipstick **(see illustration)**.

10   Drive the vehicle a few miles until the fluid is up to normal operating temperature, then recheck the fluid level (see Section 4); it should be in the range indicated on the dipstick. If not, add fluid a little at a time (cycling the shifter through each gear position between additions) until the level is correct. Tighten the dipstick/cap securely.

11   If you wish to flush the torque converter of old fluid, repeat Steps 6 through 10 one or two more times.

Four-cylinder models (6F35 transaxle)

12   Place the drain pan under the drain plug in the transaxle and remove the drain plug **(see illustration)**. Once the fluid has drained, reinstall the drain plug and tighten it to the torque listed in this Chapter's Specifications.

13   Lower the vehicle.

14   Measure the amount of fluid drained and record this figure for reference when refilling.

15   With the engine off, add new fluid to the transaxle through the fill tube **(see illustration 4.42)**. Begin the refill procedure by initially adding 1/3 of the amount drained. Then, with the engine running, add 1/2-pint at a time (cycling the shifter through each gear position between additions) until the level is correct on the dipstick.

16   Repeat Steps 12 through 15 two more times to flush any contaminated fluid from the torque converter.

17   Raise the vehicle on a hoist, keeping the vehicle in a level position, and place a drain pan under the transaxle.

18   With the engine still idling and in the Park position, remove the oil leveling plug on the side of the transaxle **(see illustration 4.41)**. Check the level of the fluid, it should be even with the bottom of the plug hole.

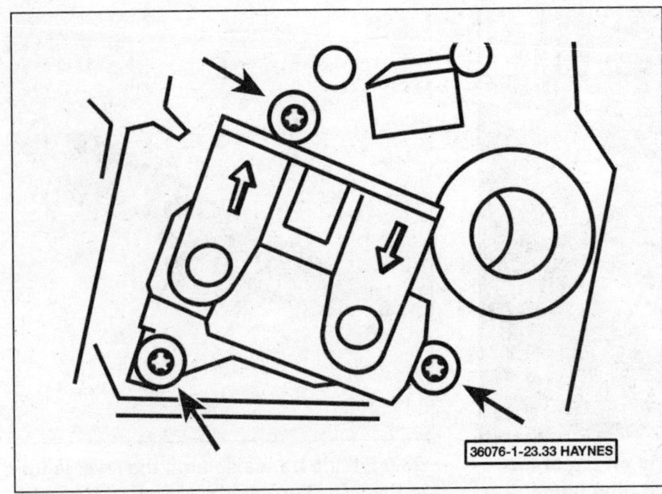

23.33 Pressure filter cover mounting bolts (CVT transaxle)

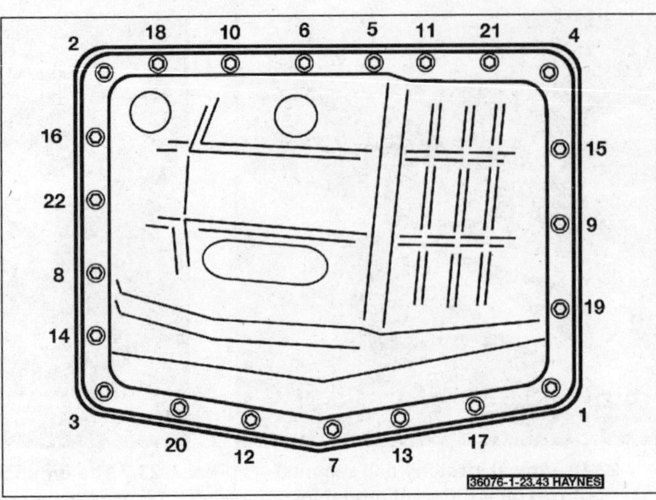

23.43 Fluid pan bolt tightening sequence

19   If the level is low, remove the filler tube cap **(see illustration 4.42)** and add the specified automatic transmission fluid through the filler tube with a funnel until the fluid starts to drip out of the oil leveling plug.
Note: *Allow all excess fluid to drip out of the plug hole.*
20   Once the fluid is even with the oil leveling plug hole, install the plug and tighten the plug to the torque listed in this Chapter's Specifications.
21   Drive the vehicle a few miles until the fluid is up to normal operating temperature, then recheck the fluid level (see Section 4); it should be in the cross-hatched range (or in the range between the hot operation lines). If not, add fluid a little at a time (cycling the shifter through each gear position between additions) until the level is correct.

Ford 500
Ford Five Hundred/Mercury Montego models

Aisin AW21 transaxle
22   Place the drain pan under the transaxle pan and remove the drain plug. Once the fluid has drained, reinstall the drain plug and tighten it to the torque listed in this Chapter's Specifications.
23   Lower the vehicle and remove the fill plug from the top of the transaxle.
24   Add 4 quarts of new fluid to the transaxle through the fill plug hole (see Recommended lubricants and fluids for the recommended fluid type), then install the fill plug and tighten it to the torque listed in this Chapter's Specifications.
25   Start the engine and, while depressing the brake pedal, cycle the shifter through each gear position and return it to PARK. With the engine running, add fluid through the dipstick tube, 1/2-pint at a time as necessary (cycling the shifter through each gear position between additions) until the level is up the COLD notch (the lowest notch) on the dipstick.

26   Drive the vehicle a few miles until the fluid is up to normal operating temperature, then recheck the fluid level (see Section 4); it should be in the range indicated in **illustration 4.49**. If not, add fluid a little at a time (cycling the shifter through each gear position between additions) until the level is correct. Be sure to tighten the fill plug to the torque listed in this Chapter's Specifications.
27   If you wish to flush the torque converter of old fluid, repeat Steps 22 through 26 one or two more times.

CVT transaxle
Refer to illustrations 23.33 and 23.43

28   Place the drain pan under the transaxle fluid pan and remove the drain plug. Once the fluid has drained, reinstall the drain plug and tighten it to the torque listed in this Chapter's Specifications.
29   Remove the transaxle fluid pan bolts and the pan. Remove the transaxle pan gasket.
30   Check the transaxle case and remove the pickup tube seal. Remove and dispose of the transmission fluid filter.
31   Remove the flange bolt and disconnect the transmission fluid cooler tubes from the pressure filter cover.
Note: *The pressure filter is located on the side of the transaxle, just forward of the left driveaxle.*
32   Remove and dispose of the four transmission fluid cooler tube seals.
33   Remove the pressure filter cover **(see illustration)**.
34   Remove the O-ring from the pressure filter cover. **Note:** *The pressure filter cover feed tube will either remain inside the cover or the case when the cover is removed.*
35   Remove the pressure filter cover feed tube. Install a new feed tube or seals depending upon type:

a) *On feed tubes with a bonded seal, install a new feed tube.*

b) *On feed tubes with o-rings seals, remove the old O-rings and replace them with new ones.*

36   Remove and discard the pressure filter.
37   Installation is the reverse of removal.
38   Be sure to install a new O-ring before installing the pressure filter cover. Install the pressure filter cover and tighten the bolts to the torque listed in this Chapter's Specifications.
39   Install four new O-rings onto the fluid cooler tubes. Note: Lubricate the O-rings with CVT transmission fluid before installing.
40   Connect the transmission fluid cooler tubes to the pressure filter cover. Be sure the cooler tubes are installed perfectly straight or leakage will occur. Tighten the flange bolt to the torque listed in this Chapter's Specifications.
41   Install a new fluid filter pickup tube seal, then install the new fluid filter.
42   Clean the gasket material off the transaxle case using a plastic scraper. Do not scratch the transaxle case. Install a new transaxle pan gasket.
43   Install the fluid pan and tighten the bolts in sequence **(see illustration)** to the torque listed in this Chapter's Specifications.
44   Add 5 quarts of new CVT transmission fluid into the fill hole and check the fluid level (see Steps 58 to 64 in Section 4).

Fluid disposal
45   The old fluid drained from the transaxle cannot be reused in its present state and should be disposed of. Check with your local auto parts store, disposal facility or environmental agency to see if they will accept the fluid for recycling. After the fluid has cooled it can be drained into a container (capped plastic jugs, topped bottles, milk cartons, etc.) for transport to one of these disposal sites. Don't dispose of the fluid by pouring it on the ground or down a drain!

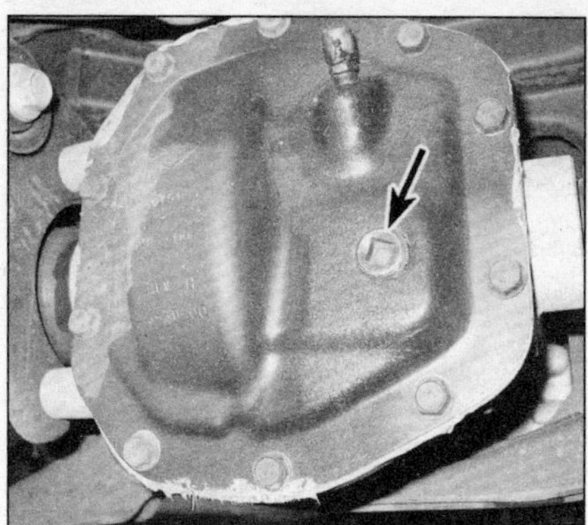

24.4 Rear differential check/fill plug

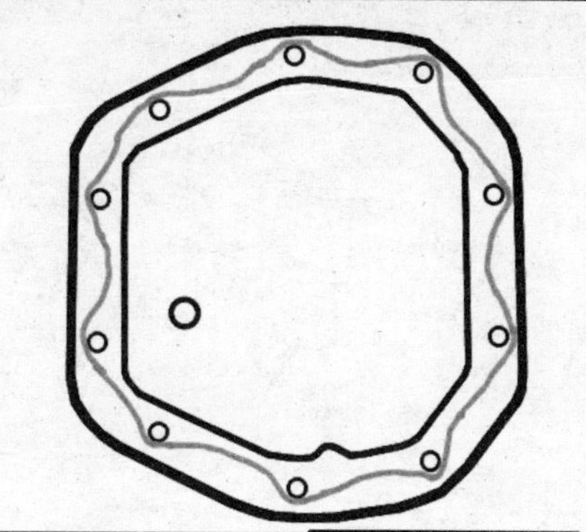

24.11 Apply a continuous bead of RTV sealant to the cover

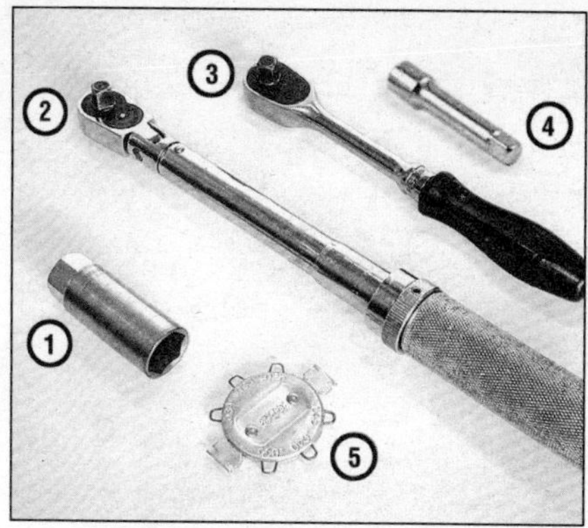

26.2 Tools required for changing spark plugs

1   *Spark plug socket - This will have special padding inside to protect the spark plug's porcelain insulator*
2   *Torque wrench - Although not mandatory, using this tool is the best way to ensure the plugs are tightened properly*
3   *Ratchet - Standard hand tool to fit the spark plug socket*
4   *Extension - Depending on model and accessories, you may need special extensions and universal joints to reach one or more of the plugs*
5   *Spark plug gap gauge - This gauge for checking the gap comes in a variety of styles. Make sure the gap for your engine is included*

24   Differential lubricant change (AWD models) (every 60,000 miles or 48 months)

Drain

1   This procedure should be performed after the vehicle has been driven so the lubricant will be warm and therefore flow out of the differential more easily.
2   Raise the vehicle and support it securely on jackstands.
3   The easiest way to drain the differential is to remove the lubricant through the filler plug hole with a suction pump. If the differential cover gasket is leaking, it will be necessary to remove the cover to drain the lubricant (which will also allow you to inspect the differential).

Changing the lubricant with a suction pump

4   Remove the filler plug from the differential **(see illustration)**.
5   Insert the flexible hose.
6   Work the hose down to the bottom of the differential housing and pump the lubricant out.

Changing the lubricant by removing the cover

7   Move a drain pan, rags, newspapers and wrenches under the vehicle.
8   Remove the bolts on the lower half of the cover. Loosen the bolts on the upper half and use them to loosely retain the cover. Allow the oil to drain into the pan, then completely remove the cover.
9   Using a lint-free rag, clean the inside of the cover and the accessible areas of the differential housing. As this is done, check for chipped gears and metal particles in the lubricant, indicating that the differential should be more thoroughly inspected and/or repaired.
10   Thoroughly clean the gasket mating surfaces of the differential housing and the cover plate. Use a gasket scraper or putty knife to remove all traces of the old gasket.
11   Apply a bead of RTV sealant to the cover flange **(see illustration)**. Make sure the bolt holes align properly, then install the cover and tighten the fasteners to the torque listed in this Chapter's Specifications.

Refill

12   Use a hand pump, syringe or funnel to fill the differential housing with the specified lubricant until it's within 1/8 to 3/16-inch (3 to 5 mm) from the bottom of the filler plug hole.
13   Install the fill plug and tighten it to the torque listed in this Chapter's Specifications.
14   The old lubricant drained from the differential cannot be reused in its present state and should be disposed of. Check with your local auto parts store, disposal facility or environmental agency to see if they will accept the lubricant for recycling. After the lubricant has cooled, it can be drained into a container (capped plastic jugs, topped bottles, milk cartons, etc.) for transport to one of these disposal sites. Don't dispose of the lubricant by pouring it on the ground or down a drain!

25   Transfer case lubricant change (AWD models)

Note: *Technically, the transfer case is filled for life; routine fluid changes aren't necessary unless the fluid somehow becomes contaminated.*

Drain

1   This procedure should be performed after the vehicle has been driven so the lubricant will be warm and therefore flow out of the transfer case more easily.
2   Raise the vehicle and support it securely on jackstands.
3   On models equipped with a drain plug, remove the drain plug and allow the fluid to drain.
4   On models without a drain plug, remove the filler plug and insert the flexible hose. Work the hose down to the bottom of the unit and pump the lubricant out.

Refill

5   Use a hand pump, syringe or funnel to fill the housing with the specified lubricant until it's within 1/8 to 3/16-inch (3 to 5 mm) from the bottom of the filler plug hole.
6   Install the fill plug and tighten it to the torque listed in this Chapter's Specifications.

7   The old lubricant cannot be reused in its present state and should be disposed of. Check with your local auto parts store, disposal facility or environmental agency to see if they will accept the lubricant for recycling. After the lubricant has cooled, it can be drained into a container (capped plastic jugs, topped bottles, milk cartons, etc.) for transport to one of these disposal sites. Don't dispose of the lubricant by pouring it on the ground or down a drain!

26   Spark plug check and replacement (see Maintenance schedule for service intervals)

1   The spark plugs are located in the center of the valve cover(s). Access to the rear cylinder bank spark plugs on V6 models requires removal of the upper intake manifold (see Chapter 2B).
2   In most cases, the tools necessary for spark plug replacement include a spark plug socket which fits onto a ratchet (spark plug sockets are padded inside to prevent damage to the porcelain insulators on the new plugs), various extensions and a gap gauge to check and adjust the gaps on the new plugs **(see illustration)**. A torque wrench should be used to tighten the new plugs.

26.5 When checking the spark plug gap, the wire should slide between the electrodes with a slight drag

26.6a All models are equipped with individual coils which must be removed to access the spark plugs (V6 shown, four-cylinder similar)

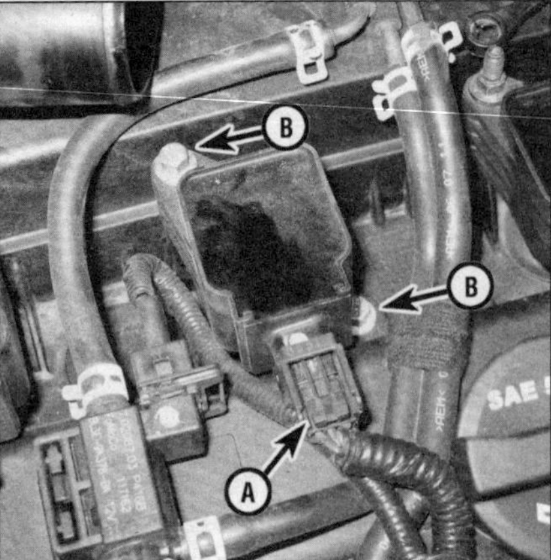

26.6b Depress the tab (A) and disconnect the electrical connector, remove the coil retaining bolts (B), then pull the coil straight up to remove it

26.8 Use a ratchet and extension to remove the spark plugs

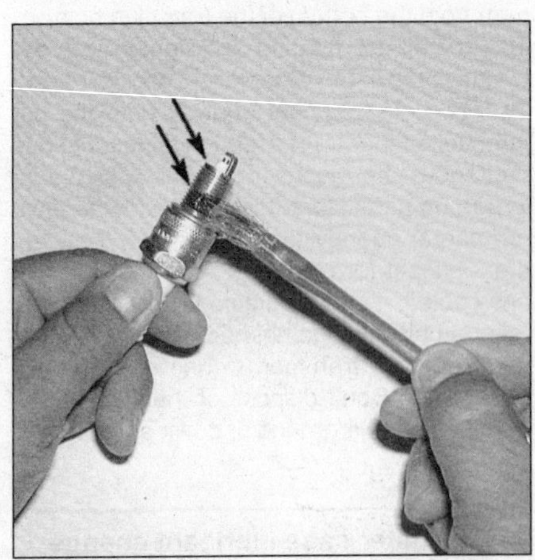

26.10a Apply a thin coat of anti-seize compound to the spark plug threads

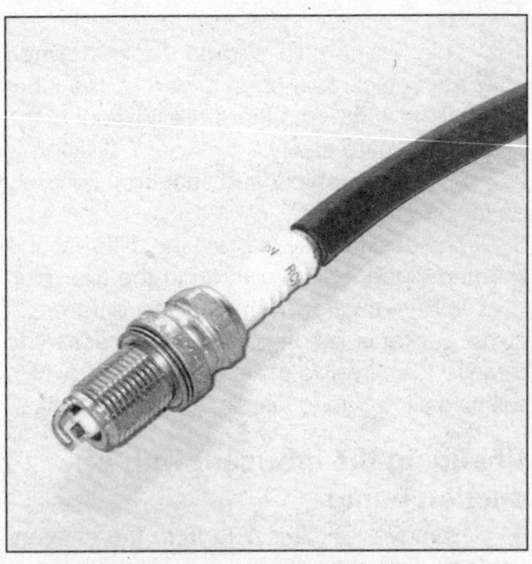

26.10b A length of snug-fitting rubber hose will save time and prevent damaged threads when installing the spark plugs

3   The best approach when replacing the spark plugs is to purchase the new ones in advance, adjust them to the proper gap and replace the plugs one at a time. When buying the new spark plugs, be sure to obtain the correct plug type for your particular engine. This information can be found in this Chapter's Specifications or in the factory owner's manual.

4   Allow the engine to cool completely before attempting to remove any of the plugs. These engines are equipped with aluminum cylinder heads, which can be damaged if the spark plugs are removed when the engine is hot. While you are waiting for the engine to cool, check the new plugs for defects and adjust the gaps.

5   The gap is checked by inserting the proper-thickness gauge between the electrodes at the tip of the plug **(see illustration)**. The gap between the electrodes should be the same as the one specified in this Chapter's Specifications. The gauge should just slide between the electrodes with a slight amount of drag. If the gap is incorrect, use the adjuster on the gauge body to bend the curved side electrode slightly until the proper gap is obtained. If the side electrode is not exactly over the center electrode, bend it with the adjuster until it is. Check for cracks in the porcelain insulator (if any are found, the plug should not be used). **Note:** *We recommend using a wire-type thickness gauge when checking platinum- or iridium-type spark plugs. Other types of gauges may scrape the thin coating from the electrodes, thus dramatically shortening the life of the plugs.*

6   All models are equipped with individual ignition coils which must be removed first to access the spark plugs **(see illustrations)**.

7   If compressed air is available, use it to blow any dirt or foreign material away from the spark plug hole. The idea here is to eliminate the possibility of debris falling into the cylinder as the spark plug is removed.

8   Place the spark plug socket over the plug and remove it from the engine by turning it in a counterclockwise direction **(see illustration)**.

9   Compare the spark plug to those shown in the photos located on the inside back cover of this book to get an indication of the general running condition of the engine.

10   Apply a small amount of anti-seize compound to the spark plug threads **(see illustration)**. Install one of the new plugs into the hole until you can no longer turn it with your fingers, then tighten it with a torque wrench (if available) or the ratchet. It is a good idea to slip a short length of rubber hose over the end of the plug to use as a tool to thread it into place **(see illustration)**. The hose will grip the plug well enough to turn it, but will start to slip if the plug begins to cross-thread in the hole - this will prevent damaged threads and the accompanying repair costs.

11   Repeat the procedure for the remaining spark plugs.

Chapter 2 Part A
Four-cylinder engine

Contents

Specifications

General

Engine type	Four-cylinder, in-line, DOHC	
Displacement	122 cubic inches	1999 cc
Engine VIN code	9	
Firing order	1-3-4-2	
Bore	3.4449 inches	87.5 mm
Stroke	3.2717 inches	83.1 mm
Compression ratio	9.3:1	
Compression pressure	See Chapter 2C	
Oil pressure	See Chapter 2C	

FRONT OF VEHICLE → ①②③④

Cylinder locations

Camshafts

Lobe height		
Intake	0.326 inch	8.3 mm
Exhaust	0.291 inch	7.4 mm
Bearing journal diameter	0.9827 to 0.9835 inch	24.96 to 24.98 mm
Journal-to-bore-clearance	0.0014 to 0.0031 inch	0.036 to 0.079 mm
Runout	0.0012 inch	0.03 mm

Valve clearances (cold)

Ideal clearance		
Intake	0.0095 inch	0.25 mm
Exhaust	0.0142 inch	0.36 mm
Acceptable clearance		
Intake	0.007 to 0.012 inch	0.19 to 0.31 mm
Exhaust	0.012 to 0.017 inch	0.30 to 0.42 mm

Warpage limits

Cylinder head gasket surfaces (head and block)	0.002 inch	0.05 mm
Exhaust manifold	0.030 inch	0.76 mm

Torque specifications

Ft-lbs (unless otherwise indicated)   **Nm**

Note: *One foot-pound (ft-lb) of torque is equivalent to 12 inch-pounds (in-lbs) of torque. Torque values below approximately 15 ft-lbs are expressed in inch-pounds, because most foot-pound torque wrenches are not accurate at these smaller values.*

	Ft-lbs (unless otherwise indicated)	Nm
Camshaft bearing cap bolts (in sequence - **see illustration 10.25**)		
Step 1, All but front bearing cap	62 in-lbs	7
Step 2, All but front bearing cap	142 in-lbs	16
Step 3, Front bearing cap (3-bolts)	62 in-lbs	7
Step 4, Front bearing cap (3-bolts)	142 in-lbs	16
Camshaft phaser and sprocket bolts		
Step 1	30	40
Step 2	Tighten an additional 60-degrees	
Crankshaft pulley bolt		
Step 1	74	100
Step 2	Tighten an additional 90-degrees	
Cylinder head bolts (in sequence - **see illustration 11.30a**)		
Step 1	62 in-lbs	7
Step 2	133 in-lbs	15
Step 3	41	56
Step 4	Tighten an additional 90-degrees	
Step 5	Tighten an additional 90-degrees	
Variable Camshaft Timing (VCT) solenoid bolt	89 in-lbs	10
Valve cover bolts (in sequence - **see illustration 4.13**)	89 in-lbs	10
Turbocharger mounting nuts	37	50
Engine mount nuts\bolts	66	89
Driveplate bolts		
Step 1	37	50
Step 2	50	68
Step 3	83	113
Intake manifold bolts	177 in-lbs	20
Crankshaft rear oil seal and retainer	89 in-lbs	10
Oil pan-to-bellhousing bolts	35	47
Timing chain cover-to-oil pan bolts	89 in-lbs	10
Oil pan-to-engine block bolts	177 in-lbs	20
Oil pick-up pipe bolts	89 in-lbs	10
Oil pump-to-cylinder block bolts		
Step 1	89 in-lbs	10
Step 2	177 in-lbs	20
Sprocket bolt	18	24
Oil pump chain tensioner and guide bolts	89 in-lbs	10
Timing chain cover (in sequence - **see illustration 8.11**)		
8 mm bolts	89 in-lbs	10
13 mm bolts	35	47
Timing chain guide bolts	89 in-lbs	10
Timing chain tensioner bolts	89 in-lbs	10
Transaxle-to-engine bolts	35	47

1 General information

How to use this Chapter

1   This Part of Chapter 2 is devoted to repair procedures for the four-cylinder engine possible while the engine is still installed in the vehicle. Since these procedures are based on the assumption that the engine is installed in the vehicle, if the engine has been removed from the vehicle and mounted on a stand, some of the preliminary dismantling steps outlined will not apply.

2   Information concerning engine/transaxle removal and replacement and engine overhaul can be found in Chapter 2C.

Engine description

3   These engines are sixteen-valve, double overhead camshaft (DOHC), four-cylinder, in-line type, mounted transversely at the front of the vehicle, with the transaxle on the left-hand end. They incorporate an aluminum cylinder head, an aluminum cylinder block, direct injection and a turbocharger.

4   The two camshafts are driven by a timing chain, each operating eight valves via conventional lifters. Each camshaft rotates in five bearings that are line-bored directly in the cylinder head and the (bolted-on) bearing caps. This means that the bearing caps are not available separately from the cylinder head, and must not be interchanged with caps from another engine. The exhaust manifold is integral with the cylinder head, and the turbocharger bolts directly to the cylinder head.

5   These engines incorporate an aluminum timing chain cover and oil pan, and the crankshaft main caps are part of a one-piece lower block support. When working on these engines, note that Torx-type (both male and female heads) and hexagon socket (Allen head) fasteners are widely used. A good selection of sockets, with the necessary adapters, will be required, so that these can be unscrewed without damage and, on reassembly, tightened to the specified torque settings.

Lubrication system

6   The oil pump is driven via a chain from the front of the crankshaft. The pump forces oil through an externally mounted full-flow cartridge-type filter. From the filter, the oil is pumped into a main gallery in the cylinder block/crankcase, from where it is distributed to the crankshaft (main bearings) and cylinder head.

7   The connecting rod bearings are supplied with oil via internal drillings in the crankshaft. Each piston crown and connecting rod is cooled by a spray of oil.

8   The cylinder head is provided with two oil galleries, one on the intake side and one on the exhaust, to ensure constant oil supply to the camshaft bearings and lifters. A retaining valve (inserted into the cylinder head's top surface, in the middle, on the intake side) prevents these galleries from being drained when the engine is switched off. The valve incor-

3.8 The marked tooth (TDC) on the crankshaft pulley at the 6 o'clock position

porates a ventilation hole in its upper end, to allow air bubbles to escape from the system when the engine is restarted.

2 Repair operations possible with the engine in the vehicle

1   Many major repair operations can be accomplished without removing the engine from the vehicle.

2   Clean the engine compartment and the exterior of the engine with some type of degreaser before any work is done. It will make the job easier and help keep dirt out of the internal areas of the engine.

3   Depending on the components involved, it may be helpful to remove the hood to improve access to the engine as repairs are performed (refer to Chapter 11 if necessary). Cover the fenders to prevent damage to the paint. Special pads are available, but an old bedspread or blanket will also work.

4   If vacuum, exhaust, oil or coolant leaks develop, indicating a need for gasket or seal replacement, the repairs can generally be made with the engine in the vehicle. The intake and exhaust manifold gaskets, oil pan gasket, crankshaft oil seals and cylinder head gasket are all accessible with the engine in place.

5   Exterior engine components, such as the intake and exhaust manifolds, the oil pan, the oil pump, the water pump, the starter motor, the alternator and the fuel system components can be removed for repair with the engine in place.

6   Since the camshaft(s) and cylinder head can be removed without pulling the engine, valve component servicing can also be accomplished with the engine in the vehicle. Replacement of the timing chain and sprockets is also possible with the engine in the vehicle.

7   In extreme cases caused by a lack of necessary equipment, repair or replacement of piston rings, pistons, connecting rods and rod bearings is possible with the engine in the

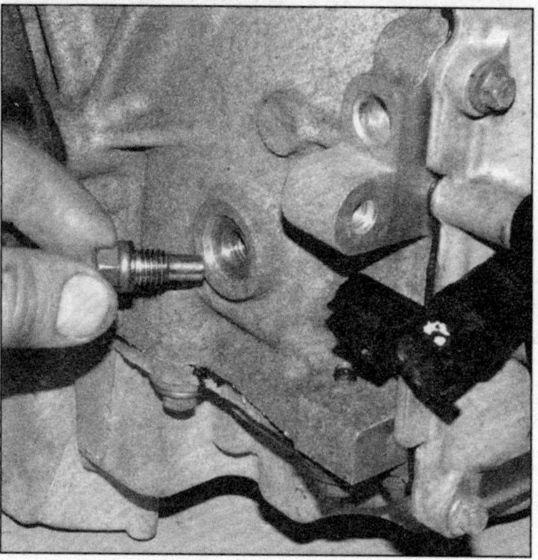

3.10 Remove the timing hole plug

vehicle. However, this practice is not recommended because of the cleaning and preparation work that must be done to the components involved.

3 Top Dead Center (TDC) for number 1 piston - locating

Note: *You will need two special tools for this procedure: the camshaft positioning tool (303-1565, or equivalent) and the timing pin (303-507).*

1   Relieve the fuel system pressure (see Chapter 4), then disconnect the negative battery cable (see Chapter 5).

2   Remove the passenger's side inner fender splash shield (see Chapter 11).

3   Remove the engine splash shield fasteners and remove the splash shield.

4   Remove the drivebelt (see Chapter 1).

5   Remove the brake vacuum pump (see Chapter 9) and the high-pressure fuel pump (see Chapter 4).

6   Remove the valve cover (see Section 4), then remove the rear intake camshaft bearing cap (see Section 10).

7   Prevent the camshaft from turning by using a wrench on the flats of the intake camshaft, then loosen and remove the brake vacuum pump adapter from the end of the camshaft.

8   Using a wrench or socket on the crankshaft pulley bolt, rotate the crankshaft clockwise until the marked tooth (TDC) on the crankshaft pulley is at the 6 o'clock position **(see illustration)**.

Note: *Counting counterclockwise, the marked tooth is twenty teeth away from the missing tooth on the crankshaft pulley.*

9   Remove the right-side driveaxle and support bracket (see Chapter 8).

10   The TDC timing hole is located near the lower right front corner of the engine block (on the firewall side), hidden behind the driveaxle support bracket; it provides a means of accurately positioning the no. 1 cylinder at TDC. When you locate this hole, remove the timing pin plug bolt **(see illustration)**.

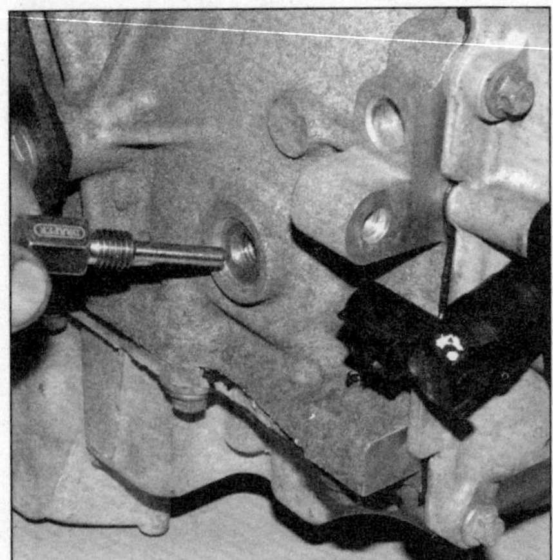

3.11 Insert the timing pin tool

3.12 The marked tooth (TDC) aligned with the center line of the Crankshaft Position (CKP) sensor

3.13a Remove the rear intake camshaft cap

3.13b Prevent the camshaft from turning by holding it with a wrench on the hex surface (A), then unscrew the vacuum pump adapter (B)

3.13c When the engine is at TDC for cylinder no. 1, the slots in the ends of the camshafts will be horizontal (and the offset portions will be even with the cylinder head surface). Manufacturer tool no. 303-1565 can then be inserted into the slots

11   Screw in the timing pin **(see illustration)**.

Caution: *We don't recommend trying to fabricate a timing pin with a bolt because while you would be able to determine the correct bolt diameter and thread pitch, it is impossible to determine what the length of the bolt should be. These pins come in several lengths, depending on the engine family. There is no way to determine the correct pin length without comparing it to a factory or aftermarket tool designed to be used with this engine. Using a bolt of the wrong length could damage the engine. Also, never use the timing pin as a means to stop the engine from rotating - tool breakage and/or engine damage can result.*

Note: *With the timing pin installed, the engine can still be rotated counterclockwise.*

12   Turn the crankshaft slowly clockwise until the crankshaft counterweight comes into contact with the timing pin, and the tooth on the crankshaft pulley is aligned with the center line of the Crankshaft Position (CKP) sensor **(see illustration)**; in this position, the engine is set to TDC for no. 1 cylinder.

13   The camshafts each have a machined slot at the transaxle end of the engine. Both slots will be completely horizontal, and at the same height as the cylinder head machined surface, when the engine is at TDC for no. 1 cylinder. Manufacturer service tool 303-1565 is used to check this position, and to positively locate the camshafts in position. The rear intake camshaft cap and the vacuum pump drive adapter will have to be removed from the intake camshaft **(see illustrations)**.

Note: *The timing slots in the camshafts are offset. If the service tool cannot be installed, remove the timing pin and carefully rotate the crankshaft three fourths of a turn clockwise and repeat Steps 12 and 13 of this procedure.*

Caution: *Never use the camshaft alignment tool as a means to stop the engine from rotating - engine damage can result.*

14   Before rotating the crankshaft again, make sure that the tools are removed. Do not forget to install the brake vacuum pump adapter and tighten it securely.

15   Once no. 1 cylinder has been positioned at TDC on the compression stroke, TDC for any of the other cylinders can then be located by rotating the crankshaft clockwise 180-degrees at a time and following the firing order (see this Chapter's Specifications).

---

4   Valve cover - removal and installation

Removal

1   Relieve the fuel system pressure (see Chapter 4).

2   Disconnect the cable from the negative battery terminal (see Chapter 5).

3   Remove the Charge Air Cooler (CAC) inlet and outlet tubes (see Chapter 4), then remove the CAC bracket fasteners and bracket.

4   Disconnect the electrical connectors for the Variable Camshaft Timing (VCT) solenoids, EVAP canister purge valve, Fuel Rail Pressure (FRP) sensor and the Manifold

Absolute Pressure (MAP) sensor.

5   Disconnect the vacuum lines and retainers, then disconnect the fuel pump supply line (see Chapter 4).

6   Remove the individual ignition coil assemblies from the spark plugs (see Chapter 5).

7   Remove the bracket for the wiring harness on the valve cover stud, then set the harness aside.

8   Remove the engine oil dipstick.

9   Working progressively, unscrew the valve cover retaining fasteners, noting the captive spacer sleeve and rubber seal, then detach the cover.

10   Discard the cover gasket. This must be replaced whenever it is disturbed. Check that the sealing faces are undamaged and that the rubber seal at each bolt hole is serviceable. Replace any worn or damaged spark plug tube seals or Variable Camshaft Timing (VCT) solenoid seals.

Installation

11   Clean the cover and cylinder head gasket faces carefully. Install a new gasket onto the valve cover, ensuring that it is located correctly by the rubber seals and spacer sleeves.

12   At the top of the timing chain cover, apply a small bead of RTV sealant to the joints where the timing chain cover meets the cylinder head **(see illustrations)**.

13   Install the cover to the cylinder head, ensuring that the gasket remains seated as the cover is tightened.

14   Tighten the cover bolts, a little at a time in sequence **(see illustration)**, to the torque listed in this Chapter's Specifications.

15   Reconnect the battery (see Chapter 5).

16   Run the engine and check for signs of oil leakage.

5   Valve clearances - check and adjustment

1   Disconnect the cable from the negative battery terminal (see Chapter 5).

2   Remove the spark plugs (see Chapter 1), then remove the valve cover (see Section 4).

4.12a Apply a bead of RTV sealant to the joints where the timing chain cover . . .

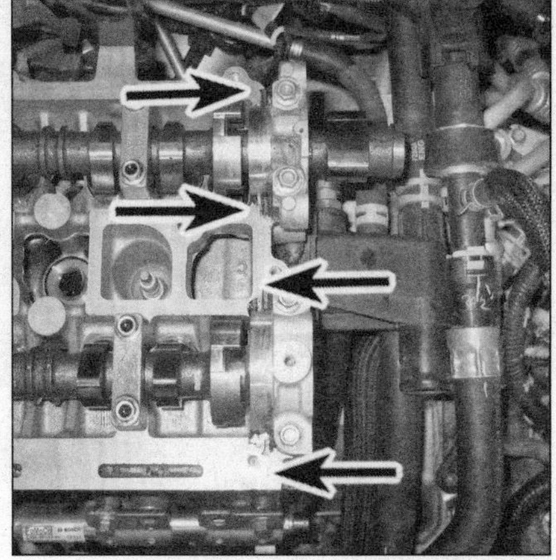

4.12b . . . meets the cylinder head

3   Loosen the right front wheel lug nuts, raise the front of the vehicle and support it securely on jackstands, then remove the wheel. Remove the fender splash shield (see Chapter 11).

4   Using a wrench or socket on the crankshaft pulley bolt, rotate the crankshaft clockwise and check each lifter when its camshaft lobe is straight up, ensuring that the measurement is between the base circle of the camshaft lobe and the top of the lifter. Use feeler gauges to measure the clearances **(see illustration)**.

5   The clearance must be checked between each camshaft lobe and the lifter it operates. Keep careful notes of the measurements recorded for each lifter.

6   If some measurements fall outside the recommended clearances in this Chapter's Specifications , the camshafts must be removed and the out-of-spec lifters removed (see Section 10). New lifters are available with various thicknesses to correct the valve clearances. Each lifter is marked with a thickness number. Only refer to the numbers after the decimal point. A "0.650" marking refers to an actual thickness of 3.650 mm.

7   To arrive at the desired thickness for

new lifters: add the thickness of the original lifter (such as 0.650 mm) to the clearance you measured. Subtract the midrange figure for ideal clearance (see the Specifications) from that number and you have the proper lifter thickness to order. Every thickness is not available, so choose the closest to your requirement.

8   Install the camshafts (see Section 10), then recheck the valve clearances.

9   The remainder of installation is the reverse of removal. Run the engine and check for oil leaks.

6   Intake manifold - removal and installation

Removal

1   Disconnect the cable from the negative battery terminal (see Chapter 5).

2   Raise the vehicle and support it securely on jackstands.

3   Remove the engine splash shield fasteners and shield.

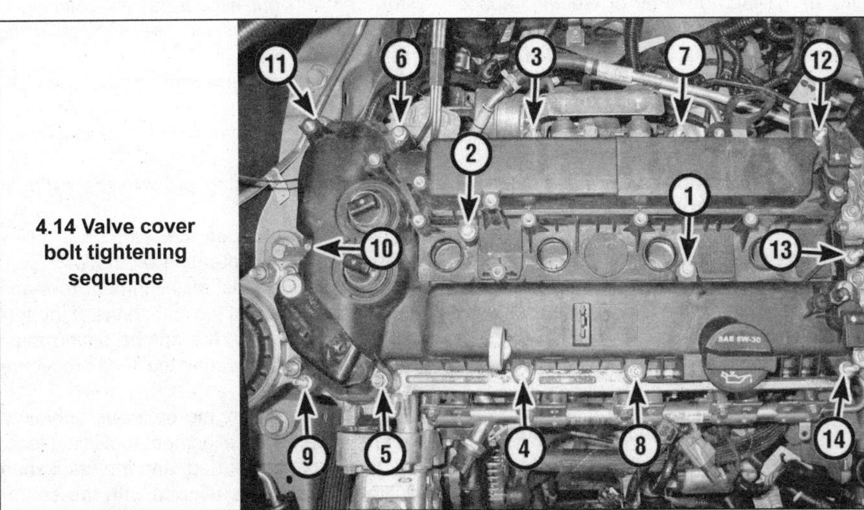

4.14 Valve cover bolt tightening sequence

5.4 Check the valve clearances with a feeler gauge of the specified thickness. If the clearance is correct, you should feel a slight drag as the feeler gauge is slid between the lifter and the camshaft

6.8 Push in on the lock ring while pulling the brake booster vacuum hose from the intake manifold

6.11 Intake manifold fasteners

4   Disconnect the EVAP tube from the Charge Air Cooler (CAC) outlet tube, then loosen the CAC outlet tube clamp and pull the tube off of the throttle body.
5   Disconnect the electrical connectors from the throttle body, Fuel Rail Pressure (FRP) sensor and Manifold Absolute Pressure (MAP) sensor.
6   Disengage the EVAP line and heater hose retainers below the manifold.
7   Remove the EVAP canister purge valve (see Chapter 6).
8   Release the power brake booster vacuum hose from the intake manifold by depressing the red quick-connect lock ring and pulling the hose outward at the same time **(see illustration)**.
9   Release the harness clips and set aside the wiring harness at the top of the intake manifold.
10   Disconnect the fuel line clips from the top of the manifold.
11   Remove the mounting bolts and pull the intake manifold away from the engine enough to access and disconnect the crankcase vent hose from the oil separator **(see illustration)**. Squeeze the two clips on the vent hose to release it.

Installation

12   There are individual gaskets for each of the four ports of the intake manifold. Using new manifold gaskets, install the intake manifold. Tighten the bolts a little at a time, working from the center out in a circular pattern, to the torque listed in this Chapter's Specifications.
13   Installation is otherwise the reverse of removal.

7   Crankshaft pulley - removal and installation

Removal

Caution: *Once the crankshaft pulley is loosened, the crankshaft (timing) sprocket will be*
loosened as well. The engine is considered out-of-time at this point. The installation procedure in this Section must be followed exactly to re-time the engine properly. Severe engine damage may occur otherwise.
Note: *You will need two special tools for this procedure: the camshaft positioning tool (303-1565, or equivalent) and the timing pin (303-507).*
1   Remove the drivebelt (see Chapter 1) and brake vacuum pump (see Chapter 9).
2   Remove the valve cover (see Section 4).
3   Remove the rear intake camshaft bearing cap bolts and cap. Prevent the camshaft from turning by placing a wrench on the flats of the camshaft, then loosen and remove the brake vacuum pump adapter from the end of the camshaft.
4   Remove the fasteners from the right driveaxle intermediate shaft bracket.
5   Set the engine to TDC using the camshaft and crankshaft positioning tools (see Section 3).
6   The crankshaft must be held to prevent its rotation while the pulley bolt is unscrewed. Use a strap wrench around the crankshaft pulley to hold it. The manufacturer recommends using an 1/2-inch drive air or electric impact gun to remove the pulley bolt.
Caution: *Failure to hold the crankshaft pulley securely while removing the pulley bolt could result in engine damage. NEVER use the timing pin or the camshaft alignment tool as a means of locking the crankshaft - they are designed for calibration only. Engine damage could occur by using these tools for anything other than their intended purpose.*
7   Unscrew the pulley bolt.
8   Remove the pulley and the diamond washer behind it. Obtain a new pulley bolt and diamond washer.

Installation

9   Install a new diamond washer onto the nose of the crankshaft.
10   Lightly coat the crankshaft front seal with
clean engine oil, then install the crankshaft pulley.
Note: *If the seal shows signs of leakage, you may want to replace it before installing the crankshaft pulley (see Section 9).*
11   Install special tool #303-1565 into the intake end of the camshaft to align the camshaft.
12   Install the Crankshaft Position (CKP) sensor alignment tool (#303-1521) onto the sensor. Install a new crankshaft pulley bolt and washer, hand tight only, and remove the tool.
13   Using the strap wrench to hold the pulley, tighten the crankshaft pulley bolt in stages, to the torque listed in this Chapter's Specifications.
Caution: *Do not use an impact gun to tighten the crankshaft pulley bolt.*
14   Remove the timing pin from the cylinder block.
15   Remove the camshaft alignment tool.
16   Remove the spark plugs and rotate the engine clockwise two complete revolutions by turning the crankshaft pulley bolt with a wrench or large socket.
Caution: *If you feel resistance at any point, stop and find out why. If the valve timing is incorrect, the valves may be contacting the pistons.*
17   Rotate the engine again to achieve TDC (see Section 3).
Note: *Rotate the engine in the clockwise direction only.*
18   Install the timing pin into the cylinder block.
19   With the tooth on the crankshaft pulley aligned with the center line on the CKP sensor, install the camshaft alignment tool and check the position of the camshafts. If the tool cannot be installed, the engine timing must be corrected by repeating the TDC procedure (see Section 3).
20   The correct engine timing is achieved when the camshaft alignment tool is in place, the timing pin is inserted, and the crankshaft pulley TDC tooth is aligned with the center

line on the CKP sensor, simultaneously.
21   Once correct engine timing is achieved, remove all the alignment tools and bolts and install the timing pin plug.
22   The remainder of installation is the reverse of removal.

8   Timing chain cover, timing chain and tensioner - removal and installation

Timing chain cover
Removal

1   Relieve the fuel system pressure (see Chapter 4), then disconnect the negative battery cable (see Chapter 5).
2   Loosen the water pump pulley bolts. Remove the drivebelt and drivebelt idler pulley (see Chapter 1), then remove the water pump pulley (see Chapter 3).
3   Remove the fuel injection high pressure pump and housing (see Chapter 4).
4   Remove the crankshaft pulley (see Section 7). After this Step, the engine must remain at TDC with the valve cover removed.
5   Disconnect the Crankshaft Position (CKP) sensor electrical connector, then remove the sensor (see Chapter 6).
Note: *Unfortunately with this engine, any time this sensor is removed, a new sensor must be installed. The new sensor is packaged with a special sensor alignment tool that is critical for installation.*
6   Remove the power steering hose bracket fastener and bracket from the bottom of cover.
7   Support the engine from above with an engine support fixture (see Chapter 7A, **illustration 5.11**). Raise the engine enough to remove the right engine mount (see Section 16).
8   Unbolt and set aside the power steering pump without disconnecting the hoses (see Chapter 10), then remove the pump bracket bolts and bracket.

9   Remove the crankshaft front oil seal (see Section 9).
10   Remove the bolts, stud bolts and the timing chain cover **(see illustration 8.11)**.

Installation
11   Installation is the reverse of removal, noting the following **(see illustration)**:
 a) *Clean the mating surfaces of all sealant.*
 b) *Install the engine cover within ten minutes of applying a 2.5 mm bead of RTV sealant.*
 c) *Tighten the bolts a little at a time, in sequence, to the torque listed in this Chapter's Specifications.*
 d) *Install a new crankshaft front oil seal.*
 e) *Verify proper crankshaft/camshaft timing (see Section 7).*
 f) *Install a new CKP sensor, which includes the necessary alignment tool (seeChapter 6). Do not tighten the sensor mounting bolts until the installation tool is in place.*

Timing chain and tensioner
Removal
12   Remove the timing chain cover (see Steps 1 through 10).
13   Compress the timing chain tensioner and place a pin (a drill bit or paper clip will work) into the hole to hold it in the compressed position **(see illustration)**.
Note: *The tensioner contacts the right-hand chain guide.*
Caution: *Compress only the round plunger on the tensioner and not the ratchet mechanism. The ratchet is next to the plunger and has square sides. If the ratchet needs to be reset, perform the following(see illustration) :*
 • *Remove the tensioner and place it lightly in a vise, with the jaws contacting the plunger and tensioner housing.*
 • *Place a pick-type tool in the hole closest to the ratchet to relieve the tension on the ratchet mechanism.*

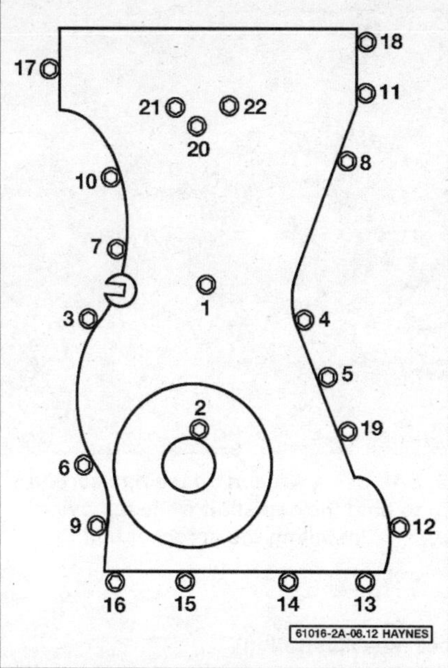

8.11 Timing chain cover bolt tightening sequence

 • *While holding the pick tool in place, move the ratchet back into the tensioner, then install a pin into the other hole to keep the plunger and ratchet compressed.*
 • *Remove the tensioner from the vise.*

14   Remove the two tensioner mounting bolts, then remove the tensioner.
15   Remove the loose timing chain guide (right), then remove the timing chain.
16   The left chain guide and camshaft sprockets can now be removed if necessary.

Installation
17   Remove the camshaft alignment tool (if installed).
18   Loosen both camshaft phaser and sprocket bolts but don't remove them. Use a wrench on the hexagonal area of the camshaft to hold it while turning the camshaft sprocket

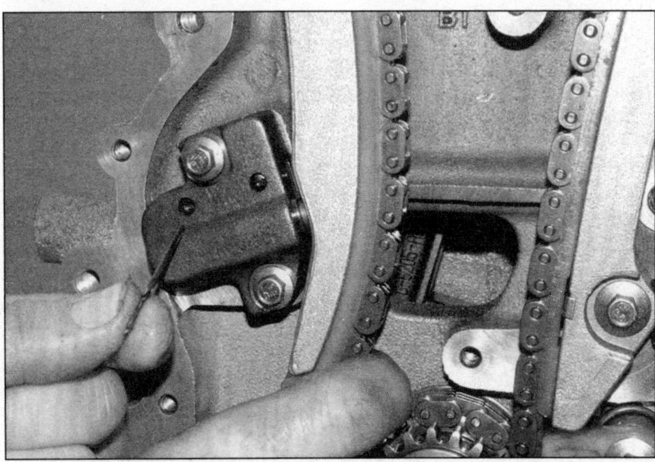

8.13a Compress the tensioner and insert the lock pin

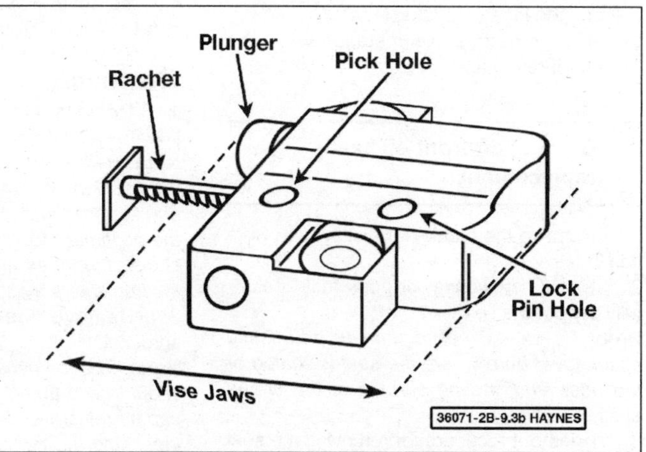

8.13b Timing chain tensioner details

8.18 Use a wrench on the hex portion to hold the camshaft while removing/ installing the sprocket bolt

8.22 Compress the tensioner to release the lock pin

9.5 Make certain that the oil seal is kept square as it is placed in the bore

bolt **(see illustration)**.
Caution: *Damage to the valves or pistons may occur if the camshafts are rotated during this procedure.*
19   Install the left chain guide (if removed).
20   Install the timing chain.
21   Install the right chain guide.
22   Install the timing chain tensioner and tighten the fasteners to the torque listed in this Chapter's Specifications. Remove the pin to release the tensioner to engage the chain guide **(see illustration)**.
23   Install the camshaft alignment tool.
24   While holding the camshafts in place with a wrench on the hex surface of the camshafts, tighten the camshaft sprocket bolts to the torque listed in this Chapter's Specifications.
Caution: *Do not rely on the camshaft alignment tool to hold the camshafts while tightening the camshaft sprocket bolts. Tool and engine damage may occur.*
25   Install the timing chain cover (see Step 11).
26   Install the fuel injection pump housing, making sure the camshaft lobe is at its lowest point on the lobe (see Chapter 4).
27   The remainder of installation is the reverse of removal.

9   Crankshaft front oil seal - replacement

1   Remove the crankshaft pulley (see Section 7).
2   Use a screwdriver or hook tool to carefully pry out the seal.
Note: *Be careful not to damage the timing chain cover bore where the seal is seated or the nose and sealing surface of the crankshaft.*
3   Another procedure for removing the seal is to drill a small hole on each side of the seal and place a self-tapping screw in each hole. Use these screws as a means of pulling the

seal out without having to pry on the seal itself.
4   Wipe the sealing surfaces in the engine cover and on the crankshaft. Clean and coat them with clean engine oil.
5   Press the new seal into the timing chain cover **(see illustration)**.
6   Use a seal driver or a suitable socket of the correct size to carefully drive the seal squarely into place **(see illustration)**.
7   The seal should be flush with the timing chain cover and remain square when installed.
8   Coat the lip of the seal (where it contacts the crankshaft) with clean engine oil.
9   Install the crankshaft pulley (see Section 7).

10   Camshafts and lifters - removal, inspection and installation

Note: *Whenever the camshafts are to be removed for a procedure, it's a good idea to check the valve clearances before disassembly (see Section 5), so any required new lifters can be ordered from a dealership.*

Removal

1   Remove the timing chain (see Section 8).
Note: *Before removing the timing chain, note the positions of the no. 1 cylinder cam lobes and the slots in the ends of the camshafts (for the alignment tool). When installing the camshafts, the lobes and the slots in the ends of the camshafts must be in the same positions.*
2   Remove the camshaft phaser and sprockets.
Note: *The camshaft phaser and sprockets should be marked with indelible ink so they can be reinstalled in the same position. When loosening the camshaft sprocket bolts, place a wrench on the hexagonal area of the camshaft to prevent it from turning (see illustration 8.18).*

9.6 A socket of the correct size can be used to install the new seal

3   Remove the Variable Camshaft Timing (VCT) solenoid fasteners and pull the solenoids out of the front camshaft bearing cap **(see illustration)**.
4   Remove the front camshaft bearing cap bolts and lift the one-piece cap from both camshafts.
5   Mark the bearing caps for each position and the direction it faces - the bearing caps must be reinstalled in their original positions.
Caution: *The camshaft bearing caps must be loosened in sequence, or the camshafts can be damaged.*
6   Loosen the camshaft bearing cap bolts, half a turn at a time, in sequence **(see illustration)**, to gradually and evenly release the pressure of the valve springs on the caps.
7   Withdraw the caps, noting their markings and the presence of the locating dowels, then remove the camshafts. There is no need to mark the camshafts; the exhaust camshaft can be identified by the reference lobe for the high pressure fuel pump on the end (and it is longer, as well).

10.3 Remove the Variable Camshaft Timing (VCT) solenoid retaining bolts

10.6 Camshaft bearing cap bolt loosening sequence - loosen each pair of bolts on the designated bearing cap in sequence

8   Obtain sixteen small, clean containers, and number them 1 to 16. Using a rubber suction tool (such as a valve-lapping tool), withdraw each lifter in turn and place them in the containers. Do not interchange the lifters.

Inspection

9   With the camshafts and lifters removed, check each for signs of obvious wear (scoring, pitting, etc.) and for roundness, and replace if necessary.

10   Measure the outside diameter of each lifter - take measurements at the top and bottom of each lifter, then a second set at right-angles to the first; if any measurement is significantly different from the others, the lifter is tapered or oval (as applicable) and must be replaced **(see illustration)**. If the necessary equipment is available, measure the inside diameter of the corresponding cylinder head bore. No manufacturer's specifications were available at the time of writing; if the lifters or the cylinder head bores are excessively worn, new lifters and/or a new cylinder head may be required.

11   If the engine's valve components have sounded noisy, it may be just that the valve clearances need adjusting (see Section 5).

12   Visually examine the camshaft lobes for score marks, pitting, galling (wear due to rubbing) and evidence of overheating (blue, discolored areas). Look for flaking away of the hardened surface layer of each lobe. If any such signs are evident, replace the component concerned.

13   Examine the camshaft bearing journals and the cylinder head bearing surfaces for signs of obvious wear or pitting. If any such signs are evident, consult an automotive machine shop for advice. Also check that the bearing oilways in the cylinder head are clear **(see illustration)**.

14   Using a micrometer, measure the diameter of each journal at several points. If the diameter of any one journal is less than the specified value, replace the camshaft.

15   To check the bearing journal running clearance, remove the lifters, use a suitable solvent and a clean lint-free rag to carefully clean all bearing surfaces, then install the camshafts and bearing caps with a strand of Plastigage across each journal. Tighten the bearing cap bolts in sequence **(see illustration 10.25)** to the torque listed in this Chapter's Specifications (do not rotate the camshafts), then remove the bearing caps and use the scale provided to measure the width of the compressed strands. Scrape off the Plastigage with your fingernail or the edge of a credit card - don't scratch or nick the journals or bearing caps.

16   If the running clearance of any bearing is found to be worn to beyond the specified service limits, install a new camshaft and repeat the check; if the clearance is still excessive, the cylinder head must be replaced.

17   To check camshaft endplay, remove the lifters, clean the bearing surfaces carefully and install the camshafts and bearing caps. Tighten the bearing cap bolts to the torque listed in this Chapter's Specifications , then measure the endplay using a dial indicator mounted on the cylinder head so that its tip bears on the camshaft right-hand end.

18   Tap the camshaft fully towards the gauge, zero the gauge, then tap the camshaft fully away from the gauge and note the gauge reading. If the endplay measured is found to be at or beyond the specified service limit, install a new camshaft and repeat the check; if the clearance is still excessive, the cylinder head must be replaced.

Installation

19   Confirm that the crankshaft is still positioned at TDC and that the timing pin is in place.

20   Liberally oil the cylinder head lifter bores and the lifters. Carefully install the lifters to the cylinder head, ensuring that each lifter is replaced to its original bore.

21   Liberally oil the camshaft bearing surfaces in the cylinder head, taking care not to get any on the camshaft cap mating surface.

22   Ensuring that each camshaft is in its original location, install the camshafts, locating each so that lobes for cylinder no. 1 are in the same position as noted in Step 1 and the slot in its left-hand end is parallel to, and just above, the cylinder head mating surface.

10.10 Measure the lifter outside diameter at several points

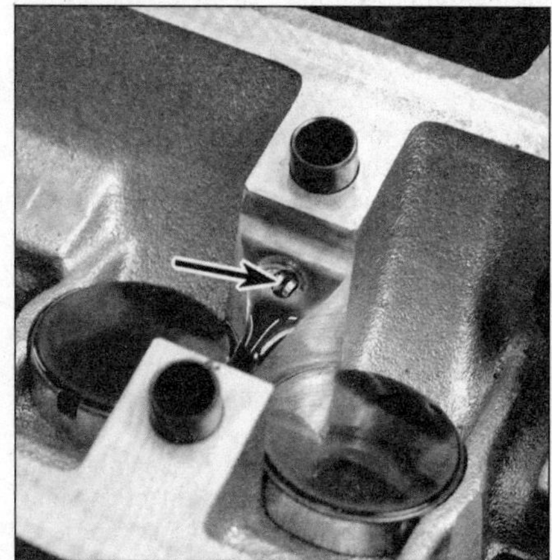

10.13 Check that the camshaft bearing oilways are not blocked with debris

10.25 Camshaft bearing cap tightening sequence

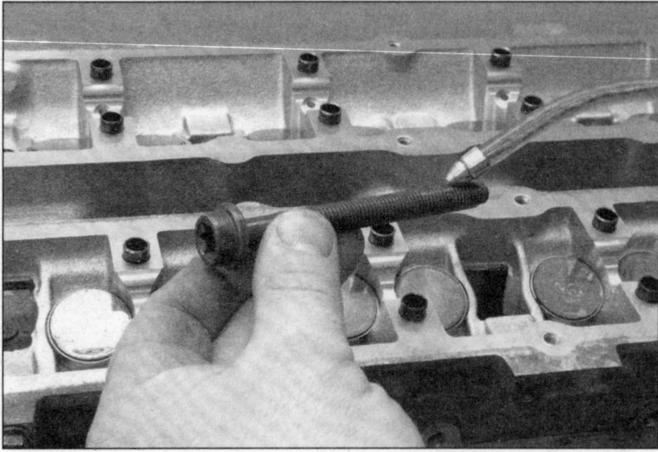

11.29 Apply a light coat of oil to the cylinder head bolt threads

Check that, as each camshaft is laid in position, the TDC setting tool will fit into the slot.
Caution: *When the camshaft bearing caps are tightened, it is imperative that the camshafts do not rotate from their TDC positions.*

23   Check that all mating surfaces are completely clean, unmarked and free from oil. Apply a 0.039-inch (1 mm) bead of RTV sealant to the exhaust camshaft rear bearing cap, making sure to keep the sealant out of the oil galleys.

24   Apply a little oil to the camshaft journals and lobes, then install each of the camshaft bearing caps to its previously-noted position, except the front bearing cap, so that its numbered side faces outwards, to the front (exhaust) or to the rear (intake).

25   Ensuring that each cap is kept square to the cylinder head as it is tightened down and working in the sequence shown, tighten the camshaft bearing cap bolts slowly and by one turn at a time, until each cap touches the cylinder head **(see illustration)**. This is the Step 1 torque.

26   Next, using the same sequence, tighten the bearing cap bolts to the Step 2 torque listed in this Chapter's Specifications.

27   Install the front bearing cap and tighten the cap in tighten the camshaft bearing cap bolts slowly and by one turn at a time, until the cap touches the cylinder head. This is the Step 3 torque then tighten the front bearing cap bolts to the Step 4 torque listed in this Chapter's Specifications.

28   Install the variable camshaft timing (VCT) solenoids into the front camshaft bearing cap and tighten the fasteners to the torque listed in this Chapter's Specifications.

29   Install the camshaft alignment tool #303-1565 then the phasers and sprockets to the camshafts, tightening the retaining bolts loosely.

30   The remainder of the reassembly procedure, including replacement of the timing chain and setting the valve timing, is as described in Section 8.

31   Before installing the valve cover, check the valve clearances (see Section 5).

11   Cylinder head - removal and installation

Warning: *Wait until the engine is completely cool before beginning this procedure.*

Removal

1   Relieve the fuel system pressure (see Chapter 4).

2   Disconnect the cable from the negative battery terminal (see Chapter 5).

3   Remove the air filter housing and charger air cooler inlet and outlet pipes (see Chapter 4).

4   Remove the alternator (see Chapter 5).

5   Drain the cooling system (see Chapter 1), then disconnect the four coolant hoses from the outlet housing on the end of the cylinder head.

6   Remove the turbocharger (see Chapter 4).

7   Remove the coolant expansion tank (see Chapter 3).

8   Remove the timing chain (see Section 8).

9   Disconnect the electrical connectors from the Cylinder Head Temperature (CHT) sensor, the Engine Coolant Temperature (ECT) sensor and the Camshaft Position (CMP) (see Chapter 6).

Note: *Whenever the camshafts are to be removed for a procedure, it's a good idea to check the valve clearances before disassembly, so any required new lifters can be ordered from a dealership.*

10   Unbolt and remove the VCT solenoid valves from the front camshaft bearing cap (see Section 10).

11   Remove the camshafts and lifters (see Section 10), keeping the lifters in order.

12   Remove the fuel rail and injectors (see Chapter 4).

13   Disconnect the hoses from the coolant outlet housing.

14   Remove the intake manifold (see Section 6).

15   If an engine support fixture or hoist is being used to hold the engine up, and it interferes with removal of the cylinder head, use a floor jack and block of wood to support the engine from below.

16   Loosen the cylinder head bolts, half a turn at a time, in the reverse of the tightening sequence **(see illustration 11.30a)**.

Caution: *The head bolts are torque-to-yield bolts that must be replaced with new ones on installation.*

17   Lift the cylinder head from the engine compartment **(see illustration)**.

18   If the head is stuck, be careful how you choose to free it. Remember that the cylinder head is made of aluminum alloy, which is easily damaged. Striking the head with tools carries the risk of damage, and the head is located on two dowels, so its movement will be limited. Do not, under any circumstances, pry the head between the mating surfaces, as this will certainly damage the sealing surfaces for the gasket, leading to leaks. Try rocking the head free, to break the seal, taking care not to damage any of the surrounding components.

19   Once the head has been removed, remove and discard the gasket. Check for the presence of locating dowels in the cylinder block and cylinder head. If dowels are present, make sure they are returned to their original locations after cleaning the components.

Inspection

20   The mating faces of the cylinder head and cylinder block must be perfectly clean before replacing the head. Use spray-on gasket remover and a hard plastic or wood scraper to remove all traces of gasket and carbon.

21   Take particular care during the cleaning operations, as aluminum alloy is easily damaged. Also, make sure that the carbon is not allowed to enter the oil and water passages - this is particularly important for the lubrication system, as carbon could block the oil supply to the engine's components.

22   To prevent carbon entering the gap between the pistons and bores, smear a little

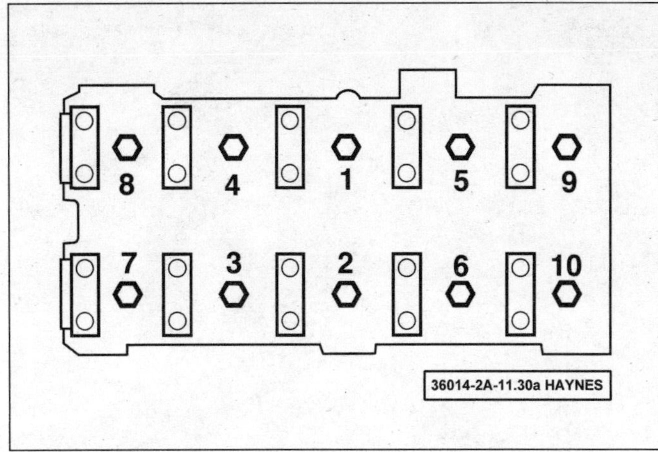

11.30a Cylinder head bolt tightening sequence

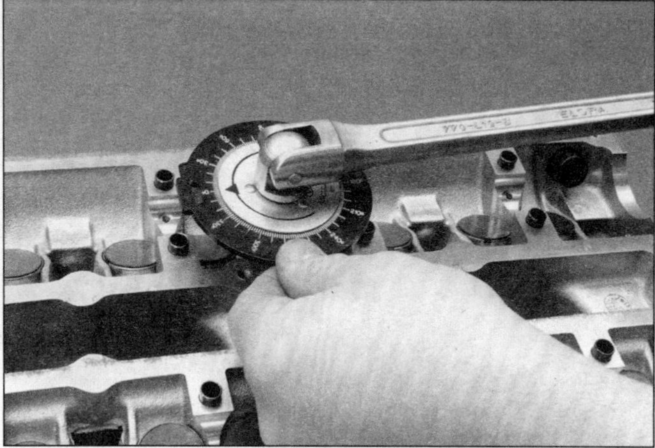

11.30b You can use a torque angle gauge, or you can carefully note the starting and stopping points of the wrench handle

grease in the gap. After cleaning each piston, use a small brush to remove all traces of grease and carbon from the gap, then wipe away the remainder with a clean rag.

23   Check the mating surfaces of the cylinder block and the cylinder head for nicks, deep scratches and other damage. Also check the cylinder head gasket surface and the cylinder block gasket surface with a precision straightedge and feeler gauges. If either surface exceeds the warpage limit listed in this Chapter's Specifications, the manufacturer states that the component out of specification must be replaced. If the gasket mating surface of your cylinder head or block is out of specification or is severely nicked or scratched, you may want to consult with an automotive machine shop for advice.

Installation

24   Wipe clean the mating surfaces of the cylinder head and cylinder block. If equipped, install the alignment dowels into their original locations.

25   The cylinder head bolt holes must be free from oil or water. This is most important, because a hydraulic lock in a cylinder head bolt hole can cause a fracture of the block casting when the bolt is tightened. Note the location of the cylinder head alignment dowels in the block.

26   Position a new gasket on the cylinder block surface, so that the "TOP" mark is facing up.

27   As the cylinder head is such a heavy and awkward assembly to install, it is helpful to make up a pair of guide studs from two 10 mm (thread size) studs approximately 90 mm long, with a screwdriver slot cut in one end - you can use two of the old cylinder head bolts with their heads cut off. Screw these guide studs, screwdriver slot upwards to permit removal, into the bolt holes at diagonally-opposite corners of the cylinder block surface; ensure that approximately 70 mm of stud protrudes above the gasket.

28   Install the cylinder head, sliding it down the guide studs (if used) and locating it on the dowels. Unscrew the guide studs (if used) when the head is in place.

29   Coat the threads with engine oil - do not apply more than a light film of oil **(see illustration)**. Install the NEW cylinder head bolts and screw them in by hand only until finger-tight.
Note: *New cylinder head bolts must be used.*

30   Tighten the cylinder head bolts, in sequence **(see illustration)** to the torque listed in this Chapter's Specifications. There are five tightening stages; the final two use the angle torque method **(see illustration)**.

31   The remainder of installation is the reverse of removal.

32   Change the engine oil and filter and refill the cooling system (see Chapter 1).

---

12   Oil pan - removal and installation

Removal

1   Raise the vehicle and support it securely on jackstands.

2   Drain the engine oil (see Chapter 1), then clean and install the engine oil drain plug, tightening it to the torque listed in the Chapter 1 Specifications. Remove and discard the oil filter, so that it can be replaced with the oil.

3   Remove the lower engine splash shield.

4   Remove the air filter housing (see Chapter 4).

5   The transaxle must be moved slightly back from the engine. Support the engine from above with a support fixture (see Chapter 2C) connected to the left end of the engine, near the transaxle, and support the transaxle with a floor jack. Loosen the upper engine-to-transaxle mounting bolts and back them off about 0.20 inch (5 mm), loosen the left-side engine-to-bellhousing bolts, then loosen the right-side bolts.
Caution: *The transaxle must not be moved back more than 0.20 inch (5 mm) or it can be damaged.*

6   Remove the transaxle roll restrictor mount through bolts and remove the mount (see Chapter 7A).

7   Remove the catalytic converter (see Chapter 4).

8   Remove the three bellhousing-to-pan bolts, and one oil pan-to-bellhousing bolt. Also remove the timing chain cover-to-oil pan fasteners. Remove the power steering hose bracket retaining nut and move the hose away from the oil pan.

9   Remove the air conditioning compressor, and tie it out of the way without disconnecting the compressor lines (see Chapter 3).

10   Use a screwdriver to pry between the engine and transaxle until the bellhousing has moved away from the block to the limit of the loosened bolts (about 0.20 inch [5 mm]).

11   Progressively unscrew the oil pan retaining bolts evenly until all the bolts are removed. Use a rubber mallet to loosen the oil pan seal, then lower the oil pan, turning it as necessary to clear the exhaust system. Unfortunately, the use of sealant can make removal of the oil pan more difficult. Be careful when prying between the mating surfaces, otherwise they will be damaged, resulting in leaks when finished. With care, a putty knife can be used to cut through the sealant.

Installation

12   Thoroughly clean and degrease the mating surfaces of the lower engine block/crankcase and oil pan, removing all traces of sealant, then use a clean rag to wipe out the oil pan.

13   Apply a 1/8-inch wide bead of sealant to the oil pan flange so that the bead is approximately 3/16-inch from the outside edge of the flange. Make sure the bead is around the inside edge of the bolt holes. Also apply sealant to the front flange of the oil pan where it meets the timing chain cover.
Note: *The oil pan must be installed within 10 minutes of applying the sealant.*

14   Install the oil pan bolts, only tightening

13.6 The oil pump pick-up tube is held by two mounting bolts (typical)

13.8 Using a holding tool on the oil pump drive sprocket to remove the retaining bolt

them finger tight at this time.

15   Install the timing chain cover-to-oil pan fasteners and tighten them to the torque listed in this Chapter's Specifications.

16   Tighten the oil pan-to engine block bolts, a little at a time, working from the center outwards in a circular pattern, to the torque listed in this Chapter's Specifications.

17   Tighten the oil pan-to-bellhousing bolts and the transaxle to engine bolts, a little at a time to draw them together evenly, to the torque listed in this Chapter's Specifications.

18   Lower the vehicle to the ground. Before refilling the engine with oil, wait at least 1 hour for the sealant to cure, or whatever time is indicated by the sealant manufacturer. Trim off the excess sealant with a sharp knife. Install a new oil filter (see Chapter 1).

13   Oil pump - removal and installation

Note: *The oil pump is serviced as a complete unit without any sub-assembly or internal inspection.*

1   Drain the engine oil and remove the oil filter (see Chapter 1).

2   Support the engine from above with a support fixture (see Chapter 2C).

3   Remove the timing chain cover (see Section 8).

4   Remove the air conditioning compressor fasteners and tie the compressor out of the way without disconnecting the compressor lines (see Chapter 3).

Note: *There is an air conditioning line bracket mounting nut just below the alternator that must be removed before trying to move the compressor.*

5   Remove the oil pan (see Section 12).

6   Remove the oil pump pick-up tube **(see illustration)** and discard the O-ring seal.

7   Use a screwdriver to pry the end of the oil pump drive chain tensioner's spring from under the shouldered bolt. Remove the two bolts and the tensioner.

8   Remove the chain from the oil pump sprocket. While holding the oil pump drive sprocket with a suitable tool, remove the sprocket bolt from the oil pump, then remove the sprocket **(see illustration)**.

9   Remove the oil pump mounting bolts, then remove the pump **(see illustration)**.

10   Installation is the reverse of removal, noting the following points:

  a) *Replace all gaskets with new ones.*
  b) *Tighten the oil pump mounting bolts, in a criss-cross pattern, to the torque listed in this Chapter's Specifications.*
  c) *After installing the oil pan, install a new oil filter and refill the crankcase with oil (see Chapter 1).*
  d) *Check for any oil warning lights in the instrument panel after the vehicle has been started and idling.*

14   Driveplate - removal, inspection and installation

Removal

1   Remove the transaxle (see Chapter 7A). Now is a good time to check components such as oil seals and replace them if necessary.

2   Use a center-punch or paint to make alignment marks on the driveplate and crankshaft to make replacement easier - the bolt holes are slightly offset, and will only line up one way, but making a mark eliminates the guesswork.

3   Hold the driveplate stationary and unscrew the bolts. To prevent the driveplate from turning, insert one of the transaxle mounting bolts into the cylinder block and have an assistant engage a wide-bladed screwdriver with the starter ring gear teeth while the driveplate bolts are loosened.

4   Loosen and remove each bolt in turn and ensure that new replacements are obtained for reassembly. These bolts are subjected to severe stresses and so must be replaced,

regardless of their apparent condition, whenever they are removed.

5   Remove the driveplate - do not drop it.

Inspection

6   Clean the driveplate to remove grease and oil. Check for cracked and broken ring gear teeth.

7   Clean and inspect the mating surfaces of the flywheel and the crankshaft. If the oil seal is leaking, replace it (see Section 15) before replacing the driveplate. If the engine has high mileage, it may be worth installing a new seal as a matter of course, given the amount of work needed to access it.

Installation

8   On installation, ensure that the engine/ transaxle adapter plate is in place (where necessary), then install the driveplate on the crankshaft so that all bolt holes align - it will fit only one way - check this using the marks made on removal. Install the new bolts, tightening them by hand.

9   Lock the driveplate by the method used on disassembly. Working in two or three

13.9 Remove the four mounting bolts for the oil pump

stages, tighten the new bolts to the torque listed in this Chapter's Specifications.
10   The remainder of installation is the reverse of removal.

15   Rear main oil seal - replacement

Note: *The one-piece rear main oil seal is pressed into a carrier mounted at the rear of the block.*
1   Remove the transaxle (see Chapter 7A) and the driveplate (see Section 14).
2   Remove the oil pan (see Section 12).
3   Unbolt and remove the oil seal and carrier.
4   Clean the oil seal carrier mating surfaces on the cylinder block and the crankshaft. Carefully remove and polish any burrs or raised edges on the crankshaft that may have caused the seal to fail.
5   Lightly coat the inside lip of the new seal with clean engine oil. Use a thin (but durable) two-inch wide plastic strip (or a two-liter plastic beverage bottle cut to size) around the inside circumference of the seal to act as a liner for installation. The manufacturer tool (#303-328) for this purpose also works well.
6   With the plastic seal liner or tool in place, carefully move the new carrier (with seal factory-installed) into position by sliding it onto the contact surface of the crankshaft.
7   Install the oil seal carrier bolts and finger tighten them while holding the carrier in place. Align the bottom of the seal carrier precisely with the bottom edge of the engine block to ensure that the surfaces are flush before tightening the carrier mounting bolts.
Caution: *The oil pan may leak if the two surfaces are not perfectly flush.*
8   Carefully remove the plastic liner or tool so that the new seal contacts the crankshaft mating surface correctly.
9   Tighten the oil seal carrier bolts in sequence **(see illustration)** to the torque listed in this Chapter's Specifications.
10   The remainder of installation is the reverse of removal.

16   Engine mount - check and replacement

1   Engine mounts seldom require attention, but broken or deteriorated mounts should be replaced immediately or the added strain placed on the driveline components may cause damage or wear.

Check

2   During the check, the engine must be raised slightly to remove the weight from the mounts.
3   Raise the vehicle and support it securely on jackstands, then position a jack under the engine oil pan. Place a large wood block between the jack head and the oil pan to prevent oil pan damage, then carefully raise the engine just enough to take the weight off the mounts.
Warning: *DO NOT place any part of your body under the engine when it's supported only by a jack!*
4   Check the mount to see if the rubber is cracked, hardened or separated from the bushing in the center of the mount.
5   Check for relative movement between the mount and the engine or chassis. Use a large screwdriver or prybar to attempt to move the mounts. If movement is noted, lower the engine and tighten the mount fasteners.

Replacement

Warning: *Wait until the engine is completely cool before beginning this procedure.*
Note: *Refer to Chapter 7A for information on the transaxle mount.*
6   Disconnect the cable from the negative terminal of the battery (see Chapter 5).

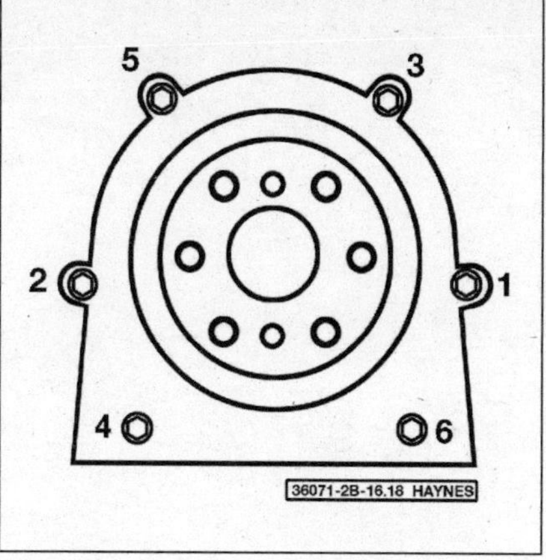

15.9 Rear main oil seal carrier bolt tightening sequence

7   Remove the engine splash shield fasteners and shield.
8   Remove the coolant expansion tank (see Chapter 3).
9   Place a floor jack under the engine with a wood block between the jack head and oil pan, then raise the engine slightly to relieve the weight from the mount.
10   Remove the power steering fluid reservoir nuts and place the reservoir out of the way.
11   Disengage the wiring harness retainer from the valve cover stud and move the harness out of the way.
12   Remove the fasteners and detach the mount from the frame and engine.
Caution: *Do not disconnect more than one mount at a time, except during engine removal.*
13   Installation is the reverse of removal. Use thread-locking compound on the mount bolts and tighten them to the torque listed in this Chapter's Specifications.

Notes

Chapter 2 Part B
V6 engines

Contents

Specifications

General

3.0L V6 engine

Engine type	Double overhead cam (DOHC) V6
Displacement	182 cubic inches
Engine VIN code	1
Bore	3.50 inches 88.9 mm
Stroke	3.13 inches 79.5 mm
Compression ratio	10:1
Compression pressure	See Chapter 2C
Firing order	1-4-2-5-3-6
Oil pressure	See Chapter 2C

3.5L V6 engine

Engine type	Double overhead cam (DOHC) V6
Displacement	214 cubic inches
Engine VIN code	
2008 through 2012 models	W
2013 and later models	8
Bore	3.64 inches 92.5 mm
Stroke	3.41 inches 86.6 mm
Compression ratio	
2008 through 2012 models	10.3:1
2013 and later models	10.8:1
Compression pressure	See Chapter 2C
Firing order	1-4-2-5-3-6
Oil pressure	See Chapter 2C

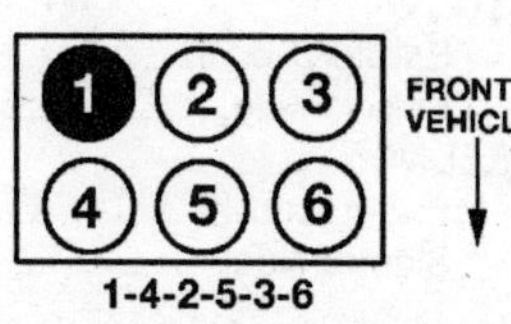

Cylinder location diagram

Camshafts

3.0L V6 engine
Lobe lift
Intake lobe .... 0.16 inch — 4.06 mm
Exhaust lobe .... 0.018 inch — 4.57 mm
Maximum lobe lift wear or loss (all) .... 0.003 inch — 0.076 mm
Journal diameter .... 1.060 to 1.061 inches — 26.924 to 26.949 mm
Bearing inside diameter .... 1.062 to 1.063 inches — 26.975 to 27.000 mm
Journal-to-bearing oil clearance
Standard .... 0.001 to 0.003 inch — 0.025 to 0.076 mm
Service limit .... 0.0047 inch — 0.119 mm
Endplay
Standard - limit .... 0.001 to 0.0064 inch — 0.025 to 0.163 mm
3.5L V6 engine
Lobe lift
2012 and earlier models (intake and exhaust)................ 0.038 inch — 0.965 mm
2013 and later models
Intake lobe.. 0.039 inch — 0.991 mm
Exhaust lobe... 0.038 inch — 0.965 mm
Maximum lobe lift wear or loss (all) .... 0.0024 inch — 0.061 mm
Journal diameter
First journal
2012 and earlier models.. 1.2202 to 1.2209 inches — 30.993 to 31.011 mm
2013 and later models... 1.535 to 1.537 inches — 38.99 to 39.01 mm
Others... 1.021 to 1.022 inches — 25.933 to 25.959 mm
Bearing inside diameter
First journal
2012 and earlier models.. 1.221 to 1.222 inches — 31.0134 to 31.0388 mm
2013 and later models... 1.537 to 1.538 inches — 39.0398 to 39.0652 mm
Others... 1.023 to 1.024 inches — 25.984 to 26.010 mm
Journal-to-bearing oil clearance (maximum)
First journal.. 0.0029 inch — 0.074 mm
Others.. 0.0030 inch — 0.0755 mm
Endplay
Standard .... 0.0012 to 0.0066 inch — 0.030 to 0.168 mm
Service limit .... 0.0075 inch — 0.191 mm
Runout - limit .... 0.0015 inch — 0.038 mm

Hydraulic lash adjuster (3.0L V6 only)

Diameter... 0.6290 to 0.6294 inch — 15.977 to 15.987 mm
Lash adjuster-to-bore clearance
Standard .... 0.0007 to 0.0027 inch — 0.018 to 0.069 mm
Minimum.. 0.0006 inch — 0.015 mm

Valve clearances (3.5L V6 engine only) - engine cold*

Intake .... 0.006 to 0.010 inch — 0.15 to 0.25 mm
Exhaust
Engines built through 10/09/2008 .... 0.011 to 0.015 inch — 0.30 to 0.40 mm
Engines built after 10/09/2008 .... 0.014 to 0.018 inch — 0.36 to 0.46 mm

On 2013 and later models, the manufacturer specifies that "engine cold" is room temperature.

Warpage limits

Head gasket surface warpage limit
3.0L V6
End-to-end... 0.005 inch — 0.127 mm
Side-to-side.. 0.002 inch — 0.051 mm
3.5L V6
End-to-end... 0.003 inch — 0.076 mm
Side-to-side.. 0.002 inch — 0.051 mm

Torque specifications

Ft-lbs (unless otherwise indicated)   **Nm**

Note: *One foot-pound (ft-lb) of torque is equivalent to 12 inch-pounds (in-lbs) of torque. Torque values below approximately 15 ft-lbs are expressed in inch-pounds, because most foot-pound torque wrenches are not accurate at these smaller values.*

	Ft-lbs (unless otherwise indicated)	Nm
Camshaft bearing cap bolts - in sequence		
3.0L V6 engines	89 in-lbs	10
3.5L V6 engines		
2010 and earlier models	89 in-lbs	10
2011 and 2012 models		
Step 1, bolts 1, 2, 3 and 4	71 in-lbs	8
Step 2, bolts 1, 2, 3 and 4	Tighten an additional 45 degrees	
Step 3, bolts 5 and 6	71 in-lbs	8
Step 4, bolts 7 and 8	71 in-lbs	8
Step 5, bolts 7 and 8	Tighten an additional 45 degrees	
Step 6, bolts 5 and 6	Loosen bolts 5 and 6	
Step 7, bolts 5 and 6	71 in-lbs	8
Step 8, bolts 5 and 6	Tighten an additional 45 degrees	
Step 9, bolts 9, 10, 11 and 12	71 in-lbs	8
Step 10, bolts 9, 10, 11 and 12	Tighten an additional 45 degrees	
Step 11, bolts 13 and 14	71 in-lbs	8
Step 12, bolts 15 and 16	71 in-lbs	8
Step 13, bolts 15 and 16	Tighten an additional 45 degrees	
Step 14, bolts 13 and 14	Loosen bolts 13 and 14	
Step 15, bolts 13 and 14	71 in-lbs	8
Step 16, bolts 13 and 14	Tighten an additional 45 degrees	
2013 and later models		
Step 1, all bolts	71 in-lbs	8
Step 2, all bolts	Tighten an additoinal 45 degrees	
Step 3, bolts 8, 9, 10 and 11 (4th cap)	Loosen bolts 8, 9, 10 and 11	
Step 4, bolts 8, 9, 10 and 11 (4th cap)	71 in-lbs	8
Step 5, bolts 8, 9, 10 and 11 (4th cap)	Tighten an additional 45 degrees	
Camshaft oil seal retainer bolts (3.0L V6 engine)	89 in-lbs	10
Camshaft sprocket bolt		
3.0L V6 engine		
2009 and earlier models		
Step 1	30	40
Step 2	Tighten an additional 90-degrees	
2010 models	159 in-lbs	18
3.5L V6 engine		
Step 1	30	40
Step 2	Loosen one turn	
Step 3	89 in-lbs	10
Step 4	Tighten an additional 90-degrees	
Crankshaft pulley bolt		
Step 1	89	121
Step 2	Loosen one full turn (360-degrees)	
Step 3	37	50
Step 4	Tighten an additional 90-degrees	
Cylinder head bolts		
3.0L engine (in sequence - **see illustration 11.23a**)		
Step 1	30	40
Step 2	66	90
Step 3	Loosen one full turn (360-degrees)	
Step 4	30	40
Step 5	Tighten an additional 90-degrees	
Step 6	Tighten an additional 90-degrees	
3.5L engine		
Main bolts (in sequence - **see illustration 11.23b**)		
Step 1	177 in-lbs	20
Step 2	26	35
Step 3	Tighten an additional 90-degrees	
Step 4	Tighten an additional 90-degrees	
Step 5	Tighten an additional 45-degrees	
M6 bolt (at front of cylinder head)	89 in-lbs	10
Drivebelt tensioner bolt	18	24
Driveplate-to-crankshaft bolts	59	80

Torque specifications	Ft-lbs (unless otherwise indicated)	Nm

Note: *One foot-pound (ft-lb) of torque is equivalent to 12 inch-pounds (in-lbs) of torque. Torque values below approximately 15 ft-lbs are expressed in inch-pounds, because most foot-pound torque wrenches are not accurate at these smaller values.*

	Ft-lbs	Nm
Exhaust manifold/catalytic converter nuts		
3.0L V6	15	20
3.5L V6		
Step 1	15	20
Step 2	18	24
Intake manifold assembly (in sequence - **see illustrations in Section 5**)		
Upper intake manifold bolts	89 in-lbs	10
Lower intake manifold bolts	89 in-lbs	10
Oil pan bolts (in sequence - **see illustrations in Section 12**)		
3.0L V6 engine		
To engine block	18	24
To transaxle	35	47
3.5L V6 engine		
Step 1, bolts 10 ,11, 13, 14	27 in-lbs	3
Step 2	Loosen 1/2-turn	
Step 3	Align oil pan with rear of cylinder block	
Step 4, bolts 10 ,11, 13, 14	27 in-lbs	3
Step 5, bolts 1 through 14	18	24
Step 6, bolts 15 and 16	89 in-lbs	10
Oil pump screen cover and tube bolts	89 in-lbs	10
Oil pump-to-engine block bolts	89 in-lbs	10
Oil pan baffle bolts		
Step 1		
Smaller nuts	44 in-lbs	5
Larger nuts	132 in-lbs	15
Step 2	Tighten all 8 nuts an additional 45-degrees	
Timing chain cover bolts		
3.0L engines (in sequence - **see illustration 8.21**)	18	24
3.5L engines (in sequence - **see illustration 8.22**)		
Step 1, bolts 17 through 20	27 in-lbs	3
Step 2, bolts 1 through 22	89 in-lbs	10
Step 3, bolts 23 through 25	133 in-lbs	15
Step 4, bolts 1 through 22	18	24
Step 5, bolts 23 through 25	55	75
Timing chain guides		
3.0L V6 engine	18	24
3.5L V6 engine	89 in-lbs	10
Timing chain tensioner arm bolts		
3.0L V6 engine	18	24
3.5L V6 engine	89 in-lbs	10
Timing chain tensioner bolts		
3.0L V6 engine	18	24
3.5L V6 engine	89 in-lbs	10
Valve cover bolts (in sequence - **see illustrations in Section 4**)	89 in-lbs	10
Variable Camshaft Timing (VCT)		
3.0L engine		
Actuator bolt		
2009 and earlier models		
Step 1	30	40
Step 2	Tighten an additional 90-degrees	
2010 models	159 in-lbs	18
Assembly (housing)	18	24
Solenoid	89 in-lbs	10
3.5L engine		
Actuator bolt		
Step 1	30	40
Step 2	Loosen one turn	
Step 3	89 in-lbs	10
Step 4	Tighten an additional 90-degrees	
Assembly (housing)	89 in-lbs	10
Solenoid	89 in-lbs	10

4.3 Disconnect the crankcase ventilation tube from the front valve cover - 3.5L engine shown

4.6 Disconnect the electrical connectors from the VCT oil control solenoids in each valve cover

1   General information

1   This Part of Chapter 2 covers in-vehicle repairs for the 3.0L, 3.5L and 3.5L Ti-VCT, Double Overhead Camshaft (DOHC) V6 Duratec engines. These engines feature aluminum engine blocks and aluminum cylinder heads with dual overhead camshafts and four valves per cylinder.

2   All information on engine removal and installation, as well as general overhaul procedures, is in Chapter 2C.

3   The following repair procedures are based on the assumption that the engine is installed in the vehicle. If the engine has been removed and mounted on a stand, many of the Steps in this Part of Chapter 2 will not apply. Some procedures on the 3.5L engine do, however, require engine removal.

4   In this Chapter, "left" and "right" are used to describe locations on the vehicle. These directions are in relation to the vehicle overall from the position of sitting in the driver's seat. However, for simplicity in describing the cylinder banks of the V6 engine, they are termed "front" (closest to the radiator) and "rear" (closest to the firewall).

2   Repair operations possible with the engine in the vehicle

1   Many major repairs can be done without removing the engine from the vehicle. Clean the engine compartment and the exterior of the engine with a pressure washer or degreaser solvent before doing any work. Cleaning the engine and engine compartment will make repairs easier and help to keep dirt out of the engine.

2   It may help to remove the hood for better access to the engine. Refer to Chapter 11, if necessary.

3   If the engine has vacuum, exhaust, oil, or coolant leaks that indicate the need for gasket replacement, repairs to the 3.0L engine can usually be done with the engine in the vehicle. The intake and exhaust manifold gaskets, the timing chain cover gasket, the oil pan gasket, crankshaft oil seals, and cylinder head gaskets are all accessible with the engine in the vehicle.

4   Exterior engine components, such as the intake and exhaust manifolds, the oil pan (3.0L V6), the water pump, the starter motor, the alternator, and many fuel system components also can be serviced with the engine installed. On 3.5L engines, the oil pan, timing chain cover, timing chain, camshaft and cylinder head procedures must be performed with the engine removed from the vehicle.

5   On 3.0L V6 engines, the timing chain and sprockets also can be replaced without removing the engine, although clearance is very limited.

3   Top Dead Center (TDC) for number one piston - locating

1   Top Dead Center (TDC) is the highest point in the cylinder that each piston reaches as it travels upward when the crankshaft turns. Each piston reaches TDC on the compression stroke and on the exhaust stroke, but TDC usually refers to piston position on the compression stroke.

2   Positioning one or more pistons at TDC is an essential part of several procedures such as rocker arm removal, valve adjustment, and timing chain replacement. These engines do not have TDC marks on the crankshaft pulley or front cover. The timing chain procedure in Section 9 describes setting the engine at TDC for cylinder Number 1.

3   After the number one piston is at TDC on the compression stroke, TDC for any of the remaining cylinders can be located by turning the crankshaft and following the firing order (refer to this Chapter's Specifications). Divide the crankshaft pulley into three equal sections with chalk marks at three points, each indicating 120-degrees of crankshaft rotation, and a corresponding mark on the timing chain cover, next to the TDC mark for cylinder number 1. For example, rotating the engine 120-degrees past TDC for number 1 piston will place the engine at TDC for cylinder number 4. Refer to the firing order for the remaining cylinder numbers.

4   Valve covers - removal and installation

Note: *The number and location of stud-bolts and standard bolts used to secure the valve covers may vary, depending on the year and build date of the vehicle. Keep track of the stud locations for reassembly.*

1   Disconnect the cable from the negative battery terminal (see Chapter 5).

2   Remove the engine access cover, if equipped.

Front valve cover

3   Disconnect the crankcase ventilation tube **(see illustration)**.

Note: *2013 and later models are equipped with a quick-disconnect type fitting (see Chapter 4).*

4   Remove upper intake manifold (see Section 5) and the ignition coils (see Chapter 5). Remove the air filter housing and duct (see Chapter 4).

5   Disconnect the wiring harness cover fasteners from the valve cover and position it off to the side. On 3.5L engines, remove the engine oil dipstick and tube.

6   Disconnect the electrical connectors from the VCT **(see illustration)**, fuel injectors and oxygen sensors (see Chapter 6).

7   Loosen the valve cover bolts/nuts gradually and evenly until all are loose. Follow the reverse of the tightening sequence **(see illustration 4.16a, 4.16b or 4.16c)**. Remove the valve cover fasteners and lift the valve cover off the engine.

8   Remove and discard the valve cover gaskets and spark plug tube seals (**see illustration**). Install new gaskets and seals during reassembly.

Note: *The spark plug tube seals can be re-used if they are in good condition and were not leaking.*

9   Make sure the bolt seals are in good condition (**see illustration**).

10   Inspect the valve cover and cylinder head sealing surfaces for nicks or other damage. Clean the sealing surfaces with brake system cleaner.

11   Install a new valve cover gasket, making sure the gasket is properly seated in the groove. Press the corner sections of the gasket in first, then the areas around the bolt holes, and finally the sections in between. If there is evidence of damage to the spark plug tube seals, replace these and the seal that surrounds the VCT solenoid.

12   Apply a 5/16-inch bead of RTV sealant where the timing cover meets the cylinder head, and on 3.0L models, where the camshaft seal retainer meets the rear of the cylinder head.

13   Lower the valve cover into position, making sure that the gaskets stay in place. Install the cover fasteners and tighten them gradu-

4.8 Check the spark plug tube seals, VCT seals and valve cover gasket. If they are in good condition they can be reused

4.9 Check the bolt seal - replace them if they're not in good condition

ally and evenly to the torque listed in this Chapter's Specifications.

14   Reconnect the wiring harness to the bracket studs.

15   Reconnect the crankcase ventilation tube to the valve cover.

16   Tighten the valve cover bolts, in sequence (**see illustrations**) to the torque listed in this Chapter's Specifications.

17   The remainder of installation is the reverse of removal.

Rear valve cover

18   On 2007 and earlier models, remove the power steering fluid reservoir (see Chapter 10). On 2008 through 2012 models, disconnect the power steering pressure switch and remove the switch bracket fastener.

19   Remove the ignition coils from the top of the valve cover (see Chapter 5).

20   Disconnect the VCT electrical connector(s), fuel injector electrical connectors and oxygen sensor connector (see Chapter 6).

21   Remove the radio/ignition interference capacitor from the stud on the valve cover (if equipped).

22   Disconnect the crankcase ventilation tube.

Note: *2013 and later models are equipped with a quick-disconnect type fitting (see Chapter 4).*

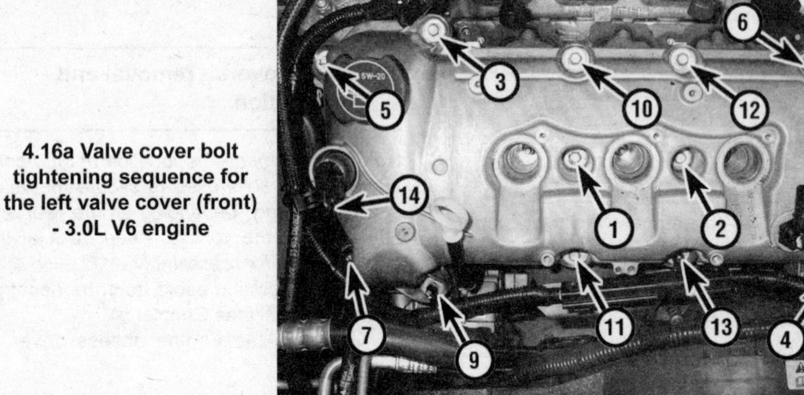

4.16a Valve cover bolt tightening sequence for the left valve cover (front) - 3.0L V6 engine

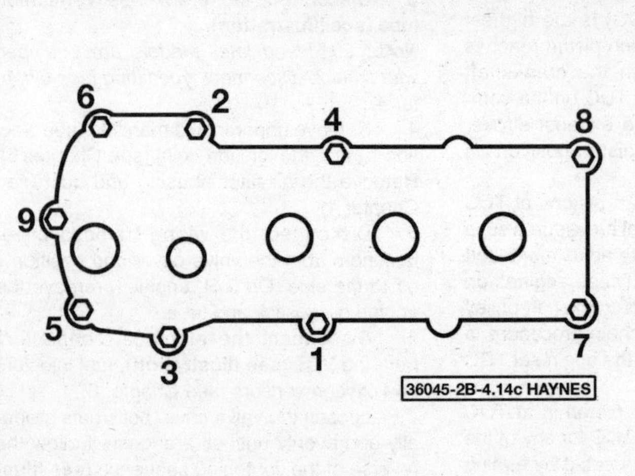

4.16b Valve cover bolt tightening sequence for the left valve cover (front) - 2012 and earlier 3.5L V6 engines

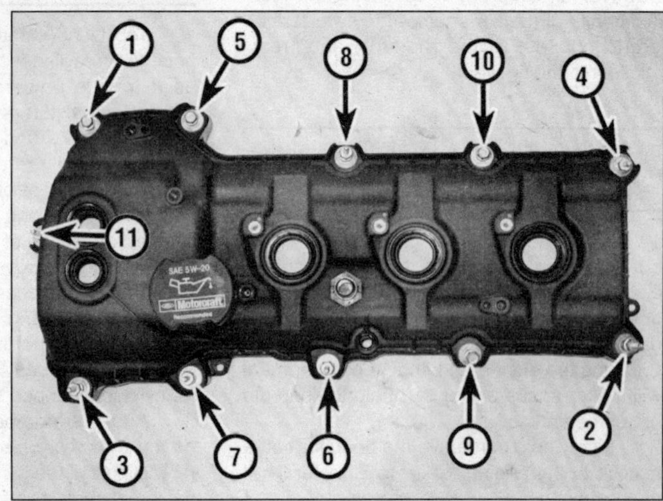

4.16c Valve cover bolt tightening sequence for the left valve cover (front) - 2013 and later 3.5L V6 engines

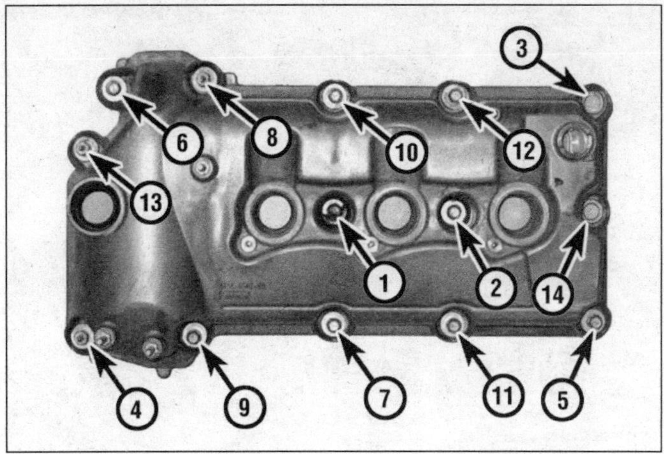

4.29a Valve cover bolt tightening sequence for the right valve cover (rear) - 3.0L V6 engine

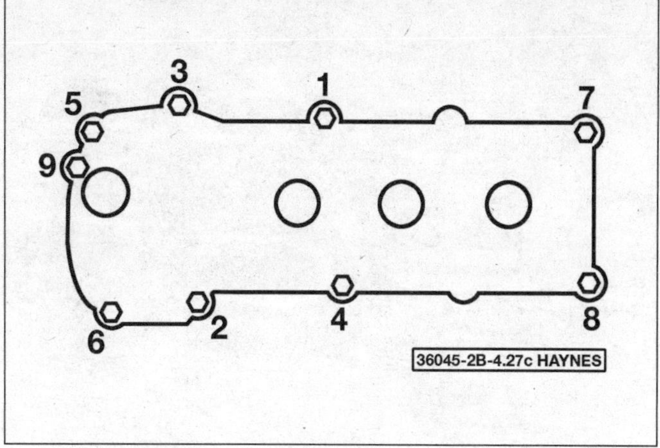

4.29b Valve cover bolt tightening sequence for the right valve cover (rear) - 2012 and earlier 3.5L V6 engines

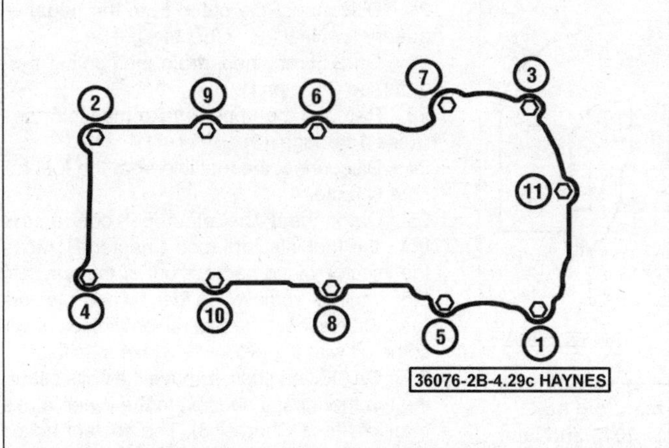

4.29c Valve cover bolt tightening sequence for the right valve cover (rear) - 2013 and later 3.5L V6 engines

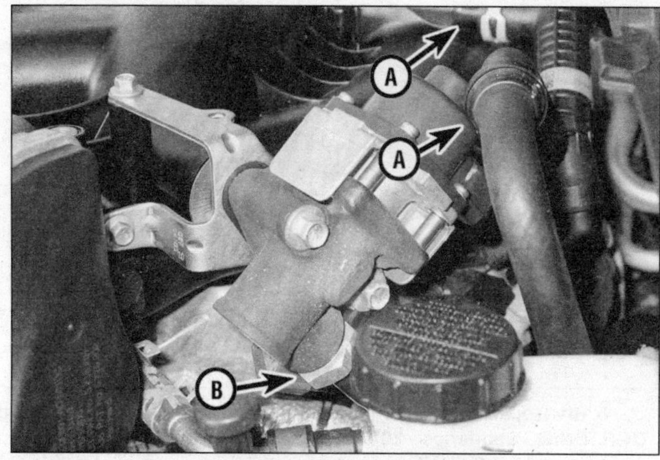

5.5 At the left end of the manifold, disconnect the hoses (A) and the EGR pipe (B)

23   On 3.5L engines, remove the bolts securing the air conditioning refrigerant pipe and move the pipe aside to clear the valve cover. **Warning:** *Do not disconnect the refrigerant line/hose connections.*

24   Loosen the valve cover fasteners gradually and evenly, until all fasteners are loose. Follow the reverse of the tightening sequence **(see illustration 4.29a, 4.29b or 4.29c).** Then, unscrew and remove the fasteners. Keep track of the stud locations for reassembly. Lift the valve cover off the cylinder head.

25   Remove the valve cover gasket and inspect the spark plug tube seals and bolt seals **(see illustrations 4.8 and 4.9).** Install new gaskets and seals during reassembly if necessary. **Note:** *The spark plug tube seals can be re-used if they are in good condition and were not leaking.*

26   Inspect the valve cover and cylinder head sealing surfaces for nicks or other damage. Clean the sealing surfaces with brake system cleaner.

27   Install a new valve cover gasket, making sure the gasket is properly seated in the groove (see Steps 7 through 10). Press the corner sections of the gasket in first, then the areas around the bolt holes, and finally the sections in between. If there is evidence of damage to the spark plug tube seals, replace these and the seal that surrounds the VCT solenoid.

28   Apply a 5/16-inch bead of RTV sealant to the head-to-front cover joints and the cam seal retainer.

29   Install the valve cover fasteners and tighten them gradually and evenly, in sequence **(see illustrations),** to the torque listed in this Chapter's Specifications.

30   Reinstall all wiring harnesses and brackets.

31   Reinstall the ignition coils (see Chapter 5).

32   Install the upper intake manifold (see Section 5).

33   The remainder of installation is the reverse of removal.

5   Intake manifold - removal and installation

Upper intake manifold

Removal

1   Disconnect the cable from the negative battery terminal (see Chapter 5).

2   Remove the air filter housing and the air intake duct (see Chapter 4).

3   Remove the cross brace fasteners and roll mount fasteners, then remove the assembly from the strut towers, if equipped.

4   Disconnect the connector at the electronic throttle body, and any coolant hoses or other connectors at the throttle body.

5   On 3.0L engines, disconnect the MAP sensor connector, the EGR valve electrical connector and the EGR pipe **(see illustration).**

6   On 3.0L engines, disconnect then plug the two coolant hoses to the PCV.

7   Disconnect the EVAP hose, brake booster vacuum hose and PCV hose.

5.13 Remove the gaskets from the upper intake manifold

5.16a Upper intake manifold bolt TIGHTENING sequence - 3.0L V6

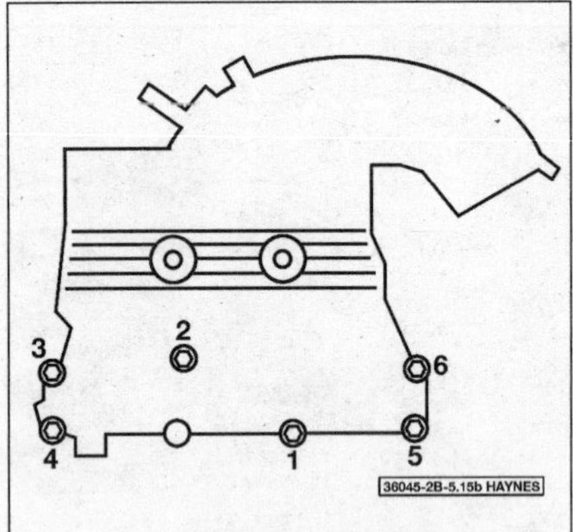

**5.16b Upper intake manifold bolt
TIGHTENING sequence - 2012 and earlier
3.5L V6**

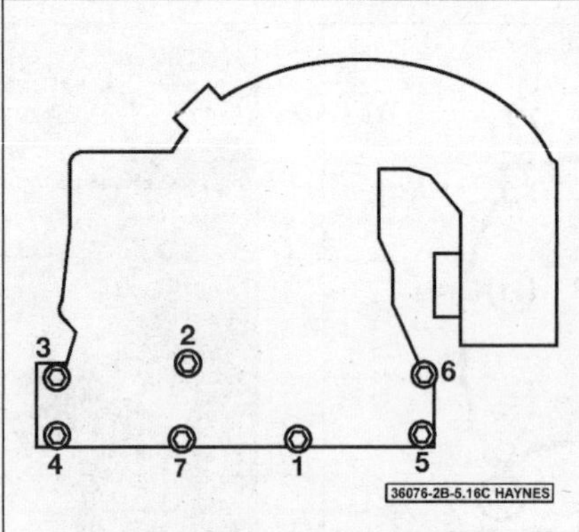

**5.16c Upper intake manifold bolt
TIGHTENING sequence - 2013 and later
3.5L V6**

8   On 3.5L engines, disconnect the heated PCV valve connector.

9   Disconnect the vacuum lines and electrical connectors from the upper intake manifold. Mark them with tape to insure correct reassembly.

10   Remove the wire harness bracket nuts and position the wiring harness off to the side. On 3.5L engines, remove the manifold brace, near the throttle body end of the manifold.

11   Remove the mounting bolt from the upper manifold brace(s). On some models, there is both a long brace and a short brace (near the throttle body).

12   Loosen the upper intake manifold bolts. Follow the opposite of the tightening sequence **(see illustration 5.16a, 5.16b or 5.16c)**. **Note:** *The bolts are captive and come out with the manifold.*

13   Remove and discard the upper intake-to-lower intake manifold gaskets **(see illustration)**.

Installation

14   If the gasket was leaking, check the mating surfaces for warpage. Check carefully around the mounting points of components such as the EGR pipe. Replace the manifold if

it is cracked or badly warped.

15   Install new gaskets. If the mating surfaces are clean and flat, new gaskets will ensure the joint is sealed. Don't use any kind of sealant on any part of the fuel system or intake manifold.

16   Locate the upper manifold on the lower manifold and install the fasteners. Tighten the fasteners in three or four steps, in sequence **(see illustrations)**, to the torque listed in this Chapter's Specifications.

17   The remainder of installation is the reverse of removal.

18   Reconnect the battery. The Powertrain Control Module (PCM) must relearn its idle and fuel trim strategy for optimum driveability and performance (see Chapter 6).

19   With the engine at operating temperature, check for fuel and vacuum leaks. Road test the vehicle and check for proper operation of all components.

Lower intake manifold
Removal

Warning: *Allow the engine to cool completely before beginning this procedure.*

20   Relieve the fuel system pressure (see

Chapter 4, Section 3).

21   Disconnect the cable from the negative battery terminal (see Chapter 5).

22   On 3.5L engines, drain the cooling system (see Chapter 1).

23   Remove the upper intake manifold (see Steps 1 through 13).

24   Disconnect the fuel line from the fuel rail (see Chapter 4).

25   Disconnect the electrical connectors from the fuel injectors (see Chapter 4). Move the injector wiring harness out of the way. On 3.5L engines, remove the fuel rail and injectors (on 3.0L engines, the fuel rail and injectors will come off with the two lower intake manifolds).

26   On 3.5L engines, remove the bolts securing the thermostat housing to the lower intake manifold (see Chapter 3). The coolant hoses can remain on the thermostat housing.

27   Loosen the lower manifold bolts gradually and evenly in the reverse of the tightening sequence **(see illustration 5.32a or 5.32b)**, then remove the bolts.

28   Lift the lower intake manifold(s) from the engine. Remove and discard the manifold gaskets.

29   Carefully clean all gasket material from the manifold and cylinder head mating surfaces. Don't nick, scratch or gouge the sealing surfaces. Inspect all parts for cracks or other damage. If the manifold gaskets were leaking, check the mating surfaces for warpage.

Caution: *Be very careful when scraping on aluminum engine parts. Aluminum is soft and gouges easily. Severely gouged parts may require replacement.*

Installation

30   Install new lower intake manifold gaskets on the cylinder heads.

31   Place the lower manifold(s) into position on the cylinder heads. Make sure the gaskets are not dislodged.

Note: *On 3.0L engines, assemble the fuel rail to the manifolds, installing the fuel rail bolts loosely. After the intake manifold bolts have been tightened in the next Step, tighten the fuel rail bolts.*

5.32a Lower intake manifold bolt TIGHTENING sequence - 3.0L V6

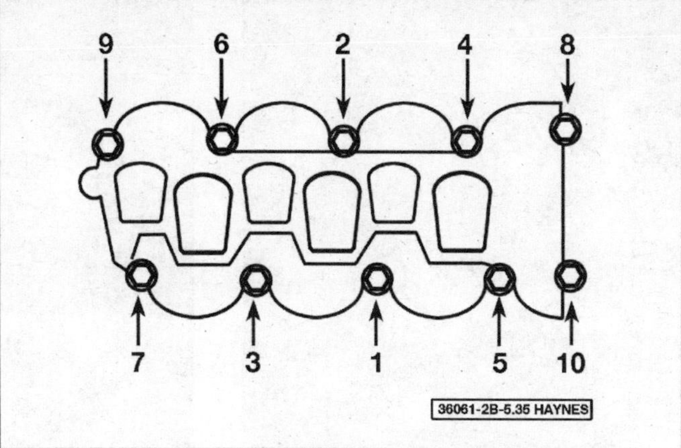

5.32b Lower intake manifold bolt TIGHTENING sequence - 3.5L V6

32   Install the lower manifold bolts. Tighten the bolts gradually and evenly, in sequence **(see illustrations)**, to the torque listed in this Chapter's Specifications.

33   The remainder of installation is the reverse of removal. Tighten the fasteners to the torque listed in this Chapter's Specifications.

34   On 3.5L engines, change the engine oil and filter, then refill and bleed the cooling system (see Chapter 1).

---

6   Exhaust manifolds - removal and installation

Note: *Before beginning this procedure, allow the engine to cool completely, then apply penetrating oil to the manifold and converter fasteners.*
Note: *On most models, the catalytic converter is an integral part of the exhaust manifold.*

Front exhaust manifold

Warning: *The engine and exhaust system must be completely cool before performing this procedure.*

1   Disconnect the cable from the negative battery terminal (see Chapter 5).

2   Disconnect the electrical connectors from the oxygen sensor and the catalytic converter monitor (see Chapter 6).

3   Raise the front of the vehicle and support it securely on jackstands. On 2013 and later models, remove the lower engine splash shield and skid plate, if equipped.

4   From below, disconnect the crossover pipe **(see illustration)**.

5   Remove the heat shield over the front exhaust manifold **(see illustration)**.

6   Remove the six nuts securing the exhaust manifold **(see illustration)**. Remove and discard the manifold gasket and the six nuts.

7   Remove the exhaust manifold.

8   Using a stud holding tool (available at auto parts stores) or a pair of nuts tightened together over a stud, extract the exhaust manifold studs and discard them.

9   Using a scraper, remove all old gasket material and carbon deposits from the manifold and cylinder head mating surfaces. If the gasket was leaking, check the manifold for warpage and have it resurfaced if necessary.
Caution: *Be very careful when scraping on aluminum engine parts such as the cylinder heads. Aluminum is soft and gouges easily. Severely gouged parts may require replacement.*

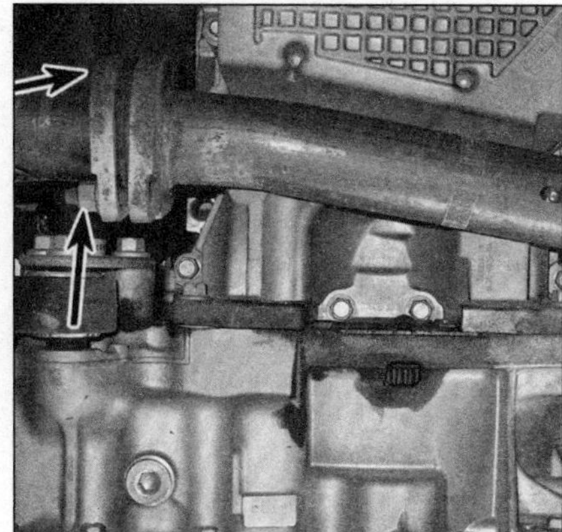

6.4 Disconnect the exhaust crossover pipe

10   Install new exhaust manifold studs with light oil on the threads, then install a new manifold gasket over the studs. Install the manifold and new self-locking nuts.

11   Tighten the nuts, starting with the center fasteners and working towards the ends, to the torque listed in this Chapter's Specifications.

12   The remainder of installation is the reverse of removal.

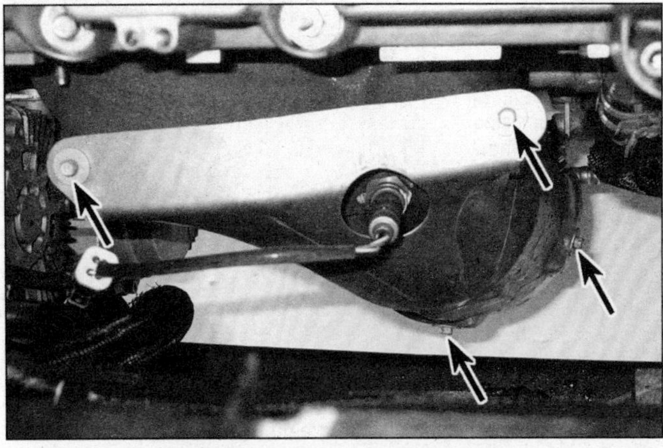

6.5 Front exhaust heat shield bolts

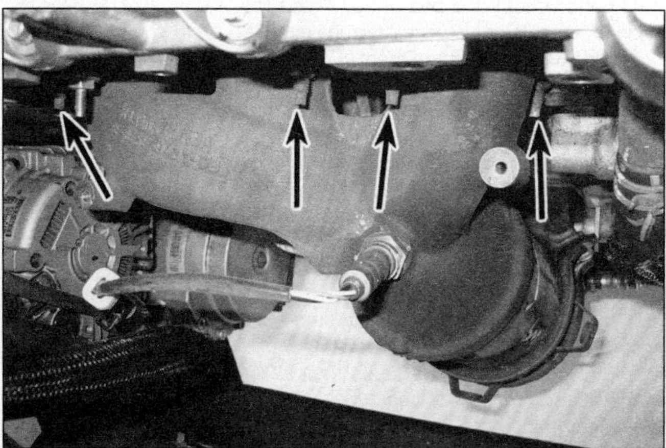

6.6 Remove the front exhaust mounting nuts from the studs (four of six shown)

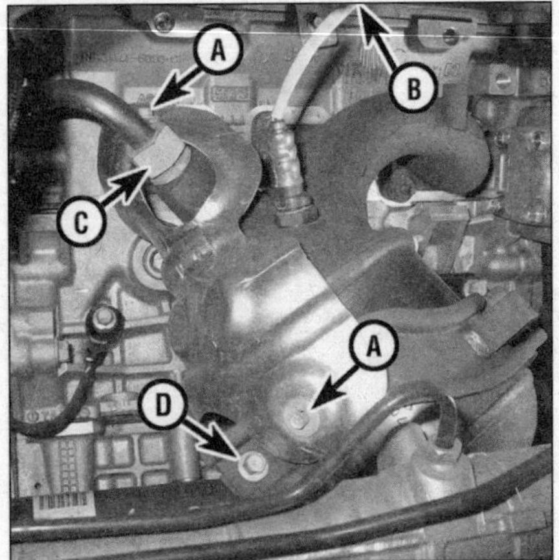

6.18 Rear exhaust heat shield bolts (A), oxygen sensor connector (B), EGR pipe (C) and catalytic converter brace bolt (D) - 3.0L V6 engine

7.5 Use a two-pin spanner to hold the pulley while removing the bolt

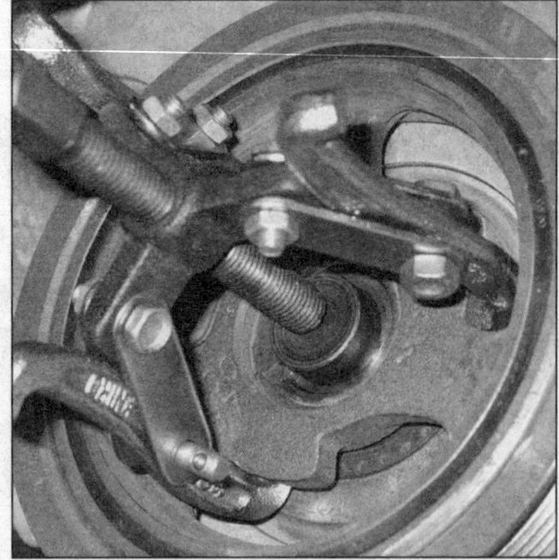

7.6 Remove the crankshaft pulley with a three-jaw puller

Rear exhaust manifold

Warning: *The engine and exhaust system must be completely cool before performing this procedure.*

13   Disconnect the cable from the negative battery terminal (see Chapter 5).

14   On 3.0L engines, remove the EGR pipe from the exhaust manifold (see Chapter 6).

15   Disconnect the connector to the rear bank oxygen sensor.

16   On 3.5L engines, remove the rear-bank catalytic converter (see Chapter 6).

Note: *The converter heat shield on 3.0L AWD models cannot be removed from the vehicle without first removing the heat shield over the steering gear. Remove the two bolts and remove the steering gear heat shield.*

17   Remove the nuts from the exhaust manifold flange and separate the crossover pipe from the manifold (see Chapter 4).

18   Remove the six exhaust manifold mounting nuts and remove the manifold from the engine **(see illustration)**. Remove and discard the manifold gasket.

19   Using a stud holding tool (available at auto parts stores) or a pair of new nuts tightened together over a stud, extract the exhaust manifold studs and discard them.

20   Using a scraper, remove all gasket material and carbon deposits from the exhaust manifold and cylinder head mating surfaces. If the gasket was leaking, check the manifold for warpage and have it resurfaced if necessary.

Caution: *Be very careful when scraping on aluminum engine parts. Aluminum is soft and gouges easily. Severely gouged parts may require replacement.*

21   Install new exhaust manifold studs with light oil on the threads, then install a new manifold gasket over the studs. Install the manifold and new self-locking nuts.

22   Tighten the nuts, starting with the center fasteners and working towards the ends, to the torque listed in this Chapter's Specifications.

23   The remainder of installation is the reverse of removal.

7   Crankshaft pulley and front oil seal - removal and installation

Removal

1   Disconnect the cable from the negative battery terminal (see Chapter 5).

2   Loosen the right front wheel lug nuts. Raise the front of the vehicle and support it securely on jackstands, then remove the wheel.

3   Remove the fender splash shield and skid plate (if equipped).

4   Remove the drivebelt (see Chapter 1).

5   Use a two-pin spanner to hold the crankshaft pulley while removing the crankshaft pulley retaining bolt **(see illustration)**.

6   Using a three-jaw puller, remove the crankshaft pulley **(see illustration)**.

Caution: *Use the proper adapter on the end of the crankshaft to prevent damage to the threads or end of the crankshaft. Also, the jaws of the puller must grasp the hub of the pulley, not the outer diameter.*

7   Using a seal puller, remove the seal from the timing chain cover. Note the depth at which the seal fits in the front cover and the orientation of the sealing lip so that the new seal will be installed in the same direction and to the same depth.

Installation

8   Inspect the front cover and the pulley seal surface for nicks, burrs, or other roughness that could damage the new seal. Correct as necessary.

9   Lubricate the new seal with clean engine oil and install it in the engine timing chain cover with a suitable seal driver which draws the seal in slowly. Be sure that the lip of the seal faces inward. If a seal driver is unavail-able, carefully tap the seal into place with a large socket and hammer until it's flush with the timing chain cover surface.

10   On 3.0L engines, apply RTV sealant to the keyway and inner bore of the pulley and lubricate the outer sealing surface of the pulley with clean engine oil. The pulley should be installed and tightened within four minutes of applying the sealant. Align the pulley keyway with the crankshaft key, and install the pulley with a suitable pulley installation tool, available at auto parts stores **(see illustration)**. Install and tighten the pulley bolt to the torque listed in this Chapter's Specifications.

Note: *The manufacturer suggests that a new pulley bolt be installed.*

11   The remainder of installation is the reverse of removal. Tighten the wheel lug nuts to the torque listed in the Chapter 1 Specifications.

12   Reconnect the battery, then start the engine and check for oil leaks.

7.10 Using a pulley installation tool, rotate the nut to drive the pulley onto the nose of the crankshaft

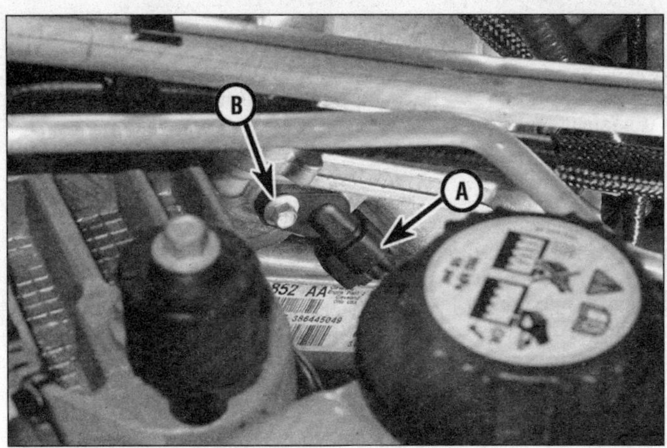

8.14 Disconnect the CMP sensor connector (A) and remove the sensor mounting bolt (B) - 3.0L engine shown

8.15 The engine must be supported from above with a support fixture and chains

8   Timing chain cover - removal and installation

Warning: *Wait until the engine is completely cool before beginning this procedure.*

Warning: *The air conditioning system is under high pressure. DO NOT loosen any fittings or remove any components until after the system has been discharged. Air conditioning refrigerant should be properly discharged into an EPA-approved container at a dealership service department or an automotive air conditioning repair facility. Always wear eye protection when disconnecting air conditioning system fittings.*

Removal

1   On 3.5L engines, have the air conditioning system discharged by an automotive air conditioning technician.

2   Relieve the fuel system pressure (see Chapter 4).

3   Disconnect the cable from the negative battery terminal (see Chapter 5).

4   Loosen the right front wheel lug nuts. Raise the front of the vehicle and support it securely on jackstands, then remove the wheel.

5   On 2013 and later models, remove the engine lower splash shield and skid plate, if equipped.

6   Remove the air filter housing inlet hose (see Chapter 4).

7   Remove the drivebelt and drivebelt tensioner, and remove the two idler pulleys from the front cover (see Chapter 1).

8   On 3.5L engines, remove the EVAP canister purge valve (see Chapter 6).

9   On 3.5L engines, disconnect, then cap or plug, the air conditioning lines to and from the receiver-drier and evaporator (see Chapter 3).

10   Remove the valve covers (see Section 4).

11   Remove the alternator and alternator mounting bracket (see Chapter 5). On 2013 and later models, remove the alternator mounting stud from the timing chain cover.

12   Remove the crankshaft pulley, then the front crankshaft oil seal (see Section 7).

Note: *The seal must be removed to create enough clearance for the cover to be removed and installed.*

13   Remove the power steering pump (see Chapter 10) and fluid lines including the mounting brackets, if equipped.

14   Disconnect the Crankshaft Position (CKP) sensor. Remove the Camshaft Position (CMP) sensors in front of each cylinder head **(see illustration)**.

15   Support the engine from above with a hoist or engine support fixture, using chains fastened to the engine lift brackets **(see illustration)**.

16   Disconnect the electrical connectors at the air conditioning compressor, then loosen the compressor mounting bolts and move the compressor aside as required for access to the engine cover. Remove the compressor bracket from the front cover. Remove the right side engine mount (see Section 17), then disconnect any remaining wires, hoses, clamps, or brackets that will interfere with engine cover removal.

Warning: *On 3.0L engines, the air conditioning system is under high pressure. Do not disconnect the hoses from the compressor.*

17   On 2013 and later models, the engine must be lowered to remove bolt #23 without letting the compressor hit the subframe, then raised to remove bolts #24 and #25 **(see illustration 8.28)**.

18   3.0L engines: Loosen the timing chain cover fasteners gradually and evenly, then remove the fasteners. Start with the oil pan-to-cover bolts, then the other bolts and studs **(see illustrations)**. Remove the timing chain cover.

Note: *Take a digital photo or draw a sketch of*

8.18a Front cover fasteners (seen from above)

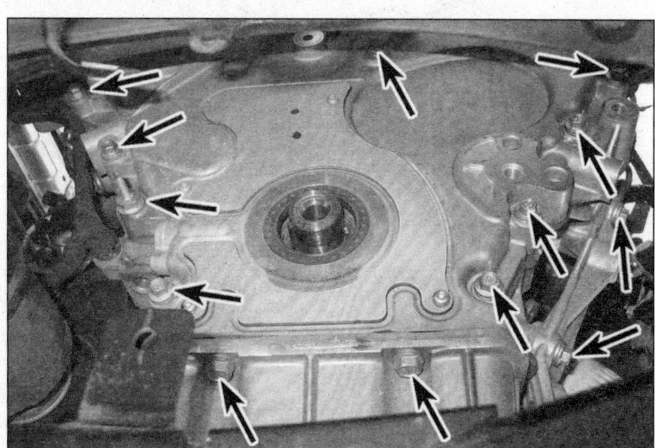

8.18b Front cover fasteners (seen from below)

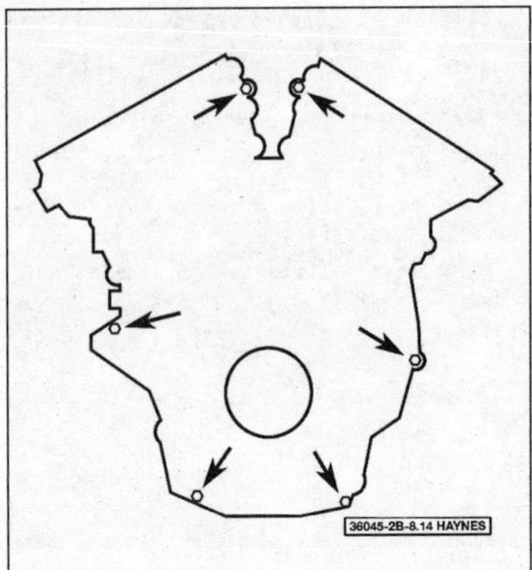

8.19 Location for inserting six bolts to push off the front cover (3.5L engines only)

the timing chain cover and fasteners. Identify the location of all stud bolts for installation in their original locations.

19   3.5L engine: Remove the cover bolts **(see illustration 8.28)**, take six of them and install them into the threaded holes in the cover **(see illustration)**. Tightening the bolts evenly a few turns will push the cover from the engine without damage.

Caution: *Make sure all of the timing chain cover bolts are removed before attempting to remove the cover.*

20   Remove and discard the cover-to-cylinder block gaskets.

Installation

21   Inspect and clean all sealing surfaces of the timing chain cover and the block.

Caution: *Be very careful when scraping on aluminum engine parts. Aluminum is soft and gouges easily. Severely gouged parts may require replacement.*

22   Replace the crankshaft seal in the front cover (see Section 7).

Caution: *The manufacturer recommends using Motorcraft High Performance Engine RTV Silicone to prevent the engine oil from foaming and causing possible engine damage.*

23   Apply a bead of RTV sealant approximately 1/8-inch wide around the sealing edges of the timing cover. Apply a 3/19-inch bead of sealant to the areas where the oil pan and cylinder heads meet at the engine block.

24   Install new front cover gaskets into the grooves on the cover. On 3.5L engines, install two dowel pins (bolts with heads cut off) into holes 21 and 22 in the engine block **(see illustration 8.28)**.

25   The manufacturer requires that bolts 17, 18, 19 and 20 **(see illustration 8.28)** be installed within the first four minutes after the timing has contacted the engine block and that all the remaining bolts be installed within 20 minutes

26   Install the timing chain cover and cover fasteners. Make sure the fasteners are in their original locations. Tighten the fasteners by hand until the cover is contacting the block and cylinder heads around its entire periphery.

27   3.0L engine: Tighten the cover bolts, in sequence **(see illustration)**, to the torque listed in this Chapter's Specifications.

28   3.5L engine: Install bolts 17 through 20 and remove the locating pins. Install the rest of the bolts, in sequence **(see illustration)**, to the torque listed in this Chapter's Specifications. Install the engine mount.

29   Install the drivebelt and tensioner. Tighten the tensioner pulley bolt to the torque listed in this Chapter's Specifications.

30   Install the crankshaft pulley (see Section 7).

31   Connect the wiring harness connectors to the CMP and CKP sensors.

32   Install the power steering pump and hoses (see Chapter 10), if equipped.

33   The remainder of installation is the reverse of removal.

34   Reconnect the battery, then start the engine and check for leaks.

9   Timing chains, tensioners, and chain guides - removal, inspection, and installation

Removal

3.0L engines

Caution: *The timing system is complex. Severe engine damage will occur if you make any mistakes. Do not attempt this procedure unless you are highly experienced with this type of repair. If you are at all unsure of your abilities, consult an expert. Double-check all your work and be sure everything is correct before you attempt to start the engine.*

1   Remove the timing chain cover (see Section 8). Slide the crankshaft position sensor trigger wheel off the crankshaft **(see illustration)**.

Caution: *The pulse (trigger) wheel has slots for more than one engine. Note the exact position of the pulse wheel to insure correct reassembly. The slot marked in orange and stamped "30 RFF" must align over the crankshaft/pulley key.*

2   Remove the spark plugs (see Chapter 1). These engines have two timing chains; the front-most chain drives the camshaft sprockets on the rear cylinder head, while the chain closest to the block drives the camshafts for the front cylinder head.

3   Install the crankshaft pulley retaining bolt, then use a wrench on the bolt to turn the crankshaft clockwise and place the crankshaft keyway at the 11 o'clock position. TDC number 1 is the starting and ending position for this procedure. Verify TDC by observing the index marks on the front of the camshaft sprockets **(see illustrations)**. If not properly aligned, turn the crankshaft exactly one full turn and again position the crankshaft keyway at 11 o'clock.

Caution: *Turning the crankshaft counterclockwise can cause the timing chains to bind and damage the chains, sprockets and tensioners. Turn the crankshaft only clockwise.*

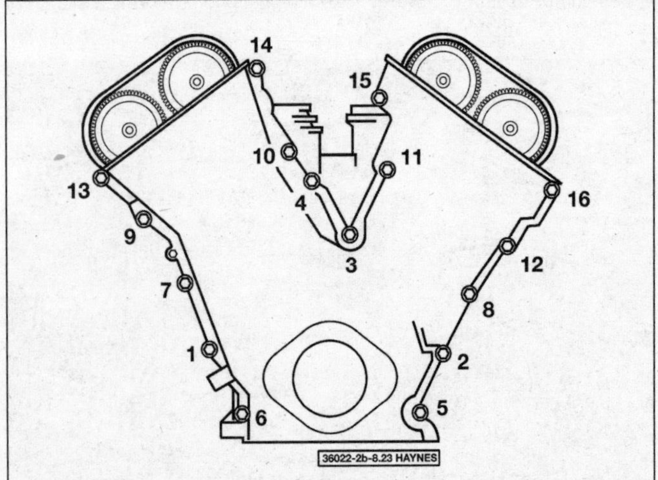

8.27 Timing chain cover bolt tightening sequence - 3.0L engine

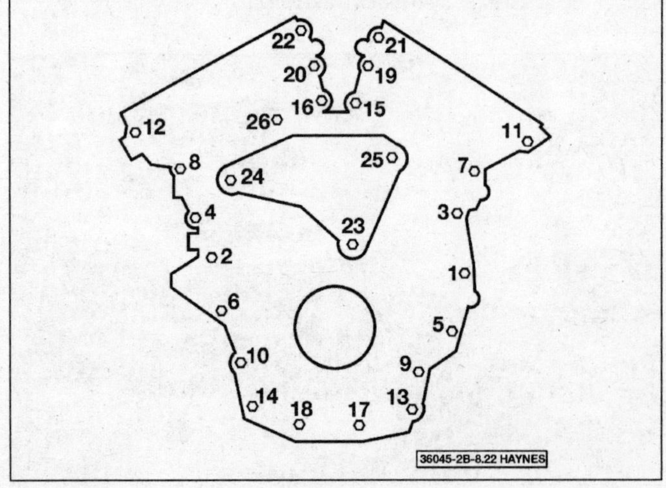

8.28 Timing chain cover bolt tightening sequence - 3.5L engine

9.1 Note the orientation of the slot and keyway on the trigger wheel

9.3a Position the crankshaft keyway at 11 o'clock; if the engine is at TDC for the number one piston . . .

9.3b . . . the rear bank exhaust camshaft sprocket timing marks will be positioned like this . . .

9.3c . . . the rear bank intake camshaft sprocket timing marks will be positioned like this . . .

9.3d . . . and the front bank camshaft sprocket timing marks will be positioned like this - intake at left, exhaust at right (3.0L engine)

9.4a Crankshaft keyway positioned at 3 o'clock for the Neutral position of the rear bank camshafts - 3.0L engine

9.4b Position of the rear bank camshaft timing marks and colored links for the Neutral position - 3.0L engine

4   Recheck the marks on the sprockets. If there are no marks on the chain links, mark the links directly above the camshaft sprocket marks. Continue to turn the crankshaft clockwise until the keyway is at the 3 o'clock position, which will set the camshafts on the rear cylinder head in their neutral position **(see illustrations)**. This ensures that the valves in the rear cylinder head will not contact the pistons. Remove the mounting bolts for the VCT assembly on the rear cylinder head.

5   Remove the two bolts securing the tim-

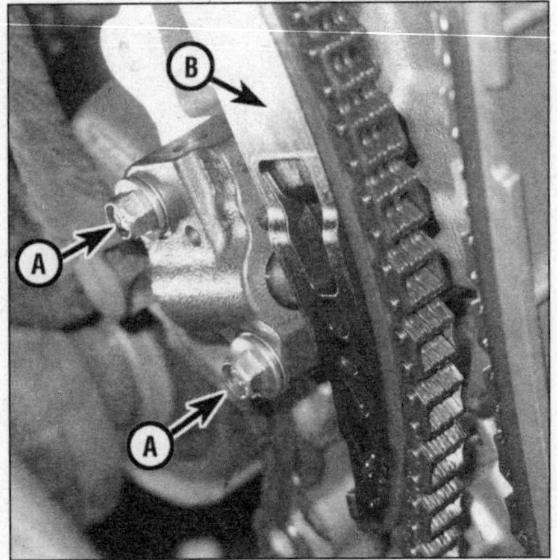

9.5 Remove the bolts (A) securing the rear timing chain tensioner and remove the tensioner, then slide the tensioner arm (B) off its pivot - 3.0L engine

9.10 Remove the front timing chain tensioner (A) and the tensioner arm (B)

9.11 Remove these bolts to remove the VCT assembly (front shown, rear similar) - 3.0L engines

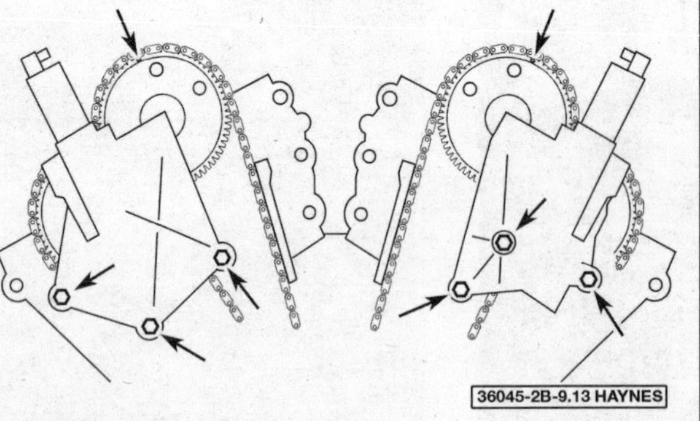

9.13 The position of the intake cam sprocket marks when the engine is set to TDC compression for cylinder no. 1 (upper arrows) - lower arrows indicate the VCT assembly mounting bolts

ing chain tensioner for the rear chain. Remove the tensioner, then remove the tensioner arm **(see illustration)**. Mark all parts that will be reused so they can be reinstalled in their original locations.

6   Lift the rear timing chain from the cam sprockets and remove the chain.

7   Remove the mounting bolts for the chain guide/VCT assembly on the rear cylinder head.

8   Slide the rear timing chain sprocket off the crankshaft.

9   Rotate the crankshaft 600-degrees (1-2/3 turns) clockwise, until the keyway is in the 11 o'clock position, setting the camshafts in the front cylinder head in their neutral position **(see illustration 9.3d)**.

10   Remove the front timing chain tensioner mounting bolts. Remove the tensioner and tensioner arm **(see illustration)**.

11   Lift the front timing chain off the sprockets and remove the chain. Remove the VCT assembly from the front cylinder head **(see illustration)**.

12   If necessary, slide the front timing chain crankshaft sprocket off the crankshaft. If you are removing the intake phaser/sprocket(s), insert a 3/8-inch-drive ratchet and extension into the hole at the back of the camshaft while loosening the phaser bolt(s).

3.5L engine

Note: *Two special camshaft holding tools (manufacturer tool no. 303-1248) are required for this procedure.*

Note: *Since the water pump on this engine is located behind the timing chain and components, it makes sense to replace the water pump while it is easily accessed during a timing chain replacement procedure.*

13   Remove the timing chain cover (see Section 8). Reinstall the crankshaft sprocket bolt and set the engine to TDC for cylinder number 1 **(see illustration)**.

Note: *At this point the TDC position will be approximate; when the special tools are installed, the TDC position will be exact.*

2012 and earlier models

14   These engines have three timing chains: The long primary chain drives the intake cam VCT sprocket on each intake camshaft and the water pump, while a smaller chain on each head drives the exhaust camshafts.

15   Install the special camshaft holding tools (manufacturer tool no. 303-1248) on each cyl-

inder head to lock the camshafts in the TDC position.

16   Remove the VCT assembly mounting bolts from the rear cylinder head, then the front cylinder head **(see illustration 9.13)**.

17   Remove the bolts and the primary timing chain tensioner and tensioner arm. Remove the lower chain guide from the front cylinder bank. Mark the chain links opposite the timing marks on the camshafts (if not already marked), and remove the primary timing chain.

18   Remove the upper chain guide from the front cylinder bank. If necessary, remove the crankshaft sprocket.

19   If the secondary timing chains and camshaft sprockets are to be removed for inspection or another procedure, compress the tensioner(s) and insert a pin into the hole in the tensioner to hold the tensioner in the retracted position. Unscrew the bolts for the intake (VCT) and exhaust camshaft sprockets, then remove both sprockets and the chain as an assembly.

Caution: *Make sure the camshaft holding tool is in place and prevents the camshafts from turning while unscrewing the bolts. Also, new bolts must be used for reassembly.*

20   Remove the bolts and the secondary chain tensioners.

Note: *The camshaft holding tool must be loosened and tilted (toward the flywheel end of the engine) to access the rearmost bolt of the tensioner.*

2013 and later models

21   Turn the engine clockwise until the VCT units (camshaft sprockets) on each intake camshaft are positioned perpendicular to the top surface of the cylinder heads (at the 12 o'clock position).

22   Remove the bolts that secure the valve train oil tubes to each cylinder head **(see illustration)**.

23   Install the special camshaft locking tools (303-1248), with the tools holding the flats on each camshaft.

9.22 Remove three of the camshaft cap bolts to remove the valvetrain oil tubes (2011 and later models)

9.27 VCT oil control solenoid mounting bolts (A and B), exhaust VCT unit (C) and intake VCT unit (D) (2011 and later models)

24   If you can't see the timing marks on the timing chain, add a paint dot to align with the marks on the VCT units and the crankshaft timing sprocket.

25   Remove the two bolts and the primary timing chain tensioner arm, then unbolt and remove the two tensioners.

26   Remove the mounting bolts and remove the lower left chain guide, then the lower right chain guide.

27   Remove the bolts securing the VCT solenoids to the cylinder heads (see illustration). You may have to twist or wiggle the solenoids to disengage them.

Note: *The intake solenoids are white, the exhaust solenoids are black.*

28   Keep the VCT solenoids in clean plastic sandwich bags, marked with their location.

29   Remove the primary timing chain.

30   The two camshafts on each cylinder head are jointly driven by a smaller secondary timing chain.

31   Depress and lock the secondary chain tensioner on each bank, using the factory tool (303-1530) inserted in the large hole at the first camshaft bearing cap, or use a length of threaded rod and nuts to hold the tensioner down, by pushing from the camshaft bearing cap.

32   With the camshafts still locked at TDC, remove the mounting bolts from the VCT units (camshaft sprockets), then remove the sprockets and secondary timing chains from the camshafts.

33   If the primary timing chain sprocket (at the center of the front of the block) is to be replaced, remove the nine bolts securing the plate that mounts the gear to the front of the block.

Inspection

Note: *Do not mix parts from the front and rear timing chains and tensioners, and on 3.5L engines, keep the primary and secondary tensioners separate.*

34   Clean all parts with clean solvent. Dry with compressed air, if available.

35   Inspect the chain tensioners and tensioner arms for excessive wear or other damage.

36   Inspect the timing chain guides for deep grooves, excessive wear, or other damage.

37   Inspect the timing chain for excessive wear or damage.

38   Inspect the camshaft and crankshaft sprockets for chipped or broken teeth, excessive wear, or damage.

39   Replace any component that is in questionable condition.

Installation

Caution: *Before starting the engine, carefully rotate the crankshaft by hand through at least two full revolutions (use a socket and breaker bar on the crankshaft pulley center bolt). If you feel anyresistance, STOP! There is something wrong - most likely, valves are contacting the pistons. You must find the problem before proceeding. Check your work and see if any updated repair information is available.*

Note: *The installation procedure is very much the reverse of the removal procedure, but refer to both the Removal and Installation Steps to ensure that you understand.*

3.0L engine

40   The timing chain tensioners must be fully compressed and locked in place before chain installation. To prepare the chain tensioners for installation:

a) *Insert a small pick into the hole in the tensioner and release the pawl mechanism.*

b) *Using a soft-jawed vise, compress the plunger into the tensioner housing until the plunger is bottomed in its bore.*

c) *Insert a 1/16-inch drill bit or a straightened paper clip into the small hole above the pawl mechanism to hold the plunger in place.*

Repeat this procedure for the other tensioner.

41   If removed, install the front timing chain crankshaft sprocket. Make sure the crankshaft keyway is still at 11 o'clock.

42   Look at the index marks on the sprockets of the front bank intake and exhaust camshafts. The marks should be at 9 o'clock (intake) and at 12 o'clock (exhaust) in relation to the top of the cylinder head **(see illustration 9.3d)**.

Caution: *The timing chains have three links that are a different color than the rest of the links. When installed, the colored links on the chain must be aligned with the index marks on the camshaft and crankshaft sprockets.*

Note: *If installing new timing chains and the colored links are not visible, mark the chain as follows:*

a) *Lay the chain on a flat surface in a circular shape. Select any link and mark it with a permanent marker.*

b) *Count 29 links counterclockwise and mark that link.*

c) *Continue counting (counterclockwise) and mark the 42nd link.*

43   Install the front timing chain guide/VCT assembly. Tighten the mounting bolts to the torque listed in this Chapter's Specifications.

44   Install the front timing chain around the camshaft and crankshaft sprockets. Make sure the index marks on the sprockets are aligned with the colored (or marked) links of the chain.

45   Install the front tensioner arm over its pivot dowel. Seat the tensioner arm firmly on the cylinder head and block.

46   Install the front timing chain tensioner. Be sure the tensioner plunger is fully compressed and locked in place. Tighten the tensioner mounting bolts to the torque listed in this Chapter's Specifications. Verify that the colored (or marked) links of the timing chain are still aligned with the index marks on the camshaft and crankshaft sprockets, and the crankshaft keyway is at 11 o'clock. If not, remove the timing chain and repeat the installation procedure.

47   Install the crankshaft sprocket for the rear timing chain on the crankshaft.

48   Rotate the crankshaft clockwise until the crankshaft keyway is in the 3 o'clock position. This will correctly position the pistons for

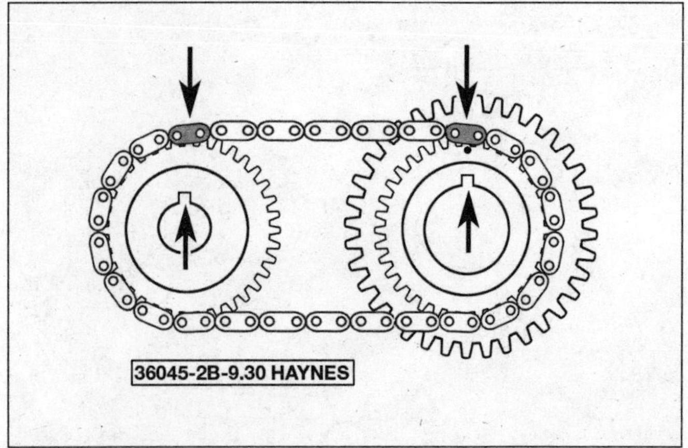

9.64 Align the secondary timing chain colored links with the keyways of the sprockets - 3.5L engine

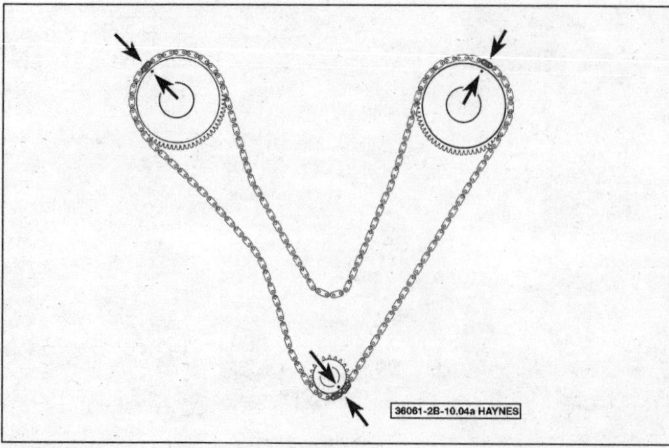

9.69 Align the colored links on the primary timing chain with the marks on the crankshaft and camshaft sprockets (VCT units)

installation of the rear timing chain.

49   Install the rear timing chain guide/VCT assembly. Tighten the mounting bolts to the torque listed in this Chapter's Specifications.

50   Double-check the position of the rear camshafts so the index marks on the sprockets are at (approximately) 3 o'clock (intake) and at 12 o'clock (exhaust) in relation to the top of the cylinder head **(see illustration 9.4b)**.

Caution: *The timing chains have three links that are a different color than the rest of the links. When installed, the colored (or marked) links on the chain must be aligned with the index marks on the camshaft and crankshaft sprockets.*

51   Install the rear timing chain around the camshaft and crankshaft sprockets. Make sure the colored (or marked) links of the chain are aligned with the index marks on the front of the camshaft and crankshaft sprockets.

52   Install the rear tensioner arm over its pivot dowel. Seat the tensioner arm firmly on the cylinder head and block.

53   Install the rear timing chain tensioner. Be sure the tensioner plunger is fully compressed and locked in place. Tighten the tensioner mounting bolts to the torque listed in this Chapter's Specifications. Verify that the colored (or marked) links of the timing chain are still aligned with the index marks on the camshaft and crankshaft sprockets, and the crankshaft keyway is at 3 o'clock. If not, remove the timing chain and repeat the installation procedure.

54   Remove the drill bits or wires (locking pins) from the timing chain tensioners.

55   Rotate the crankshaft counterclockwise back to the 11 o'clock position (the Number 1 TDC position). Verify the timing marks on the camshaft sprockets and the crankshaft sprocket are still aligned with the colored links **(see illustrations 9.3a, 9.3b, 9.3c and 9.4)**.

56   Install the crankshaft position sensor pulse (trigger) wheel on the crankshaft.

Caution: *Make sure the pulse wheel is installed with the crankshaft key in the slot marked "30 RFF"* **(see illustration 9.1)**.

57   Rotate the engine by hand at least two revolutions and verify that there is no binding.

Caution: *If any resistance is felt, STOP; double-check your work and find out why.*

58   Install the timing chain cover (see Section 8).

59   The remainder of installation is the reverse of removal.

60   Fill the crankcase with the recommended oil (see Chapter 1).

61   Reconnect the battery (see Chapter 5), then start the engine and check for leaks.

3.5L engine

2012 and earlier models

62   Install the primary timing chain guide for the rear (right) cylinder bank and tighten the bolts to the torque listed in this Chapter's Specifications.

63   Tilt the rear (right) cylinder bank camshaft holding tool to the rear and install the secondary timing chain tensioner, tightening the bolts to the torque listed in this Chapter's Specifications. Don't remove the lock pin from the tensioner yet.

64   Install the secondary timing chains onto the camshaft sprockets. The colored links on the chain must align with the marks/camshaft keyway slots in the sprockets **(see illustration)**.

65   Install the sprockets/VCT actuator (phaser)/secondary timing chain onto the rear camshafts. When installing the camshaft sprocket bolts, NEW bolts must be used. Tighten the bolts to the torque listed in this Chapter's Specifications.

66   Tilt the front (left) cylinder bank camshaft holding tool to the rear and install the secondary timing chain tensioner, tightening the bolts to the torque listed in this Chapter's Specifications. Don't remove the lock pin from the tensioner yet.

67   Install the sprockets/VCT actuator (phaser)/secondary timing chain (with the marks aligned as shown in **illustration 9.64**) onto the front camshafts. When installing the camshaft sprocket bolts, NEW bolts must be used. Tighten the bolts to the torque listed in this Chapter's Specifications. Remove the lock pin from the tensioner.

68   Install the crankshaft sprocket.

69   When the secondary chains and VCT units are installed and aligned, install the primary timing chain, aligning the colored links with the marks on the sprockets **(see illustration)**. When all components are installed and aligned, pull the pins holding back the two primary chain tensioners

70   Install the upper chain guide on the front (left) cylinder bank, tightening the bolts to the torque listed in this Chapter's Specifications.

71   Install the lower chain guide for the front cylinder bank, tightening the bolts to the torque listed in this Chapter's Specifications.

72   Install the primary timing chain tensioner arm to the rear cylinder bank.

73   Place the timing chain tensioner in a soft-jawed vise, with the jaws bearing on the tensioner body and the plunger. Swing the lever on the tensioner counterclockwise, then tighten the vise until the tensioner plunger has been retracted. Swing the lever clockwise, aligning the hole in the lever with the hole in the tensioner body, then install a lock pin made of heavy wire, a drill bit, or small Allen wrench. Remove the tensioner from the vise.

74   Install the primary timing chain tensioner, tightening the bolts to the torque listed in this Chapter's Specifications. Remove the lock pin from the tensioner.

Note: *It might be necessary to rotate the crankshaft slightly to create a little slack in the chain to enable the tensioner to be installed.*

75   Recheck the timing marks to make sure they are all in proper alignment.

76   Check the seals on the VCT housing, replacing them if necessary.

77   Install the VCT housings, making sure the dowels engage completely with their corresponding holes in the cylinder head. Install the bolts and tighten them a little at a time to the torque listed in this Chapter's Specifications.

78   Remove the camshaft holding tools, then rotate the engine by hand at least two revolutions and verify that there is no binding.

Caution: *If any resistance is felt, STOP; double-check your work and find out why.*

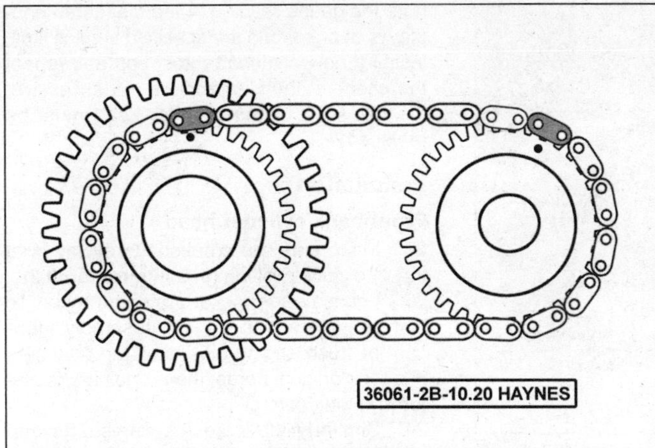

9.84 Align the colored links of the secondary timing chain with the marks on the back of the sprockets (VCT units) - 2013 and later models

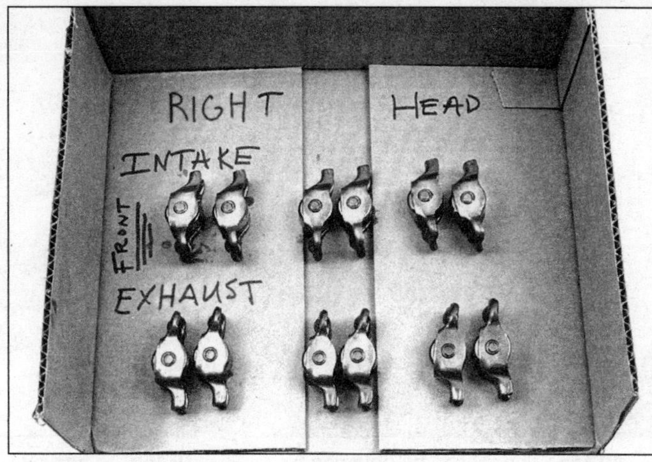

10.6 Place all the parts in a container so they can be separated and identified for installation in their original locations - 3.0L shown

79   Install the timing chain cover (see Section 8).
80   Refill the engine with oil (install a new filter) and coolant (see Chapter 1).

2013 and later models

81   If the primary chain gear and its plate were removed, clean the mounting surface and the block, then install the sprocket and plate with a new gasket. Prepare the primary chain tensioners by pushing in the release button and compressing the plunger until a nail or large paper clip can be inserted to hold the plunger.
82   If the secondary timing chain tensioners were removed, they cannot be reused. New tensioners must be installed.
Warning: *Do not remove the plastic clip that is keeping the new tensioner compressed.*
83   The tensioner is installed to the correct depth when you hear a snap. Install the tensioner shoe. The plastic clip can now be removed with pliers.
84   Align the colored links with the marks on the VCT units and install the chain on the backside of the VCT units **(see illustration)**. Align the two VCT units with the dowel pins on the front of the camshafts.
85   New bolts must be used to install the VCT units. Tighten the bolts to the torque listed in this Chapter's Specifications.
86   When the secondary chains and VCT units are installed and aligned, install the primary timing chain, aligning the colored links with the marks on the sprockets **(see illustration 9.69)**. When all components are installed and aligned, pull the pins holding back the two primary chain tensioners.
87   The remainder of installation is the reverse of removal.
88   Carefully rotate the crankshaft by hand through at least two full revolutions (use a socket and breaker bar on the crankshaft pulley center bolt).
Caution: *If you feel any resistance, STOP! There is something wrong - most likely, valves are contacting the pistons. You must find the problem before proceeding.*

89   Install a new oil filter, then add engine oil and coolant (see Chapter 1).
90   Run the engine and check for leaks.

10   Camshafts and valvetrain - removal inspection, and installation

3.0L V6 engine
Removal
Rear bank cylinder head

1   Remove the rear cylinder bank timing chain (see Section 9).
2   Note the location of each camshaft cap. Use a marker on each cap or make notes if they're not marked. Do not mix any of the camshaft caps.
3   Working in the reverse of the tightening sequence **(see illustration 10.31)**, gradually loosen the bolts that secure the camshaft bearing caps to the cylinder head, then remove the camshaft caps. It may be necessary to tap the caps lightly with a soft-faced mallet to loosen them from the locating dowels.
Caution: *The camshaft bearing caps and cylinder heads are numbered to identify the locations of the caps. The caps must be installed in their original locations. Keep all parts from each camshaft together; never mix parts from one camshaft with those for another.*
4   Mark the intake and exhaust camshafts to prevent reinstalling them in the wrong locations, then lift the camshafts straight up and out of the cylinder head.
5   Mark the positions of the rocker arms so they can be reinstalled in their original locations, then remove the rocker arms.
6   Place the rocker arms in a suitable container so they can be separated and identified **(see illustration)**.
7   Lift the hydraulic lash adjusters from their bores in the cylinder head. Identify and separate the adjusters so they can be reinstalled in their original locations.

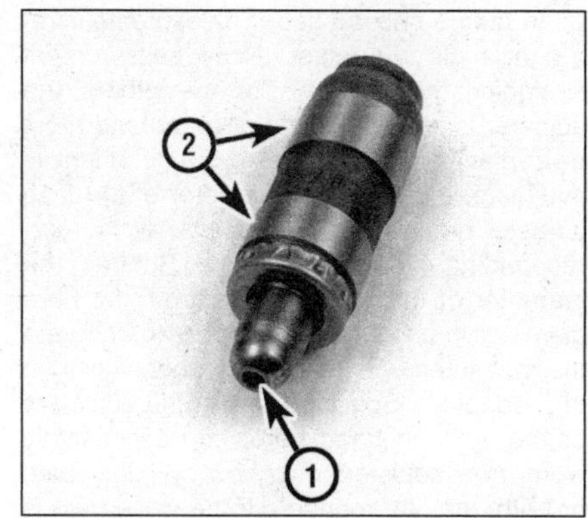

10.11 Inspect the lash adjusters for signs of excessive wear or damage, such as pitting, scoring or signs of overheating (bluing or discoloration), where the tip contacts the rocker arm (1) and the side surfaces that contact the bore in the cylinder head (2) - 3.0L models

Front bank cylinder head

8   To place the front bank camshafts in the neutral position turn the crankshaft 1-2/3 turns (clockwise) until the crankshaft keyway is at 11 o'clock **(see illustration 9.3a)**.
9   Remove the timing chain for the front cylinder bank (see Section 9). Also remove the water pump pulley and oil seal retainer from the rear of the exhaust camshaft.
Note: *Refer to Chapter 3 for the pulley removal procedure.*
10   Follow Steps 3 through 7 to remove the front (left side) camshafts, rocker arms and lash adjusters. Loosen the bearing caps on the front camshafts in the reverse of the tightening sequence **(see illustration 10.25)**.

Inspection

11   Check each hydraulic lash adjuster for excessive wear, scoring, pitting, or an out-of-round condition **(see illustration)**. Replace as necessary.

10.15a Lobe lift can be obtained by measuring camshaft lobe height . . .

10.15b . . . and by measuring the camshaft base circle - the difference between the two measurements equals lobe lift

12   Measure the outside diameter of each adjuster at the top and bottom of the adjuster. Then take a second set of measurements at a right angle to the first. If any measurement is significantly different from the others, the adjuster is tapered or out of round and must be replaced. If the necessary equipment is available, measure the diameter of the lash adjuster and the inside diameter of the corresponding cylinder head bore. Subtract the diameter of the lash adjuster from the bore diameter to obtain the oil clearance. Compare the measurements obtained to those given in this Chapter's Specifications. If the adjusters or the cylinder head bores are excessively worn, new adjusters or a new cylinder head, or both, may be required. If the valve train is noisy, particularly if the noise persists after a cold start, you can suspect a faulty hydraulic adjuster.

13   Inspect the rocker arms for signs of wear or damage. The areas of wear are the tip that contacts the valve stem, the socket that contacts the lash adjuster and the roller that contacts the camshaft.

14   Examine the camshaft lobes for scoring, pitting, galling (wear due to rubbing), and evidence of overheating (blue, discolored areas). Look for flaking of the hardened surface layer of each lobe. If any such wear is evident, replace the camshaft.

15   Calculate the camshaft lobe lift by measuring the lobe height and the diameter of the base circle of the lobe **(see illustrations)**. Subtract the base circle measurement from the lobe height to determine the lobe lift. If the lobe lift is less than that listed in this Chapter's Specifications the camshaft lobe is worn and should be replaced.

16   Inspect the camshaft bearing journals and the cylinder head bearing surfaces for pitting or excessive wear. If any such wear is evident, replace the component concerned. Using a micrometer, measure the diameter of each camshaft bearing journal at several points. If the diameter of any journal is less than specified, replace the camshaft.

17   To check the bearing journal oil clearance, remove the rocker arms and hydraulic lash adjusters (if not already done), use a suitable solvent and a clean lint-free rag to clean all bearing surfaces, then install the camshafts and bearing caps with a piece of Plastigage across each journal. Tighten the bearing cap bolts to the specified torque. Don't rotate the camshafts.

18   Remove the bearing caps and measure the width of the flattened Plastigage with the Plastigage scale. Scrape off the Plastigage with your fingernail or the edge of a credit card. Don't scratch or nick the journals or bearing caps.

19   If the oil clearance of any bearing is worn beyond the specified service limit, install a new camshaft and repeat the check. If the clearance is still excessive, replace the cylinder head.

20   To check camshaft endplay, clean the bearing surfaces and install the camshafts (without the lash adjusters or rocker arms) and bearing caps. Tighten the bearing cap bolts to the specified torque, then measure the endplay using a dial indicator mounted on the cylinder head so that its tip bears on the camshaft end.

21   Lightly but firmly tap the camshaft fully toward the gauge, zero the gauge, then tap the camshaft fully away from the gauge and note the gauge reading. If the measured endplay is at or beyond the specified service limit, install a new camshaft thrust cap and repeat the check. If the clearance is still excessive, the camshaft or the cylinder head must be replaced.

Installation

Front bank cylinder head

22   Make sure the crankshaft keyway is at the 11 o'clock position **(see illustration 9.2)**.

23   Lubricate the rocker arms and hydraulic lash adjusters with engine assembly lubricant or fresh engine oil. Install the adjusters into their original bores, then install the rocker arms in their correct locations.

24   Similarly lubricate the camshafts and install them in their correct locations.

25   Install the camshaft bearing caps in their correct locations. Install the cap bolts and tighten by hand until snug. Install the camshaft thrust caps and bolts. Tighten the bolts in four to five steps, following the sequence shown **(see illustration)**, to the torque listed in this Chapter's Specifications.

26   Install the seal retainer with a new seal over the left end of the exhaust camshaft. Tighten the bolts to the torque listed in this Chapter's Specifications.

27   Install the front timing chain sprocket on the crankshaft. Install the front timing chain (see Section 9). Install the water pump pulley onto the left end of the exhaust camshaft. **Note:** *Refer to Chapter 3 for the pulley installation procedure.*

Rear bank cylinder head

28   Turn the crankshaft clockwise and position the crankshaft keyway at the 3 o'clock position.

29   Lubricate the rocker arms and hydraulic lash adjusters with engine assembly lubricant or fresh engine oil. Install the adjusters into their original bores, then install the rocker arms in their correct locations.

30   Similarly lubricate the camshafts and install them in their correct locations.

31   Install the camshaft bearing caps in their correct locations. Install the cap bolts and tighten by hand until snug, then install the camshaft thrust caps and bolts. Tighten the bolts in four to five steps, in sequence **(see**

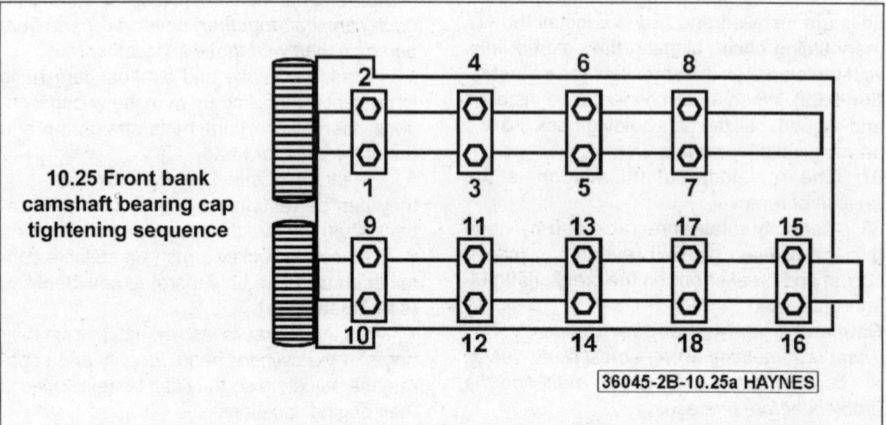

10.25 Front bank camshaft bearing cap tightening sequence

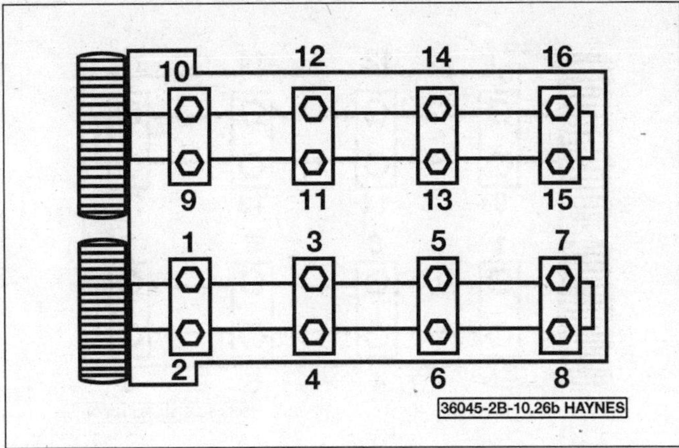

10.31 Rear bank camshaft bearing cap tightening sequence - 3.0L models

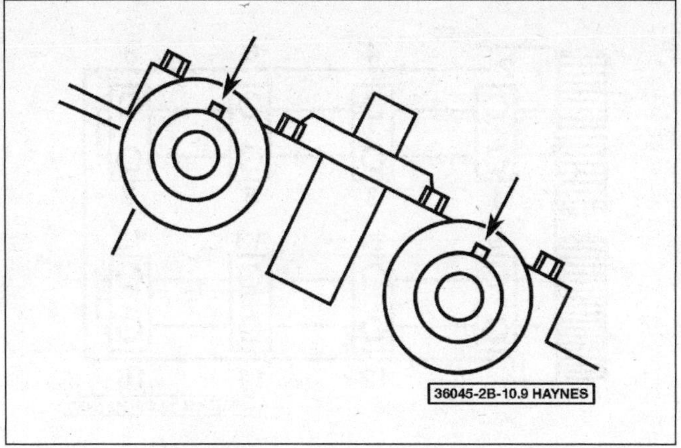

10.38 Front (left) bank camshaft timing marks (keyways) in the neutral position - 2012 and earlier 3.5L engine

illustration), to the torque listed in this Chapter's Specifications.

32   Install the rear timing chain (see Section 9).

33   Install the timing chain cover (see Section 8).

34   The remainder of installation is the reverse of removal.

35   Fill the crankcase with the recommended oil, fill the power steering reservoir with the correct fluid, and refill the cooling system (see Chapter 1).

36   Reconnect the battery, then start the engine and check for leaks.

3.5L V6 engine

Note: *Two special camshaft holding tools (manufacturer tool no. 303-1248) are required for this procedure.*

Removal

37   Check the valve clearances (see Section 16).

2012 and earlier models

38   Remove the primary timing chain and the front (left) cylinder bank VCT assembly/camshaft sprockets/secondary timing chain (see Section 9), then remove the camshaft holding tool from the front (left) cylinder bank camshafts. Confirm that the camshafts are in the neutral positions after the holding tool has been removed **(see illustration)**.

39   Note the location of each camshaft cap. Use a marker on each cap or make notes if they're not marked.

40   Working in the reverse of the tightening sequence **(see illustration 10.55)**, remove the camshaft bearing cap bolts. Remove the caps, then lift the camshafts from the cylinder head. Lay all of the parts out in order to prevent mixing them up.

41   Remove the primary timing chain and the rear (right) cylinder bank VCT assembly/camshaft sprockets/secondary timing chain (see Section 9), then remove the camshaft holding tool from the rear (right) cylinder bank camshafts. Confirm that the camshafts are in

the neutral positions after the holding tool has been removed **(see illustration)**.

42   Note the location of each camshaft cap. Use a marker on each cap or make notes if they're not marked.

43   Working in the reverse of the tightening sequence **(see illustration 10.57)**, remove the camshaft bearing cap bolts. Remove the caps, then lift the camshafts from the cylinder head. Lay all of the parts out in order to prevent mixing them up.

44   Remove the lifters from their bores and lay them out in order. A magnet or suction cup can be used.

2013 and later models

45   Remove the primary timing chain and camshaft VCT units (see Section 9).

46   Loosen the camshaft cap and mega-cap mounting bolts and remove the caps.

Caution: *Keep the caps in order and don't mix them up.*

47   Remove the camshafts from the cylinder head.

48   With the camshafts removed, the lifters can be removed using a magnet.

Caution: *The lifters must be stored in an egg carton or other divided and marked container, so they can be restored to their original locations during reassembly.*

Inspection

Lifters

49   Inspect the contact and sliding surfaces of each lifter for wear and scratches.

Note: *If the lifter face is worn, be sure to check the corresponding camshaft lobe carefully.*

50   Verify that each lifter moves up and down freely in its bore.

Camshafts

51   Inspect the camshafts as described in Steps 13 through 21.

Installation

52   Turn the crankshaft counterclockwise to place the keyway in the 9 o'clock position.

Caution: *The crankshaft must remain in this position until the camshafts are installed and the valve clearances are checked and, if necessary, adjusted.*

53   Lubricate the lifters with clean engine oil and reinstall them in their original locations. If any valve clearances were out-of-specification, replace the lifter(s) with new ones of the proper thickness to achieve the desired clearance.

2012 and earlier models

54   Lubricate the camshafts and bearing saddles in the cylinder head for the front (left)

10.41 Rear (right) bank camshaft timing marks (keyways) in the neutral position - 2012 and earlier 3.5L engine

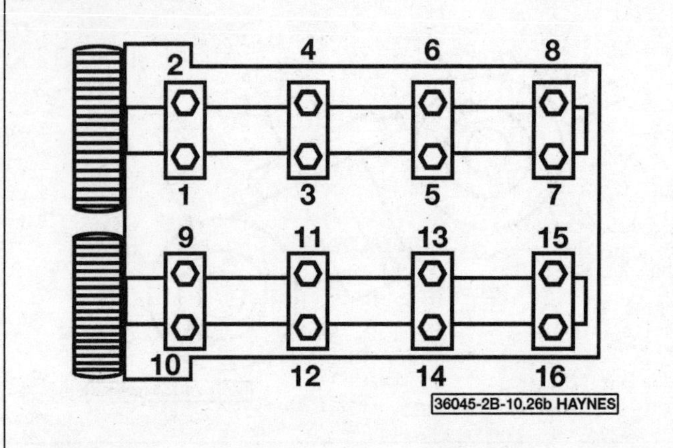

10.55 Front (left) bank camshaft bearing cap tightening sequence - 2012 and earlier 3.5L engines

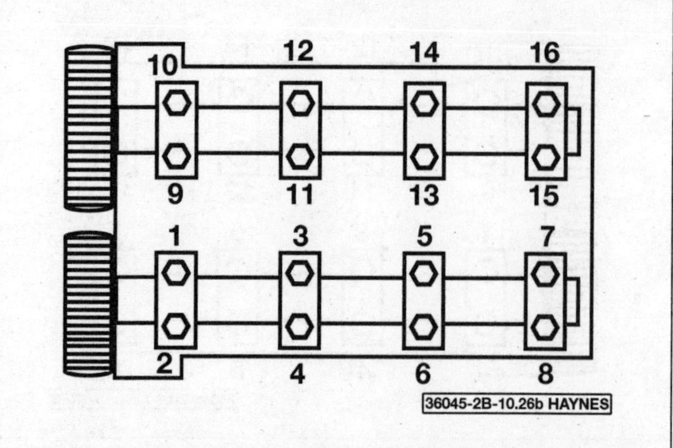

10.57 Rear (right) bank camshaft bearing cap tightening sequence - 2012 and earlier 3.5L engines

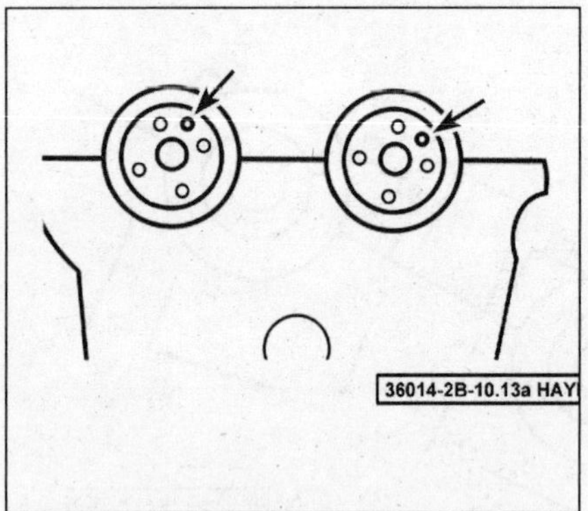

10.65a When installing the rear (right) bank cylinder head camshafts, position the dowel pins like this - 2013 and later models

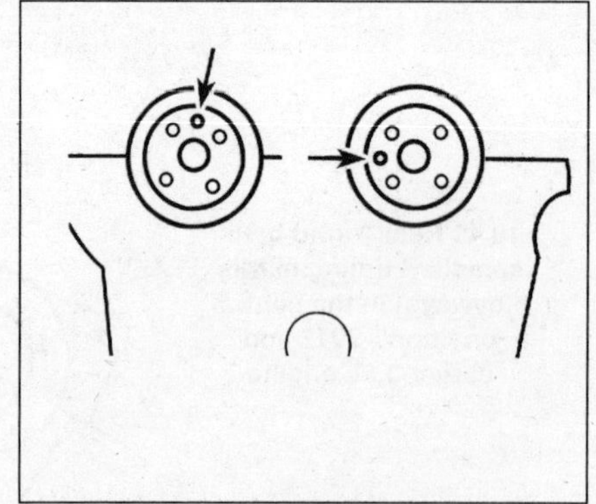

10.65b When installing the left (front) bank cylinder head camshafts, position the dowel pins like this - 2013 and later models

cylinder bank with clean engine oil or camshaft installation lube. Set the camshafts in the cylinder head, making sure they are in their neutral positions **(see illustration 10.38)**.

55   Lubricate the friction surfaces of the camshaft bearing caps with clean engine oil or camshaft installation lube and install them in their proper positions. Install the bolts and tighten them, in sequence **(see illustration)**, to the torque listed in this Chapter's Specifications.

56   Lubricate the camshafts and bearing saddles in the cylinder head for the rear (right) cylinder bank with clean engine oil or camshaft installation lube. Set the camshafts in the cylinder head, making sure they are in their neutral positions **(see illustration 10.41)**.

57   Lubricate the friction surfaces of the camshaft bearing caps with clean engine oil or camshaft installation lube and install them in their proper positions. Install the bolts and tighten them, in sequence **(see illustration)**, to the torque listed in this Chapter's Specifications.

58   Check and if necessary, adjust the valve clearances (see Section 16).

Note: *Since the crankshaft is in its neutral position, the camshafts can be turned without the*

danger of the valves contacting the pistons. Insert a bolt into the front of the camshaft to turn it.

59   Return the camshafts to their positions shown in **illustrations 10.38 and 10.41**, then install the camshaft holding tools.

60   Install the secondary timing chains, VCT actuator and camshaft sprockets (see Section 9).

61   Turn the crankshaft clockwise 60-degrees until the keyway is in the 11 o'clock position.

62   Install the primary timing chain and timing chain cover (see Section 9).

2013 and later models

63   At the front of each camshaft, there are two grooves to hold seals. Obtain new seals and install them in the camshaft grooves.

Note: *The split where the ends of each seal come together must face UP (12 o'clock position) on the camshafts when they are installed.*

64   Lubricate the camshaft bearing journals and cam lobes with moly-based grease or camshaft installation lubricant.

65   Position the camshafts in the cylinder head in their neutral positions **(see illustrations)**.

66   Install the camshaft bearing caps (in their original locations), and tighten the bolts, in sequence **(see illustration)**, to the torque listed in this Chapter's Specifications.

67   Recheck the valve clearances (see Section 16). Since the crankshaft is in the neutral position, the camshafts can be turned without the valves contacting the pistons.

68   Remove the camshaft cap bolts that

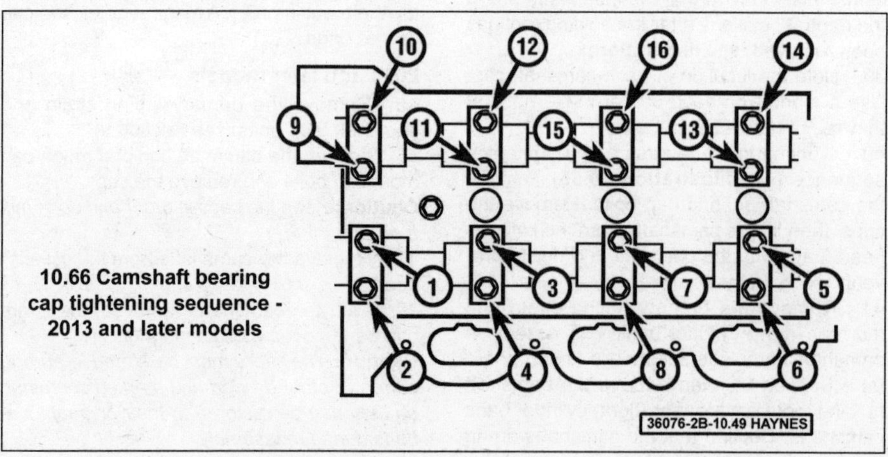

10.66 Camshaft bearing cap tightening sequence - 2013 and later models

secure the valve train oil tubes. Remove the oil tubes.

69   Rotate the camshafts to position the dowel pins in their proper positions for installing the VCT units and secondary timing chains **(see illustrations)**. Install the camshaft holding tools.

All models

70   Install the VCT units (see Section 9).
71   Rotate the crankshaft clockwise to position the keyway in the 11 o'clock position.
72   Install the primary timing chain (see Section 9).
73   Reinstall the valve train oil tubes and tighten the bearing cap bolts to the torque listed in this Chapter's Specifications.
74   The remainder of installation is the reverse of removal.
75   Before starting and running the engine, refill the cooling system, change the oil and install a new oil filter (see Chapter 1).

---

11   Cylinder heads - removal and installation

Warning: *Wait until the engine is completely cool before beginning this procedure.*
Note: *On 3.5L V6 engines, this procedure can only be performed with the engine removed (see Chapter 2C). Ignore the steps which don't apply.*

Removal

1   Relieve the fuel system pressure (see Chapter 4, Section 3), then disconnect the cable from the negative battery terminal (see Chapter 5).
2   Drain the cooling system (see Chapter 1).
3   Remove the upper and lower intake manifolds (see Section 5).
4   With the vehicle raised and supported securely on jackstands, disconnect the front oxygen sensors and the catalytic converters (see Chapter 6).
5   Remove the two Camshaft Position (CMP) sensors at the rear of each cylinder head then disconnect the Cylinder Head Tem-

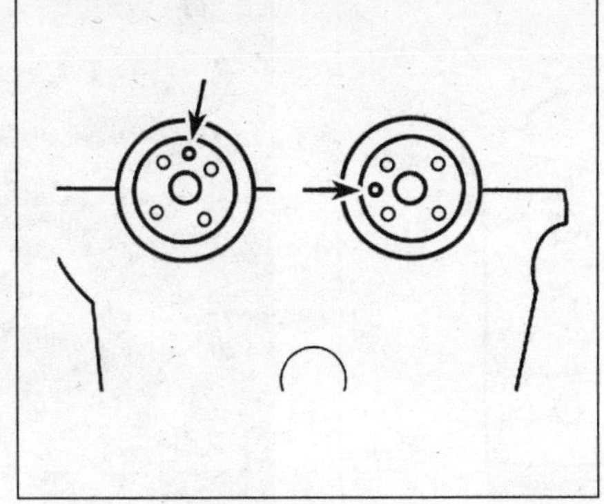

10.69a Rotate the left (front) bank cylinder head camshafts so the dowel pins are positioned like this (TDC position), then install the camshaft holding tool – 2013 and later models

perature (CHT) sensor, catalytic converter monitor sensor, and Camshaft Position (CMP) sensors (see Chapter 6).
6   Remove the camshafts from the cylinder head to be removed (see Section 10).
7   Where applicable, disconnect bolts or clips that secure wiring harnesses or ground straps to the cylinder heads.
8   Remove the exhaust manifold(s) (see Section 6).
9   Remove any additional components that might interfere with cylinder head removal, referring to the appropriate Chapters of this manual.
10   Remove the hoses and any electrical connectors from the coolant bypass tube. Remove the two fasteners securing the coolant bypass tube, then remove the tube.
11   Loosen the cylinder head bolts in 1/4-turn increments until they can be removed by hand. Work from bolt-to-bolt in the reverse of the tightening sequence **(see illustration 11.20a)**.
Note: *Remove the bolts and discard them - new bolts must be used when installing the cylinder head(s).*
12   Lift the cylinder head(s) off the engine. If resistance is felt, DO NOT pry between the cylinder head and engine block as damage to

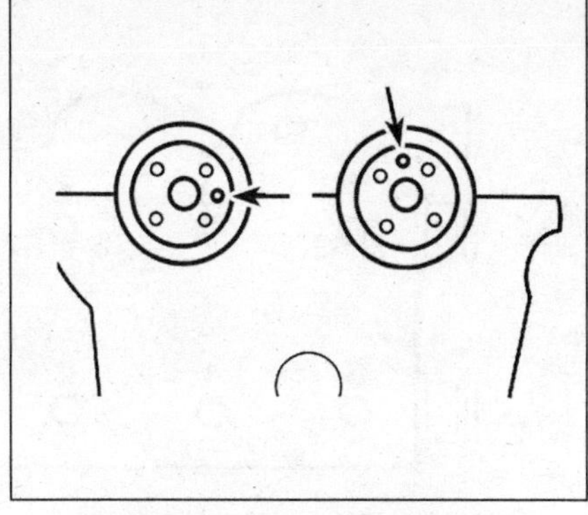

10.69b Rotate the right (rear) bank cylinder head camshafts so the dowel pins are positioned like this (TDC position), then install the camshaft holding tool – 2013 and later models

the mating surfaces will result. To dislodge the cylinder head, place a wood block against the end of it and strike the wood block with a hammer or pry against a casting protrusion. Store the cylinder heads on blocks of wood to prevent damage to the gasket sealing surfaces.
13   Cylinder head disassembly and inspection procedures should be performed by a qualified automotive machine shop.

Installation

14   The mating surfaces of the cylinder heads and engine block must be perfectly clean when the cylinder heads are installed. Cover all openings with shop rags to keep debris out of the engine. Use a vacuum cleaner to remove any debris that falls into the valley or intake ports.
Caution: *Do not use a scraper of any kind or abrasive discs to remove old gasket material, as the block, heads and intake manifold(s) are aluminum.*
15   Check the engine block and cylinder head mating surfaces for nicks, deep scratches and other damage. If damage is slight, it can be removed with a file - if it's excessive, machining may be the only alternative. Use a straightedge and feeler gauges to check for warpage **(see illustration)**. If the warpage is beyond Specifications, have the head checked to see if it can be machined at an automotive machine shop.
16   Use a tap of the correct size to chase the threads in the block head bolt holes. Dirt, corrosion, sealant and damaged threads will affect torque readings.
17   Position the new gasket(s) over the dowel pins in the engine block; make sure it's facing the right way. If the cylinder head is to be replaced, a new secondary timing chain tensioner will be required.
18   Carefully position the cylinder head(s) on the engine block without disturbing the gasket(s).
19   Lightly oil the new cylinder head bolts and turn down by hand until snug.
Caution: *The cylinder head bolts are the torque-to-yield type and are stretched during tightening.*

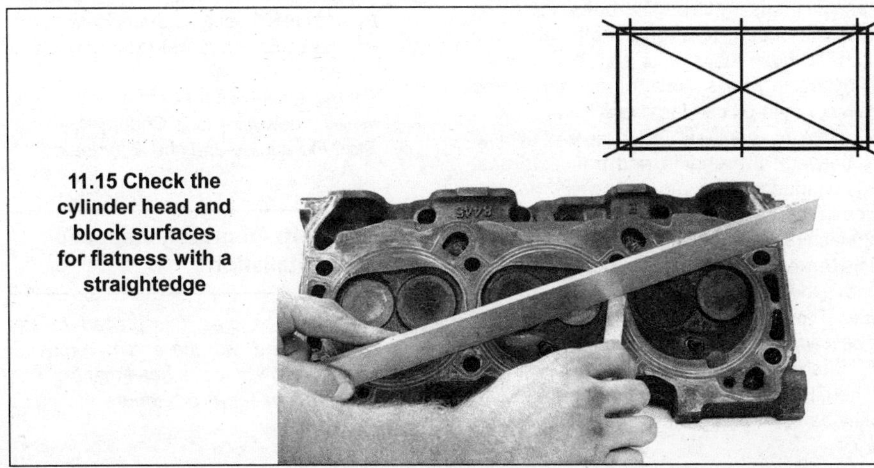

11.15 Check the cylinder head and block surfaces for flatness with a straightedge

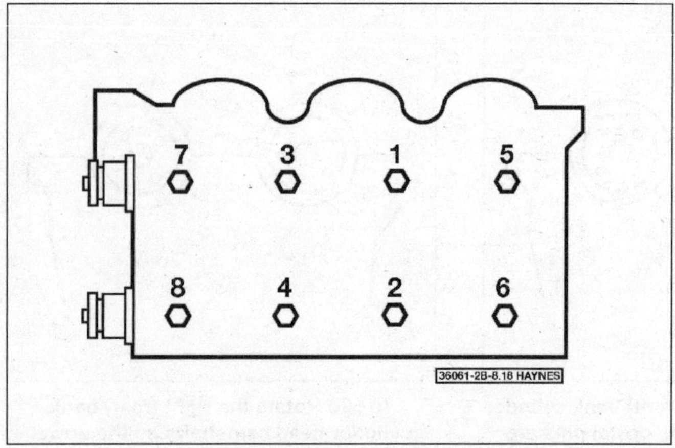

11.20a Cylinder head bolt tightening sequence

11.20b An angle gauge takes the guesswork out of tightening the torque-to-yield cylinder head bolts

Therefore, the original bolts must be discarded and new bolts installed during assembly.

20   Tighten the bolts, in sequence **(see illustration)**, to the torque and angle of rotation **(see illustration)** listed in this Chapter's Specifications.

Note: *The method used for the cylinder head bolt tightening procedure is referred to as the "torque angle" or "torque-to-yield" method; follow the procedure exactly. Tighten the bolts using a torque wrench, then use a breaker bar and a special torque angle adapter (available at auto parts stores) to tighten the bolts the required angle.*

21   The remainder of installation is the reverse of removal. Tighten fasteners to the torque listed in this Chapter's Specifications.

22   Change the engine oil and filter, then fill and bleed the cooling system (see Chapter 1).

23   Start the engine and check for leaks.

12   Oil pan - removal and installation

Removal

1   Raise the vehicle and support it securely on jackstands.

2   Drain the engine oil (see Chapter 1), then clean and install the engine oil drain plug, tightening it to the torque listed in the Chapter 1 Specifications. Remove and discard the oil filter, so that it can be replaced with the oil.

3   On 2013 and later models, remove the battery and battery tray (see Chapter 5).

4   On 2013 and later models, remove the air filter inlet tube and filter housing (see Chapter 4).

5   Remove the lower engine splash shield fasteners and splash shield, then remove the skid plate fasteners and plate, if equipped.

6   Remove the crossover and Y-pipe and converter assembly from the vehicle (see Chapter 4).

7   On 3.0L engines, remove the catalytic converter support bracket fasteners and bracket.

8   On 3.5L engines, remove the nut and stud from the alternator.

9   On 3.5L engines, the transaxle must be moved slightly back from the engine. Support the engine from above with a support fixture (see Chapter 2C) connected to the left end of the engine, near the transaxle, and support the transaxle with a floor jack. Loosen the upper engine-to-transaxle mounting bolts and back them off about 0.20 inch (5 mm), loosen the left-side engine-to-bellhousing bolts, then loosen the right-side bolts.

Caution: *The transaxle must not be moved back more than 0.20 inch (5 mm) or the transaxle can be damaged.*

10   On 3.5L engines, remove the transaxle roll restrictor mount through bolts and remove the mount (see Section 17).

11   On All-Wheel Drive (AWD) models, remove the right exhaust manifold-converter (see Section 6), then remove the power transfer unit (PTU) support bracket fasteners and bracket (see).

12   On 3.5L engines, remove the air conditioning compressor and tie it out of the way, without disconnecting the compressor lines (see Chapter 3), then remove the compressor stud from the side of the oil pan.

13   Remove the driveplate inspection cover fasteners and cover.

14   On 3.5L engines, remove the three upper bellhousing-to-engine bolts, the three side bellhousing-to-engine bolts, the one engine-to-bellhousing bolt and four oil pan-to-bellhousing bolts. Also remove the timing chain cover-to-oil pan fasteners.

15   On 3.5L engines, use a screwdriver to pry between the engine and transaxle until the bellhousing has moved away from the block to the limit of the loosened bolts (about 0.20-inch [5 mm]).

16   Remove the oil pan fasteners and remove the oil pan.

Note: *There are 15 mounting bolts on 3.0L models and 16 mounting bolts on 3.5L models.*

17   There are notches at the top rear corners of the oil pan where a large screwdriver can safely be used to pry the pan loose, if necessary.

18   Thoroughly clean the mating surfaces of the pan, the engine, timing chain cover and transaxle of all traces of RTV sealant using lacquer thinner or acetone. The surfaces must be free of any residue that will keep the sealant from adhering properly. Clean the oil pan inside and out with solvent and dry with compressed air. Use RTV sealant remover rather than scraping the pan or block surfaces.

Installation

19   Apply a 7/32-inch (5.5 mm) bead of RTV sealant at the junctures of the rear main seal housing and the block, and also where the pan meets the front cover.

20   Apply a 1/8-inch (3 mm) bead of RTV sealant around the inner perimeter of the oil pan's mounting surface and install the oil pan. Install the four corner bolts within four minutes of applying the RTV sealant. Install and tighten the remaining bolts within an hour.

21   When all of the pan-to-engine bolts are started, tighten the bolts, in sequence, to the torque listed in this Chapter's Specifications. After the pan-to-engine bolts are tightened, install and tighten the pan-to-transmission bolts, and all fasteners loosened in Step 9.

22   The remainder of installation is the reverse of removal, noting the following:

a) *Tighten all fasteners to the torque values listed in this Chapter's Specifications.*

b) *Always replace any self-locking nuts disturbed on removal.*

c) *Fill the engine with fresh engine oil and install a new filter (see Chapter 1).*

d) *Start the engine and check for leaks.*

13   Oil pump - removal, inspection and installation

Note: *On 3.5L engines, this procedure can only be performed with the engine removed. In the Steps below, it is assumed that the 3.5L engine has been removed; ignore the steps which don't apply.*

Removal

1   Remove the oil pan and the oil screen pick-up tube assembly (see Section 12).
2   Remove the timing chain cover (see Section 8), timing chains and crankshaft sprockets (see Section 9).
3   Loosen each of the four oil pump mounting bolts one turn (three bolts on 3.5L engines), then gradually and evenly loosen each bolt in several steps. When all bolts are loose, remove the bolts and oil pump. On 3.5L engines, rotate the oil pump housing clockwise to separate it from the oil pickup tube.

Inspection

4   Remove the oil pump cover from the pump body.
5   Note any identification marks on the rotors and withdraw the rotors from the pump body.
6   Thoroughly clean and dry the components.
7   Inspect the rotors for obvious wear or damage. If either rotor, the pump body or the cover is scored or damaged, the complete oil pump assembly must be replaced.
8   If the oil pump components are in acceptable condition, dip the rotors in clean engine oil and install them into the pump body with any identification marks positioned as noted during disassembly.
9   Install the cover and tighten the screws securely.

Installation

10   Rotate the oil pump inner rotor so it aligns with the flats on the crankshaft. Install the oil pump over the crankshaft and fit it firmly against the cylinder block. On 3.5L engines, rotate the pump assembly counterclockwise to seat it against the oil pickup tube's O-ring.
11   Install the oil pump bolts and tighten by hand until snug, then tighten them gradually and evenly, in a criss-cross pattern, to the torque listed in this Chapter's Specifications.
12   The remainder of installation is the reverse of removal.
13   Fill the engine with fresh engine oil and install a new filter (see Chapter 1).
14   Start the engine and check for leaks.

---

14   Rear main oil seal - replacement

1   The one-piece rear main oil seal is pressed into a rear main oil seal carrier mounted at the rear of the block. On 3.0L models, remove the transaxle (see Chapter 7A).
Note: *On 3.5L engines, the engine must be lifted out of the vehicle and supported on an engine hoist.*
Note: *On 3.5L V6 engines, two rear seal retaining plates are used. An aluminum plate on early models or steel plate on later models, if the engine is equipped with a steel plate the plate and seal must be replaced as an assembly and can not be replaced separately.*

Replacement

2   Remove the oil pan (see Section 12).
3   On 3.0L engines, use a seal removal tool to remove the rear seal.
4   On 3.5L engines with aluminum seal retainer plates, remove the CKP sensor (see Chapter 6) and sensor ring, and remove the 8 bolts securing the oil seal carrier to the block. Remove the two oil pan-to carrier bolts and insert them into the two threaded holes in the carrier. Tighten them evenly (a few turns should do it) until the carrier is forced off the engine.
5   Clean the oil seal carrier mating surfaces on the cylinder block and crankshaft. Carefully remove and polish any burrs or raised edges on the crankshaft that may have caused the seal to fail.

3.0L V6 models

6   Lightly coat the inside lip of the new seal with clean engine oil. Use a thin (but durable) two-inch wide plastic strip (or a two-liter plastic beverage bottle cut to size) around the inside circumference of the seal to act as a liner for installation.
7   With the plastic seal liner in place, carefully move the new seal into position by sliding it onto the contact surface of the crankshaft. A special seal installer can be used (manufacturer tool #303-178) which uses two studs threaded into the crankshaft and two nuts (which when tightened on the studs will force the seal evenly into place), or a large socket or piece of pipe the correct size can be used with a small hammer to tap the seal in place on the block.
8   Carefully remove the plastic liner or tool so that the new seal contacts the crankshaft mating surface correctly.
9   Tighten the oil seal carrier bolts to the torque listed in this Chapter's Specifications, alternating from left to right evenly.
10   Check for signs of oil leakage when the engine is operable.

3.5L V6 models

11   The seal installation can be performed more easily by unbolting and removing the seal retainer plate. Remove all the mounting bolts, then use two of the retainer-to-oil pan bolts and start them into the two threaded holes in the retainer plate. Tightening these two bolts alternately will push the retainer from the engine. Remove all traces of RTV sealant. Apply a 3/16-inch bead of RTV where the block and oil pan flanges meet.
12   Install the oil seal carrier bolts and finger tighten them while holding the carrier in place. Align the bottom of the seal carrier precisely with the bottom edge of the engine block to ensure that the surfaces are flush before tightening the carrier mounting bolts.
Caution: *The oil pan may leak if the two surfaces are not perfectly flush.*
13   Install the retainer to the engine and install all the bolts within 10 minutes of applying the sealant.
14   Make sure the bore is clean, then apply a film of clean engine oil to the outer edge

16.5 Measure the valve clearance for each valve with a feeler gauge of the specified thickness - if the clearance is correct, you should be able to feel a slight drag on the gauge as you pull it out

and the lips of the new seal. The seal must be pressed squarely into the bore; a special seal installation tool (#303-1250 and 205-153) should be used. Hammering it into place is not recommended.
15   Install the CKP sensor ring and sensor (see Chapter 6).
16   Check for signs of oil leakage when the engine is operable.

---

15   Driveplate - removal and installation

This procedure is essentially the same as the driveplate removal procedure for the four-cylinder engine. Refer to Chapter 2A, and follow the procedure outlined there. However, use the bolt torque listed in this Chapter's Specifications.
Note: *On 3.5L engines, the bolt pattern of the driveplate will only align one way with the crankshaft flange.*

---

16   Valve clearance - check and adjustment

Caution: *The engine must be cold before checking the valve clearances.*
Note: *Checking and, if necessary, adjusting the valve clearance is only necessary after replacement of the camshaft(s) or other valve-related parts, or if the valve train is making excessive noise.*
1   Disconnect the cable from the negative terminal of the battery (see Chapter 5).
2   Remove the spark plugs (see Chapter 1).
3   Remove the valve covers (see Section 4).
4   Using a socket and a breaker bar on the crankshaft pulley center bolt, rotate the engine until the cam lobes on the cylinder to be checked are pointing away from the lifters.
5   Measure the clearance of the valves with a feeler gauge **(see illustration)**. Record

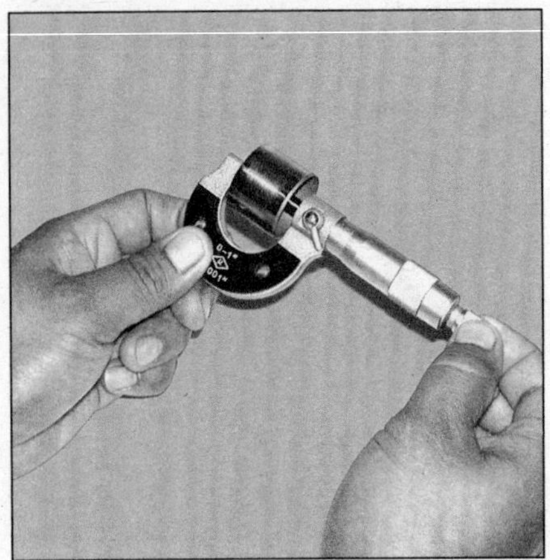

16.8 Use a micrometer to measure the thickness of the head of the lifter

17.1a Remove the two bolts (A) and the roll restrictor (B) from the frame bracket

17.1b Remove the engine mount bracket nuts (A) and the bracket-to-mount bolt (B)

each measurement and compare your measurements with the desired valve clearance found in this Chapter's Specifications. Note which ones are out of specification, as this data will be used later to determine the required replacement lifters.

6   Repeat Steps 4 and 5 until the clearances for all valves have been measured.

7   If a clearance is out of specification, the lifter must be replaced with a new lifter that has a different thickness head to correct the clearance. Remove the camshafts to access the lifters (see Section 10).

8   Mark the lifters that are to be replaced, and record which valve they came from. Use a micrometer to measure the thickness of the head of the lifter, making sure the measure-

ment is precise and on the center projection on the underside of the lifter **(see illustration)**.

9   To calculate the correct thickness for a replacement lifter that will place the valve clearance within the specified value, use this formula:

$N = R + (M1 - M2)$
N = *thickness of the new lifter*
R = *thickness of the old lifter*
$M1$ = *measured valve clearance*
$M2$ = *standard valve clearance*

10   Lifters are marked on the underside as to their size. A marking of 3.310 on the underside of the lifter indicates a thickness value of 3.31 mm, or 0.13 inch.

11   Mark the new lifters as to their destina-

tion, lubricate them with engine assembly lube and install them. After replacing the lifters, reinstall the camshafts and the timing chains (see Sections 9 and 10), then re-check the valve clearances.

17   Engine mounts - inspection and replacement

This procedure is essentially the same as for the four cylinder engine. The engine must be fully supported when removing/installing engine mounts. Refer to Chapter 2A and follow the procedure outlined there, but refer to the illustrations for this Section.

Chapter 2 Part C
General engine overhaul procedures

Contents

Specifications

General

Cylinder compression	Lowest cylinder must be within 75% of the highest cylinder	
Oil pressure		
Four-cylinder engines, hot, at 2000 rpm	29 to 39 psi	200 to 268 kPa
V6 engine, at 1500 rpm	30 psi	206 kPa
Balance shaft assembly backlash (four-cylinder engines)	0.0008 to 0.0047 inch	0.020 to 0.119 mm

Torque specifications

Note: *One foot-pound (ft-lb) of torque is equivalent to 12 inch-pounds (in-lbs) of torque. Torque values below approximately 15 ft-lbs are expressed in inch-pounds, because most foot-pound torque wrenches are not accurate at these smaller values.*

	Ft-lbs (unless otherwise indicated)	Nm
Balance shaft assembly mounting bolts (four-cylinder engines)		
Step 1	18	24
Step 2	31	42
Connecting rod bolts*		
Four-cylinder engines		
Step 1	89 in-lbs	10
Step 2	21	28
Step 3	Tighten an additional 90 degrees	
3.0L V6 engines		
Step 1	17	23
Step 2	32	43
3.5L V6 engines		
Step 1	17	23
Step 2	32	43
Step 3	Tighten an additional 90 degrees	

* Use new bolts

Torque specifications

Ft-lbs (unless otherwise indicated)   **Nm**

Note: *One foot-pound (ft-lb) of torque is equivalent to 12 inch-pounds (in-lbs) of torque. Torque values below approximately 15 ft-lbs are expressed in inch-pounds, because most foot-pound torque wrenches are not accurate at these smaller values.*

	Ft-lbs (unless otherwise indicated)	Nm
Main bearing bolts*		
Four-cylinder engines		
Step 1	44 in-lbs	5
Step 2	18	24
Step 3	Tighten an additional 90 degrees	
3.0L V6 engines		
Step 1, bolts 1 through 8	18	24
Step 2, bolts 9 through 16	30	40
Step 3, bolts 1 through 16	Tighten an additional 90 degrees	
Step 4, bolts 17 through 22 (side bolts)	18	24
3.5L V6 engines		
2012 and earlier models		
Step 1, bolts 1 through 8	44	60
Step 2, bolts 1 through 8	Tighten an additional 90 degrees	
2013 and later models		
Step 1, bolts 1 through 8	24	32
Step 2, bolts 1 through 8	Tighten an additional 135 degrees	
Step 3, side bolts 10 through 16	33	45
Step 4, side bolts 10 through 16	Tighten an additional 90 degrees	
Main bearing cap support brace (3.5L V6 engines)		
Step 1	18	24
Step 2	Tighten an additional 180 degrees	

** Use new bolts*

1.10a An engine block being bored. An engine rebuilder will use special machinery to recondition the cylinder bores

1.10b If the cylinders are bored, the machine shop will normally hone the engine on a machine like this

1　General information - engine overhaul

1　Included in this portion of Chapter 2 are general information and diagnostic testing procedures for determining the overall mechanical condition of your engine.

2　The information ranges from advice concerning preparation for an overhaul and the purchase of replacement parts and/or components to detailed, step-by-step procedures covering removal and installation.

3　The following Sections have been written to help you determine whether your engine needs to be overhauled and how to remove and install it once you've determined it needs to be rebuilt. For information concerning in-vehicle engine repair, see Chapter 2A or 2B.

4　The Specifications included in this Part are general in nature and include only those necessary for testing the oil pressure and checking the engine compression. Refer to Chapter 2A or 2B for additional engine Specifications.

5　It's not always easy to determine when, or if, an engine should be completely overhauled, because a number of factors must be considered.

6　High mileage is not necessarily an indication that an overhaul is needed, while low mileage doesn't preclude the need for an overhaul. Frequency of servicing is probably the most important consideration. An engine that's had regular and frequent oil and filter changes, as well as other required maintenance, will most likely give many thousands of miles of reliable service. Conversely, a neglected engine may require an overhaul very early in its service life.

7　Excessive oil consumption is an indication that piston rings, valve seals and/or valve guides are in need of attention. Make sure that oil leaks aren't responsible before deciding that the rings and/or guides are bad. Perform a cylinder compression check to determine the extent of the work required (see Section 3). Also check the vacuum readings

1.10c A crankshaft having a main bearing journal ground

under various conditions (see Section 4).

8　Check the oil pressure with a gauge installed in place of the oil pressure sending unit and compare it to this Chapter's Specifications (see Section 2). If it's extremely low, the bearings and/or oil pump are probably worn out.

9　Loss of power, rough running, knocking or metallic engine noises, excessive valve train noise and high fuel consumption rates may also point to the need for an overhaul, especially if they're all present at the same time. If a complete tune-up doesn't remedy the situation, major mechanical work is the only solution.

10　An engine overhaul involves restoring the internal parts to the specifications of a new engine. During an overhaul, the piston rings are replaced and the cylinder walls are reconditioned (rebored and/or honed) **(see illustrations)**. If a rebore is done by an automotive machine shop, new oversize pistons will also be installed. The main bearings, connecting rod bearings and camshaft bearings are generally replaced with new ones and, if necessary, the crankshaft may be reground to

1.11a A machinist checks for a bent connecting rod, using specialized equipment

restore the journals **(see illustration)**. Generally, the valves are serviced as well, since they're usually in less-than-perfect condition at this point. While the engine is being overhauled, other components, such as the starter and alternator, can be rebuilt or replaced as well. The end result should be similar to a new engine that will give many trouble free miles.

Note: *Critical cooling system components such as the hoses, drivebelts, thermostat and water pump should be replaced with new parts when an engine is overhauled. The radiator should be checked carefully to ensure that it isn't clogged or leaking (see Chapter 3). If you purchase a rebuilt engine or short block, some rebuilders will not warranty their engines unless the radiator has been professionally flushed. Also, we don't recommend overhauling the oil pump - always install a new one when an engine is rebuilt.*

11　Overhauling the internal components on today's engines is a difficult and time-consuming task which requires a significant amount of specialty tools and is best left to a professional engine rebuilder **(see illustrations)**.

A competent engine rebuilder will handle the inspection of your old parts and offer advice concerning the reconditioning or replacement of the original engine, never purchase parts or have machine work done on other components until the block has been thoroughly inspected by a professional machine shop. As a general rule, time is the primary cost of an overhaul, especially since the vehicle may be tied up for a minimum of two weeks or more. Be aware that some engine builders only have the capability to rebuild the engine you bring them while other rebuilders have a large inventory of rebuilt exchange engines in stock. Also be aware that many machine shops could take as much as two weeks time to completely rebuild your engine depending on shop workload. Sometimes it makes more sense to simply exchange your engine for another engine that's already rebuilt to save time.

1.11b A bore gauge being used to check the main bearing bore

1.11c Uneven piston wear like this indicates a bent connecting rod

2   Oil pressure check

1   Low engine oil pressure can be a sign of an engine in need of rebuilding. A low oil pressure indicator (often called an "idiot light") is not a test of the oiling system. Such indicators only come on when the oil pressure is dangerously low. Even a factory oil pressure gauge in the instrument panel is only a relative indication, although much better for driver information than a warning light. A better test is with a mechanical (not electrical) oil pressure gauge.

2   Locate the oil pressure sending unit. On four-cylinder engines, it is located on the front of the engine, threaded into the oil filter adapter (see illustration); on V6 engines, the sending unit is located on the front side of the block.

3   Unscrew the oil pressure sending unit and screw in the hose for your oil pressure gauge (see illustration). If necessary, install an adapter fitting. Use Teflon tape or thread sealant on the threads of the adapter and/or the fitting on the end of your gauge's hose.

4   Connect an accurate tachometer to the engine, according to the tachometer manufacturer's instructions.

5   Check the oil pressure with the engine running (normal operating temperature) at the specified engine speed, and compare it to this Chapter's Specifications. If it's extremely low, the bearings and/or oil pump are probably worn out.

3   Cylinder compression check

1   A compression check will tell you what mechanical condition the upper end of your engine (pistons, rings, valves, head gaskets) is in. Specifically, it can tell you if the compression is down due to leakage caused by worn piston rings, defective valves and seats or a blown head gasket.

Note: *The engine must be at normal operating temperature and the battery must be fully charged for this check.*

2   Begin by cleaning the area around the ignition coils before you remove them (compressed air should be used, if available). The idea is to prevent dirt from getting into the cylinders as the compression check is being done.

3   Remove all of the spark plugs from the engine (see Chapter 1).

4   Remove the air intake duct from the throttle body, then block the throttle wide open.

5   Disable the fuel pump (see Chapter 4, Section 3).

6   Install a compression gauge in the spark plug hole (see illustration).

7   Crank the engine over at least seven compression strokes and watch the gauge. The compression should build up quickly in a healthy engine. Low compression on the first stroke, followed by gradually increasing pressure on successive strokes, indicates worn piston rings. A low compression reading on the first stroke, which doesn't build up during successive strokes, indicates leaking valves or a blown head gasket (a cracked head could also be the cause). Deposits on the undersides of the valve heads can also cause low compression. Record the highest gauge reading obtained.

8   Repeat the procedure for the remaining cylinders and compare the results to this Chapter's Specifications.

9   Add some engine oil (about three squirts from a plunger-type oil can) to each cylinder, through the spark plug hole, and repeat the test.

2.2 The oil pressure sending unit is located on the oil filter adapter (four-cylinder engine shown)

2.3 The oil pressure can be checked by removing the sending unit and installing a pressure gauge in its place

3.6 Use a compression gauge with a threaded fitting for the spark plug hole, not the type that requires hand pressure to maintain the seal

4.4 A simple vacuum gauge can be handy in diagnosing engine condition and performance

10 If the compression increases after the oil is added, the piston rings are definitely worn. If the compression doesn't increase significantly, the leakage is occurring at the valves or head gasket. Leakage past the valves may be caused by burned valve seats and/or faces or warped, cracked or bent valves.

11 If two adjacent cylinders have equally low compression, there's a strong possibility that the head gasket between them is blown. The appearance of coolant in the combustion chambers or the crankcase would verify this condition.

12 If one cylinder is slightly lower than the others, and the engine has a slightly rough idle, a worn lobe on the camshaft could be the cause.

13 If the compression is unusually high, the combustion chambers are probably coated with carbon deposits. If that's the case, the cylinder head(s) should be removed and decarbonized.

14 If compression is way down or varies greatly between cylinders, it would be a good idea to have a leak-down test performed by an automotive repair shop. This test will pinpoint exactly where the leakage is occurring and how severe it is.

15 After performing the test, don't forget to unblock the throttle plate.

4 Vacuum gauge diagnostic checks

1 A vacuum gauge provides inexpensive but valuable information about what is going on in the engine. You can check for worn rings or cylinder walls, leaking head or intake manifold gaskets, incorrect carburetor adjustments, restricted exhaust, stuck or burned valves, weak valve springs, improper ignition or valve timing and ignition problems.

2 Unfortunately, vacuum gauge readings are easy to misinterpret, so they should be used in conjunction with other tests to confirm the diagnosis.

3 Both the absolute readings and the rate of needle movement are important for accurate interpretation. Most gauges measure vacuum in inches of mercury (in-Hg). The following references to vacuum assume the diagnosis is being performed at sea level. As elevation increases (or atmospheric pressure decreases), the reading will decrease. For every 1,000 foot increase in elevation above approximately 2,000 feet, the gauge readings will decrease about one inch of mercury.

4 Connect the vacuum gauge directly to the intake manifold vacuum, not to ported (throttle body) vacuum **(see illustration)**. Be sure no hoses are left disconnected during the test or false readings will result.

5 Before you begin the test, allow the engine to warm up completely. Block the wheels and set the parking brake. With the transaxle in Park, start the engine and allow it to run at normal idle speed.

Warning: *Keep your hands and the vacuum gauge clear of the fans.*

6 Read the vacuum gauge; an average, healthy engine should normally produce about 17 to 22 in-Hg with a fairly steady needle **(see illustration)**. Refer to the following vacuum gauge readings and what they indicate about the engine's condition:

7 A low steady reading usually indicates a leaking gasket between the intake manifold and cylinder head(s) or throttle body, a leaky vacuum hose, late ignition timing or incorrect camshaft timing. Check ignition timing with a timing light and eliminate all other possible causes, utilizing the tests provided in this Chapter before you remove the timing chain cover to check the timing marks.

8 If the reading is three to eight inches below normal and it fluctuates at that low reading, suspect an intake manifold gasket leak at an intake port or a faulty fuel injector.

9 If the needle has regular drops of about two-to-four inches at a steady rate, the valves are probably leaking. Perform a compression check or leak-down test to confirm this.

10 An irregular drop or down-flick of the needle can be caused by a sticking valve or

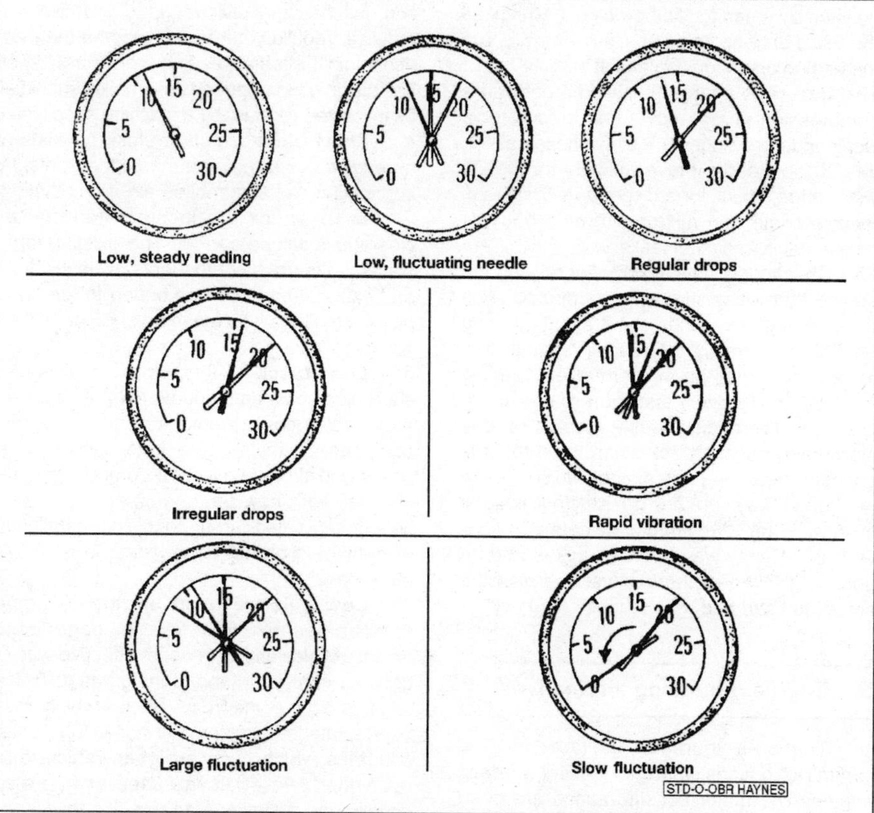

4.6 Typical vacuum gauge readings

6.3a After tightly wrapping water-vulnerable components, use a spray cleaner on everything, with particular concentration on the greasiest areas, usually around the valve cover and lower edges of the block. If one section dries out, apply more cleaner

6.3b Depending on how dirty the engine is, let the cleaner soak in according to the directions and then hose off the grime and cleaner. Get the rinse water down into every area you can get at; then dry important components with a hair dryer or paper towels

an ignition misfire. Perform a compression check or leak-down test and read the spark plugs.

11   A rapid vibration of about four in-Hg vibration at idle combined with exhaust smoke indicates worn valve guides. Perform a leak-down test to confirm this. If the rapid vibration occurs with an increase in engine speed, check for a leaking intake manifold gasket or head gasket, weak valve springs, burned valves or ignition misfire.

12   A slight fluctuation, say one inch up and down, may mean ignition problems. Check all the usual tune-up items and, if necessary, run the engine on an ignition analyzer.

13   If there is a large fluctuation, perform a compression or leak-down test to look for a weak or dead cylinder or a blown head gasket.

14   If the needle moves slowly through a wide range, check for a clogged PCV system, incorrect idle fuel mixture, throttle body or intake manifold gasket leaks.

15   Check for a slow return after revving the engine by quickly snapping the throttle open until the engine reaches about 2,500 rpm and let it shut. Normally the reading should drop to near zero, rise above normal idle reading (about 5 in-Hg over) and then return to the previous idle reading. If the vacuum returns slowly and doesn't peak when the throttle is snapped shut, the rings may be worn. If there is a long delay, look for a restricted exhaust system (often the muffler or catalytic converter). An easy way to check this is to temporarily disconnect the exhaust ahead of the suspected part and redo the test.

5   Engine rebuilding alternatives

1   The do-it-yourselfer is faced with a number of options when purchasing a rebuilt engine. The major considerations are cost, warranty, parts availability and the time required for the rebuilder to complete the proj-

ect. The decision to replace the engine block, piston/connecting rod assemblies and crankshaft depends on the final inspection results of your engine. Only then can you make a cost effective decision whether to have your engine overhauled or simply purchase an exchange engine for your vehicle.

2   Some of the rebuilding alternatives include:

3   **Individual parts** - If the inspection procedures reveal that the engine block and most engine components are in reusable condition, purchasing individual parts and having a rebuilder rebuild your engine may be the most economical alternative. The block, crankshaft and piston/connecting rod assemblies should all be inspected carefully by a machine shop first.

4   **Short block** - A short block consists of an engine block with a crankshaft and piston/connecting rod assemblies already installed. All new bearings are incorporated and all clearances will be correct. The existing camshafts, valve train components, cylinder head and external parts can be bolted to the short block with little or no machine shop work necessary.

5   **Long block** - A long block consists of a short block plus an oil pump, oil pan, cylinder head, valve cover, camshaft and valve train components, timing sprockets and chain or gears and timing cover. All components are installed with new bearings, seals and gaskets incorporated throughout. The installation of manifolds and external parts is all that's necessary.

6   **Low mileage used engines** - Some companies now offer low mileage used engines which are a very cost effective way to get your vehicle up and running again. These engines often come from vehicles which have been totaled in accidents or come from other countries which have a higher vehicle turn over rate. A low mileage used engine also usually has a similar warranty like the newly remanufactured engines.

7   Give careful thought to which alternative is best for you and discuss the situation with local automotive machine shops, auto parts dealers and experienced rebuilders before ordering or purchasing replacement parts.

6   Engine removal - methods and precautions

1   If you've decided that an engine must be removed for overhaul or major repair work, several preliminary steps should be taken. Read all removal and installation procedures carefully prior to committing to this job. These engines are removed by lowering the engine to the floor, along with the transaxle, and then raising the vehicle sufficiently to slide the assembly out; this will require a vehicle hoist as well as an engine hoist. Make sure the engine hoist is rated in excess of the combined weight of the engine and transaxle. A transmission jack is also very helpful. Safety is of primary importance, considering the potential hazards involved in removing the engine from the vehicle.

2   Locating a suitable place to work is extremely important. Adequate work space, along with storage space for the vehicle, will be needed. If a shop or garage isn't available, at the very least a flat, level, clean work surface made of concrete or asphalt is required.

3   Cleaning the engine compartment and engine before beginning the removal procedure will help keep tools clean and organized **(see illustrations)**.

4   If you're a novice at engine removal, get at least one helper. One person cannot easily do all the things you need to do to remove a big heavy engine and transaxle assembly from the engine compartment. Also helpful is to seek advice and assistance from someone who's experienced in engine removal.

5   Plan the operation ahead of time. Arrange for or obtain all of the tools and

equipment you'll need prior to beginning the job **(see illustration)**. Some of the equipment necessary to perform engine removal and installation safely and with relative ease are (in addition to a vehicle hoist and an engine hoist) a heavy duty floor jack (preferably fitted with a transmission jack head adapter), complete sets of wrenches and sockets, wooden blocks, plenty of rags and cleaning solvent for mopping up spilled oil, coolant and gasoline.

6   Plan for the vehicle to be out of use for quite a while. A machine shop can do the work that is beyond the scope of the home mechanic. Machine shops often have a busy schedule, so before removing the engine, consult the shop for an estimate of how long it will take to rebuild or repair the components that may need work.

7   Engine - removal and installation

Warning: *The models covered by this manual are equipped with Supplemental Restraint Systems (SRS), more commonly known as airbags. Always disable the airbag system before working in the vicinity of airbag system components to avoid the possibility of accidental deployment of the airbag, which could cause personal injury (see Chapter 12).*

Warning: *Gasoline is extremely flammable, so take extra precautions when you work on any part of the fuel system. Don't smoke or allow open flames or bare light bulbs near the work area, and don't work in a garage where a gas-type appliance (such as a water heater or clothes dryer) is present. Since gasoline is carcinogenic, wear fuel-resistant gloves when there's a possibility of being exposed to fuel, and, if you spill any fuel on your skin, rinse it off immediately with soap and water. Mop up any spills immediately and do not store fuel-soaked rags where they could ignite. The fuel system is under constant pressure, so, if any fuel lines are to be disconnected, the fuel pressure in the system must be relieved first (see Chapter 4 for more information). When you perform any kind of work on the fuel system, wear safety glasses and have a Class B type fire extinguisher on hand.*

Warning: *The engine must be completely cool before beginning this procedure.*

Warning: *The air conditioning system is under high pressure. DO NOT loosen any fittings or remove any components until after the system has been discharged. Air conditioning refrigerant should be properly discharged into an EPA-approved container at a dealership service department or an automotive air conditioning repair facility. Always wear eye protection when disconnecting air conditioning system fittings.*

Note: *Engine removal on these models is a difficult job, especially for the do-it-yourself mechanic working at home. Because of the vehicle's design, the manufacturer states that the engine and transaxle have to be removed as a unit from the bottom of the vehicle, not the top. With a floor jack and jackstands, the*

6.5 Get an engine stand sturdy enough to firmly support the engine while you're working on it. Stay away from three-wheeled models; they have a tendency to tip over more easily, so get a four-wheeled unit

vehicle can't be raised high enough and supported safely enough for the engine/transaxle assembly to slide out from underneath. The manufacturer recommends that removal of the engine/transaxle assembly only be performed on a vehicle hoist.

Removal

1   Have the air conditioning system discharged by an automotive air conditioning technician.

2   Park the vehicle on a frame-contact type vehicle hoist. The pads of the hoist arms must contact the body welt along each side of the vehicle.

3   Relieve the fuel system pressure (see Chapter 4), then disconnect the cable from the negative battery terminal (see Chapter 5).

4   Place protective covers on the fenders and cowl and remove the hood (see Chapter 11).

5   Remove the air filter housing (see Chapter 4).

6   Remove the cowl panels (see Chapter 11).

7   Remove the battery and battery tray (see Chapter 5).

8   Loosen the front wheel lug nuts and the driveaxle/hub nuts, then raise the vehicle on the hoist. Drain the cooling system and engine oil and remove the drivebelt (see Chapter 1).

9   Clearly label, then disconnect all vacuum lines, coolant and emissions hoses, wiring harness connectors, ground straps and fuel lines. Masking tape and/or a touch up paint applicator work well for marking items **(see illustration)**. Take instant photos or sketch the locations of components and brackets.

10   On V6 models, remove the upper intake manifold (see Chapter 2B).

11   On 3.5L V6 models, disconnect the oxgen sensors (see Chapter 6), then remove the right side catalytic converter (see Chapter 6).

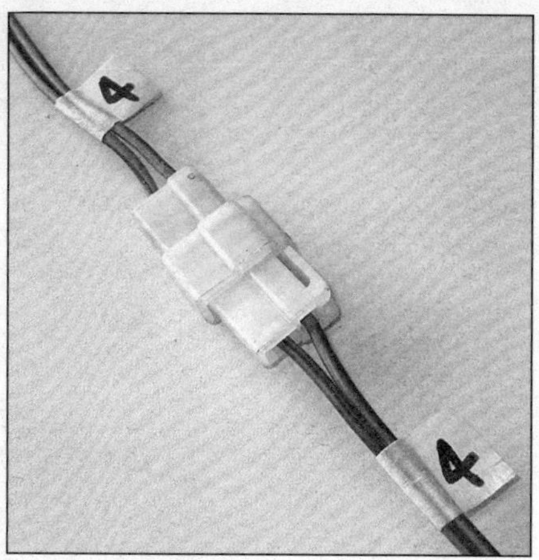

7.9 Label both ends of each wire before unplugging the connector

12   On four-cylinder models, disconnect the high pressure fuel pump quick disconnect line (see Chapter 4).

13   On 2008 and later models, remove the strut tower brace nuts and brace.

14   Remove the alternator and the starter (see Chapter 5).

15   On 2008 and later V6 models, disconnect the air conditioning tubes from the firewall to the condenser. Discard the O-rings and plug or cap the tubes and fittings.

16   Remove the power steering pump and all hose retainers, if equipped (see Chapter 10).

17   Remove the heater hoses and radiator hoses (see Chapter 3).

18   On four-cylinder models, disconnect and remove the charge air cooler inlet and outlet pipes (see Chapter 4).

19   Remove the coolant expansion tank, engine cooling fan and radiator (see Chapter 3).

Note: *This step is not absolutely necessary, but it will help avoid damage to the cooling fans and radiator as the engine is lowered out of the vehicle. If the radiator is not taken out it will still be necessary to detach the transaxle oil cooler lines from the bottom of the radiator.*

20   Remove the skid plate mounting bolts and lower the skid plate, if equipped.

21   Disconnect the shift cable(s) from the transaxle (see Chapter 7A).

22   Disconnect any wiring harness connectors from the transaxle.

23   Remove the air conditioning compressor (see Chapter 3), and cap all the lines to prevent dirt and moisture from entering the system.

24   Place the wheels in the straight-ahead position, then lock the steering wheel in place and detach the steering column shaft from the steering gear (see Chapter 10).

Note: *It may be necessary to use a steering wheel holding tool to prevent the wheel from moving.*

25   Disconnect the PCM harness connectors and place the connectors out of the way (see Chapter 6).

26   On four-cylinder models, disconnect the Transmission Control Module (TCM) electrical

9.1 Before you try to remove the pistons, use a ridge reamer to remove the raised material (ridge) from the top of the cylinders

connector and harness retainers, then place the harness out of the way.

27   On later models, disconnect and remove the engine wiring harness from the firewall by pushing the wiring harness locking tab in, then pushing the harness upwards and off of the firewall.

28   Detach the exhaust pipe(s) from the exhaust manifold(s) (see Chapter 4).

29   Detach all wiring harnesses and hoses from between the engine/transaxle and the chassis. Mark all connectors to facilitate reassembly.

30   Remove the wheels, then remove the brake calipers. Tie the calipers out of the way with a piece of wire (see Chapter 9).

31   Remove the driveaxles (see Chapter 8). On AWD vehicles, make matching marks for the driveshaft, then remove the rear driveshaft and discard the bolts.

32   Disconnect the EVAP line quick disconnect connectors at the rear of the subframe.

33   Detach the stabilizer bar links from the bar and separate the lower control arms from the steering knuckles. Also detach the tie-rod ends from the steering knuckles (see Chapter 10).

34   Mark the relationship of the torque converter to the driveplate, then remove the torque converter-to-driveplate nuts (see Chapter 7A).

35   Remove the roll restrictor between the lower rear part of the engine and the subframe.

36   Remove the subframe-to-bumper nuts and separate the bumper from the subframe.

37   Remove the subframe brace bolts and remove the brace.

38   Attach a lifting sling or chain to the engine. Position an engine hoist and connect the sling to it. If no lifting hooks or brackets are present, you'll have to fasten the chains or slings to some substantial part of the engine - ones that are strong enough to take the weight, but in locations that will provide good balance. Take up the slack until there is slight tension on the sling or chain. Position the chain on the hoist so it balances the engine and the transaxle level with the vehicle.

39   Mark the position of each corner of the subframe to the chassis. Support the sub-

frame with two floor jacks, then remove the fasteners and lower the subframe. Remove the subframe from underneath the vehicle.

40   Remove the transaxle mount (see Chapter 7A) and the right-side engine mount (see Chapter 2A or 2B).

41   Recheck to be sure nothing is still connecting the engine or transaxle to the vehicle. Disconnect and label anything still remaining.

42   Slowly lower the engine/transaxle from the vehicle.

Note: *Placing a sheet of hardboard or paneling between the engine and the floor makes moving the powertrain easier.*

43   Once the powertrain is on the floor, disconnect the engine lifting hoist and raise the vehicle hoist until the powertrain can be slid out from underneath.

Note: *A helper will be needed to move the powertrain.*

44   Reconnect the chain or sling and raise the engine/transaxle with the hoist. Support the transaxle with a jack (preferably one with a transmission jack head adapter). Separate the engine from the transaxle (see Chapter 7A).

45   Remove the driveplate and the crankshaft sensor ring, then mount the engine on a stand.

Installation

Note: *The manufacturer recommends replacing all subframe and suspension fasteners with new ones whenever they are loosened or removed.*

46   Installation is the reverse of removal, noting the following:

a) *Check the engine/transaxle mounts. If they're worn or damaged, replace them.*

b) *Attach the transaxle to the engine (see Chapter 7A).*

c) *Add coolant, oil, power steering and transmission fluids as needed (see Chapter 1).*

d) *Align the subframe reference marks before tightening the bolts.*

e) *Tighten the subframe mounting fasteners to the torque listed in the Chapter 10 Specifications.*

f) *Reconnect the negative battery cable (see Chapter 5).*

g) *Run the engine and check for proper operation and leaks. Shut off the engine and recheck fluid levels.*

h) *Have the air conditioning system recharged and leak tested by the shop that discharged it.*

8   Engine overhaul - disassembly sequence

1   It's much easier to remove the external components if it's mounted on a portable engine stand. A stand can often be rented quite cheaply from an equipment rental yard. Before the engine is mounted on a stand, the driveplate should be removed from the engine.

2   If a stand isn't available, it's possible to remove the external engine components with it blocked up on the floor. Be extra careful not to tip or drop the engine when working without a stand.

3   If you're going to obtain a rebuilt engine, all external components must come off first, to be transferred to the replacement engine. These components include:

Turbocharger (four-cylinder engines)
Driveplate
Emissions-related components
Engine mounts and mount brackets
Intake/exhaust manifolds
Fuel injection components
Oil filter
Ignition coils and spark plugs
Thermostat and housing assembly
Water pump

Note: *When removing the external components from the engine, pay close attention to details that may be helpful or important during installation. Note the installed position of gaskets, seals, spacers, pins, brackets, washers, bolts and other small items.*

4   If you're going to obtain a short block (assembled engine block, crankshaft, pistons and connecting rods), remove the timing chain, cylinder head, oil pan, oil pump pick-up tube, oil pump and water pump from your engine so that you can turn in your old short block to the rebuilder as a core. See Section 5 for additional information regarding the different possibilities to be considered.

9   Pistons and connecting rods - removal and installation

Removal

Note: *Prior to removing the piston/connecting rod assemblies, remove the cylinder head and oil pan (see Chapter 2A or 2B).*

1   Use your fingernail to feel if a ridge has formed at the upper limit of ring travel (about 1/4-inch down from the top of each cylinder). If carbon deposits or cylinder wear have produced ridges, they must be completely removed with a special tool **(see illustration)**. Follow the manufacturer's instructions provided with the tool. Failure to remove the

9.3 Checking the connecting rod endplay (side clearance)

9.4 If the connecting rods and caps are not marked, use permanent ink or paint to mark the caps to the rods by cylinder number (for example, this would be the No. 4 connecting rod)

ridges before attempting to remove the piston/connecting rod assemblies may result in piston breakage.

2   After the cylinder ridges have been removed, turn the engine so the crankshaft is facing up. On four-cylinder engines, remove the balance shaft assembly (see Section 13). On 3.5L engines, remove the main bearing cap support brace.

3   Before the main bearing caps or main-bearing support bridge and connecting rods are removed, check the connecting rod endplay with feeler gauges. Slide them between the first connecting rod and the crankshaft throw until the play is removed **(see illustration)**. Repeat this procedure for each connecting rod. The endplay is equal to the thickness of the feeler gauge(s). Check with an automotive machine shop for the endplay service limit (a typical end play limit should measure between 0.005 to 0.015 inch [0.127 to 0.381 mm]). If the play exceeds the service limit, new connecting rods will be required. If new rods (or a new crankshaft) are installed, the endplay may fall under the minimum allowable. If it does, the rods will have to be machined to restore it. If necessary, consult an automotive machine shop for advice.

4   Check the connecting rods and caps for identification marks. If they aren't plainly marked, use paint or marker to clearly identify each rod and cap (1, 2, 3, etc., depending on the cylinder they're associated with) **(see illustration)**.

5   Loosen each of the connecting rod cap bolts 1/2-turn at a time until they can be removed by hand.

Note: *New connecting rod cap bolts must be used when reassembling the engine, but save the old bolts for use when checking the connecting rod bearing oil clearance.*

6   Remove the number one connecting rod cap and bearing insert. Don't drop the bearing insert out of the cap.

7   Remove the bearing insert and push the connecting rod/piston assembly out through the top of the engine. Use a wooden or plastic hammer handle to push on the upper bearing surface in the connecting rod. If resistance is felt, double-check to make sure that all of the ridge was removed from the cylinder.

8   Repeat the procedure for the remaining cylinders.

9   After removal, reassemble the connecting rod caps and bearing inserts in their respective connecting rods and install the cap bolts finger tight. Leaving the old bearing inserts in place until reassembly will help prevent the connecting rod bearing surfaces from being accidentally nicked or gouged.

10   The pistons and connecting rods are now ready for inspection and overhaul at an automotive machine shop.

Piston ring installation

11   Before installing the new piston rings, the ring end gaps must be checked. It's assumed that the piston ring side clearance has been checked and verified correct.

12   Lay out the piston/connecting rod assemblies and the new ring sets so the ring sets will be matched with the same piston and cylinder during the end gap measurement and engine assembly.

13   Insert the top (number one) ring into the first cylinder and square it up with the cylinder walls by pushing it in with the top of the piston **(see illustration)**. The ring should be near the bottom of the cylinder, at the lower limit of ring travel.

14   To measure the end gap, slip feeler gauges between the ends of the ring until a gauge equal to the gap width is found **(see illustration)**. The feeler gauge should slide between the ring ends with a slight amount of drag. A typical ring gap should fall between 0.010 and 0.020 inch (0.25 to 0.50 mm) for compression rings and up to 0.030 inch (0.76 mm) for the oil ring steel rails. If the gap is larger or smaller than specified, double-check to make sure you have the correct rings before proceeding.

15   If the gap is too small, it must be enlarged or the ring ends may come in contact with each other during engine operation, which

9.13 Install the piston ring into the cylinder then push it down into position using a piston so the ring will be square in the cylinder

9.14 With the ring square in the cylinder, measure the ring end gap with a feeler gauge

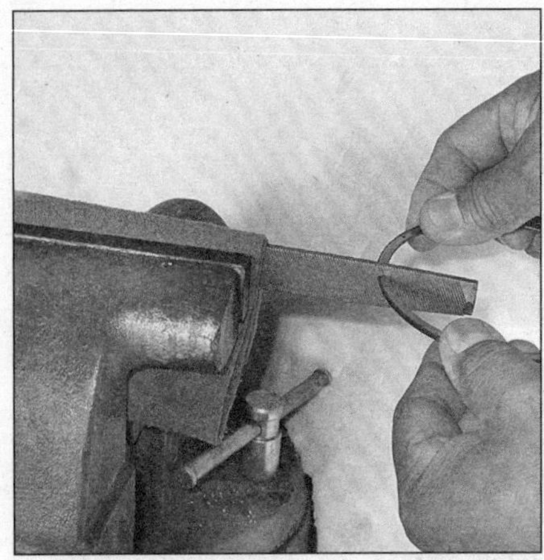

9.15 If the ring end gap is too small, clamp a file in a vise as shown and file the piston ring ends - be sure to remove all raised material

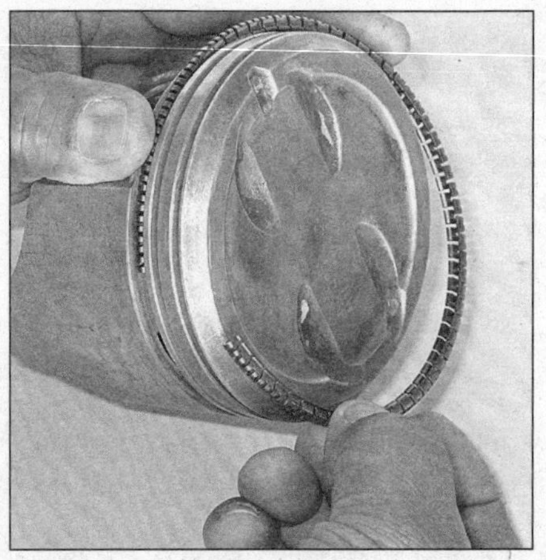

9.19a Installing the spacer/expander in the oil ring groove

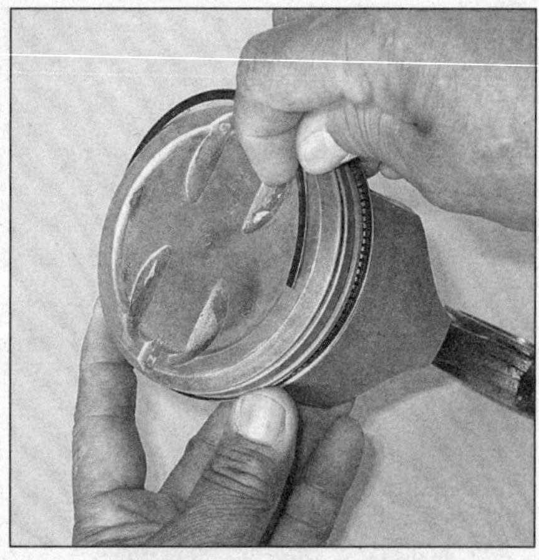

9.19b DO NOT use a piston ring installation tool when installing the oil control side rails

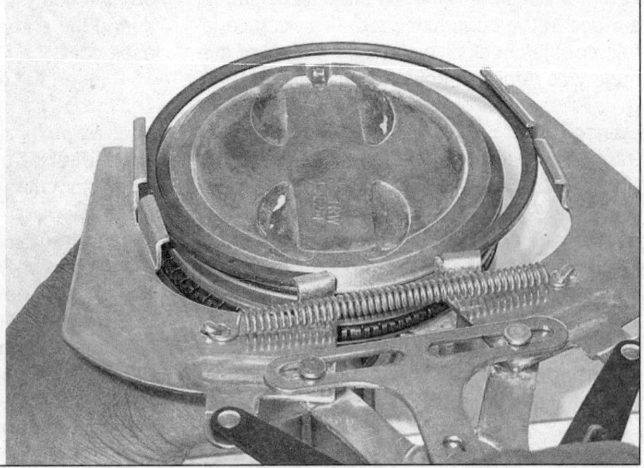

9.22 Use a piston ring installation tool to install the number 2 and the number 1 (top) rings - be sure the directional mark on the piston ring(s) is facing toward the top of the piston

can cause serious damage to the engine. If necessary, increase the end gaps by filing the ring ends very carefully with a fine file. Mount the file in a vise equipped with soft jaws, slip the ring over the file with the ends contacting the file face and slowly move the ring to remove material from the ends. When performing this operation, file only by pushing the ring from the outside end of the file towards the vise **(see illustration)**.

16 Excess end gap isn't critical unless it's greater than 0.040 inch (1.01 mm). Again, double-check to make sure you have the correct ring type.

17 Repeat the procedure for each ring that will be installed in the first cylinder and for each ring in the remaining cylinders. Remember to keep rings, pistons and cylinders matched up.

18 Once the ring end gaps have been checked/corrected, the rings can be installed on the pistons.

19 The oil control ring (lowest one on the piston) is usually installed first. It's composed of three separate components. Slip the spacer/expander into the groove **(see illustration)**. If an anti-rotation tang is used, make sure it's

inserted into the drilled hole in the ring groove. Next, install the upper side rail in the same manner **(see illustration)**. Don't use a piston ring installation tool on the oil ring side rails, as they may be damaged. Instead, place one end of the side rail into the groove between the spacer/expander and the ring land, hold it firmly in place and slide a finger around the piston while pushing the rail into the groove. Finally, install the lower side rail.

20 After the three oil ring components have been installed, check to make sure that both the upper and lower side rails can be rotated smoothly inside the ring grooves.

21 The number two (middle) ring is installed next. It's usually stamped with a mark which must face up, toward the top of the piston. Do not mix up the top and middle rings, as they have different cross-sections.

Note: *Always follow the instructions printed on the ring package or box - different manufacturers may require different approaches.*

22 Use a piston ring installation tool and make sure the identification mark is facing the top of the piston, then slip the ring into the middle groove on the piston **(see illustration)**. Don't expand the ring any more than

necessary to slide it over the piston.

23 Install the number one (top) ring in the same manner. Make sure the mark is facing up. Be careful not to confuse the number one and number two rings.

24 Repeat the procedure for the remaining pistons and rings.

Installation

25 Before installing the piston/connecting rod assemblies, the cylinder walls must be perfectly clean, the top edge of each cylinder bore must be chamfered, and the crankshaft must be in place.

26 Remove the cap from the end of the number one connecting rod (refer to the marks made during removal). Remove the original bearing inserts and wipe the bearing surfaces of the connecting rod and cap with a clean, lint-free cloth. They must be kept spotlessly clean.

Connecting rod bearing oil clearance check

27 Clean the back side of the new upper bearing insert, then lay it in place in the connecting rod.

28 Make sure the tab on the bearing fits into the recess in the rod. Don't hammer the bearing insert into place and be very careful not to nick or gouge the bearing face. Don't lubricate the bearing at this time.

29 Clean the back side of the other bearing insert and install it in the rod cap. Again, make sure the tab on the bearing fits into the recess in the cap, and don't apply any lubricant. It's critically important that the mating surfaces of the bearing and connecting rod are perfectly clean and oil free when they're assembled.

30 Position the piston ring gaps at 90-degree intervals around the piston as shown **(see illustration)**.

31 Lubricate the piston and rings with clean engine oil and attach a piston ring compressor to the piston. Leave the skirt protruding about 1/4-inch to guide the piston into the cylinder.

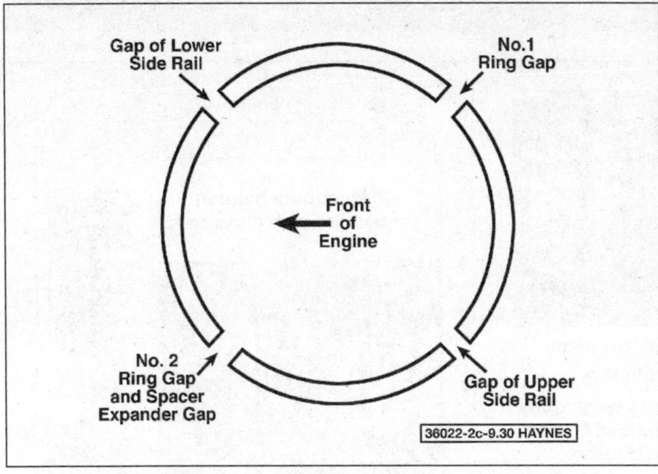

9.30 Position the piston ring end gaps as shown

9.35 Use a plastic or wooden hammer handle to push the piston into the cylinder

The rings must be compressed until they're flush with the piston.

32   Rotate the crankshaft until the number one connecting rod journal is at BDC (bottom dead center) and apply a liberal coat of engine oil to the cylinder walls.

33   With the mark on top of the piston facing the front (timing belt or chain end) of the engine, gently insert the piston/connecting rod assembly into the number one cylinder bore and rest the bottom edge of the ring compressor on the engine block.

34   Tap the top edge of the ring compressor to make sure it's contacting the block around its entire circumference.

35   Gently tap on the top of the piston with the end of a wooden or plastic hammer handle **(see illustration)** while guiding the end of the connecting rod into place on the crankshaft journal. The piston rings may try to pop out of the ring compressor just before entering the cylinder bore, so keep some downward pressure on the ring compressor. Work slowly, and if any resistance is felt as the piston enters the cylinder, stop immediately. Find out what's hanging up and fix it before proceeding. Do not, for any reason, force the piston into the cylinder - you might break a ring and/or the piston.

36   Once the piston/connecting rod assembly is installed, the connecting rod bearing oil clearance must be checked before the rod cap is permanently installed.

37   Cut a piece of the appropriate size Plastigage slightly shorter than the width of the connecting rod bearing and lay it in place on the number one connecting rod journal, parallel with the journal axis **(see illustration)**.

38   Clean the connecting rod cap bearing face and install the rod cap. Make sure the mating mark on the cap is on the same side as the mark on the connecting rod **(see illustration 9.4)**.

39   Install the old rod bolts, at this time, and tighten them to the torque listed in this Chapter's Specifications.

Note: *Use a thin-wall socket to avoid erro-*

9.37 Place Plastigage on each connecting rod bearing journal parallel to the crankshaft centerline

neous torque readings that can result if the socket is wedged between the rod cap and the bolt head. If the socket tends to wedge itself between the fastener and the cap, lift up on it slightly until it no longer contacts the cap. DO NOT rotate the crankshaft at any time during this operation.

40   Remove the fasteners and detach the rod cap, being very careful not to disturb the Plastigage.

41   Compare the width of the crushed Plastigage to the scale printed on the Plastigage envelope to obtain the oil clearance **(see illustration)**. The connecting rod oil clearance is usually about 0.001 to 0.002 inch (0.025 to 0.05 mm). Consult an automotive machine shop for the clearance specified for the rod bearings on your engine. One the covered vehicles, code numbers on the block and crankshaft are used to select the proper bearings, using a chart at a dealership service/parts department.

42   If the clearance is not as specified, the bearing inserts may be the wrong size (which means different ones will be required). Before

9.41 Use the scale on the Plastigage package to determine the bearing oil clearance - be sure to measure the widest part of the Plastigage and use the correct scale; it comes with both standard and metric scales

deciding that different inserts are needed, make sure that no dirt or oil was between the bearing inserts and the connecting rod or cap when the clearance was measured. Also, recheck the journal diameter. If the Plastigage was wider at one end than the other, the journal may be tapered. If the clearance still exceeds the limit specified, the bearing will have to be replaced with an undersize bearing.

Caution: *When installing a new crankshaft always use a standard size bearing.*

Final installation

43   Carefully scrape all traces of the Plastigage material off the rod journal and/or bearing face. Be very careful not to scratch the bearing - use your fingernail or the edge of a plastic card.

44   Make sure the bearing faces are perfectly clean, then apply a uniform layer of clean moly-base grease or engine assembly

ENGINE BEARING ANALYSIS

Debris

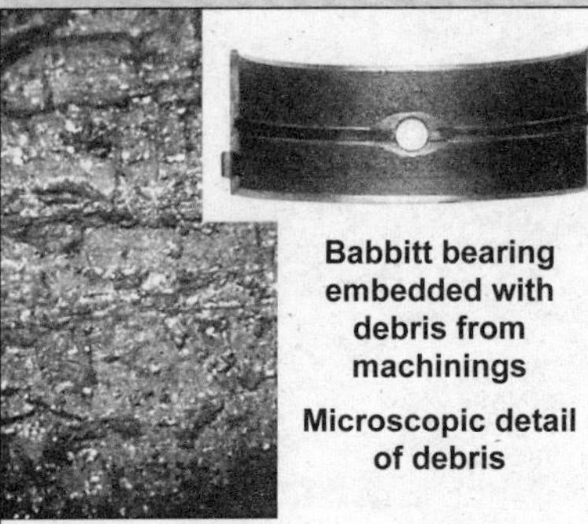

Babbitt bearing embedded with debris from machinings

Microscopic detail of debris

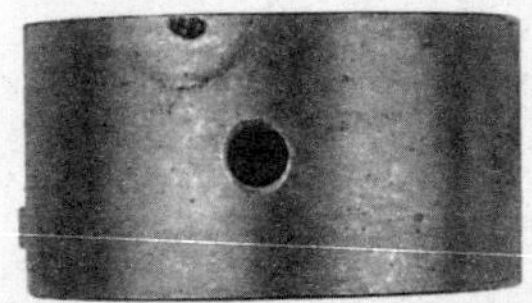

Microscopic detail of gouges

Overplated copper alloy bearing gouged by cast iron debris

Aluminum bearing embedded with glass beads

Microscopic detail of glass beads

Damaged lining caused by dirt left on the bearing back

Misassembly

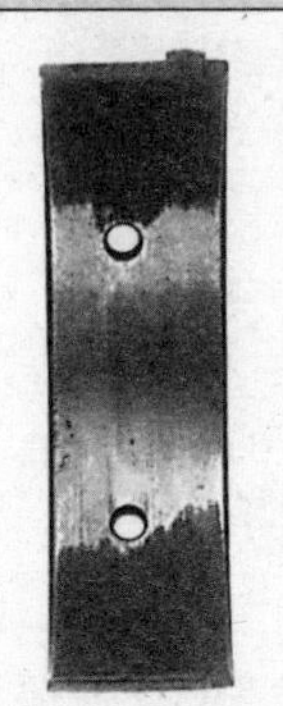

Result of a lower half assembled as an upper - blocking the oil flow

Excessive oil clearance is indicated by a short contact arc

Polished and oil-stained backs are a result of a poor fit in the housing bore

Result of a wrong, reversed, or shifted cap

Overloading

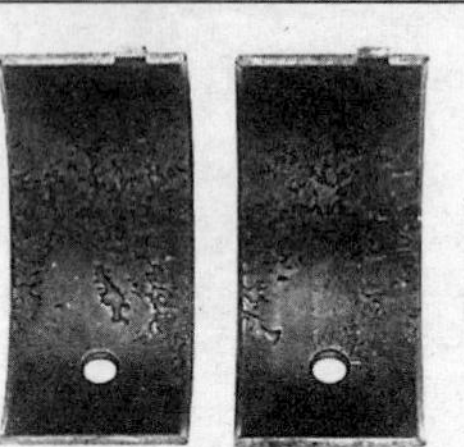

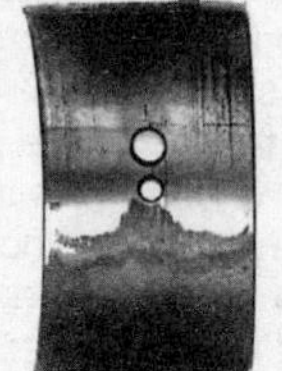

Damage from excessive idling which resulted in an oil film unable to support the load imposed

Damaged upper connecting rod bearings caused by engine lugging; the lower main bearings (not shown) were similarly affected

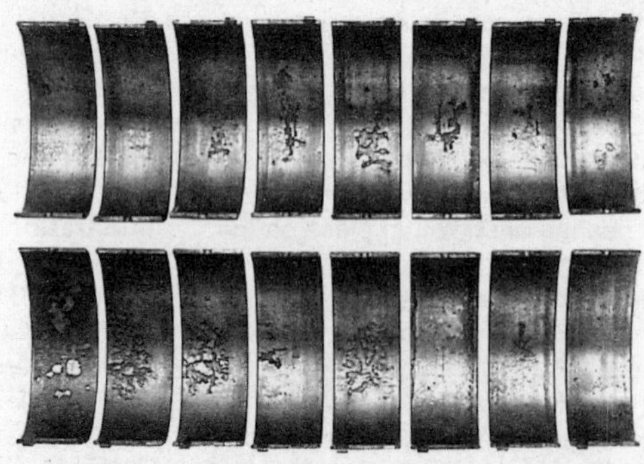

The damage shown in these upper and lower connecting rod bearings was caused by engine operation at a higher-than-rated speed under load

Misalignment

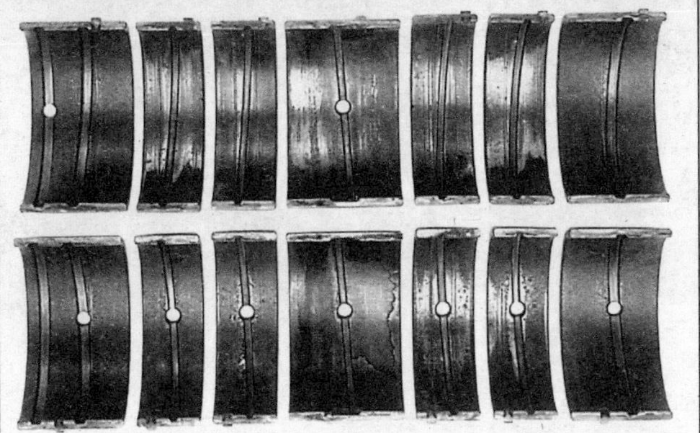

A warped crankshaft caused this pattern of severe wear in the center, diminishing toward the ends

A poorly finished crankshaft caused the equally spaced scoring shown

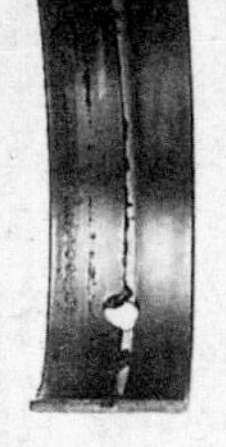

A tapered housing bore caused the damage along one edge of this pair

A bent connecting rod led to the damage in the "V" pattern

Lubrication

Result of dry start: The bearings on the left, farthest from the oil pump, show more damage

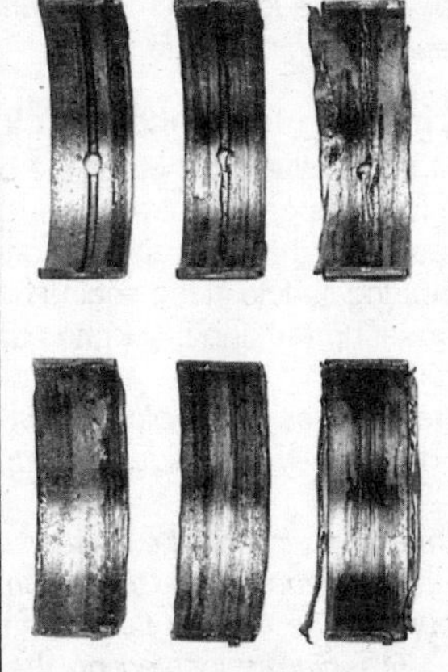

Result of a low oil supply or oil starvation

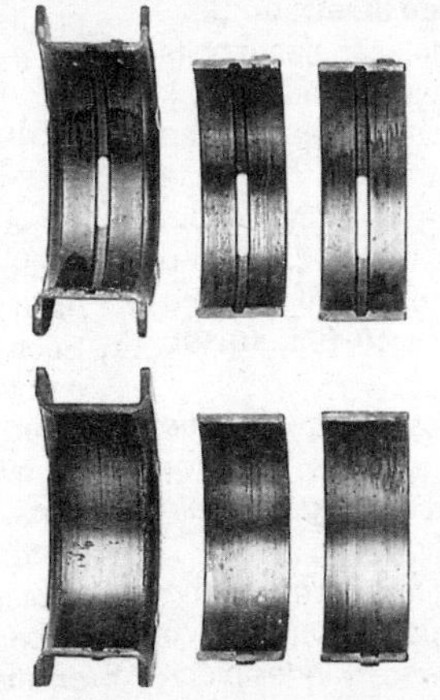

Severe wear as a result of inadequate oil clearance

Corrosion

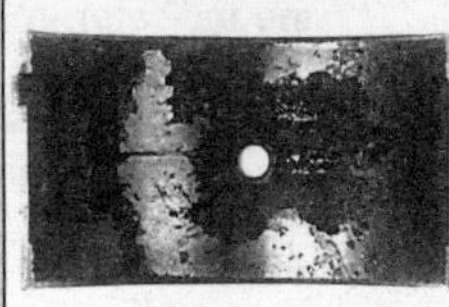

Microscopic detail of corrosion

Corrosion is an acid attack on the bearing lining generally caused by inadequate maintenance, extremely hot or cold operation, or inferior oils or fuels

Microscopic detail of cavitation

Example of cavitation - a surface erosion caused by pressure changes in the oil film

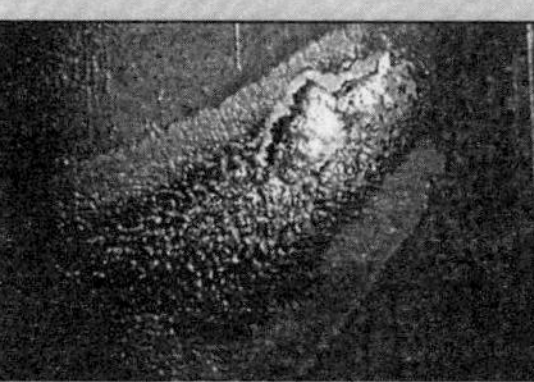

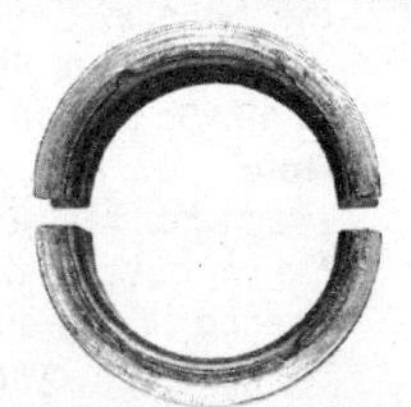

Damage from excessive thrust or insufficient axial clearance

Bearing affected by oil dilution caused by excessive blow-by or a rich mixture

10.1 Checking crankshaft endplay with a dial indicator

10.3 Checking the crankshaft endplay with feeler gauges at the thrust bearing journal

lube to both of them. You'll have to push the piston into the cylinder to expose the face of the bearing insert in the connecting rod.

45   Slide the connecting rod back into place on the journal, install the rod cap, install the new bolts and tighten them to the torque listed in this Chapter's Specifications.

Caution: *Install new connecting rod cap bolts. Do NOT reuse old bolts - they have stretched and cannot be reused. Again, work up to the torque in three steps.*

46   Repeat the entire procedure for the remaining pistons/connecting rods.

47   The important points to remember are: Keep the back sides of the bearing inserts and the insides of the connecting rods and caps perfectly clean when assembling them. Make sure you have the correct piston/rod assembly for each cylinder.

   a) *The mark on the piston must face the front (timing chain) of the engine.*
   b) *Lubricate the cylinder walls liberally with clean oil.*
   c) *Lubricate the bearing faces when installing the rod caps after the oil clearance has been checked.*

48   After all the piston/connecting rod assemblies have been correctly installed, rotate the crankshaft a number of times by hand to check for any obvious binding.

49   As a final step, check the connecting rod endplay, as described in Step 3. If it was correct before disassembly and the original crankshaft and rods were reinstalled, it should still be correct. If new rods or a new crankshaft were installed, the endplay may be inadequate. If so, the rods will have to be removed and taken to an automotive machine shop for resizing.

10   Crankshaft - removal and installation

Removal

Note: *The crankshaft can be removed only after the engine has been removed from the vehicle. It's assumed that the driveplate,* *crankshaft pulley, timing chain, oil pan, oil pump body, oil filter and piston/connecting rod assemblies have already been removed. The rear main oil seal retainer must be unbolted and separated from the block before proceeding with crankshaft removal.*

1   Before the crankshaft is removed, measure the endplay. Mount a dial indicator with the indicator in line with the crankshaft and just touching the end of the crankshaft as shown **(see illustration)**.

2   Pry the crankshaft all the way to the rear and zero the dial indicator. Next, pry the crankshaft to the front as far as possible and check the reading on the dial indicator. The distance traveled is the endplay. A typical crankshaft endplay will fall between 0.003 to 0.010 inch (0.076 to 0.254 mm). If it is greater than that, check the crankshaft thrust surfaces for wear after it's removed. If no wear is evident, new main bearings should correct the endplay.

3   If a dial indicator isn't available, feeler gauges can be used. Gently pry the crankshaft all the way to the front of the engine. Slip feeler gauges between the crankshaft and the front face of the thrust bearing or washer to determine the clearance **(see illustration)**.

4   Loosen the main bearing cap beam bolts (four-cylinder engines), lower cylinder block bolts (3.0L V6 engines) or main bearing cap support brace and main bearing cap bolts (3.5L V6 engines) 1/4-turn at a time each, until they can be removed by hand. Loosen the bolts in the reverse of the tightening sequence **(see illustrations 10.19a, 10.19b or 10.19c and 10.19d)**.

Note: *New main bearing cap bolts must be used when reassembling the engine, but save the old bolts for use when checking the main bearing oil clearance.*

5   On four-cylinder engines, remove the main bearing cap support beam. On 3.0L V6 engines, gently tap the lower cylinder block with a soft-face hammer around its perimeter and pull the lower cylinder block straight up and off the cylinder block. On 3.5L V6 engines, remove the main bearing caps. Try not to drop the bearing inserts if they come out with the assembly.

6   Carefully lift the crankshaft out of the engine. It may be a good idea to have an assistant available, since the crankshaft is quite heavy and awkward to handle. With the bearing inserts in place inside the engine block and main bearing caps or lower cylinder block, reinstall the main bearing caps or lower cylinder block onto the engine block and tighten the bolts finger tight.

Installation

7   Crankshaft installation is the first step in engine reassembly. It's assumed at this point that the engine block and crankshaft have been cleaned, inspected and repaired or reconditioned.

8   Position the engine block with the bottom facing up.

9   Remove the bolts and lift off the support beam, main bearing caps or lower cylinder block, as applicable.

10   If they're still in place, remove the original bearing inserts. Wipe the bearing surfaces of the block and main bearing cap assembly with a clean, lint-free cloth. They must be kept spotlessly clean. This is critical for determining the correct bearing oil clearance.

Main bearing oil clearance check

11   Without mixing them up, clean the back sides of the new upper main bearing inserts (with grooves and oil holes) and lay one in each main bearing saddle in the engine block. Each upper bearing (engine block) has an oil groove and oil hole in it.

Caution: *The oil holes in the block must line up with the oil holes in the upper bearing inserts.*

Note: *The thrust bearing on the four-cylinder engine is located on the engine block number 3 (center) journal. The flanged thrust bearing on the 3.0L V6 engine is located on the 4th journal on the lower cylinder block and thrust washer at the rear of the rear (number four) main saddle on the cylinder block. The thrust bearings on the 3.5L V6 engine are located on the fourth journal (two upper on each side of the main saddle, one lower on the rear of the*

10.17 Place the Plastigage onto the crankshaft bearing journal as shown

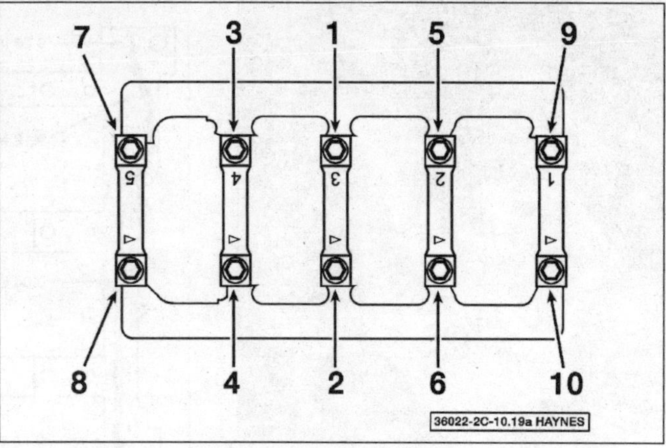

10.19a Main bearing cap beam bolt tightening sequence (four-cylinder engines)

main bearing cap). The grooves on shim-type thrust washers must face the crankshaft (not the main bearing saddle).

12   Clean the back sides of the lower main bearing inserts and lay them in the corresponding location in the main bearing caps or the lower cylinder block. Make sure the tab on the bearing insert fits into its corresponding recess. **Caution:** *Do not hammer the bearing insert into place and don't nick or gouge the bearing faces. DO NOT apply any lubrication at this time.*

13   Clean the faces of the bearing inserts in the block and the crankshaft main bearing journals with a clean, lint-free cloth then check or clean the oil holes in the crankshaft, as any dirt here can go only one way - straight through the new bearings.

14   Once you're certain the crankshaft is clean, carefully lay it in position in the cylinder block.

15   Before the crankshaft can be permanently installed, the main bearing oil clearance must be checked.

16   Cut several strips of the appropriate size of Plastigage. They must be slightly shorter than the width of the main bearing journal.

17   Place one piece on each crankshaft main bearing journal, parallel with the journal

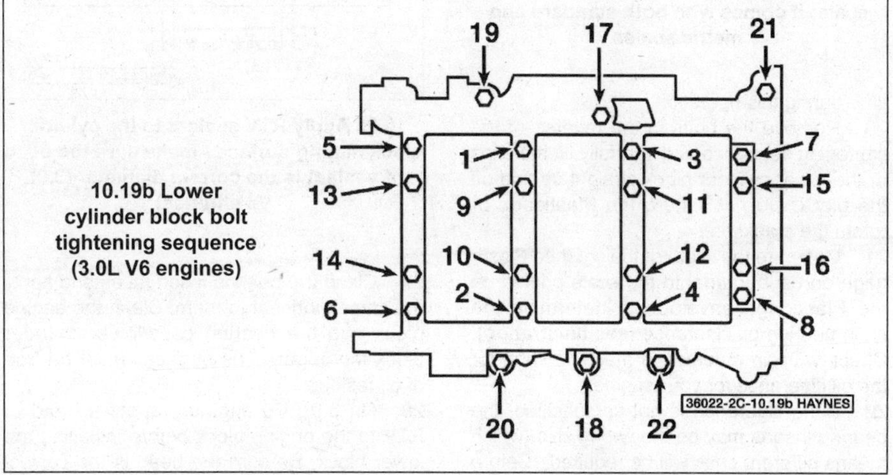

10.19b Lower cylinder block bolt tightening sequence (3.0L V6 engines)

axis as shown **(see illustration)**.

18   Clean the faces of the bearing inserts in the main bearing caps or the lower cylinder block. Hold the bearing inserts in place and install the caps or the lower cylinder block onto the crankshaft and cylinder block. DO NOT disturb the Plastigage.

Note: *Use the old bolts at this time.*

19   Apply clean engine oil to all bolt threads prior to installation, then install all bolts finger-tight. Tighten the bolts in the sequence shown **(see illustrations)** progressing in steps, to the torque listed in this Chapter's Specifications. DO NOT rotate the crankshaft at any

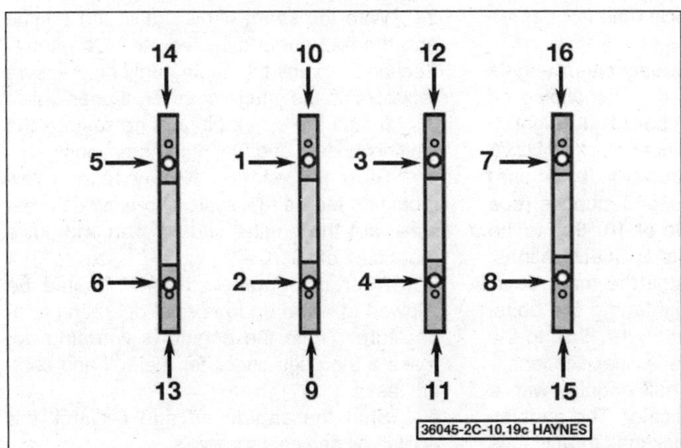

10.19c Main bearing cap support brace, bolt tightening sequence (3.5L V6 engines)

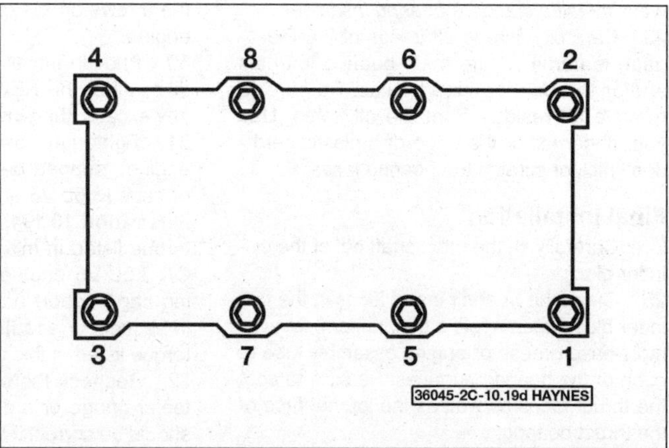

10.19d Main bearing cap support brace bolt tightening sequence (3.5L V6 engines)

10.21 Use the scale on the Plastigage package to determine the bearing oil clearance - be sure to measure the widest part of the Plastigage and use the correct scale; it comes with both standard and metric scales

time during this operation.

20   Remove the bolts in the reverse of the tightening sequence and carefully lift the caps or the lower cylinder block straight up and off the block. Do not disturb the Plastigage or rotate the crankshaft.

21   Compare the width of the crushed Plastigage on each journal to the scale printed on the Plastigage envelope to determine the main bearing oil clearance **(see illustration)**. Check with an automotive machine shop for the oil clearance for your engine.

22   If the clearance is not as specified, the bearing inserts may be the wrong size (which means different ones will be required). Before deciding if different inserts are needed, make sure that no dirt or oil was between the bearing inserts and the cap assembly or block when the clearance was measured. If the Plastigage was wider at one end than the other, the crankshaft journal may be tapered. If the clearance still exceeds the limit specified, the bearing insert(s) will have to be replaced with an undersize bearing insert(s).

Caution: *When installing a new crankshaft always install a standard bearing insert set.*

23   Carefully scrape all traces of the Plastigage material off the main bearing journals and/or the bearing insert faces. Be sure to remove all residue from the oil holes. Use your fingernail or the edge of a plastic card - don't nick or scratch the bearing faces.

Final installation

24   Carefully lift the crankshaft out of the cylinder block.

25   Clean the bearing insert faces in the cylinder block, then apply a thin, uniform layer of moly-base grease or engine assembly lube to each of the bearing surfaces. Be sure to coat the thrust faces as well as the journal face of the thrust bearing.

26   Make sure the crankshaft journals are clean, then lay the crankshaft back in place in the cylinder block.

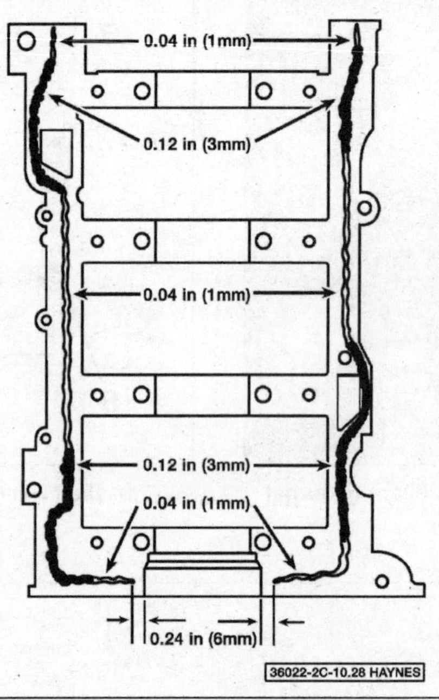

10.28 Apply RTV sealant to the cylinder block mating surface - make sure the bead of sealant is the correct diameter (3.0L V6 engines)

27   Clean the bearing insert faces and apply the same lubricant to them. Clean the engine block and the bearing caps/lower cylinder block thoroughly. The surfaces must be free of oil residue.

28   On 3.0L V6 engines, apply a bead of RTV to the engine block before installing the lower block. Be sure the bead is the correct thickness **(see illustration)**.

Caution: *The lower block mounting bolts and studs must be installed within four minutes of applying the sealant. If it takes longer the lower block will have to be removed, cleaned of all sealant, and installation procedure repeated.*

29   On V6 engines, install the lower cylinder block onto the crankshaft and cylinder block. On four-cylinder engines, install the main bearing caps in their proper locations, with the arrows on the caps facing the front of the engine.

30   Prior to installation, apply clean engine oil to all of the NEW bolt threads, wiping off any excess, then install all bolts finger-tight.

31   Tighten the lower cylinder block (3.0L V6 engine), support beam (four-cylinder engine) or caps (3.5L V6 engines), in sequence **(see illustration 10.19a, 10.19b or 10.19c)**, to the torque listed in this Chapter's Specifications. On 3.5L V6 engines, install the main bearing cap support brace, tightening the bolts, in sequence **(see illustration 10.19d)**, to the torque listed in this Chapter's Specifications.

32   Recheck the crankshaft endplay with a feeler gauge or a dial indicator. The endplay should be correct if the crankshaft thrust faces aren't worn or damaged and if new bearings have been installed.

33   Rotate the crankshaft a number of times

by hand to check for any obvious binding. It should rotate with a running torque of 50 in-lbs or less. If the running torque is too high, correct the problem at this time.

34   Install a new rear main oil seal (see Chapter 2A or 2B).

11   Engine overhaul - reassembly sequence

1   Before beginning engine reassembly, make sure you have all the necessary new parts, gaskets and seals as well as the following items on hand:

Common hand tools
A 1/2-inch drive torque wrench
New engine oil
Gasket sealant
Thread locking compound

2   If you obtained a short block it will be necessary to install the cylinder head, the oil pump and pick-up tube, the oil pan, the water pump, the timing belt and timing cover, and the valve cover (see Chapter 2A or 2B). In order to save time and avoid problems, the external components must be installed in the following general order:

Thermostat and housing cover
Water pump
Intake/exhaust manifolds
Turbocharger (four-cylinder models)
Fuel injection components
Emission control components
Spark plugs
Ignition coils
Oil filter
Engine mounts and mount brackets
Driveplate

12   Initial start-up and break-in after overhaul

Warning: *Have a fire extinguisher handy when starting the engine for the first time.*

1   Once the engine has been installed in the vehicle, double-check the engine oil and coolant levels.

2   With the spark plugs out of the engine and the fuel pump disabled (see Chapter 4, Section 3), crank the engine until oil pressure registers on the gauge or the light goes out.

3   Install the spark plugs, and restore the ignition system and fuel pump functions.

4   Start the engine. It may take a few moments for the fuel system to build up pressure, but the engine should start without a great deal of effort.

5   After the engine starts, it should be allowed to warm up to normal operating temperature. While the engine is warming up, make a thorough check for fuel, oil and coolant leaks.

6   Shut the engine off and recheck the engine oil and coolant levels.

7   Drive the vehicle to an area with minimum traffic, accelerate from 30 to 50 mph, then allow the vehicle to slow to 30 mph with the throttle

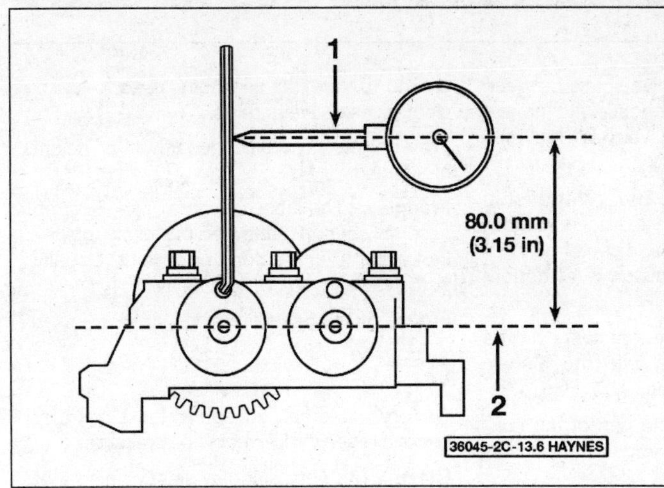

13.6 Method of checking the backlash in the balancer assembly

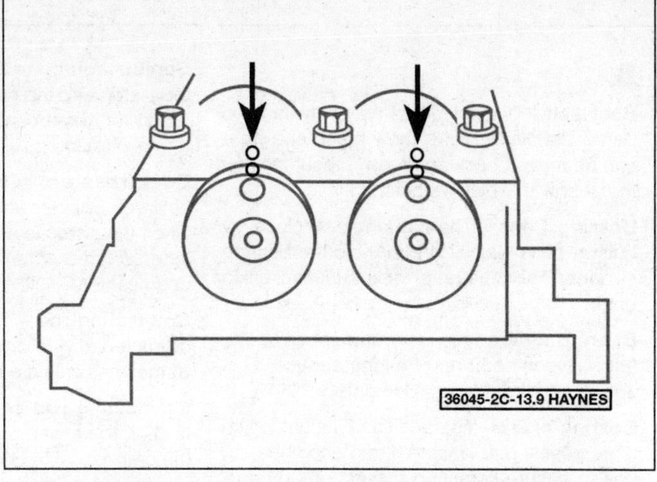

13.9 Remove/install the balance shaft assembly bolts only when the crank is at TDC and these balancer dots align

closed. Repeat the procedure 10 or 12 times. This will load the piston rings and cause them to seat properly against the cylinder walls. Check again for oil and coolant leaks.

8　Drive the vehicle gently for the first 500 miles (no sustained high speeds) and keep a constant check on the oil level. It is not unusual for an engine to use oil during the break-in period.

9　At approximately 500 to 600 miles, change the oil and filter.

10　For the next few hundred miles, drive the vehicle normally. Do not pamper it or abuse it.

11　After 2,000 miles, change the oil and filter again and consider the engine broken in.

13　Balance shaft assembly (four-cylinder engine) - removal and installation

---

1　The balance shaft assembly is bolted to the crankshaft main bearing support beam. A gear on the crankshaft meshes with a gear on the balance shaft assembly. When the engine is operating, the assembly smoothes engine vibrations.

2　The balancer is a precision-machined assembly, there are no serviceable parts inside and it should not be disassembled. If the backlash is out of Specification (see Steps 5 through 8), the assembly must be replaced as a complete unit.

Removal

3　Position the crankshaft at TDC (see Chapter 2A). Remove the four mounting bolts.

4　With the engine turned crankshaft side up on the engine stand, lift the assembly straight up from the engine.

Inspection

5　When the balance shaft assembly is in place, the backlash between the drive gear (on the crankshaft) and the driven gear on the assembly can be checked. Remove the timing peg.

6　Attach a 5 mm Allen wrench to the top of the driveshaft with the long end of the wrench pointing straight up. Secure a dial-indicator fixture to the engine so that the tip of the indicator is against the top of the wrench **(see illustration)**.

7　Use a pry tool against the crankshaft front counterweight to apply thrust pressure, while turning the crankshaft back-and-forth. Record the measurements of the dial-indicator. Measurements should be taken at the following degrees of engine rotation: 10, 30, 100, 190, 210 and 280 degrees. Compare your results with the allowable range of backlash given in this Chapter's Specifications.

8　If the backlash is out of range, the assembly must be replaced.

Installation

9　When installing the balance shaft assembly, the engine must set to TDC for cylinder number 1. Before installing the assembly, rotate it to align the timing marks on both shafts of the assembly **(see illustration)**. Bolt the assembly to the engine and recheck that the timing marks are still aligned and that the crankshaft has not moved. Tighten the bolts in a criss-cross pattern to the torque listed in this Chapter's Specifications.

10　The crankshaft timing peg should remain installed to keep the engine at TDC until installation of the timing chain and sprockets is completed.

COMMON ENGINE OVERHAUL TERMS

B

Backlash - The amount of play between two parts. Usually refers to how much one gear can be moved back and forth without moving the gear with which it's meshed.

Bearing Caps - The caps held in place by nuts or bolts which, in turn, hold the bearing surface. This space is for lubricating oil to enter.

Bearing clearance - The amount of space left between shaft and bearing surface. This space is for lubricating oil to enter.

Bearing crush - The additional height which is purposely manufactured into each bearing half to ensure complete contact of the bearing back with the housing bore when the engine is assembled.

Bearing knock - The noise created by movement of a part in a loose or worn bearing.

Blueprinting - Dismantling an engine and reassembling it to EXACT specifications.

Bore - An engine cylinder, or any cylindrical hole; also used to describe the process of enlarging or accurately refinishing a hole with a cutting tool, as to bore an engine cylinder. The bore size is the diameter of the hole.

Boring - Renewing the cylinders by cutting them out to a specified size. A boring bar is used to make the cut.

Bottom end - A term which refers collectively to the engine block, crankshaft, main bearings and the big ends of the connecting rods.

Break-in - The period of operation between installation of new or rebuilt parts and time in which parts are worn to the correct fit. Driving at reduced and varying speed for a specified mileage to permit parts to wear to the correct fit.

Bushing - A one-piece sleeve placed in a bore to serve as a bearing surface for shaft, piston pin, etc. Usually replaceable.

C

Camshaft - The shaft in the engine, on which a series of lobes are located for operating the valve mechanisms. The camshaft is driven by gears or sprockets and a timing chain. Usually referred to simply as the cam.

Carbon - Hard, or soft, black deposits found in combustion chamber, on plugs, under rings, on and under valve heads.

Cast iron - An alloy of iron and more than two percent carbon, used for engine blocks and heads because it's relatively inexpensive and easy to mold into complex shapes.

Chamfer - To bevel across (or a bevel on) the sharp edge of an object.

Chase - To repair damaged threads with a tap or die.

Combustion chamber - The space between the piston and the cylinder head, with the piston at top dead center, in which air-fuel mixture is burned.

Compression ratio - The relationship between cylinder volume (clearance volume) when the piston is at top dead center and cylinder volume when the piston is at bottom dead center.

Connecting rod - The rod that connects the crank on the crankshaft with the piston. Sometimes called a con rod.

Connecting rod cap - The part of the connecting rod assembly that attaches the rod to the crankpin.

Core plug - Soft metal plug used to plug the casting holes for the coolant passages in the block.

Crankcase - The lower part of the engine in which the crankshaft rotates; includes the lower section of the cylinder block and the oil pan.

Crank kit - A reground or reconditioned crankshaft and new main and connecting rod bearings.

Crankpin - The part of a crankshaft to which a connecting rod is attached.

Crankshaft - The main rotating member, or shaft, running the length of the crankcase, with offset throws to which the connecting rods are attached; changes the reciprocating motion of the pistons into rotating motion.

Cylinder sleeve - A replaceable sleeve, or liner, pressed into the cylinder block to form the cylinder bore.

D

Deburring - Removing the burrs (rough edges or areas) from a bearing.

Deglazer - A tool, rotated by an electric motor, used to remove glaze from cylinder walls so a new set of rings will seat.

E

Endplay - The amount of lengthwise movement between two parts. As applied to a crankshaft, the distance that the crankshaft can move forward and back in the cylinder block.

F

Face - A machinist's term that refers to removing metal from the end of a shaft or the face of a larger part, such as a flywheel.

Fatigue - A breakdown of material through a large number of loading and unloading cycles. The first signs are cracks followed shortly by breaks.

Feeler gauge - A thin strip of hardened steel, ground to an exact thickness, used to check clearances between parts.

Free height - The unloaded length or height of a spring.

Freeplay - The looseness in a linkage, or an assembly of parts, between the initial application of force and actual movement. Usually perceived as slop or slight delay.

Freeze plug - See Core plug.

G

Gallery - A large passage in the block that forms a reservoir for engine oil pressure.

Glaze - The very smooth, glassy finish that develops on cylinder walls while an engine is in service.

H

Heli-Coil - A rethreading device used when threads are worn or damaged. The device is installed in a retapped hole to reduce the thread size to the original size.

I

Installed height - The spring's measured length or height, as installed on the cylinder head. Installed height is measured from the spring seat to the underside of the spring retainer.

J

Journal - The surface of a rotating shaft which turns in a bearing.

K

Keeper - The split lock that holds the valve spring retainer in position on the valve stem.

Key - A small piece of metal inserted into matching grooves machined into two parts fitted together - such as a gear pressed onto a shaft - which prevents slippage between the two parts.

Knock - The heavy metallic engine sound, produced in the combustion chamber as a result of abnormal combustion - usually detonation. Knock is usually caused by a loose or worn bearing. Also referred to as detonation, pinging and spark knock. Connecting rod or main bearing knocks are created by too much oil clearance or insufficient lubrication.

L

Lands - The portions of metal between the piston ring grooves.

Lapping the valves - Grinding a valve face and its seat together with lapping compound.

Lash - The amount of free motion in a gear train, between gears, or in a mechanical assembly, that occurs before movement can begin. Usually refers to the lash in a valve train.

Lifter - The part that rides against the cam to transfer motion to the rest of the valve train.

M

Machining - The process of using a machine to remove metal from a metal part.

Main bearings - The plain, or babbit, bearings that support the crankshaft.

Main bearing caps - The cast iron caps, bolted to the bottom of the block, that support the main bearings.

O

O.D. - Outside diameter.

Oil gallery - A pipe or drilled passageway in the engine used to carry engine oil from one area to another.

Oil ring - The lower ring, or rings, of a piston; designed to prevent excessive amounts of oil from working up the cylinder walls and into the combustion chamber. Also called an oil-control ring.

Oil seal - A seal which keeps oil from leaking out of a compartment. Usually refers to a dynamic seal around a rotating shaft or other moving part.

O-ring - A type of sealing ring made of a special rubberlike material; in use, the O-ring is compressed into a groove to provide the sealing action.

Overhaul - To completely disassemble a unit, clean and inspect all parts, reassemble it with the original or new parts and make all adjustments necessary for proper operation.

P

Pilot bearing - A small bearing installed in the center of the flywheel (or the rear end of the crankshaft) to support the front end of the input shaft of the transmission.

Pip mark - A little dot or indentation which indicates the top side of a compression ring.

Piston - The cylindrical part, attached to the connecting rod, that moves up and down in the cylinder as the crankshaft rotates. When the fuel charge is fired, the piston transfers the force of the explosion to the connecting rod, then to the crankshaft.

Piston pin (or wrist pin) - The cylindrical and usually hollow steel pin that passes through the piston. The piston pin fastens the piston to the upper end of the connecting rod.

Piston ring - The split ring fitted to the groove in a piston. The ring contacts the sides of the ring groove and also rubs against the cylinder wall, thus sealing space between piston and wall. There are two types of rings: Compression rings seal the compression pressure in the combustion chamber; oil rings scrape excessive oil off the cylinder wall.

Piston ring groove - The slots or grooves cut in piston heads to hold piston rings in position.

Piston skirt - The portion of the piston below the rings and the piston pin hole.

Plastigage - A thin strip of plastic thread, available in different sizes, used for measuring clearances. For example, a strip of plastigage is laid across a bearing journal and mashed as parts are assembled. Then parts are disassembled and the width of the strip is measured to determine clearance between journal and bearing. Commonly used to measure crankshaft main-bearing and connecting rod bearing clearances.

Press-fit - A tight fit between two parts that requires pressure to force the parts together. Also referred to as drive, or force, fit.

Prussian blue - A blue pigment; in solution, useful in determining the area of contact between two surfaces. Prussian blue is commonly used to determine the width and location of the contact area between the valve face and the valve seat.

R

Race (bearing) - The inner or outer ring that provides a contact surface for balls or rollers in bearing.

Ream - To size, enlarge or smooth a hole by using a round cutting tool with fluted edges.

Ring job - The process of reconditioning the cylinders and installing new rings.

Runout - Wobble. The amount a shaft rotates out-of-true.

S

Saddle - The upper main bearing seat.

Scored - Scratched or grooved, as a cylinder wall may be scored by abrasive particles moved up and down by the piston rings.

Scuffing - A type of wear in which there's a transfer of material between parts moving against each other; shows up as pits or grooves in the mating surfaces.

Seat - The surface upon which another part rests or seats. For example, the valve seat is the matched surface upon which the valve face rests. Also used to refer to wearing into a good fit; for example, piston rings seat after a few miles of driving.

Short block - An engine block complete with crankshaft and piston and, usually, camshaft assemblies.

Static balance - The balance of an object while it's stationary.

Step - The wear on the lower portion of a ring land caused by excessive side and back-clearance. The height of the step indicates the ring's extra side clearance and the length of the step projecting from the back wall of the groove represents the ring's back clearance.

Stroke - The distance the piston moves when traveling from top dead center to bottom dead center, or from bottom dead center to top dead center.

Stud - A metal rod with threads on both ends.

T

Tang - A lip on the end of a plain bearing used to align the bearing during assembly.

Tap - To cut threads in a hole. Also refers to the fluted tool used to cut threads.

Taper - A gradual reduction in the width of a shaft or hole; in an engine cylinder, taper usually takes the form of uneven wear, more pronounced at the top than at the bottom.

Throws - The offset portions of the crankshaft to which the connecting rods are affixed.

Thrust bearing - The main bearing that has thrust faces to prevent excessive endplay, or forward and backward movement of the crankshaft.

Thrust washer - A bronze or hardened steel washer placed between two moving parts. The washer prevents longitudinal movement and provides a bearing surface for thrust surfaces of parts.

Tolerance - The amount of variation permitted from an exact size of measurement. Actual amount from smallest acceptable dimension to largest acceptable dimension.

U

Umbrella - An oil deflector placed near the valve tip to throw oil from the valve stem area.

Undercut - A machined groove below the normal surface.

Undersize bearings - Smaller diameter bearings used with re-ground crankshaft journals.

V

Valve grinding - Refacing a valve in a valve-refacing machine.

Valve train - The valve-operating mechanism of an engine; includes all components from the camshaft to the valve.

Vibration damper - A cylindrical weight attached to the front of the crankshaft to minimize torsional vibration (the twist-untwist actions of the crankshaft caused by the cylinder firing impulses). Also called a harmonic balancer.

W

Water jacket - The spaces around the cylinders, between the inner and outer shells of the cylinder block or head, through which coolant circulates.

Web - A supporting structure across a cavity.

Woodruff key - A key with a radiused backside (viewed from the side).

Notes

Chapter 3
Cooling, heating and air conditioning systems

Contents

Specifications

General

Expansion tank cap pressure rating	13 to 18 psi	89 to 124 kPa
Cooling system capacity	See Chapter 1	
Refrigerant type	R-134a	
Refrigerant capacity	Refer to HVAC specification tag	

Torque specifications

Ft-lbs (unless otherwise indicated)   **Nm**

Note: *One foot-pound (ft-lb) of torque is equivalent to 12 inch-pounds (in-lbs) of torque. Torque values below approximately 15 ft-lbs are expressed in inch-pounds, because most foot-pound torque wrenches are not accurate at these smaller values.*

Thermostat housing mounting bolts	89 in-lbs	10
Water pump mounting bolts		
Four-cylinder engines	89 in-lbs	10
V6 engines (see text)	89 in-lbs	10
Water pump pulley bolts (four-cylinder engines)	177 in-lbs	20

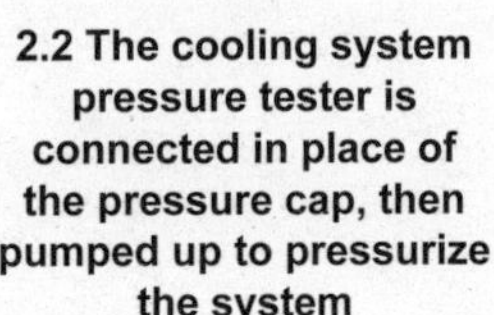

2.2 The cooling system pressure tester is connected in place of the pressure cap, then pumped up to pressurize the system

1   General information

Warning: *Do not allow antifreeze to come in contact with your skin or painted surfaces of the vehicle. Rinse off spills immediately with plenty of water. Antifreeze is highly toxic if ingested. Never leave antifreeze lying around in an open container or in puddles on the floor; children and pets are attracted by it's sweet smell and may drink it. Check with local authorities about disposing of used antifreeze. Many communities have collection centers which will see that antifreeze is disposed of safely. Never dump used antifreeze on the ground or pour it into drains.*

Engine cooling system

1   All modern vehicles employ a pressurized engine cooling system with thermostatically controlled coolant circulation. The cooling system consists of a radiator, an expansion tank or coolant reservoir, a pressure cap (located on the expansion tank or radiator), a thermostat, a cooling fan, and a water pump.

2   The water pump circulates coolant through the engine. The coolant flows around each cylinder and around the intake and exhaust ports, near the spark plug areas and in close proximity to the exhaust valve guides.

3   A thermostat controls engine coolant temperature. During warm up, the closed thermostat prevents coolant from circulating through the radiator. As the engine nears normal operating temperature, the thermostat opens and allows hot coolant to travel through the radiator, where it's cooled before returning to the engine.

Heating system

4   The heating system consists of a blower fan and heater core located in a housing under the dash, the hoses connecting the heater core to the engine cooling system and the heater/air conditioning control head on the dashboard. Hot engine coolant is circulated through the heater core. When the heater mode is activated, a flap door in the housing opens to expose the heater core to the passenger compartment through air ducts. A fan switch on the control head activates the blower motor, which forces air through the core, heating the air.

Air conditioning system

5   The air conditioning system consists of a condenser mounted in front of the radiator, an evaporator mounted adjacent to the heater core, a compressor mounted on the engine, a receiver-drier or accumulator and the plumbing connecting all of the above components.

6   A blower fan forces the warmer air of the passenger compartment through the evaporator core (sort of a radiator-in-reverse), transferring the heat from the air to the refrigerant. The liquid refrigerant boils off into low pressure vapor, taking the heat with it when it leaves the evaporator.

2   Troubleshooting

Coolant leaks

1   A coolant leak can develop anywhere in the cooling system, but the most common causes are:

 A loose or weak hose clamp
 A defective hose
 A faulty pressure cap
 A damaged radiator
 A bad heater core
 A faulty water pump
 A leaking gasket at any joint that carries coolant

2   Coolant leaks aren't always easy to find. Sometimes they can only be detected when the cooling system is under pressure. Here's where a cooling system pressure tester comes in handy. After the engine has cooled completely, the tester is attached in place of the pressure cap, then pumped up to the pressure value equal to that of the pressure cap rating **(see illustration)**. Now, leaks that only exist when the engine is fully warmed up will become apparent. The tester can be left connected to locate a nagging slow leak.

Coolant level drops, but no external leaks

3   If you find it necessary to keep adding coolant, but there are no external leaks, the probable causes include:

 • A blown head gasket
 • A leaking intake manifold gasket (only on engines that have coolant passages in the manifold)
 • A cracked cylinder head or cylinder block

4   Any of the above problems will also usually result in contamination of the engine oil, which will cause it to take on a milkshake-like appearance. A bad head gasket or cracked head or block can also result in engine oil contaminating the cooling system.

5   Combustion leak detectors (also known as block testers) are available at most auto parts stores. These work by detecting exhaust gases in the cooling system, which indicates a compression leak from a cylinder into the coolant. The tester consists of a large bulb-type syringe and bottle of test fluid **(see illustration)**. A measured amount of the fluid is added to the syringe. The syringe is placed over the cooling system filler neck and, with the engine running, the bulb is squeezed and a sample of the gases present in the cooling system are drawn up through the test fluid **(see illustration)**. If any combustion gases are present in the sample taken, the test fluid will change color.

6   If the test indicates combustion gas is present in the cooling system, you can be sure that the engine has a blown head gasket or a crack in the cylinder head or block, and will require disassembly to repair.

Pressure cap

Warning: *Wait until the engine is completely cool before beginning this check.*

7   The cooling system is sealed by a spring-loaded cap, which raises the boiling point of the coolant. If the cap's seal or spring are worn out, the coolant can boil and escape past the cap. With the engine completely cool, remove the cap and check the seal; if it's cracked, hardened or deteriorated in any way, replace it with a new one.

8   Even if the seal is good, the spring might not be; this can be checked with a cooling system pressure tester **(see illustration)**. If the cap can't hold a pressure within approximately 1-1/2 lbs of its rated pressure (which is marked on the cap), replace it with a new one.

9   The cap is also equipped with a vacuum relief spring. When the engine cools off, a vacuum is created in the cooling system. The vacuum relief spring allows air back into the system, which will equalize the pressure and prevent damage to the radiator (the radiator tanks could collapse if the vacuum is great enough). If, after turning the engine off and allowing it to cool down you notice any of the cooling system hoses collapsing, replace the pressure cap with a new one.

2.5a The combustion leak detector consists of a bulb, syringe and test fluid

2.5b Place the tester over the cooling system filler neck and use the bulb to draw a sample into the tester

Thermostat

10   Before assuming the thermostat **(see illustration)** is responsible for a cooling system problem, check the coolant level (see Chapter 1), drivebelt tension (see Chapter 1), and temperature gauge (or light) operation.

11   If the engine takes a long time to warm up (as indicated by the temperature gauge or heater operation), the thermostat is probably stuck open. Replace the thermostat with a new one.

12   If the engine runs hot or overheats, a thorough test of the thermostat should be performed.

13   Definitive testing of the thermostat can only be made when it is removed from the vehicle. If the thermostat is stuck in the open position at room temperature, it is faulty and must be replaced.

Caution: *Do not drive the vehicle without a thermostat. The computer may stay in open loop and emissions and fuel economy will suffer.*

14   To test a thermostat, suspend the (closed) thermostat on a length of string or wire in a pot of cold water.

15   Heat the water on a stove while observing the thermostat. The thermostat should fully open before the water boils.

16   If the thermostat doesn't open and close as specified, or sticks in any position, replace it.

Cooling fan

Electric cooling fan

17   If the engine is overheating and the cooling fan is not coming on when the engine temperature rises to an excessive level, unplug the fan motor electrical connector(s) and connect the motor directly to the battery with fused jumper wires. If the fan motor doesn't come on, replace the motor.

18   If the fan motor is okay, but it isn't coming on when the engine gets hot, the cooling fan control module or the Powertrain Control Module (PCM) might be defective.

19   These control circuits are fairly complex, and checking them should be left to a qualified automotive technician.

20   Check all wiring and connections to the fan motor. Refer to the wiring diagrams at the end of Chapter 12.

21   If no obvious problems are found, the problem could be the Cylinder Head Temperature (CHT) sensor or the Powertrain Control Module (PCM). Have the cooling fan system and circuit diagnosed by a dealer service department or repair shop with the proper diagnostic equipment.

Belt-driven cooling fan

22   Disconnect the cable from the negative battery terminal and rock the fan back and forth by hand to check for excessive bearing play.

23   With the engine cold (and not running), turn the fan blades by hand. The fan should turn freely.

24   Visually inspect for substantial fluid leakage from the clutch assembly. If problems are noted, replace the clutch assembly.

25   With the engine completely warmed up, turn off the ignition switch and disconnect the cable from the negative battery terminal. Turn the fan by hand. Some drag should be evident. If the fan turns easily, replace the fan clutch.

Water pump

26   A failure in the water pump can cause serious engine damage due to overheating.

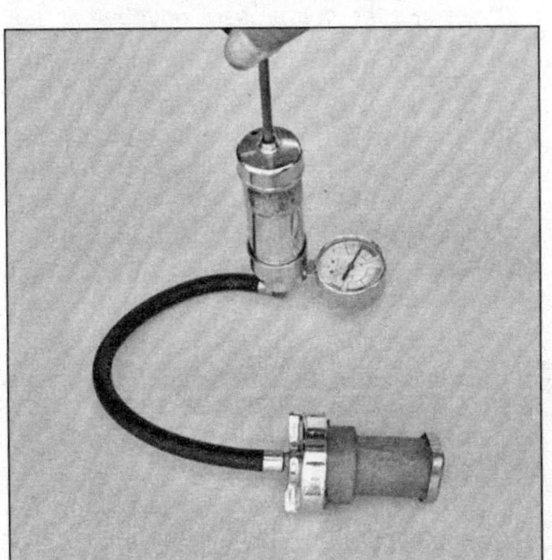

2.8 Checking the cooling system pressure cap with a cooling system pressure tester

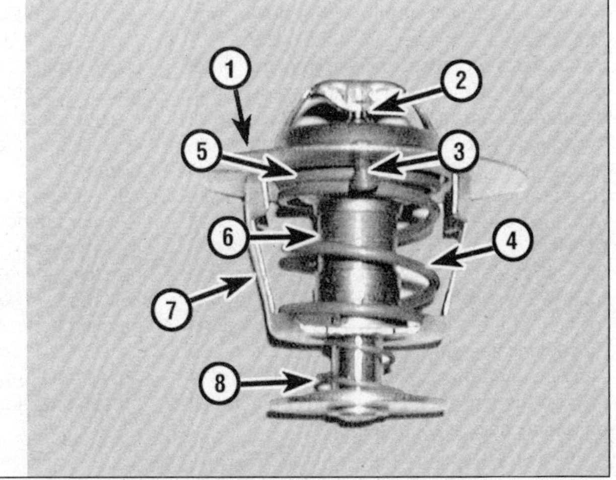

2.10 Typical thermostat

1   Flange
2   Piston
3   Jiggle valve
4   Main coil spring
5   Valve seat
6   Valve
7   Frame
8   Secondary coil spring

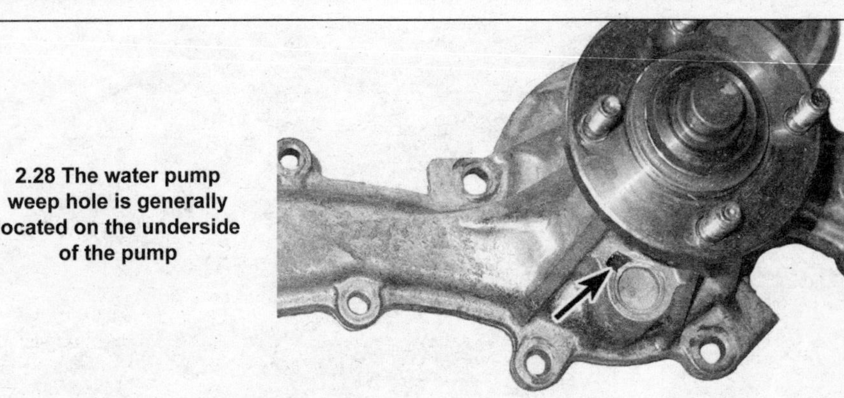

2.28 The water pump weep hole is generally located on the underside of the pump

Drivebelt-driven water pump

27   There are two ways to check the operation of the water pump while it's installed on the engine. If the pump is found to be defective, it should be replaced with a new or rebuilt unit.

28   Water pumps are equipped with weep (or vent) holes **(see illustration)**. If a failure occurs in the pump seal, coolant will leak from the hole.

29   If the water pump shaft bearings fail, there may be a howling sound at the pump while it's running. Shaft wear can be felt with the drivebelt removed if the water pump pulley is rocked up and down (with the engine off). Don't mistake drivebelt slippage, which causes a squealing sound, for water pump bearing failure.

Timing chain or timing belt-driven water pump

30   Water pumps driven by the timing chain or timing belt are located underneath the timing chain or timing belt cover.

31   Checking the water pump is limited because of where it is located. However, some basic checks can be made before deciding to remove the water pump. If the pump is found to be defective, it should be replaced with a new or rebuilt unit.

32   One sign that the water pump may be failing is that the heater (climate control) may not work well. Warm the engine to normal operating temperature, confirm that the coolant level is correct, then run the heater and check for hot air coming from the ducts.

33   Check for noises coming from the water pump area. If the water pump impeller shaft or bearings are failing, there may be a howling sound at the pump while the engine is running.

Note: *Be careful not to mistake drivebelt noise (squealing) for water pump bearing or shaft failure.*

34   It you suspect water pump failure due to noise, wear can be confirmed by feeling for play at the pump shaft. This can be done by rocking the drive sprocket on the pump shaft up and down. To do this you will need to remove the tension on the timing chain or belt as well as access the water pump.

All water pumps

35   In rare cases or on high-mileage vehicles, another sign of water pump failure may be the presence of coolant in the engine oil. This condition will adversely affect the engine in varying degrees.

Note: *Finding coolant in the engine oil could indicate other serious issues besides a failed water pump, such as a blown head gasket or a cracked cylinder head or block.*

36   Even a pump that exhibits no outward signs of a problem, such as noise or leakage, can still be due for replacement. Removal for close examination is the only sure way to tell. Sometimes the fins on the back of the impeller can corrode to the point that cooling efficiency is diminished significantly.

Heater system

37   Little can go wrong with a heater. If the fan motor will run at all speeds, the electrical part of the system is okay. The three basic heater problems fall into the following general categories:

- *Not enough heat*
- *Heat all the time*
- *No heat*

38   If there's not enough heat, the control valve or door is stuck in a partially open position, the coolant coming from the engine isn't hot enough, or the heater core is restricted. If the coolant isn't hot enough, the thermostat in the engine cooling system is stuck open, allowing coolant to pass through the engine so rapidly that it doesn't heat up quickly enough. If the vehicle is equipped with a temperature gauge instead of a warning light, watch to see if the engine temperature rises to the normal operating range after driving for a reasonable distance.

39   If there's heat all the time, the control valve or the door is stuck wide open.

40   If there's no heat, coolant is probably not reaching the heater core, or the heater core is plugged. The likely cause is a collapsed or plugged hose, core, or a frozen heater control valve. If the heater is the type that flows coolant all the time, the cause is a stuck door or a broken or kinked control cable.

Air conditioning system

41   If the cool air output is inadequate: Inspect the condenser coils and fins to make sure they're clear

a) *Check the compressor clutch for slippage*
b) *Check the blower motor for proper operation*
c) *Inspect the blower discharge passage for obstructions*
d) *Check the system air intake filter for clogging*

42   If the system provides intermittent cooling air:

a) *Check the circuit breaker, blower switch and blower motor for a malfunction*
b) *Make sure the compressor clutch isn't slipping*
c) *Inspect the plenum door to make sure it's operating properly*
d) *Inspect the evaporator to make sure it isn't clogged*
e) *If the unit is icing up, it may be caused by excessive moisture in the system, incorrect super heat switch adjustment, or low thermostat adjustment*

43   If the system provides no cooling air:

a) *Inspect the compressor drivebelt; make sure it isn't loose or broken*
b) *Make sure the compressor clutch engages; if it doesn't, check for a blown fuse*
c) *Inspect the wire harness for broken or disconnected wires*
d) *If the compressor clutch doesn't engage, bridge the terminals of the AC pressure switch(es) with a jumper wire; if the clutch now engages, and the system is properly charged, the pressure switch is bad*
e) *Make sure the blower motor is not disconnected or burned out*
f) *Make sure the compressor isn't partially or completely seized*
g) *Inspect the refrigerant lines for leaks*
h) *Check the components for leaks*
i) *Inspect the receiver-drier/accumulator or expansion valve/tube for clogged screens*

44   If the system is noisy:

a) *Look for loose panels in the passenger compartment*
b) *Inspect the compressor drivebelt; it may be loose or worn*
c) *Check the compressor mounting bolts; they should be tight*
d) *Listen carefully to the compressor; it may be worn out*
e) *Listen to the idler pulley and bearing, and the clutch; either may be defective*
f) *The winding in the compressor clutch coil or solenoid may be defective*
g) *The compressor oil level may be low*
h) *The blower motor fan bushing or the motor itself may be worn out*
i) *If there is an excessive charge in the system, you'll hear a rumbling noise in the high pressure line, a thumping noise in the compressor, or see bubbles or cloudiness in the sight glass*

3.9 Insert a thermometer in the center vent, turn on the air conditioning system and wait for it to cool down; depending on the humidity, the output air should be 35 to 40 degrees cooler than the ambient air temperature

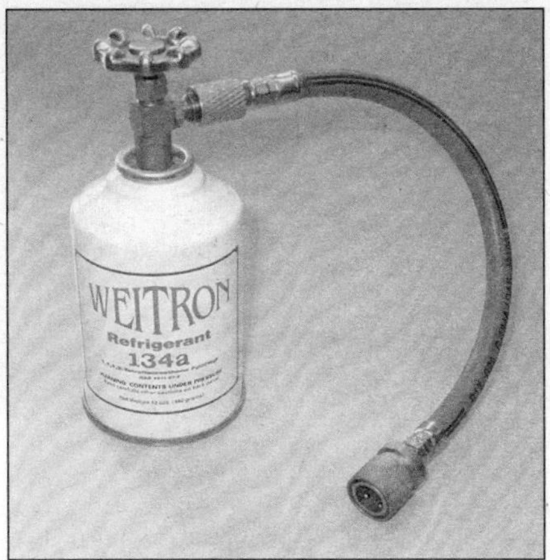

3.11 R-134a automotive air conditioning charging kit

3.13 Location of the low-side charging port

j)   If there is a low charge in the system, you might hear hissing in the evaporator case at the expansion valve, or see bubbles or cloudiness in the sight glass

3   Air conditioning and heating system - check and maintenance

Air conditioning system

Warning: *The air conditioning system is under high pressure. Do not loosen any hose fittings or remove any components until after the system has been discharged. Air conditioning refrigerant should be properly discharged into an EPA-approved recovery/recycling unit at a dealer service department or an automotive air conditioning repair facility. Always wear eye protection when disconnecting air conditioning system fittings.*

Caution: *All models covered by this manual use environmentally friendly R-134a. This refrigerant (and its appropriate refrigerant oils) are not compatible with R-12 refrigerant system components and must never be mixed or the components will be damaged.*

Caution: *When replacing entire components, additional refrigerant oil should be added equal to the amount that is removed with the component being replaced. Read the can before adding any oil to the system, to make sure it is compatible with the R-134a system.*

1   The following maintenance checks should be performed on a regular basis to ensure that the air conditioning continues to operate at peak efficiency.

a)   Inspect the condition of the compressor drivebelt. If it is worn or deteriorated, replace it (see Chapter 1).

b)   Check the drivebelt tension (see Chapter 1).

c)   Inspect the system hoses. Look for cracks, bubbles, hardening and deterioration. Inspect the hoses and all fittings for oil bubbles or seepage. If there is any evidence of wear, damage or leakage, replace the hose(s).

d)   Inspect the condenser fins for leaves, bugs and any other foreign material that may have embedded itself in the fins. Use a fin comb or compressed air to remove debris from the condenser.

e)   Make sure the system has the correct refrigerant charge.

2   It's a good idea to operate the system for about ten minutes at least once a month. This is particularly important during the winter months because long term non-use can cause hardening, and subsequent failure, of the seals. Note that using the Defrost function operates the compressor.

3   If the air conditioning system is not working properly, proceed to Step 6 and perform the general checks outlined below.

4   Because of the complexity of the air conditioning system and the special equipment necessary to service it, in-depth troubleshooting and repairs beyond checking the refrigerant charge and the compressor clutch operation are not included in this manual. However, simple checks and component replacement procedures are provided in this Chapter. For more complete information on the air conditioning system, refer to the Haynes Automotive Heating and Air Conditioning Manual.

5   The most common cause of poor cooling is simply a low system refrigerant charge. If a noticeable drop in system cooling ability occurs, one of the following quick checks will help you determine if the refrigerant level is low.

Checking the refrigerant charge

6   Warm the engine up to normal operating temperature.

7   Place the air conditioning temperature selector at the coldest setting and put the blower at the highest setting.

8   After the system reaches operating temperature, feel the larger pipe exiting the evaporator at the firewall. The outlet pipe should be cold (the tubing that leads back to the compressor). If the evaporator outlet pipe is warm, the system probably needs a charge.

9   Insert a thermometer in the center air distribution duct **(see illustration)** while operating the air conditioning system at its maximum setting - the temperature of the output air should be 35 to 40 degrees F below the ambient air temperature (down to approximately 40 degrees F). If the ambient (outside) air temperature is very high, say 110 degrees F, the duct air temperature may be as high as 60 degrees F, but generally the air conditioning is 35 to 40 degrees F cooler than the ambient air.

10   Further inspection or testing of the system requires special tools and techniques and is beyond the scope of the home mechanic.

Adding refrigerant

Caution: *Make sure any refrigerant, refrigerant oil or replacement component you purchase is designated as compatible with R-134a systems.*

11   Purchase an R-134a automotive charging kit at an auto parts store **(see illustration)**. A charging kit includes a can of refrigerant, a tap valve and a short section of hose that can be attached between the tap valve and the system low side service valve.

Caution: *Never add more than one can of refrigerant to the system. If more refrigerant than that is required, the system should be evacuated and leak tested.*

12   Back off the valve handle on the charging kit and screw the kit onto the refrigerant can, making sure first that the O-ring or rubber seal inside the threaded portion of the kit is in place.

Warning: *Wear protective eyewear when dealing with pressurized refrigerant cans.*

13   Remove the dust cap from the low-side charging port and attach the hose's quick-connect fitting to the port **(see illustration)**.

Warning: *DO NOT hook the charging kit hose to the system high side! The fittings on the charging kit are designed to fit only on the low side of the system.*

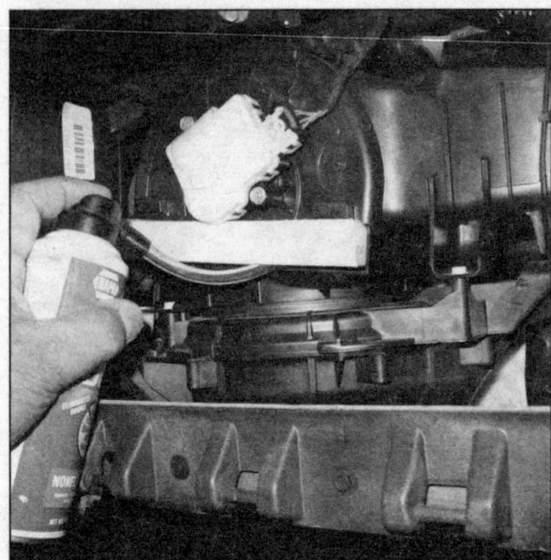

3.24 Insert the nozzle of the disinfectant can into the return-air intake behind the glove box

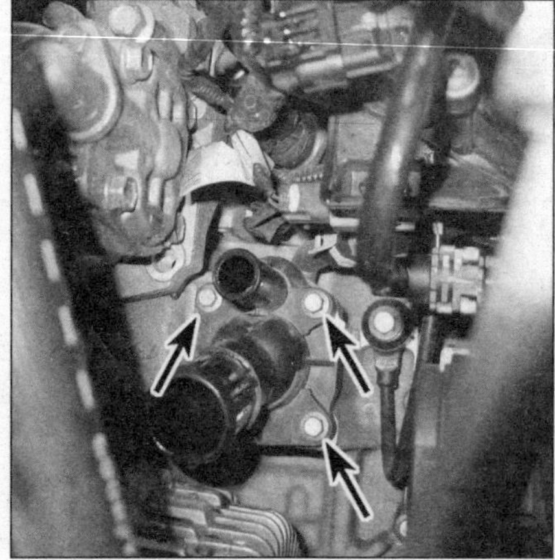

4.5 Thermostat housing bolt locations - four-cylinder engine

14   Warm up the engine and turn On the air conditioning. Keep the charging kit hose away from the fan and other moving parts.

Note: *The charging process requires the compressor to be running. If the clutch cycles off, you can put the air conditioning switch on High and leave the car doors open to keep the clutch on and compressor working. The compressor can be kept on during the charging by removing the connector from the pressure switch and bridging it with a paper clip or jumper wire during the procedure.*

15   Turn the valve handle on the kit until the stem pierces the can, then back the handle out to release the refrigerant. You should be able to hear the rush of gas. Keep the can upright at all times, but shake it occasionally. Allow stabilization time between each addition.

Note: *The charging process will go faster if you wrap the can with a hot-water-soaked rag to keep the can from freezing up.*

16   If you have an accurate thermometer, you can place it in the center air conditioning duct inside the vehicle and keep track of the output air temperature. A charged system that is working properly should cool down to approximately 40 degrees F. If the ambient (outside) air temperature is very high, say 110 degrees F, the duct air temperature may be as high as 60 degrees F, but generally the air conditioning is 35 to 40 degrees F cooler than the ambient air.

17   When the can is empty, turn the valve handle to the closed position and release the connection from the low-side port. Reinstall the dust cap.

18   Remove the charging kit from the can and store the kit for future use with the piercing valve in the UP position, to prevent inadvertently piercing the can on the next use.

Heating systems

19   If the carpet under the heater core is damp, or if antifreeze vapor or steam is coming through the vents, the heater core is leaking. Remove it (see Section 12) and install a new unit (most radiator shops will not repair a leaking heater core).

20   If the air coming out of the heater vents isn't hot, the problem could stem from any of the following causes:

- *The thermostat is stuck open, preventing the engine coolant from warming up enough to carry heat to the heater core. Replace the thermostat (see Section 4).*
- *There is a blockage in the system, preventing the flow of coolant through the heater core. Feel both heater hoses at the firewall. They should be hot. If one of them is cold, there is an obstruction in one of the hoses or in the heater core, or the heater control valve is shut. Detach the hoses and back flush the heater core with a water hose. If the heater core is clear but circulation is impeded, remove the two hoses and flush them out with a water hose.*
- *If flushing fails to remove the blockage from the heater core, the core must be replaced (see Section 12).*

Eliminating air conditioning odors

21   Unpleasant odors that often develop in air conditioning systems are caused by the growth of a fungus, usually on the surface of the evaporator core. The warm, humid environment there is a perfect breeding ground for mildew to develop.

22   The evaporator core on most vehicles is difficult to access, and factory dealerships have a lengthy, expensive process for eliminating the fungus by opening up the evaporator case and using a powerful disinfectant and rinse on the core until the fungus is gone. You can service your own system at home, but it takes something much stronger than basic household germ-killers or deodorizers.

23   Aerosol disinfectants for automotive air conditioning systems are available in most auto parts stores, but remember when shopping for them that the most effective treatments are also the most expensive. The basic procedure for using these sprays is to start by running the system in the RECIRC mode for ten minutes with the blower on its highest speed. Use the highest heat mode to dry out the system and keep the compressor from engaging by disconnecting the wiring connector at the compressor.

24   The disinfectant can usually comes with a long spray hose. Insert the nozzle into an intake port inside the cabin, and spray according to the manufacturer's recommendations **(see illustration)**. Try to cover the whole surface of the evaporator core, by aiming the spray up, down and sideways. Follow the manufacturer's recommendations for the length of spray and waiting time between applications.

Automatic heating and air conditioning systems

25   Some vehicles are equipped with an optional automatic climate control system. This system has its own computer that receives inputs from various sensors in the heating and air conditioning system. This computer, like the PCM, has self-diagnostic capabilities to help pinpoint problems or faults within the system. Vehicles equipped with automatic heating and air conditioning systems are very complex and considered beyond the scope of the home mechanic. Vehicles equipped with automatic heating and air conditioning systems should be taken to dealer service department or other qualified facility for repair.

---

4   Thermostat - replacement

Warning: *Wait until the engine is completely cool before performing this procedure.*

Removal

Note: *The thermostat and thermostat housing on four-cylinder models are replaced as an assembly.*

1   Disconnect the cable from the negative battery terminal (see Chapter 5).

2   Drain the cooling system (see Chapter 1). If the coolant is relatively new and still in good condition, save it and reuse it.

Caution: *On 2013 and later four cylinder engines, cover the alternator in a plastic bag or other waterproof material to keep it dry and prevent alternator damage.*

3   If the outer surface of the thermostat housing cover, which mates with the hose, is already corroded, pitted, or otherwise deteriorated, it may be damaged even more by removal. If it is, replace the thermostat housing cover.

Four-cylinder models

4   Disconnect the heater hose from the thermostat housing.

5   Remove the thermostat housing bolts **(see illustration)**, then detach the housing from the engine.

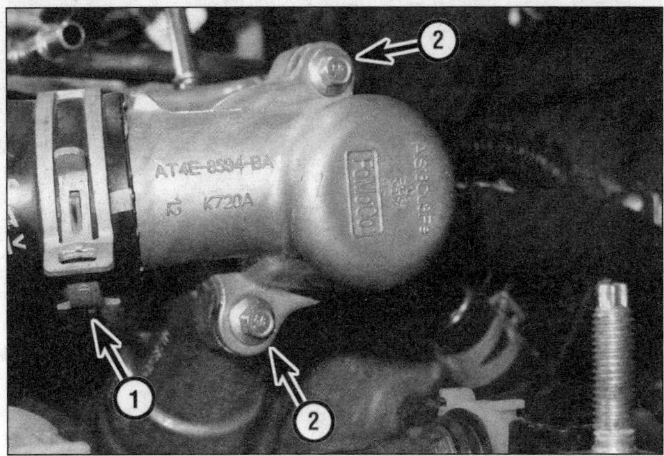

**4.7 Heater hose (1) and thermostat inlet cover bolts (2) -
V6 engines**

5.6 Lower radiator splash shield fastener locations

V6 models

Thermostat

6   Remove the air filter housing and outlet pipe (see Chapter 4).

7   Disconnect the heater hose from the thermostat housing **(see illustration)**.

8   Remove the two inlet cover bolts **(see illustration 4.7)**. If the cover is stuck, tap it with a soft-face hammer to jar it loose. Be prepared for some coolant to spill as the gasket seal is broken. Remove the inlet cover from the vehicle.

9   Take note of the thermostat orientation and O-ring in the thermostat housing, and remove the thermostat.

Thermostat housing

10   Remove the air filter housing and outlet pipe (see Chapter 4).

11   Remove the following coolant hoses from the thermostat housing. If the hose clamp is stuck, grasp it near the end with a pair of adjustable pliers and twist it to break the seal, then pull it off. If the hose is old or if it has deteriorated, cut it off and install a new one.

a) Throttle body
b) Upper radiator hose
c) Coolant expansion tank
d) Bypass tube
e) Heater hose

12   Remove the thermostat housing cover bolts and separate the thermostat housing covers.

Note: *On 2009 and earlier 3.5L V6 engines, note how the thermostat bridge is aligned with the marks on the thermostat housing; this is how the new thermostat unit will need to be aligned in the housing.*

Installation

13   Clean the sealing surfaces of the thermostat housing covers. Also inspect the hoses, replacing them as necessary.

14   Discard all old O-rings and replace with new ones. Lubricate the new O-ring seal with clean coolant and install the O-ring seal onto the thermostat housing.

15   On 2008 and earlier 3.5L V6 engines, install the thermostat into the upper thermostat housing so that the thermostat bridge is in-line with the marks on the upper thermostat housing. Assemble the thermostat housing covers together and tighten the housing cover bolts to the torque listed in this Chapter's Specifications.

16   Tighten the thermostat mounting bolts to the torque listed in this Chapter's Specifications.

V6 models

17   Install a new thermostat gasket on the thermostat housing and install the housing.

18   Install the thermostat housing cover and tighten the mounting bolts to the torque listed in this Chapter's Specifications.

19   Reattach the radiator hoses, heater hose, expansion tank and bypass hoses to the thermostat housing, ensuring all clamps are tight. Replace clamps with new ones as necessary.

All models

20   Refill the cooling system (see Chapter 1).

21   Start the engine and allow it to reach normal operating temperature, then check for leaks and proper thermostat operation.

---

5   Engine cooling fans - replacement

Warning: *To avoid possible injury or damage, DO NOT operate the engine with a damaged fan. Do not attempt to repair fan blades - replace a damaged fan with a new one.*

Note: *Check for blown fuses before attempting to diagnose an electrical circuit problem.*

Note: *Cooling fans are controlled by a fan module controlled by the PCM.*

1   If the engine is overheating and the cooling fan is not coming on when the engine temperature rises to an excessive level, see Section 2. Check the fuses in the underhood fuse/relay box (see Chapter 12).

2   If the fuses are okay, check all wiring and connections to the fan motor. Refer to the wiring diagrams in Chapter 13. If no obvious problems are found, the problem could be the Cylinder Head Temperature (CHT) sensor, the cooling fan control module or the Powertrain Control Module (PCM). Have the cooling fan system and circuit diagnosed by a dealer service department or repair shop with the proper diagnostic equipment.

Warning: *Wait until the engine is completely cool before performing this procedure.*

Warning: *These models have an airbag sensor mounted near the radiator support bracket. It will be necessary to disarm the system prior to performing any work around the radiator, fans or other components in this area (see Chapter 12).*

3   Disconnect the cable from the negative battery terminal (see Chapter 5).

4   Drain the cooling system (see Chapter 1). If the coolant is relatively new and still in good condition, save it and reuse it. Detach the upper radiator hose from the radiator and position it aside.

5   Raise the vehicle and support it securely on jackstands.

6   Remove the splash shield underneath the radiator **(see illustration)**.

7   Remove the air filter housing and duct (see Chapter 4).

2.0L four-cylinder engines

8   Remove and discard the charge air adapter cooler gasket and charge air adapter heat shield.

Note: *A new charge air adapter gasket and heat shield must be used on installation.*

V6 engines

9   On 2007 and earlier models, disconnect the upper coolant hose retainer from the fan shroud and position aside.

10   If equipped, detach the block heater wire

5.12 Press the tab through the access hole to release the upper coolant hose retainer (2008 and later models)

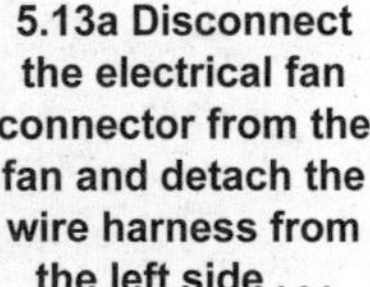

5.13a Disconnect the electrical fan connector from the fan and detach the wire harness from the left side . . .

harness clip from the engine electrical wire harness.

11   Detach the electrical wire harness from the fan shroud and move it aside.

All models

12   On 2008 and later models, the upper coolant hose is held by hose supports. To release the upper coolant hose from the hose supports, use a flat head screwdriver to press the tab through the access hole in the hose support and remove the support **(see illustration)**.

13   Disconnect the electrical wire harness clips from the fan motors. Detach all clips holding the wire harness to the fan shroud assembly on the left and right sides of the fan shroud **(see illustrations)**. Move the wire harness aside.

14   On 2010 and later models, detach the hood release cable from the fan shroud and move the cable aside **(see illustration)**.

15   Remove the fan shroud mounting bolts **(see illustrations)** and lift the fan shroud assembly out of the vehicle.

5.13b . . . and right side of the fan shroud

5.14 Detach the hood release cable from the fan shroud and move it aside

Installation

16   Installation is the reverse of removal.

Note: *On 2.0L four-cylinder engines, use a new charge air adapter gasket and heat shield.*

17   Reconnect the battery, refill the cooling system and bleed the air from the system (see Chapter 1).

18   Start the engine and allow it to reach normal operating temperature, then check for leaks and proper operation.

5.15a Remove the fan shroud mounting bolts from the driver's side . . .

5.15b . . . and the passenger's side of the vehicle

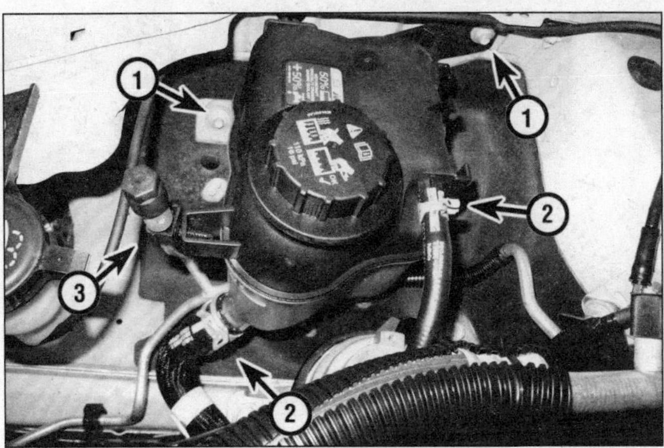

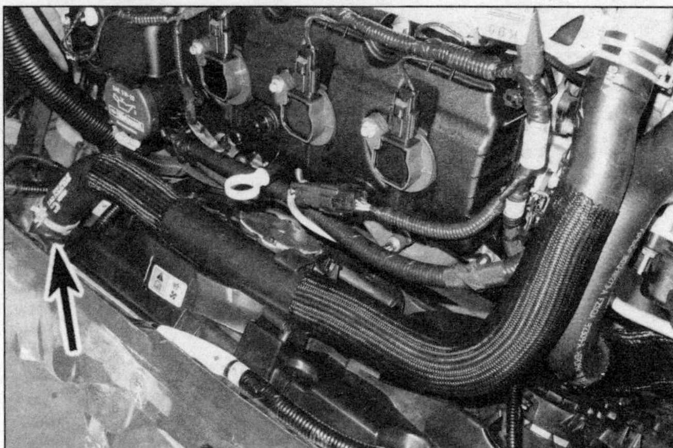

6.4 Expansion tank mounting fasteners (1), coolant hoses (2), and pin type retainer (3 - if equipped)

7.4a Disconnect and move aside the upper radiator hose . . .

7.4b . . . and the lower radiator hose

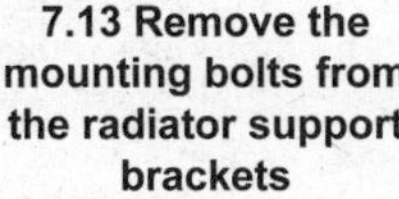

7.13 Remove the mounting bolts from the radiator support brackets

6 Coolant expansion tank - removal and installation

Removal

Warning: *Wait until the engine is completely cool before beginning this procedure.*

1　Release pressure from the cooling system by slowly turning the expansion tank cap one-half turn counterclockwise. Remove the coolant expansion tank cap.

2　Using suitable hose clamp pliers, clamp the lower coolant hose connected to the coolant expansion tank.

3　Remove the coolant in the coolant expansion tank using a suitable suction device. If the coolant is relatively new and in good condition, save and reuse it.

4　Disconnect the upper coolant hose and lower coolant hoses from the coolant expansion tank and move them aside **(see illustration)**.

5　If equipped, detach the pin-type retainer from the expansion tank **(see illustration 6.4)**.

6　On some models, the power steering fluid reservoir will need to be separated from the coolant expansion tank (see Chapter 10).

7　Remove the coolant expansion tank mounting bolts **(see illustration 6.4)**.

8　Position the coolant expansion tank aside to access the electrical connector. Disconnect the electrical connector and remove the coolant expansion tank from the vehicle.

9　Clean out the tank with soapy water and a brush to remove any deposits inside. Inspect the coolant expansion tank carefully for cracks. If you find a crack, replace the coolant expansion tank.

Installation

10　Installation is the reverse of removal.

7 Radiator - removal and installation

Warning: *Wait until the engine is completely cool before beginning this procedure.*
Warning: *These models have an airbag sensor mounted near the radiator support. It will be necessary to disarm the airbag system prior to performing any work around the radiator, fans or other components in this area (see Chapter 12).*

Removal

1　Disconnect the cable from the negative battery terminal (see Chapter 5).

2　Drain the cooling system (see Chapter 1). If the coolant is relatively new and in good condition, save it and reuse it. Detach the radiator hose from the bottom of the radiator.

3　Remove the cooling fan/shroud assembly from the radiator (see Section 5).

4　Disconnect the upper and lower radiator hoses and move them aside **(see illustrations)**.

5　Remove the front bumper cover (see Chapter 11).
Note: *This is not required for all models, but will aid in the radiator removal procedure.*

6　Remove the front grille and grille shutter assembly (see Chapter 11) (if equipped).

7　Remove the upper radiator cover (if equipped).

8　On 2007 and earlier 3.5L V6 engines, remove air filter housing assembly (see Chapter 3).

9　On 2007 and earlier 3.5L V6 engines, remove the horn assembly (see Chapter 12).

10　On 2007 and earlier 3.5L V6 models, remove the transaxle cooler bracket bolts. Lift the transaxle cooler from the retainers and position it aside.

11　On 2008 and later models, detach the lower coolant expansion tank hose from the radiator.

12　On 2008 and later models, detach the transaxle cooler hose from the radiator (if equipped).

13　Remove the radiator support brackets mounting bolts **(see illustration)**.

7.16a Driver's side radiator air dam

7.16b Passenger's side radiator air dam

14   Position the radiator towards the front of the vehicle.

15   On some models, the radiator support bracket are held by tabs; disengage the tabs by lifting them up, then position the radiator towards the engine.

16   Remove the radiator air dams from each side of the vehicle **(see illustrations)**.

17   Remove the air conditioning condenser mounting bolts and position the air conditioning condenser aside **(see illustration)**.

18   Remove the radiator from the vehicle.
Warning: *Do not to bend the fins, or damage the air conditioning condenser and radiator during re-positioning or removal.*

Installation

19   Remove bugs and dirt from the radiator with compressed air and a soft brush. Don't bend the cooling fins. Inspect the radiator for leaks and damage. If it needs repair, have a radiator shop or a dealer service department do the work.

20   Inspect the rubber insulators in the lower radiator support for cracks and deterioration. Make sure that they're free of dirt and gravel.

21   When installing the radiator, make sure that it's correctly seated on the insulators **(see illustration)**.

22   Installation is otherwise the reverse of removal. Fill the cooling system with the correct mixture of antifreeze and water (see Chapter 1).

23   Start the engine and check for leaks. Allow the engine to reach normal operating temperature, indicated by the upper radiator hose becoming hot. Check the coolant level and add more if required.

24   Check and add automatic transmission fluid as needed (see Chapter 1).

---

8   Water pump - replacement

Warning: *Wait until the engine is completely cool before beginning this procedure.*

Removal

1   Disconnect the cable from the negative battery terminal (see Chapter 5).

2   Drain the cooling system (see Chapter 1).

3.5L V6 engines

2007 and earlier models

3   Disconnect and move aside the thermostat housing to bypass tube coolant hose.

4   Remove the thermostat housing mounting bolts and position the thermostat housing aside.

5   Disconnect the water pump coolant hose and position it aside.

6   Remove the water pump mounting bolts.

7   Completely unscrew and remove the center mounting bolt from the water pump. Discard the center water pump mounting bolt sealing washer.

8   Remove the water pump from the vehicle; remove all traces of gasket and sealant from the mating surfaces on the water pump and the engine.

2008 and later models

9   On these models, the water pump is mounted to the front of the engine and driven by the timing chain. Remove the timing chain to access the water pump (see Chapter 2B).

2.0L four-cylinder engines

Note: *Cover the accessory drivebelt with plastic to prevent coolant from spilling on it.*

10   Remove the water pump pulley bolts and separate the pulley from the water pump **(see illustration)**.

11   Remove the water pump mounting bolts

7.17 Air conditioning condenser mounting bolts - V6 model shown

7.21 Ensure that the rubber insulators are in good condition and correctly seated in the retainers

and remove the water pump from the engine **(see illustration)**. If the water pump is stuck, gently tap it with a soft face hammer to break the seal.

12   Remove all traces of gasket and sealant from the mating surfaces on the water pump and the engine. Discard the old sealing gasket.

Installation

13   Compare the new pump to the old one to make sure that they're identical.

14   Replace all old gaskets and O-rings with new ones.

15   Apply a thin film of RTV sealant to hold the new gaskets and O-rings in place during installation. Gaskets and O-rings should be coated with clean coolant.

16   Correctly position the gasket on the water pump; make sure the mating surfaces are clean and free of old gasket material.

17   Carefully mate the pump to the water pump housing.

18   On 2007 and earlier 3.5L V6 models, tighten the water pump mounting bolts in the following sequence:

- *Center water pump bolt (35 in-lbs)*
- *Remaining three water pump mounting bolts (finger tight)*
- *Center water pump bolt (see this Chapter's Specifications)*
- *Remaining three water pump mounting bolts (see this Chapter's Specifications)*

19   On 2008 and later 3.5L V6 models, ensure that any coolant that has accumulated into the oil pan is drained completely. Clean any spilled coolant on the engine and oil pan. **Warning:** *Failure to remove all traces of coolant will result in oil contamination, which may result in engine damage.*

20   On 3.5L V6 engines, tighten the water pump bolts, in sequence **(see illustration)**, to the torque listed in this Chapter's Specifications. On 2008 and later V6 engines, tighten the bolts an additional 45 degrees.

21   On all other models, install the water pump bolts and tighten them to the torque listed in this Chapter's Specifications.

8.10 Remove the water pump pulley bolts - four cylinder engine

22   The remainder of installation is the reverse of removal. Refill and bleed the cooling system (see Chapter 1).

23   Run the engine and check for leaks.

9   Engine Coolant Temperature (ECT)/Cylinder Head Temperature (CHT) sensor - replacement

Note: *The removal and installation procedure for the ECT and CHT sensor is located in Chapter 6.*

10   Blower motor resistor and blower motor - replacement

Warning: *The models covered by this manual are equipped with Supplemental Restraint Systems (SRS), more commonly known as airbags. Always disable the airbag system before working in the vicinity of any airbag system component to avoid the possibility of accidental deployment of the airbag, which could cause personal injury (see Chapter 12).*

8.11 Remove the water pump mounting bolts - four cylinder engine

1   Remove the scuff plate, trim panel and panel insulator from the passenger's footwell, below the glove box (see Chapter 11).

Blower motor resistor and motor speed control

Note: *On 2009 and earlier models, the resistor and speed control are two separate units located near each other. In 2010 and later models the resistor and speed control are combined into a single unit. These components vary the speed of the blower motor.*

2   Disconnect the electrical connector from the blower motor resistor/speed control **(see illustration)**.

3   Remove the resistor/speed control mounting screws **(see illustration 10.2)** and remove the resistor/speed control.

4   Installation is the reverse of removal.

Blower motor

5   Disconnect the blower motor electrical connector **(see illustration 10.7)**.

6   On 2008 and later models, remove the blower motor vent tube clips and disconnect the vents from the heating and air conditioning evaporator core.

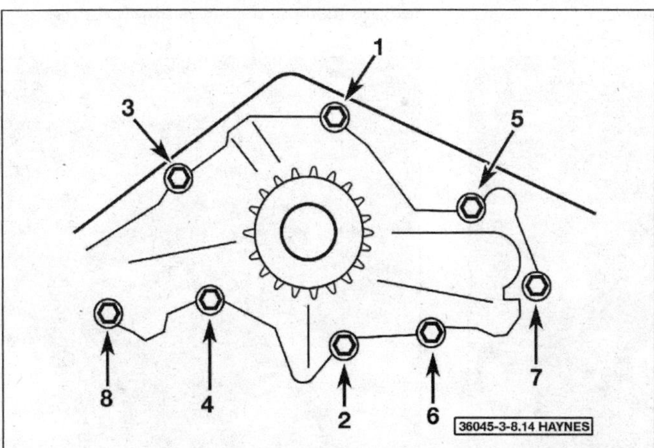

8.20 Water pump mounting bolt tightening sequence - 3.5L V6 engines

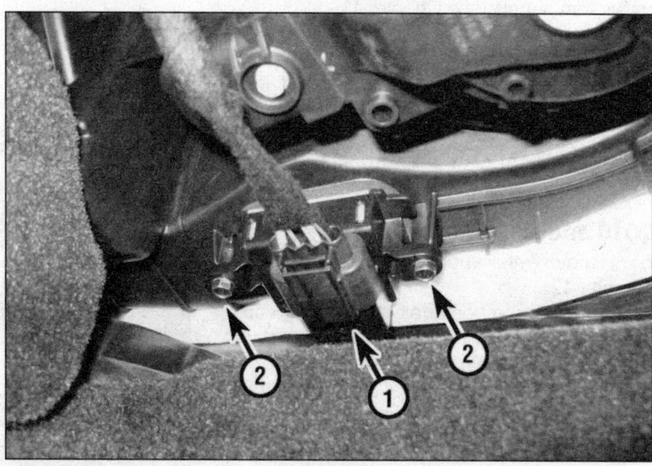

10.2 Resistor/speed control electrical connector (1) and mounting screws (2)

10.7 Blower motor electrical connector (1) and mounting fastener (2)

11.6 Heater/air conditioning control assembly retaining fastener

12.3 Disconnect the heater hoses from the heater core inlet and outlet pipes at the firewall

7   Remove the blower motor mounting fastener **(see illustration)**.
8   Rotate the blower motor to release it, and remove the blower motor.
9   Installation is the reverse of removal.

11   Heater/air conditioner control assembly - removal and installation

Removal

Warning: *The models covered by this manual are equipped with Supplemental Restraint Systems (SRS), more commonly known as airbags. Always disable the airbag system before working in the vicinity of any airbag system component to avoid the possibility of accidental deployment of the airbag, which could cause personal injury (see Chapter 12).*

Note: *The heater/air conditioner control assembly is incorporated into the Front Controls Interface Module (FCIM); if there is a problem, the entire module must be replaced.*

1   Disconnect the cable from the negative battery terminal (see Chapter 5).
2   Remove the left and right floor console upper trim panels (see Chapter 11).

2009 and earlier models

3   Remove the center instrument panel (see Chapter 11).
4   Remove the heater/air conditioner control assembly mounting screws and remove the control assembly.

2010 and later models

5   Remove the audio control module (see Chapter 12).
6   Remove the heater/air conditioning control assembly retaining fastener **(see illustration)** and move the control assembly aside.
7   Disconnect the electrical connectors from the heater/air conditioning control assembly and remove the control assembly.

Installation

8   Installation is the reverse of removal.

12   Heater core - replacement

Warning: *The models covered by this manual are equipped with Supplemental Restraint Systems (SRS), more commonly known as airbags. Always disarm the airbag system before working in the vicinity of any airbag system component to avoid the possibility of accidental deployment of the airbag, which could cause personal injury (see Chapter 12).*

Warning: *The air conditioning system is under high pressure. DO NOT loosen any fittings or remove any components until after the system has been discharged. Air conditioning refrigerant must be properly discharged into an EPA-approved container at a dealer service department or an automotive air conditioning repair facility. Always wear eye protection when disconnecting air conditioning system fittings.*

Warning: *Wait until the engine is completely cool before beginning this procedure.*

Note: *This is a difficult procedure for the home mechanic, involving numerous hard-to-find fasteners, clips and electrical connectors.*

1   Have the air conditioning system recovered by a dealer service department or an automotive air conditioning shop before proceeding (see **Warning** above).

2   Disconnect the cable from the negative battery terminal (see Chapter 5).
3   Drain the cooling system (see Chapter 1). Disconnect the heater hoses from the heater core inlet and outlet pipes at the firewall **(see illustration)**.
4   Remove the instrument panel (see Chapter 11).

2007 and earlier models

5   Remove the dash panel sealing from the heater core tubes.
6   Remove the heater core tube bracket fasteners and remove the brackets.
7   Disconnect the discharge air temperature sensor electrical connector and move it aside.
8   Remove the passenger's side temperature blend actuator mounting screws and remove the actuator.
9   Remove the heater core cover screws and remove the cover.

2008 and later models

10   Remove the instrument panel insulator fasteners and move the insulator aside.
11   Remove the floor duct fasteners and remove the floor duct **(see illustrations)**.

12.11a Remove the floor duct fasteners . . .

12.11b . . . and remove the floor duct

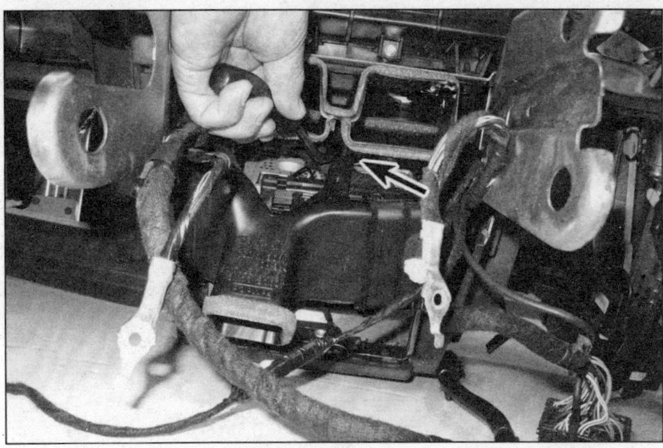

12.14a Detach the pin retainer holding the console Y-duct adapter . . .

12.14b . . . and remove the console Y-duct adapter

12.15a Heater core and evaporator core housing mounting bolt - 1 of 4 . . .

12.15b . . . bolt 2 of 4 . . .

12.15c . . . bolt 3 of 4 . . .

12.15d . . . and bolt 4 of 4

12.16a Remove the floor duct adapter fasteners . . .

12.16b . . . and remove the floor duct adapter

12   If equipped, remove the Remote Function Actuator module fasteners, and move the module aside.

13   If equipped, disconnect the temperature sensor aspirator from the heater core and evaporator core housing.

14   Detach the pin retainer holding the console duct Y-adapter and remove the Y-adapter **(see illustrations)**.

15   Remove the heater core and evaporator core housing mounting bolts **(see illustrations)**.

16   Remove the floor duct adapter fasteners and remove the adapter from the heater core and evaporator core housing **(see illustrations)**.

17   Disconnect the electrical connectors and the pin type wire harness retainers from the

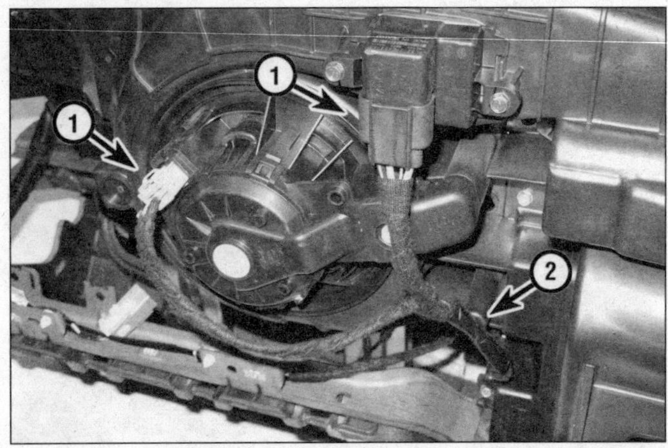

12.17 Heater/evaporator core housing electrical connectors (1) and pin-type wiring harness (2)

12.18 Disconnect any connections from the wire harness and detach the pin connectors holding the harness along the heater core and evaporator core housing

12.20 Remove the dash panel seal from the heater core tube support

12.21 Heater core tube support bracket fasteners

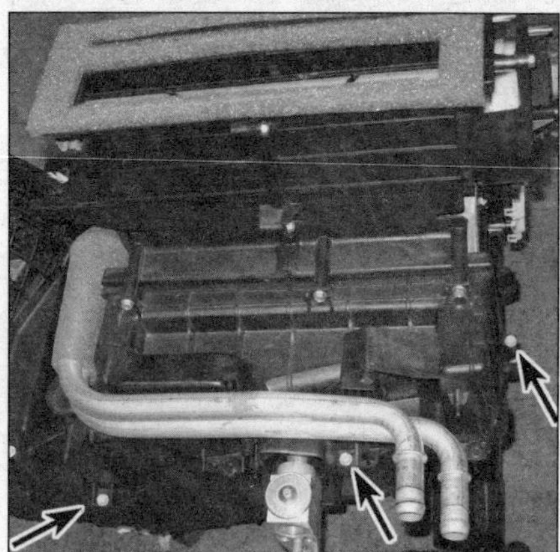

12.22 Plenum chamber screws (not all shown)

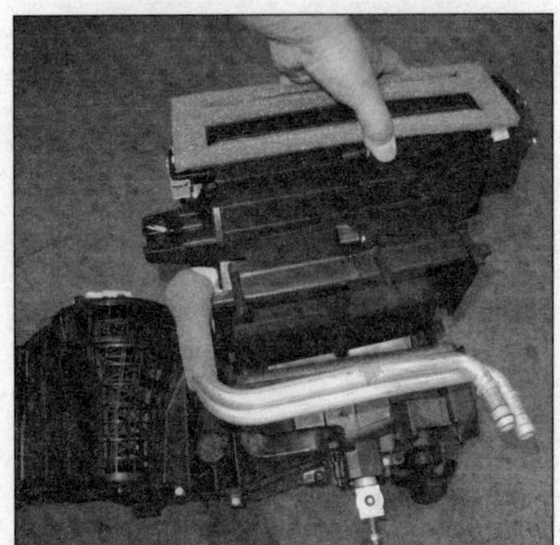

12.23a Separate the heater core from the housing . . .

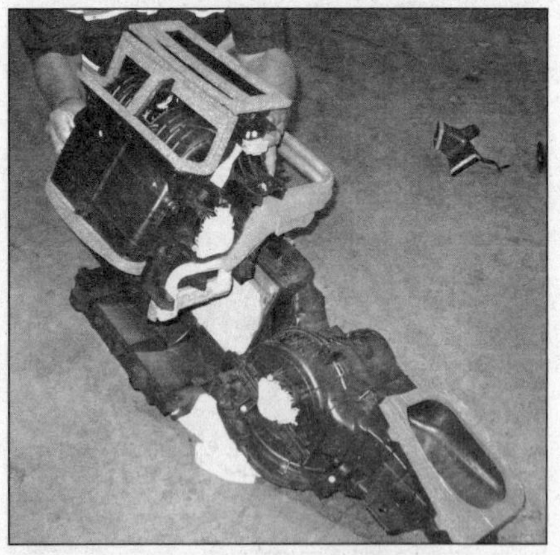

12.23b . . . lift up the heater core assembly . . .

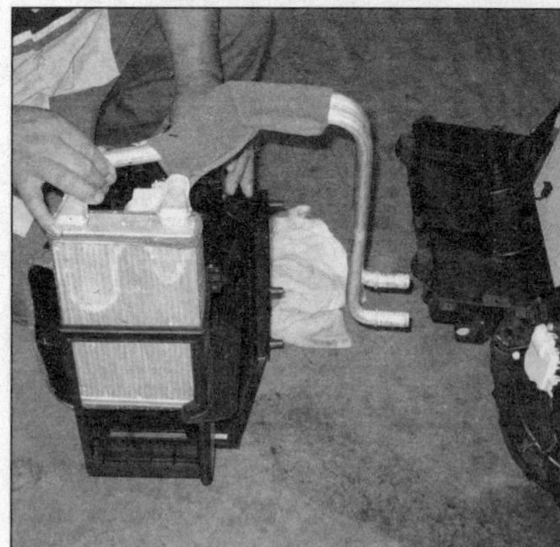

12.23c . . . and remove the heater core

heater core and evaporator core housing **(see illustration)**.

18   Detach all electrical connectors and wire harnesses from the heater core and evaporator core housing **(see illustration)**.

19   Remove the heater core and evaporator housing from the vehicle.

Caution: *To prevent damage to the vehicle interior, use rags and old towels to cover the interior during removal of the heater core and evaporator core housing.*

20   Remove the dash panel seal from the heater core tube support **(see illustration)**.

21   Remove the heater core tube support

bracket fasteners and remove the bracket **(see illustration)**.

22   Remove the plenum chamber mounting fasteners **(see illustration)**.

23   Remove the heater core **(see illustrations)**.

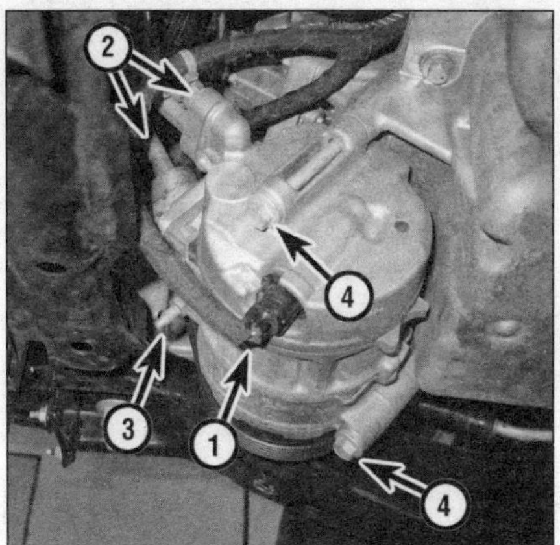

13.7 Air conditioning compressor details:

1 *Wiring harness*
2 *Refrigerant inlet/outlet line nuts*
3 *Compressor mounting nut/stud*
4 *Compressor mounting bolts*

Installation

24 Installation is the reverse of removal.
25 Refill and bleed the cooling system (see Chapter 1). Have the system evacuated, recharged and leak-tested by the shop that discharged it.

13 Air conditioning compressor - removal and installation

Warning: *The air conditioning system is under high pressure. DO NOT loosen any fittings or remove any components until after the system has been discharged. Air conditioning refrigerant must be properly discharged into an EPA-approved container at a dealer service department or an automotive air conditioning repair facility. Always wear eye protection when disconnecting air conditioning system fittings.*
Caution: *If the compressor is being replaced due to failure, the rest of the system should be flushed by a technician to remove particles or contaminants.*

Removal

1 Have the air conditioning system recovered by a dealer service department or an automotive air conditioning shop before proceeding (see **Warning** above).
2 Raise the vehicle and support it securely on jackstands.
3 Remove the lower radiator splash shield and engine splash shield (if equipped).
4 Remove the drivebelt (see Chapter 1).
5 On 2007 and earlier models, remove the cooling fan assembly (see Section 5).
6 If equipped, remove the air conditioning compressor shield fasteners and remove the shield.

Four-cylinder models

7 Detach the wiring harness from the air conditioning compressor and move it aside **(see illustration)**.

13.11 Compressor clutch field coil electrical connector (1) and pin-type wire harness (4) (2013 and later models)

8 Remove the refrigerant line nuts **(see illustration 13.7)**. Disconnect the refrigerant inlet and outlet lines from the compressor. Remove and discard the old O-rings.
9 Remove the compressor mounting nut **(see illustration 13.7)**.
10 Completely loosen the air conditioning compressor mounting stud and bolt **(see illustration 13.7)** and remove the compressor from the vehicle.

V6 models

11 Disconnect the electrical connector from the compressor clutch field coil **(see illustration)**.
12 Disconnect the pressure transducer electrical connector, if equipped.
13 Remove the refrigerant line mounting nuts **(see illustration)**. Disconnect the refrigerant inlet and outlet lines from the compressor. Remove and discard the old O-rings.
14 On 2013 and later models, detach the wire harness from the air conditioning compressor and move it aside.
15 On 2012 and earlier models, the harness may be held by a bracket; remove the mounting bracket bolt and move the harness aside.
16 Remove the lower compressor mounting nut and completely loosen the stud **(see illustration)**.
17 Completely remove the air conditioning compressor mounting bolts and remove the compressor from the vehicle.

Installation

18 If a new compressor is being installed, follow the directions that came with the compressor regarding the draining of excess oil prior to installation.
19 The clutch may have to be transferred from the original to the new compressor.
20 Before reconnecting the inlet and outlet lines to the compressor, replace all O-rings and lubricate them with refrigerant oil.
21 Installation is otherwise the reverse of removal.
22 Have the system evacuated, recharged and leak-tested by the shop that discharged it.

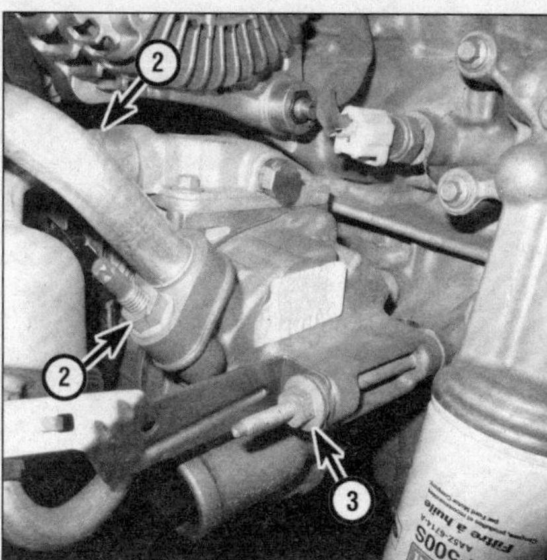

13.13 Refrigerant line mounting nuts (2) and compressor mounting bolt (3)

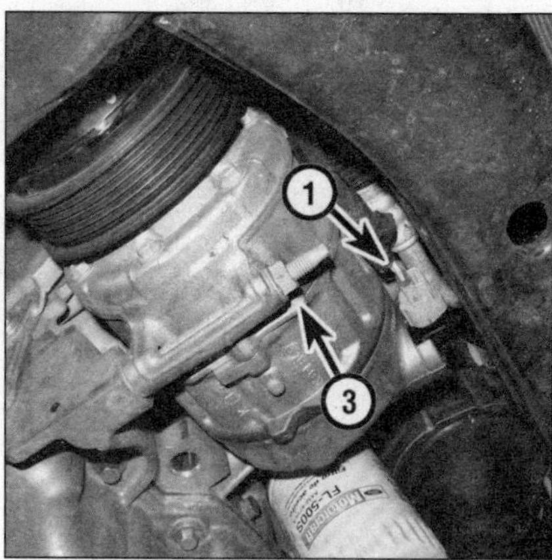

13.16 Secondary electrical connector (1) and lower compressor mounting nut (3)

14 Air conditioning condenser - removal and installation

Warning: *The air conditioning system is under high pressure. DO NOT loosen any fittings or remove any components until after the system has been discharged. Air conditioning refrigerant must be properly discharged into an EPA-approved container at a dealer service department or an automotive air conditioning repair facility. Always wear eye protection when disconnecting air conditioning system fittings.*
Note: *The air conditioning condenser has an integrated receiver/drier, equipped with a receiver/drier desiccant bag. The receiver/drier desiccant bag may be removed and replaced with a new one (available from the dealer).*

Removal

1 Have the air conditioning system discharged by a dealer service department or an automotive air conditioning shop before proceeding (see **Warning** above).
2 Remove the upper radiator grill and sight shield (if equipped).
3 On 2007 and earlier models, unbolt the horn assembly and move it aside (see Chapter 12, if necessary).

14.7 Disconnect the refrigerant inlet and outlet pipes from the condenser

14.15 Remove the threaded plug at the bottom left of the condenser

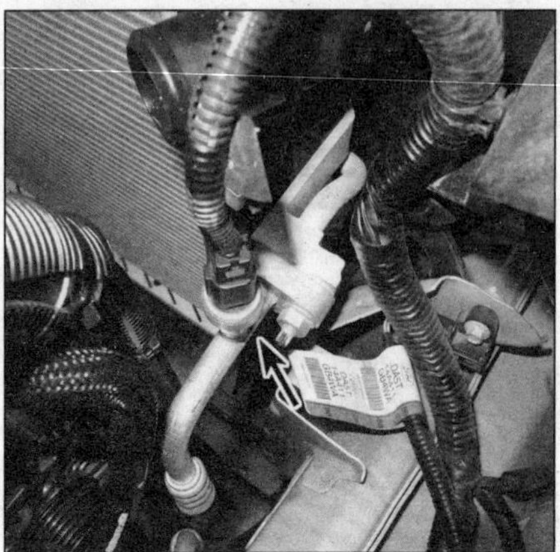

15.5 Disconnect the pressure cycling switch electrical connector

4   On four-cylinder models, remove the radiator grille shutter (see Chapter 11).

5   On V6 models, remove the radiator (see Section 7).

6   On 2008 and later models, disconnect the transaxle cooler line clamps and disconnect the lines from the condenser core.

7   Disconnect the refrigerant inlet and outlet pipes from the condenser, capping the lines to prevent contamination **(see illustration)**. Remove the bolt or nut securing the pipe fitting to the condenser.

8   Remove the condenser. If reinstalling the original condenser, store it with the line fittings facing up to prevent oil from draining out.

Installation

9   If installing a new condenser, pour one ounce of refrigerant oil of the correct type into it prior to installation.

10   Before reconnecting the refrigerant lines to the condenser, coat a pair of new O-rings with refrigerant oil, install them in the refrigerant line fittings and tighten the condenser inlet and outlet nuts securely.

11   Refill the transmission fluid as needed to the correct level (see Chapter 1).

12   Installation is otherwise the reverse of removal.

13   Have the system evacuated, recharged and leak tested by the shop that discharged it.

Receiver/drier desiccant bag - replacement

14   Remove the condenser as previously described in this Section.

15   Remove the threaded plug at the bottom left of the condenser **(see illustration)**.

16   Using needle nose pliers, pull the desiccant bag out of the receiver/drier.

17   Insert a new bag into the receiver drier.

18   Install the plug and tighten it securely.

15   Air conditioning pressure cycling switch - replacement

Warning: *The air conditioning system is under high pressure. DO NOT loosen any fittings or*

remove any components until after the system has been discharged. Air conditioning refrigerant must be properly discharged into an EPA-approved container at a dealer service department or an automotive air conditioning repair facility. Always wear eye protection when disconnecting air conditioning system fittings.

1   The pressure cycling switch is located on top of the hard line from the condenser to the air conditioning thermostatic expansion valve (TXV).

2   The pressure cycling switch detects low refrigerant line pressure, and switches the A/C system off, then back on again to provide higher pressure. If the pressure increases too high, the pressure cut-off switch (located in the high-pressure side of the system) shuts the system off.

Removal

3   Have the air conditioning system recovered by a dealer service department or an automotive air conditioning shop before proceeding (see **Warning** above).

4   On four-cylinder models, remove the under engine splash shield (if equipped), and the splash shield below the radiator.

5   Unplug the electrical connector from the pressure cycling switch **(see illustration)**.

6   Unscrew and remove the pressure cycling switch.

Installation

7   Lubricate the switch O-ring with clean refrigerant oil of the correct type.

8   Screw the new switch into place until hand tight, then tighten it securely.

9   Reconnect the electrical connector. On four-cylinder models, install the splash shields.

10   Have the system evacuated, recharged and leak tested by the shop that discharged it.

16   Air conditioning thermostatic expansion valve (TXV) - removal and installation

Warning: *The air conditioning system is under high pressure. DO NOT loosen any hose*

fittings or remove any components until the system has been discharged. Air conditioning refrigerant must be properly discharged into an EPA-approved recovery/recycling unit by a dealer service department or an automotive air conditioning repair facility. Always wear eye protection when disconnecting air conditioning system fittings.

Removal

1   Have the air conditioning system discharged by a dealer service department or an automotive air conditioning shop before proceeding (see **Warning** above).

2   Remove the strut tower brace mounting bolts and remove the brace.

3   On 2007 and earlier models, remove the strut tower brace bracket bolts and remove the bracket.

4   On 2008 models, remove the evaporator inlet line fitting bracket bolt.

5   On 2008 models, remove the evaporator inlet and outlet line mounting nuts and disconnect the lines.

6   Remove the auxiliary evaporator inlet and outlet line mounting nuts (if equipped), disconnect the lines, and position them aside.

7   Remove the TXV fitting nuts and disconnect the refrigerant lines from the TXV at the firewall.

8   Remove the two bolts securing the valve, then remove the valve.

Note: *Remove and discard all O-rings from all disconnected refrigerant lines.*

Installation

9   Replace all refrigerant line O-rings and lubricate the new ones with refrigerant oil prior to installation.

10   Installation is otherwise the reverse of removal.

11   Have the system evacuated, recharged and leak tested by the shop that discharged it.

Chapter 4
Fuel and exhaust systems

Contents

Specifications

General

Fuel system pressure

  2.0L engines

    Key on, engine off..   55 psi   379 kPa

    Key on, engine running..   51 to 75 psi   351 to 517 kPa

  3.0L engines (engine running) ....   40 psi   276 kPa

  3.5L engines (engine off and engine running)

    2008 through 2012 models.....................................   65 psi   448 kPa

    2013 and later models ....   55 psi   379 kPa

Torque specifications   Ft-lbs (unless otherwise indicated)   Nm

Note: *One foot-pound (ft-lb) of torque is equivalent to 12 inch-pounds (in-lbs) of torque. Torque values below approximately 15 ft-lbs are expressed in inch-pounds, because most foot-pound torque wrenches are not accurate at these smaller values.*

Throttle body mounting fasteners...   89 in-lbs   10

Fuel rail mounting bolts

  Four-cylinder models

    Step 1 ....   71 in-lbs   8

    Step 2 ....   Tighten an additional 26-degrees

  V6 models ....   89 in-lbs   10

Torque specifications

	Ft-lbs (unless otherwise indicated)	Nm

Note: *One foot-pound (ft-lb) of torque is equivalent to 12 inch-pounds (in-lbs) of torque. Torque values below approximately 15 ft-lbs are expressed in inch-pounds, because most foot-pound torque wrenches are not accurate at these smaller values.*

High-pressure fuel pump mounting bolts (four-cylinder)

Step 1	44 in-lbs	5
Step 2	Tighten an additional 55-degrees	

High-pressure fuel tube flare nuts (four-cylinder)

Step 1	133 in-lbs	15
Step 2	Tighten an additional 30-degrees	

High-pressure fuel tube bracket bolts (four-cylinder and V6 turbocharged)

	89 in-lbs	10

Turbocharger

Coolant line banjo bolts	21	28
Oil line banjo bolts	18	24
Oil drain tube bolts	89 in-lbs	10
Turbocharger mounting studs	150 in-lbs	17
Turbocharger mounting nuts	37	50

1   General information

Fuel system warnings

1   Gasoline is extremely flammable and repairing fuel system components can be dangerous. Consider your automotive repair knowledge and experience before attempting repairs which may be better suited for a professional mechanic.

- *Don't smoke or allow open flames or bare light bulbs near the work area*
- *Don't work in a garage with a gas-type appliance (water heater, clothes dryer)*
- *Use fuel-resistant gloves. If any fuel spills on your skin, wash it off immediately with soap and water*
- *Clean up spills immediately*
- *Do not store fuel-soaked rags where they could ignite*
- *Prior to disconnecting any fuel line, you must relieve the fuel pressure (see Section 3)*
- *Wear safety glasses*
- *Have a proper fire extinguisher on hand*

Fuel system

2   The fuel system consists of the fuel tank, electric fuel pump/fuel level sending unit (located in the fuel tank), fuel rail, fuel injectors and, on four-cylinder models, a high-pressure fuel pump mounted to the end of the cylinder head. The fuel injection system is a multi-port system; multi-port fuel injection uses timed impulses to inject the fuel directly into the intake port of each cylinder. The Powertrain Control Module (PCM) controls the injectors. The PCM monitors various engine parameters and delivers the exact amount of fuel required into the intake ports.

3   Fuel is circulated from the fuel pump to the fuel rail through fuel lines running along the underside of the vehicle. Various sections of the fuel line are either rigid metal or nylon, or flexible fuel hose. The various sections of the fuel hose are connected either by quick-connect fittings or threaded metal fittings.

Exhaust system

4   The exhaust system consists of the exhaust manifold(s), catalytic converter(s), muffler(s), tailpipe and all connecting pipes, flanges and clamps. The catalytic converters are an emission control device added to the exhaust system to reduce pollutants.

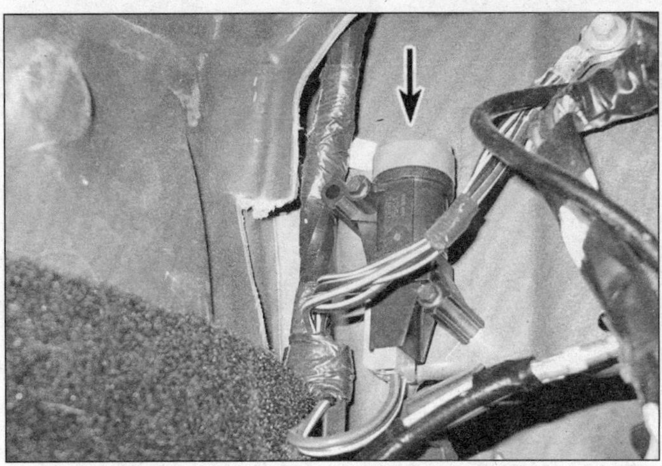

2.2 The fuel pump inertia switch is located behind the right-front passenger's kick panel. To reset it, push the button on top (typical 2009 and earlier models)

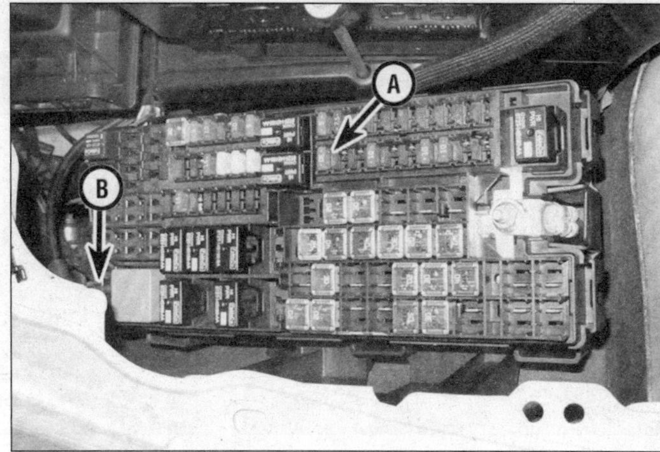

2.4 The fuel pump fuse (A) is located in the engine compartment fuse box along with the fuel pump relay (B, obscured by fender in this photo) (2013 model shown). The location of the fuse and relay varies with model and year - refer to the guide in your owner's manual

2   Troubleshooting

Electric fuel pump

1   The electric fuel pump is located inside the fuel tank. Sit inside the vehicle with the windows closed, turn the ignition key to ON (not START) and listen for the sound of the fuel pump as it's briefly activated. You will only hear the sound for a second or two, but that sound tells you that the pump is working. Alternatively, have an assistant listen at the fuel filler cap.

2   On 2009 and earlier models, if the pump does not come on, make sure that the inertia switch **(see illustration)** has not opened the fuel pump circuit. The inertia switch is a reset-table circuit breaker that automatically opens the fuel pump circuit in the event of an acci-dent. To access it, remove the right panel in the passenger's fotwell (see Chapter 11).

3   On 2010 and later models, a fuel-cut off system is used in case of an accident. If there has been an accident, the restraint system sends a signal to the Fuel Pump Control Mod-ule (FPCM) and shuts the module off. To reset the FPCM, turn the ignition key to the "OFF" position, then to the "ON" position and start the engine.

Note: *This may take a few attempts.*

4   Check the fuel pump fuse and relay **(see illustration)**. If the fuse and relay are okay, check the wiring back to the fuel pump. If the fuse, relay, wiring and (on 2009 and earlier models) inertia switch are okay, the fuel pump is probably defective. If the pump runs contin-uously with the ignition key in the ON position, the Powertrain Control Module (PCM) is prob-ably defective. Have the PCM checked by a professional mechanic.

Fuel injection system

Note: *The following procedure is based on the assumption that the fuel pump is working and*

the fuel pressure is adequate *(see Section 4).*

5   Check all electrical connectors that are related to the system. Check the ground wire connections for tightness. Verify that the bat-tery is fully charged (see Chapter 5).

6   Inspect the air filter element (see Chap-ter 1).

7   Check all fuses related to the fuel sys-tem (see Chapter 12).

8   Check the air induction system between the throttle body and the intake manifold for air leaks. Also inspect the condition of all vac-uum hoses connected to the intake manifold and to the throttle body.

9   Remove the air intake duct from the throttle body and look for dirt, carbon, varnish, or other residue in the throttle body, particu-larly around the throttle plate. If it's dirty, clean it with carb cleaner, a toothbrush and a clean shop towel.

10   Check to see if any trouble codes are stored in the PCM (see Chapter 6).

3   Fuel pressure relief procedure

Warning: *Gasoline is extremely flammable. See* **Fuel system warnings** *in Section 1.*

2007 and earlier models

1   Remove the fuel pump fuse from the underhood fuse/relay box; it's fuse number F1.27, 15 amp.

Note: *Consult your owner's manual or the un-derside of the fuse/relay box lid for the fuse layout legend.*

2   Proceed to Step 8.

2008 and 2009 models

3   Remove the kick panel trim from the right front passenger's footwell. Disconnect the electrical connector from the fuel pump inertia switch **(see illustration 2.2)**.

4   Proceed to Step 8.

2010 and later models

Note: *The Fuel Pump Control Module (FPCM) or Fuel Pump Driver Module (FPDM) is mount-ed to the panel behind the right rear seat-back cushion.*

5   Fold the right rear seat-back down and peel back the trim panel to gain access to the FPCM/FPDM.

6   Disconnect the electrical connector from the module **(see illustration)**.

7   Proceed to the next Step.

All models

8   Start the engine and allow it to idle until it stalls.

9   Turn the ignition switch to the OFF posi-tion. Fuel system pressure is now relieved.

Warning: *On four-cylinder models, the fuel pressure must also be released from the high pressure fuel pump prior to disconnecting any fuel lines in the delivery (low pressure) system (see Steps 10 through 12).*

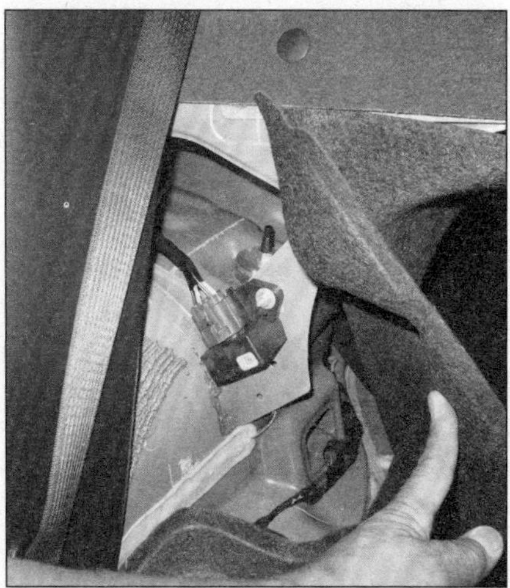

3.6 The FPCM/FPDM is located behind the right-rear seat back

3.10 Loosen the high pressure fuel tube with a flare-nut wench while covering it with a shop towel

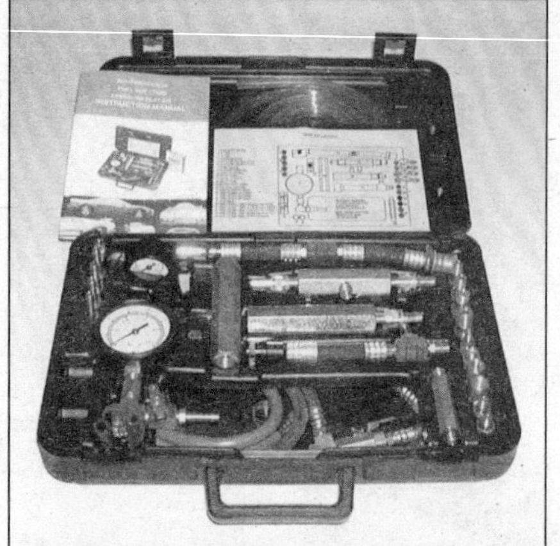

4.1 This fuel pressure testing kit contains all the necessary fittings and adapters, along with the fuel pressure gauge, to test most automotive systems

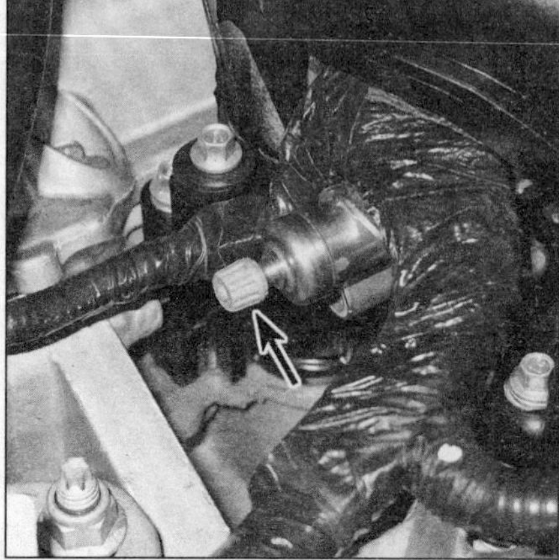

4.2 Some models are equipped with a fuel pressure test port on the fuel rail (3.0L V6 engine shown)

High-pressure fuel system (2.0L four-cylinder models)

Warning: *Wrap a shop towel around the high-pressure line flare nut prior to loosening the flare nut to absorb fuel when relieving fuel pressure.*

10   Place a flare-nut wrench on the high-pressure fuel tube at the high-pressure pump **(see illustration)**, then wrap the wrench and nut with a shop towel to absorb any remaining fuel pressure while loosening the nut.

11   Loosen the high-pressure fuel tube-to-fuel injection pump flare nut and release the remaining pressure.

Warning: *The manufacturer states that the high-pressure fuel tube must be replaced with a new one whenever it is loosened or removed.*

12   When installing the new fuel tube, tighten the fitting nuts to the torque listed in this Chapter's Specifications.

---

4   Fuel pressure - check

Warning: *Gasoline is extremely flammable. See* **Fuel system warnings** *in Section 1.*
Note: *The following procedure assumes that the fuel pump is receiving voltage and runs.*

1   A fuel pressure gauge, with the proper adapter(s) and capable of reading fuel pressures within the range listed in this Chapter's Specifications, will be required **(see illustration)**.

Models with a test port on the fuel rail

2   Locate the fuel pressure test port on the fuel rail, unscrew the cap and connect a fuel pressure gauge **(see illustrations)**.

3   Start the engine and allow it to idle. Note the gauge reading as soon as the pressure stabilizes, and compare it with the pressure listed in.

4   If the fuel pressure is not within specifi-

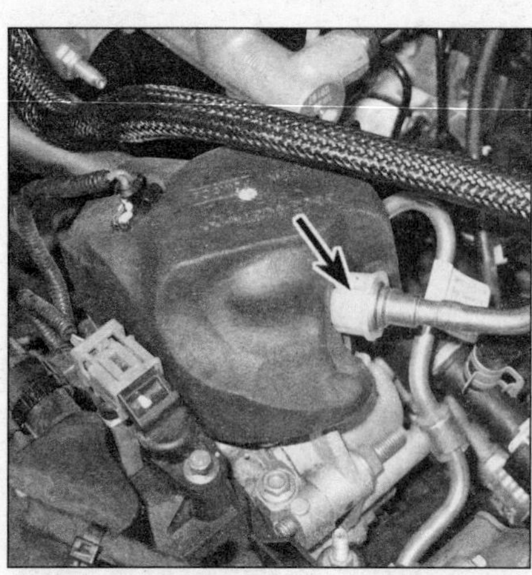

4.8a On four-cylinder models, detach the fuel feed line from the high-pressure fuel pump and connect a fuel pressure gauge between the line and the pump

cations, check the following:

a)   *Check for a restriction in the fuel system (kinked fuel line, plugged fuel pump inlet strainer or clogged fuel filter). If no restrictions are found, replace the fuel pump module (see Section 7).*

b)   *If the fuel pressure is higher than specified, replace the fuel pump module (see Section 7).*

5   Turn off the engine. Fuel pressure should not fall more than 8 psi over five minutes. If it does, the problem could be a leaky fuel injector, fuel line leak, or faulty fuel pump module.

6   Disconnect the fuel pressure gauge. Wipe up any spilled gasoline.

Models without a test port on the fuel rail

7   Relieve the fuel system pressure (see Section 3).

8   Disconnect the fuel supply line at the high-pressure fuel pump (four-cylinder engine)

4.8b On models with a 3.5L V6 engine, detach the fuel feed line from the fuel rail pipe at the right end of the engine and install a fuel pressure gauge between the line and the pipe

or at the fuel rail (3.5L V6 engine) (see Section 5), then use an adapter to connect the fuel pressure gauge between the fuel line and the fuel rail.

9   Refer to Steps 2 through 4 for the fuel pressure check.

10   Relieve the fuel system pressure (see Section 3), then disconnect the fuel pressure gauge.

11   Reconnect the fuel line to the fuel rail.

12   Reconnect the battery (see Chapter 5). Turn the ignition key to the On position and check for fuel leaks.

---

5   Fuel lines and fittings - general information and disconnection

Warning: *Gasoline is extremely flammable. See* **Fuel system warnings** *in Section 1.*

1   Relieve the fuel pressure before servicing fuel lines or fittings (see Section 3), then

Disconnecting Fuel Line Fittings

Two-tab type fitting; depress both tabs with your fingers, then pull the fuel line and the fitting apart

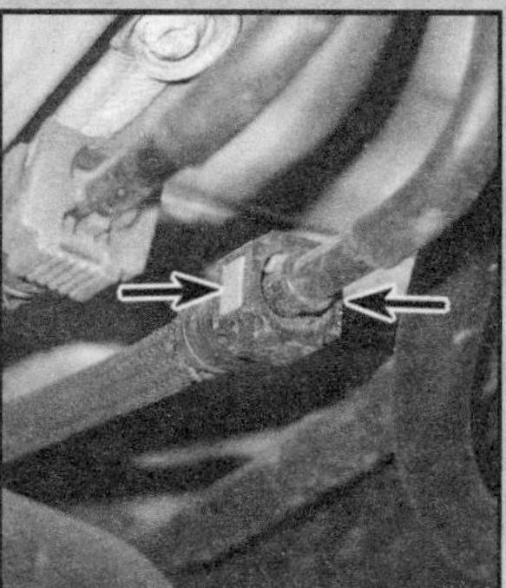

On this type of fitting, depress the two buttons on opposite sides of the fitting, then pull it off the fuel line

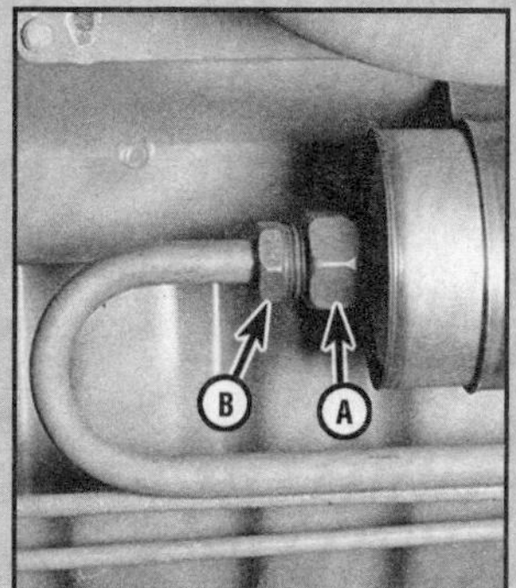

Threaded fuel line fitting; hold the stationary portion of the line or component (A) while loosening the tube nut (B) with a flare-nut wrench

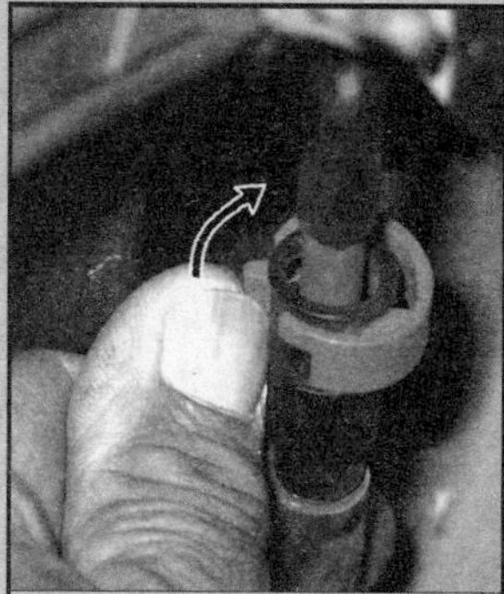

Plastic collar-type fitting; rotate the outer part of the fitting

Metal collar quick-connect fitting; pull the end of the retainer off the fuel line and disengage the other end from the female side of the fitting . . .

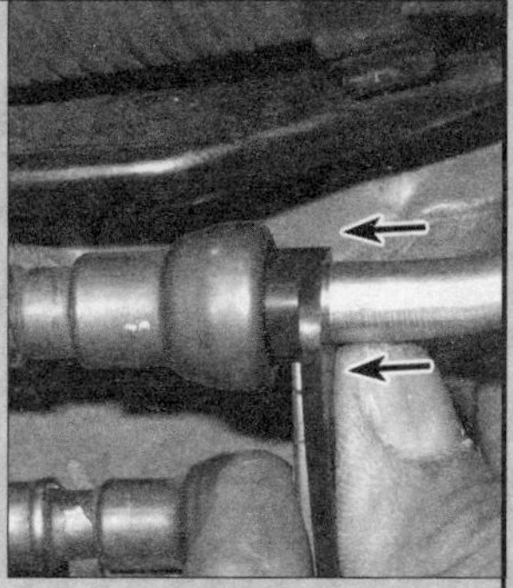

. . . insert a fuel line separator tool into the female side of the fitting, push it into the fitting and pull the fuel line off the pipe

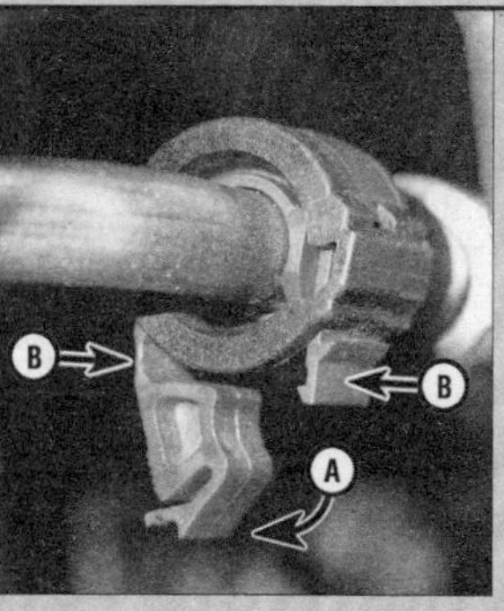

Some fittings are secured by lock tabs. Release the lock tab (A) and rotate it to the fully-opened position, squeeze the two smaller lock tabs (B) . . .

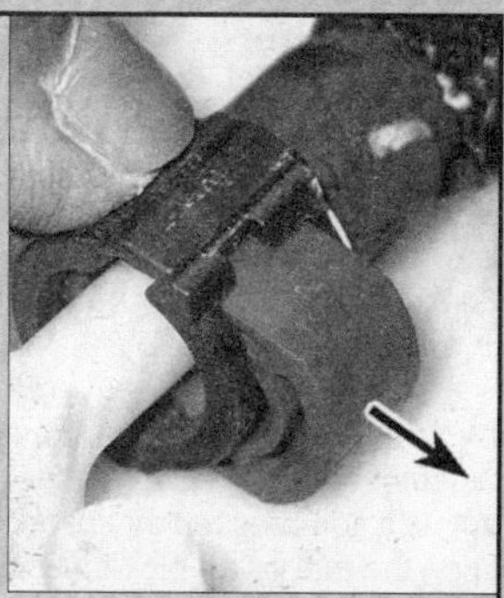

. . . then push the retainer out and pull the fuel line off the pipe

Spring-lock coupling; remove the safety cover, install a coupling release tool and close the tool around the coupling . . .

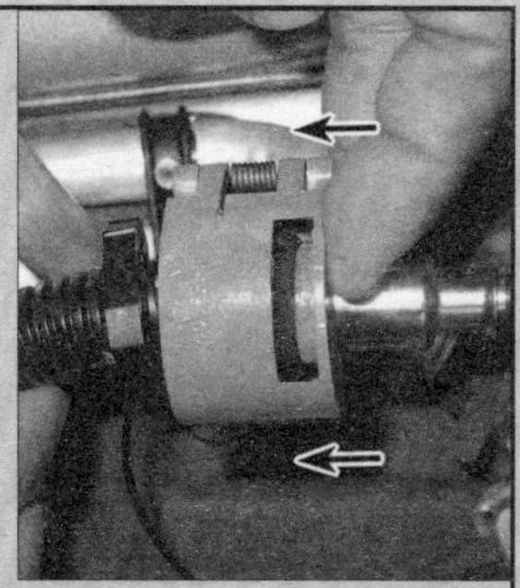

. . . push the tool into the fitting, then pull the two lines apart

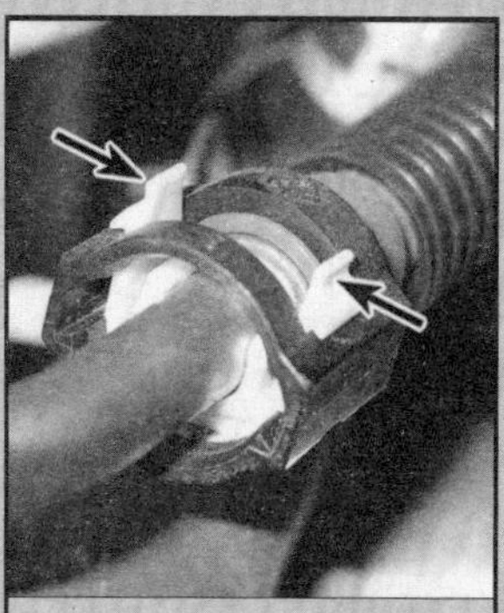

Hairpin clip type fitting: push the legs of the retainer clip together, then push the clip down all the way until it stops and pull the fuel line off the pipe

6.1a A typical exhaust system hanger. Inspect regularly and replace at the first sign of damage or deterioration

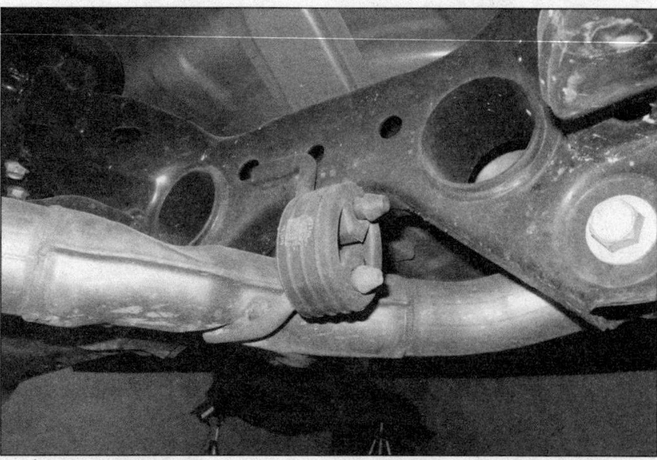

6.1b A damaged exhaust system hanger can cause the exhaust pipe to rub on the underside of the body

disconnect the cable from the negative battery terminal (see Chapter 5) before proceeding.

2　The fuel supply line connects the fuel pump in the fuel tank to the fuel rail on the engine. The Evaporative emission (EVAP) system lines connect the fuel tank to the EVAP canister, and connects the canister to the intake manifold.

3　Whenever you're working under the vehicle, inspect all fuel and EVAP lines for leaks, kinks, dents and other damage. Always replace a damaged fuel or EVAP line immediately.

4　If you find signs of dirt in the lines during disassembly, disconnect all lines and blow them out with compressed air. Inspect the fuel strainer on the fuel pump pick-up unit for damage and deterioration.

Steel tubing

5　It is critical that the fuel lines be replaced with lines of equivalent type and specification.
6　Some steel fuel lines have threaded fittings. When loosening these fittings, hold the stationary fitting with a wrench while turning the tube nut.

Plastic tubing

7　When replacing fuel system plastic tubing, use only original equipment replacement plastic tubing.

Caution: *When removing or installing plastic fuel line tubing, be careful not to bend or twist it too much, which can damage it. Also, plastic fuel tubing is NOT heat resistant, so keep it away from excessive heat.*

Flexible hoses

8　When replacing fuel system flexible hoses, use only original equipment replacements.

9　Don't route fuel hoses (or metal lines) within four inches of the exhaust system or within ten inches of the catalytic converter. Make sure that no rubber hoses are installed directly against the vehicle, particularly in places where there is any vibration. If allowed to touch some vibrating part of the vehicle, a hose can easily become chafed and it might start leaking. A good rule of thumb is to maintain a minimum of 1/4-inch clearance around a hose (or metal line) to prevent contact with the vehicle underbody.

6　Exhaust system servicing - general information

Warning: *Allow exhaust system components to cool before inspection or repair. Also, when working under the vehicle, make sure it is securely supported on jackstands.*

1　The exhaust system consists of the exhaust manifolds, catalytic converter, muffler, tailpipe and all connecting pipes, flanges and clamps. The exhaust system is isolated from the vehicle body and from chassis components by a series of rubber hangers **(see illustrations)**. Periodically inspect these hangers for cracks or other signs of deterioration, replacing them as necessary.

Note: *On 2011 and later V6 engines, the front manifold and front catalytic converter have been combined into a single unit.*

2　Conduct regular inspections of the exhaust system to keep it safe and quiet. Look for any damaged or bent parts, open seams, holes, loose connections, excessive corrosion or other defects which could allow exhaust fumes to enter the vehicle. Do not repair deteriorated exhaust system components; replace them with new parts.

3　If the exhaust system components are extremely corroded, or rusted together, a cutting torch is the most convenient tool for removal. Consult a properly-equipped repair shop. If a cutting torch is not available, you can use a hacksaw, or if you have compressed air, there are special pneumatic cutting chisels that can also be used. Wear safety goggles to protect your eyes from metal chips and wear work gloves to protect your hands.

4　Here are some simple guidelines to follow when repairing the exhaust system:
Work from the back to the front when removing exhaust system components.

  a)　Apply penetrating oil to the exhaust system component fasteners to make them easier to remove.
  b)　Use new gaskets, hangers and clamps.
  c)　Apply anti-seize compound to the threads of all exhaust system fasteners during reassembly.
  d)　Allow sufficient clearance between newly installed parts and all points on the underbody to avoid overheating the floor pan and possibly damaging the interior carpet and insulation. Pay particularly close attention to the catalytic converter and heat shield.

7　Fuel pump module - removal and installation

Warning: *Gasoline is extremely flammable. See **Fuel system warnings** in Section 1.*

Fuel pump module

Note: *The fuel pump module includes the fuel pump, the fuel level sending unit and a fuel filter, it's located on the passenger's side of the fuel tank. The fuel level sending unit is the only item that can be serviced separately.*

1　Relieve the fuel system pressure (see Section 3). Disconnect the cable from the negative battery terminal (see Chapter 5).

Warning: *The fuel tank should be less than half full before removing the fuel pump (the top of the pump is below the fuel level when the tank is full). Use a hose, siphon pump and an approved container to drain fuel from the tank.*

2　Remove the rear seat cushion (see Chapter 11).

3　Disconnect the electrical connector from the fuel pump module **(see illustration)**.

4　Disconnect the fuel supply and vapor control lines.

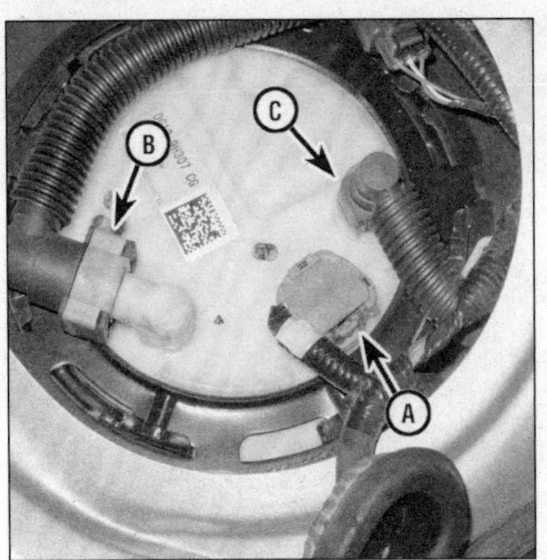

7.3 Disconnect the electrical connector (A), the fuel feed line (B) and the vapor control line (C)

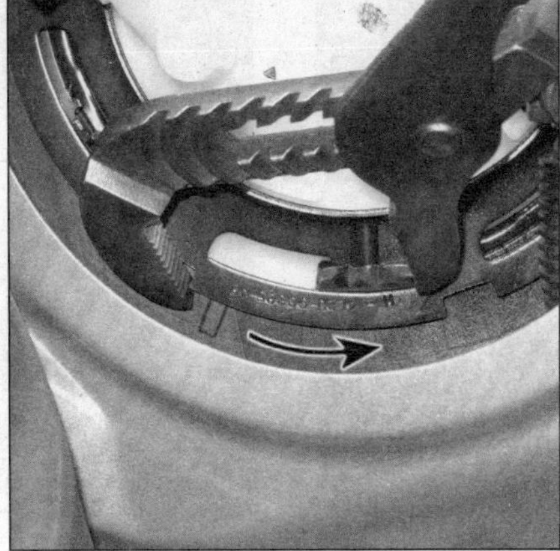

7.12 A pair of pliers can be used to unscrew the fuel pump module lock ring

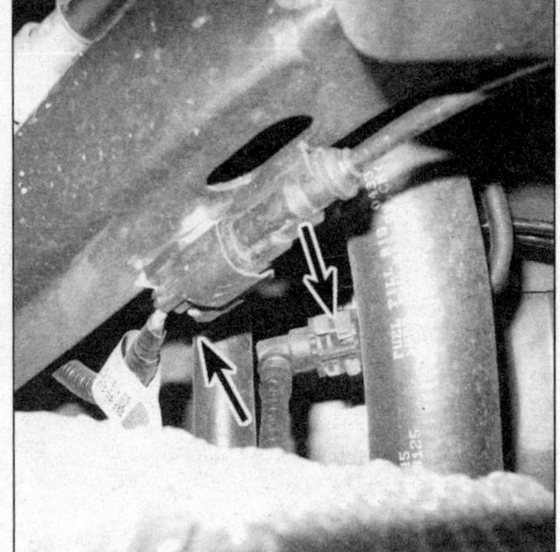

8.7 EVAP hose quick-connect fitting and fuel tank harness electrical connector (fuel supply line fitting not shown)

2008 through 2012 all-wheel drive models

5   Raise the rear of the vehicle and support it securely on jackstands.

6   Remove the driveshaft (see Chapter 8).

7   Disconnect the quick-connect fitting at the fuel tank jumper line.

8   Remove the EVAP canister (see Chapter 6).

9   Support the fuel tank with a floor jack and wood plank, or with a floor jack equipped with a transmission adapter head. Remove the bolts from the front of the fuel tank straps (see Section 8).

10   Lower the front of the fuel tank just far enough to remove the fuel pump module shield.

11   After the shield has been removed, raise the tank and temporarily install the fuel tank strap bolts.

All models

12   Remove the pump module lock ring using a lock ring removal tool (available at most auto parts stores) or use a pair of large water pump pliers to unscrew the lock ring by turning it counterclockwise **(see illustration)**.

13   Carefully pull the fuel pump module out of the tank enough to disconnect the fuel vapor hose quick-connect fitting, and separate the hose. Lift the module out of tank completely, angling it as necessary to protect the fuel level sensor float arm.

Note: *On AWD models, the fuel vapor hose quick connect fitting and line are located at the base of the module.*

14   Inspect the O-ring and replace it if it shows any sign of deterioration.

15   Installation is the reverse of removal.

Fuel level sending unit

16   Remove the fuel pump module.

17   Press the locking tab inwards and slide the fuel level sender up and off of the sensor.

18   Installation is the reverse of removal.

Fuel level sensor (AWD models)

Note: *AWD models are equipped with a saddle-shaped fuel tank that has two fuel level sensors; one is mounted on the fuel pump module (on the passenger's side of the fuel tank) and the other is located on the driver's side of the fuel tank.*

19   Remove the rear seat cushion.

20   Unscrew the lock ring **(see illustration 7.12)**.

21   Pull the fuel level sensor out of the tank, disconnect the fuel hose quick-connect fitting, and separate the hose. Lift the module completely out of tank, angling it as necessary to protect the fuel level sensor float arm.

22   Inspect the O-ring and replace it if it shows any sign of deterioration.

23   Installation is the reverse of removal.

8   Fuel tank - removal and installation

Warning: *Gasoline is extremely flammable. See **Fuel system warnings** in Section 1.*

Note: *The following procedure is much easier*

8.8 Fuel tank filler neck hose clamp (A) and fresh air vent hose cap (B)

to perform if the fuel tank is empty.

1   Remove the fuel tank filler cap to relieve fuel tank pressure.

2   Relieve the fuel system pressure (see Section 3).

3   Disconnect the cable from the negative battery terminal (see Chapter 5).

4   Raise the rear of the vehicle and support it securely on jackstands.

5   On AWD models, remove the driveshaft (see Chapter 8).

6   Remove the rear portion of the exhaust system (see Section 6).

7   Disconnect the EVAP and fuel supply line quick-connect fittings, and unplug the fuel tank harness electrical connector **(see illustration)**.

8   Loosen the hose clamp and disconnect the fuel filler neck hose and the fresh air hose vent cap **(see illustration)**.

9   Support the fuel tank securely, then remove the fuel tank retaining strap bolts **(see illustration)**. Remove the straps and carefully lower the fuel tank.

Note: *On AWD models, the fuel tank must be moved forward as it is lowered to clear the rear differential.*

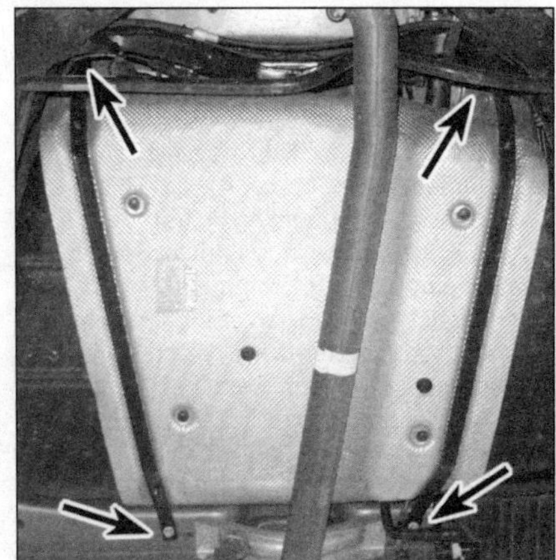

8.9 Fuel tank strap bolts

9.3 Loosen the hose clamp and carefully remove the air duct (3.5L V6 shown)

10.3 Loosen the charge air cooler pipe clamp (four-cylinder models)

10   Installation is the reverse of removal. Tighten the fuel tank strap bolts securely.

11   Reconnect the cable to the negative battery terminal (see Chapter 5), then start the engine and check for fuel leaks.

9   Air intake duct and air filter housing - removal and installation

Air intake duct

1   Disconnect the PCV fresh air hose from the air intake duct.

2   On turbocharged four-cylinder models, loosen the clamp at the air intake duct and the charge air cooler inlet tube and remove the intake duct.

Note: *When removing the turbocharger air intake system components, always cover open ports to protect them from debris, or the turbocharger compressor vanes may be damaged.*

3   On V6 models, loosen the clamps at the air filter housing and the throttle body and remove the air intake duct **(see illustration)**.

4   Installation is the reverse of removal.

Air filter housing

5   Remove the air intake duct (see Steps 1 through 3).

6   Disconnect the electrical connector from the MAF sensor (see Chapter 6).

7   Remove the air filter housing cover and filter element (see Chapter 4).

8   Remove the mounting bolt(s).

9   Pull up on the housing to detach the locating pins from the grommets.

10   Inspect the condition of the filter housing mounting grommets. If they're cracked, torn or deteriorated, replace them.

11   Installation is the reverse of removal.

10   Throttle body - removal and installation

Warning: *Wait until the engine is completely cool before beginning this procedure.*

1   Disconnect the cable from the negative battery terminal (see Chapter 5).

2   Remove the air intake duct (see Section 9).

3   On four-cylinder models, loosen the clamps and remove the charge air cooler outlet pipe from the throttle body; remove the upper charge air cooler outlet tube.

4   Disconnect the electrical connector from the throttle body.

5   Remove the throttle body mounting fasteners and detach the throttle body from the intake manifold **(see illustration)**. Discard the gasket; it should be replaced with a new one. Cover the intake manifold opening with a clean shop towel.

6   Installation is the reverse of removal. Use a new gasket and tighten the throttle body fasteners to the torque listed in this Chapter's Specifications.

11   Fuel rail and injectors - removal and installation

Warning: *Gasoline is extremely flammable. See* ***Fuel system warnings*** *in Section 1.*

1   Relieve the fuel system pressure (see Section 3).

2   Disconnect the cable from the negative battery terminal (see Chapter 5).

Four-cylinder models

3   Remove the intake manifold (see Chapter 2A).

4   Disconnect the high pressure fuel line from the fuel pump and fuel rail (see Section 12).

Warning: *The manufacturer recommends replacing the fuel lines any time they are removed.*

5   Disconnect the electrical connectors for all wiring that shares the harness with the fuel injectors, then disconnect the four fuel injector electrical connectors. Using a trim removal tool, disengage the two pin-type retainers that secure the wiring harness and harness insulator to the fuel rail, then push the harness aside.

10.5 Throttle body mounting fasteners (3.5L V6 model shown)

6   Clean the area around each injector using compressed air.

7   Remove and discard the fuel rail mounting fasteners **(see illustration)**, then remove the fuel rail and injectors. Use new fuel rail bolts on installation.

Note: *The fuel injectors may remain in the fuel rails when the rail is removed, but normally they remain in the cylinder heads and require the use of a removal tool.*

8   Remove each fuel injector retaining clip with a pair of needle-nose pliers, then remove the injector from its bore in the fuel rail. Remove and discard the upper injector O-rings. Repeat this procedure for each injector.

Note: *Even if you only removed the fuel rail assembly to replace a single injector or a leaking O-ring, replace all of the fuel injector retaining clips and O-rings.*

9   If any injectors stick in the cylinder head, use special tool #310-206 attached to a slide hammer to remove the injector(s).

10   Remove the old combustion chamber Teflon sealing ring, upper O-ring and support ring from each injector **(see illustration)**.

Caution: *Be extremely careful not to damage*

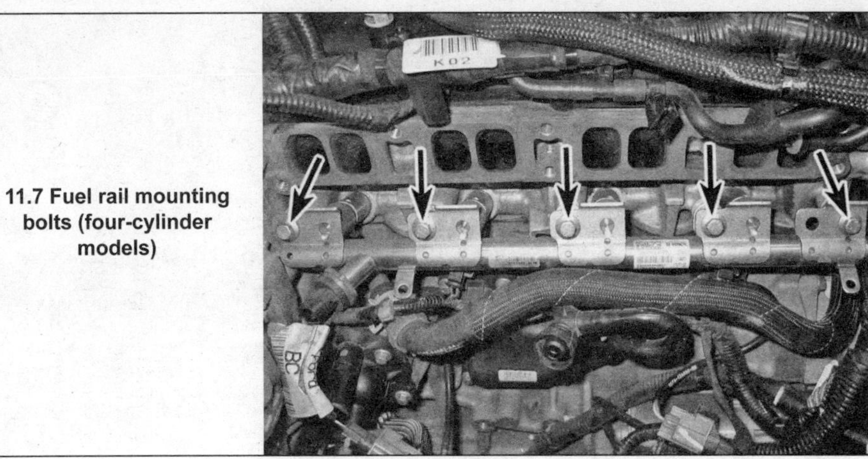

11.7 Fuel rail mounting bolts (four-cylinder models)

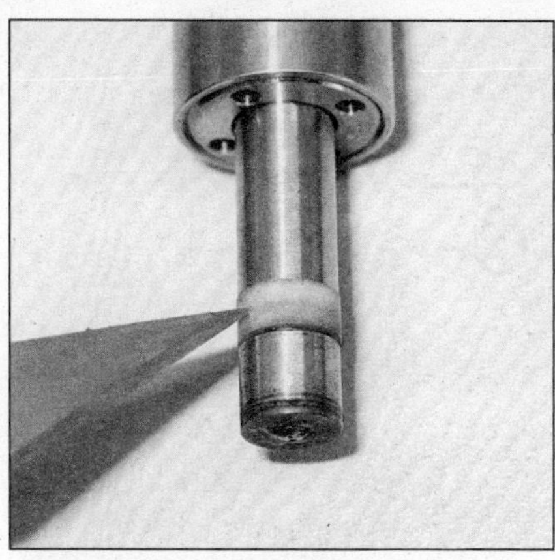

11.10 To remove the Teflon sealing ring, cut it off with a hobby knife (be careful not to scratch the injector groove)

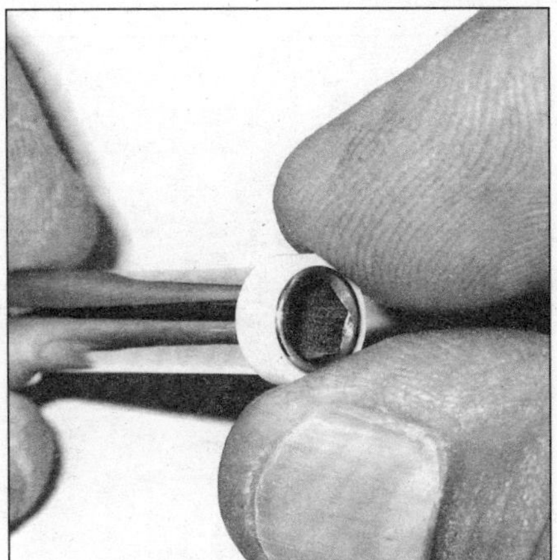

11.15 Slide the new Teflon seal onto the end of a socket that's the same diameter as the end of the fuel injector . . .

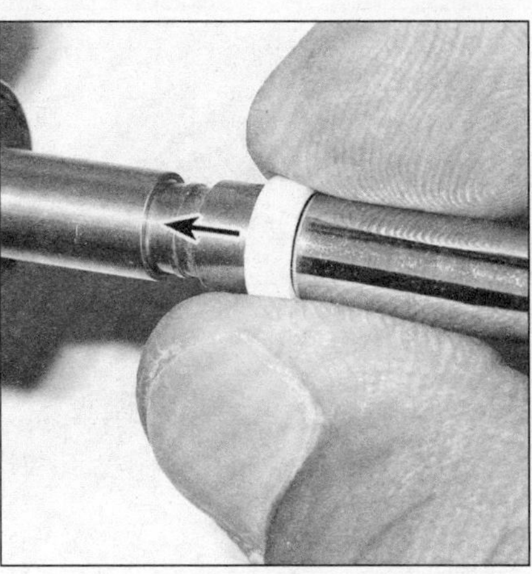

11.16 . . . and align the socket with the end of the injector; slide the seal onto the injector and into its mounting groove

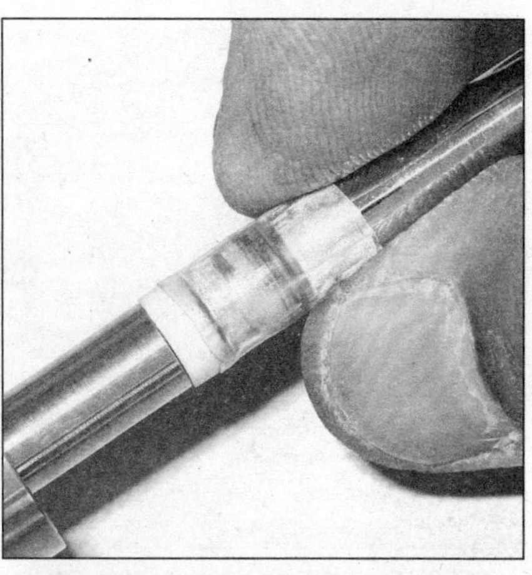

11.17a Use the socket to push a short section of plastic tubing onto the end of the injector and over the new seal . . .

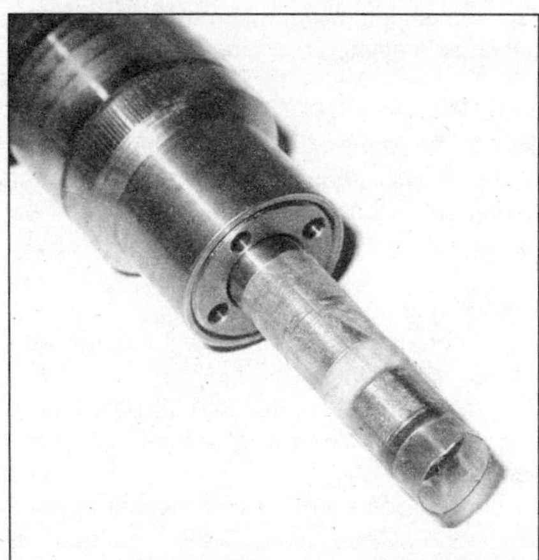

11.17b . . . then leave the plastic tubing in place for several hours to compress the new seal

the groove for the seal or the rib in the floor of the groove. If you damage the groove or the rib, you must replace the injector.

11   Before installing the new Teflon seal on each injector, thoroughly clean the groove for the seal and the injector shaft. Remove all combustion residue and varnish with a clean shop rag.

Teflon seal installation using the special tools

12   The manufacturer recommends that you use the tools included in the special injector tool set to install the Teflon lower seals on the injectors: Install the special seal assembly cone on the injector, install the special sleeve on the injector and use the sleeve to push on the assembly cone, which pushes the Teflon seal into place on its groove. Do NOT use any lubricants to do so.

13   Pushing the Teflon seal into place in its groove expands it slightly. There are three sizing sleeves in the special tool set with progressively smaller inside diameters. Using a clockwise rotating motion of about 180 degrees, install the slightly larger sleeve onto the injector and over the Teflon seal until the sleeve hits its stop, then carefully turn the sleeve counterclockwise as you pull it off the

injector. Use the slightly smaller sizing sleeve the same way, followed by the smallest sizing ring. The seal is now sized. Repeat this step for each injector.

Teflon seal installation without special tools

14   If you don't have the special injector tool set, the Teflon seal can be installed using this method: First, find a socket that is equal or very close in diameter to the diameter of the end of the fuel injector.

15   Work the new Teflon seal onto the end of the socket **(see illustration)**.

16   Place the socket against the end of the injector **(see illustration)** and slide the seal from the socket onto the injector. Do NOT use any lubricants to do so. Continue pushing the seal onto the injector until it seats into its mounting groove.

17   Because the inside diameter of the seal has to be stretched open to fit over the bore of the socket and the injector, its outside diameter is now slightly too large - it is no longer flush with the surface of the injector. It must be shrunk back to its original size. To do so, push a piece of plastic tubing with an interference fit onto the end of the socket; a plastic straw that fits tightly on the injector will work.

After pushing the plastic tubing onto the socket about an inch, snip off the rest of the tubing, then use the socket to push the tubing onto the end of the injector **(see illustration)**, sliding it onto the injector until it completely covers the new seal **(see illustration)**. Leave

11.18 Note that the upper O-ring (1) is installed above the support ring (2)

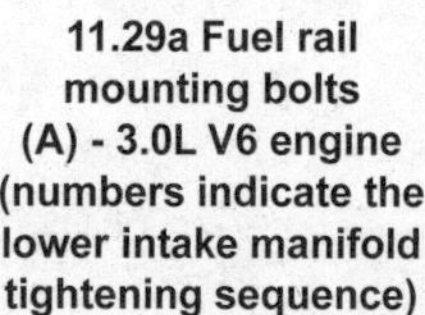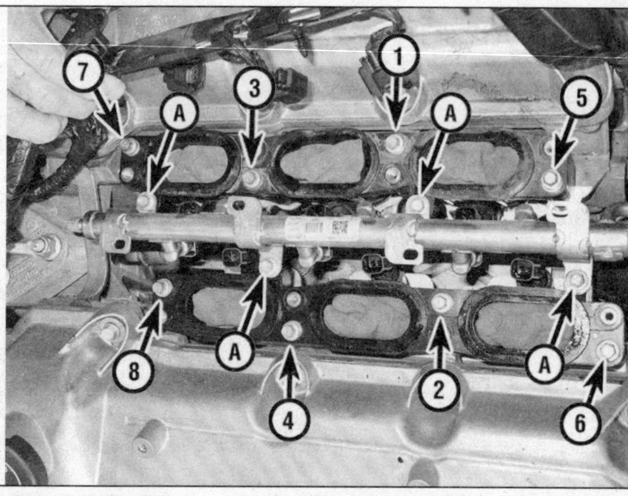

11.29a Fuel rail mounting bolts (A) - 3.0L V6 engine (numbers indicate the lower intake manifold tightening sequence)

11.29b Fuel rail mounting bolts - 3.5L V6 engine

11.30 Before removing the injector retaining clips, note how they're installed to ensure that they're correctly reinstalled

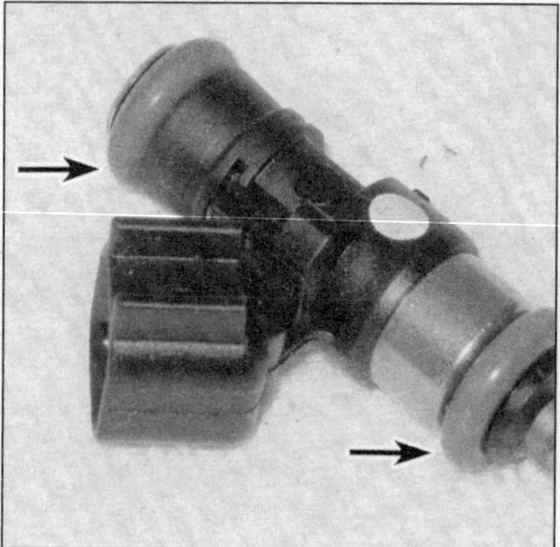

11.31 Fuel injector O-rings

the tubing on for a few hours, then remove it. The seal should now be shrunk back its original outside diameter, or close to it.

Injector and fuel rail installation

18   Install a new support ring on the top of the injector, then lubricate the new upper O-ring with clean engine oil and install it on the injector. Do NOT oil the new Teflon seal. Note that the O-ring is installed above the support ring **(see illustration)**.

19   Thoroughly clean the injector bores with a small nylon brush.

20   Insert each injector into its bore in the fuel rail. Install the new retaining clips on the injectors.

21   Install the injectors and fuel rail assembly on the cylinder head. Tighten the fuel rail mounting fasteners to the torque listed in this Chapter's Specifications , starting with the center bolt and working outwards.

22   The remainder of installation is the reverse of removal.

23   If removed, install a new fuel rail pressure sensor (see Chapter 6).

V6 models

24   On 3.5L engines, remove the upper intake manifold (see Chapter 2B).

25   On 3.0L engines, remove the lower intake manifold (see Chapter 2B).

26   Disconnect the fuel supply line at the fuel rail (see Section 5).

27   Disconnect the electrical connector from each fuel injector.

28   Detach the three pin-type retainers from the fuel rail, push the wiring harness aside and remove the other three injector electrical connectors.

29   Remove the four fuel rail mounting bolts, then remove the fuel rail and injectors as a single assembly.

30   Release the fuel injector retaining clip **(see illustration)** and remove each injector from its bore in the fuel rail.

31   Remove and discard the upper and lower injector O-rings **(see illustration)** from each injector.

Note: *Even if you only removed the fuel rail assembly to replace a single injector or a leaking O-ring, it's a good idea to remove all of the injectors from the fuel rail and replace all of the O-rings at the same time.*

32   Coat the new upper O-rings with clean engine oil and slide them into place on each of the fuel injectors. Coat the new lower O-rings with clean engine oil and install them on the

lower ends of the injectors.

33   Coat the outside surface of each upper O-ring with clean engine oil, then insert each injector into its bore in the fuel rail. Secure the injectors to the fuel rail with the injector retaining clips.

34   On 3.0L models, remove the intake manifold gaskets and install new ones **(see illustration)**.

35   On 3.0L models, install the intake manifolds on the injectors, then attach the fuel rail

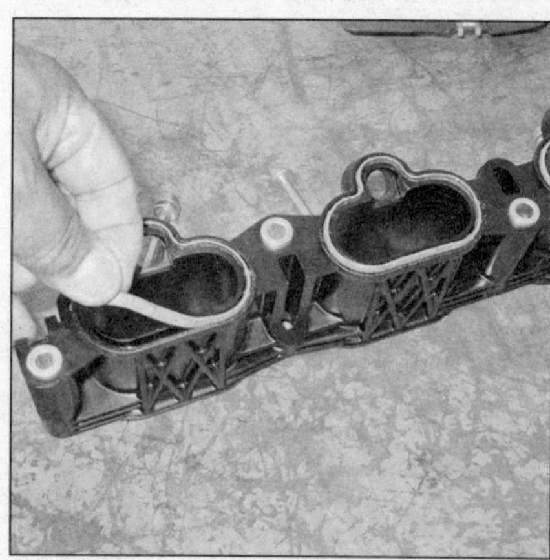

11.34 Replace the intake manifold gaskets (3.0L engine)

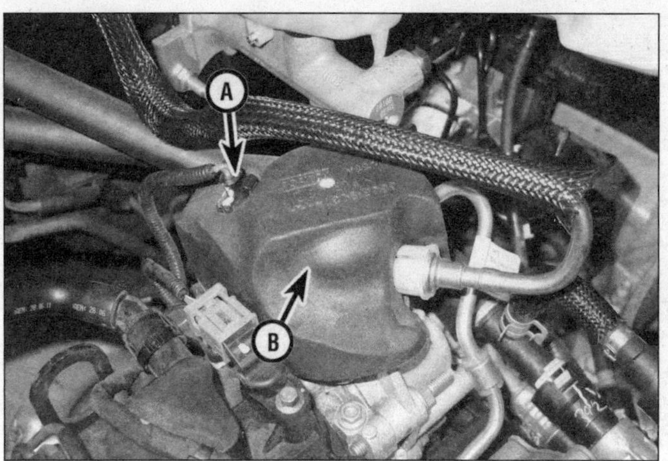

12.4 High-pressure fuel pump electrical connector (A) and
insulator (B)

12.9 High-pressure fuel pump details

1	Fuel feed line	3	Fuel pump mounting bolts
2	High-pressure fuel line		

assembly to the intake manifolds, tightening the bolts by hand. Install the fuel rail and intake manifolds as a single assembly. Be sure to tighten the intake manifold bolts in the correct sequence **(see illustration 11.29a)** to the torque listed inthe Chapter 2B Specifications.

36   On 3.5L models, guide the injectors into their bores, then install the fuel rail bolts.

37   Tighten the fuel rail bolts to the torque listed in this Chapter's Specifications. The remainder of installation is the reverse of removal.

38   Reconnect the cable to the negative battery terminal (see Chapter 5), then turn the ignition switch to ON (but don't operate the starter). This activates the fuel pump for about two seconds, which builds up fuel pressure in the fuel lines and the fuel rail. Repeat this step two or three times, then check the fuel lines, fuel rails and injectors for fuel leaks.

12   High-pressure fuel pump (four-cylinder engine) – removal and installation

Warning: *Gasoline is extremely flammable. SeeFuel system warningsin Section 1.*

Removal

1   Relieve the fuel system pressure (see Section 3).

2   Disconnect the cable from the negative battery terminal (see Chapter 5).

3   Remove the air filter housing intake duct (see Section 9).

4   Disconnect the fuel injection pump electrical connector **(see illustration)**.

5   Carefully remove the pump insulator from around the outside of the pump (see illustration 12.4).

Note: *Spreading the openings of the fuel in-*

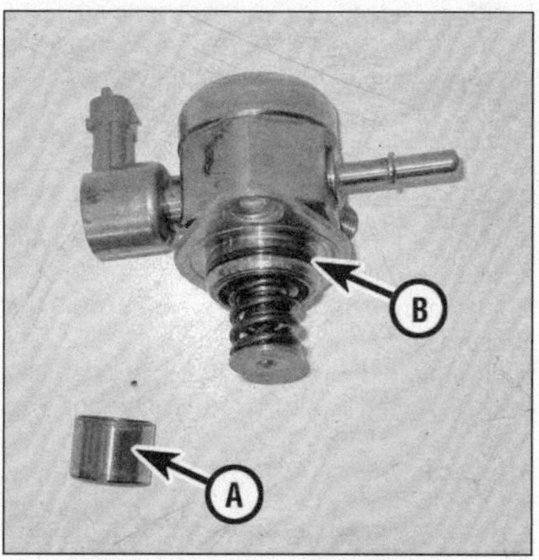

12.11 High-pressure fuel pump tappet (A)
and O-ring (B)

jection pump noise insulator will reduce the risk of damage to the insulator.

6   Disconnect the quick disconnect line and remove the fuel line from the fuel pump.

7   Loosen, then remove the fuel lines with a flare nut wrench.

Warning: *The manufacturer recommends replacing the fuel line anytime it is removed.*

8   Slide the heater hose clip forward then up to expose the fuel pump shield bolts. Remove the shield bolts and shield.

9   Loosen the fuel pump mounting bolts **(see illustration)**, alternating one turn at a time, until the bolts and pump can be removed. The bolts must be replaced after they have been removed.

Caution: *The fuel pump is under extreme pressure - if the bolts are not loosened evenly (one complete turn at a time), the pump or housing will be damaged.*

10   Remove and discard the fuel pump O-ring.

12.13 The cam lobe (and tappet) must
be at its lowest point before installing
the pump

Installation

11   Before installing the pump, check the pump tappet in the pump body for wear or damage **(see illustration)**.

12   Install a new O-ring on the pump, then apply clean oil to the pump tappet and the O-ring.

13   Rotate the engine until the cam lobe for the fuel injection pump is on the lowest point, or Bottom Dead Center (BDC) **(see illustration)**. The pump tappet will be as low as it can go for installation.

14   Set the pump in the housing, then install the new bolts hand tight.

15   Tighten the bolts in even stages, alternating between the bolts, to the torque listed in this Chapter's Specifications.

16   The remainder of installation is the reverse of removal.

13.3a Disconnect the charge air cooler inlet tube . . .

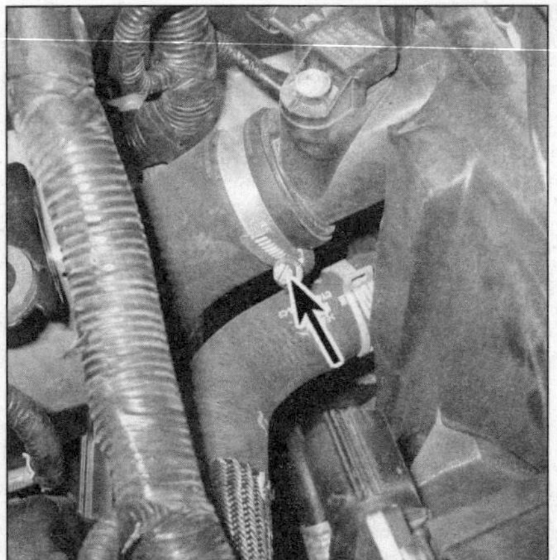

13.3b . . . and the outlet tube clamps

13.4 The charge air cooler is secured by two bolts on each end (left side shown)

13   Charge air cooler - removal and installation

Caution: *Whenever the turbocharger, charge air cooler or cooler tubes are removed, always cover any opening to prevent debris from falling in. The system is easily damaged, so carefully clean all openings before reassembling.*

1   Remove the cooling fan shroud (see Chapter 3).

2   Remove the Manifold Absolute Pressure Temperature (MAPT) sensor (see Chapter 6).

3   Loosen the clamps securing the inlet and outlet tubes to the charge air cooler **(see illustrations)**, then disconnect the tubes.

4   Remove the charge air cooler bolts **(see illustration)**. Slide the cooler to the left while pulling the left side out, and carefully remove the cooler from the vehicle.

5   Installation is the reverse of removal.

14   Turbocharger - removal and installation

Warning: *Wait until the engine is completely cool before beginning this procedure.*

Caution: *Do not disassemble the turbocharger or try to adjust the wastegate actuator. The turbocharger, or possibly even the engine, could be damaged.*

Caution: *Whenever the turbocharger, charge air cooler or cooler tubes are removed, always cover any opening to prevent debris from falling in. The system is easily damaged, so carefully clean all openings before reassembling.*

Removal

1   Raise the vehicle and support it securely on jackstands.

2   Remove the catalytic converter (see Chapter 6).

3   Remove the charge air cooler inlet tube (see Section 13) and the turbocharger inlet pipe.

4   Drain the cooling system (see Chapter 1).

5   Remove the turbocharger heat shield mounting bolts and remove the shield **(see illustration)**.

6   From above, squeeze and slide back the hose clamps on the coolant line **(see illustration)**. From below, remove the coolant outlet line banjo bolt and disconnect the line from the turbocharger **(see illustration)**.

14.5 Remove the turbocharger heat shield mounting bolts

Note: *Always replace the linked sealing washers to the banjo bolts and coolant lines.*

7   Remove the oil supply line banjo bolts and discard the sealing washers **(see illustrations)**, then pull the inline oil supply filter out of the engine block and replace it with a new one.

14.6a Detach the hoses at each end of the coolant pipe

14.6b Disconnect the coolant outlet line from the turbocharger and the engine block

14.7a Oil supply line banjo bolt

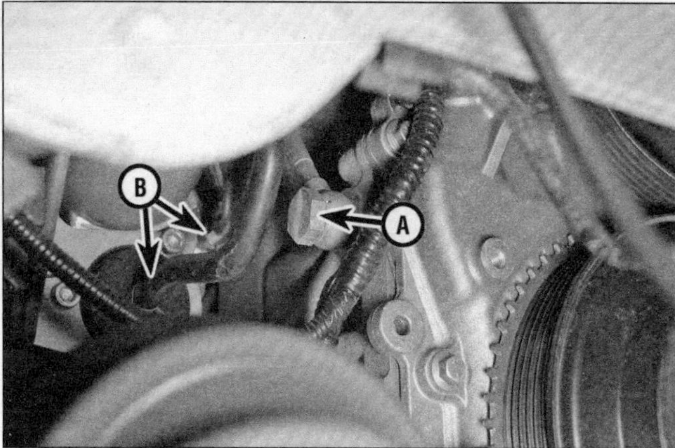

14.7b Oil supply line banjo bolt (A) and coolant lines (B)

8   Disconnect the vacuum lines and electrical connectors from the turbocharger.

9   Detach the coolant lines from the right end of the turbocharger **(see illustration 14.6b)**.

10   Remove the oil drain tube mounting bolts and drain tube, then discard the gasket and drain tube **(see illustration)**.

Note: *The factory requires the oil drain tube be replaced whenever it is removed.*

11   Remove and discard the turbocharger mounting nuts **(see illustration)**, then carefully maneuver the turbocharger from the vehicle.

12   Use a stud removal tool (available from most auto parts stores) to remove the turbocharger studs from the cylinder head. Discard the studs.

Installation

13   Install the four new studs in the cylinder head.

14   Install the turbocharger and tighten the new nuts to the torque listed in this Chapter's Specifications.

15   Install the new oil drain tube and new drain tube gaskets, then install and tighten the bolts to the torque listed in this Chapter's Specifications.

16   Install new oil feed line sealing washers and coolant line washers. Tighten the banjo bolts to the torque listed in this Chapter's Specifications.

17   The remainder of installation is the reverse of removal.

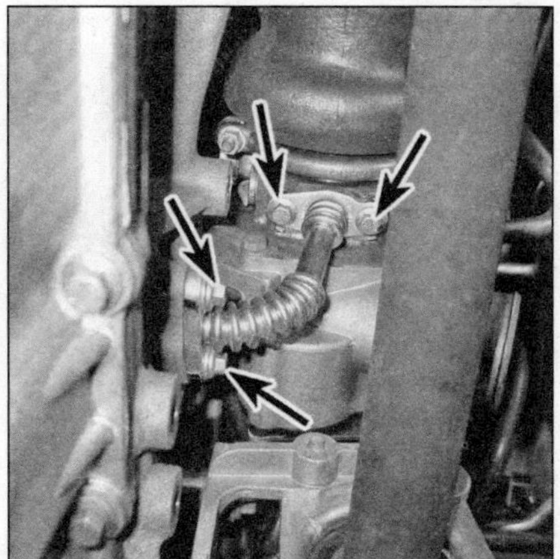

14.10 Turbocharger oil drain tube bolts

18   Refill the cooling system and change the engine oil and filter (see Chapter 1).

---

15   Fuel Pump Control Module (FPCM)/Fuel Pump Driver Module (FPDM) - removal and installation

Note: *The fuel pump module's speed, and therefore the output and pressure, is controlled by the FPCM (also known as the FPDM), which is located behind the right-rear seat back and trim panel.*

14.11 Remove the turbocharger mounting nuts

1   Remove (or fold down, as applicable) the right-rear seat back cushion and pull back the trim panel for access to the module **(see illustration 3.6)**.

2   Disconnect the electrical connector from the FPCM.

3   Remove the pin-type retainers or nuts, as applicable, and remove the FPCM.

4   Installation is the reverse of removal.

Notes

Chapter 5
Engine electrical systems

Contents

Specifications

Torque specifications

	Ft-lbs	Nm
Alternator mounting bolts/nuts		
Four-cylinder engine	18	24
V6 engines	35	47
Starter motor mounting bolts		
Four-cylinder engine	35	47
V6 engines		
2007 and earlier	18	24
2008 through 2012 models	20	27
2013 and later models	35	47

1 General information and precautions

General information

Ignition system

1   The electronic ignition system consists of the Crankshaft Position (CKP) sensor, the Camshaft Position (CMP) sensor, the Knock Sensor (KS), the Powertrain Control Module (PCM), the ignition switch, the battery, the individual ignition coils, and the spark plugs. For more information on the CKP, CMP and KS sensors, as well as the PCM, refer to Chapter 6.

Charging system

2   The charging system includes the alternator (with an integral voltage regulator), the Powertrain Control Module (PCM), the Body Control Module (BCM), a charge indicator light on the dash, the battery, a fuse or fusible link and the wiring connecting all of these components. The charging system supplies electrical power for the ignition system, the lights, the radio, etc. The alternator is driven by a drivebelt.

Starting system

3   The starting system consists of the battery, the ignition switch, the starter relay, the Powertrain Control Module (PCM), the Body Control Module (BCM), the Transmission Range (TR) switch, the starter motor and solenoid assembly, and the wiring connecting all of the components.

Precautions

4   Always observe the following precautions when working on the electrical system:

a) *Be extremely careful when servicing engine electrical components. They are easily damaged if checked, connected or handled improperly.*

b) *Never leave the ignition switched on for long periods of time when the engine is not running.*

c) *Never disconnect the battery cables while the engine is running.*

d) *Maintain correct polarity when connecting battery cables from another vehicle during jump starting - see the "Booster battery (jump) starting" Section at the front of this manual.*

e) *Always disconnect the cable from the negative battery terminal before working on the electrical system, but read the battery disconnection procedure first (see Section 3).*

5   It's also a good idea to review the safety-related information regarding the engine electrical systems located in the *Safety first!* Section at the front of this manual before beginning any operation included in this Chapter.

2   Troubleshooting

Ignition system

1   If a malfunction occurs in the ignition system, do not immediately assume that any particular part is causing the problem. First, check the following items:

a) *Make sure that the cable clamps at the battery terminals are clean and tight.*

b) *Test the condition of the battery (see Steps 15 through 19). If it doesn't pass all the tests, replace it.*

c) *Check the ignition coil or coil pack connections.*

d) *Check any relevant fuses in the engine compartment fuse and relay box (see Chapter 12). If they're burned, determine the cause and repair the circuit.*

Check

Warning: *Because of the high voltage generated by the ignition system, use extreme care when performing a procedure involving ignition components.*

Note: *The ignition system components on these vehicles are difficult to diagnose. In the event of ignition system failure that you can't diagnose, have the vehicle tested at a dealer service department or other qualified auto repair facility.*

Note: *You'll need a spark tester for the following test. Spark testers are available at most auto supply stores.*

2   If the engine turns over but won't start, verify that there is sufficient ignition voltage to fire the spark plugs as follows.

3   Remove a coil and install the tester between the boot at the lower end of the coil and the spark plug **(see illustration)**.

4   Crank the engine and note whether or not the tester flashes.

Caution: *Do NOT crank the engine or allow it to run for more than five seconds; running the engine for more than five seconds may set a Diagnostic Trouble Code (DTC) for a cylinder misfire.*

5   If the tester flashes during cranking, the coil is delivering sufficient voltage to the spark plug to fire it. Repeat this test for each cylinder to verify that the other coils are OK.

6   If the tester doesn't flash, remove a coil from another cylinder and swap it for the one being tested. If the tester now flashes, you know that the original coil is bad. If the tester still doesn't flash, the PCM or wiring harness is probably defective. Have the PCM checked out by a dealer service department or other qualified repair shop (testing the PCM is beyond the scope of the do-it-yourselfer because it requires expensive special tools).

7   If the tester flashes during cranking but a misfire code (related to the cylinder being tested) has been stored, the spark plug could be fouled or defective.

Charging system

8   If a malfunction occurs in the charging system, do not automatically assume the alternator is causing the problem. First check the following items:

a) *Check the drivebelt tension and condition, as described in Chapter 1. Replace it if it's worn or deteriorated.*

b) *Make sure the alternator mounting bolts are tight.*

c) *Inspect the alternator wiring harness and the connectors at the alternator and voltage regulator. They must be in good condition, tight and have no corrosion.*

d) *Check the fusible link (if equipped) or main fuse in the underhood fuse/relay box. If it is burned, determine the cause, repair the circuit and replace the link or fuse (the vehicle will not start and/or the accessories will not work if the fusible link or main fuse is blown).*

e) *Start the engine and check the alternator for abnormal noises (a shrieking or squealing sound indicates a bad bearing).*

f) *Check the battery. Make sure it's fully charged and in good condition (one bad cell in a battery can cause overcharging by the alternator).*

g) *Disconnect the battery cables (negative first, then positive). Inspect the battery posts and the cable clamps for corrosion. Clean them thoroughly if necessary (see Chapter 1). Reconnect the cables (positive first, negative last).*

Alternator - check

9   Use a voltmeter to check the battery voltage with the engine off. It should be at least 12.6 volts **(see illustration 2.16)**.

10   Start the engine and check the battery voltage again. It should now be approximately 13.5 to 15 volts.

11   If the voltage reading is more or less than the specified charging voltage, the voltage regulator is probably defective, which will require replacement of the alternator (the voltage regulator is not replaceable separately). Remove the alternator and have it bench tested (most auto parts stores will do this for you).

12   The charging system (battery) light on the instrument cluster lights up when the ignition key is turned to ON, but it should go out when the engine starts.

13   If the charging system light stays on after the engine has been started, there is a problem with the charging system. Before replacing the alternator, check the battery condition, alternator belt tension and electrical cable connections.

14   If replacing the alternator doesn't restore voltage to the specified range, have the charging system tested by a dealer service department or other qualified repair shop.

Battery - check

15   Check the battery state of charge. Visually inspect the indicator eye on the top of the battery (if equipped with one); if the indicator eye is black in color, charge the battery as described in Chapter 1. Next perform an open circuit voltage test using a digital voltmeter.

Note: *The battery's surface charge must be removed before accurate voltage measurements can be made. Turn on the high beams for ten seconds, then turn them off and let the vehicle stand for two minutes.*

16   With the engine and all accessories Off, touch the negative probe of the voltmeter to the negative terminal of the battery and the positive probe to the positive terminal of the battery **(see illustration)**. The battery voltage should be 12.6 volts or slightly above. If the battery is less than the specified voltage, charge the battery before proceeding to the next test. Do not proceed with the battery load test unless the battery charge is correct.

17   Disconnect the negative battery cable, then the positive cable from the battery.

18   Perform a battery load test. An accurate check of the battery condition can only be performed with a load tester **(see illustration)**. This test evaluates the ability of the battery to operate the starter and other accessories dur-

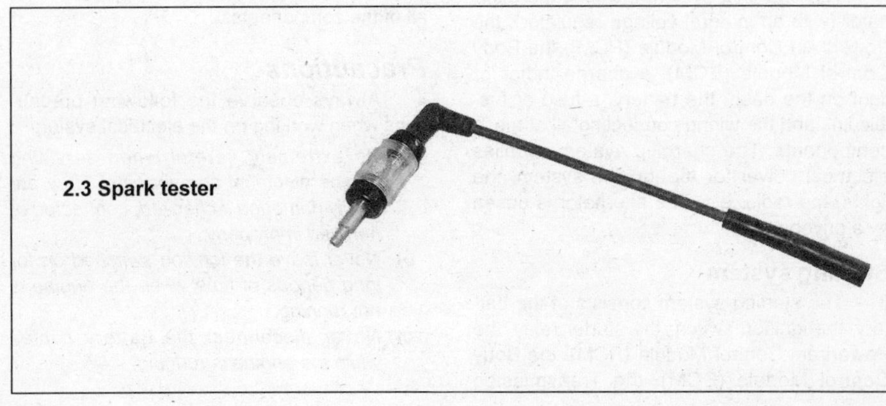

2.3 Spark tester

2.16 To test the open circuit voltage of the battery, touch the black probe of the voltmeter to the negative terminaland the red probe to the positive terminal of the battery; a fully charged battery should be at least 12.6 volts

2.18 Connect a battery load tester to the battery and check the battery condition under load following the toolmanufacturer's instructions

ing periods of high current draw. Connect the load tester to the battery terminals. Load test the battery according to the tool manufacturer's instructions. This tool increases the load demand (current draw) on the battery.

19   Maintain the load on the battery for 15 seconds and observe that the battery voltage does not drop below 9.6 volts. If the battery condition is weak or defective, the tool will indicate this condition immediately.

Note: *Cold temperatures will cause the minimum voltage reading to drop slightly. Follow the chart given in the manufacturer's instructions to compensate for cold climates. Minimum load voltage for freezing temperatures (32 degrees F) should be approximately 9.1 volts.*

Starting system

The starter rotates, but the engine doesn't

20   Remove the starter (see Section 8). Check the overrunning clutch and bench test the starter to make sure the drive mechanism extends fully for proper engagement with the flywheel ring gear. If it doesn't, replace the starter.

21   Check the flywheel ring gear for missing teeth and other damage. With the ignition turned off, rotate the flywheel so you can check the entire ring gear.

The starter is noisy

22   If the solenoid is making a chattering noise, first check the battery (see Steps 15 through 19). If the battery is okay, check the cables and connections.

23   If you hear a grinding, crashing metallic sound when you turn the key to Start, check for loose starter mounting bolts. If they're tight, remove the starter and inspect the teeth on the starter pinion gear and flywheel ring gear. Look for missing or damaged teeth.

24   If the starter sounds fine when you first turn the key to Start, but then stops rotating the engine and emits a zinging sound, the problem is probably a defective starter drive that's not staying engaged with the ring gear. Replace the starter.

The starter rotates slowly

25   Check the battery (see Steps 15 through 19).

26   If the battery is okay, verify all connections (at the battery, the starter solenoid and motor) are clean, corrosion-free and tight. Make sure the cables aren't frayed or damaged.

27   Check that the starter mounting bolts are tight so it grounds properly. Also check the pinion gear and flywheel ring gear for evidence of a mechanical bind (galling, deformed gear teeth or other damage).

The starter does not rotate at all

28   Check the battery (see Steps 15 through 19).

29   If the battery is okay, verify all connections (at the battery, the starter solenoid and motor) are clean, corrosion-free and tight. Make sure the cables aren't frayed or damaged.

30   Check all of the fuses in the underhood fuse/relay box.

31   Check that the starter mounting bolts are tight so it grounds properly.

32   Check for voltage at the starter solenoid "S" terminal when the ignition key is turned to the start position. If voltage is present, replace the starter/solenoid assembly. If no voltage is present, the problem could be the starter relay, the Transmission Range (TR) switch (see Chapter 6), or with an electrical connector somewhere in the circuit (see the wiring diagrams at the end of Chapter 12). Also, on many modern vehicles, the Powertrain Control Module (PCM) and the Body Control Module (BCM) control the voltage signal to the starter solenoid; on such vehicles a special scan tool is required for diagnosis.

3   Battery - disconnection

Caution: *Always disconnect the cable from the negative battery terminal FIRST and hook it up LAST or the battery may be shorted by the tool being used to loosen the cable clamps.*

1   Some systems on the vehicle require battery power to be available at all times, either to maintain continuous operation (alarm system, power door locks, etc.), or to maintain control unit memory (radio station presets, Powertrain Control Module (PCM) and other control units). When the battery is disconnected, the power that maintains these systems is cut. So, before you disconnect the battery, please note that on a vehicle with power door locks, it's a wise precaution to remove the key from the ignition and to keep it with you, so that it does not get locked inside if the power door locks should engage accidentally when the battery is reconnected!

2   Devices known as "memory-savers" can be used to avoid some of these problems. Precise details vary according to the device used. The typical memory saver is plugged into the cigarette lighter and is connected to a spare battery. Then the vehicle battery can be disconnected from the electrical system. The memory saver will provide sufficient current to maintain audio unit security codes, PCM memory, etc. and will provide power to always hot circuits such as the clock and radio memory circuits.

Warning: *Some memory savers deliver a considerable amount of current in order to keep vehicle systems operational after the main battery is disconnected. If you're using a memory saver, make sure that the circuit concerned is actually open before servicing it.*

Warning: *If you're going to work near any of the airbag system components, the battery MUST be disconnected and a memory saver must NOT be used. If a memory saver is used, power will be supplied to the airbag, which*

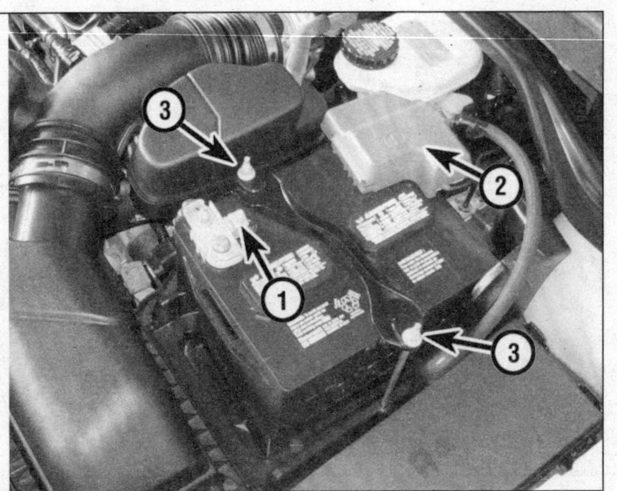

4.1 Battery details (2013 model shown)

1   *Negative battery terminal nut*
2   *Positive battery terminal (under cover)*
3   *Hold-down clamp nuts*

4.8 Battery tray mounting bolts

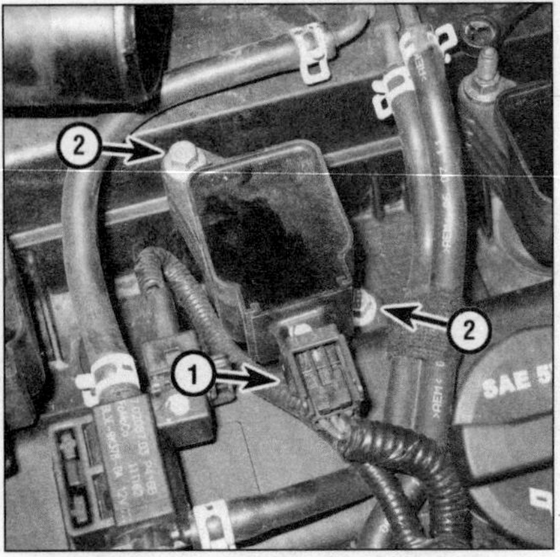

6.4a Ignition coil details (4-cylinder engine shown)

1   *Electrical connector*
2   *Mounting fasteners*

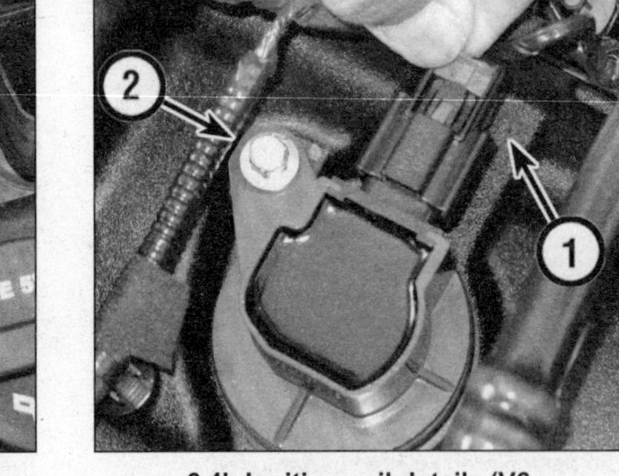

6.4b Ignition coil details (V6 engine shown)

1   *Electrical connector*
2   *Mounting fasteners*

means that it could accidentally deploy and cause serious personal injury.

3   To disconnect the battery for service procedures requiring power to be cut from the vehicle, loosen the cable end bolt and disconnect the cable from the negative battery terminal. Isolate the cable end to prevent it from coming into accidental contact with the battery terminal.

4   Battery and battery tray - removal and installation

1   Disconnect the cable from the negative battery terminal first, then disconnect the cable from the positive battery terminal **(see illustration)**.
2   Remove the battery hold-down clamp.
3   Lift out the battery. Be careful - it's heavy.
Note: *Battery straps and handlers are available at most auto parts stores for reasonable prices. They make it easier to remove and carry the battery.*

4   If you are replacing the battery, make sure you get one that's identical, with the same dimensions, amperage rating, cold cranking rating, etc. Also, if the battery was equipped with a heat shield, remove it from the old battery and install it on the new one.
5   If necessary for access to other components, remove the battery tray.
6   Remove the air cleaner housing, if necessary, for access to remove the battery tray (see Chapter 4).
7   Disconnect any electrical harness or connectors from the battery tray
8   Remove the battery tray mounting bolts and or nuts and the battery tray from the vehicle **(see illustration)**.
9   Installation is the reverse of removal. Connect the positive cable first and the negative cable last.

5   Battery cables - replacement

1   When removing the cables, always disconnect the cable from the negative battery

terminal first and hook it up last, or you might accidentally short out the battery with the tool you're using to loosen the cable clamps. Even if you're only replacing the cable for the positive terminal, be sure to disconnect the negative cable from the battery first.
2   Disconnect the old cables from the battery, then trace each of them to their opposite ends and disconnect them. Note the routing of each cable before disconnecting it to ensure correct installation.
3   If you are replacing any of the old cables, take them with you when buying new cables. It is vitally important that you replace the cables with identical parts.
4   Clean the threads of the solenoid or ground connection with a wire brush to remove rust and corrosion. Apply a light coat of battery terminal corrosion inhibitor or petroleum jelly to the threads to prevent future corrosion.
5   Attach the cable to the solenoid or ground connection and tighten the mounting nut/bolt securely.
6   Before connecting a new cable to the battery, make sure that it reaches the battery post without having to be stretched.
7   Connect the cable to the positive battery terminal first, then connect the ground cable to the negative battery terminal.

6   Ignition coils - replacement

1   Disconnect the cable from the negative battery terminal (see Section 3).
2   On four-cylinder models, remove the air filter outlet duct (see Chapter 4), then remove the EVAP canister purge valve fastener. Using care not to damage any hoses, move the EVAP canister purge valve out of the way.
3   On V6 models, remove the upper intake manifold to access the rear (Right) bank ignition coils (see Chapter 2B). If necessary for access to the front (Left) bank coils, disconnect the crankcase vent tube.
4   Disconnect the electrical connector from the ignition coil **(see illustrations)**.

6.6 Grasp the top of the coil and twist the coil while pulling it up and off of the spark plug (V6 shown, others similar)

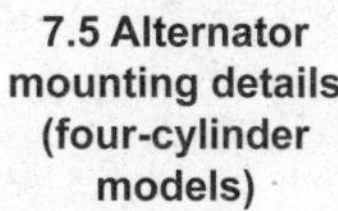

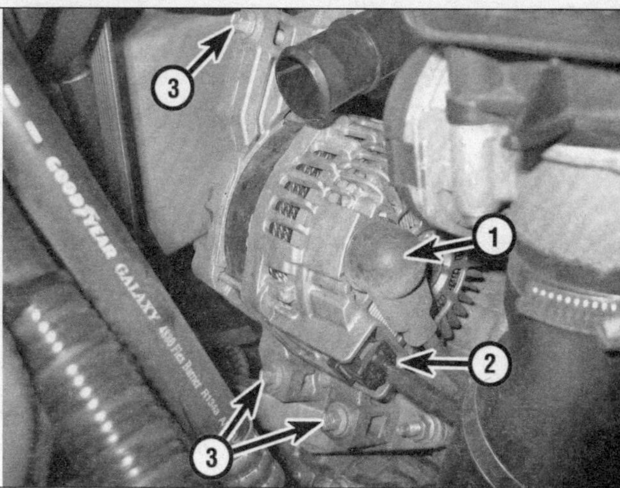

7.5 Alternator mounting details (four-cylinder models)

1 B+ terminal
2 Electrical connector
3 Mounting bolts

5   Remove the mounting fastener(s) from the ignition coil.
During the next step, twist the coil left and right to break the boot free of the spark plug.
6   Grasp the coil firmly and pull it off the spark plug **(see illustration)**.
7   Installation is the reverse of removal. Place a small amount of dielectric grease on the inside of the coil boot prior to installation.

7   Alternator - removal and installation

1   Disconnect the cable from the negative battery terminal (see Section 3).
2   Remove the engine cover as necessary to allow access.
3   Remove the drivebelt (see Chapter 1).

Four-cylinder models

4   Remove the Charge Air Cooler (CAC) upper pipe (see Chapter 4).
5   Pull back the protective cover from the alternator's battery terminal, remove the nut and disconnect the battery cable from the alternator **(see illustration)**. Set the battery cable aside. Disconnect the electrical connector from the alternator.
6   Remove the alternator mounting fasteners **(see illustration)** and remove the alternator from the vehicle.

V6 models

2007 and earlier models

7   Raise the front of the vehicle and support it securely on jackstands.
8   Remove the right front splash shield to allow access to the alternator.
9   Disconnect the crankshaft position sensor and detach the harness clips from the shield when removing.
10   Remove the alternator cover retaining pins and position the cover out of the way.
11   Push back the protective cover from the alternator's battery terminal, remove the nut and disconnect the battery cable from the alternator. Also disconnect the electrical connector from the alternator **(see illustration)**.
12   Remove the alternator mounting fasteners **(see illustrations)** and if necessary, remove the mounting studs and remove the alternator from the vehicle.

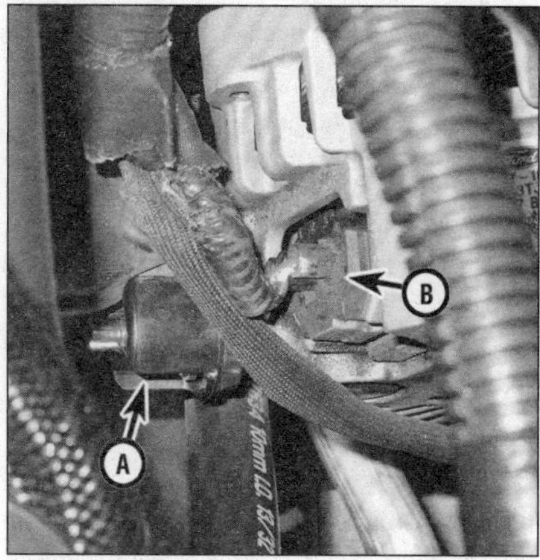

7.11 Alternator battery terminal (A) and electrical connector (B) (3.0L V6 engine)

2008 and later models

Warning: *Wait until the engine is completely cool before beginning this procedure.*
13   One 2012 and earlier models, remove the upper radiator hose support.
14   On 2013 and later models, remove the cooling fan and shroud assembly (see Chapter 3).

7.12a Alternator upper mounting bolt (3.0L V6 engine)

7.12b Alternator lower mounting bolts (3.0L V6 engine)

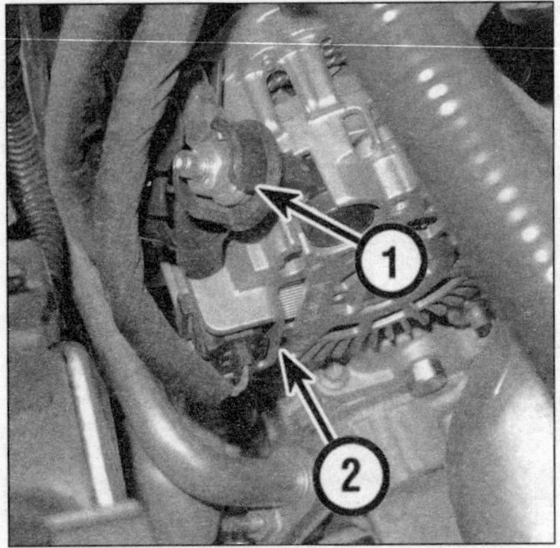

7.15 Alternator electrical connections (2008 and later V6 models)

1   B+ Terminal
2   Electrical connector

7.16 Alternator mounting details (2008 and later V6 models)

1   Upper mounting nut
2   Lower mounting bolt

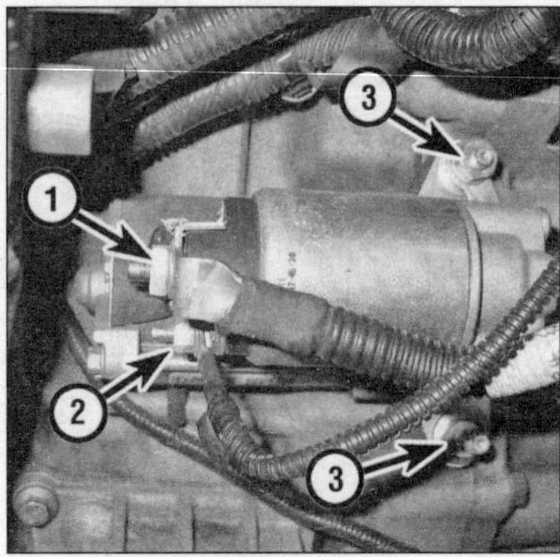

8.3 Starter motor details - four-cylinder models

1   Starter motor battery terminal
2   Starter solenoid terminal
3   Mounting stud-bolts

15   Push back the protective cover from the alternator's battery terminal, remove the nut and disconnect the battery cable from the alternator. Disconnect the electrical connector from the alternator **(see illustration)**.
16   Remove the alternator upper mounting nut **(see illustration)**.
17   Remove the alternator lower mounting bolt and remove the alternator from the vehicle towards the front of the engine.

All models

18   If you're replacing the alternator, take the old one with you when purchasing the replacement unit. Make sure that the new/rebuilt unit looks identical to the old alternator. Look at the electrical terminals on the backside of the alternator. They should be the same in number, size and location as the terminals on the old alternator. Finally, look at the identification numbers. They will be stamped into the housing or printed on a tag attached to the housing. Make sure that the ID numbers are the same on both alternators.

19   Many new/rebuilt alternators DO NOT have a pulley installed, so you might have to swap the pulley from the old unit to the new/rebuilt one. When buying an alternator, find out the store's policy regarding pulley swaps. Some stores perform this service free of charge. If your local auto parts store doesn't offer this service, you'll have to purchase a puller for removing the pulley and do it yourself.
20   Installation is the reverse of removal. Tighten the alternator mounting bolts securely.
21   Reconnect the cable to the negative terminal of the battery. Check the charging voltage (see Section 2) to verify that the alternator is operating correctly.

8   Starter motor - removal and installation

1   Detach the cable from the negative terminal of the battery (see Section 3).

2   Raise the vehicle and support it securely on jackstands. Remove the underbody cover as necessary.

Four-cylinder models

Note: *The coolant hoses will need to be repositioned as necessary to remove the starter.*
3   Disconnect the starter motor solenoid wire nut and the starter motor battery cable nut, and disconnect both wires from the starter **(see illustration)**.
4   Remove the nut that secures the ground wire to the starter mounting stud and disconnect the ground wire from the stud. Remove the mounting stud bolts and remove the starter.
5   Installation is the reverse of removal. Tighten the starter mounting stud-bolts securely.

V6 models

6   Remove the air filter housing (see Chapter 4). Also, on models where it would interfere, remove the battery and the battery tray (see Section 4).
7   On 2006 and earlier 6-speed models, remove the transaxle torque arm assembly mounting bolts and the torque arm.
8   On all EXCEPT 2006 and earlier 6-speed models, disconnect the transaxle shift cable, then remove the manual shift lever nut and lever from the transaxle (see Chapter 7A).
9   On all models, remove the starter motor solenoid wire nut and the starter motor battery cable nut, then disconnect the wire and cable from the starter motor **(see illustration)**.
10   Remove the starter motor mounting fasteners **(see illustration)** and remove the starter motor.
11   Installation is the reverse of removal.

8.9 Starter motor details - V6 models

1   Starter motor battery terminal
2   Starter solenoid terminal

8.10 Starter motor mounting bolts - V6 models

Chapter 6
Emissions and engine control systems

Contents

Specifications

Torque specifications

Ft-lbs (unless otherwise indicated)   **Nm**

Note: *One foot-pound (ft-lb) of torque is equivalent to 12 inch-pounds (in-lbs) of torque. Torque values below approximately 15 ft-lbs are expressed in inch-pounds, because most foot-pound torque wrenches are not accurate at these smaller values.*

	Ft-lbs	Nm
Cylinder Head Temperature (CHT) sensor		
Four-cylinder engine	97 in-lbs	11
V6 engines	89 in-lbs	10
Fuel Rail Pressure (FRP) sensor (four-cylinder engine)		
Step 1	53 in-lbs	6
Step 2	Tighten an additional 5-degrees	
Step 3	Loosen 90-degrees	
Step 4	53 in-lbs	6
Step 5	Tighten an additional 21-degrees	

Torque specifications

Ft-lbs (unless otherwise indicated)　　**Nm**

Note: *One foot-pound (ft-lb) of torque is equivalent to 12 inch-pounds (in-lbs) of torque. Torque values below approximately 15 ft-lbs are expressed in inch-pounds, because most foot-pound torque wrenches are not accurate at these smaller values.*

	Ft-lbs (unless otherwise indicated)	Nm
Camshaft Position Sensor (CMP)		
Four-cylinder engine	53 in-lbs	6
V6 engines	89 in-lbs	10
Crankshaft Position Sensor (CKP)		
Four-cylinder engine	62 in-lbs	7
V6 engines	89 in-lbs	10
Knock sensor mounting bolt	177 in-lbs	20
Oxygen sensor/catalyst monitor sensor	35	48
Catalytic converter-to-turbocharger outlet flange	177 in-lbs	20
Catalytic converter-to-bracket nuts	18	24
Variable camshaft timing valve mounting bolts		
Four-cylinder engine	89 in-lbs	10
3.5L V6 engines		
Step 1	71 in-lbs	8
Step 2	Tighten an additional 20 degrees	
Turbine shaft speed sensor bolt (2008 and later models)	106 in-lbs	12
Transaxle main control cover (2008 and later models)	106 in-lbs	12
Crankcase vent oil separator bolts (four-cylinder engine)	89 in-lbs	10

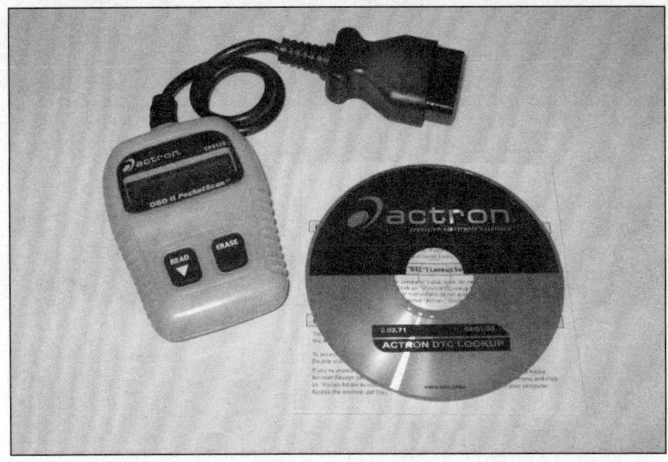

2.4a Simple code readers are an economical way to extract trouble codes when the CHECK ENGINE light comes on

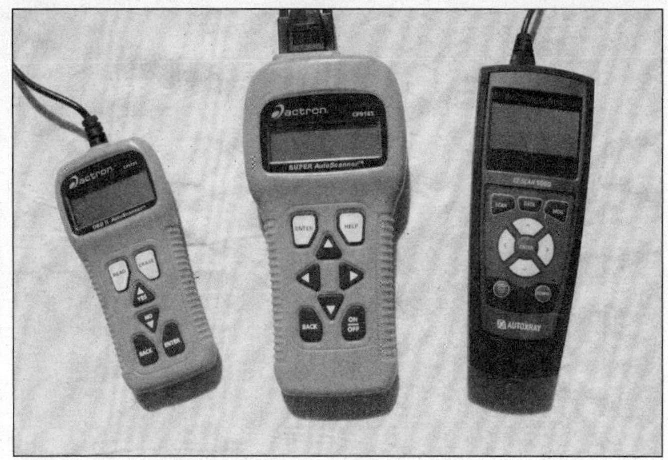

2.4b Hand-held scan tools like these can extract computer codes and also perform diagnostics

1 General information

1   To prevent pollution of the atmosphere from incompletely burned and evaporating gases, and to maintain good driveability and fuel economy, a number of emission control systems are incorporated. They include the:

Catalytic converter

2   A catalytic converter is an emission control device in the exhaust system that reduces certain pollutants in the exhaust gas stream. There are two types of converters: oxidation converters and reduction converters.

3   Oxidation converters contain a monolithic substrate (a ceramic honeycomb) coated with the semi-precious metals platinum and palladium. An oxidation catalyst reduces unburned hydrocarbons (HC) and carbon monoxide (CO) by adding oxygen to the exhaust stream as it passes through the substrate, which, in the presence of high temperature and the catalyst materials, converts the HC and CO to water vapor (H_2O) and carbon dioxide (CO_2).

4   Reduction converters contain a monolithic substrate coated with platinum and rhodium. A reduction catalyst reduces oxides of nitrogen (NOx) by removing oxygen, which in the presence of high temperature and the catalyst material produces nitrogen (N) and carbon dioxide (CO_2).

5   Catalytic converters that combine both types of catalysts in one assembly are known as three-way catalysts or TWCs. A TWC can reduce all three pollutants.

Evaporative Emissions Control (EVAP) system

6   The Evaporative Emissions Control (EVAP) system prevents fuel system vapors (which contain unburned hydrocarbons) from escaping into the atmosphere. On warm days, vapors trapped inside the fuel tank expand until the pressure reaches a certain threshold. Then the fuel vapors are routed from the fuel tank through the fuel vapor vent valve and the fuel vapor control valve to the EVAP canister, where they're stored temporarily until the next time the vehicle is operated. When the conditions are right (engine warmed up, vehicle up to speed, moderate or heavy load on the engine, etc.) the PCM opens the canister purge valve, which allows fuel vapors to be drawn from the canister into the intake manifold. Once in the intake manifold, the fuel vapors mix with incoming air before being drawn through the intake ports into the combustion chambers where they're burned up with the rest of the air/fuel mixture. The EVAP system is complex and virtually impossible to troubleshoot without the right tools and training.

Powertrain Control Module (PCM)

7   The Powertrain Control Module (PCM) is the brain of the engine management system. It also controls a wide variety of other vehicle systems. In order to program the new PCM, the dealer needs the vehicle as well as the new PCM. If you're planning to replace the PCM with a new one, there is no point in trying to do so at home because you won't be able to program it yourself.

Positive Crankcase Ventilation (PCV) system

8   The Positive Crankcase Ventilation (PCV) system reduces hydrocarbon emissions by scavenging crankcase vapors, which are rich in unburned hydrocarbons. A PCV valve or orifice regulates the flow of gases into the intake manifold in proportion to the amount of intake vacuum available.

9   The PCV system generally consists of the fresh air inlet hose, the PCV valve or orifice and the crankcase ventilation hose (or PCV hose). The fresh air inlet hose connects the air intake duct to a pipe on the valve cover. The crankcase ventilation hose (or PCV hose) connects the PCV valve or orifice in the valve cover or crankcase vent oil separator to the intake manifold.

2 On Board Diagnosis (OBD) system

General description

1   All models are equipped with the second generation OBD-II system. This system consists of an on-board computer known as the Powertrain Control Module (PCM), and information sensors, which monitor various functions of the engine and send data to the PCM. This system incorporates a series of diagnostic monitors that detect and identify fuel injection and emissions control system faults and store the information in the computer memory. This system also tests sensors and output actuators, diagnoses drive cycles, freezes data and clears codes.

2   The PCM is the brain of the electronically controlled fuel and emissions system. It receives data from a number of sensors and other electronic components (switches, relays, etc.). Based on the information it receives, the PCM generates output signals to control various relays, solenoids (fuel injectors) and other actuators. The PCM is specifically calibrated to optimize the emissions, fuel economy and driveability of the vehicle.

3   It isn't a good idea to attempt diagnosis or replacement of the PCM or emission control components at home while the vehicle is under warranty. Because of a Federally mandated warranty which covers the emissions system components and because any owner-induced damage to the PCM, the sensors and/or the control devices may void this warranty, take the vehicle to a dealer service department if the PCM or a system component malfunctions.

Scan tool information

4   Because extracting the Diagnostic Trouble Codes (DTCs) from an engine management system is now the first step in troubleshooting many computer-controlled systems and components, a code reader, at the very least, will be required **(see illustration)**. More

Information Sensors

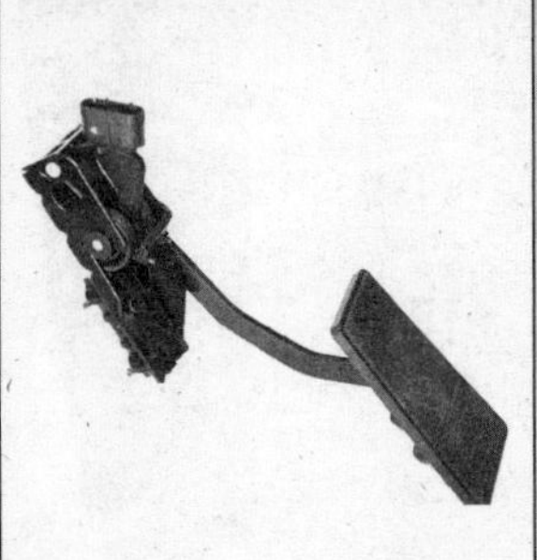

Accelerator Pedal Position (APP) sensor - as you press the accelerator pedal, the APP sensor alters its voltage signal to the PCM in proportion to the angle of the pedal, and the PCM commands a motor inside the throttle body to open or close the throttle plate accordingly

Camshaft Position (CMP) sensor - produces a signal that the PCM uses to identify the number 1 cylinder and to time the firing sequence of the fuel injectors

Crankshaft Position (CKP) sensor - produces a signal that the PCM uses to calculate engine speed and crankshaft position, which enables it to synchronize ignition timing with fuel injector timing, and to detect misfires

Engine Coolant Temperature (ECT) sensor - a thermistor (temperature-sensitive variable resistor) that sends a voltage signal to the PCM, which uses this data to determine the temperature of the engine coolant

Fuel tank pressure sensor - measures the fuel tank pressure and controls fuel tank pressure by signaling the EVAP system to purge the fuel tank vapors when the pressure becomes excessive

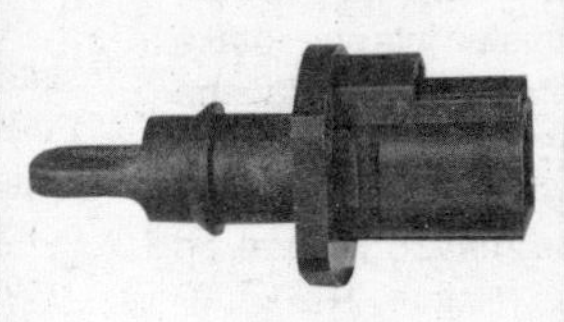

Intake Air Temperature (IAT) sensor - monitors the temperature of the air entering the engine and sends a signal to the PCM to determine injector pulse-width (the duration of each injector's on-time) and to adjust spark timing (to prevent spark knock)

Knock sensor - a piezoelectric crystal that oscillates in proportion to engine vibration which produces a voltage output that is monitored by the PCM. This retards the ignition timing when the oscillation exceeds a certain threshold

Manifold Absolute Pressure (MAP) sensor - monitors the pressure or vacuum inside the intake manifold. The PCM uses this data to determine engine load so that it can alter the ignition advance and fuel enrichment

Mass Air Flow (MAF) sensor - measures the amount of intake air drawn into the engine. It uses a hot-wire sensing element to measure the amount of air entering the engine

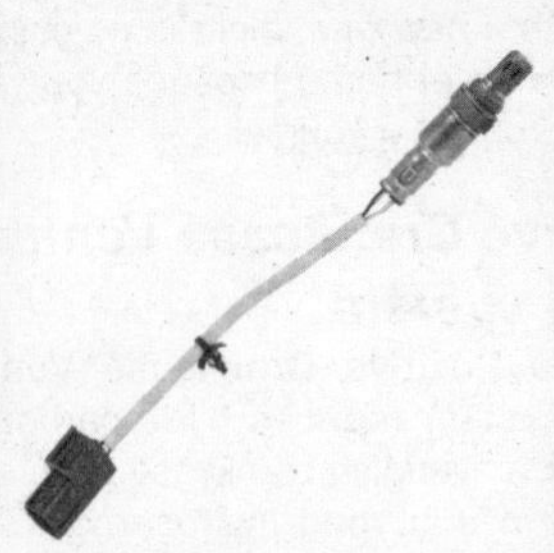

Oxygen sensors - generates a small variable voltage signal in proportion to the difference between the oxygen content in the exhaust stream and the oxygen content in the ambient air. The PCM uses this information to maintain the proper air/fuel ratio. A second oxygen sensor monitors the efficiency of the catalytic converter

Throttle Position (TP) sensor - a potentiometer that generates a voltage signal that varies in relation to the opening angle of the throttle plate inside the throttle body. Works with the PCM and other sensors to calculate injector pulse width (the duration of each injector's on-time)

Photos courtesy of Wells Manufacturing, except APP and MAF sensors.

powerful scan tools can also perform many of the diagnostics once associated with expensive factory scan tools **(see illustration)**. If you're planning to obtain a generic scan tool for your vehicle, make sure that it's compatible with OBD-II systems. If you don't plan to purchase a code reader or scan tool and don't have access to one, you can have the codes extracted by a dealer service department or an independent repair shop.

Note: *Some auto parts stores even provide this service.*

3 Obtaining and clearing Diagnostic Trouble Codes (DTCs)

1   All models covered by this manual are equipped with on-board diagnostics. When the PCM recognizes a malfunction in a monitored emission or engine control system, component or circuit, it turns on the Malfunction Indicator Light (MIL) on the dash. The PCM will continue to display the MIL until the problem is fixed and the Diagnostic Trouble Code (DTC) is cleared from the PCM's memory. You'll need a scan tool to access any DTCs stored in the PCM.

2   Before outputting any DTCs stored in the PCM, thoroughly inspect ALL electrical connectors and hoses. Make sure that all electrical connections are tight, clean and free of corrosion. And make sure that all hoses are correctly connected, fit tightly and are in good condition (no cracks or tears).

Accessing the DTCs

3   The Diagnostic Trouble Codes (DTCs) can only be accessed with a code reader or scan tool. Professional scan tools are expensive, but relatively inexpensive generic code readers or scan tools **(see illustrations 2.4a and 2.4b)** are available at most auto parts stores. Simply plug the connector of the scan tool into the diagnostic connector **(see illustration)**. Then follow the instructions included with the scan tool to extract the DTCs.

4   Once you have outputted all of the stored DTCs, look them up on the accompanying DTC chart.

5   After troubleshooting the source of each DTC, make any necessary repairs or replace the defective component(s).

Clearing the DTCs

6   Clear the DTCs with the code reader or scan tool in accordance with the instructions provided by the tool's manufacturer.

Diagnostic Trouble Codes

7   The accompanying tables are a list of the Diagnostic Trouble Codes (DTCs) that can be accessed by a do-it-yourselfer working at home (there are many, many more DTCs

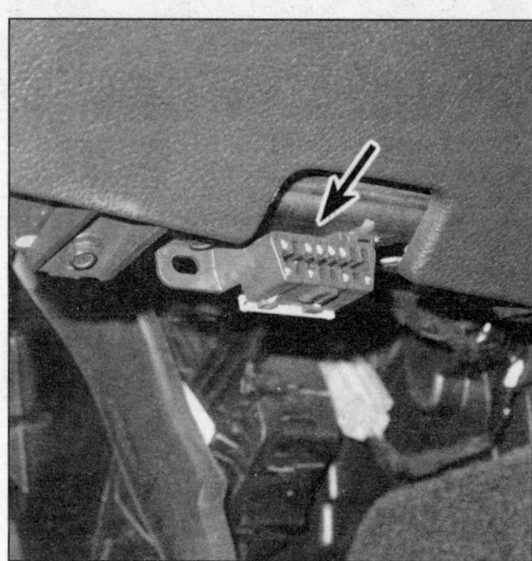

3.3 The Data Link Connector (DLC) is located at the lower edge of the dash, below the steering column

available to professional mechanics with proprietary scan tools and software, but those codes cannot be accessed by a generic scan tool). If, after you have checked and repaired the connectors, wire harness and vacuum hoses (if applicable) for an emission-related system, component or circuit, the problem persists, have the vehicle checked by a dealer service department or other qualified repair shop.

OBD-II trouble codes

Note: *Not all trouble codes apply to all models.*

Code	Probable cause
P0010	Intake camshaft position actuator, open circuit (Bank 1)
P0011	Intake camshaft position timing over-advanced (Bank 1)
P0012	Intake camshaft position timing, over-retarded (Bank 1)
P013A	Oxygen sensor slow response, rich to lean (Bank 1, Sensor 2)
P013C	Oxygen sensor slow response, rich to lean (Bank 2, Sensor 2)
P013E	Oxygen sensor delayed response, rich to lean (Bank 1, Sensor 2)
P014A	Oxygen sensor delayed response, rich to lean (Bank 2, Sensor 2)
P0016	Crankshaft position-to-camshaft position correlation (Bank 1)
P0018	Crankshaft position-to-camshaft position correlation (Bank 2)
P0020	Intake camshaft position actuator, open circuit (Bank 2)
P0021	Intake camshaft position timing over-advanced (Bank 2)
P0022	Intake camshaft position timing over-retarded (Bank 2)

OBD-II trouble codes (continued)

Note: *Not all trouble codes apply to all models.*

Code	Probable cause
P025A	Fuel pump module control circuit open
P025B	Fuel pump module control circuit range or performance problem
P0030	Oxygen sensor heater control circuit (Bank 1, Sensor 1)
P0040	Oxygen sensor signals swapped (Bank 1, Sensor 1/Bank 2, Sensor 1)
P0041	Oxygen sensor signals swapped (Bank 1, Sensor 2/Bank 2, Sensor 2)
P0050	Oxygen sensor heater control circuit (Bank 2, Sensor 1)
P050A	Cold start idle air control performance
P050B	Cold start ignition timing performance
P050E	Cold start engine exhaust temperature out of range
P052A	Cold start camshaft position timing over-advanced (Bank 1)
P052B	Cold start camshaft position timing over-retarded (Bank 1)
P052C	Cold start camshaft position timing over-advanced (Bank 2)
P052D	Cold start camshaft position timing over-retarded (Bank 2)
P0053	Oxygen sensor heater resistance (Bank 1, Sensor 1)
P053A	Positive Crankcase Ventilation (PCV) heater control circuit open
P0054	Oxygen sensor heater resistance (Bank 1, Sensor 2)
P0055	Oxygen sensor heater resistance (Bank 1, Sensor 3)
P0059	Oxygen sensor heater resistance (Bank 2, Sensor 1)
P0060	Oxygen sensor heater resistance (Bank 2, Sensor 2)
P060A	Internal control module monitoring processor performance
P060B	Internal control module analog/digital processing performance
P060C	Internal control module main processor performance
P060D	Internal control module accelerator pedal position performance
P061B	Internal control module torque calculation performance
P061C	Internal control module engine rpm performance
P061D	Internal control module engine air mass performance
P061F	Internal control module throttle actuator controller performance
P062C	Internal control module vehicle speed performance
P064D	Internal control module oxygen sensor processor performance (Bank 1)

Code	Probable cause
P064E	Internal control module oxygen sensor processor performance (Bank 2)
P065B	Alternator control circuit range or performance problem
P0068	Manifold Absolute Pressure (MAP) sensor/Mass Air Flow (MAF) sensor-to-throttle position correlation
P0097	Intake Air Temperature (IAT) sensor 2 circuit, low voltage
P0098	Intake Air Temperature (IAT) sensor 2 circuit, high voltage
P0102	Mass or volume air flow A circuit, low voltage
P0104	Mass Air Flow (MAF) sensor A circuit, intermittent or erratic signal
P0106	Manifold Absolute Pressure (MAP) sensor circuit, range or performance problem
P0107	Manifold Absolute Pressure (MAP) sensor circuit, low voltage
P0108	Manifold Absolute Pressure (MAP) sensor circuit, high voltage
P0109	Manifold Absolute Pressure (MAP) sensor circuit, intermittent signal
P0111	Intake Air Temperature (IAT) sensor circuit, range or performance problem
P0112	Intake Air Temperature (IAT) sensor circuit, low voltage
P0113	Intake Air Temperature (IAT) sensor circuit, high voltage
P0114	Intake Air Temperature (IAT) sensor circuit, intermittent or erratic signal
P0116	Engine Coolant Temperature (ECT) sensor circuit, range or performance problem
P0117	Engine Coolant Temperature (ECT) sensor circuit, low voltage
P0118	Engine Coolant Temperature (ECT) sensor circuit, high voltage
P0119	Engine Coolant Temperature (ECT) sensor circuit, intermittent or erratic signal
P0121	Throttle Position (TP) sensor A circuit, range or performance problem
P0122	Throttle Position (TP) sensor A circuit, low voltage
P0123	Throttle Position (TP) sensor A circuit, high voltage
P0125	Insufficient coolant temperature for closed loop fuel control
P0128	Coolant temperature below coolant thermostat's regulating temperature
P0130	Oxygen sensor circuit malfunction (Bank 1, Sensor 1)
P0132	Oxygen sensor circuit, high voltage (Bank 1, Sensor 1)
P0133	Oxygen sensor circuit, slow response (Bank 1, Sensor 1)
P0134	Oxygen sensor circuit, no activity detected (Bank 1, Sensor 1)
P0135	Oxygen sensor heater circuit malfunction (Bank 1, Sensor 1)
P0138	Oxygen sensor circuit, high voltage (Bank 1, Sensor 2)
P0139	Oxygen sensor circuit, slow response (Bank 1, Sensor 2)

OBD-II trouble codes (continued)

Note: *Not all trouble codes apply to all models.*

Code	Probable cause
P0144	Oxygen sensor circuit, high voltage (Bank 1, Sensor 3)
P0147	Oxygen sensor heater circuit malfunction (Bank 1, Sensor 3)
P0148	Fuel delivery error
P0150	Oxygen sensor circuit malfunction (Bank 2, Sensor 1)
P0152	Oxygen sensor circuit, high voltage (Bank 2, Sensor 1)
P0153	Oxygen sensor circuit, slow response (Bank 2, Sensor 1)
P0154	Oxygen sensor circuit, no activity detected (Bank 2, Sensor 1)
P0155	Oxygen sensor heater circuit malfunction (Bank 2, Sensor 1)
P0158	Oxygen sensor circuit, high voltage (Bank 2, Sensor 2)
P0159	Oxygen sensor circuit, slow response (Bank 2, Sensor 2)
P0161	Oxygen sensor heater circuit malfunction (Bank 2, Sensor 2)
P0171	System too lean (Bank 1)
P0172	System too rich (Bank 1)
P0174	System too lean (Bank 2)
P0175	System too rich (Bank 2)
P0180	Fuel temperature sensor circuit malfunction
P0181	Fuel temperature sensor circuit, range or performance problem
P0182	Fuel temperature sensor circuit, low voltage
P0183	Fuel temperature sensor circuit, high voltage
P0191	Fuel rail pressure sensor circuit, range or performance problem
P0192	Fuel rail pressure sensor circuit, low voltage
P0193	Fuel rail pressure sensor circuit, high voltage
P0196	Engine Oil Temperature (EOT) sensor circuit, range or performance problem
P0197	Engine Oil Temperature (EOT) sensor circuit, low voltage
P0198	Engine Oil Temperature (EOT) sensor circuit, high voltage
P0201	Injector open circuit, cylinder 1
P0202	Injector open circuit, cylinder 2
P0203	Injector open circuit, cylinder 3
P0204	Injector open circuit, cylinder 4

Code	Probable cause
P0205	Injector open circuit, cylinder 5
P0206	Injector open circuit, cylinder 6
P0217	Engine coolant over-temperature condition
P0218	Transaxle fluid temperature over-temperature condition
P0219	Engine over-speed condition
P0221	Throttle Position (TP) sensor circuit, range or performance problem
P0222	Throttle Position (TP) sensor circuit, low voltage
P0223	Throttle Position (TP) sensor circuit, high voltage
P0230	Fuel pump primary circuit malfunction
P0231	Fuel pump secondary circuit, low voltage
P0232	Fuel pump secondary circuit, high voltage
P0298	Engine oil over-temperature condition
P0300	Random misfire detected
P0301	Cylinder 1 misfire
P0302	Cylinder 2 misfire
P0303	Cylinder 3 misfire
P0304	Cylinder 4 misfire
P0305	Cylinder 5 misfire
P0306	Cylinder 6 misfire
P0315	Crankshaft position system variation not learned
P0316	Misfire detected on start-up (first 1000 revolutions)
P0320	Ignition/distributor engine speed input circuit
P0325	Knock sensor 1 circuit malfunction (Bank 1)
P0326	Knock sensor 1 circuit, range or performance problem (Bank 1)
P0330	Knock sensor 2 circuit malfunction (Bank 2)
P0331	Knock sensor 2 circuit, range or performance problem (Bank 2)
P0340	Camshaft Position (CMP) sensor circuit malfunction (Bank 1 or single sensor)
P0341	Camshaft Position (CMP) sensor circuit, range or performance problem (Bank 1 or single sensor)
P0344	Camshaft Position (CMP) sensor circuit, intermittent signal (Bank 1 or single sensor)
P0345	Camshaft Position (CMP) sensor circuit malfunction (Bank 2)
P0346	Camshaft Position (CMP) sensor circuit, range or performance problem (Bank 2)

OBD-II trouble codes (continued)

Note: *Not all trouble codes apply to all models.*

Code	Probable cause
P0349	Camshaft Position (CMP) sensor circuit, intermittent signal (Bank 2)
P0350	Ignition coil primary/secondary circuit malfunction
P0351	Ignition coil A primary/secondary circuit malfunction
P0352	Ignition coil B primary/secondary circuit malfunction
P0353	Ignition coil C primary/secondary circuit malfunction
P0354	Ignition coil D primary/secondary circuit malfunction
P0355	Ignition coil E primary/secondary circuit malfunction
P0356	Ignition coil F primary/secondary circuit malfunction
P0400	Exhaust Gas Recirculation (EGR) system flow
P0401	Exhaust Gas Recirculation (EGR) system, insufficient flow detected
P0402	Exhaust Gas Recirculation (EGR) system, excessive flow detected
P0403	Exhaust Gas Recirculation (EGR) system control circuit malfunction
P0405	Exhaust Gas Recirculation (EGR) system, differential pressure feedback sensor circuit, low voltage
P0406	Exhaust Gas Recirculation (EGR) system, differential pressure feedback sensor circuit, high voltage
P0410	Secondary Air Injection (AIR) system
P0412	Secondary Air Injection (AIR) system, switching valve circuit malfunction
P0420	Catalyst system efficiency below threshold (Bank 1)
P0430	Catalyst system efficiency below threshold (Bank 2)
P0442	Evaporative Emission (EVAP) system, small leak detected
P0443	Evaporative Emission (EVAP) system, purge control valve circuit malfunction
P0446	Evaporative Emission (EVAP) system, vent control circuit malfunction
P0451	Evaporative Emission (EVAP) system, pressure sensor range or performance problem
P0452	Evaporative Emission (EVAP) system, pressure sensor, low voltage
P0453	Evaporative Emission (EVAP) system, pressure sensor, high voltage
P0454	Evaporative Emission (EVAP) system, pressure sensor, intermittent signal
P0455	Evaporative Emission (EVAP) system, gross leak detected/no flow
P0456	Evaporative Emission (EVAP) system, very small leak detected
P0457	Evaporative Emission (EVAP) system, leak detected (fuel cap loose or off)
P0460	Fuel level sensor circuit malfunction

Code	Probable cause
P0461	Fuel level sensor circuit, range or performance problem
P0462	Fuel level sensor circuit, low voltage
P0463	Fuel level sensor circuit, high voltage
P0480	Fan 1 control circuit malfunction
P0481	Fan 2 control circuit malfunction
P0483	Fan performance
P0491	Secondary Air Injection (AIR) system, insufficient flow (Bank 1)
P0500	Vehicle Speed Sensor (VSS)
P0503	Vehicle Speed Sensor (VSS), intermittent, erratic or high signal
P0505	Idle Air Control (IAC) system
P0506	Idle Air Control (IAC) system, rpm lower than expected
P0507	Idle Air Control (IAC) system, rpm higher than expected
P050A	Cold start idle air control performance
P050B	Cold start ignition timing performance
P050E	Cold start engine exhaust temperature out of range
P0511	Idle Air Control (IAC) system circuit malfunction
P0512	Starter request circuit malfunction
P052A	Cold start camshaft position timing over-advanced (Bank 1)
P052B	Cold start camshaft position timing over-retarded (Bank 1)
P052C	Cold start camshaft position timing over-advanced (Bank 2)
P052D	Cold start camshaft position timing over-retarded (Bank 2)
P0528	Fan speed sensor circuit, no signal
P0532	Air conditioning refrigerant pressure sensor circuit, low voltage
P0533	Air conditioning refrigerant pressure sensor circuit, high voltage
P0534	Air conditioning refrigerant charge loss
P0537	Air conditioning evaporator temperature sensor circuit, low voltage
P0538	A/C evaporator temperature sensor circuit, high voltage
P053A	Positive Crankcase Ventilation (PCV) heater control circuit open
P0552	Power Steering Pressure (PSP) sensor circuit, low voltage
P0553	Power Steering Pressure (PSP) sensor circuit, high voltage
P0562	System voltage low

OBD-II trouble codes (continued)

Note: *Not all trouble codes apply to all models.*

Code	Probable cause
P0563	System voltage high
P0571	Brake switch circuit malfunction
P0572	Brake switch circuit, low voltage
P0573	Brake switch circuit, high voltage
P0579	Cruise control multifunction input circuit, ranger or performance problem
P0581	Cruise control multifunction input circuit, high voltage
P0600	Serial communication link
P0601	Powertrain Control Module (PCM), memory checksum error
P0602	Powertrain Control Module (PCM) programming error
P0603	Powertrain Control Module (PCM), Keep Alive Memory (KAM) error
P0604	Powertrain Control Module (PCM), Random Access Memory (RAM) error
P0605	Powertrain Control Module (PCM), Read Only Memory (ROM) error
P0606	Powertrain Control Module (PCM) processor
P0607	Powertrain Control Module (PCM) performance
P060A	Internal control module monitoring processor performance
P060B	Internal control module analog/digital processing performance
P060C	Internal control module main processor performance
P060D	Internal control module accelerator pedal position performance
P0610	Powertrain Control Module (PCM) options error
P061B	Internal control module torque calculation performance
P061C	Internal control module engine rpm performance
P061D	Internal control module engine air mass performance
P061F	Internal control module throttle actuatorcontroller performance
P0620	Alternator control circuit malfunction
P0622	Alternator field terminal, circuit malfunction
P0625	Alternator field terminal, low circuit voltage
P0626	Alternator field terminal, high circuit voltage
P0627	Fuel pump, open control circuit
P062C	Internal control module vehicle speed performance

Code	Probable cause
P062F	Internal control module EEPROM error
P0642	Sensor reference voltage (VREF) circuit below VREF minimum voltage
P0643	Sensor reference voltage (VREF) circuit, high voltage
P0645	Air conditioning clutch relay control circuit malfunction
P064D	Internal control module oxygen sensor processor performance (Bank 1)
P064E	Internal control module oxygen sensor processor performance (Bank 2)
P0657	Actuator supply voltage, open circuit
P065B	Alternator control circuit range or performance problem
P0660	Intake Manifold Tuning Valve (IMTV) control circuit, open circuit (Bank 1)
P0663	Intake Manifold Tuning Valve (IMTV) control circuit, open circuit (Bank 2)
P0685	Powertrain Control Module (PCM) power relay control circuit open
P0689	Powertrain Control Module (PCM) power relay sense circuit, low voltage
P0690	Powertrain Control Module (PCM) power relay sense circuit, high voltage
P06B8	Internal control module Non-volatile random access memory (NVRAM) error
P0703	Brake switch input circuit malfunction
P0704	Clutch switch input circuit malfunction
P0705	Transmission Range (TR) sensor circuit (PRNDL) input problem
P0706	Transmission Range (TR) sensor circuit, range or performance problem
P0707	Transmission Range (TR) sensor circuit, low voltage
P0708	Transmission range sensor circuit, high voltage
P0711	Transmission fluid temperature sensor circuit, range or performance problem
P0712	Transmission fluid temperature sensor circuit, low input
P0713	Transmission fluid temperature sensor circuit, high input
P0715	Input/turbine speed sensor circuit malfunction
P0716	Input/turbine speed sensor circuit, range or performance problem
P0717	Input/turbine speed sensor circuit, no signal
P0720	Output Shaft Speed (OSS) sensor circuit malfunction
P0721	Output Shaft Speed (OSS) sensor circuit, range or performance problem
P0722	No signal from Output Shaft Speed (OSS) sensor
P0723	Output Shaft Speed (OSS) sensor circuit, intermittent signal
P06B8	Internal control module Non-volatile random access memory (NVRAM) error

OBD-II trouble codes (continued)

Note: *Not all trouble codes apply to all models.*

Code	Probable cause
P0729	Gear 6 incorrect ratio
P072C	Stuck in Gear 1
P072E	Stuck in Gear 3
P072F	Stuck in Gear 4
P0730	Incorrect gear ratio
P0731	Incorrect gear ratio, first gear
P0732	Incorrect gear ratio, second gear
P0733	Incorrect gear ratio, third gear
P0734	Incorrect gear ratio, fourth gear
P0735	Incorrect gear ratio, fifth gear
P0736	Incorrect gear ratio, reverse gear
P0740	Torque converter clutch solenoid circuit, open
P0741	Torque converter clutch, circuit performance problem or stuck in Off position
P0742	Torque converter clutch circuit, stuck in On position
P0743	Torque converter clutch solenoid circuit, electrical malfunction
P0744	Torque converter clutch circuit, intermittent
P0745	Pressure control solenoid malfunction
P0748	Pressure control solenoid malfunction
P0750	Shift solenoid A, performance problem
P0751	Shift solenoid A, performance problem or stuck in Off position
P0752	Shift solenoid A, stuck in On position
P0753	Shift solenoid A, electrical problem
P0755	Shift solenoid B, performance problem
P0756	Shift solenoid B, performance problem or stuck in Off position
P0757	Shift solenoid B, stuck in On position
P0758	Shift solenoid B, electrical problem
P0760	Shift solenoid C, performance problem
P0761	Shift solenoid C, performance problem or stuck in Off position
P0762	Shift solenoid C, stuck in On position

Code	Probable cause
P0763	Shift solenoid C, electrical problem
P0765	Shift solenoid D, performance problem
P0766	Shift solenoid D, performance problem or stuck in Off position
P0767	Shift solenoid D, stuck in On position
P0768	Shift solenoid D, electrical problem
P0769	Shift solenoid D, intermittent problem
P0770	Shift solenoid E, performance
P0771	Shift solenoid E, performance problem or stuck in Off position
P0772	Shift solenoid E, stuck in On position
P0773	Shift solenoid E, electrical problem
P0774	Shift solenoid E, intermittent electrical problem
P0777	Pressure control solenoid "B" stuck On
P0778	Pressure control solenoid "B" electrical
P0780	Shift malfunction
P0791	Intermediate shaft speed sensor circuit malfunction
P0812	Reverse input circuit malfunction
P0815	Upshift switch circuit malfunction
P0816	Downshift switch circuit malfunction
P0817	Starter disable circuit malfunction
P0830	Clutch pedal switch circuit malfunction
P0840	Transmission fluid pressure sensor circuit malfunction
P0841	Transmission fluid pressure sensor/switch "A" circuit range/performance problem
P0850	Park/neutral switch input circuit malfunction
P0882	Transmission control module (TCM) power input signal low
P0894	Transmission component slipping
P0960	Pressure Control (PC) solenoid A - control circuit open
P0961	Pressure control (PC) solenoid A - control circuit range/performance problem
P0962	Pressure control (PC) solenoid A - control circuit low
P0963	Pressure control (PC) solenoid A - control circuit high
P0973	Shift solenoid (SS) A - control circuit low
P0974	Shift solenoid (SS) A - control circuit high

OBD-II trouble codes (continued)

Note: *Not all trouble codes apply to all models.*

Code	Probable cause
P0976	Shift solenoid (SS) B - control circuit low
P0977	Shift solenoid (SS) B - control circuit high
P0978	Shift solenoid (SS) C - control circuit range/performance problem
P0979	Shift solenoid (SS) C - control circuit low
P0980	Shift solenoid (SS) C - control circuit high
P0981	Shift solenoid (SS) D - control circuit range/performance problem
P0982	Shift solenoid (SS) D - control circuit low
P0983	Shift solenoid (SS) D - control circuit high
P0984	Shift solenoid (SS) E - control circuit range/performance problem
P0985	Shift solenoid (SS) E - control circuit low
P0986	Shift solenoid (SS) E - control circuit high
P0997	Shift solenoid (SS) F - control circuit range/performance problem
P0998	Shift solenoid (SS) F - control circuit low
P0999	Shift solenoid (SS) F - control circuit high

4.1 APP sensor details

1   *Electrical connector (slide the lock up then depress the tab to unplug)*
2   *Mounting bolts*

4   Accelerator Pedal Position (APP) sensor - replacement

1   Disconnect the electrical connector from the upper end of the APP sensor assembly **(see illustration)**.
2   Remove the pedal/sensor assembly mounting fasteners and remove the assembly.
3   Installation is the reverse of removal.

5   Camshaft Position (CMP) sensor – replacement

1   Disconnect the cable from the negative battery terminal (see Chapter 5).

Four-cylinder models

Note: *The CMP sensors are located at the top corners of the valve cover, above the left end of the intake and exhaust camshafts.*

2   Remove the air filter outlet duct (see Chapter 4).
3   Disconnect the CMP sensor electrical connector **(see illustration)**.
4   Remove the CMP sensor mounting bolt and remove the sensor from the valve cover.
5   Inspect the condition of the CMP sensor O-ring. If it's cracked, torn or deteriorated, replace it.
6   Installation is the reverse of removal.

V6 models

Note: *On 3.0L engines, a single CMP sensor is located above and to the left of the air conditioning compressor on the front bank cylinder head.*
Note: *On 3.5 non-VCT engines (2008 through 2012 models), there are two CMP sensors, located in the ends of each cylinder head at the driver's side of the engine.*
Note: *On 3.5L VCT (variable cam timing) engines (2013 and later models), there are four CMP sensors, two on the end of each cylinder head.*

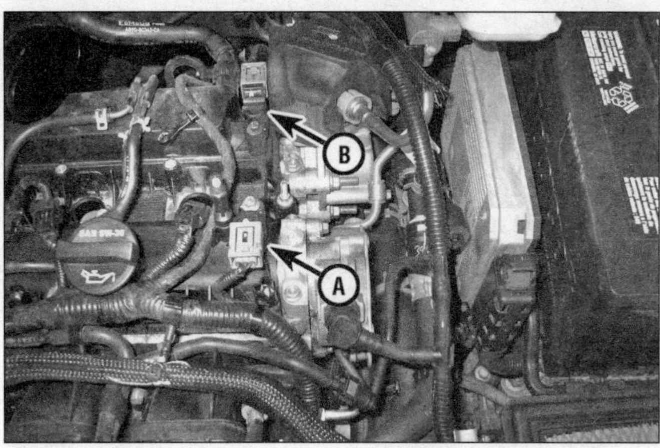

5.3 Intake CMP sensor (A) and exhaust CMP sensor (B) locations (four-cylinder engine)

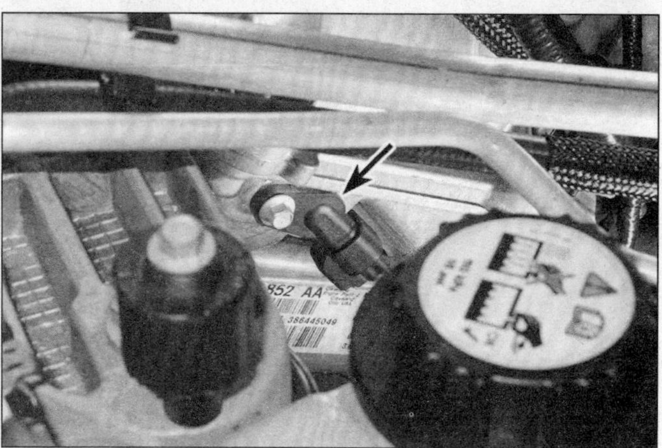

5.8a The CMP sensor on 3.0L engines is at the right end (passenger side) of the front bank cylinder head

5.8b The CMP sensor(s) are located at the left ends of the cylinder heads (2013 3.5L engine, front cylinder bank shown)

6.4 CKP sensor details (four-cylinder models):

1   Electrical connector   3   CKP sensor
2   Mounting bolts

7   If you're working on a 2008 or later model, remove the air filter housing and duct (see Chapter 4).

8   Disconnect the CMP sensor electrical connector(s) **(see illustration)**.

9   Remove the mounting bolt(s) and remove the sensor(s).

10   Remove the CMP sensor O-ring and inspect its condition. If it's cracked, torn or otherwise deteriorated, replace it.

11   Lubricate the sensor O-ring with clean engine oil. Installation is otherwise the reverse of removal. Tighten the CMP sensor mounting bolt to the torque listed in this Chapter's Specifications.

6   Crankshaft Position (CKP) sensor - replacement

Note: *Replacing the CKP sensor might set a Diagnostic Trouble Code (DTC). If it does, and you have a generic scan tool that can clear codes, erase the code and see if it reappears. If it does,* *drive the vehicle to a dealer service department to perform a Misfire Monitor Neutral Profile Correction procedure with a factory scan tool.*

1   Disconnect the cable from the negative battery terminal (see Chapter 5).

2   On four-cylinder models and 3.0L V6 models (2007 and earlier), loosen the right front wheel lug nuts. Raise the front of the vehicle and support it securely on jackstands. Remove the right front wheel, then remove the inner fender splash shield (see Chapter 11).

3   Remove the engine under-cover.

Four-cylinder models
Removal

Note: *The CKP sensor is located at the lower front corner of the timing chain cover.*

4   Position the no. 1 cylinder at Top Dead Center (TDC) (see Chapter 2A), then disconnect the electrical connector from the CKP sensor **(see illustration)**.

5   Unscrew the CKP sensor mounting bolts and remove the sensor.

Installation

Note: *If you're installing a new CKP sensor, the new sensor comes with a special alignment jig (#303-1521) that, according to the manufacturer, is available only with a new sensor. However, you might be able to find an aftermarket tool that does the same thing. If you removed the CKP sensor simply to access some other component, like the timing chain, use the alternate method of aligning the CKP sensor included here.*

6   Install the CKP sensor but don't tighten the sensor mounting bolts.

7   If you're installing a new CKP sensor, align the sensor with the special alignment jig (included with the new sensor) in accordance with the manufacturer's instructions. With the alignment jig in place, tighten the CKP sensor bolts securely, then remove the alignment jig.

8   If you're installing the old CKP sensor, look at the sensor trigger wheel, or timing plate, that's mounted on the backside of the crankshaft pulley. Note the small teeth that stick out from the circumference of the timing

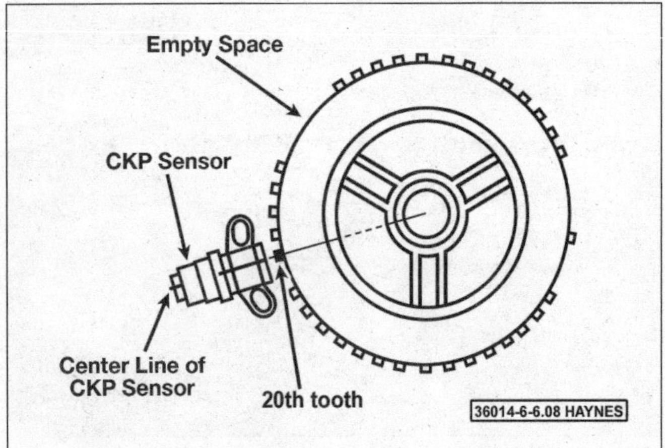

6.8 CKP sensor alignment details (four-cylinder models)

6.10 On 3.0L V6 models, the CKP sensor is located at the lower rear edge of the timing chain cover

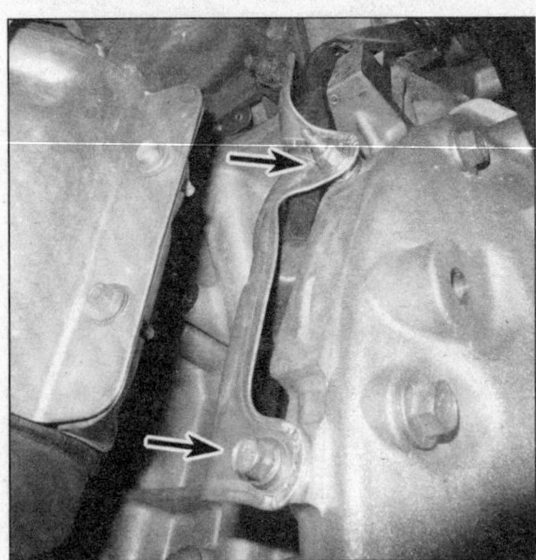

6.15 Remove the heat shield retaining bolts

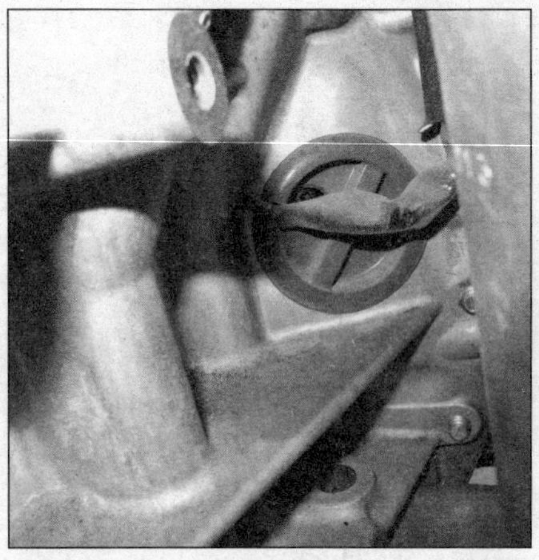

6.16 Pry the rubber grommet out of the engine block to access the CKP sensor

6.18 CKP sensor mounting bolt

plate. There is a blank spot on the edge of the timing plate, where there are no teeth. From this blank area, count 20 teeth in a counter-clockwise direction, then use a straightedge to draw a straight line from the center of the 20th tooth through the center of the crank-shaft pulley **(see illustration)**. Position the centerline of the CKP sensor with the line that you made, then tighten the sensor bolts to the torque listed in this Chapter's Specifications.

9   The remainder of installation is the reverse of removal.

V6 models

Note: *On 3.0L engines, the CKP sensor is located on the firewall-side of the timing chain cover, just below the alternator.*

Note: *On 3.5L engines, the CKP sensor is located on the left front side of the engine block, near the transaxle.*

3.0L V6 engine

10   Disconnect the CKP sensor electrical connector **(see illustration)**.

11   Unscrew the CKP sensor mounting bolt and remove the sensor.

12   Inspect the CKP sensor O-ring for dam-age and lubricate it with oil prior to installa-tion.

13   Installation is the reverse of removal. Tighten the sensor mounting bolt to the torque listed in this Chatper's Specifications.

3.5L V6 engine

14   On 3.5L non-VCT engines (2008 through 2012 models), remove the front cylinder bank catalytic converter (see Section 19).

15   Remove the CKP sensor heat shield mounting bolt and nut, then remove the heat shield **(see illustration)**.

16   Remove the rubber grommet cover (if applicable) **(see illustration)**.

Caution: *On 3.5L VCT engines, remove the mounting bolt before disconnecting the electri-cal connector to prevent the sensor from fall-ing into the bellhousing.*

17   Disconnect the CKP sensor electrical connector.

18   Remove the CKP sensor mounting bolt and remove the sensor.

19   Inspect the CKP sensor O-ring for dam-age and lubricate it with oil prior to installa-tion.

20   Installation is the reverse of removal.

Tighten the mounting bolt to the torque listed in this Chapter's Specifications.

---

7   Cylinder Head Temperature (CHT) sensor - replacement

Warning: *Wait until the engine has cooled completely before beginning this procedure.*
Note: *3.0L V6 engines do not use a CHT sen-sor.*

Four-cylinder models

1   Disconnect the cable from the negative battery terminal (see Chapter 5).

2   Remove the air filter outlet duct, then disconnect the charge air cooler inlet pipe (see Chapter 4).

3   Pull back the insulator (if equipped) from the CHT sensor electrical connector and dis-connect the connector **(see illustration)**.

4   Unscrew the CHT sensor from the cylin-der head.

5   When installing the CHT sensor, tighten it to the torque listed in this Chapter's Specifi-cations. Installation is the reverse of removal.

7.3 On four-cylinder engines the CHT sensor is located on the back side of the cylinder head

7.8 Location of the CHT sensor on 3.5L engines

3.5L V6 models

Note: *The CHT sensor is screwed into the rear cylinder head below the intake manifold.*

6   Disconnect the cable from the negative battery terminal (see Chapter 5).

7   Remove the lower intake manifold (see Chapter 2B).

8   Disconnect the CHT sensor electrical connector.

9   Unscrew and remove the CHT sensor.

10   Installation is the reverse of removal. Tighten the sensor to the torque listed in this Chapter's Specifications.

8   Engine Coolant Temperature (ECT) sensor - replacement

Warning: *Wait until the engine is completely cool before beginning this procedure.*

Four-cylinder engine

1   Drain the cooling system (see Chapter 3).

2   The ECT sensor is located on the water outlet housing on left end of the cylinder head **(see illustration)**.

3   Disconnect the electrical connector from the sensor.

4   Remove the retaining clip.

5   Remove the sensor and discard the O-ring

6   Installation is the reverse of removal. Use a new O-ring.

7   Refill the cooling system (see Chapter 1).

3.0L V6 engine

8   Drain the engine coolant (see Chapter 1).

9   Disconnect the electrical connector from the ECT sensor **(see illustration)**.

10   To remove the ECT sensor, pull out the locking tab, rotate the sensor counterclockwise, then pull it out of the coolant passage **(see illustration)**.

11   Remove and inspect the sensor O-ring. If it's cut, torn, damaged or otherwise deteriorated, replace it.

12   To install the ECT sensor, insert it into the coolant passage, then turn it clockwise

8.2 The ECT sensor is located on the back of the water outlet housing at the left end of the cylinder head (four-cylinder models)

until the locking tab snaps into place. Installation is otherwise the reverse of removal.

13   Refill the cooling system (see Chapter 1).

8.9 The ECT sensor is located at the left end of the engine (3.0L V6 engine)

8.10 Pull out the locking tab (A), rotate the sensor counterclockwise, then pull it out of the coolant passage

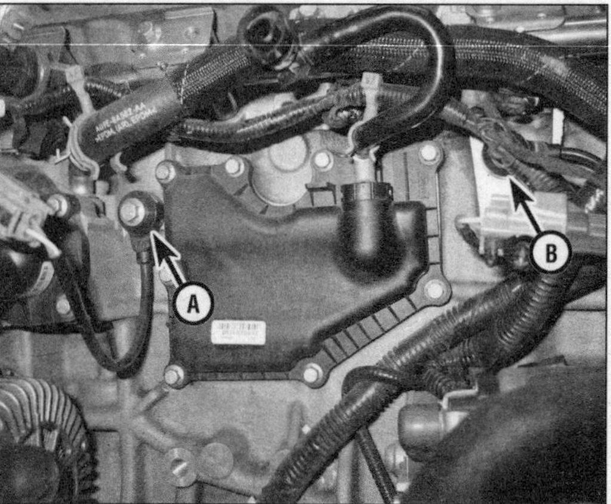

9.4 The right hand knock sensor (A), must be installed with the wire end of the sensor pointing towards the 6 o'clock position and the left side knock sensor (B - not visible) must be installed with the wire end pointing towards the 3 o'clock position (four-cylinder model shown)

9.8 The knock sensor is located on the left rear side of the engine block (3.0L V6 engine)

9   Knock sensors - replacement

1   Disconnect the cable from the negative battery terminal (see Chapter 5).

Four-cylinder models

Note: *The two knock sensors are located on the front side of the block, behind the intake manifold.*

2   Remove the intake manifold (see Chapter 2A).

3   Disconnect the electrical connector from the knock sensor.

4   Remove the knock sensor bolt and remove the knock sensor **(see illustration)**.

Note: *The right hand knock sensor must be installed with the wire end of the sensor pointing towards the 6 o'clock position, and the left side knock sensor must be installed with the wire end pointing towards the 3 o'clock position.*

5   Installation is the reverse of removal. Tighten the knock sensor bolt to the torque listed in this Chapter's Specifications.

V6 models

3.0L engine

Note: *3.0L engines use a single knock sensor located on the left rear side of the engine block.*

6   Raise the rear of the vehicle and support it securely on jackstands.

7   Loosen the knock sensor heat shield and position it aside.

8   Disconnect the knock sensor electrical connector, remove mounting bolt and remove the sensor.

9   Installation is the reverse of removal. Tighten the knock sensor bolt to the torque listed in this Chapter's Specifications.

3.5L engines

Warning: *Wait until the engine is completely cool before beginning this procedure.*

Note: *The knock sensors are located in the valley between the cylinder heads, under the coolant pipe. They share the same wiring harness and must be replaced as a pair.*

10   Remove the upper and lower intake manifold (see Chapter 2B).

11   Remove the thermostat housing and coolant tube (see Chapter 3).

12   Disconnect the knock sensor electrical connector.

13   Remove the knock sensor bolts and remove the knock sensors.

14   Installation is the reverse of removal. Tighten the knock sensor bolts to the torque listed in this Chapter's Specifications.

10   Turbocharger Boost Pressure (TCBP)/Charge Air Cooler Temperature (CACT) sensor (four-cylinder models only) - replacement

Note: *The TCBP/CACT sensor is located on the lower left duct fitting of the charge air cooler.*

1   Disconnect the cable from the negative battery terminal (see Chapter 5).

2   Disconnect the electrical connector from the sensor.

3   Remove the sensor retaining bolt and remove the sensor from the charge air cooler.

4   Installation is the reverse of removal.

11   Mass Air Flow (MAF)/Intake Air Temperature (IAT) sensor - replacement

Note: *These sensors are both located on the duct portion of the air filter housing cover. Not all models are equipped with an IAT sensor.*

1   Disconnect the cable from the negative battery terminal (see Chapter 5).

2   Disconnect the electrical connector from the MAF or IAT sensor **(see illustration)**.

3   MAF sensor: Remove the MAF sensor mounting fasteners and remove the sensor from the air filter housing.

4   IAT sensor: Lift up the tab on the sensor, then turn the sensor counterclockwise, then pull it out.

5   Installation is the reverse of removal.

12   Oxygen sensors - replacement

Note: *Because it is installed in the exhaust manifold or pipe, both of which contract when cool, an oxygen sensor might be very difficult to loosen when the engine is cold. Rather than risk damage to the sensor or its mounting threads, start and run the engine for a minute or two, then shut it off. Be careful not to burn*

9.13 The knock sensors are located underneath the coolant tube

11.2 The MAF sensor is located on the air filter housing cover (3.5L V6 shown, others similar)

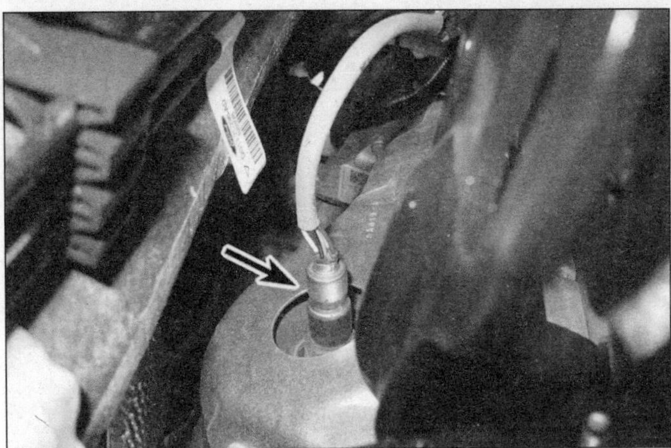

12.4a Upstream oxygen sensor location - V6 engine, Bank 1

12.4b Upstream oxygen sensor location - V6 engine, bank 2

yourself during the following procedure.

1   Be particularly careful when servicing an oxygen sensor:

a) *Oxygen sensors have a permanently attached pigtail and an electrical connector that cannot be removed. Damaging or removing the pigtail or electrical connector will render the sensor useless.*

b) *Keep grease, dirt and other contaminants away from the electrical connector and the louvered end of the sensor.*

c) *Do not use cleaning solvents of any kind on an oxygen sensor.*

d) *Oxygen sensors are extremely delicate. Do not drop a sensor or handle it roughly.*

e) *Make sure that the silicone boot on the sensor is installed in the correct position. Otherwise, the boot might melt and it might prevent the sensor from operating correctly.*

Replacement

2   Disconnect the cable from the negative battery terminal (see Chapter 5).

3   To access downstream sensors on all models, raise the front of the vehicle and place it securely on jackstands. Remove the engine under-cover.

Upstream oxygen sensor

4   Locate the upstream oxygen sensor (**see illustration**), then trace the sensor's electrical lead to its electrical connector and disconnect the connector. Disengage any harness clips.

5   Using a wrench or an oxygen sensor socket, unscrew the upstream oxygen sensor.

6   If you're going to install the old sensor, apply anti-seize compound to the threads of the sensor to facilitate future removal. If you're going to install a new oxygen sensor, it's not necessary to apply anti-seize compound to the threads; the threads on new sensors already have anti-seize compound on them.

7   Installation is the reverse of removal. Tighten the oxygen sensor to the torque listed in this Chapter's Specifications.

Downstream oxygen sensor (catalyst monitor sensor)

8   Locate the downstream oxygen sensor (**see illustration**), then trace the lead up to the electrical connector and disconnect the connector. Disengage any harness clips.

9   Using a wrench or an oxygen sensor socket, unscrew the downstream oxygen sensor.

10   If you're going to install the old sensor,

12.4c Upstream oxygen sensor location - four-cylinder engine

apply anti-seize compound to the threads of the sensor to facilitate future removal. If you're going to install a new oxygen sensor, it's not necessary to apply anti-seize compound to the threads. The threads on new sensors already have anti-seize compound on them.

11   Installation is the reverse of removal. Tighten the oxygen sensor to the torque listed in this Chapter's Specifications.

12.8a Downstream oxygen sensor location - V6 engine, bank 1

12.8b Downstream oxygen sensor location - V6 engine, bank 2

12.8c Downstream oxygen sensor - four-cylinder engine

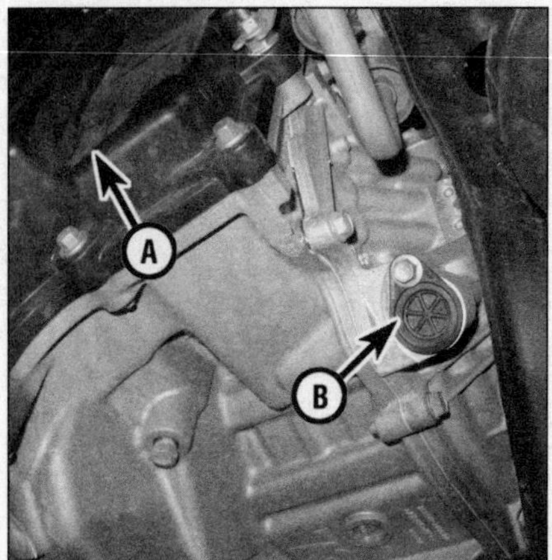

16.3 Transaxle main control cover (A) and Turbine Shaft Speed (TSS) sensor (B)

13   Power Steering Pressure (PSP) switch (2008 and 2009 models) - replacement

Note: *The PSP switch is located on the power steering pressure line.*

1   Disconnect the electrical connector from the PSP switch.

2   Unscrew the PSP switch from the fitting on the pressure line.

3   Installation is the reverse of removal.

14   Throttle Position (TP) sensor - replacement

The TP sensor is an integral component of the electronic throttle body, and is not separately serviceable. If you need to replace the TP sensor, you must replace the throttle body (see Chapter 4).

15   Transmission Range (TR) sensor - removal and installation

2007 and earlier models

1   The TR sensor on these models is part of the Transmission Control Module. See Section 17 for the removal and installation procedure.

2008 and later models

2   The TR sensor on these models is located in the valve body and repair is beyond the scope of the home mechanic. If you need to replace the TR sensor, we recommend taking the vehicle to your local dealer or other qualified repair shop for repair.

16   Turbine Shaft Speed (TSS) sensor/Output Shaft Speed (OSS) sensor - replacement

2007 and earlier models

Note: *On these models the sensor is located*

in the valve body of the transaxle and should be taken to your local dealer or other qualified repair shop for repair.

2008 and later models

Note: *2008 and later models have two speed sensors: the Turbine Shaft Speed (TSS) sensor and the Output Shaft Speed (OSS) sensor. The TSS sensor is located on the bottom of the transaxle. The OSS sensor is located in the valve body of the transaxle and should be taken to your local dealer or other qualified repair shop for repair.*

1   Raise the vehicle and support it securely on jackstands. Remove the engine undercover, then drain the transaxle fluid (see Chapter 1) and remove the main control cover from the front of the transaxle.

2   Disconnect the sensor's electrical connector from the valve body.

3   Remove the sensor mounting bolt and remove the sensor from the transaxle case **(see illustration)**.

4   Lubricate the O-ring of the new sensor with clean transmission fluid. Attach a length of wire to the sensor's electrical connector and guide it through the transaxle case. Pull the sensor's wiring harness through the case and plug the electrical connector into its terminal on the valve body.

5   Push the sensor into the case and install the bolt, tightening it to the torque listed in this Chapter's Specifications.

6   Install the main control cover, tightening the bolts to the torque listed in this Chapter's Specifications.

7   Lower the vehicle and fill the transaxle with the proper type and amount of transmission fluid (see Chapter 1).

17   Transmission Control Module (TCM) - removal and installation

2007 and earlier models

Note: *On these models the Transmission Range (TR) sensor is incorporated into the TCM.*

Note: *On this transaxle, the TR sensor is an integral component of the Transaxle Control Module (TCM) and is not separately service-*

able. If you need to replace the TR sensor, you must replace the TCM. The TCM cannot be replaced at home, because the replacement unit must be programmed with a factory scan tool before it will operate properly. The following procedure assumes that you are simply removing the current TCM unit from the old transaxle and installing it on a replacement transaxle.

Note: *The TCM is located on top of the transaxle.*

Removal

1   Remove the air filter housing (see Chapter 4).

2   Disconnect the electrical connector from the TCM **(see illustration)**.

3   Using a trim removal tool or a screwdriver, carefully pry the end of the shift cable off the ballstud on the manual control lever.

4   Remove the manual control lever nut and remove the lever.

5   Remove the TCM mounting bolts and remove the TCM.

Installation

6   Before installing the TCM, verify that the manual control lever is in the NEUTRAL position by aligning the mark on the control lever with the stationary mark on the TCM **(see illustration)**.

17.6 TCM manual control lever NEUTRAL position alignment marks (6-speed transaxle)

18.3 Rotate the locking levers up . . .

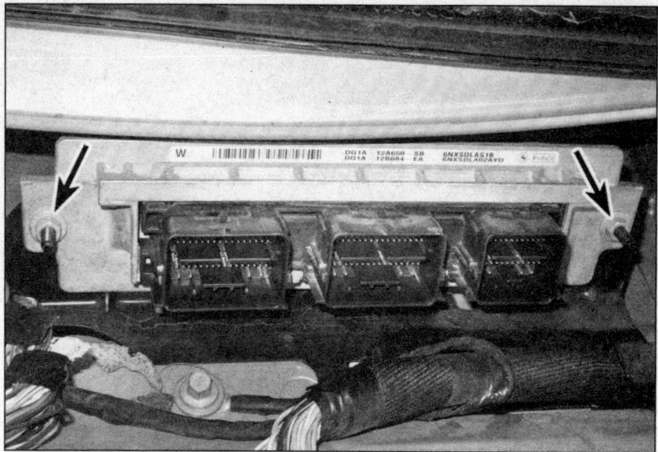

18.4 . . . then remove the nuts and pull the PCM from the cowl

7   Install the TCM and tighten the TCM mounting bolts securely.

8   Install the manual control lever, install the lever nut and tighten it securely.

9   Reconnect the electrical connector to the TCM.

10   Reconnect the shift cable to the ballstud on the manual control lever. adjust the cable as described in Chapter 7A.

11   The remainder of installation is the reverse of removal. Verify that the engine will only start in PARK or NEUTRAL.

2008 and later models

12   The transmission control functions on these models are handled by the Powertrain Control Module (PCM); there is no separate TCM. Refer to Section 18 for information on the PCM.

18   Powertrain Control Module (PCM) - removal and installation

Caution: *To avoid electrostatic discharge damage to the PCM, handle the PCM only by its case. Do not touch the electrical terminals during removal and installation. If possible, ground yourself to the vehicle with an anti-static ground strap, available at computer supply stores.*

Note: *This procedure applies only to disconnecting, removing and installing the PCM that is already installed in your vehicle. If the PCM is defective and has to be replaced, it must be programmed with new software and calibrations. This procedure requires the use of Vehicle Communication Module (VCM) and Integrated Diagnostic System (IDS) software with appropriate hardware, or equivalent scan tool, so you WILL NOT BE ABLE TO REPLACE THE PCM AT HOME.*

1   Disconnect the cable from the negative battery terminal (see Chapter 5).

2   Remove the cowl panel (see Chapter 11).

3   Rotate the lock locking levers up and disconnect the electrical connectors from the PCM **(see illustration)**.

4   Remove the PCM mounting nuts **(see illustration)** and remove the PCM.

5   Installation is the reverse of removal.

19   Catalytic converter - replacement

Warning: *Wait until the engine has cooled completely before beginning this procedure.*

Note: *Exhaust fasteners are of a torque prevailing design. Use only new fasteners with the same part number as the original. Torque values must be used as specified during reassembly to ensure correct retention of exhaust components.*

Four-cylinder engines

1   Raise the vehicle and place it securely on jackstands.

2   Remove the downstream oxygen sensor/catalyst sensor from the catalyst (see Section 12).

3   Loosen the clamp fasteners securing the front end of the catalyst to the turbocharger. If the threads are severely damaged or rusted, apply some penetrant to the threads and wait awhile before loosening them.

4   Remove the nuts and bolts that secure the flange at the rear end of the catalyst to the exhaust pipe. If the threads are severely damaged or rusted, apply some penetrant to the threads and wait awhile before loosening them.

5   Remove the catalytic converter.

Note: *Removing the catalytic converter-to-turbocharger outlet flange clamp may be difficult. Use care not to scratch or gouge the catalytic converter or turbocharger flanges or sealing surfaces. Scratches and gouges may cause exhaust leaks*

6   Remove and discard the old gasket between the exhaust down pipe and the catalyst mounting flange.

7   Installation is the reverse of removal. Use a new gasket and, if necessary, new fasteners. Tighten fasteners to the torque listed in this Chapter's Specifications.

V6 engines

3.0L

8   Remove and discard the two upper catalytic converter-to-exhaust manifold bolts and gasket from the front or rear catalytic converter

9   Raise the front of the vehicle and place it securely on jackstands. Remove the engine under-cover

10   If removing the front catalytic converter, remove the bracket bolt.

11   Remove and discard the two lower catalytic converter nuts and remove the front or rear catalytic converter.

12   If removing the front catalytic converter, inspect the bracket clamp and install a new clamp if necessary.

13   Installation is the reverse of removal. Use a new flange gasket.

3.5L

14   Raise the front of the vehicle and place it securely on jackstands. Remove the engine under-cover.

15   Locate the upstream and downstream oxygen sensors, trace their electrical leads to their respective connectors and disconnect them. Remove both oxygen sensors (see Section 12).

16   If the catalyst and/or exhaust manifold is equipped with a heat shield, remove the heat shield bolts and remove the heat shield from the exhaust manifold. On some models, there is another heat shield protecting the steering gear assembly. If necessary, remove this heat shield as well.

17   Remove the heat shield mounting bracket fasteners and remove the bracket.

Note: *On the left side converter, remove the bolts and position aside the Electronic Power Assist Steering (EPAS) shield. On AWD models, remove the transaxle support insulator - anti-roll cover.*

18   Remove the catalyst upper mounting flange-to-exhaust manifold fasteners. If the threads are severely damaged or rusted, apply some penetrant to the threads and wait awhile before loosening them.

19   If equipped, remove the skid plate retainers and remove the skid plate.

20.2a The EVAP canister purge valve is located above the right end of the valve cover on four-cylinder models

20.2b EVAP canister purge valve (A) and electrical connector (B) (3.5L V6 engine)

20　Remove the lower mounting flange-to-exhaust pipe fasteners. If the threads are severely damaged or rusted, apply some penetrant to the threads and wait awhile before loosening them.

21　Pull the exhaust pipe down far enough to clear the lower end of the catalyst.

22　Remove the catalyst from the exhaust manifold.

23　Remove and discard the old gaskets between the exhaust manifold flange and the upper catalyst flange and, if equipped, between the lower catalyst flange and the exhaust pipe flange.

24　Installation is the reverse of removal. Use new flange gaskets.

20　Evaporative Emissions Control (EVAP) system - component replacement

EVAP canister purge valve

Note: *The canister purge valve on 2007 and earlier models (3.0L V6 engine) is located no a* *bracket near the power steering fluid reservoir.*

1　Disconnect the cable from the negative battery terminal (see Chapter 5).

2　Disconnect the electrical connector from the canister purge valve **(see illustrations)**.

3　Disconnect the EVAP line quick-connect fittings (see Chapter 4 for information on quick-connect fittings).

4　Remove the purge valve mounting fasteners and remove the assembly.

5　Installation is the reverse of removal. On V6 engines, use a new O-ring.

EVAP canister

Note: *The EVAP canister is located under the vehicle, towards the rear.*

6　Disconnect the cable from the negative battery terminal (see Chapter 5).

7　Raise the vehicle and support it securely on jackstands.

8　Remove the splash shield fasteners and remove the shield, if equipped **(see illustration)**.

9　Disconnect the electrical connector **(see illustration 20.10)** and the vapor hose from the EVAP canister vent solenoid dust separator.

10　Disconnect the two EVAP line quick-connect fittings **(see illustration)** from the EVAP canister (see Chapter 4 for information on quick-connect fittings).

11　Remove the canister mounting fasteners and remove the canister.

12　Installation is the reverse of removal.

EVAP canister vent solenoid and dust separator assembly

Note: *The EVAP canister vent solenoid is mounted on the EVAP canister. On 3.0L engines remove the EVAP canister vent tube-to-EVAP canister vent solenoid assembly.*

13　Remove the EVAP canister (see Steps 6 through 11).

14　Release the two lock tabs and remove the EVAP canister vent solenoid heat shield from the canister by pushing it straight down.

15　Disconnect the fuel vapor hose from the vent solenoid.

16　Release the lock tab and detach the vent solenoid and dust separator assembly from the EVAP canister.

17　Installation is the reverse of removal.

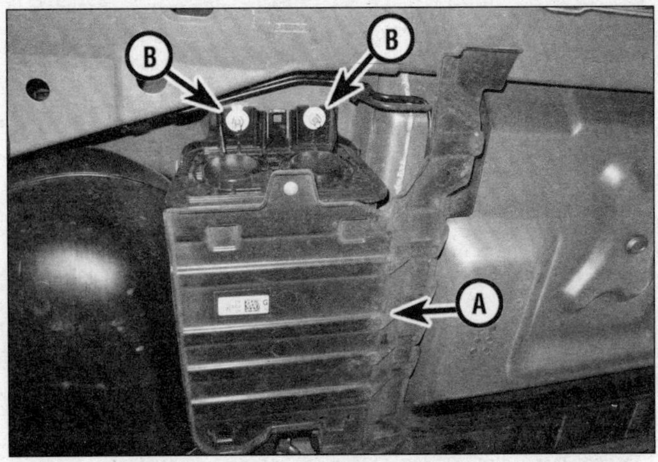

20.8 Remove the EVAP splash shield (A) and fasteners (B)

20.10 EVAP line quick-connect fittings (A) and EVAP canister vent solenoid electrical connector (B)

21.3 Location of the Fuel Rail Pressure (FRP) sensor - manifold removed for clarity

22.2 Location of the vent oil separator (four-cylinder engine)

22.8a On 3.0L V6 engines the hose is secured to the valve by a quick-connect fitting

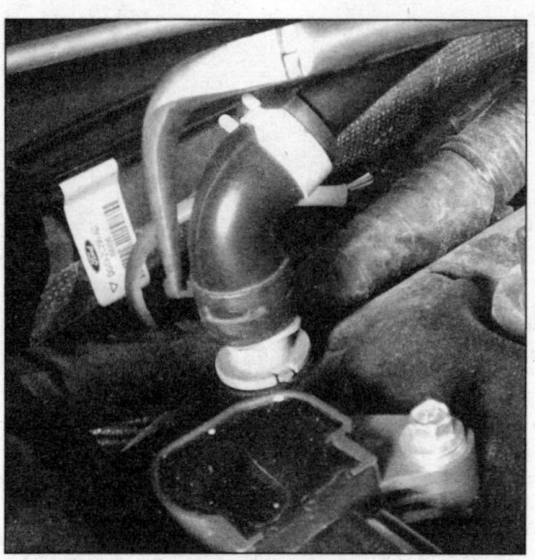

22.8b On 3.6L V6 engines the hose is secured to the valve with a clamp

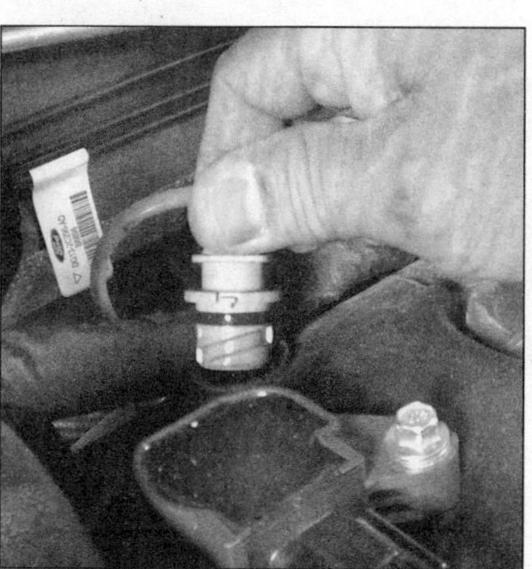

22.9 Twist the PCV valve counterclockwise and pull it from the vavle cover (3.5L engine shown, upper intake manifold removed for clarity)

21 Fuel Rail Pressure (FRP) sensor (four-cylinder models) - replacement

1   Relieve the fuel system pressure (see Chapter 4).
2   Remove the charge air cooler inlet tube (see Chapter 4).
3   Disconnect the FRP sensor electrical connector **(see illustration)**.
4   Unscrew and remove the FRP sensor.
5   Installation is the reverse of removal. Tighten the sensor to the torque listed in this Chapter's Specifications.

22 Positive Crankcase Ventilation (PCV) valve - replacement

Four-cylinder models

Note: *The PCV valve is an integral part of the crankcase vent oil separator, which is located on the front side of the engine block.*

1   Remove the intake manifold (see Chapter 2A).
2   Remove the oil vent separator mounting bolts **(see illustration)** and gasket.
3   Clean the engine block and install a new gasket to the separator.
4   Installation is the reverse of removal. Tighten the oil vent separator bolts to the torque listed in this Chapter's Specifications.

V6 models

Note: *On 3.0L engines, the PCV valve is located next to the EGR valve at the top of the engine.*
Note: *On 3.5L engines, the PCV valve is located on the rear valve cover. According to the manufacturer, the PCV valve must be replaced if it's removed.*

5   If you're working on a 3.5L V6 engine, access to the valve is easier if you remove the upper intake manifold (see Chapter 2B), but it is not absolutely necessary; it can be done by feel.
6   On 3.0L engines, remove the transaxle roll restrictor brace.
7   Disconnect the electrical connector from the valve, if equipped.

8   Disconnect the hose from the valve **(see illustration)**.
9   Turn the PCV valve counterclockwise and remove it from the valve cover.
10   Every time the PCV valve is removed, it must be replaced with a new unit, because the locking mechanism of the PCV valve is damaged by removal.
11   When installing the new PCV valve, make sure that the new valve is oriented correctly before screwing it into place, so that the terminal faces toward the wiring harness. If you install the new PCV valve so that it's facing in the wrong direction, you will have to unscrew it and once you do that, you must replace it again.

23 Exhaust Gas Recirculation (EGR) valve (3.0L engine) - replacement

Note: *The EGR valve is located at the left end of the intake manifold, behind the throttle body.*
1   Disconnect the cable from the negative battery terminal (see Chapter 5).

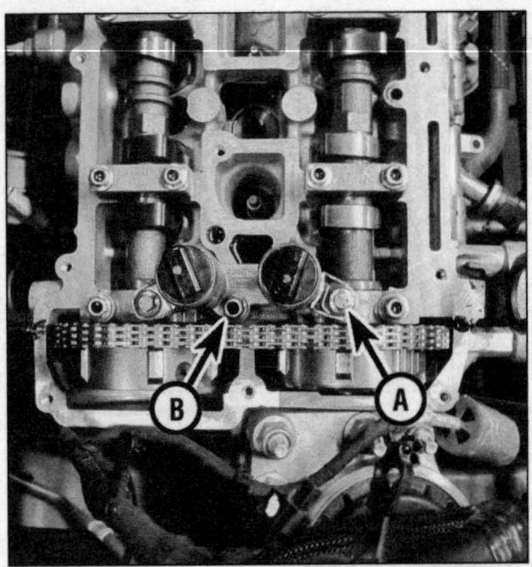

24.5 Intake (A) and Exhaust (B) VVT solenoid mounting bolts (four-cylinder engine shown)

2   Disconnect the electrical connector from the EGR valve.

3   Unscrew the tube nut fitting and disconnect the EGR pipe from the EGR valve.

4   Remove the EGR valve mounting bolts and remove the EGR valve.

5   Remove and discard the EGR valve gasket and clean the gasket mating surfaces of the intake manifold and EGR valve.

6   Installation is the reverse of removal. Use a new EGR valve gasket, and tighten the EGR valve mounting nuts securely.

24   Variable Valve Timing (VVT) system - description and solenoid replacement

1   The VVT system controls intake valve timing to increase engine torque in the low and mid-speed range, and to increase horsepower in the high-speed range.

2   The VVT system consists of the PCM-controlled Oil Control Valves (OCV), which are mounted on top of the cylinder head, and the VVT actuators, which are mounted on the front end of the camshafts.

3   The PCM-controlled OCVs vary the oil pressure in the VVT actuators, which continually varies the timing of both cams.

Note: *2.0L engines have two variable valve timing solenoids located under the valve cover. 3.5L engines have four solenoids, two located under each valve cover.*

4   Remove the valve cover(s).

5   Remove the solenoid mounting bolt(s) and remove the solenoid(s).

6   Installation is the reverse of removal. Tighten the valve solenoid mounting bolts to the torque listed in this Chapter's Specifications.

Chapter 7 Part A
Automatic transaxle

Contents

Specifications

General

Fluid type and capacity .... See Chapter 1

Torque specifications

Ft-lbs (unless otherwise indicated) **Nm**

Note: *One foot-pound (ft-lb) of torque is equivalent to 12 inch-pounds (in-lbs) of torque. Torque values below approximately 15 ft-lbs are expressed in inch-pounds, because most foot-pound torque wrenches are not accurate at these smaller values.*

	Ft-lbs	Nm
Subframe mounting bolts	See Chapter 10	
Fluid pan bolts	80 in-lbs	9
Torque converter-to-driveplate fasteners		
2007 and earlier models	27	37
2008 through 2012 models (slotted hole first)	41	56
2013 and later models		
Four-cylinder engine	30	40
V6 engine		
6F35 transaxle	30	40
6F50/55 transaxle (slotted hole first)	41	56
Transaxle-to-engine bolts	35	47
Transaxle mount		
2007 and earlier models	41	56
2008 and later models		
Mount-to-subframe bolts	41	56
Mount through-bolt	129	175
Bracket-to-transaxle		
Bolt	59	80
Nuts	46	62
Torque rod bolts		
2009 and earlier models	66	89
2010 and later models	76	103

1   General information

1   All information on the automatic transaxle is included in this Part of Chapter 7. The transfer case portion of the transaxle is covered in Chapter 7B.

2   Because of the complexity of the automatic transaxles and the specialized equipment necessary to perform most service operations, this Chapter contains only those procedures related to general diagnosis, adjustment and removal and installation.

3   If the transaxle requires major repair work, it should be left to a dealer service department or an automotive or transmission repair shop. Once properly diagnosed you can, however, remove and install the transaxle yourself and save the expense, even if the repair work is done by a transmission shop.

2   Diagnosis - general

1   Automatic transaxle malfunctions may be caused by five general conditions:

a) *Poor engine performance*
b) *Improper adjustments*
c) *Hydraulic malfunctions*
d) *Mechanical malfunctions*
e) *Malfunctions in the computer or its signal network*

2   Diagnosis of these problems should always begin with a check of the easily repaired items: fluid level and condition (see Chapter 1), shift cable adjustment and shift lever installation. Next, perform a road test to determine if the problem has been corrected or if more diagnosis is necessary. If the problem persists after the preliminary tests and corrections are completed, additional diagnosis should be performed by a dealer service department or other qualified transmission repair shop. On modern electronically-controlled automatic transaxles, a scan tool is helpful in retrieving trouble codes relating to the transaxle. Refer to the "Troubleshooting" Section at the front of this manual for information on symptoms of transaxle problems.

Preliminary checks

3   Drive the vehicle to warm the transaxle to normal operating temperature.

4   Check the fluid level as described in Chapter 1 :

- *If the fluid level is unusually low, add enough fluid to bring the level within the designated area of the dipstick, then check for external leaks (see following).*
- *If the fluid level is abnormally high, drain off the excess, then check the drained fluid for contamination by coolant. The presence of engine coolant in the automatic transmission fluid indicates that a failure has occurred in the internal radiator oil cooler walls that separate the coolant from the transmission fluid (see Chapter 3).*

- *If the fluid is foaming, drain it and refill the transaxle, then check for coolant in the fluid, or a high fluid level.*

5   Check the engine idle speed.

Note: *If the engine is malfunctioning, do not proceed with the preliminary checks until it has been repaired and runs normally.*

6   Check and adjust the shift cable, if necessary (see Section 4).

7   If hard shifting is experienced, inspect the shift cable under the steering column and at the manual lever on the transaxle (see Section 4).

Fluid leak diagnosis

8   Most fluid leaks are easy to locate visually. Repair usually consists of replacing a seal or gasket. If a leak is difficult to find, the following procedure may help.

9   Identify the fluid. Make sure it's transmission fluid and not engine oil or brake fluid (automatic transmission fluid is a deep red color).

10   Try to pinpoint the source of the leak. Drive the vehicle several miles, then park it over a large sheet of cardboard. After a minute or two, you should be able to locate the leak by determining the source of the fluid dripping onto the cardboard.

11   Make a careful visual inspection of the suspected component and the area immediately around it. Pay particular attention to gasket mating surfaces. A mirror is often helpful for finding leaks in areas that are hard to see.

12   If the leak still cannot be found, clean the suspected area thoroughly with a degreaser or solvent, then dry it thoroughly.

13   Drive the vehicle for several miles at normal operating temperature and varying speeds. After driving the vehicle, visually inspect the suspected component again.

14   Once the leak has been located, the cause must be determined before it can be properly repaired. If a gasket is replaced but the sealing flange is bent, the new gasket will not stop the leak. The bent flange must be straightened.

15   Before attempting to repair a leak, check to make sure that the following conditions are corrected or they may cause another leak.

Note: *Some of the following conditions cannot be fixed without highly specialized tools and expertise. Such problems must be referred to a qualified transmission shop or a dealer service department.*

Gasket leaks

16   Check the pan periodically. Make sure the bolts are tight, no bolts are missing, the gasket is in good condition and the pan is flat (dents in the pan may indicate damage to the valve body inside).

17   If the pan gasket is leaking, the fluid level or the fluid pressure may be too high, the vent may be plugged, the pan bolts may be too tight, the pan sealing flange may be warped, the sealing surface of the transaxle housing may be damaged, the gasket may be damaged or the transaxle casting may be cracked or porous. If sealant instead of gasket material has been used to form a seal between the pan and the transaxle housing, it may be the wrong type of sealant.

Seal leaks

18   If a transaxle seal is leaking, the fluid level or pressure may be too high, the vent may be plugged, the seal bore may be damaged, the seal itself may be damaged or improperly installed, the surface of the shaft protruding through the seal may be damaged or a loose bearing may be causing excessive shaft movement.

19   Make sure the dipstick tube seal is in good condition and the tube is properly seated. Periodically check the area around the sensors for leakage. If transmission fluid is evident, check the seals for damage.

Case leaks

20   If the case itself appears to be leaking, the casting is porous and will have to be repaired or replaced.

21   Make sure the oil cooler hose fittings are tight and in good condition.

Fluid comes out vent pipe or fill tube

22   If this condition occurs the possible causes are: the transaxle is overfilled; there is coolant in the fluid; the case is porous; the dipstick is incorrect; the vent is plugged or the drain-back holes are plugged.

3   Shift lever - replacement

Warning: *These models are equipped with a Supplemental Restraint System (SRS), more commonly known as airbags. Always disable the airbag system before working in the vicinity of any airbag system component to avoid the possibility of accidental deployment of the airbag(s), which could cause personal injury (see Chapter 12).*

Warning: *Do not use a memory saving device to preserve the PCM or radio memory when working on or near airbag system components.*

Floor shifter

Shift knob

2007 and earlier models

1   Move the shift knob lower bezel down and remove the screw on the front of the shift knob.

2   Lift upward on the shift knob and remove it.

3   Installation is the reverse of removal.

2008 through 2012 models

4   Remove the upper bezel of the floor console around the shifter (see Chapter 11).

5   If equipped with Traction Control System (TCS), disconnect the TCS electrical connector located below the indicator side of the shift lever assembly.

6   Slide the shift knob lower cover down to expose the screws. Remove the two screws in the knob assembly, then remove the

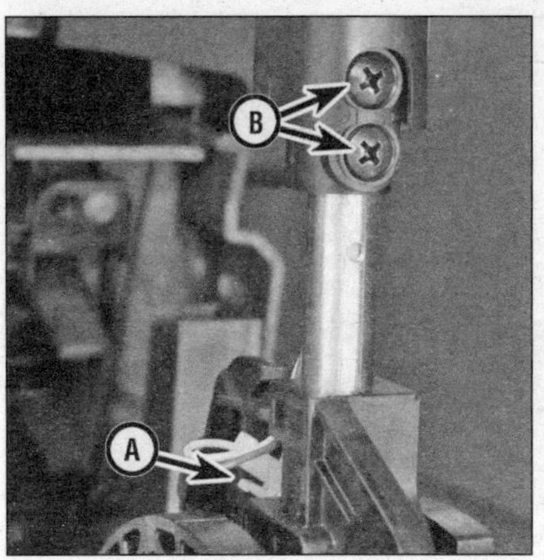

3.9 Shift lever electrical connector (A) and mounting screws (B)

3.13 Pry the cable end from the ballstud on the shifter

3.14 Pry the tabs forward to release the cable retainer from the console

knob while pulling out the TCS harness (if equipped).

7   Installation is the reverse of removal.

2013 and later models

8   Remove the upper shift lever bezel (see Chapter 11).

9   Pull up the shift knob boot and disconnect the electrical connector. Remove the two screws and pull the knob off the shaft **(see illustration)**.

10   Installation is the reverse of removal.

Shift lever assembly

11   Disconnect the cable from the negative battery terminal (see Chapter 5). Wait at least two minutes before proceeding.

12   Remove the floor console and center trim covers as needed to access the shift lever assembly components (see Chapter 11).

13   Use a trim tool to pry the cable end from the ballstud on the shifter **(see illustration)**.

14   Release the tabs on the sides of the shift cable and detach it from the console **(see illustration)**.

15   Disconnect the electrical connector and wire harness clips. Remove the carpet retainers from both sides of the shift lever assembly.

16   Remove the four shifter base bolts and remove the shift lever assembly from the vehicle.

17   Installation is the reverse of removal.

18   Check the shift cable adjustment (see Section 4) and adjust as necessary. Ensure the vehicle starts in Park and Neutral, and the back-up lights illuminate when in Reverse.

Column shifter

Shift lever

19   Remove the upper and lower steering column covers (see Chapter 11).

20   Disconnect the shift lever connector and harness clip.

21   Remove the shift lever screw and remove the shift lever from the vehicle, using care when removing the harness.

22   Installation is the reverse of removal.

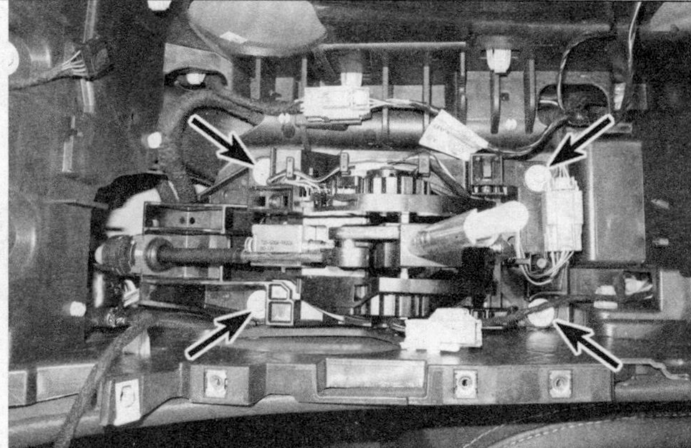

3.16 Remove the shift lever assembly bolts to remove the shifter

Shift lever assembly

23   Remove the shift lever (see Steps 19 through 21).

24   Remove the shift interlock cable from the shift lever assembly. Disconnect the shift cable from the shift lever assembly.

25   Remove the shift lever assembly mounting bolts and remove shift lever assembly.

26   Installation is the reverse of removal.

27   Check the shift cable adjustment (see Section 4) and adjust as necessary. Make sure the vehicle only starts in Park and Neutral, and the back-up lights come on when shifted into Reverse.

Paddle shifter

28   Disconnect the cable from the negative battery terminal (see Chapter 5). Wait at least two minutes before proceeding.

29   Remove the airbag module from the steering wheel (see Chapter 10).

30   Remove the steering wheel switch trim panel screws.

31   Disconnect the electrical connectors from the switch trim panel, then remove the trim panel.

32   Disconnect the electrical connectors from the paddle shifter.

33   Remove the two mounting screws and remove the paddle shifter.

34   Installation is the reverse of removal.

4   Shift cable - replacement and adjustment

Warning: *The models covered by this manual are equipped with Supplemental Restraint Systems (SRS), more commonly known as airbags. Always disarm the airbag system before working in the vicinity of any airbag system component to avoid the possibility of accidental deployment of the airbag, which could cause personal injury (see Chapter 12). Do not use a memory saving device to preserve the PCM or radio memory when working on or near airbag system components.*
Note: *This is a difficult procedure for the home mechanic, since replacement of the cables requires removal of the instrument panel and the HVAC housing under the instrument panel.*

Replacement

1   If the vehicle has just been driven, wait several hours to allow the engine to cool down before beginning this procedure. Disconnect both the negative and positive cables from the battery (see Chapter 5). Wait at least two minutes before proceeding.

2   Place the shifter in neutral.

3   Raise the vehicle on a hoist, or raise the front of the vehicle and support it securely on jackstands.

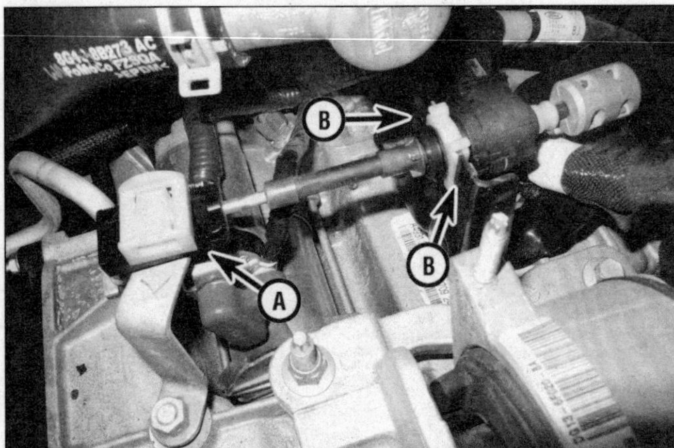

4.15 Pry the cable end from the ballstud on the shift control lever (A), then depress the tabs (B) and slide the cable housing out of the bracket

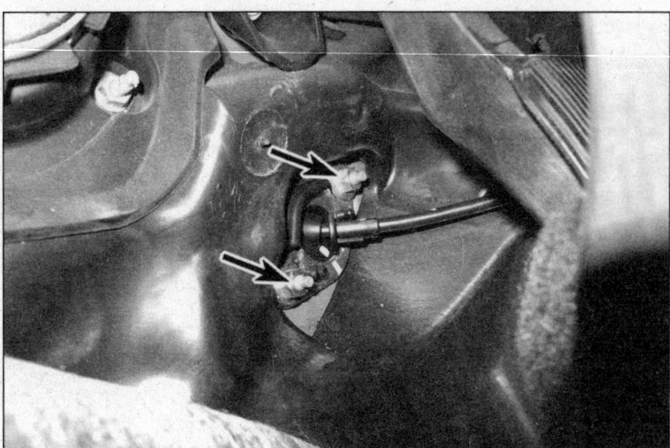

4.18 Shift cable grommet plate nuts

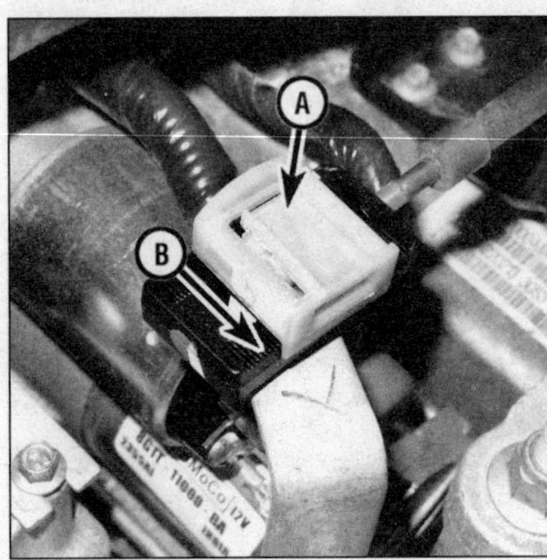

4.27 Pry up the release tab (A), then slide the lock tab out (B) to release (2008 and later models)

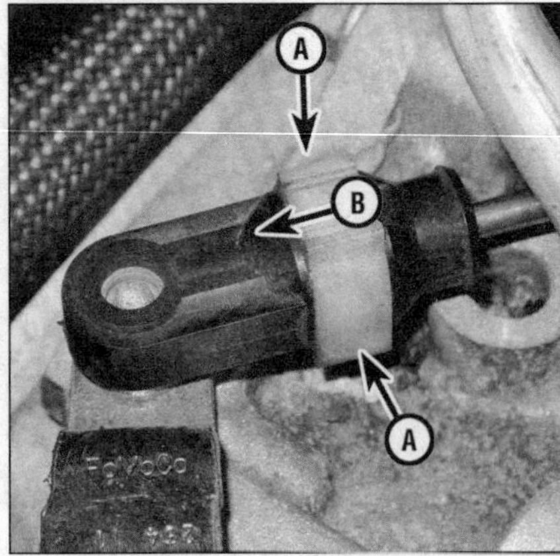

4.28 Pry the lock tabs out (A) then slide the lock forward (B) to release

4   Remove the air filter housing (see Chapter 4).

Floor shifter

5   Remove the center console and trim to access the shift cable to disconnect from the shift lever (see Chapter 11).
6   Remove the driver's side knee bolster (see Chapter 11).
7   Use a trim tool to pry the cable eye from the ballstud on the shifter (see Section 3).
8   Release the tabs on the sides of the shift cable and detach it from the console (see Section 3).
9   On 2007 and earlier models, remove the two instrument panel brace bolts at the floor, then slide the cable under the brace and remove it.

Column shifter

10   Remove the upper and lower steering column covers (see Chapter 11).
11   Remove the center dash bezel and driver's side trim panel (see Chapter 11).
12   Use a trim tool to pry the cable eye from the ballstud on the shifter.

13   Release the tabs on the sides of the shift cable and detach it from the bracket.

All models

14   Remove the insulation from the floor area under the center of the instrument panel to access the fasteners securing the cable grommet to the floorpan. Remove the fasteners securing the transaxle cable plate/grommet.
15   To disconnect the shift cable at the transaxle control lever, pop the cable end off of the lever ballstud **(see illustration)**.
16   Squeeze the retaining tab(s) and detach the cable housing from the mounting bracket on the transaxle.
17   Disconnect any cable retainers along the length of the cable.
18   Remove the grommet plate nuts from the floorpan studs below the HVAC housing **(see illustration)**.
19   Pull the shift cable through the floor from the inside, passing it under and to the left of the air duct that leads to the rear seats.
Note: *The grommet is integral to the cable assembly.*
20   Installation is the reverse of removal. Adjust the new cable after installation (see following).

Adjustment

Note: *The transaxle end of the shift cable is equipped with an adjuster mechanism.*
21   Set the parking brake, then disconnect the cable from the negative battery terminal (see Chapter 5).
22   Remove the air filter housing (see Chapter 4).
23   Place the shifter in Drive.
24   Pop the cable off of the shift lever ballstud **(see illustration 4.15)**.
25   Manually move the shift arm at the transaxle clockwise until it stops, then rotate the lever counterclockwise one click.
26   On 2007 and earlier models, slide the release tab toward the cable end to unlock it and pull out the adjusting tab.
27   On 2008 and later models, carefully pry up on the the release tab, then pull up the lock tab **(see illustration)**.
28   On 2013 and later models without paddle shift, pry the lock tabs out and slide the lock forward to release **(see illustration)**.
29   Slide the shift lever cable end until the cable is aligned with the control lever.
30   Reconnect the cable end to the manual lever ballstud, with the lock still released.
31   Slide back the lock on the adjuster.
Note: *Make sure the adjuster is locked and the cable is securely seated onto the ball stud.*
32   Install any remaining components, then apply the parking brake, start the engine, and shift into each range to verify the adjustment is correct.

---

5   Automatic transaxle - removal and installation

Warning: *Wait until the engine is completely cool before beginning this procedure.*

Removal

1   Loosen the front wheel lug nuts. Place the vehicle on a hoist or raise and support the front of the vehicle on jackstands. Remove the

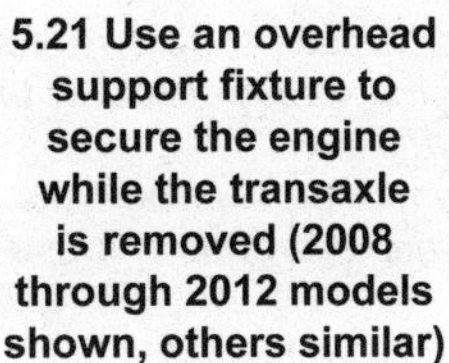

5.21 Use an overhead support fixture to secure the engine while the transaxle is removed (2008 through 2012 models shown, others similar)

5.32 Torque converter cover retainers (2013 and later model shown, others similar)

wheels. Have an assistant depress the brake pedal, then loosen the driveaxle/hub nuts.

2   Drain the transaxle fluid into a suitable container for recycling (see Chapter 1).

3   Drain the cooling system (see Chapter 1).

4   Remove the battery and battery tray (see Chapter 5).

5   Remove the air filter housing and duct (see Chapter 4), then remove the housing bracket bolts and bracket. Remove the throttle body intake hose.

6   Disconnect the shift cable from the shift lever and housing from the bracket (see Section 4). If possible, remove the bracket from the transaxle with the cable attached.

2007 and earlier models

7   Remove the wiper arms and wiper cowl panel (see Chapter 11).

8   Remove the upper engine torque rod bracket.

9   On non-CVT vehicles, disconnect the Transaxle Control Module (TCM) harness electrical connector at the transmission range sensor.

10   Disconnect the ground straps and remove the bolts holding the electrical harness to the transaxle.

11   On CVT vehicles, unbolt the auxiliary electric coolant pump and secure it to the side without disconnecting the coolant hoses.

12   Remove the upper engine torque rod mount from the engine.

13   Remove the PCV hose and disconnect the throttle body vacuum lines. Remove the bolt securing the power steering hose bracket to the engine.

14   Remove the starter (see Chapter 5).

15   Remove the bolt and disconnect the large ground cable from the transaxle.

16   On CVT vehicles, disconnect the transaxle connector at the firewall by rotating counterclockwise and disconnect the harness from the transaxle.

17   Remove the four upper transaxle bolts.

18   Remove the driveaxles (see Chapter 8).

19   Disconnect the oxygen sensor connectors and remove the exhaust y-pipe (see Chapter 4).

20   Remove the knock sensor(s) (see Chapter 6). Remove the knock sensor harness from the transaxle.

21   Attach an engine support fixture to the lifting hook at the transaxle end of the engine **(see illustration)**. If no hook is provided, use a bolt of the proper size and thread pitch to attach the support fixture chain to a hole at the end of the cylinder head.

22   Disconnect the charcoal canister purge valve lines.

23   Disconnect any power steering hose brackets from the transaxle or subframe.

24   Drain the cooling system (see Chapter 1), then disconnect the lower radiator hose and secure it out of the way.

25   Remove the steering gear-to-subframe mounting bolts and secure the steering gear to the vehicle body (see Chapter 10).

26   Remove the left and right inner fender liners and disconnect all electrical harnesses from the subframe.

27   Remove the right and left motor mount nuts from the subframe, and remove the transaxle torque rod bracket from the transaxle. Remove the transaxle mount subframe bolts.

28   Disconnect the stabilizer bar end links from the struts, and disconnect the lower control arm balljoints from the steering knuckle (see Chapter 10).

29   Support the subframe with two floor jacks. Remove the subframe brackets the subframe mounting bolts.

30   Slowly lower the subframe, checking for any harnesses, hoses or components still attached and disconnect them as necessary. Remove the subframe from the vehicle.

31   Remove the two upper bolts and bracket bolts and remove the catalytic converter.

32   Remove the torque converter access cover retainers and remove the cover **(see illustration)**.

33   Mark the relationship of the torque converter to the driveplate **(see illustration)**. Remove the converter mounting nuts.

34   Remove the bolt(s) and disconnect the transaxle cooling lines from the transaxle and remove the cooling line bracket.

35   Support the transaxle with a jack - preferably a transmission jack made for this purpose (available at most tool rental yards). Safety chains will help steady the transaxle on the jack.

36   Remove the remaining bolts securing the transaxle to the engine.

37   Move the transaxle away from the engine to disengage it from the engine block dowel pins. Carefully lower the transmission jack to the floor and remove the transaxle. Ensure the torque converter is secure in the transaxle and does not fall out. Transfer the transaxle components to the new transaxle before installation.

2008 and later V6 models

38   Remove the upper intake manifold (see Chapter 2B).

39   Remove the starter (see Chapter 5).

40   Disconnect the auxiliary coolant pump bracket, without disconnecting the hoses, and secure the pump out of the way.

41   Disconnect the transaxle connector and harness retainer from the transaxle.

42   Remove the transaxle dipstick tube nut, rotate the tube counterclockwise and remove it.

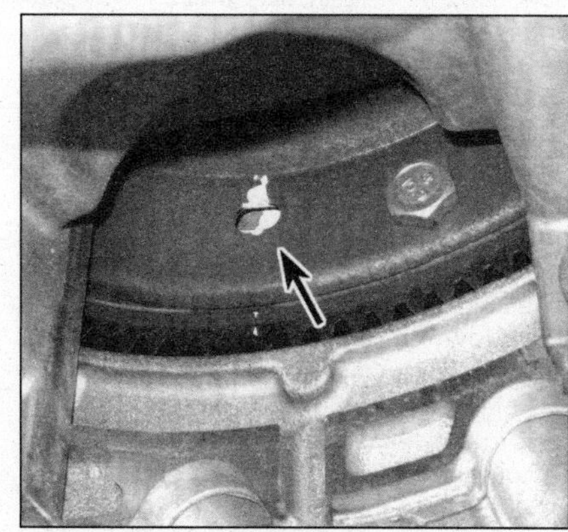

5.33 Mark the torque converter and the driveplate for alignment during installation (2013 and later model shown, others similar)

43   Remove the upper transaxle-to-engine bolts.

44   Attach an engine support fixture to the lifting hook at the transaxle end of the engine **(see illustration 5.21)**. If no hook is provided, use a bolt of the proper size and thread pitch to attach the support fixture chain to a hole at the end of the cylinder head.

45   Remove the front wheels, inner fender liners and splash shield.

46   Detach the power steering line retainers from the subframe. Remove the left and right half-shafts (see Chapter 8).

47   Disconnect the oxygen sensor connectors and harnesses and remove the exhaust y-pipe (see Chapter 4).

48   Remove the bolts attaching the steering gear to the subframe and secure it to the vehicle (see Chapter 10).

49   Remove the stabilizer bar brackets from the subframe and secure the stabilizer bar to the vehicle (see Chapter 10).

50   Disconnect the torque rod bracket from the transaxle (see Section 8).

51   On AWD models, remove the transfer case (see Chapter 8).

52   Disconnect the lower control arm balljoints from the steering knuckles (see Chapter 10).

53   Support the subframe using two floor jacks. Remove the subframe brackets and the subframe mounting bolts.

54   Slowly lower the subframe, checking for any harnesses, hoses or components still attached and disconnect them as necessary. Remove the subframe from the vehicle.

55   Slowly lower the subframe and check for any harnesses, hoses or components still attached and disconnect them as necessary. Remove the subframe from the vehicle.

56   Remove the torque converter access cover by removing the two retainers **(see illustration 5.32)**.

57   Mark the relationship of the torque converter to the driveplate **(see illustration 5.33)**. Remove the converter mounting bolts.

58   Remove the transaxle cooler line covers and disconnect the cooler lines from the bypass valve using a cooler line disconnect tool or equivalent.

59   Support the transaxle with a jack - preferably a transmission jack made for this purpose (available at most tool rental yards). Safety chains will help steady the transaxle on the jack.

60   Remove the transaxle mount through-bolt. Lower the transaxle about 2 inches, then remove the mount bracket from the transaxle.

61   Remove the remaining transaxle-to-engine bolts.

62   Move the transaxle away from the engine to disengage it from the engine block dowel pins. Carefully lower the transmission jack to the floor and remove the transaxle. Ensure the torque converter is secure in the transaxle and does not fall out. Transfer transaxle components to the new transaxle before installation.

2013 and later four-cylinder models

63   Remove the transaxle cooler line-to-transaxle nuts and disconnect the lines.

Note: *Ensure the cooling line seals do not get stuck in the transaxle. Inspect the transaxle case and remove any seals stuck inside.*

64   Remove the temperature control valve and transaxle fluid warmer mounting nuts and secure them out of the way.

65   Disconnect any harness clips from top of the transaxle and remove the upper transaxle-to-engine bolts.

66   Remove the starter (see Chapter 5), then remove the insulator.

67   Mark the relationship of the torque converter to the driveplate **(see illustration 5.33)**. Remove the converter mounting nuts.

Caution: *Only rotate the engine in a clockwise direction or engine damage may occur.*

68   Disconnect the torque rod bracket from the transaxle.

69   Disconnect the steering column coupler at the steering gear.

70   Remove the stabilizer bar links from the strut assemblies.

71   Remove the nuts and disconnect the tie-rod ends from the steering arms.

72   Disconnect the lower control arm balljoints from the steering knuckle (see Chapter 10).

73   Support the subframe using a pair of floor jacks. Remove the subframe brackets and the subframe mounting bolts.

74   Slowly lower the subframe, checking for any harnesses, hoses or components still attached and disconnect them as necessary. Remove the subframe from the vehicle.

75   Remove the driveaxles (see Chapter 8).

76   Disconnect any brackets securing the transaxle cooling lines. Remove the catalytic converter bracket nuts and remove the bracket.

77   Support the transaxle with a jack - preferably a transmission jack made for this purpose (available at most tool rental yards). Safety chains will help steady the transaxle on the jack.

78   Remove the transaxle mount through-bolt, then remove the mount bracket from the transaxle.

79   Remove the remaining transaxle-to-engine bolts.

80   Move the transaxle away from the engine to disengage it from the engine block dowel pins. Carefully lower the transmission jack to the floor and remove the transaxle. Ensure the torque converter is secure in the transaxle and does not fall out. Transfer transaxle components to the new transaxle before installation.

Installation

81   Installation is the reverse of removal, noting the following:

a) *As the torque converter is reinstalled, ensure that the drive tangs at the center of the torque converter hub engage with the recesses in the automatic transaxle fluid pump inner gear. This can be confirmed by turning the torque converter while pushing it towards the transaxle. If it isn't fully engaged, it will clunk into place.*

b) *When installing the transaxle, make sure the matchmarks you made on the torque converter and driveplate line up.*

c) *Install all of the driveplate-to-torque converter nuts before tightening any of them.*

d) *Tighten the driveplate-to-torque converter nuts to the torque listed in this Chapter's Specifications.*

e) *Tighten the transaxle mounting bolts to the torque listed in this Chapter's Specifications.*

f) *Tighten the subframe mounting bolts to the torque listed in the Chapter 10 Specifications.*

g) *Tighten the driveaxle/hub nuts to the torque listed in the Chapter 8 Specifications.*

h) *Tighten the wheel lug nuts to the torque listed in the Chapter 1 Specifications.*

i) *Fill the transaxle with the correct type and amount of automatic transmission fluid (see Chapter 1).*

j) *Adjust the shift cable (see Section 4).*

---

6   Automatic transaxle overhaul - general information

1   In the event of a problem occurring, it will be necessary to establish whether the fault is electrical, mechanical or hydraulic in nature, before repair work can be contemplated. Diagnosis requires detailed knowledge of the transaxle's operation and construction, as well as access to specialized test equipment, and so is deemed to be beyond the scope of this manual. It is therefore essential that problems with the automatic transaxle are referred to a dealer service department or other qualified repair facility for assessment.

2   Note that a faulty transaxle should not be removed before the vehicle has been diagnosed by a knowledgeable technician equipped with the proper tools, as troubleshooting must be performed with the transaxle installed in the vehicle.

---

7   Driveaxle oil seals - replacement

1   Oil leaks frequently occur due to wear of the driveaxle oil seals. Replacement of these seals is relatively easy, since the repair can be performed without removing the transaxle from the vehicle.

2   Driveaxle oil seals are located at the sides of the transaxle, where the driveaxles are attached. If leakage at the seal is suspected, raise the vehicle and support it securely on jackstands. If the seal is leaking, lubricant will be found on the sides of the transaxle, below the seals.

3   Remove the driveaxles (see Chapter 8).

4   Use a screwdriver or prybar to carefully pry the oil seal out of the transaxle bore.

5   If the oil seal cannot be removed with a screwdriver or prybar, a special oil seal

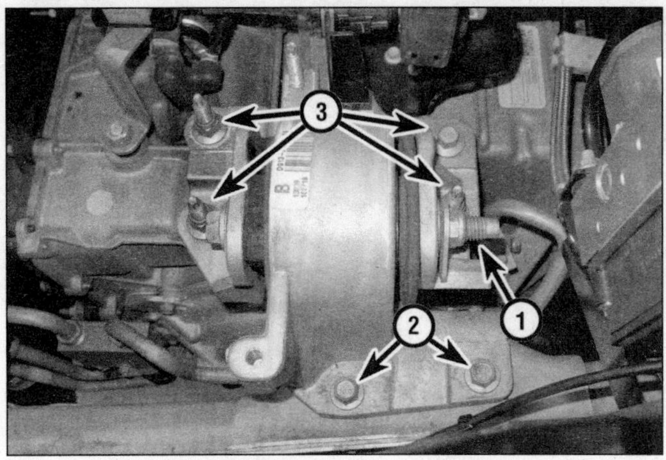

8.8 Transaxle mount details

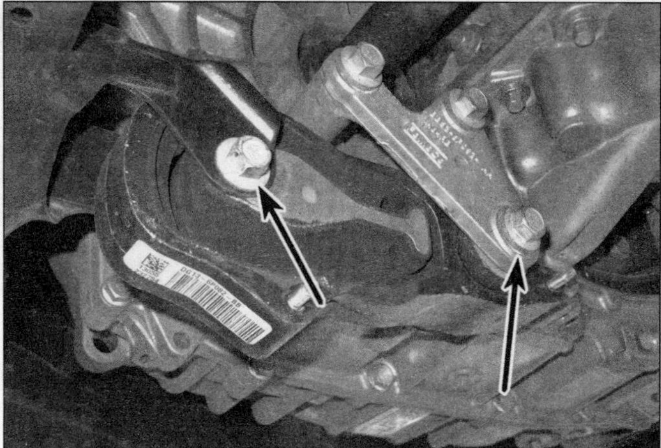

8.13 Torque rod mounting bolts (2010 and later models shown, others similar)

1   *Through-bolt/nut*
2   *Mount-to-chassis bolts*

3   *Mount bracket-to-transaxle nuts*

removal tool (available at auto parts stores) will be required.

6   Using a large section of pipe or a large deep socket (slightly smaller than the outside diameter of the seal) as a drift, install the new oil seal. Drive it into the bore squarely and make sure it's completely seated. Coat the seal lip with transaxle lubricant.

7   Install the driveaxle(s). Be careful not to damage the lip of the new seal with the inboard splines of the driveaxle.

---

8   Transaxle mount - replacement

---

1   Insert a large screwdriver or prybar between the mount and the transaxle and pry up/down (mount) or left/right (torque rod).

2   The transaxle should not move excessively away from the mount. If it does, replace the mount.

Mount

2007 and earlier models

3   Loosen the left front wheel lug nuts. Raise the front of the vehicle and support it securely on jackstands. Remove the left front wheel and inner fender liner (see Chapter 11).

4   Remove the transaxle mount-to-subframe and mount-to-transaxle case mounting bolts, and remove the mount.

5   Installation is the reverse of removal.

2008 and later models

6   Remove the battery and battery tray (see Chapter 5).

7   Remove the air filter housing (see Chapter 4)

8   Supporting the transaxle with a floor jack or engine support, remove the through-bolt nut and bolt and the mount-to-chassis bolts, then remove the mount **(see illustration)**. It may be necessary to raise the transaxle slightly to provide enough clearance to remove the mount.

9   Remove the remaining mount bolts.

10   Installation is the reverse of removal.

Note: *Install all of the mount fasteners before tightening any of them.*

Torque rod

11   Raise the front of the vehicle and support it securely on jackstands. Remove the splash shield.

12   Disconnect and lower the exhaust y-pipe (see Chapter 10 , **illustration 19.22)**.

13 Remove the torque rod bolts and remove the torque rod **(see illustration)**.

14 Installation is the reverse of removal.

Notes

Chapter 7 Part B
Transfer case

Contents

Specifications

Transfer case fluid type .... See Chapter 1

Torque specifications — Ft-lbs (unless otherwise indicated) — Nm

Note: *One foot-pound (ft-lb) of torque is equivalent to 12 inch-pounds (in-lbs) of torque. Torque values below approximately 15 ft-lbs are expressed in inch-pounds, because most foot-pound torque wrenches are not accurate at these smaller values.*

	Ft-lbs (unless otherwise indicated)	Nm
Transfer case output shaft flange nut		
2007 and earlier models	74	100
2008 and later mdoels	See Section 2	
Transfer case-to-transaxle bolts	66	89
Transfer case support bracket bolts		
2007 and earlier models	41	56
2008 and later models	35	47
Roll-restrictor bracket bolts	66	89
Roll-restrictor through-bolt	76	103
Transfer case fill plug		
2007 and earlier models	36	49
2008 and later models	177 in-lbs	20
Transfer case cooler fasteners		
Housing-to-transfer case	106 in-lbs	12
Housing-to-cooler lines	18	24

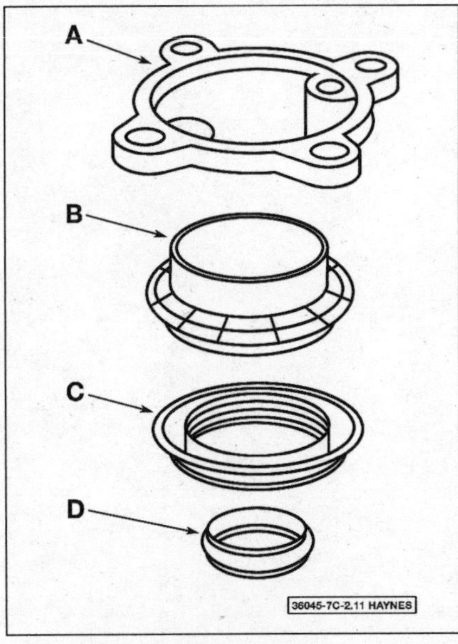

2.15 Rear output shaft seal details

A   *Driveshaft companion flange*
B   *Output shaft seal*
C   *Seal deflector*
D   *Collapsible bearing spacer*

1   General information

1   Some models equipped with V6 engines are equipped with optional All Wheel Drive (AWD). The transfer case sends power through a driveshaft that delivers the torque to a rear differential and two rear driveaxles. The AWD control module will shift into AWD when the PCM initiates the need due to differences in wheelslip speed between the front and rear wheels. The system requires no driver input to operate, thus there is no select button on the instrument panel.
2   Due to the complexity of the transfer case covered in this manual and the need for specialized equipment to perform most service operations, this Chapter contains only seal replacement and removal and installation procedures.
3   If a leak is noticed, remember that a red leak is from the transaxle and black/brown gear lube is from the transfer case. Fresh transfer case fluid has a harsh smell - do not mistake that for contaminated fluid.
4   The transfer case fluid is not normally serviced, so there is no drain plug. To completely drain the transfer case, it must be removed from the vehicle.
5   If the transfer case requires major repair work, it must be replaced as a unit.

2   Transfer case rear output shaft oil seal - removal and installation

1   Raise the vehicle and support it securely on jackstands.

2007 and earlier models

2   Remove the driveshaft (see Chapter 8).
3   Mark the relative positions of the pinion, nut and flange.
4   Remove the nut and companion flange. If necessary, use a puller whose bolt-holes can be attached to two, three or all four of the flange's driveshaft bolt holes. Tighten the puller center bolt to press the flange off the shaft.
5   Pry out the seal with a screwdriver or a seal removal tool. Don't damage the seal bore.
6   Lubricate the lips of the new seal with multi-purpose grease and tap it evenly into position using a seal installer or a large deep socket as a drift, install the new oil seal. Drive it into the bore squarely and make sure it's completely seated.
7   Align the mating marks made before disassembly and install the companion flange. If necessary, tighten the pinion nut to draw the flange into place.
8   Tighten the output flange nut to the torque listed in this Chapter's Specifications
9   Match the mating marks on the flange and install the driveshaft (see Chapter 8). Top-off the transfer case fluid as necessary (see Chapter 1).

2008 and later models

10   Disconnect the muffler-to-"y" exhaust pipe and support the resonator.
11   Mark the positions of the output shaft and driveshaft flange and remove the driveshaft (see Chapter 8).
12   Using a beam or dial type inch-pound torque wrench, measure the torque required to rotate the pinion (vehicle in neutral). Record the torque reading for later.
13   Count the number of threads visible between the end of the nut and the end of the pinion shaft and record it for use later.
14   Remove the flange mounting nut using a two-pin spanner to hold the pinion flange while loosening the lock nut.
15   Remove the companion flange **(see illustration)**. If necessary, use a puller whose bolt-holes can be attached to two, three or all four of the flange's driveshaft bolt holes. Tighten the puller center bolt to press the flange off the shaft.
16   Pry out the seal with a screwdriver or a seal removal tool. Don't damage the seal bore. Remove the seal deflector.
17   Remove the collapsible bearing spacer.
18   Install a new collapsible spacer.
19   Install the seal deflector. Lubricate the lips of the new seal with multi-purpose grease and tap it evenly into position using a seal installer or a large deep socket as a drift. Drive it into the bore squarely and make sure it's completely seated.
20   Align the mating marks and install the flange on the output shaft and install a NEW nut.
21   Tighten the NEW nut carefully until the original number of threads are exposed.
22   Referring to the rotational torque mea-

sured in Step 12, tighten the nut, in small increments, until the recorded rotational torque reading is achieved.
Caution: *If you exceed the original torque reading by more than 3 in-lbs, the assembly will need to be taken apart again to install a new collapsible spacer.*
23   Align the mating marks on the flange and install the driveshaft (see Chapter 8). Top-off the transfer case fluid as necessary (see Chapter 1).
Caution: *All driveshaft flange and support bolts must be replaced with NEW fasteners.*

3   Transfer case driveaxle oil seal (right side) - removal and installation

Note: *The driveaxle oil seal may also be referred to as the cover seal (for parts purposes).*
1   Loosen the right front wheel lug nuts, raise the vehicle and support it securely on jackstands.
2   Have an assistant depress the brake pedal, then break the hub nut loose with a socket and large breaker bar.
3   Remove the right front wheel and the inner fender splash shield (see Chapter 11).
4   Remove the right driveaxle and intermediate shaft (see Chapter 8).
5   Carefully remove the seal deflector and seal. There are several types of seal removal tools. The manufacturer recommends using a slide-hammer tool with an internal-expanding type of seal-puller. Using a long, threaded extension on the slide-hammer allows the seal to be removed without removing the exhaust system.
Note: *On 2008 and later models, there is a non-servicable bearing behind the deflector.*
6   Lubricate the lips of the new seal with multi-purpose grease and tap it evenly into position using a seal installer or a large deep socket as a drift. Drive it into the bore squarely and make sure it's completely seated.
7   Install a new seal deflector.
8   Install the intermediate shaft and driveaxle (see Chapter 8).
9   The remainder of installation is the reverse of removal. Top-off the transfer case fluid, if necessary (see Chapter 1).

4   Transfer case driveaxle cover seal - removal and installation

Note: *This procedure applies to 2008 and later models only.*
1   Remove the right side transfer case driveaxle oil seal (see Section 3).
2   Carefully remove the cover seal. There are several types of seal removal tools. The manufacturer recommends using a slide-hammer tool with an internal-expanding type of seal-puller. Using a long, threaded extension on the slide-hammer allows the seal to

be removed without removing the exhaust system.

Note: *There is a non-servicable bearing behind the deflector.*

3   Lubricate the lips of the new seal with multi-purpose grease and tap it evenly into position using a seal installer or a large deep socket as a drift. Drive it into the bore squarely and make sure it's completely seated.

4   Install a NEW transfer case driveaxle oil seal and deflector (see Section 3).

5   The remainder of installation is the reverse of removal. Top-off the transfer case fluid, if necessary (see Chapter 1).

5   Transfer case input shaft oil seal - removal and installation

1   Remove the transfer case (see Section 7).

2   Carefully remove the oil slinger and seal. There are several types of seal removal tools. The manufacturer recommends using a slide-hammer tool with an internal-expanding type of seal-puller. Using a long, threaded extension on the slide-hammer allows the seal to be removed without removing the exhaust system.

3   Lubricate the lips of the new seal with multi-purpose grease and tap it evenly into position using a seal installer or a large deep socket as a drift. Drive it into the bore squarely and make sure it's completely seated.

4   Lubricate the lip of the new seal with multi-purpose grease, then install a new oil slinger.

5   Install the transfer case (see Section 7).

6   The remainder of installation is the reverse of removal. Check the transfer case lubricant level and add some, if necessary, to bring it to the appropriate level (see Chapter 1).

6   Transfer case cooler - removal and installation

Note: *This procedure applies to 2013 and later models only.*

1   Raise the vehicle and support it securely on jackstands.

2   Remove the rear bank catalytic converter (see Chapter 4).

3   Remove the transfer case temperature sensor harness cover fasteners and remove the cover.

4   Disconnect the harness from the transfer case cooler housing, and remove the transfer case temperature sensor at the bottom of the cooler housing.

5   Using a drain pan to catch any fluid, remove the transfer case cooler line mounting bolts and disconnect the lines from the cooler.

6   Remove the remaining cooler housing-to-transfer case fasteners and remove the cooler housing.

7   Discard the cooler housing gasket.

8   Clean and inspect the cooler housing and transfer case mating surfaces.

9   Installation is the reverse of removal, noting the following:

 a) *Install a NEW gasket for the cooler housing.*

 b) *Tighten the fasteners to the torque listed in this Chapter's Specifications.*

 c) *Install new cooler line seals.*

 d) *Refill the transfer case with the proper type and amount of fluid (see Chapter 1).*

7   Transfer case - removal and installation

Removal

1   Loosen the front wheel lug nuts (on 2008 and later models, only loosen the right front wheel lug nuts). Raise the front of the vehicle and support it securely on jackstands.

2   Have an assistant depress the brake pedal. On 2007 and earlier models, break the left and right driveaxle/hub nuts loose with a socket and large breaker bar. On 2008 and later models, only break the right driveaxle/hub nut loose.

3   Remove both wheels (2007 and earlier models) or the right wheel (2008 and later models).

4   Remove the engine undercover and splash shields as necessary for access.

2007 and earlier models

5   Remove the driveaxles (see Chapter 8).

6   Remove the front and rear exhaust pipe nuts and remove the catalytic converter and pipe.

7   Mark the positions of the driveshaft and output shaft flanges before removal. Unbolt the driveshaft center support bracket and front portion of the driveshaft (see Chapter 8); suspend it from a piece of wire (don't let it hang from the center support bearing).

8   If equipped, remove the upper transfer case bracket bolts and bracket.

9   Remove the four transfer case bolts.

10   To remove the transfer case from the vehicle, push the output flange upwards, then rotate the output flange while removing the transfer case from the transaxle.

2008 and later models

11   Mark the positions of the driveshaft and output shaft flanges before removal. Unbolt the front portion of the driveshaft (see Chapter 8) and suspend it from a piece of wire (don't let it hang from the center support bearing).

12   Remove the right driveaxle and intermediate shaft (see Chapter 8). Remove the right-side catalytic converter (see Chapter 6).

13   If equipped, disconnect the oil cooler lines from the oil cooler housing.

14   Disconnect any electrical connectors or harnesses attached to the transfer case.

15   Remove the roll-restrictor mount fasteners and mount.

16   Remove the two bolts securing the transfer case to the support bracket.

17   Remove the three bolts securing the transfer case support bracket to the engine.

18   Support the transfer case with a suitable jack.

19   Working on the right side of the transfer case, remove the three transfer case-to-transaxle mounting bolts.

20   Working on the left side, remove the final two mounting bolts (bellhousing-to-transfer case).

21   To remove the transfer case from the vehicle, push the output flange upwards, then rotate the output flange while removing the transfer case from the transaxle.

Installation

22   Installation is the reverse of removal, noting the following:

 a) *Install a new compression seal to the case.*

 b) *Tighten the NEW driveshaft fasteners to the torque listed in the Chapter 8 Specifications.*

 c) *Tighten the transfer case fasteners to the torque listed in this Chapter's Specifications.*

 d) *Refill the transfer case with the proper type and amount of lubricant (see Chapter 1).*

 e) *Tighten the wheel lug nuts to the torque listed in the Chapter 1 Specifications.*

Notes

Chapter 8   Driveline

Contents

Specifications

Torque specifications

Ft-lbs (unless otherwise indicated)   **Nm**

Note: *One foot-pound (ft-lb) of torque is equivalent to 12 inch-pounds (in-lbs) of torque. Torque values below approximately 15 ft-lbs are expressed in inch-pounds, because most foot-pound torque wrenches are not accurate at these smaller values.*

Driveaxles

	Ft-lbs	Nm
Driveaxle/hub nut		
Front driveaxle	258	350
Rear driveaxle (AWD models)		
2007 and earlier models	148	200
2008 and later models	258	350
Intermediate shaft support bearing bracket nuts		
2007 and earlier models	20	27
2008 and later models	18	25

Driveshaft (AWD models)

	Ft-lbs	Nm
Driveshaft flange bolts at transfer case	18	25
Driveshaft center support bearing		
Bracket-to-vehicle	22	30
Bracket-to-bearing	177 lb-in	20
Driveshaft-to-differential pinion flange bolts	18	25
Exhaust crossmember bolts	22	30

Rear differential (AWD models)

	Ft-lbs	Nm
2007 and earlier models		
Differential cross-bracket bolts	46	63
Differential-to-front insulator bolt	66	90
Differential-to-rear insulator bolts	81	110
Differential pinion nut	74	100
2008 and later models		
Differential-to-front insulator bracket bolts	66	90
Differential-to-side insulator bracket bolts	66	90
Differential insulator bracket-to-subframe	66	90
Differential pinion nut	180	244

2.5 Using a drive hub remover to push the driveaxle out of the hub splines

2.7a Remove the nuts attaching the right-side intermediate shaft support bearing to the bracket

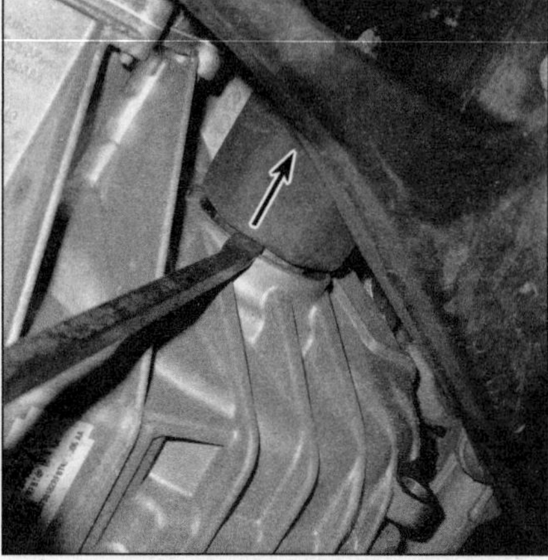

2.7b Carefully pry the inner end of the left-side driveaxle from the transaxle

1 General Information

1   The information in this Chapter deals with the components from the rear of the engine to the drive wheels, except for the transaxle, which is dealt with in the previous Chapter.
2   Since nearly all the procedures covered in this Chapter involve working under the vehicle, make sure it's securely supported on sturdy jackstands or on a hoist where the vehicle can be easily raised and lowered.

2 Driveaxles - removal and installation

Warning: *Wait until the engine is completely cool before beginning this procedure.*
Note: *It is recommended to replace the drive-axle seal when the driveaxle is replaced.*

Front
Removal
1   Loosen the wheel lug nuts, raise the vehicle and support it securely on jackstands. Remove the wheel. If necessary for access to the inner CV joint of the driveaxle, remove the pushpins securing the splash shield in the fenderwell and remove the splash shield.
2   With the brakes applied to keep the driveaxle from turning, remove the driveaxle/hub nut. Obtain a new nut, but but do not discard the old one yet.
3   Disconnect the brake hose bracket and the wheel speed sensor wiring harness from the shock absorber.
Note: *If necessary for additional clearance, remove the brake caliper and bracket and support using wire or similar to prevent damage to the brake hose (see Chapter 9).*
Note: *If necessary for additional clearance, remove the nut and remove the tie-rod end from the steering knuckle (see Chapter 10).*
4   Separate the control arm from the steering knuckle (see Chapter 10).

5   Use a drive hub remover or other suitable puller to separate the driveaxle from the hub **(see illustration)**.
6   Swing the knuckle/hub assembly out (away from the vehicle) until the end of the driveaxle is free of the hub. Use a length of wire to secure the knuckle out of the way to the rear. Support the outer end of the driveaxle with a piece of wire to avoid unnecessary strain on the inner CV joint.
7   If you are removing the right side driveaxle, remove the nuts attaching the intermediate shaft support bearing to the bracket **(see illustration)**. If you are removing the left side driveaxle, use a driveaxle remover and slide hammer to remove the driveaxle from the transaxle. If a removal tool is not available, pry the inner CV joint out of the transaxle using a large screwdriver or pry bar positioned between the transaxle and the CV joint housing **(see illustration)**. Be careful not to damage the differential seal.
8   Support the CV joints and carefully remove the driveaxle from the vehicle.

Installation
9   Pry the old spring clip from the inner end of the driveaxle and install a new one.
10   Lubricate the differential or transfer case shaft seal with multi-purpose grease and raise the driveaxle into position while supporting the CV joints.
Note: *Position the spring clip with the opening facing down; this will ease insertion of the driveaxle and prevent damage to the clip.*
11   Push the splined end of the inner CV joint into the differential side gear and make sure the spring clip locks in its groove.
Caution: *Be careful to not let the sharp edges on the driveaxle splines cut or damage the oil seal when inserting the driveaxle.*
12   Check that the spring clip has engaged by tugging outward on the inboard CV joint housing.
13   For the right side driveaxle, install the intermediate shaft support bearing bracket nuts and tighten them to the torque listed in

this Chapter's Specifications
Note: *To make insertion of the left-side driveaxle easier, position the gap in the spring clip in the 6 o-clock position.*
14   Apply a light coat of multi-purpose grease to the outer CV joint splines, pull out on the steering knuckle assembly and install the stub axle into the hub.
15   Reconnect the control arm to the steering knuckle and tighten all fasteners to the torque listed in the Chapter 10 Specifcations.
16   If removed, reinstall the brake caliper and bracket. If disconnected, connect the tie rod to the steering knuckle.
17   Seat the driveaxle using the old driveaxle/hub nut. Apply the brake to prevent the driveaxle from rotating, tighten the old driveaxle nut to the speciied torque listed in this Chapter's Specifications, then remove and discard the old nut. Install a new nut and tighten it to the torque listed in this Chapter's Specifications.
Caution: *The driveaxle/hub nut must be tightened before lowering the vehicle or damage to the wheel bearings may occur.*
Note: *The driveaxle nut is coated with a one-use locking chemical and cannot be re-used for final assembly. The locking chemical is activated by heat created during tightening. The nut must be tightened to the specified torque within five minutes of starting it on the threads or the locking chemical will not activate properly.*
18   Install the wheel and lug nuts, then lower the vehicle.
19   Tighten the lug nuts to the torque listed in the Chapter 1 Specifications.

Rear (AWD models)
Warning: *The manufacturer recommends replacing all suspension fasteners with new ones during installation.*

Removal
20   Block the front wheels to prevent the vehicle from rolling. Loosen the wheel lug nuts, raise the rear of the vehicle and support

it securely on jackstands. Remove the wheel.

21 Remove the wheel speed sensor and brake line bracket from the wheel knuckle. Remove the brake caliper and brake disc (see Chapter 9). Hang the caliper with a length of wire and do not disconnect the brake hose.

22 Have an assistant depress the brake pedal, then remove the driveaxle/hub nut.

23 Use a drive hub remover to separate the driveaxle from the wheel hub **(see illustration 2.5)**.

2007 and earlier models

24 Remove the hub and bearing assembly (see Chapter 10) then proceed to Step 28.

2008 and later models

25 While supporting the lower control arm with a jack, unbolt the upper control arm and the shock absorber lower bolt from the rear knuckle (see Chapter 10).

26 Disconnect the outer toe link and upper stabilizer bar link (see Chapter 10).

27 Support the wheel knuckle and loosen the nut and bolt for the lower arm from the knuckle.

All models

28 Pry the inner end of the driveaxle out of the differential **(see illustration 2.7b)**.

29 On 2007 and earlier models, remove the driveaxle from the vehicle by passing the outer end of the shaft up through the opening in the wheel knuckle.

30 On 2008 and later models, swing the knuckle outward to separate the outer end of the driveaxle from the hub and pull the driveaxle out.

Installation

31 Pry the old spring clip from the inner end of the driveaxle and install a new one.

32 Apply a light film of grease to the area on the inner CV joint stub shaft where the seal rides, then insert the splined end of the inner CV joint into the differential. Make sure the spring clip locks in its groove.

Caution: *Take care not to damage the differential seal with the driveaxle splines. It is recommended to use a plastic seal protector (manufacturer tool #205-816).*

Note: *To make insertion of the driveaxle easier, position the gap in the spring clip in the 6 o'clock position.*

2007 and earlier models

33 Apply a light film of grease to the outer CV joint splines, then install the hub and bearing assembly and tighten the bolts to the torque listed in the Chapter 10 Specifications.

34 Seat the driveaxle using the old driveaxle/hub nut. With the brake applied to prevent the driveaxle from rotating, tighten the old driveaxle/hub nut to the specified torque, then remove and discard the old nut.

2008 and later models

35 Apply a light film of grease to the outer CV joint splines, swing the knuckle outward and insert the outer end of the driveaxle into the hub.

36 Seat the driveaxle using the old driveaxle/hub nut. With the brake applied to prevent the driveaxle from rotating, tighten the old driveaxle/hub nut to the torque listed in this Chapter's Specifications, then remove and discard the old nut.

37 Install the bolts to connect the upper and lower control arms to the wheel knuckle and tighten them to the torque listed in the Chapter 10 Specifications.

All models

38 Re-install the wheel speed sensor.

Note: *The new driveaxle/hub nut(s) must be tightened before lowering the vehicle or damage to the wheel bearings may occur.*

Note: *The driveaxle/hub nuts are coated with a one-use locking chemical and cannot be re-used for final assembly. The locking chemical is activated by heat created during tightening. The nut must be tightened to the specified torque within five minutes of starting it on the threads or the locking chemical will not activate properly.*

39 Install a new driveaxle nut. With the brake applied to keep the driveaxle from turning, tighten the nut to the torque listed in this Chapter's Specifications.

40 The remainder of installation is the reverse of removal. Use new suspension fasteners and tighten them to the torque listed in the Chapter 10 Specifications. Tighten the brake fasteners to the torque listed in the Chapter 9 Specifications.

41 Install the wheel and lug nuts, then lower the vehicle. Tighten the lug nuts to the torque listed in the Chapter 1 Specifications.

---

3 Driveaxle boot - replacement

Note: *If the CV joints are worn, indicating the need for an overhaul (usually due to torn boots), explore all options before beginning the job. Complete rebuilt driveaxles are available on an exchange basis, which eliminates much time and work.*

Note: *The driveaxles are equipped with ABS sensor rings on the outer CV joints. Inspect the sensor rings for chipped or missing teeth.*

1 Remove the driveaxle from the vehicle (see Section 2).

2 Mount the driveaxle in a vise. The jaws of the vise should be lined with wood or rags to prevent damage to the driveaxle.

Front

Note: *The outboard CV joint is not removable. The outboard boot can only be replaced if the inboard CV joint is disassembled.*

Removal

3 Remove and discard the boot clamps.

4 Remove the retainer clip and pull the boot back from the inner CV joint. Mark the relationship of the tri-pod to the outer housing.

5 Be careful not to let the bearings slide off the tri-pod as you separate the joint housing from the driveaxle.

3.19 Equalize the pressure inside the boot by inserting a small, dull screwdriver between the boot and the outer race

6 Remove the retaining clip and use a puller to remove the tri-pod from the shaft.

7 Slide the old inboard boot off the shaft.

8 The outer CV joint boot can now be removed by removing the two boot clamps and sliding the outer boot off at the inboard end of the shaft.

Inspection

9 Clean the old grease from the outer race and the tri-pod bearing assembly. Carefully disassemble each section of the tri-pod assembly, one at a time so as not to mix up the parts. Clean the needle bearings with solvent.

10 Inspect the rollers, tri-pod, bearings and outer race for scoring, pitting or other signs of abnormal wear, which will warrant the replacement of the inner CV joint.

Reassembly

11 If you are replacing the outboard CV joint boot, slide a new boot onto the shaft. Pack half the grease provided in the sealing boot kit into the outboard CV joint and spread the remaining grease in the sealing boot.

12 Seat the small end of the outboard boot into the groove in the axleshaft and tighten the boot clamps.

13 Slide a new inboard boot clamp (small end), then the inboard sealing boot onto the axleshaft.

14 Slide the tri-pod with the roller bearings onto the axle shaft and install a new snap ring. Again, be careful to not let the bearings fall off the tri-pod.

15 Pack the bearing with half the grease provided in the kit and spread the remaining grease inside the boot.

16 Slide the outer housing over the bearing assembly and install the outer bearing retaining ring.

17 Seat the large end of the boot into the groove in the outer housing.

18 Place the two boot clamps in position on the boot but do not tighten them yet.

19 Position the CV joint mid-way through its travel, then equalize the air pressure in the boot **(see illustration)**.

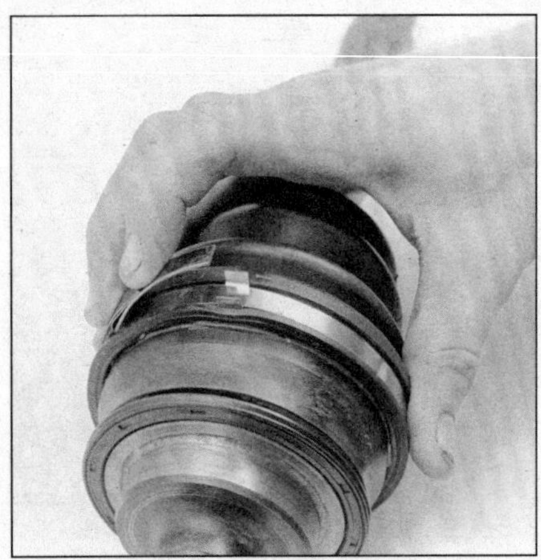

3.20a To install new fold-over type clamps, bend the tang down . . .

3.20b . . . and flatten the tabs to hold it in place

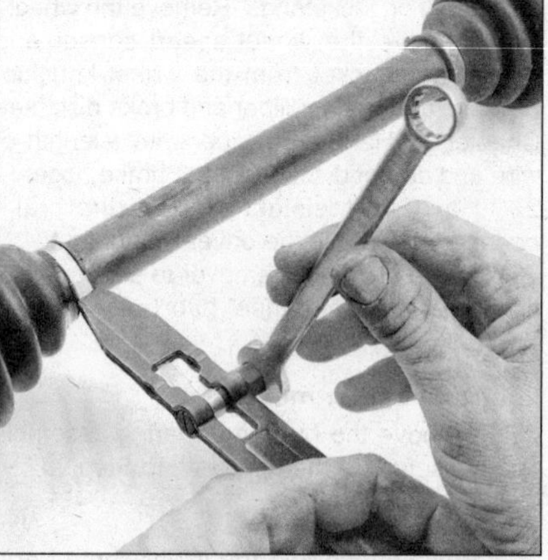

3.20c To install band-type clamps you'll need a special tool; install the band with its end pointing in the direction of axle rotation and tighten it securely, then pivot the tool up 90-degrees and tap the center of the clip with a center punch . . .

20   Tighten the boot clamps **(see illustrations)**.
21   Install the driveaxle as outlined in Section 2.

Rear (AWD models)

Note: *The outboard CV joint is not removable. The outboard boot can only be replaced if the inboard CV joint is disassembled.*

Removal

22   Remove the driveaxle from the vehicle (see Section 2).
23   Mount the driveaxle in a vise. The jaws of the vise should be lined with wood or rags to prevent damage to the driveaxle.
24   Remove the two clamps from the inboard boot.
25   With the boot cover pulled back from the CV joint housing, remove and discard the retaining ring from the outer housing and remove the balls and bearing cage.
26   Remove the retaining clip from the axle splines.
27   Remove the inner bearing race and slide the boot off the axle.
28   The outer CV joint boot can now be

removed by removing the two boot clamps and sliding the outer boot off at the inboard end of the shaft.

Inspection

29   Thoroughly clean all components with solvent until the old grease is completely removed. Inspect the bearing surfaces of the inner races and housings for cracks, pitting, scoring, and other signs of wear. If any part of the CV joint is worn, you must replace the entire driveaxle assembly (inner CV joint, axleshaft and outer CV joint).

Reassembly

30   If you are replacing the outboard CV joint boot, slide a new boot onto the shaft. Pack half the grease provided in the sealing boot kit into the outboard CV joint and spread the remaining grease in the sealing boot.
31   Seat the outboard boot into the groove in the outboard CV joint housing and tighten the boot clamps.
32   Slide a new inboard boot clamp (small end), then the inboard sealing boot onto the axleshaft.
33   Slide the inner race onto the axle shaft

and install a new snap-ring.
34   Place the bearing cage and the eight balls onto the inner race.
35   Pack the bearing with half the grease provided in the kit and spread the remaining grease inside the boot.
36   Slide the outer housing over the bearing assembly and install the outer bearing retaining ring.
37   Seat the large end of the boot into the groove in the outer housing.
38   Place the two boot clamps in position on the boot but do not tighten them yet.
39   Position the CV joint mid-way through its travel, then equalize the air pressure in the boot **(see illustration 3.19)**.
40   Tighten the boot clamps **(see illustrations 3.20a through 3.20e)**.
41   Replace the retaining clip on the inboard end of the assembly where it engages the transaxle gear.
42   Install the driveaxle as outlined in Section 2.

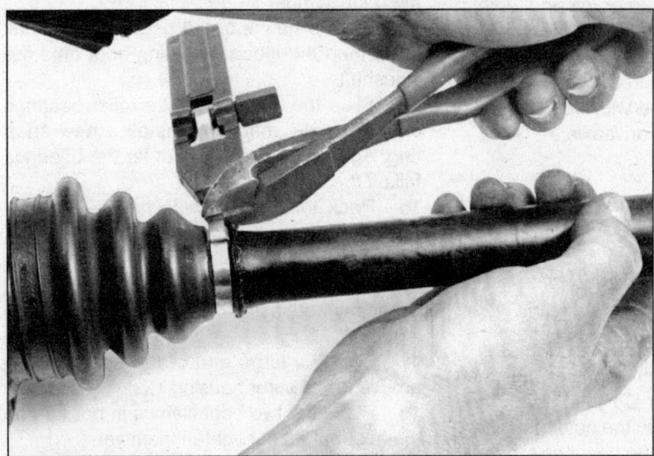

3.20d . . . then bend the end of the clamp back over the clip and cut off the excess

3.20e If you're installing crimp-type boot clamps, you'll need a pair of special crimping pliers (available at most auto parts stores)

4 Driveshaft (AWD models) - removal and installation

Caution: *The manufacturer recommends replacing driveshaft fasteners with new ones when installing the driveshaft.*

1   Raise the vehicle and support it securely on jackstands. Place the shift lever in Neutral.

2   Use chalk or a scribe to mark the relationship of the driveshaft flange to the differential pinion yoke. Do the same at the front U-joint flange where it bolts to the transfer case yoke. This ensures correct alignment when the driveshaft is reinstalled.

3   Remove the muffler and exhaust as necessary to provide clearance for removal of the driveshaft.

4   Remove the exhaust crossmember bolts and remove the crossmember.

5   Working at the front of the driveshaft, remove the bolts securing the driveshaft to the transfer case.

6   Remove the bolts securing the universal joint flange to the differential pinion yoke.

7   Remove the nuts securing the center support bearing.

8   With help from an assistant, carefully remove the driveshaft from the vehicle.

9   Installation is the reverse of removal. Use your index marks to keep the U-joints in alignment and make sure the mating surfaces are clean so the universal joint flanges seat properly in the yokes. Tighten the fasteners to the torque listed in this Chapter's Specifications.

5 Rear driveaxle oil seals (AWD models) - replacement

1   Raise the rear of the vehicle and support it securely on jackstands. Place the transaxle in Neutral with the parking brake off. Block the front wheels to prevent the vehicle from rolling.

2   Remove the driveaxle(s) (see Section 2).

3   Carefully pry out the driveaxle oil seal with a seal removal tool, a large screwdriver or a slide hammer and attachment. Be careful not to damage or scratch the seal bore or the bearing inside the case.

4   Using a seal installer or a large deep socket as a drift, install the new oil seal. Drive it into the bore squarely and make sure it's completely seated.

5   Lubricate the lip of the new seal with multi-purpose grease, then install the drive-axle. Be careful not to damage the lip of the new seal.

6   Check the differential lubricant level and add some, if necessary, to bring it to the appropriate level (see Chapter 1).

6 Differential (AWD models) - removal and installation

Note: *On AWD models, the manufacturer uses an Active Torque Control Coupling (ATCC) to manage power distribution to the front and rear wheels. Normally, the front wheels receive the majority of the torque produced by the engine. When the ATCC system senses wheel slip, it automatically increases the torque to the rear wheels. The system is always active, continuously monitoring vehicle conditions and adjusting the torque being delivered to the rear wheels by controlling the current sent to an electric clutch device inside the rear axle. The ATCC system has no mode selector nor does it require any driver input. The ATCC solenoid in the rear axle is not repairable and must be replaced with the rear axle assembly as a unit.*

1   Raise the rear of the vehicle and support it securely on jackstands. Block the front wheels to prevent the vehicle from rolling.

2   Remove the driveshaft (see Section 4).

3   Remove the driveaxles (see Section 2).

4   Remove the rear stabilizer bar (see Chapter 10).

Note: *On Five Hundred and Montego models, the stabilizer does not need to be removed completely, only slid forward for clearance.*

5   Support the differential with a floor jack.

6   Disconnect the any electrical connectors for the differential.

2007 and earlier models

7   Remove the differential cross-bracket bolts and bracket.

8   Remove the differential front insulator bolt.

9   Remove the two differential rear insulator bolts.

Note: *The passenger rear insulator bolt cannot be removed until the differential is removed.*

2008 and later models

10   There are four rear differential mounting brackets securing the differential to the subframe, one at either side at the top-front of the assembly and two at the top-rear. Remove the four bolts (two each side) securing the front of the differential to each front bracket.

11   Loosen the two front mounting brackets from the subframe and swing the brackets out to allow clearance to lower the rear differential.

12   Remove the six bolts securing the differential to the rear mounting brackets.

13   Lower the differential slightly and disconnect any remaining connectors.

All models

14   Lower the differential with the floor jack.

15   Installation is the reverse of removal. Tighten all fasteners to the torque listed in this Chapter's Specifications.

7 Differential pinion oil seal - replacement

1   Loosen the wheel lug nuts. Raise the rear of the vehicle and support it securely on jackstands. Block the opposite set of wheels to keep the vehicle from rolling off the stands. Remove the wheels.

2   Disconnect the driveshaft from the differential companion flange and fasten it out of the way (see Section 4).

3   Mark the relationship of the pinion flange to the shaft, then count and write down the number of exposed threads on the shaft.

4   A flange holding tool will be required to keep the companion flange from moving while the self-locking pinion nut is loosened. A chain wrench will also work.

5   Remove the pinion nut.

6   Withdraw the flange. It may be necessary to use a two-jaw puller engaged behind the flange to draw it off. Do not attempt to pry or hammer behind the flange or hammer on the end of the pinion shaft.

7   Pry out the old seal and discard it.

8   Inspect the seal bore to ensure it is clean and smooth.

9   Lubricate the lips of the new seal and fill the space between the seal lips with wheel bearing grease, then tap it evenly into position with a seal installation tool or a large socket. Make sure it enters the housing squarely and is tapped in to its full depth.

10   Install the pinion flange, lining up the marks made in Step 3. If necessary, tighten the pinion nut to draw the flange into place. Do not try to hammer the flange into position.

11   Install a new pinion nut, then tighten it to the torque listed in this Chapter's Specifications.

12   The remainder of installation is the reverse of removal.

Notes

Chapter 9   Brakes

Contents

Specifications

General
Brake fluid type .... See Chapter 1

Disc brakes
Minimum pad lining thickness	See Chapter 1	
Disc lateral runout limit	0.002 inch	0.050 mm
Disc minimum thickness	Cast into disc	

Torque specifications

Ft-lbs (unless otherwise indicated)   **Nm**

Note: *One foot-pound (ft-lb) of torque is equivalent to 12 inch-pounds (in-lbs) of torque. Torque values below approximately 15 ft-lbs are expressed in inch-pounds, because most foot-pound torque wrenches are not accurate at these smaller values.*

	Ft-lbs	Nm
Brake line banjo bolt		
Front		
2007 and earlier models	22	30
2008 and 2009 models	26	35
2010 and later models	35	47
Rear (2010 and later models)	22	30
Rear caliper brake line fitting	150 in-lbs	17
Bleeder screw		
Front	97 in-lbs	11
Rear	89 in-lbs	10

Torque specifications

Ft-lbs (unless otherwise indicated)   **Nm**

Note: *One foot-pound (ft-lb) of torque is equivalent to 12 inch-pounds (in-lbs) of torque. Torque values below approximately 15 ft-lbs are expressed in inch-pounds, because most foot-pound torque wrenches are not accurate at these smaller values.*

	Ft-lbs	Nm
Caliper mounting bracket bolts		
2007 and earlier models		
Front	74	100
Rear	81	110
2008 and 2009 models		
Front	111	150
Rear	81	110
2010 through 2012 models		
Front	111	150
Rear	76	103
2013 and later models		
Front	122	165
Rear	76	103
Caliper bolts		
2007 and earlier models		
Front	44	60
Rear	23	31
2008 and 2009 models		
Front	44	60
Rear	21	28
2010 and later models		
Front		
Models with 13-inch brakes	53	72
Models with 14 inch brakes	55	75
Rear	24	32
Brake disc retaining screw		
2008 and earlier models		
Front	108 in-lbs	12
Rear	15	20
2009 and later models		
Front	15	20
Rear	15	20
Master cylinder mounting nuts	15	20
Brake line nuts (to master cylinder)		
Models with ABS	156 in-lbs	17.5
Models with ABS/Stability and Traction Control	16	22
Power brake booster mounting nuts	18	24
Brake booster vacuum pump mounting bolts	18	24
Wheel lug nuts	See Chapter 1	

1 General information

1   The vehicles covered by this manual are equipped with hydraulically operated front and rear brake systems. The front and rear brakes are disc type. Both the front and rear brakes are self adjusting. The disc brakes automatically compensate for pad wear.

Hydraulic system

2   The hydraulic system consists of two separate circuits. The master cylinder has separate reservoirs for the two circuits, and, in the event of a leak or failure in one hydraulic circuit, the other circuit will remain operative.

Power brake booster

3   On non-turbocharged models, the power brake booster uses engine manifold vacuum to boost the effort applied by the driver at the brake pedal and transmits this increased effort to the master cylinder pistons. On turbocharged models, a camshaft-driven vacuum pump is used to supply vacuum to the power brake booster.

Parking brake

4   The parking brake operates the rear brakes only and is activated by a pedal in the driver's foot well. Depressing the pedal puts tension on the parking brake cables. The cables are connected to levers on the rear brake calipers which mechanically actuate the rear caliper pistons.

Service

5   After completing any operation involving disassembly of any part of the brake system, always test drive the vehicle to check for proper braking performance before resuming normal driving. When testing the brakes, perform the tests on a clean, dry, flat surface. Conditions other than these can lead to inaccurate test results.

6   Test the brakes at various speeds with both light and heavy pedal pressure. The vehicle should stop evenly without pulling to one side or the other. Avoid locking the brakes, because this slides the tires and diminishes braking efficiency and control of the vehicle.

7   Tires, vehicle load and wheel alignment are factors which also affect braking performance.

Precautions

8   There are some general cautions and warnings involving the brake system on this vehicle:

Use only brake fluid conforming to DOT 3 or DOT 4 standards as listed in the Chapter 1 Specifications for your model year.

The brake pads contain fibers which are hazardous to your health if inhaled. Whenever you work on brake system components, clean all parts with brake system cleaner. Do not allow the fine dust to become airborne. Also, wear an approved filtering mask.

Safety should be paramount whenever any servicing of the brake components is performed. Do not use parts or fasteners which are not in perfect condition, and be sure that all clearances and torque specifications are adhered to. If you are at all unsure about a certain procedure, seek professional advice. Upon completion of any brake system work, test the brakes carefully in a controlled area before putting the vehicle into normal service. If a problem is suspected in the brake system, don't drive the vehicle until it's fixed.

2 Troubleshooting

PROBABLE CAUSE	CORRECTIVE ACTION

No brakes - pedal travels to floor

PROBABLE CAUSE	CORRECTIVE ACTION
1 Low fluid level	1 and 2 Low fluid level and air in the system are symptoms of another problem a leak somewhere in the hydraulic system. Locate and repair the leak.
2 Air in system	
3 Defective seals in master cylinder	3 Replace master cylinder
4 Fluid overheated and vaporized due to heavy braking	4 Bleed hydraulic system (temporary fix). Replace brake fluid (proper fix)

Brake pedal slowly travels to floor under braking or at a stop

PROBABLE CAUSE	CORRECTIVE ACTION
1 Defective seals in master cylinder	1 Replace master cylinder
2 Leak in a hose, line, caliper or wheel cylinder	2 Locate and repair leak
3 Air in hydraulic system	3 Bleed the system, inspect system for a leak

Brake pedal feels spongy when depressed

PROBABLE CAUSE	CORRECTIVE ACTION
1 Air in hydraulic system	1 Bleed the system, inspect system for a leak
2 Master cylinder or power booster loose	2 Tighten fasteners
3 Brake fluid overheated (beginning to boil)	3 Bleed the system (temporary fix). Replace the brake fluid (proper fix)
4 Deteriorated brake hoses (ballooning under pressure)	4 Inspect hoses, replace as necessary (it's a good idea to replace all of them if one hose shows signs of deterioration)

Troubleshooting (continued)

| PROBABLE CAUSE | CORRECTIVE ACTION |

Brake pedal feels hard when depressed and/or excessive effort required to stop vehicle

PROBABLE CAUSE	CORRECTIVE ACTION
1 Power booster faulty	1 Replace booster
2 Engine not producing sufficient vacuum, or hose to booster clogged, collapsed or cracked	2 Check vacuum to booster with a vacuum gauge. Replace hose if cracked or clogged, repair engine if vacuum is extremely low
3 Brake linings contaminated by grease or brake fluid	3 Locate and repair source of contamination, replace brake pads or shoes
4 Brake linings glazed	4 Replace brake pads or shoes, check discs and drums for glazing, service as necessary
5 Caliper piston(s) or wheel cylinder(s) binding or frozen	5 Replace calipers or wheel cylinders
6 Brakes wet	6 Apply pedal to boil-off water (this should only be a momentary problem)
7 Kinked, clogged or internally split brake hose or line	7 Inspect lines and hoses, replace as necessary

Excessive brake pedal travel (but will pump up)

PROBABLE CAUSE	CORRECTIVE ACTION
1 Drum brakes out of adjustment	1 Adjust brakes
2 Air in hydraulic system	2 Bleed system, inspect system for a leak

Excessive brake pedal travel (but will not pump up)

PROBABLE CAUSE	CORRECTIVE ACTION
1 Master cylinder pushrod misadjusted	1 Adjust pushrod
2 Master cylinder seals defective	2 Replace master cylinder
3 Brake linings worn out	3 Inspect brakes, replace pads and/or shoes
4 Hydraulic system leak	4 Locate and repair leak

Brake pedal doesn't return

PROBABLE CAUSE	CORRECTIVE ACTION
1 Brake pedal binding	1 Inspect pivot bushing and pushrod, repair or lubricate
2 Defective master cylinder	2 Replace master cylinder

Brake pedal pulsates during brake application

PROBABLE CAUSE	CORRECTIVE ACTION
1 Brake drums out-of-round	1 Have drums machined by an automotive machine shop
2 Excessive brake disc runout or disc surfaces out-of-parallel	2 Have discs machined by an automotive machine shop
3 Loose or worn wheel bearings	3 Adjust or replace wheel bearings
4 Loose lug nuts	4 Tighten lug nuts

Brakes slow to release

PROBABLE CAUSE	CORRECTIVE ACTION
1 Malfunctioning power booster	1 Replace booster
2 Pedal linkage binding	2 Inspect pedal pivot bushing and pushrod, repair/lubricate
3 Malfunctioning proportioning valve	3 Replace proportioning valve
4 Sticking caliper or wheel cylinder	4 Repair or replace calipers or wheel cylinders
5 Kinked or internally split brake hose	5 Locate and replace faulty brake hose

Brakes grab (one or more wheels)

PROBABLE CAUSE	CORRECTIVE ACTION
1 Grease or brake fluid on brake lining	1 Locate and repair cause of contamination, replace lining
2 Brake lining glazed	2 Replace lining, deglaze disc or drum

PROBABLE CAUSE **CORRECTIVE ACTION**

Vehicle pulls to one side during braking

PROBABLE CAUSE	CORRECTIVE ACTION
1 Grease or brake fluid on brake lining	1 Locate and repair cause of contamination, replace lining
2 Brake lining glazed	2 Deglaze or replace lining, deglaze disc or drum
3 Restricted brake line or hose	3 Repair line or replace hose
4 Tire pressures incorrect	4 Adjust tire pressures
5 Caliper or wheel cylinder sticking	5 Repair or replace calipers or wheel cylinders
6 Wheels out of alignment	6 Have wheels aligned
7 Weak suspension spring	7 Replace springs
8 Weak or broken shock absorber	8 Replace shock absorbers

Brakes drag (indicated by sluggish engine performance or wheels being very hot after driving)

PROBABLE CAUSE	CORRECTIVE ACTION
1 Brake pedal pushrod incorrectly adjusted	1 Adjust pushrod
2 Master cylinder pushrod (between booster and master cylinder) incorrectly adjusted	2 Adjust pushrod
3 Obstructed compensating port in master cylinder	3 Replace master cylinder
4 Master cylinder piston seized in bore	4 Replace master cylinder
5 Contaminated fluid causing swollen seals throughout system	5 Flush system, replace all hydraulic components
6 Clogged brake lines or internally split brake hose(s)	6 Flush hydraulic system, replace defective hose(s)
7 Sticking caliper(s) or wheel cylinder(s)	7 Replace calipers or wheel cylinders
8 Parking brake not releasing	8 Inspect parking brake linkage and parking brake mechanism, repair as required
9 Improper shoe-to-drum clearance	9 Adjust brake shoes
10 Faulty proportioning valve	10 Replace proportioning valve

Brakes fade (due to excessive heat)

PROBABLE CAUSE	CORRECTIVE ACTION
1 Brake linings excessively worn or glazed	1 Deglaze or replace brake pads and/or shoes
2 Excessive use of brakes	2 Downshift into a lower gear, maintain a constant slower speed (going down hills)
3 Vehicle overloaded	3 Reduce load
4 Brake drums or discs worn too thin	4 Measure drum diameter and disc thickness, replace drums or discs as required
5 Contaminated brake fluid	5 Flush system, replace fluid
6 Brakes drag	6 Repair cause of dragging brakes
7 Driver resting left foot on brake pedal	7 Don't ride the brakes

Brakes noisy (high-pitched squeal)

PROBABLE CAUSE	CORRECTIVE ACTION
1 Glazed lining	1 Deglaze or replace lining
2 Contaminated lining (brake fluid, grease, etc.)	2 Repair source of contamination, replace linings
3 Weak or broken brake shoe hold-down or return spring	3 Replace springs
4 Rivets securing lining to shoe or backing plate loose	4 Replace shoes or pads
5 Excessive dust buildup on brake linings	5 Wash brakes off with brake system cleaner
6 Brake drums worn too thin	6 Measure diameter of drums, replace if necessary
7 Wear indicator on disc brake pads contacting disc	7 Replace brake pads
8 Anti-squeal shims missing or installed improperly	8 Install shims correctly

Troubleshooting (continued)

PROBABLE CAUSE	CORRECTIVE ACTION

Brakes noisy (scraping sound)

PROBABLE CAUSE	CORRECTIVE ACTION
1 Brake pads or shoes worn out; rivets, backing plate or brake shoe metal contacting disc or drum	1 Replace linings, have discs and/or drums machined (or replace)

Brakes chatter

PROBABLE CAUSE	CORRECTIVE ACTION
1 Worn brake lining	1 Inspect brakes, replace shoes or pads as necessary
2 Glazed or scored discs or drums	2 Deglaze discs or drums with sandpaper (if glazing is severe, machining will be required)
3 Drums or discs heat checked	3 Check discs and/or drums for hard spots, heat checking, etc. Have discs drums machined or replace them
4 Disc runout or drum out-of-round excessive	4 Measure disc runout and/or drum out-of-round, have discs or drums machined or replace them
5 Loose or worn wheel bearings	5 Adjust or replace wheel bearings
6 Loose or bent brake backing plate (drum brakes)	6 Tighten or replace backing plate
7 Grooves worn in discs or drums	7 Have discs or drums machined, if within limits (if not, replace them)
8 Brake linings contaminated (brake fluid, grease, etc.)	8 Locate and repair source of contamination, replace pads or shoes
9 Excessive dust buildup on linings	9 Wash brakes with brake system cleaner
10 Surface finish on discs or drums too rough after machining (especially on vehicles with sliding calipers)	10 Have discs or drums properly machined
11 Brake pads or shoes glazed	11 Deglaze or replace brake pads or shoes

Brake pads or shoes click

PROBABLE CAUSE	CORRECTIVE ACTION
1 Shoe support pads on brake backing plate grooved or excessively worn	1 Replace brake backing plate
2 Brake pads loose in caliper	2 Loose pad retainers or anti-rattle clips
3 Also see items listed under Brakes chatter	

Brakes make groaning noise at end of stop

PROBABLE CAUSE	CORRECTIVE ACTION
1 Brake pads and/or shoes worn out	1 Replace pads and/or shoes
2 Brake linings contaminated (brake fluid, grease, etc.)	2 Locate and repair cause of contamination, replace brake pads or shoes
3 Brake linings glazed	3 Deglaze or replace brake pads or shoes
4 Excessive dust buildup on linings	4 Wash brakes with brake system cleaner
5 Scored or heat-checked discs or drums	5 Inspect discs/drums, have machined if within limits (if not, replace discs or drums)
6 Broken or missing brake shoe attaching hardware	6 Inspect drum brakes, replace missing hardware

Rear brakes lock up under light brake application

PROBABLE CAUSE	CORRECTIVE ACTION
1 Tire pressures too high	1 Adjust tire pressures
2 Tires excessively worn	2 Replace tires
3 Defective proportioning valve	3 Replace proportioning valve

PROBABLE CAUSE

CORRECTIVE ACTION

Brake warning light on instrument panel comes on (or stays on)

Probable Cause	Corrective Action
1 Low fluid level in master cylinder reservoir (reservoirs with fluid level sensor)	1 Add fluid, inspect system for leak, check the thickness of the brake pads and shoes
2 Failure in one half of the hydraulic system	2 Inspect hydraulic system for a leak
3 Piston in pressure differential warning valve not centered	3 Center piston by bleeding one circuit or the other (close bleeder valve as soon as the light goes out)
4 Defective pressure differential valve or warning switch	4 Replace valve or switch
5 Air in the hydraulic system	5 Bleed the system, check for leaks
6 Brake pads worn out (vehicles with electric wear sensors - small probes that fit into the brake pads and ground out on the disc when the pads get thin)	6 Replace brake pads (and sensors)

Brakes do not self adjust

Disc brakes

Probable Cause	Corrective Action
1 Defective caliper piston seals	1 Replace calipers. Also, possible contaminated fluid causing soft or swollen seals (flush system and fill with new fluid if in doubt)
2 Corroded caliper piston(s)	2 Same as above

Drum brakes

Probable Cause	Corrective Action
1 Adjuster screw frozen	1 Remove adjuster, disassemble, clean and lubricate with high-temperature grease
2 Adjuster lever does not contact star wheel or is binding	2 Inspect drum brakes, assemble correctly or clean or replace parts as required
3 Adjusters mixed up (installed on wrong wheels after brake job)	3 Reassemble correctly
4 Adjuster cable broken or installed incorrectly (cable-type adjusters)	4 Install new cable or assemble correctly

Rapid brake lining wear

Probable Cause	Corrective Action
1 Driver resting left foot on brake pedal	1 Don't ride the brakes
2 Surface finish on discs or drums too rough	2 Have discs or drums properly machined
3 Also see Brakes drag	

3.2 The ABS hydraulic unit/ECU are located under the master cylinder

3.10a Front wheel speed sensor mounting bolt

3.10b Rear wheel speed sensor mounting bolt

3   Anti-lock Brake System (ABS) - general information

General information

1   The anti-lock brake system is designed to maintain vehicle steerability, directional stability and optimum deceleration under severe braking conditions on most road surfaces. It does so by monitoring the rotational speed of each wheel and controlling the brake line pressure to each wheel during braking. This prevents the wheels from locking up.

2   The ABS system has three main components - the wheel speed sensors, the ABS Module and the Hydraulic Control Unit (HCU) **(see illustration)**. Four wheel-speed sensors - one at each wheel - send a variable voltage signal to the ABS Module, which monitors these signals, compares them to its program and determines whether a wheel is about to lock up. When a wheel is about to lock up, the ABS Module signals the HCU to reduce hydraulic pressure (or not increase it further) at that wheel's brake caliper. Pressure modulation is handled by electrically operated solenoid valves.

3   If a problem develops within the system, an "ABS" warning light will glow on the dashboard. Sometimes, a visual inspection of the ABS system can help you locate the problem. Carefully inspect the ABS wiring harness. Pay particularly close attention to the harness and connections near each wheel. Look for signs of chafing and other damage caused by incorrectly routed wires. If a wheel sensor harness is damaged, the sensor must be replaced.

Warning: *Do NOT try to repair an ABS wiring harness. The ABS system is sensitive to even the smallest changes in resistance. Repairing the harness could alter resistance values and cause the system to malfunction. If the ABS wiring harness is damaged in any way, it must be replaced.*

Caution: *Turn the ignition off before unplugging or reattaching any electrical connections.*

4   Some vehicles come equipped with traction control, which helps prevent wheelspin under acceleration. The traction control system (TCS) utilizes some of the same components as the ABS system. The wheel sensors monitor wheel rotation and transmit data through the same wiring to the ABS control module. The control module compares rotation speeds, then controls the amount of power supplied to the wheels by adjusting fuel settings to the engine.

Diagnosis and repair

5   If a dashboard warning light comes on and stays on while the vehicle is in operation, the ABS system requires attention. Although special electronic ABS diagnostic testing tools are necessary to properly diagnose the system, you can perform a few preliminary checks before taking the vehicle to a dealer service department.

   a) *Check the brake fluid level in the reservoir.*
   b) *Verify that the computer electrical connectors are securely connected.*
   c) *Check the electrical connectors at the hydraulic control unit.*
   d) *Check the fuses.*
   e) *Follow the wiring harness to each wheel and verify that all connectors are secure and that the wiring is undamaged.*

6   If the above preliminary checks do not rectify the problem, the vehicle should be diagnosed by a dealer service department or other qualified repair shop. Due to the complex nature of this system, all actual repair work must be done by a qualified automotive technician.

Wheel speed sensor - removal and installation

7   Loosen the wheel lug nuts, raise the vehicle and support it securely on jackstands. Remove the wheel.

8   Make sure the ignition key is turned to the Off position.

9   Trace the wiring back from the sensor, detaching all brackets and clips while noting its correct routing, then disconnect the electrical connector.

10   Remove the mounting bolt and carefully pull the sensor out from the knuckle or wheel bearing housing **(see illustrations)**.

11   Installation is the reverse of removal. Tighten the mounting bolt securely.

12   Install the wheel and lug nuts, tightening them securely. Lower the vehicle and tighten the lug nuts to the torque listed in the Chapter 1 Specifications.

4   Disc brake pads - replacement

Warning: *Disc brake pads must be replaced on both front or both rear wheels at the same time - never replace the pads on only one wheel. Also, the dust created by the brake system is harmful to your health. Never blow it out with compressed air and don't inhale any of it. An approved filtering mask should be worn when working on the brakes. Do not, under any circumstances, use petroleum-based solvents to clean brake parts. Use brake system cleaner only!*

1   Remove the cap from the brake fluid reservoir. To prevent brake fluid from possibly overflowing the reservoir when the calipers are fully retracted, use a syringe or suction gun to remove brake fluid until the reservoir is approximately half full.

2   Loosen the wheel lug nuts, raise the vehicle and support it securely on jackstands. Block the wheels at the opposite end.

3   Remove the wheels. Work on one brake assembly at a time, using the assembled brake for reference if necessary.

4   Inspect the brake disc carefully (see Section 6). If machining is necessary, follow the information in that Section to remove the disc, at which time the pads can be removed as well.

5   Before disassembling the brake, wash it thoroughly with brake system cleaner and

allow it to dry **(see illustration)**. Position a drain pan under the brake to catch the residue - DO NOT use compressed air to blow off the brake dust.
Caution: *Do not allow oil, grease, brake fluid or contaminates of any kind to contact the new brake pads. If a brake pad becomes contaminated it must be discarded and replaced.*

Front brake pads

6   For the front brake pad replacement sequence, follow the accompanying photos **(see illustrations 4.6a through 4.6g and 4.8a through 4.8c)**. Be sure to stay in order and read the caption under each illustration.
Note: *On 2009 and earlier models, the manufacturer states that brake pads are a one-time use only. Once the brake pad has been separated from the caliper, new brake pads must be installed even if they are not worn out.*

4.5 Always wash the brakes with brake cleaner before disassembling anything

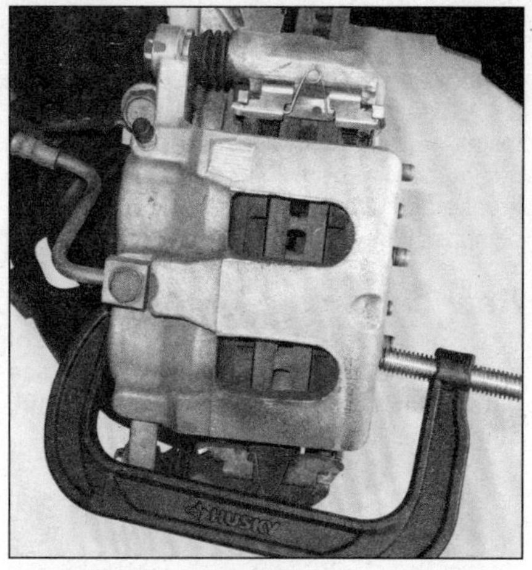

4.6a Depress the piston into the bottom of its bore in the caliper with a large C-clamp to make room for the new pads. Check the fluid level in the master cylinder reservoir to make sure it doesn't overflow

4.6b Remove the caliper lower mounting bolt

4.6c On 2010 and later models, use pliers to remove the upper and lower coiled wire springs

4.6d Rotate the caliper up for access to the pads. You may need to use a flat screwdriver to separate the inner pad from the caliper

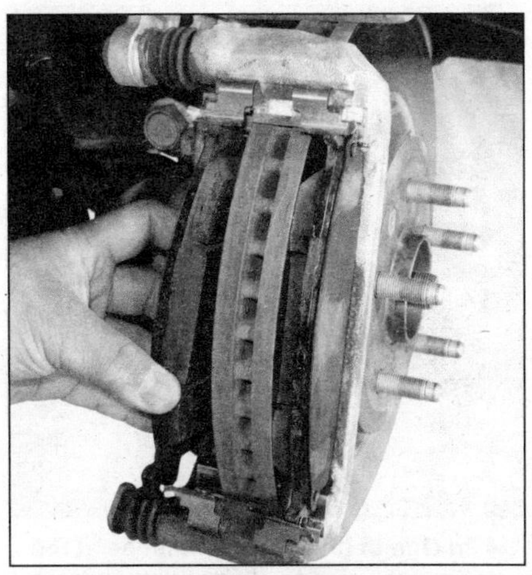

4.6e Remove the inner and outer brake pads from the caliper mounting bracket

4.6f Remove and discard the lower support plate

4.6g Remove and discard the upper support plate

7   Clean and inspect the caliper and other components including the rubber boots for wear or damage. Replace as necessary.

8   Installation is the reverse of removal. Install new support plates. Lubrcate the caliper guide pins with high-temperature brake grease and use new clips and wire springs (if equipped) **(see illustrations)**.

Rear brake pads

9   For the brake pad replacement sequence, follow Steps 1 through 5, then **see illustrations 4.9a through 4.9g, and 4.10a and 4.10b**. Note the following:

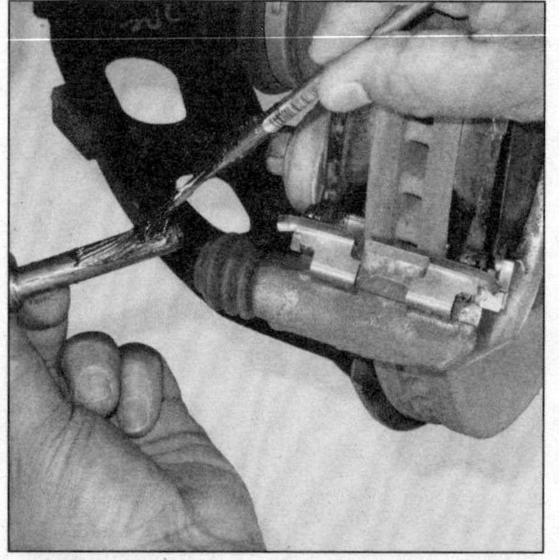

4.8a Clean the caliper guide pins (slide the upper pin from the mounting bracket along with the caliper), then apply a coat of high-temperature brake grease to the sliding surface. Swing the caliper down, install the caliper mounting bolt and tighten it to the torque listed in this Chapter's Specifications

4.8b The center coils of the wire springs (if equipped) must rest against the mounting bracket. If the coil does not rest against the bracket, it is installed incorrectly and must be re-installed properly

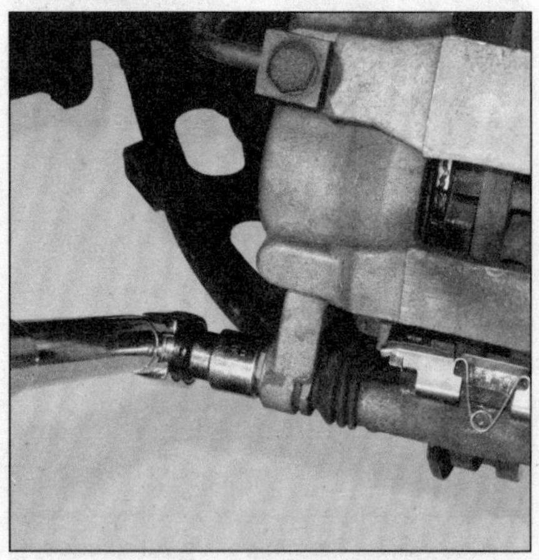

4.8c Tighten the mounting bolt to the torque listed in this Chapter's Specifications

4.9a Hold the caliper guide pins with one wrench while loosening the caliper mounting bolts

4.9b Remove the caliper and hang it with a length of wire - don't let it hang by the hose

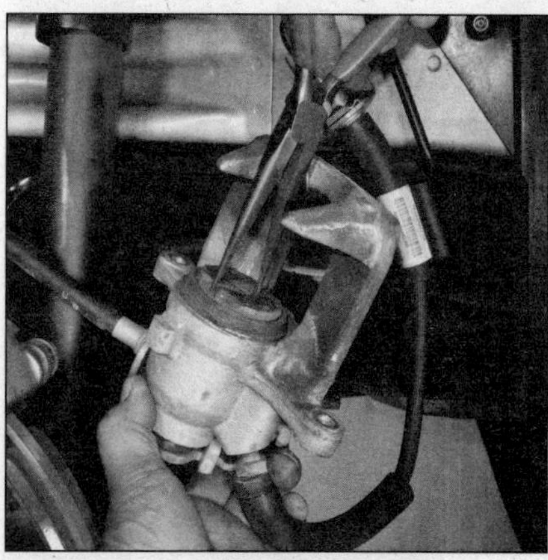

4.9c Use a caliper piston tool to rotate and compress the caliper piston into the caliper bore. Make sure the fluid in the master cylinder reservoir doesn't overflow. Note: *On 2009 and earlier models, turn the left side caliper piston clockwise and the right side caliper piston counterclockwise to compress the piston into the caliper bore. On 2010 and later models, both left and right side caliper pistons turn clockwise to compress*

4.9d One of the notches must be at the bottom position to align with the pin on the inner pad. Use needle-nose pliers to rotate the piston to the proper alignment

4.9e Remove the outer brake pad

4.9f Remove the inner brake pad

**4.9g Remove and discard the
support plates**

a) *The parking brake cable is attached to the caliper. The cable does not have to be separated from the caliper in order to change the pads, but be careful not to twist or damage the cable ends when positioning and supporting the caliper to the side.*

b) *The manufacturer states that the brake pads are one-time use only. Anytime the brake pads are separated from the caliper, they must be replaced with new pads even if they are not worn out. Brake shudder and noise will occur if pads are reused.*

c) *The caliper guide pins are pressed into the mounting bracket (anchor plate). Do not try to remove them or they will be damaged and the mounting bracket will have to be replaced.*

d) *The inboard brake pad has a pin on the back. Turn the caliper piston so the notch will line-up with the pin on the backside of the pad.*

10   Installation is the reverse of removal. Inspect the caliper and other components for wear or damage. Replace as necessary. Install new support plates. Use a wire brush to clean the area of the caliper bracket where the brake pads rest. Lubrcate the caliper guide pins with high-temperature brake grease **(see illustrations)**.

Note: *On 2013 and later models equipped with 13.5 inch brake discs, note the position of the inner and outer pads. New outer pads will be labeled "OTR" on the top of the backing.*

Front or rear pads

11   After the job has been completed, firmly depress the brake pedal a few times to bring the pads into contact with the disc. Hold the brake pedal down for approximately one minute to allow the adhesive to activate and adhere the pads to the caliper. Check the level of the brake fluid, adding some if necessary. Check the operation of the brakes carefully before placing the vehicle into normal service.

5   Disc brake caliper - removal and installation

Warning: *Dust created by the brake system is harmful to your health. Never blow it out with* compressed air and don't inhale any of it. An approved filtering mask should be worn when working on the brakes. Do not, under any circumstances, use petroleum-based solvents to clean brake parts. Use brake system cleaner only.

Note: *If replacement is indicated (usually because of fluid leakage or damage to a piston boot), it is recommended that the calipers be replaced, not overhauled. New and factory rebuilt units are available on an exchange basis, which makes this job quite easy. Always replace the calipers in pairs (both fronts or both rears) - never replace just one of them.*

Removal

1   Loosen the wheel lug nuts, raise front or rear of the vehicle and support it securely on jackstands. Remove the wheels.

2   Remove the cap from the brake fluid reservoir. To prevent brake fluid from possibly overflowing the reservoir when the calipers are fully retracted, use a syringe or suction gun to remove brake fluid until the reservoir is approximately half full.

4.10a Pull out the caliper guide pins and clean them, then apply a coat of high-temperature grease to the pins andreinstall them in the caliper bracket

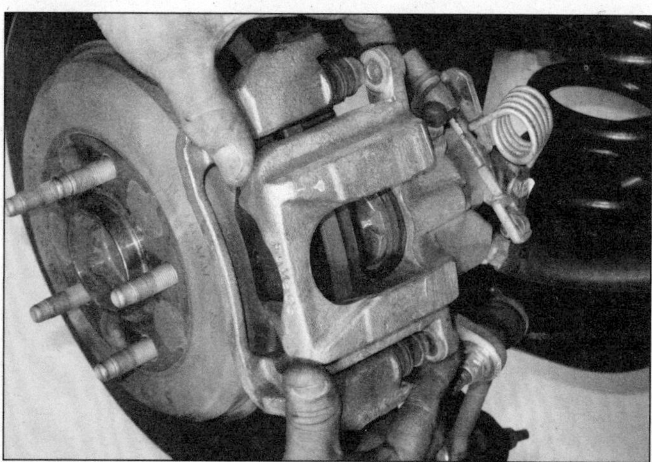

4.10b Install the new support plates and pads. Install the caliper, tightening the caliper mounting bolts to the torque listed in this Chapter's Specifications

5.6 Depress the retaining tangs on the parking brake cable casing and pull the cable through the bracket then unhook the cable end from the lever

6.3 The brake pads on this vehicle were obviously neglected, as they wore down completely and cut deep grooves into the disc - wear this severe means the disc must be replaced

Note: *Compressing the caliper piston will separate the outer pad from the caliper. On 2009 and earlier models this will require replacement of the brake pads (see Section 4).*

3   Use a large C-clamp to compress the caliper piston into the caliper bore **(see illustration 4.6a)** Make sure the brake fluid does not overflow from the master cylinder.

4   Remove the banjo fitting bolt and disconnect the brake hose from the caliper. Discard the sealing washers from each side of the hose fitting. Plug the brake hose to keep contaminants out of the brake system and to prevent losing any more brake fluid than is necessary.

Note: *If the caliper is being removed for access to another component, don't disconnect the hose.*

5   Remove the two caliper bolts. On rear calipers, use a second wrench to hold the caliper guide pin.

Note: *On rear calipers, the caliper guide pins are pressed into the mounting bracket (anchor plate). Do not try to remove them or they will be damaged and the mounting bracket will*

have to be replaced.

6   If you're working on a rear caliper, disconnect the parking brake cable from the bracket on the subframe, then disconnect the cable end from the caliper **(see illustration)**.

7   Start at **illustration 4.6a** (front) or **illustration 4.9a** (rear) for the caliper removal procedure. If the caliper is being removed just to access another component, use a piece of wire to securely hang it out of the way **(see illustration 4.9b)**.

Caution: *Do not let the caliper hang by the brake hose.*

Installation

8   Installation is the reverse of removal. Tighten the mounting bolts to the torque listed in this Chapter's Specifications. Use new sealing washers and tighten the banjo fitting bolt to the torque listed in this Chapter's Specifications.

9   Bleed the brake circuit (see Section 9). Make sure there are no leaks from the hose connections. Test the brakes carefully before returning the vehicle to normal service.

6   Brake disc - inspection, removal and installation

Inspection

1   Loosen the wheel lug nuts, raise the vehicle and support it securely on jackstands.

2   Remove the brake caliper (see Section 5). It isn't necessary to disconnect the brake hose. After removing the caliper bolts, suspend the caliper out of the way with a piece of wire **(see illustration 4.9b)**.

3   Visually inspect the disc surface for score marks and other damage. Light scratches and shallow grooves are normal after use and may not always be detrimental to brake operation, but deep scoring requires disc removal and refinishing by an automotive machine shop. Be sure to check both sides of the disc **(see illustration)**. If pulsating has been noticed during application of the brakes, suspect disc runout.

4   To check disc runout, place a dial indicator at a point about 1/2-inch from the outer edge of the disc **(see illustration)**. Set the indicator to zero and turn the disc. The indicator reading should not exceed the specified allowable runout limit. If it does, the disc should be refinished by an automotive machine shop.

Note: *The discs should be resurfaced regardless of the dial indicator reading, as this will impart a smooth finish and ensure a perfectly flat surface, eliminating any brake pedal pulsation or other undesirable symptoms related to questionable discs. At the very least, if you elect not to have the discs resurfaced, remove the glaze from the surface with emery cloth or sandpaper, using a swirling motion* **(see illustration)**.

5   It's absolutely critical that the disc not be machined to a thickness under the specified minimum thickness. The minimum (or discard) thickness is cast or stamped into the inside of the disc **(see illustration)**. The disc thickness can be checked with a micrometer **(see illustration)**.

6.4a To check disc runout, mount a dial indicator as shown and rotate the disc

6.4b Using a swirling motion, remove the glaze from the disc surface with sandpaper or emery cloth

6.5a The minimum thickness dimension is cast into the front or back side of the disc

6.5b Use a micrometer to measure disc thickness

6.6a Caliper mounting bracket-to-knuckle bolts

Removal

6   Remove and discard the caliper mounting bracket bolts and remove the bracket (see illustration).
Note: *The caliper mounting bracket bolts are one-time use. Always use new caliper mounting bracket bolts when installing the caliper*
7   Remove and discard the disc retaining screw and remove the disc (see illustration).

Installation

8   While the disc is off, wire-brush the backside of the center portion that contacts the wheel hub. Also clean off any rust or dirt on the hub face.
9   Apply small dots of high-temperature anti-seize around the circumference of the hub, and around the raised center portion.
10   Place the disc in position over the threaded studs, install a new disc retaining screw and tighten to the torque listed in this Chapter's Specifications.
11   Install the caliper mounting bracket and caliper; use new bolts and tighten them to the torque listed in this Chapter's Specifications.

12   Install the wheel, then lower the vehicle to the ground. Tighten the lug nuts to the torque listed in the Chapter 1 Specifications. Depress the brake pedal a few times to bring the brake pads into contact with the disc. Bleeding won't be necessary unless the brake hose was disconnected from the caliper. Check the operation of the brakes carefully before driving the vehicle.
13   If new or resurfaced rear discs are being installed, check the operation of the parking brake.

7   Master cylinder - removal and installation

Removal

1   The master cylinder is located in the engine compartment, mounted to the power brake booster.
2   With the engine OFF, deplete the vacuum from the power brake booster by depressing the brake pedal several times.

3   Remove the battery and the battery tray (see Chapter 5).
4   Remove the air filter housing and intake duct (see Chapter 4).
5   Remove as much fluid as you can from the reservoir with a syringe, such as an old turkey baster.
Warning: *If a baster is used to remove brake fluid, never again use it for food preparation.*
6   Disconnect the electrical connector at the brake fluid level switch on the master cylinder reservoir (see illustration).
7   Place rags under the fluid fittings and prepare caps or plastic bags to cover the ends of the lines once they are disconnected.
Caution: *Brake fluid will damage paint. Cover all body parts and be careful not to spill fluid during this procedure.*
8   Loosen the fittings at the ends of the brake lines where they enter the master cylinder (see illustration 7.6). To prevent rounding off the corners on these nuts, the use of a flare-nut wrench, which wraps around the nut, is preferred. Pull the brake lines slightly away from the master cylinder and plug the ends to prevent contamination.

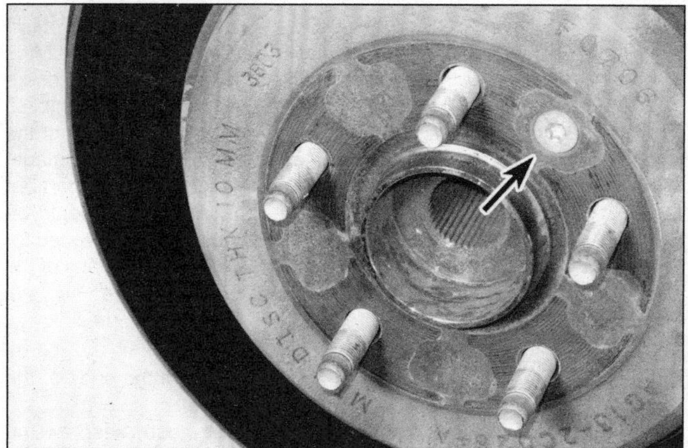

6.7 Remove the screw that secures the disc to the hub

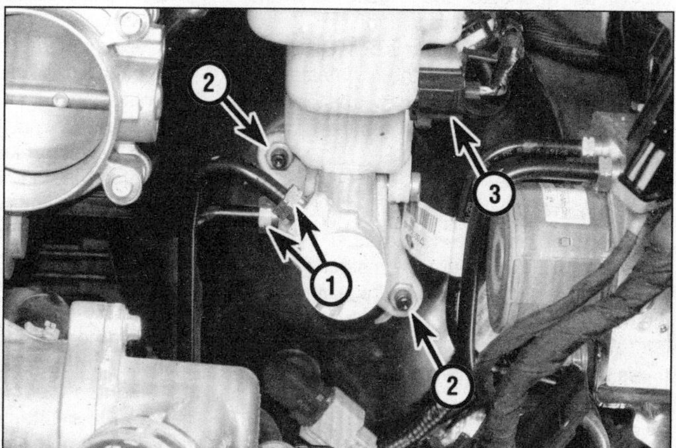

7.6 Master cylinder mounting details

1   Brake line fittings
2   Mounting nuts
3   Electrical connector

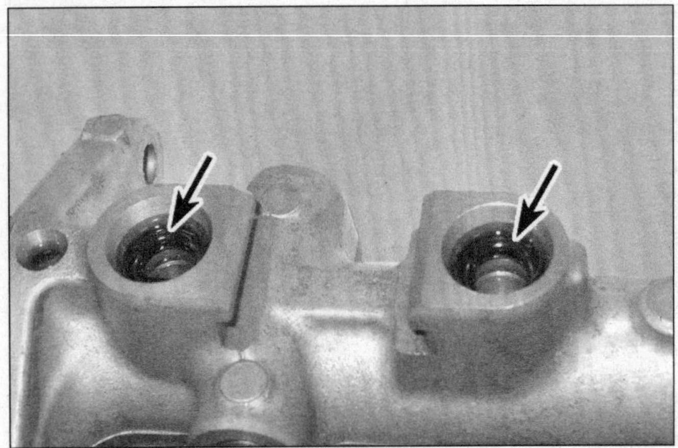

7.10 After the reservoir has been removed, replace the O-rings with new ones

7.12 The best way to bleed air from the master cylinder before installing it on the vehicle is with a pair of bleeder tubes that direct brake fluid into the reservoir during bleeding

7.17 Install a new O-ring onto the master cylinder sleeve

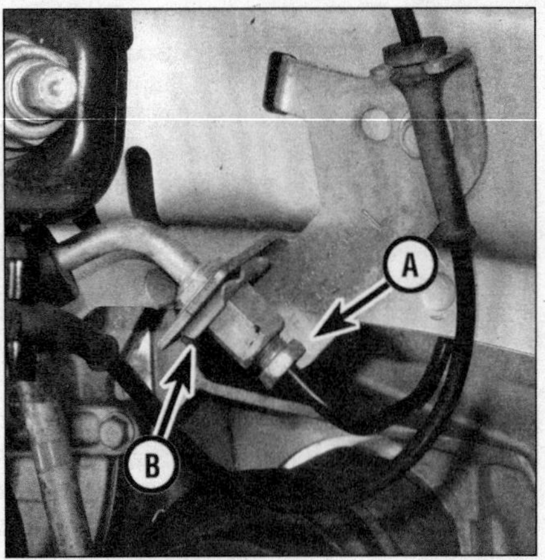

8.3 Brake line fitting (A) and retaining clip (B)

9   Remove and discard the nuts attaching the master cylinder to the power booster. Pull the master cylinder off the studs and out of the engine compartment along with the master cylinder-to-booster seal. Again, be careful not to spill the fluid as this is done.

10   If a new master cylinder is being installed, remove the reservoir from the old master cylinder and transfer it to the new master cylinder. Install new seals when transferring the reservoir **(see illustration)**.

Installation

11   Bench bleed the new master cylinder before installing it. Mount the master cylinder in a vise, with the jaws of the vise clamping on the mounting flange.

12   Attach a pair of master cylinder bleeder tubes to the outlet ports of the master cylinder **(see illustration)**.

13   Fill the reservoir with brake fluid of the recommended type (see Chapter 1).

14   Slowly push the pistons into the master cylinder (a large Phillips screwdriver can be used for this) - air will be expelled from the pressure chambers and into the reservoir.

Because the tubes are submerged in fluid, air can't be drawn back into the master cylinder when you release the pistons.

15   Repeat the procedure until no more air bubbles are present.

16   Remove the bleed tubes, one at a time, and install plugs in the open ports to prevent fluid leakage and air from entering. Install the reservoir cap.

17   Install the master cylinder over the studs on the power brake booster. Use new nuts and tighten them only finger tight at this time. Install a new seal into the sleeve of the master cylinder **(see illustration)**.

18   Thread the brake line fittings into the master cylinder. Since the master cylinder is still a bit loose, it can be moved slightly in order for the fittings to thread in easily. Do not strip the threads as the fittings are tightened.

19   Tighten the mounting nuts to the torque listed in this Chapter's Specifications, then tighten the brake line fittings securely.

20   Fill the master cylinder reservoir with fluid, then bleed the master cylinder and the brake system (see Section 9). To bleed the cylinder on the vehicle, have an assistant

depress the brake pedal and hold the pedal to the floor. Loosen the fitting to allow air and fluid to escape. Repeat this procedure on both fittings until the fluid is clear of air bubbles.

Caution: *Have plenty of rags on hand to catch the fluid - brake fluid will ruin painted surfaces. After the bleeding procedure is completed, rinse the area under the master cylinder with clean water.*

21   Test the operation of the brake system carefully before placing the vehicle into normal service.

Warning: *Do not operate the vehicle if you are in doubt about the effectiveness of the brake system. It is possible for air to become trapped in the anti-lock brake system hydraulic control unit, so, if the pedal continues to feel spongy after repeated bleedings or the BRAKE or ANTI-LOCK light stays on, have the vehicle towed to a dealer service department or other qualified shop to be bled with the aid of a scan tool.*

8   Brake hoses and lines - inspection and replacement

1   About every six months, with the vehicle raised and placed securely on jackstands, the flexible hoses which connect the steel brake lines with the front and rear brake assemblies should be inspected for cracks, chafing of the outer cover, leaks, blisters and other damage. These are important and vulnerable parts of the brake system and inspection should be complete. A light and mirror will be needed for a thorough check. If a hose exhibits any of the above defects, replace it with a new one.

Flexible hoses

2   Clean all dirt away from the ends of the hose.

3   To remove a brake hose, unscrew the tube nut with a flare-nut wrench, if available, to prevent rounding-off the corners of the nut, then remove the bolt(s) or clip(s) securing the hose to the body (and any suspension components) **(see illustrations)**.

4   Disconnect the hose from the caliper, discarding the sealing washers on either side of the fitting.

Note: *On some models, the rear brake hose threads directly into the caliper. On these models, unscrew the brake line fitting at the frame bracket, remove the retaining clip, then unscrew the hose from the caliper.*

5   Using new sealing washers, attach the new brake hose to the caliper. Tighten the banjo fitting bolt to the torque listed in this Chapter's Specifications.

6   Install the hose, making sure it isn't twisted.

7   Carefully check to make sure the suspension or steering components don't make contact with the hose. Have an assistant push down on the vehicle and also turn the steering wheel lock-to-lock during inspection.

8   Bleed the brake system (see Section 9).

Metal brake lines

9   When replacing brake lines, be sure to use the correct parts. Don't use copper tubing for any brake system components. Purchase steel brake lines from a dealer parts department or auto parts store.

10   Prefabricated brake line, with the tube ends already flared and fittings installed, is available at auto parts stores and dealer parts departments. These lines can be bent to the proper shapes using a tubing bender.

11   When installing the new line make sure it's well supported in the brackets and has plenty of clearance between moving or hot components.

12   After installation, check the master cylinder fluid level and add fluid as necessary. Bleed the brake system (see Section 9) and test the brakes carefully before placing the vehicle into normal operation.

---

9   Brake hydraulic system - bleeding

Warning: *If air has found its way into the hydraulic control unit, the system must be bled with the use of a scan tool. If the brake pedal feels spongy even after bleeding the brakes, or the ABS light on the instrument panel does not go off, or if you have any doubts whatsoever about the effectiveness of the brake system, have the vehicle towed to a dealer service department or other repair shop equipped with the necessary tools for bleeding the system.*

Warning: *Wear eye protection when bleeding the brake system. If the fluid comes in contact with your eyes, immediately rinse them with water and seek medical attention.*

Note: *Bleeding the brake system is necessary to remove any air that's trapped in the system when it's opened during removal and installation of a hose, line, caliper, wheel cylinder or master cylinder.*

1   If a brake line was disconnected only at a wheel, then only that caliper or wheel cylinder must be bled.

2   If a brake line is disconnected at a fitting located between the master cylinder and any of the brakes, that part of the system served by the disconnected line must be bled.

3   Remove any residual vacuum (or hydraulic pressure) from the brake power booster by applying the brake several times with the engine off.

4   Remove the master cylinder reservoir cap and fill the reservoir with brake fluid. Reinstall the cap.

Note: *Check the fluid level often during the bleeding operation and add fluid as necessary to prevent the fluid level from falling low enough to allow air bubbles into the master cylinder.*

5   Have an assistant on hand, as well as a supply of new brake fluid, an empty clear plastic container, a length of tubing (preferably clear) to fit over the bleeder valve and a wrench to open and close the bleeder valve.

6   Beginning at the right rear wheel, loosen the bleeder screw slightly, then tighten it to a point where it's snug but can still be loosened quickly and easily.

7   Place one end of the tubing over the bleeder screw fitting and submerge the other end in brake fluid in the container **(see illustration)**.

8   Have the assistant slowly depress the brake pedal and hold it in the depressed position.

9   While the pedal is held depressed, open the bleeder screw just enough to allow a flow of fluid to leave the valve. Watch for air bubbles to exit the submerged end of the tube. When the fluid flow slows after a couple of seconds, tighten the screw and have your assistant release the pedal.

10   Repeat Steps 8 and 9 until no more air is seen leaving the tube, then tighten the bleeder screw and proceed to the left rear wheel, the right front wheel and the left front wheel, in that order, and perform the same procedure. Check the fluid in the master cylinder reservoir frequently.

11   Never use old brake fluid. It contains moisture which can boil, rendering the brake system inoperative.

12   Refill the master cylinder with fluid at the end of the operation.

13   Check the operation of the brakes. The pedal should feel solid when depressed, with no sponginess. If necessary, repeat the entire process.

Warning: *Do not operate the vehicle if you are in doubt about the effectiveness of the brake system. It is possible for air to become trapped in the anti-lock brake system hydraulic control unit, so, if the pedal continues to feel spongy after repeated bleedings or the BRAKE or ANTI-LOCK light stays on, have the vehicle towed to a dealer service department or other qualified shop to be bled with the aid of a scan tool.*

---

10   Power brake booster - check, removal and installation

Operating check

1   Depress the brake pedal several times with the engine off and make sure that there is no change in the pedal reserve distance.

9.7 When bleeding the brakes, a hose is connected to the bleed screw at the caliper and submerged in brake fluid - air will be seen as bubbles in the tube and container (all air must be expelled before moving to the next wheel)

2   Depress the pedal and start the engine. If the pedal goes down slightly, operation is normal.

Airtightness check

3   Start the engine and turn it off after one or two minutes. Depress the brake pedal several times slowly. If the pedal goes down farther the first time but gradually rises after the second or third depression, the booster is airtight.

4   Depress the brake pedal while the engine is running, then stop the engine with the pedal depressed. If there is no change in the pedal reserve travel after holding the pedal for 30 seconds, the booster is airtight.

Removal and installation

5   Disassembly of the power unit requires special tools and is not ordinarily performed by the home mechanic. If a problem develops, it's recommended that a new or factory rebuilt unit be installed.

Caution: *Before disconnecting the brake pedal, brake booster or booster pushrod, the brake light switch and speed control deactivator switch (if equipped) must be removed. With the brake pedal in the at-rest position, pull very lightly rearward on the brake pedal, compress the plunger then rotate the switch clockwise 45-degrees and remove the switch.*

6   Remove the four bolts securing the transaxle roll resistor cross brace to the left and right front strut towers.

7   Remove the bolt securing the cross brace to the transaxle (2009 and earlier models) and remove the cross brace.

8   On 2010 and later models, remove the air filter outlet pipe (see Chapter 4). On turbocharged models, remove any ducting that would interfere.

9   Remove the vacuum hose fitting from the power booster and position it out of the way.

10   Remove the master cylinder (see Section 7).

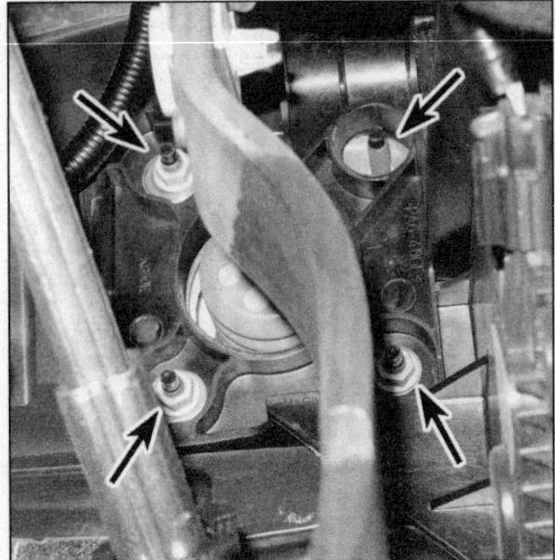

10.14 To detach the power brake booster from the firewall, remove the four nuts

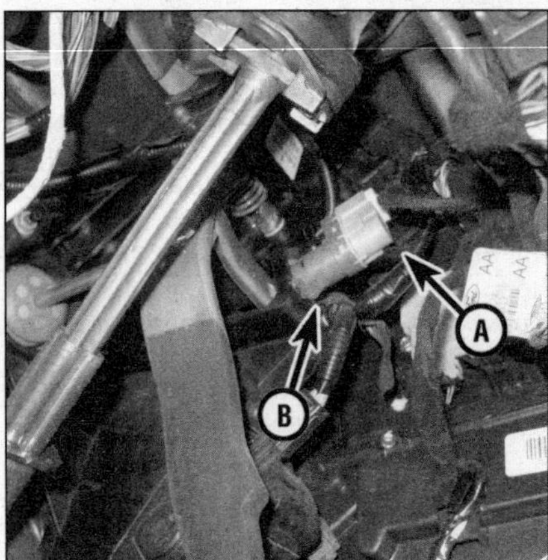

11.1 Disconnect the electrical connector (A) then rotate the switch (B) 45-degrees clockwise to remove it

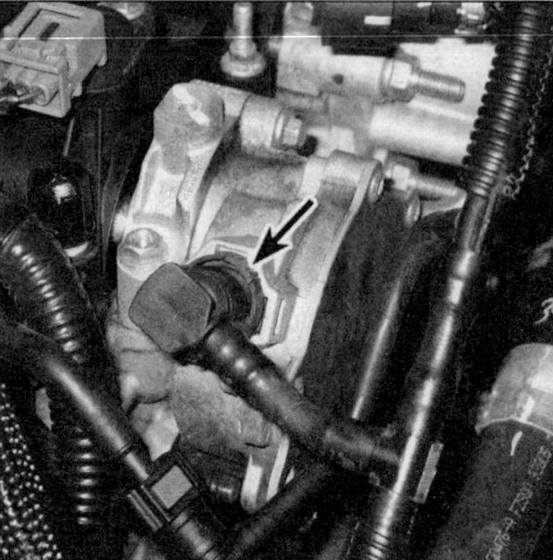

12.2 Squeeze the sides of the connector and detach the vacuum hose from the brake booster pump

12.3 Brake booster vacuum pump bolts

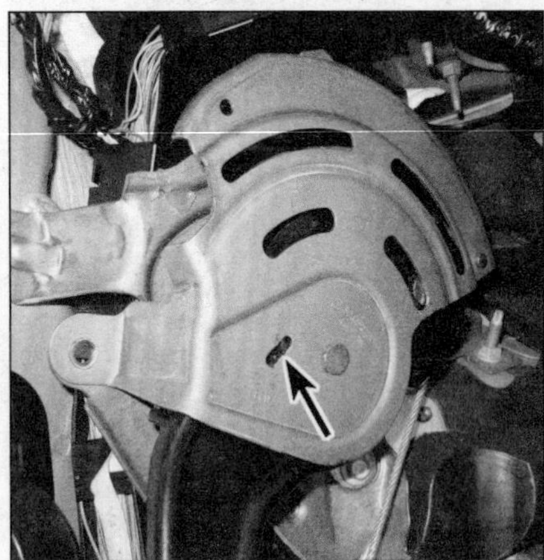

13.3 With an assistant pulling down on the parking brake cable, insert a pin into this hole to hold the automatic adjuster in the tensioned position. The parking brake cable(s) can now be disconnected

11   Without disconnecting any brake lines, unbolt the ABS Hydraulic Control Unit (HCU) mounting bracket so it can be positioned out of the way as the booster is removed.

12   In the driver's footwell, unlock the pin cover on the brake pedal arm and remove the retaining pin.

13   Remove the washer and the brake booster pushrod.

Note: *2010 and later models utilize a one-piece clevis locking pin to connect the push-rod to the brake pedal. Use a 12-point, 11 mm wrench or socket to release the tabs on the pin. The pin is a one-time-use part and must be dis-carded and replaced whenever it is removed.*

14   Remove and discard the brake booster mounting nuts **(see illustration)**, then care-fully lift the booster unit away from the firewall and out of the engine compartment.

15   Installation is the reverse of removal. Use new booster mounting nuts and test the operation of the brakes before placing the vehicle in normal service.

16   On 2010 and later models, install the brake booster pushrod before installing the brake light switch and speed control deactiva-tor switch (if equipped). When installing the

switch(es), insert the switch into the bracket and rotate the switch 45-degrees counter-clockwise. Be careful not to move the brake pedal when installing the switch or damage to the switch can occur.

11   Brake light switch - replacement

1   Disconnect the electrical connector at the switch **(see illustration)**.

2   With the brake pedal in the at-rest posi-tion, pull very lightly rearward on the brake pedal, rotate the switch clockwise 45-degrees and remove the switch.

3   Insert the switch into the bracket and rotate the switch 45-degrees counterclock-wise. Be careful not to move the brake pedal when installing the switch or damage to the switch can occur. The brake light switch is self-adjusting.

Note: *Do not press on the brake pedal during installation of the switch.*

4   Connect the switch electrical connector.

12   Brake booster vacuum pump - removal and installation

1   Remove the air outlet duct (see Chap-ter 4).

2   Detach the vacuum hose from the fitting on the pump **(see illustration)**.

3   Remove the mounting bolts and detach the pump from the cylinder head **(see illus-tration)**.

4   Check the condition of the pump O-ring; if it's in good condition, it can be re-used.

5   Installation is the reverse of removal. Align the pump with the slot on the camshaft, and tighten the bolts to the torque listed in this Chapter's Specifications.

13   Parking brake - cable tension release

Note: *On these models the parking brake cable is self-adjusting, via the parking brake control unit located at the parking brake pedal. Manual adjustment is not necessary or pos-sible.*

Note: *Several procedures in this manual re-quire the tension on the parking brake cable to be released.*

1   Remove the left kick panel or pull back the carpet as applicable) for access to the parking brake control.

2   Under the vehicle, have an assistant pull down on the front parking brake cable at the union where it connects to the rear cable. Pull down on the cable as far as possible.

Note: *If necessary, raise the vehicle and sup-port it securely on jackstands.*

3   Insert a 5/32-inch (4 mm) pin into the hole in the parking brake control **(see illustra-tion)**.

4   After work has been performed, have you assistant pull down on the cable again while you remove the pin from the parking brake control, then have your assistant slowly release tension on the cable.

Chapter 10
Suspension and steering systems

Contents

Specifications

Torque specifications

Ft-lbs (unless otherwise indicated) **Nm**

Note: *One foot-pound (ft-lb) of torque is equivalent to 12 inch-pounds (in-lbs) of torque. Torque values below approximately 15 ft-lbs are expressed in inch-pounds, because most foot-pound torque wrenches are not accurate at these smaller values.*

Front suspension

	Ft-lbs	Nm
Control arm		
Balljoint-to-steering knuckle nut		
2009 and earlier models	111	150
2010 and later models	148	200
Control arm-to-subframe		
Forward pivot bolt		
2005, 2006 and 2009 models	111	150
2007, 2008 and 2010 and later models	136	184
Rear bushing-to-subframe bolt/nuts	73	99
Stabilizer bar		
Bracket bolts		
2006 and earlier models	37	50
2007 and later models	41	55
Strut/coil spring assembly		
Upper mounting nuts		
2007 and earlier models	22	30
2007 through 2009 models	26	35
2010 and later models	22	30
Strut-to-steering knuckle bolts/nuts	129	175
Strut piston rod nut	98	133

Torque specifications

Ft-lbs (unless otherwise indicated)   **Nm**

Note: *One foot-pound (ft-lb) of torque is equivalent to 12 inch-pounds (in-lbs) of torque. Torque values below approximately 15 ft-lbs are expressed in inch-pounds, because most foot-pound torque wrenches are not accurate at these smaller values.*

Front suspension (continued)

	Ft-lbs	Nm
Subframe		
Main bolts		
Front	148	200
Rear	111	150
Subframe bracket bolts	41	55
Hub and bearing assembly bolts		
2008 and earlier models	81	110
2009 and later models	98	133
Driveaxle/hub nut	See Chapter 8	

Rear suspension

	Ft-lbs	Nm
Shock absorber		
Upper mounting nut		
2007 and earlier models	61	83
2008 and 2009 models	38	51
2010 and later models	41	55
Lower mounting bolt		
2007 and earlier models	81	110
2008 and 2009 models		
Front-wheel drive	81	110
All-wheel drive	77	105
2010 and later models	129	175
Upper suspension arm		
To subframe		
2008 and earlier models	81	110
2009 models	81	110
2010 and later models	111	150
To rear knuckle		
2007 and earlier models	77	105
2008 and 2009 models		
Front-wheel drive	77	105
All-wheel drive	81	110
2010 and later models	148	200
Lower suspension arm		
2009 and earlier models		
To rear knuckle	81	110
To subframe	98	133
2010 and later models		
To rear knuckle	196	266
To subframe	159	215
Toe link		
To rear knuckle		
2009 and earlier models	74	100
2010 and later models	59	80
To subframe	100	
2009 and earlier models	74	100
2010 and later models	52	70
Trailing arm		
To rear knuckle		
2009 and earlier models	77	104
2010 and later models	66	89
To subframe		
2009 and earlier models	81	110
2010 and later models	122	165
Stabilizer bar		
Link nuts		
2007 and earlier models		
Upper	28	37
Lower	41	55
2009 models (upper and lower)	41	55
2010 and later models		
Upper	41	55
Lower	46	62
Bushing bracket bolts	41	55

Torque specifications	**Ft-lbs** (unless otherwise indicated)	**Nm**
Steering		
Power steering pump mounting fasteners	18	24
Power steering pressure line-to-pump		
2009 and earlier models	48	65
2010 and later models	55	74
Intermediate shaft pinch bolts	18	25
Steering column mounting bolts		
2009 and earlier models	156 in-lbs	18
2010 and later models	18	25
Steering wheel bolt		
2005 models	30	40
2006 and later models	35	47
Tie-rod end-to-steering knuckle nut		
2009 and earlier models	85	115
2010 and later models	111	150
Steering gear mounting fasteners		
2007 and earlier models	86	117
2008 and 2009 models		
Step 1	30	40
Step 2	Tighten an additional 180 degrees	
2010 and later models		
With hydraulic power steering		
Step 1	66	90
Step 2	Tighten an additional 90 degrees	
With electronic power steering		
Step 1	122	165
Step 2	Tighten an additional 90 degrees	

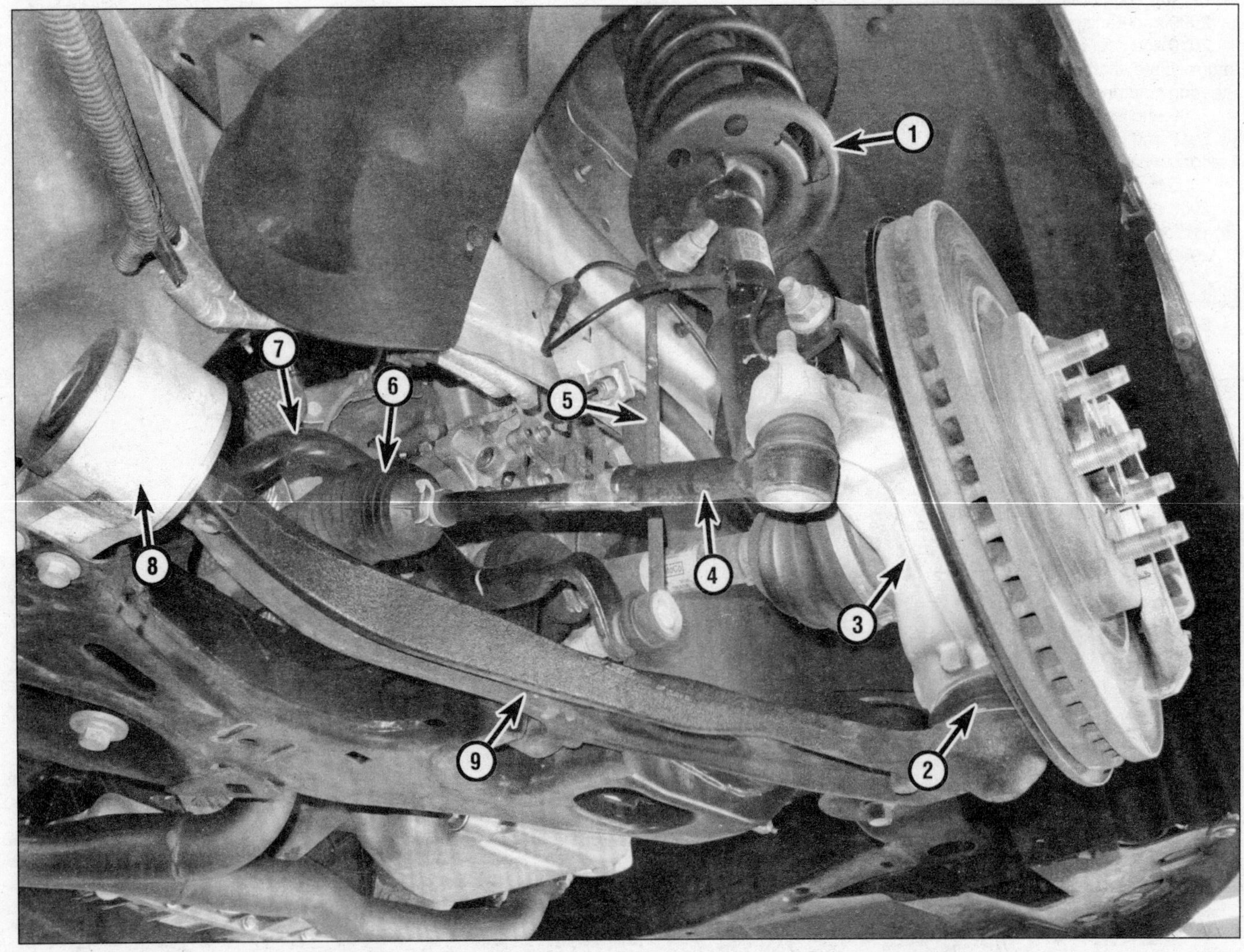

1.1 Front suspension and steering components (2013 and later models shown)

1	Strut/coil spring assembly	4	Tie-rod end	7	Stabilizer bar
2	Balljoint	5	Stabilizer bar link	8	Control arm rear bushing
3	Steering knuckle	6	Steering gear boot	9	Control arm

1   General Information

1   The front suspension is made up of a strut assembly, lower control arm, steering knuckle/hub assembly and a stabilizer bar **(see illustration)**. The strut assembly is made up of a shock absorber and a coil spring. The strut combines several functions into one by supporting the weight of the vehicle, functioning as the spring dampener and providing the pivot point for the steering knuckle.

2   The rear suspension employs upper and lower control arms, a trailing arm, a toe link, and a coil spring and shock absorber on each side **(see illustration)**.

3   The rack-and-pinion steering gear is located on the front suspension subframe and actuates the tie-rods, which are attached to the steering knuckles. The inner ends of the tie-rods are protected by rubber boots which should be inspected periodically for secure attachment, tears and leaking lubricant (which would indicate a failed rack seal).

4   The power assist system on some models consists of a belt-driven pump and associated lines and hoses. The fluid level in the power steering pump reservoir should be checked periodically (see Chapter 1). Other models are equipped with an Electricronic Power Assist Steering (EPAS) system.

5   The steering wheel operates the steering shaft, which actuates the steering gear through universal joints. Looseness in the steering can be caused by wear in the steering shaft universal joints, the steering gear, the tie-rod ends and loose retaining bolts.

Precautions

6   Frequently, when working on the suspension or steering system components, you may come across fasteners which seem impossible to loosen. These fasteners on the underside of the vehicle are continually subjected to water, road grime, mud, etc., and can become

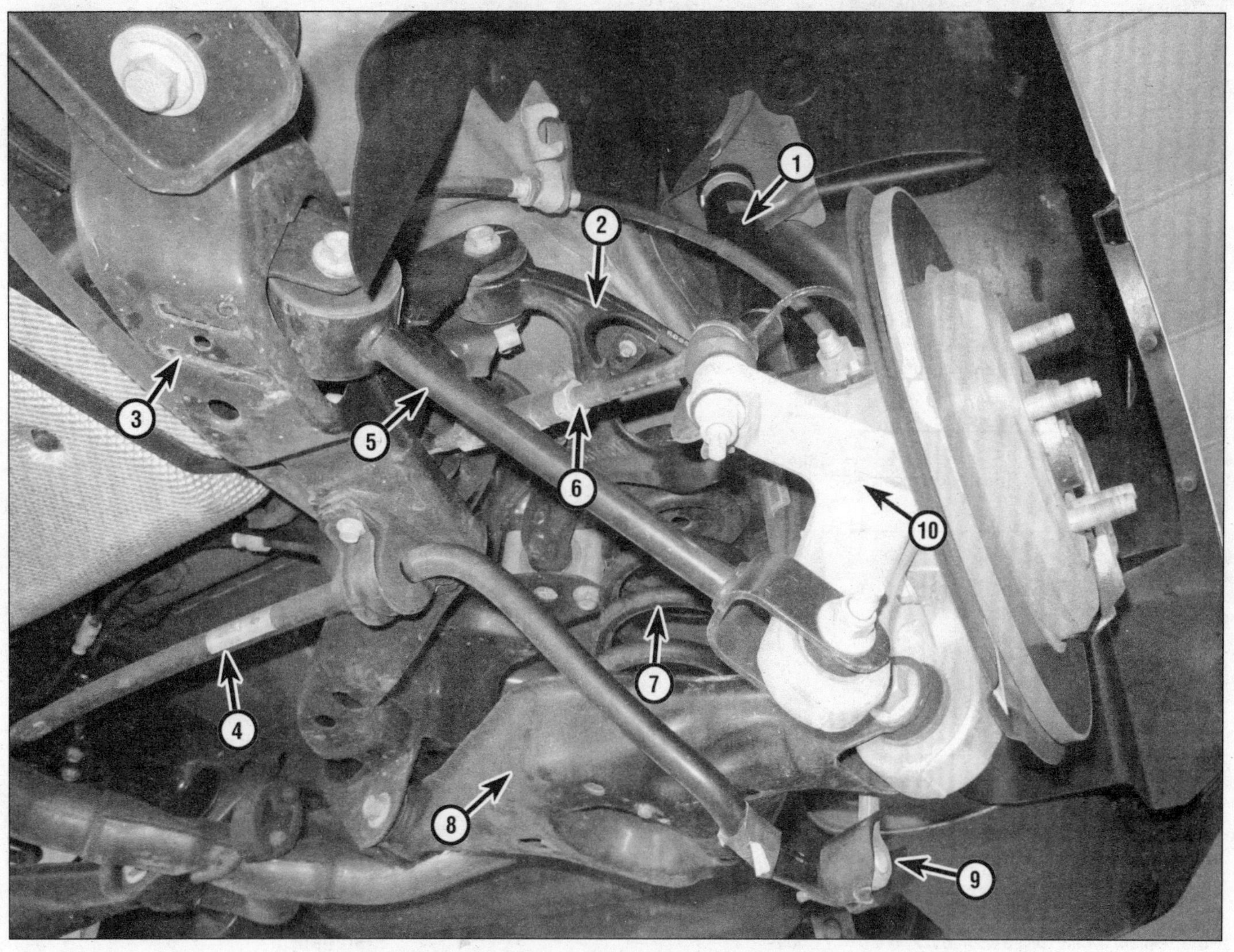

1.2 Rear suspension components (2010 and later models shown)

1	Shock absorber	5	Trailing arm	8	Lower suspension arm
2	Upper suspension arm	6	Toe link	9	Stabilizer bar link
3	Subframe	7	Coil spring	10	Rear knuckle
4	Stabilizer bar				

rusted or frozen, making them extremely difficult to remove. In order to unscrew these stubborn fasteners without damaging them (or other components), be sure to use lots of penetrating oil and allow it to soak in for a while. Using a wire brush to clean exposed threads will also ease removal of the nut or bolt and prevent damage to the threads. Sometimes a sharp blow with a hammer and punch will break the bond between a nut and bolt threads, but care must be taken to prevent the punch from slipping off the fastener and ruining the threads. Heating the stuck fastener and surrounding area with a torch sometimes helps too, but isn't recommended because

of the obvious dangers associated with fire. Long breaker bars and extension, or cheater, pipes will increase leverage, but never use an extension pipe on a ratchet - the ratcheting mechanism could be damaged. Sometimes tightening the nut or bolt first will help to break it loose. Fasteners that require drastic measures to remove should always be replaced with new ones.

7   Since most of the procedures dealt with in this Chapter involve jacking up the vehicle and working underneath it, a good pair of jackstands will be needed. A hydraulic floor jack is the preferred type of jack to lift the vehicle, and it can also be used to support certain

components during various operations.
Warning: *Never, under any circumstances, rely on a jack to support the vehicle while working on it. Whenever any of the suspension or steering fasteners are loosened or removed they must be inspected and, if necessary, replaced with new ones of the same part number or of original equipment quality and design. Torque specifications must be followed for proper reassembly and component retention. Never attempt to heat or straighten any suspension or steering components. Instead, replace any bent or damaged part with a new one.*

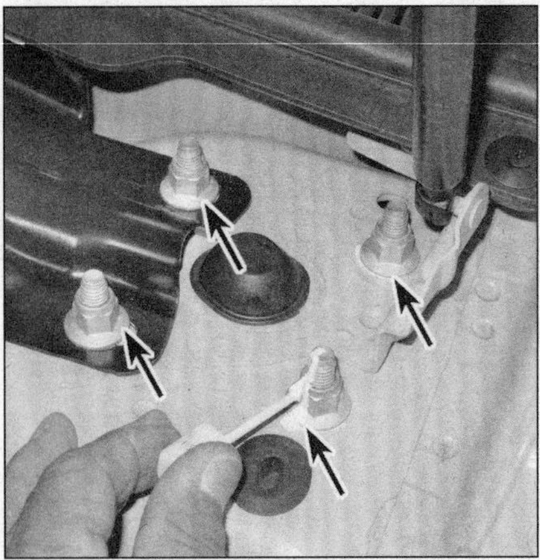

2.28 Mark the relationship of one of the mounting studs to the strut tower, then loosen the upper mounting nuts

2.32 Unscrew the nuts, then drive the bolts out with a hammer (don't turn the bolts - they have serrated shoulders)

2   Strut/coil spring assembly (front) - removal, inspection and installation

Warning: *The manufacturer recommends replacing all fasteners with new ones during installation.*

2012 and earlier models
Removal
Note: *Before starting the removal ensure the steering is unlocked.*

1   In the engine compartment, loosen the strut upper mounting nuts but do not remove them **(see illustration 2.28)**.

2   Loosen the wheel lug nuts, raise the vehicle and support it securely on jackstands. Remove the wheel.

3   Have an assistant depress the brake pedal, then remove the driveaxle/hub nut.
Note: *Obtain a new driveaxle/hub nut, but do not discard this nut yet.*

4   Remove the brake disc (see Chapter 9).

5   Separate the the tie-rod end from the steering knuckle (see Section 17).

6   Detach the stabilizer bar link from the strut (see Section 4).

7   Detach the wheel speed sensor harness from the strut, then remove the bolt and pull the wheel speed sensor from the steering knuckle.

8   Separate the control arm balljoint from the steering knuckle (see Section 5).

9   Using a front wheel hub remover, press the driveaxle from the hub splines (see Chapter 8).
Note: *DO NOT allow the driveaxle to move outward. This can cause damage to the inner CV joint. Also, DO NOT allow the splines on the wheel bearing/hub side fall against any other part of the vehicle. Use a piece of wire or strap to hold the shaft in a level position.*

10   Remove the upper mounting nuts and remove the strut and steering knuckle as an assembly.

11   Remove and nut and pinch bolt securing the steering knuckle to the strut, then slide the knuckle off of the strut.

Inspection
12   Check the shock body for leaking fluid, dents, cracks and other obvious damage which would warrant replacement.

13   Check the coil spring for chips or cracks in the spring coating (this will cause premature spring failure due to corrosion). Inspect the spring seat for cuts, hardness and general deterioration.

14   If any undesirable conditions exist, proceed to the shock absorber/coil spring disassembly procedure (see Section 3).

Installation
15   Position the steering knuckle onto the strut and install a NEW strut to steering knuckle nut and pinch bolt. Tighten the nut to the torque listed in this Chapter's Specifications.

16   Guide the assembly up into the fenderwell, align the previously made matchmarks and insert the upper mounting studs through the holes in the body. Once the studs protrude, install the new nuts so the strut won't fall back through but don't tighten them yet. This is most easily accomplished with the help of an assistant, as the strut is quite heavy and awkward.

17   With the driveaxle supported in the level position, guide the shaft into the wheel hub/bearing assembly.

18   Connect the control arm balljoint to the steering knuckle. Tighten the balljoint nut to the torque listed in this Chapter's Specifications

19   Install the wheel speed sensor and attach the sensor harness to the strut.

20   Connect the stabilizer bar link to the strut and install a new nut, tightening it to the torque listed in this Chapter's Specifications.

21   Connect the tie-rod end to the steering knuckle and install a new nut, tightening it to the torque listed in this Chapter's Specifications.

22   Install the brake discs (see Chapter 9)

23   Install the old hub nut onto the driveaxle and tighten to the torque listed in the Chapter 8 Specifications.
Caution: *This nut must be tightened before lowering the vehicle; have an assistant apply the brakes to keep the driveaxle from turning.*

24   Remove the driveaxle/hub nut and install the new one. Tighten the nut to the torque listed in the Chapter 8 Specifications.

25   Install the wheel and lug nuts, then lower the vehicle and tighten the lug nuts to the torque listed in the Chapter 1 Specifications.

26   Tighten the strut upper mounting nuts to the torque listed in this Chapter's Specifications.

27   Have the front end alignment checked, and if necessary, adjusted.

2013 and later models
Removal
28   In the engine compartment, mark the relationship of one of the mounting studs to the body, then loosen (but don't remove) the four upper mounting nuts **(see illustration)**.

29   Loosen the wheel lug nuts, raise the vehicle and support it securely on jackstands. Remove the wheel.

30   Detach the ABS wheel speed sensor harness from the strut.

31   Support the outer end of the lower control arm with a floor jack.

32   Unscrew the nuts securing the strut to the steering knuckle, then tap the bolts out with a hammer **(see illustration)**.

33   Use the floor jack to lower the knuckle to allow room to remove the shock absorber/coil spring assembly, but be careful not to overextend the inner CV joint.

Inspection
34   See Steps 12 through 14 for the inspection procedures.

Installation
35   Guide the assembly up into the fenderwell, align the previously made matchmarks and insert the upper mounting studs through the holes in the body. Once the studs protrude, install the new nuts so the shock won't fall back through but don't tighten them yet. This is most easily accomplished with the help of an assistant, as the strut is quite heavy and awkward.

36   Use the jack to position the steering knuckle and install the two lower mounting bolts and nuts, then tighten the nuts to the torque listed in this Chapter's Specifications.

37   Connect the wheel speed sensor harness to the strut.

38   Install the wheel and lug nuts, then lower the vehicle and tighten the lug nuts to the torque listed in the Chapter 1 Specifications.

39   Tighten the upper mounting nuts to the torque listed in this Chapter's Specifications.

40   Have the front end alignment checked, and if necessary, adjusted.

3.3 Make sure the spring compressor tool is on securely

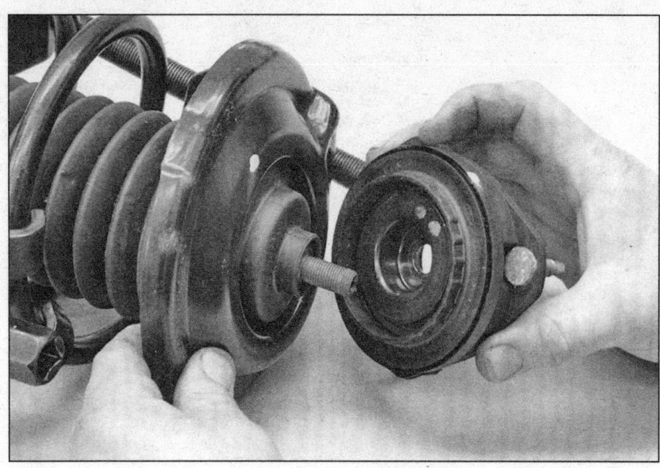

3.5a Remove the upper mount and spring seat . . .

3 Strut/coil spring assembly (front) - replacement

Warning: *Before attempting to disassemble the shock absorber/coil spring assembly, a tool to hold the coil spring in compression must be obtained. Do not attempt to use makeshift methods. Uncontrolled release of the spring could cause damage and personal injury or even death. Use a high-quality spring compressor, and carefully follow the tool manufacturer's instructions provided with it. After removing the coil spring with the compressor still installed, place it in a safe, isolated area. The strut is pressurized; do not apply heat or flame to the assembly or it could explode.*

Warning: *The manufacturer recommends replacing all fasteners with new ones during installation.*

1   If the front suspension shock absorber/coil springs exhibit signs of wear (leaking fluid, loss of damping capability, sagging or cracked coil springs) then they should be disassembled and overhauled as necessary. The shock absorbers themselves cannot be serviced, and should be replaced if faulty; the springs and related components can be replaced individually. To maintain balanced characteristics on both sides of the vehicle, the components on both sides should be replaced at the same time.

2   With the assembly removed from the vehicle (see Section 2), clean away all external dirt but be careful not to damage or remove the protective coating from the spring as this helps prevent corrosion damage.

3   Install the coil spring compressor tools (ensuring that they are fully engaged), and compress the spring until all tension is relieved from the upper mount **(see illustration)**.

4   Hold the shock absorber piston rod with a wrench and unscrew the nut. Do not use an impact wrench as this could damage the shock absorber.

5   Remove the upper mount and spring, followed by the boot, bump stop and lower spring seat **(see illustrations)**.

6   If a new spring is to be installed, the original spring must now be carefully released from the compressor. If it is to be re-used, the spring can be left in compression.

7   With the strut assembly now completely disassembled, examine all the components for wear and damage. Replace components as necessary.

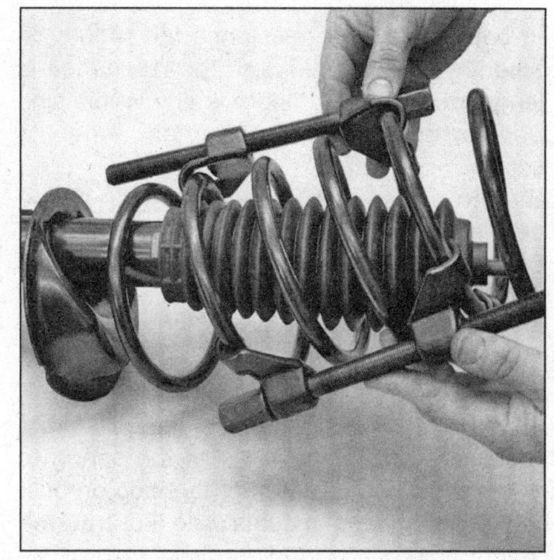

3.5b . . . then remove the spring . . .

8   Examine the shock for signs of fluid leakage. Check the piston rod for signs of pitting along its entire length, and check the shock body for signs of damage. Test the operation of the shock, while holding it in an upright position, by moving the piston through a full stroke, then through short strokes of 2 to 4 inches.

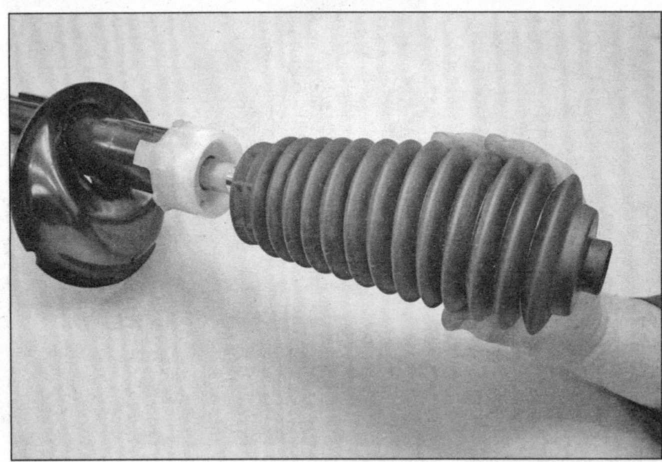

3.5c . . . followed by the boot . . .

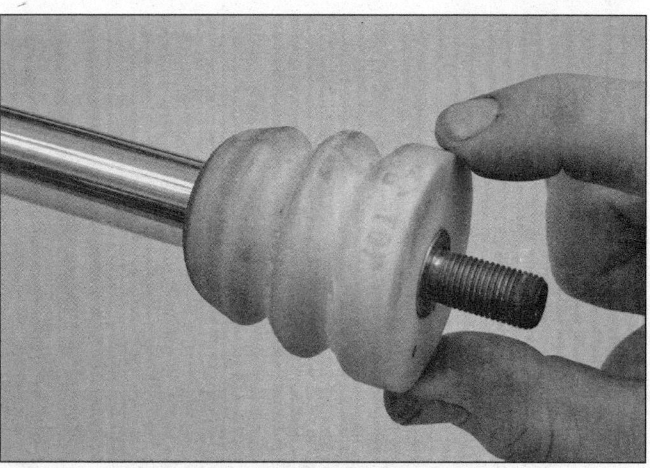

3.5d . . . and the bump stop

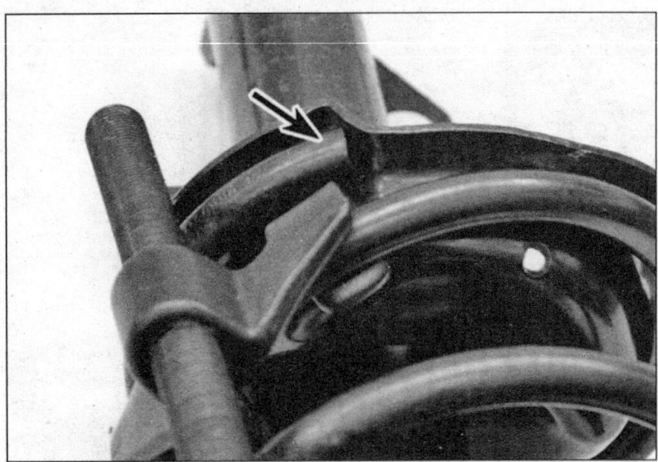

3.10 When installing the spring, make sure the ends fit into the recessed portion of the seats, and keep the gap at 0.39-inch or less

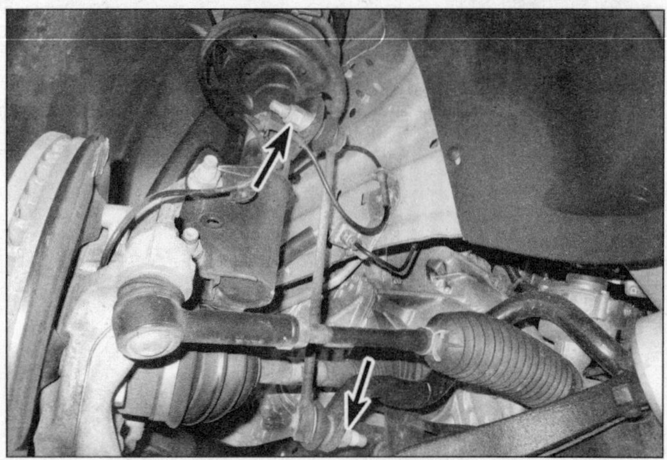

4.5 Stabilizer bar link nuts (2013 and later models shown)

In both cases, the resistance felt should be smooth and continuous. If the resistance is jerky or uneven, or if there is any visible sign of wear or damage, replacement is necessary.

9   To reassemble, install the lower spring seat first, then the bump stop and dust boot onto the shock absorber. Next install the spring and upper mount/upper seat. The arrow (2010 and earlier models) or notch (2011 and later models) on the upper mount must be aligned with the lower mount (pointing out).

10   With the spring compressed, install the rod nut. Position the ends of the spring to within 0.39-inch (10 mm) of the step on both the top and bottom mounts **(see illustration)**. Tighten the nut to the specified torque while maintaining the position at both ends.

11   Release the tension on the spring and re-install the spring assembly in the vehicle.

4   Stabilizer bar and bushings (front) - removal and installation

Warning: *The manufacturer recommends replacing all fasteners with new ones during installation.*

Note: *The bushings and brackets are part of the stabilizer bar and are not replaceable.*

1   Place the shifter in the Neutral position.

2   Detach the oxygen sensor harness from the rear of the subframe, then disconnect the electrical connector.

3   If you're working on an all-wheel drive model, remove the exhaust Y pipe and the front catalytic converter.

4   If you're working on a 2007 or earlier model, remove the rear catalytic converter.

5   Remove the the lower nut from the stabilizer link lower nut **(see illustration)**.

Caution: *DO NOT use power tools to remove the stabilizer link nuts.*

6   Separate the tie-rods ends from the steering knuckle (see Section 17).

7   Detach the control arms from the subframe (see Section 5).

8   Support the rear of the subframe utilizing a floor jack positioned in the center.

9   Remove the power steering bracket bolt from the return line and position the line out of the way.

10   Remove the steering gear nuts and bolts (see Section 19). Support the steering gear from above with a length of rope or wire.

11   Remove and subframe bracket bolts and the subframe rear bolts **(see illustration)**, then lower the subframe about two inches.

12   Remove the left and right stabilizer bar bracket bolts **(see illustration)**.

13   Remove the stabilizer bar by guiding it towards the right side of the vehicle between the subframe and steering gear.

14   Installation is the reverse of the removal procedure. Replace all nuts and bolts with NEW fasteners and tighten them to the torque values listed in this Chapter's Specifications.

5   Control arm (front) - removal, inspection and installation

Warning: *The manufacturer recommends replacing all fasteners with new ones during installation.*

Removal

1   Loosen the wheel lug nuts on the side to be disassembled, raise the front of the vehicle, support it securely on jackstands and remove the wheel.

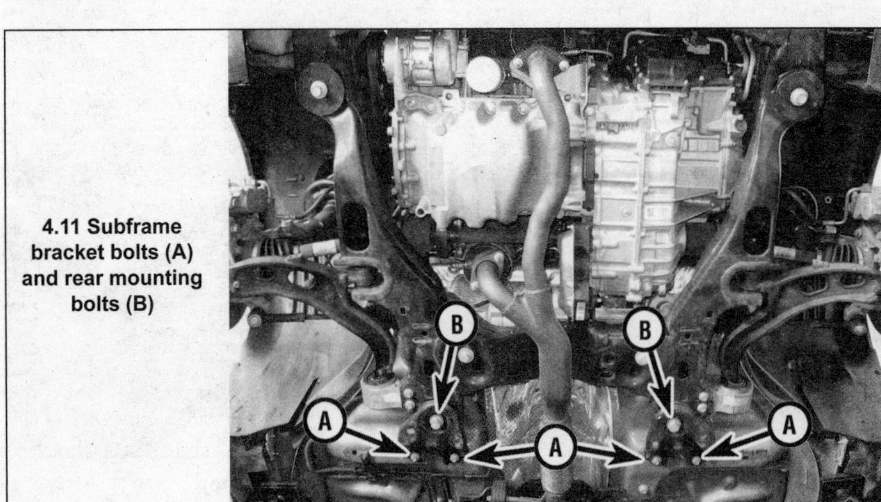

4.11 Subframe bracket bolts (A) and rear mounting bolts (B)

4.12 Stabilizer bar bracket bolts (left side shown, right side identical)

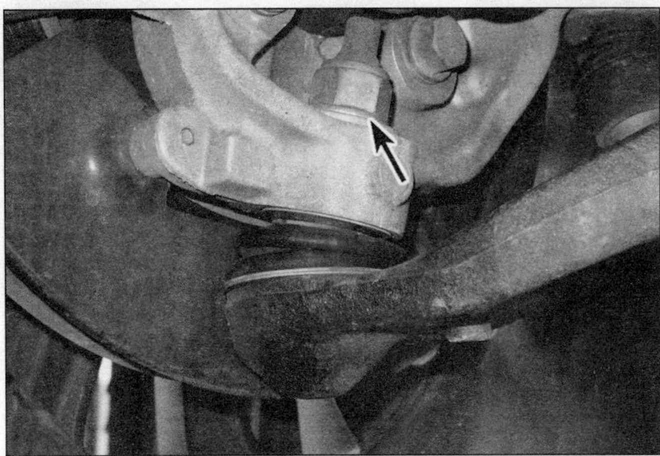

5.2 Control arm balljoint nut. If the stud turns as you loosen the nut, hold it with a wrench placed on the hex

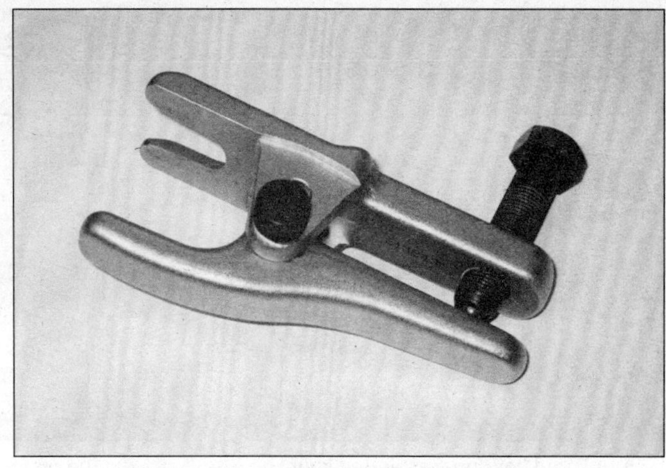

5.3 Balljoint separators like this are available at most auto parts stores

2   Remove the control arm balljoint nut **(see illustration)**.

3   Push the lower control arm down until the balljoint releases from the knuckle. If the balljoint stud sticks in the knuckle, use a balljoint separator to force the components apart **(see illustration)**.

4   Remove the control arm front pivot bolt and the rear bushing bracket bolts and detach the control arm from the subframe **(see illustration)**.

Inspection

5   Check the control arm for distortion and the bushings for wear, replacing parts as necessary. Do not attempt to straighten a bent control arm.

Installation

6   Installation is the reverse of removal. When installing the control arm, leave the control arm-to-subframe bolts finger tight until the balljoint has been connected to the steering knuckle. Tighten the balljoint nut to the torque listed in this Chapter's Specifications.

7   Raise the outer end of the control arm with a floor jack to simulate normal ride height, then tighten the control arm-to-subframe fasteners to the torque listed in this Chapter's Specifications.

8   It's a good idea to have the front wheel alignment checked and, if necessary, adjusted after this job has been performed.

6   Control arm bushing - replacement

1   Replacement of the control arm bushing requires a press and adapters of the proper size. Remove the control arm (see Section 5) and take it to an automotive machine shop or other qualified repair shop to have the bushing replaced.

7   Steering knuckle and hub - removal and installation

Warning: *Dust created by the brake system is harmful to your health. Never blow it out with compressed air and don't inhale any of it. Do not, under any circumstances, use petroleum-based solvents to clean brake parts. Use brake system cleaner only.*

Warning: *The manufacturer recommends replacing all fasteners with new ones during installation.*

2012 and earlier models

1   Refer to Section 2 for the steering knuckle removal and installation procedure (it's part of the strut removal procedure).

2013 and later models

Removal

2   Loosen the wheel lug nuts. Raise the vehicle and support it securely on jackstands, then remove the wheel.

3   With the brake applied to prevent the driveaxle from rotating, remove the driveaxle/ hub nut. Obtain a new nut, but do not discard the old nut yet.

4   Separate the tie rod from the steering knuckle (see Section 17).

5   Remove the brake disc (see Chapter 9).

6   Remove the ABS wheel speed sensor and the wiring harness bracket bolt (see Chapter 9)

7   Separate the lower arm from the steering knuckle (see Section 5).

8   Separate the driveaxle from the hub using a drive hub remover or an equivalent puller (see Chapter 8).

9   Remove the strut-to-steering knuckle bolts and separate the knuckle from the strut (see Section 2).

Installation

10   Guide the steering knuckle and hub assembly into position, inserting the driveaxle into the hub.

11   Install and tighten the strut-to-knuckle bolts and nuts.

12   Connect the balljoint to the steering knuckle and tighten the nut to the torque listed in this Chapter's Specifications.

13   Attach the tie-rod end to the steering

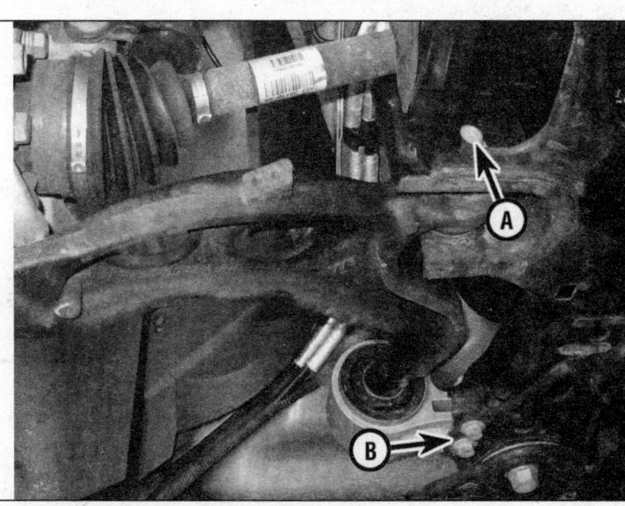

5.4 Control arm (A) and bushing bracket bolts (B)

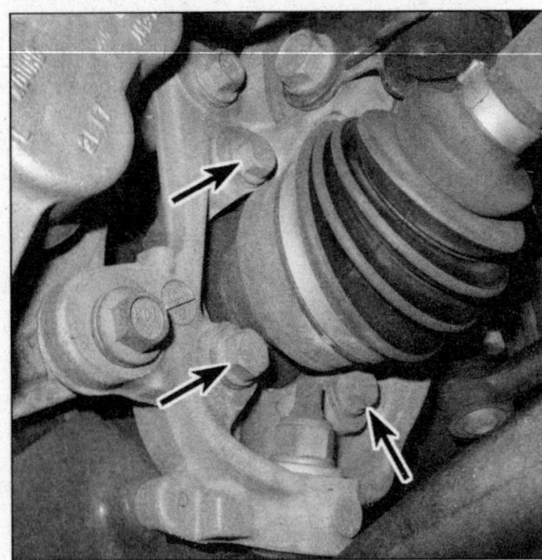

8.5 Hub and bearing-to-steering knuckle bolts (one bolt not visible here)

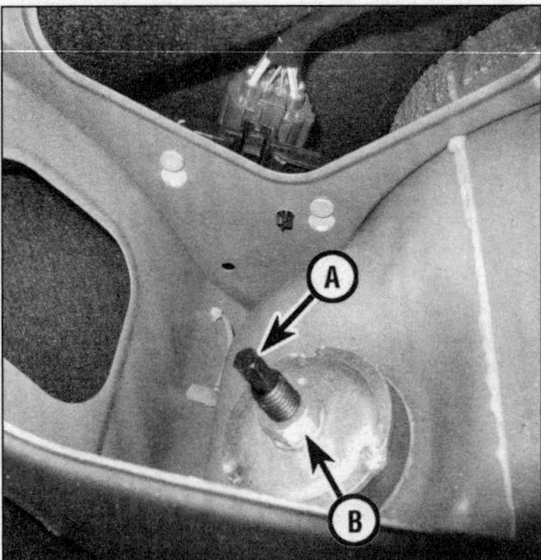

9.20 Hold the piston rod (A) with a wrench to prevent it from turning while loosening the shock absorber upper mounting nut (B)

knuckle arm (see Section 17). Tighten the nut to the torque listed in this Chapter's Specifications.

14   Install the wheel speed sensor and harness bracket.

15   Install the brake disc and caliper/mounting bracket assembly (see Chapter 9).

16   With the brake applied to prevent the driveaxle from rotating, seat the driveaxle by using the old driveaxle/hub nut and washer and tighten the nut to the torque listed in the Chapter 8 Specifications. Remove and discard the old nut, replace it with the new nut and tighten to the specified torque.

Note: *The driveaxle/hub nut must be tightenedbeforelowering the vehicle or damage to the wheel bearings may occur.*

Note: *The driveaxle/hub nut is coated with a one-use locking chemical and cannot be reused for final assembly. The locking chemical is activated by heat created during tightening. The nut must be tightened to the specified torque within five minutes of starting it on the threads or the locking chemical will not activate properly.*

17   Install the wheel and lug nuts. Lower the vehicle and tighten the lug nuts to the torque listed in then Chapter 1 Specifications.

18   Have the front-end alignment checked and, if necessary, adjusted.

8   Hub and bearing assembly (front) - removal and installation

Warning: *The manufacturer recommends replacing all fasteners with new ones during installation.*

1   Loosen the wheel lug nuts. Raise the vehicle and support it securely on jackstands, then remove the wheel.

2   With an assistant applying the brake to prevent the driveaxle from rotating, remove the driveaxle/hub nut. Obtain a new nut but do not discard the old nut yet.

3   Remove the brake caliper, the caliper mounting bracket and the brake disc from the hub (see Chapter 9).

Caution: *Suspend the caliper to the strut coil spring with a piece of wire. DO NOT let the caliper hang by the brake hose.*

4   Push the driveaxle into the hub using a drive hub remover or an equivalent puller (see Chapter 8).

Caution: *Just push it into the hub as far as necessary to allow you to put a socket on the hub and bearing assembly bolts.*

5   Remove the hub and bearing-to-steering knuckle bolts **(see illustration)**. Separate the hub and bearing assembly from the knuckle as you draw the assembly off of the driveaxle.

Caution: *Be careful not to overextend the inner CV joint.*

6   Make sure that the mounting surface inside the steering knuckle and on the driveaxle splines is smooth and free of burrs and nicks prior to installing the hub/bearing assembly.

7   Install the hub/bearing assembly to the steering knuckle using NEW mounting bolts. Tighten the bolts to the torque listed in this Chapter's Specifications.

8   Install the brake disc, the caliper mounting bracket and the caliper; tighten the fasteners to the torque listed in the Chapter 9 Specifications.

9   With the brake applied to prevent the driveaxle from rotating, seat the driveaxle by using the old driveaxle/hub nut and washer and tighten the nut to the torque listed in the Chapter 8 Specifications. Remove and discard the old nut, replace it with the new nut and tighten to the specified torque.

10   Install the wheel and lug nuts, lower the vehicle and tighten the lug nuts to the torque listed in the Chapter 1 Specifications.

9   Shock absorber (rear) - removal and installation

Warning: *The manufacturer recommends replacing all fasteners with new ones during installation.*

Caution: *New shock absorbers are gas-filled and come compressed and retained with a fi-* berglass strap. Do NOT remove the strap until the shock is installed.

2012 and earlier models

1   With the vehicle at rest, measure the distance from the center of the wheel hub to the lip of the fender.

2   Open the trunk and pull back the interior quarter trim panel (see Chapter 11).

3   Loosen the wheel lug nuts, raise the vehicle and support it securely on jackstands. Block the front wheels to prevent the vehicle from rolling and remove the rear wheel.

4   Support the lower suspension arm with a floor jack.

5   Remove the brake caliper and mounting bracket as an assembly (see Chapter 9).

Caution: *Support the caliper with a length of wire - don't let it hang by the brake hose.*

6   Remove the upper shock absorber mounting nut.

7   Index the spring position on the shock absorber and the upper spring isolator.

8   Raise the floor jack enough to slightly compress the coil spring.

9   Remove the trailing arm-to-rear knuckle bolt (see Section 10).

10   If you're working on an all-wheel drive model, loosen the trailing arm to subframe bolt. if you're working on a front-wheel drive model, remove the trailing arm-to-subframe bolt and remove the arm

11   Remove the lower arm-to-rear knuckle bolt.

12   If you're working on a front-wheel drive model, loosen the lower arm-to-subframe bolt.

13   Slowly lower the floor jack and remove it.

14   Remove the shock absorber lower mounting bolt. Maneuver the shock absorber and coil spring out from between the lower arm and the subframe.

15   Installation is the reverse of the removal procedure, noting the following points:

- *Transfer the match marks to the new components, then align them on assembly.*
- *Before tightening any of the fasteners, raise the lower suspension arm with a floor jack to simulate normal ride height (measured in Step 1), then tighten the fasteners to the torque listed in this Chapter's Specifications.*
- *Install the wheel and lug nuts. Lower the vehicle and tighten the nuts to the torque listed in the Chapter 1 Specifications.*

2013 and later models

16   Loosen the wheel lug nuts, raise the vehicle and support it securely on jackstands. Block the front wheels to prevent the vehicle from rolling and remove the rear wheel.

17   Open the trunk and pull back the interior quarter trim panel (see Chapter 11).

18   Detach the stabilizer bar link from the rear knuckle (see Section 14).

19   Support the lower suspension arm with a floor jack placed under the spring pocket.

20   Remove the shock absorber upper mounting nut **(see illustration)**.

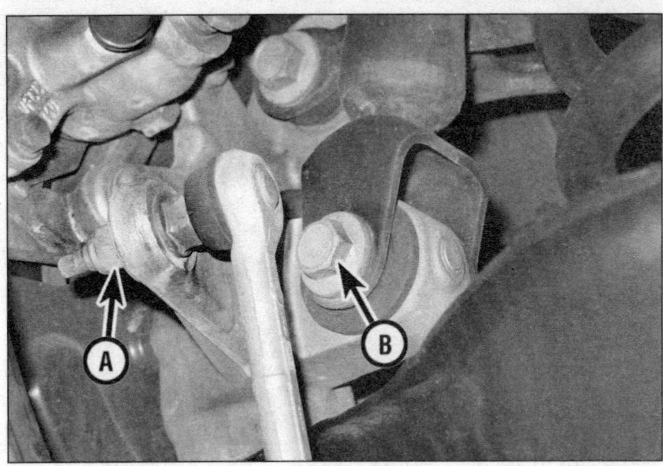

9.21 Stabilizer bar link upper mounting nut (A, remove first) and shock absorber lower mounting bolt (B)

10.6 Upper suspension arm-to-rear knuckle nut and bolt

21   Remove the shock absorber lower mounting bolt **(see illustration)** and remove the shock absorber.

22   Installation is the reverse of the removal procedure. Use new fasteners and tighten them to the torque values listed in this Chapter's Specifications.

23   Before tightening the shock absorber lower muonting bolt, raise the lower suspension arm with a floor jack to simulate normal ride height, then tighten the fasteners to the torque listed in this Chapter's Specifications.

24   Install the wheel and lug nuts. Lower the vehicle and tighten the nuts to the torque listed in the Chapter 1 Specifications.

10   Suspension arms (rear) - removal and installation

Warning: *The manufacturer recommends replacing all fasteners with new ones during installation.*

Note: *To prevent possible damage to the bushings, always tighten bushing fasteners while the full weight of the vehicle is resting on the wheels (or alternatively, with the suspension raised with a floor jack to simulate normal ride height).*

Upper suspension arm
2009 and earlier models

Note: *Upper suspension arm removal and installation on these models requires removing the subframe (see Section 22) and the use of special tools (bearing splitter, drawbolt-type extractor, and the necessary adapters). For this reason it is recommended that this procedure be left to a qualified repair shop. If desired, the subframe/rear suspension assembly can be removed and taken to a shop to have the procedure performed, saving the expense of subframe removal and installation.*

2010 and later models

1   With the vehicle at rest, measure the distance from the center of the wheel hub to the lip of the fender.

2   Loosen the wheel lug nuts, raise the vehicle and support it securely on jackstands. Block the front wheels to prevent the vehicle from rolling and remove the rear wheel.

3   Unbolt the parking brake cable brackets from the chassis.

4   Remove the left and right brake calipers and mounting brackets (as assemblies) and support them with wire or rope (see Chapter 9).

5   Position a floor jack under each rear knuckle. Raise the jacks just enough to make contact.

6   Detach the upper arm from the rear knuckle **(see illustration)**.

7   Remove the rear upper arm-to-subframe bushing bolts **(see illustration)**.

8   Detach the upper ends of the stabilizer bar links from the rear knuckles (see Section 14).

9   Unbolt the lower ends of the shock absorbers from the rear knuckles (see Section 9).

10   Remove the subframe bracket bolts and forward mounting bolts, then remove the subframe rear mounting bolts (see Section 22).

11   Slowly and evenly lower the subframe with the floor jacks just enough to allow removal of the upper arm mounting bolt.

12   Remove the upper arm to subframe bolt **(see illustration)**.

13   To replace the rear bushing, remove the bolt and slide the bushing off the arm.

14   Installation is the reverse of removal, noting the following points:

a) *If a new rear bushing is being installed, make sure it is positioned with the markings TOP OF PART facing upwards and ARM TO THIS SIDE arrow is pointing inward, toward the arm. Tighten the bolt to the torque listed in this Chapter's Specifications.*

b) *Raise the subframe into place and tighten the subframe mounting bolts to the torque listed in this Chapter's Specifications.*

c) *Using the floor jacks, raise the steering knuckles to simulate normal ride height (the measurement recorded in Step 1), then tighten the upper control arm fasteners and the shock absorber lower mounting bolts to the torque values listed in this Chapter's Specifications.*

d) *Install the wheel and lug nuts. Lower the vehicle and tighten the nuts to the torque listed in the Chapter 1 Specifications.*

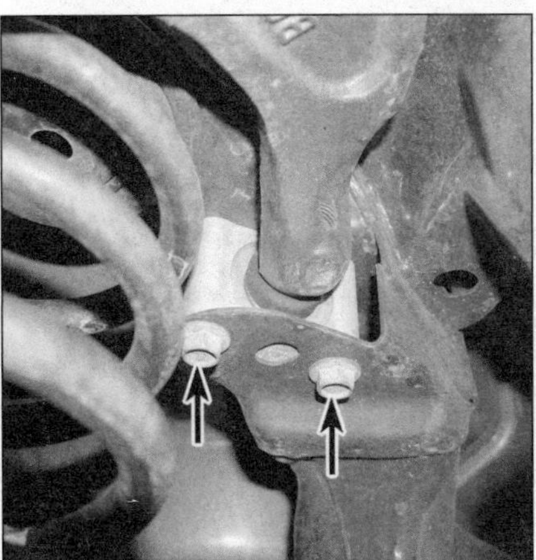

10.7 Upper suspension arm rear bushing bolts

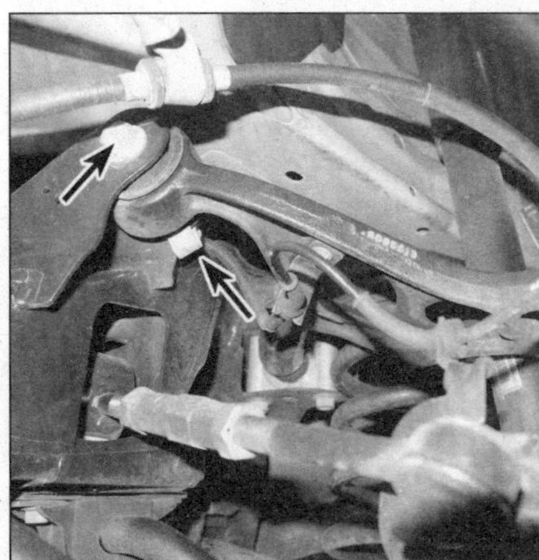

10.12 Upper arm-to-subframe bolt and nut

10.35 Lower control arm-to-rear knuckle bolt/nut

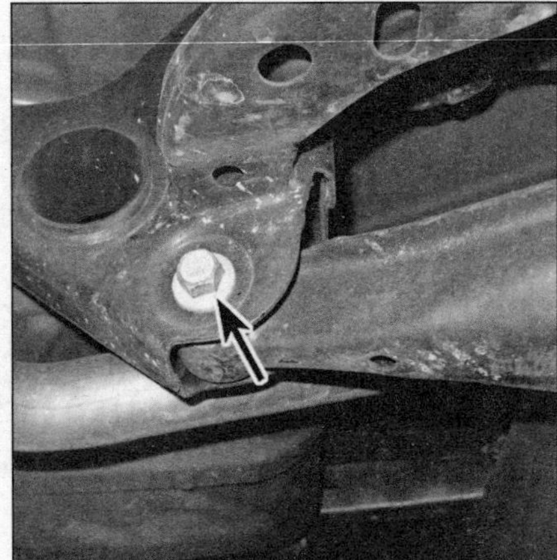

10.36 Lower arm-to-subframe bolt (the nut on the other side is captive; don't try to turn it)

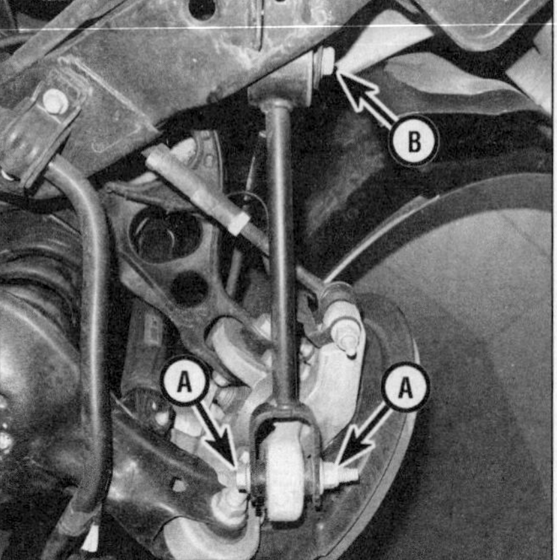

10.44 Trailing arm-to-rear knuckle nut and bolt (A) and trailing arm-to-subframe bolt (B) (2010 and later models shown)

Lower suspension arm

2009 and earlier models

15   Measure the distance front the center of the rear wheel hub to the fender lip with the vehicle sitting on level ground, under its own weight.

16   Loosen the wheel lug nuts, raise the vehicle and support it securely on jackstands. Block the front wheels to prevent the vehicle from rolling and remove the rear wheel.

17   Remove the trailing arm-to-rear knuckle bolt.

18   Loosen the trailing arm to subframe bolt. The trailing arm will swing down, but do not allow the arm to swing down violently.

19   Remove the ABS wheel speed sensor harness from the toe link.

20   Mark the relationship of the cam on the toe link nut to the arm, then loosen the nut.

21   Remove the toe link-to-rear knuckle nut and bolt.

22   If you're working on a front-wheel drive model, remove the four stabilizer bar bracket bolts.

23   Support the lower arm with a floor jack.

24   Remove the lower arm-to-rear knuckle bolt.

25   Remove the shock absorber lower bolt.

26   Slowly lower the floor jack until the coil spring is no longer under compression, then remove the shock absorber and coil spring.

27   Remove the lower arm-to-subframe bolt and remove the lower arm.

28   Installation is the reverse of the removal procedure. Tighten the fasteners to the torque listed in this Chapter's Specifications but only after the outer end of the lower arm is raised with a floor jack to simulate normal ride height (as recorded in Step 15).

29   Install the wheel and lug nuts. Lower the vehicle and tighten the nuts to the torque listed in the Chapter 1 Specifications.

30   Have the wheel alignment checked and, if necessary, adjusted.

2010 and later models

31   Measure the distance front the center of the rear wheel hub to the fender lip with the vehicle sitting on level ground, under its own weight.

32   Loosen the wheel lug nuts, raise the vehicle and support it securely on jackstands. Block the front wheels to prevent the vehicle from rolling and remove the rear wheel.

33   Detach the stabilizer bar links from the steering knuckles (both sides; see Section 14).

34   Support the lower arm with a floor jack positioned underneath the spring pocket.

35   Remove the lower arm-to-rear knuckle nut and bolt **(see illustration)**.

36   Loosen (but don't remove) the lower arm-to-subframe bolt **(see illustration)**.

37   Slowly lower the floor jack until the coil spring is extended, then remove the spring.

38   Remove the lower arm-to-subframe bolt and detach the arm.

39   Installation is the reverse of the removal procedure. Tighten the fasteners to the torque listed in this Chapter's Specifications but only after the outer end of the lower arm is raised with a floor jack to simulate normal ride height (as recorded in Step 31).

40   Install the wheel and lug nuts. Lower the vehicle and tighten the nuts to the torque listed in the Chapter 1 Specifications.

Trailing arm

41   Measure the distance between the center of the wheel hub and fender lip with the vehicle on level ground and under its own weight.

42   Loosen the wheel lug nuts, raise the vehicle and support it securely on jackstands. Block the front wheels to prevent the vehicle from rolling and remove the rear wheel.

43   Support the lower arm with a floor jack. Raise the jack until the distance between the center of the hub and the lip of the fender is the same as measured in Step 41.

44   Remove the trailing arm-to-knuckle bolt **(see illustration)**.

45   Remove the trailing arm-to-subframe bolt and remove the arm.

46   Installation is the reverse of the removal procedure. Tighten the fasteners to the torque listed in this Chapter's Specifications, then lower the floor jack supporting the lower arm.

47   Install the wheel and lug nuts. Lower the vehicle and tighten the nuts to the torque listed in the Chapter 1 Specifications.

Toe link

48   Measure the distance between the center of the wheel hub and fender lip with the vehicle on level ground and under its own weight.

49   Loosen the wheel lug nuts, raise the vehicle and support it securely on jackstands. Block the front wheels to prevent the vehicle from rolling and remove the rear wheel.

50   Support the lower arm with a floor jack. Raise the jack until the distance between the center of the hub and the lip of the fender is the same as measured in Step 48.

51   If you're working on a 2009 or earlier model, disconnect the wheel speed sensor wire harness from the toe link. Also on 2009 and earlier models mark the relationship of the inner toe link cam bolt to the arm.

52   Remove the toe link-to-steering knuckle nut and bolt **(see illustration)**. If you're work-

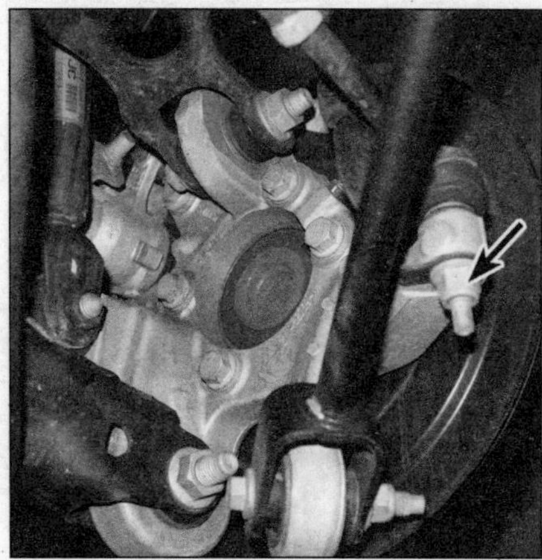

10.52 Toe link-to-steering knuckle nut and bolt (2010 and later models shown)

ing on a 2013 or later model and the link balljoint sticks in the knuckle, force it out with a two-jaw puller or balljoint separator.

53   Remove the toe link-to-subframe nut and bolt (2009 and earlier models) or bolt (2010 and later models) **(see illustration)**.

Note: *On 2010 and later models the nut is captive; don't try to loosen it.*

54   Installation is the reverse of the removal procedure. Tighten the fasteners to the torque listed in this Chapter's Specifications , then lower the floor jack supporting the lower arm.

55   Install the wheel and lug nuts. Lower the vehicle and tighten the nuts to the torque listed in the Chapter 1 Specifications.

56   Have the wheel alignment checked and, if necessary, adjusted.

11 Coil spring (rear) - removal and installation

Warning: *Always replace the springs as a set - never replace just one of them.*

Warning: *The manufacturer recommends replacing all fasteners with new ones during installation.*

2009 and earlier models

1   Coil spring removal and installation is part of the rear shock absorber removal and installation procedure (see Section 9).

2010 and later models

2   Coil spring removal and installation on these models is part of the lower arm removal and installation procedure. See Section 10, but note that is isn't necessary to detach the lower arm from the subframe (just loosen the fastener).

12 Hub and bearing assembly (rear) - removal and installation

Warning: *The manufacturer recommends replacing all fasteners with new ones during installation.*

Removal

1   Loosen the rear wheel lug nuts. Raise the rear of the vehicle and support it securely on jackstands, then remove the wheel.

2   If you're working on an all-wheel drive model, have an assistant apply the brakes while you remove the driveaxle/hub nut.

3   Remove the brake disc (see Chapter 9).

4   Remove the wheel speed sensor (see Chapter 9).

5   Remove the bolts and detach the wheel bearing and hub assembly from the wheel knuckle **(see illustration)**. If you're working on an all-wheel drive model, simultaneously push the driveaxle from the hub with a suitable puller (see Chapter 8).

Installation

6   Install the wheel hub/bearing assembly onto the rear knuckle. If you're working on an

10.53 Toe-link-to-subframe bolt (2010 and later models shown)

all-wheel drive model, guide the end of the driveaxle into the splines as the hub is being installed. Tighten the hub assembly-to-rear knuckle bolts to the torque listed in this Chapter's Specifications.

7   The remainder of installation is the reverse of removal. Tighten the brake fasteners to the torque values listed in the Chapter 9 Specifications. If you're working on an all-wheel drive model, tighten the driveaxle/hub nut to the torque listed in the Chapter 8 Specifications.

8   Install the wheel and lug nuts, then lower the vehicle. Tighten the lug nuts to the torque listed in the Chapter 1 Specifications.

13 Rear knuckle - removal and installation

Warning: *The manufacturer recommends replacing all fasteners with new ones during installation.*

1   Measure the distance front the center of the rear wheel hub to the fender lip with the vehicle sitting on level ground, under its own weight.

2   Loosen the rear wheel lug nuts. Raise the rear of the vehicle and support it securely on jackstands, then remove the wheel.

3   Support the lower arm with a floor jack. Raise the jack until the distance between the center of the hub and the lip of the fender is the same as measured in Step 1.

4   If you're working on an all-wheel drive model, have an assistant apply the brakes while you remove the driveaxle/hub nut.

5   Remove the brake caliper (see Chapter 9) but leave the brake line attached. Use wire to support the caliper - don't let it hang by the hose.

6   Remove the hub and bearing assembly (see Section 12).

7   Disconnect the lower end of the shock absorber from the knuckle (see Section 9).

8   Detach the outer end of the upper control arm from the knuckle (see Section 10).

9   Detach the toe link from the knuckle (see Section 10).

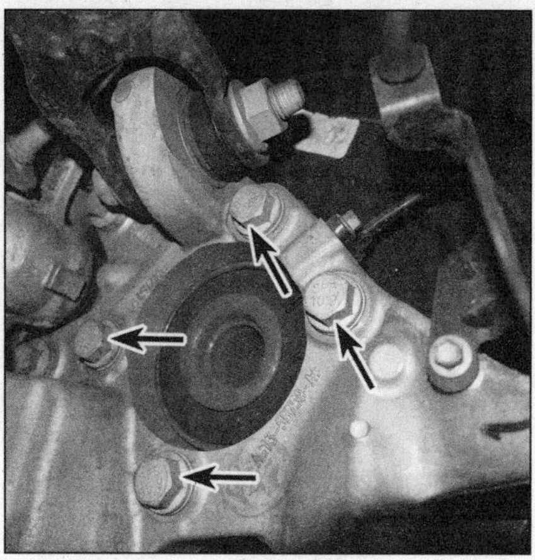

12.5 Hub and bearing assembly-to-rear knuckle bolts

10   Detach the trailing arm from the knuckle (see Section 10).

11   Detach the lower arm from the knuckle (see Section 10), and remove the knuckle.

12   Installation is the reverse of the removal procedure, tightening all suspension fasteners to the torque values listed in this Chapter's Specifications with the suspension at normal ride height (as measured in Step 1). Tighten the brake fasteners to the torque values listed in the Chapter 9 Specifications. If you're working on an all-wheel drive model, tighten the driveaxle/hub nut(s) to the torque listed in the Chapter 8 Specifications.

13   Install the wheel and lug nuts, then lower the vehicle. Tighten the lug nuts to the torque listed in the Chapter 1 Specifications.

14 Stabilizer bar and bushings (rear) - removal and installation

Warning: *The manufacturer recommends replacing all fasteners with new ones during installation.*

Note: *The bushings and brackets are part of the stabilizer bar and are not replaceable.*

2009 and earlier front-wheel drive models

1   Loosen the rear wheel lug nuts. Raise the rear of the vehicle and support it securely on jackstands, then remove the wheels.

2   Lower the exhaust system from the rear of the flex pipe by removing the insulators and supporting the exhaust with a jack or jack stand.

3   Remove the stabilizer bar link to stabilizer bar nuts (both sides).

4   Remove the bolts holding the stabilizer bar bushing brackets and remove the brackets and the stabilizer bar.

5   While the stabilizer bar is off the vehicle, inspect the bushings, if cracked, worn or deteriorated the stabilizer bar must be replaced.

6   Installation is the reverse of removal. Tighten the fasteners to the torque values

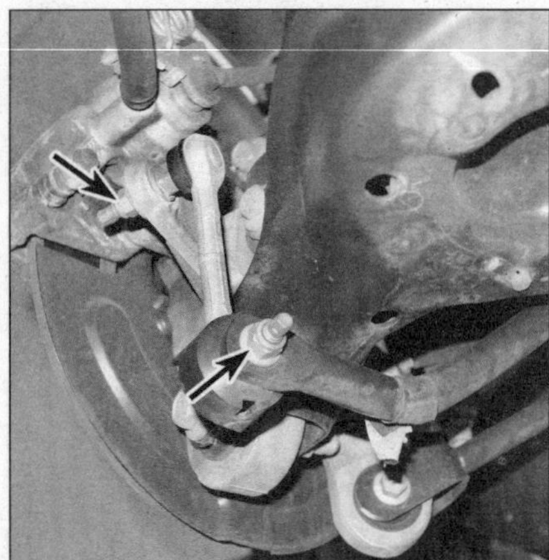

14.39 Stabilizer bar link nuts. If the ballstud spins while loosening the nut, hold it with a wrench (2010 and later models)

14.40 Stabilizer bar bracket bolts (2010 and later models)

listed in this Chapter's Specifications.

7   Install the wheel and lug nuts, then lower the vehicle. Tighten the lug nuts to the torque listed in the Chapter 1 Specifications.

2007 and earlier all-wheel drive models

8   Measure the distance front the center of the rear wheel hub to the fender lip with the vehicle sitting on level ground, under its own weight.

9   Loosen the rear wheel lug nuts. Raise the rear of the vehicle and support it securely on jackstands, then remove the wheels.

10   Remove the rear section of the exhaust system.

11   Have an assistant apply the brake while you unscrew the left side driveaxle/hub nut.

12   Remove the left side brake caliper and caliper mounting bracket as an assembly (see Chapter 9). Don't disconnect the brake hose.

Caution: *Support the caliper with a length of wire or rope - don't let it hang by the brake hose.*

13   Push the driveaxle stub shaft into the hub with a drive hub remover (see Chapter 8).

14   Push the driveaxle stub shaft into the hub with a drive hub remover (see Chapter 8).

15   Remove the left side upper arm-to-rear knuckle nut, then use a balljoint separator and separate the arm from the knuckle.

16   Support the lower suspension arm with a floor jack. Raise the jack to slightly compress the coil spring.

17   Loosen the left-side trailing arm-to-sub-frame bolt, then detach the trailing arm from the knuckle.

18   Detach the left-side toe link from the knuckle.

19   Loosen the left side shock absorber lower mounting bolt. Lower the floor jack until the coil spring si almost fully extended, then remove the shock absorber lower mounting bolt.

20   Remove the nuts and detach the stabilizer bar links from the stabilizer bar.

21   Remove the bolts holding the stabilizer bar bushing brackets and remove the brackets and the stabilizer bar. Guide the bar out from the left side of the vehicle.

22   While the stabilizer bar is off the vehicle, inspect the bushings, if cracked, worn or deteriorated the stabilizer bar must be replaced.

23   Installation is the reverse of removal. Tighten the fasteners to the torque values listed in this Chapter's Specifications.

Caution: *Before tightening any of the fasteners, raise the lower control arm to simulate normal ride height (as measured in Step 8).*

24   Install the wheel and lug nuts, then lower the vehicle. Tighten the lug nuts to the torque listed in the Chapter 1 Specifications.

2008 and 2009 all-wheel drive models

25   Measure the distance front the center of the rear wheel hub to the fender lip with the vehicle sitting on level ground, under its own weight.

26   Loosen the rear wheel lug nuts. Raise the rear of the vehicle and support it securely on jackstands, then remove the wheels.

27   Remove the rear driveaxles (see Chapter 8).

28   Remove the rear section of the exhaust system.

29   Support the right-side lower suspension arm with a floor jack.

30   Remove the right-side upper arm-to-rear knuckle nut, then use a balljoint separator and separate the arm from the knuckle.

31   Remove the cross brace under the differential.

32   Remove the nuts and detach the stabilizer bar links from the bar.

33   Remove the stabilizer bracket bolts and guide the stabilizer bar out from the right side of the vehicle.

34   While the stabilizer bar is off the vehicle, inspect the bushings, if cracked, worn or deteriorated the stabilizer bar must be replaced.

35   Installation is the reverse of removal. Tighten the fasteners to the torque values

listed in this Chapter's Specifications.

Caution: *Before tightening any of the fasteners, raise the lower control arm to simulate normal ride height (as measured in Step 25).*

36   Install the wheel and lug nuts, then lower the vehicle. Tighten the lug nuts to the torque listed in the Chapter 1 Specifications.

2010 and later models

37   Loosen the rear wheel lug nuts. Raise the rear of the vehicle and support it securely on jackstands, then remove the wheels.

38   Support the exhaust system with a floor jack, then detach the two rear exhaust system hangers from their anchors. Lower the exhaust system about two inches.

39   Remove the nuts and detach the stabilizer bar links from the bar **(see illustration)**.

40   Remove the stabilizer bar bracket bolts, then remove the bar **(see illustration)**.

41   While the stabilizer bar is off the vehicle, inspect the bushings, if cracked, worn or deteriorated the stabilizer bar must be replaced.

42   Installation is the reverse of removal. Tighten the fasteners to the torque values listed in this Chapter's Specifications.

43   Install the wheel and lug nuts, then lower the vehicle. Tighten the lug nuts to the torque listed in the Chapter 1 Specifications.

15   Steering wheel - removal and installation

Warning: *These models are equipped with a Supplemental Restraint System (SRS), more commonly known as airbags. Always disable the airbag system before working in the vicinity of any airbag system component to avoid the possibility of accidental deployment of the airbag(s), which could cause personal injury (see Chapter 12).*

Warning: *Do not use a memory saving device to preserve the PCM or radio memory when working on or near airbag system components.*

Removal

1   Turn the ignition key to Off, then disconnect the cable from the negative terminal of the battery (see Chapter 5). Wait at least two minutes before proceeding.

2   Turn the steering wheel so the wheels are pointing straight ahead.

2007 and earlier models

3   Remove the access panel from the underside of the steering wheel.

4   One at a time, pry each retaining spring end up and over the post until they overlap each other.

5   Detach the airbag module from the steering wheel.

2008 through 2012 models

6   Remove the knee bolster trim panel from underneath the steering column, then remove

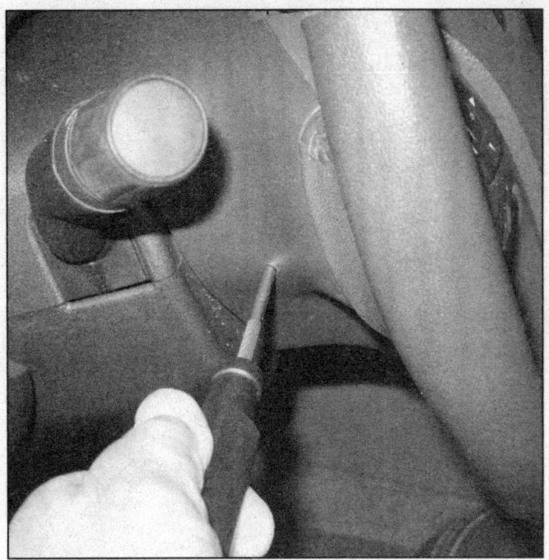

15.9 Depress the clips through the holes on each side of the steering wheel to release the airbag (2013 and later models)

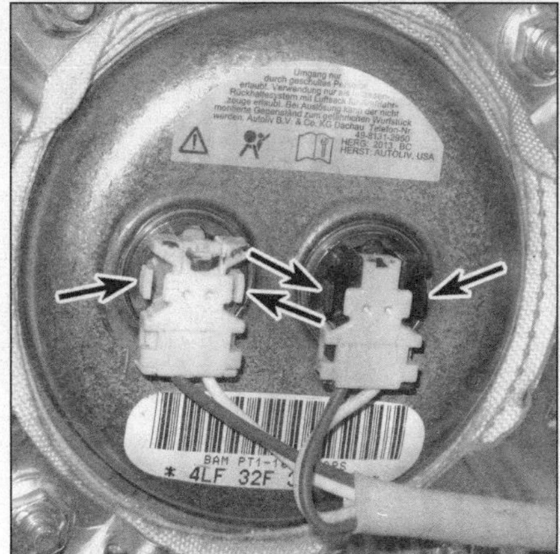

15.10 Squeeze the locking tabs, then disconnect the airbag connectors

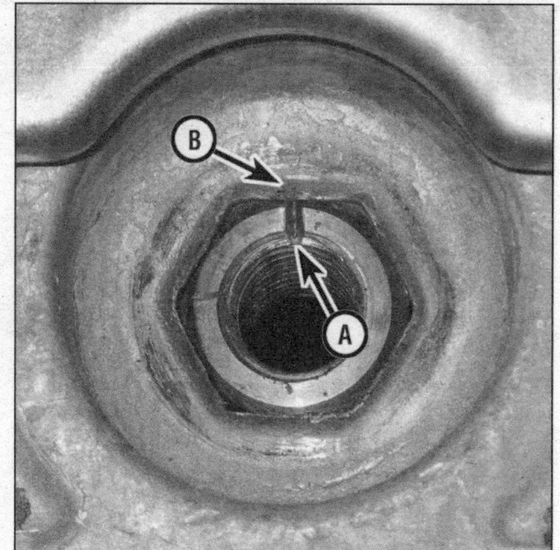

15.12 Mark (A) is usually a factory mark, make your mark at point (B) to ensure correct location during assembly

the steering column covers (see Chapter 11). **Note:** *On 2008 and 2009 models, remove the instrument cluster bezel along with the steering column upper cover.*

7   Turn the steering wheel 90-degrees, then insert a screwdriver through the upper access hole to disengage the upper airbag module retaining spring clip.

8   Repeat the procedure and disengage the lower clip, then remove the airbag module from the steering wheel.

2013 and later models

9   Use a small screwdriver or a 3 mm Allen wrench through the holes in the side of the steering wheel to release the airbag module clips **(see illustration)**. Gently pull the airbag module away from the wheel on the side you have released, then repeat this Step on the other side of the wheel.

All models

10   Disconnect the airbag module electrical connectors **(see illustration)**.

11   Remove the airbag and set the module in a safe, isolated area.

Warning: *Carry the airbag module with the trim side facing away from you, and set the steering wheel/airbag module down with the trim side facing up. Don't place anything on top of the steering wheel/airbag module.*

12   Remove the steering wheel bolt. Make match marks on the wheel and the steering shaft, then disconnect the electrical connector(s) **(see illustration)**.

13   You will need to route the connectors through the steering wheel.

14   Try rocking the wheel lightly to remove it from the shaft. If this does not work, use a suitable puller to remove the steering wheel. Do not hit the steering shaft with a hammer or you will damage the shaft.

15   Tape the clockspring so that it cannot rotate **(see illustration)**.

Caution: *Do not rotate the steering shaft at any time while the wheel and airbag are removed or the clockspring could be damaged.*

16   If it is necessary to remove the airbag

clockspring, remove the steering column covers (see Chapter 11), disconnect the electrical connectors, then remove the screws and take the clockspring off the steering column.

Installation

17   If the clockspring was removed, install it onto the steering column, making sure the pins on the back of the clockspring engage with the holes in the steering wheel rotation sensor. Install the screws, tightening them securely.

18   New clocksprings come equipped with an anti-rotation pin that holds them in the pre-centered position. If you are installing a new clockspring, don't remove the pin until you are ready to install the steering wheel after the steering column covers have been installed. If you are installing the old clockspring, or are not sure whether or not the clockspring has become uncentered, center the clockspring:

2007 and earlier models

a) *Turn the inner hub of the clockspring counterclockwise until you feel resistance. Don't apply too much force to the hub or you could damage the clockspring ribbon.*

b) *Turn the clockspring hub approximately three turns clockwise until the clockspring ribbon appears in the window at the 2 o'clock position and the arrow on the hub lines up with the arrow on the bottom left part of the housing.*

2008 through 2012 models

a) *Turn the inner hub of the clockspring counterclockwise until you feel resistance. Don't apply too much force to the hub or you could damage the clockspring ribbon.*

b) *Turn the hub to the 12 o'clock position, then rotate it clockwise three turns, returning it to the 12 o'clock position.*

2013 and later models

a) *Turn the inner hub of the clockspring counterclockwise until you feel resistance.*

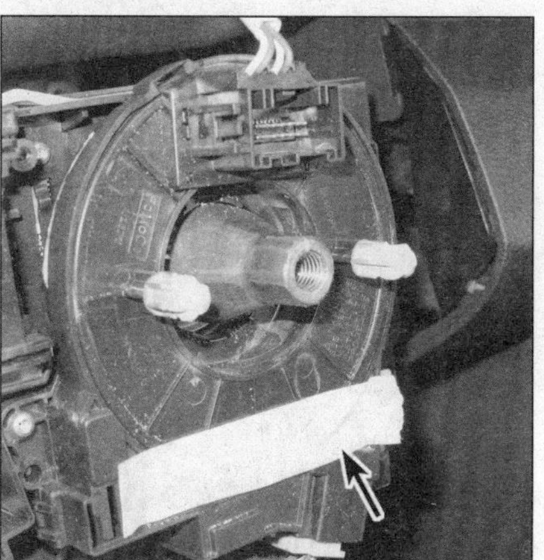

15.15 Apply a piece of tape to the clockspring to prevent it from rotating (arrow points to the tape strip)

Don't apply too much force to the hub or you could damage the clockspring ribbon.

b) *Position the electrical connector of the clockspring in the 12 o'clock position.*

c) *Turn the hub of the clockspring clockwise five turns, returning the electrical connector to the 12 o'clock position.*

d) *Turn the hub of the clockspring counterclockwise two turns, returning the electrical connector to the 12 o'clock position.*

All models

19   Install the steering column covers, if removed. If you installed a new clockspring, remove the anti-rotation pin.

20   Install the steering wheel by reversing the removal procedure. When placing the steering wheel onto the shaft, be sure to align the match marks.

21   Tighten the NEW steering wheel bolt to the torque listed in this chapters Specifications.

Caution: *Make sure the connectors fit correctly on the airbag module (with the safety tabs still UP). When connecting the airbag connectors,*

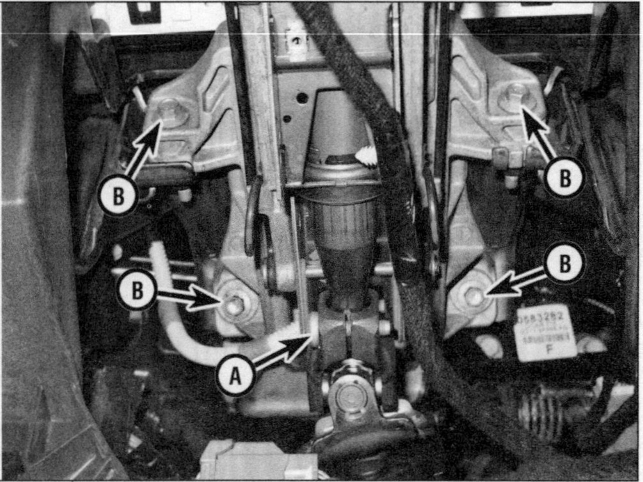

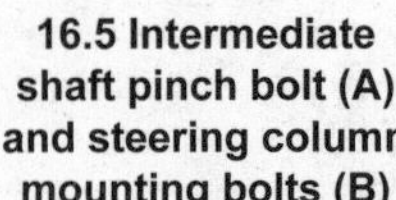

16.5 Intermediate shaft pinch bolt (A) and steering column mounting bolts (B)

17.2a Loosen the jam nut . . .

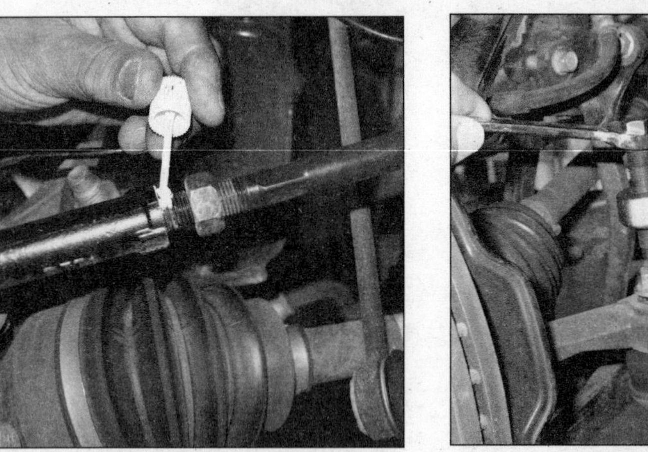

17.2b . . . then mark the position of the tie-rod end

17.3 If necessary, use a puller to separate the tie-rod end from the steering knuckle arm

match the key on the connector to the corresponding keyway on the module. Do not push the connectors on if the clips are down. After the clips are secured, push the airbag module down toward the wheel until the retaining clips lock. When seated properly, the gap between the airbag module trim cover and the steering wheel should be even and consistent.

16 Steering column - removal and installation

Warning: *These models are equipped with a Supplemental Restraint System (SRS), more commonly known as airbags. Always disable the airbag system before working in the vicinity of any airbag system component to avoid the possibility of accidental deployment of the airbag(s), which could cause personal injury (see Chapter 12).*
Warning: *Do not use a memory saving device to preserve the PCM or radio memory when working on or near airbag system components.*
Warning: *The manufacturer recommends replacing all fasteners with new ones during installation.*

Removal

1   Park the vehicle with the wheels pointing straight ahead. Disconnect the cable from the negative terminal of the battery (see Chapter 5).
2   Remove the steering wheel (see Section 15) and tape the airbag clockspring to prevent it from turning.
Caution: *If this is not done, the airbag clockspring could be damaged.*
3   Remove the steering column covers (see Chapter 11).
4   Remove the lower shroud, on models so equipped.
5   Remove the steering column intermediate shaft pinch bolt and disconnect the shaft from the column **(see illustration)**.
6   Disconnect the electrical connectors from all of the components on the steering column, the detach the wire harness from the column .
7   Remove the four steering column mounting fasteners **(see illustration 16.5)**. Lower the column and pull it to the rear, making sure nothing is still connected, then remove the column.

Installation

8   Guide the steering column into position, engaging the intermedaite shaft U-joint with the bottom of the steering shaft, then install the steering column mounting fasteners and tighten them to the torque listed in this Chapter's Specifications.
Note: *An assistant will be very helpful in this procedure.*
9   Tighten the intermediate shaft pinch bolt to the torque listed in this Chapter's Specifications.
10   The remainder of installation is the reverse of removal.

17 Tie-rod ends - removal and installation

Warning: *The manufacturer recommends replacing all fasteners with new ones during installation.*

Removal

1   Loosen the front wheel lug nuts. Apply the parking brake, raise the front of the vehicle and support it securely on jackstands. Remove the front wheel.
2   Hold the tie-rod with a pair of locking pliers or wrench and loosen the jam nut enough to mark the position of the tie-rod end in relation to the threads **(see illustrations)**.
3   Remove the nut on the tie-rod end stud and disconnect the tie-rod end from the steering knuckle arm. If the ballstud sticks in the steering knuckle arm, separate it from the arm with a puller **(see illustration)**.
4   Unscrew the tie-rod end from the tie-rod.

Installation

5   Thread the tie-rod end on to the marked position and insert the stud into the steering knuckle arm. Install the nut on the stud and tighten it to the torque listed in this Chapter's Specifications. Tighten the jam nut securely.
6   Install the wheel and lug nuts. Lower the vehicle and tighten the lug nuts to the torque listed in the Chapter 1 Specifications.
7   Have the wheel alignment checked and, if necessary, adjusted.

18.3 The outer ends of the steering gear boots are secured by band-type clamps (A); they're easily removed with a pair of pliers. The inner ends are retained by boot clamps (B) which must be cut off and discarded

18   Steering gear boots - replacement

1   Loosen the lug nuts, raise the vehicle and support it securely on jackstands. Remove the wheel.
2   Remove the tie-rod end and jam nut (see Section 17).
3   Remove the outer steering gear boot clamp with a pair of pliers **(see illustration)**. Cut off the inner boot clamp with a pair of diagonal cutters. Slide off the boot.
4   Before installing the new boot, wrap the threads and serrations on the end of the steering rod with a layer of tape so the small end of the new boot isn't damaged.
5   Slide the new boot into position on the steering gear until it seats in the groove in the steering rod and install new clamps.
6   Remove the tape and install the tie-rod end (see Section 17).
7   Install the wheel and lug nuts. Lower the vehicle and tighten the lug nuts to the torque listed in the Chapter 1 Specifications.

19   Steering gear - removal and installation

Warning: *These models are equipped with airbags. Always disable the airbag system before working in the vicinity of airbag system components (see Chapter 12). Make sure the steering column shaft is not turned while the steering gear is removed or you could damage the airbag system clockspring. To prevent the shaft from turning, turn the ignition key to the lock position with the steering wheel in the straight ahead position before beginning work.*
Warning: *The manufacturer recommends replacing all fasteners with new ones during installation.*

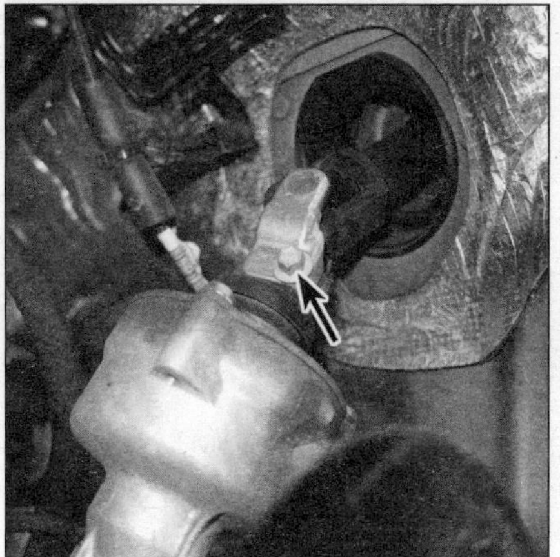

19.11 Remove the pinch bolt and disconnect the intermediate shaft from the steering gear

Removal

1   Disconnect the cable from the negative terminal of the battery (see Chapter 5).
2   On models with hydraulic power steering, remove as much fluid from the power steering fluid reservoir as possible.
3   Loosen the front wheel lug nuts. Raise the vehicle and place it securely on jackstands. Remove both front wheels. Also remove the under-vehicle splash shield.
4   Position the steering wheel in the straight ahead position. It is advised that a steering wheel holder be used while performing this operation. Alternatively, run the seat belt through the steering wheel and click it into its buckle.
5   Detach the tie-rod ends from the steering knuckles (see Section 17)

Models with hydraulic power steering

6   Place a container under the pressure line fittings to catch any remaining fluid.
7   Remove the pressure line bracket.
8   Remove the power steering line clamp bolt from the steering gear.
9   Gently rotate the clamp plate and detach the pressure lines.
Note: *The O-rings must be discarded and replaced with new ones.*
10   On 2007 and earlier models, loosen the column shaft boot clamp from the shaft boot.
11   Remove the steering gear bolt and disconnect the intermediate shaft **(see illustration)**. On 2007 and earlier models this is done from under the instrument panel. On 2008 and later models it's done from the engine compartment.

2007 and earlier models

12   If you're working on an all-wheel drive model, raise the transaxle and engine, as an assembly, about 1/4-inch.
13   Remove the steering gear fasteners and remove the steering gear.

2008 and later models

14   Remove the stabilizer bar link upper nuts (see Section 4).
15   If you're working on an all-wheel drive model, unbolt the Y-pipe and lower the front

19.22 Exhaust Y-pipe-to-manifold fasteners

19.23 Roll restrictor bolts

portion of the exhaust system.
Caution: *DO NOT twist or bend the flex pipe excessively - it will break the pipe.*
16   Remove the roll restrictor bracket to transaxle bolt.
17   Place a jack under the roll restrictor bracket and raise the transaxle/engine assembly about 1-inch.
Caution: *DO NOT let the jack touch the engine or transaxle as pressure here will damage the engine or transaxle.*
18   Remove the stabilizer bar bracket bolts (see Section 4).
19   Remove the steering gear fasteners and remove the steering gear out from the left side of the vehicle.

Models with electric power steering

20   Remove the pinch bolt and disconnect the intermediate shaft from the steering gear **(see illustration 19.11)**.
21   Remove the stabilizer bar link upper nuts (see Section 4).
22   Remove the front section of the exhaust system **(see illustration)**.
23   Remove the bolts from the roll restrictor **(see illustration)**.
24   Support the rear of the subframe utilizing a floor jack positioned in the center.
25   Remove and subframe bracket bolts

19.27 Steering gear mounting bolts (models with electric power steering)

and the subframe rear bolts **(see illustration 4.11)**. Loosen the subframe front mounting bolts, then lower the rear of the subframe fot access to the steering gear.

26   Unscrew the steering wiring harness bracket bolt and disconnect the electrical connectors to the steering gear assist motor.

27   Remove the steering gear bolts **(see illustration)** and maneuver the steering gear out from the right side of the vehicle.

Installation

28   Installation is the reverse of removal, noting the following points:

a) *New fasteners should be used during reassembly. Tighten all fasteners to the torque values listed in this Chapter's Specifications.*

b) *The O-rings on the pressure lines must be replaced.*

c) *Fill the power steering reservoir with the recommended fluid (see Chapter 1). Bleed the power steering hydraulic system as described in Section 21.*

d) *Install the wheel and lug nuts. Lower the vehicle and tighten the lug nuts to the torque listed in the Chapter 1 Specifications.*

e) *Have the front end alignment checked and, if necessary, adjusted.*

20   Power steering pump - removal and installation

Warning: *The manufacturer recommends replacing all fasteners with new ones during installation.*

Removal

1   Disconnect the cable from the negative battery terminal (see Chapter 5).

2   Remove the coolant expansion tank and reposition it without disconnecting the hoses.

3   Disconnect the following electrical connectors:, Power Steering Pressure switch Camshaft Position Sensor, oxygen sensor, A/C pressure switch, and the cooling fan, as applicable, and

any others that would interfere with removal.

4   Remove the nuts that hold the wire harness to the engine, position the harness aside.

5   Detach any hose brackets that would interfere with removal of the pump.

6   Using a large syringe or suction gun, suck as much fluid out of the power steering fluid reservoir as possible. Place a drain pan under the vehicle to catch any fluid that spills out when the hoses are disconnected.

7   Remove the drivebelt (see Chapter 1).

8   Unbolt the power steering fluid reservoir and position it aside.

9   Disconnect the supply hose and the pressure line fitting from the pump.

Note: *To disconnect the pressure line fitting from the pump body on later models, insert a punch into the mounting cavity to secure the pump body in place, then pull on the pressure line with your hand.*

10   Remove the pump mounting bolts: rotate the pulley for access to the bolts.

Installation

11   Installation is the reverse of removal, noting the following points:

a) *The O-ring seals must be replaced with new ones*

b) *Tighten all fasteners to the torque listed in this Chapter's Specifications.*

c) *Fill the power steering reservoir with the recommended fluid (see Chapter 1). Bleed the power steering hydraulic system as described in Section 21.*

21   Power steering system - bleeding

1   The power steering system must be bled whenever a line is disconnected. Bubbles can be seen in power steering fluid that has air in it and the fluid will often have a tan or milky appearance. Low fluid level can cause air to mix with the fluid, resulting in a noisy pump as well as foaming of the fluid.

2   Open the hood and check the fluid level in the reservoir, adding the specified fluid necessary to bring it up to the proper level (see Chapter 1).

3   Start the engine and slowly turn the steering wheel several times from left-to-right and back again. Do not turn the wheel completely from lock-to-lock. Check the fluid level, topping it up as necessary until it remains steady and no more bubbles are visible.

22   Subframe - removal and installation

Warning: *The manufacturer recommends replacing all fasteners with new ones during installation.*

1   Disconnect the cable from the negative terminal of the battery (see Chapter 5).

Front

2   Loosen the front wheel lug nuts. Raise the vehicle and place it securely on

jackstands. Remove both front wheels. Also remove the under-vehicle splash shield.

3   Position the steering wheel in the straight ahead position. It is advised that a steering wheel holder be used while performing this operation. Alternatively, run the seat belt through the steering wheel and click it into its buckle.

2007 and earlier models

4   Support the engine and transaxle assembly from above with an engine support fixture.
Note: *Engine support fixtures are available at many auto parts stores and most equipment rental yards.*

5   Remove the air filter housing and duct (see Chapter 4).

6   Remove the cowl panel (see Chapter 11).

7   Remove the upper roll restrictor bolt and the cross-brace.

8   Remove the high-pressure power steering line bracket bolts.

9   Remove the Positive Crankcase Ventilation line.

10   If you're working on an all-wheel drive model, unbolt the transfer case bracket from the subframe.

11   Remove the front section of the exhaust system.

12   Detach the coolant hose clamps at the subframe.

13   Unscrew the lower roll restrictor fasteners.

14   Detach the control arm balljoints from the steering knuckles (see Section 5).

15   Detach the stabilizer bar links from the front struts (see Section 4).

16   Remove the power steering line bracket at the rear of the subframe.

17   Detach the intermediate shaft from the steering gear (see Section 19).

18   Unbolt the steering gear from the subframe and support it from above with a length of wire or rope.

19   Unbolt the transaxle and engine mounts from the subframe.

20   Detach any remaining sires or hoses from the subframe.

21   Detach the inner fender splash shields from the subframe.

22   Remove the right-side driveaxle (see Chapter 8).

23   Support the subframe with two floor jacks (one positioned on each side).

24   Remove the subframe bracket bolts and the main subframe mounting bolts. Slowly lower the subframe, making sure nothing is still connected.

25   Installation is the reverse of the removal procedure, noting the following points:

a) *Use new fasteners, tightening them to the torque values listed in this Chapter's Specifications.*

b) *Install the wheel and lug nuts, then lower the vehicle and tighten the lug nuts to the torque listed in the Chapter 1 Specifications.*

c) *Have the wheel alignment checked and, if necessary, adjusted.*

22.37 Subframe mounting details (2013 and later model shown)

1　Front mounting bolts　　3　Rear mounting bolts
2　Subframe bracket bolts

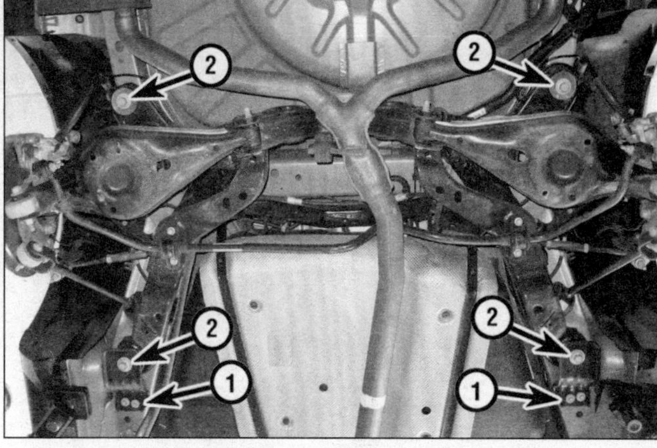

22.63 Rear subframe details

1　Subframe bracket bolts　　2　Subframe mounting bolts

2008 and later models

26　Remove the front section of the exhaust system.
27　Unbolt the roll restrictor from the subframe **(see illustration 19.23)**.
28　Detach the control arm balljoints from the steering knuckles (see Section 5).
29　If you're working on a 2010 or later model, detach the stabilizer bar links from the front struts (see Section 4).
30　If you're working on a 2008 or 2009 model, remove the stabilizer bar bracket bolts (see Section 4).
31　If you're working on a 2008 or 2008 model, unbolt the steering gear from the subframe. Support the steering gear and stabilizer bar from above with a length of rope or wire.
32　If you're working on a 2010 or later model, detach the tie-rod ends from the steering knuckle arms (see Section 17).
33　If you're working on a 2010 or later model, detach the steering column intermediate shaft from the steering gear **(see illustration 19.11)**.
34　Detach the inner fender splash shields from the subframe.
35　Detach all hoses, lines and wiring harness from the subframe.
36　Support the subframe with two floor jacks (one positioned on each side).
37　Remove the subframe bracket bolts and the main subframe mounting bolts **(see illustration)**. Slowly lower the subframe, making sure nothing is still connected.
38　Installation is the reverse of the removal procedure, noting the following points:

a)　*Use new fasteners, tightening them to the torque values listed in this Chapter's Specifications.*
b)　*Install the wheel and lug nuts, then lower the vehicle and tighten the lug nuts to the torque listed in the Chapter 1 Specifications.*
c)　*Have the wheel alignment checked and, if necessary, adjusted.*

Rear

39　Measure the distance front the center of the rear wheel hub to the fender lip with the vehicle sitting on level ground, under its own weight.
40　Release the tension from the parking brake cables (see Chapter 9).
41　Loosen the rear wheel lug nuts. Raise the vehicle and place it securely on jackstands. Remove both rear wheels.
42　Remove the rear section of the exhaust system.
43　If you're working on an all-wheel drive model, mark the driveshaft to the diffential flange, then disconnect the driveshaft from the rear differential.
44　Mark the relationship of the subframe to the chassis at each mounting point.
45　Detach the front parking brake cable from the connector where it attaches to the intermediate parking brake cable, then detach the intermediate cable from the bracket on the chassis.
46　Detach the rear parking brake cables from the equalizer.
47　Detach the parking brake cables from the brake calipers and brackets.
48　Remove the rear brake calipers (without disconnecting the hoses) (see Chapter 9). Hang the calipers out of the way with a length of wire or rope.

2012 and earlier models

49　Loosen the trailing arm-to-rear knuckle bolts.
50　Support each rear knuckle with a floor jack. Remove the trailing arm-to-knuckle bolts and allow the arm to hang down.
51　Remove the shock absorber lower mounting bolts.
52　Follow the wiring harnesses from the ABS wheel speed sensors, then disconnect the electrical connectors.
53　Disconnect any other wiring harness electrical connectors from the subframe.
54　If you're working on a 2007 or earlier all-wheel drive model, remove the rear differen-

tial (see Chapter 8).
55　Support the rear suspension/subframe assembly with a pair of floor jacks or a floor jack with a transmission adapter.
56　Remove the subframe bracket bolts (all-wheel drive models) and the four subframe mounting bolts.
57　Carefully lower the subframe, making sure nothing is still attached.
58　Installation is the reverse of the removal procedure, noting the following points:

a)　*When installing the subframe, align the marks you made in Step 44.*
b)　*Before tightening any suspension arm or shock absorber fasteners, raise the rear knuckles with floor jack to simulate normal ride height (as measured in Step 39).*
c)　*Use new fasteners, tightening them to the torque values listed in this Chapter's Specifications.*
d)　*Install the wheel and lug nuts, then lower the vehicle and tighten the lug nuts to the torque listed in the Chapter 1 Specifications.*
e)　*Have the wheel alignment checked and, if necessary, adjusted.*

2013 and later models

59　Detach the stabilizer bar links from the rear knuckles (see Section 14).
60　Remove the shock absorber lower mounting bolts (see Section 9).
61　Disconnect the subframe wiring harness electrical connector.
62　Support the rear suspension/subframe assembly with a pair of floor jacks or a floor jack with a transmission adapter.
63　Remove the subframe bracket bolts and the four subframe mounting bolts.
64　Carefully lower the subframe, making sure nothing is still attached.
65　Installation is the reverse of the removal procedure, noting the following points:

a)　*When installing the subframe, align the marks you made in Step 44.*

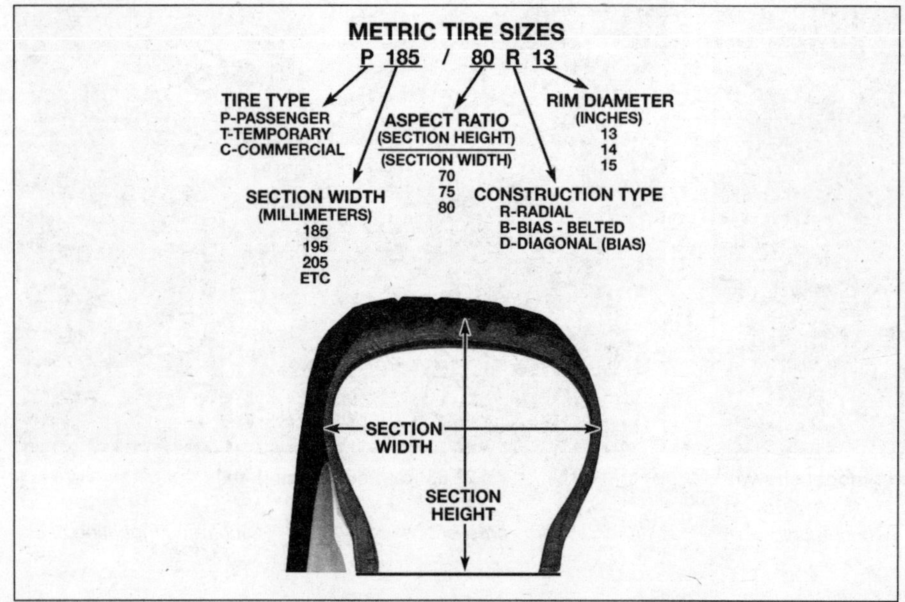

23.1 Metric tire size code

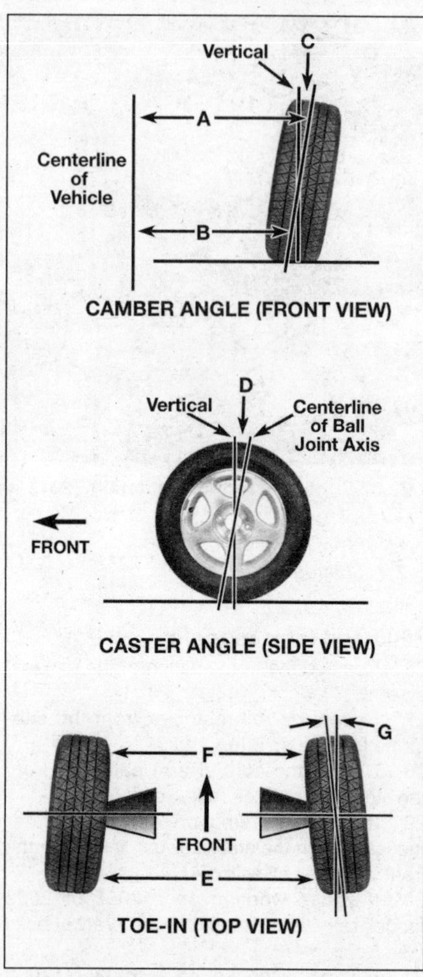

24.1 Camber, caster and toe-in angles

A minus B = C (degrees camber)
D = degrees caster
E minus F = toe-in (measured in inches)
G = toe-in (expressed in degrees)

b) *Before tightening any suspension arm or shock absorber fasteners, raise the rear knuckles with floor jack to simulate normal ride height (as measured in Step 39).*

c) *Use new fasteners, tightening them to the torque values listed in this Chapter's Specifications.*

d) *Install the wheel and lug nuts, then lower the vehicle and tighten the lug nuts to the torque listed in the Chapter 1 Specifications.*

e) *Have the wheel alignment checked and, if necessary, adjusted.*

23   Wheels and tires - general information

1   All vehicles covered by this manual are equipped with metric-sized fiberglass or steel belted radial tires **(see illustration)**. Use of other size or type of tires may affect the ride and handling of the vehicle. Don't mix different types of tires, such as radials and bias belted, on the same vehicle as handling may be seriously affected. It's recommended that tires be replaced in pairs on the same axle, but if only one tire is being replaced, be sure it's the same size, structure and tread design as the other.

2   Because tire pressure has a substantial effect on handling and wear, the pressure on all tires should be checked at least once a month or before any extended trips (see Chapter 1).

3   Wheels must be replaced if they are bent, dented, leak air, have elongated bolt holes, are heavily rusted, out of vertical symmetry or if the lug nuts won't stay tight. Wheel repairs that use welding or peening are not recommended.

4   Tire and wheel balance is important in the overall handling, braking and performance of the vehicle. Unbalanced wheels can adversely affect handling and ride characteristics as well as tire life. Whenever a tire is installed on a wheel, the tire and wheel should be balanced by a shop with the proper equipment.

24   Wheel alignment - general information

1   A wheel alignment refers to the adjustments made to the wheels so they are in proper angular relationship to the suspension and the ground. Wheels that are out of proper alignment not only affect vehicle control, but also increase tire wear. The front end angles normally measured are camber, caster and toe-in **(see illustration)**. Toe-in and camber are adjustable; if the caster is not correct, check for bent components. Rear toe-in is also adjustable.

2   Getting the proper wheel alignment is a very exacting process, one in which complicated and expensive machines are necessary to perform the job properly. Because of this, you should have a technician with the proper equipment perform these tasks. We will, however, use this space to give you a basic idea of what is involved with a wheel alignment so you can better understand the process and deal intelligently with the shop that does the work.

3   Toe-in is the turning in of the wheels. The purpose of a toe specification is to ensure parallel rolling of the wheels. In a vehicle with zero toe-in, the distance between the front edges of the wheels will be the same as the distance between the rear edges of the wheels. The actual amount of toe-in is normally only a fraction of an inch. On the front end, toe-in is controlled by the tie-rod end position on the tie-rod. On the rear end, it's controlled by a cam bolt on the inner end of the toe-link (early models) or by turning the turnbuckle on the toe-link (later models). Incorrect toe-in will cause the tires to wear improperly by making them scrub against the road surface.

4   Camber is the tilting of the wheels from vertical when viewed from one end of the vehicle. When the wheels tilt out at the top, the camber is said to be positive (+). When the wheels tilt in at the top the camber is negative (-). The amount of tilt is measured in degrees from vertical and this measurement is called the camber angle. This angle affects the amount of tire tread which contacts the road and compensates for changes in the suspension geometry when the vehicle is cornering or traveling over an undulating surface. On the front end it is adjustable by removing the strut upper mount and repositioning it 180-degrees. On the rear end on 2013 and later models, it's adjusted by altering the position of the rear knuckle in relation to the upper suspension arm. On 2012 and earlier models it isn't adjustable.

5   Caster is the tilting of the front steering axis from the vertical. A tilt toward the rear is positive caster and a tilt toward the front is negative caster. Caster isn't adjustable on these vehicles.

Chapter 11 Body

Contents

1 General information

Warning: *The models covered by this manual are equipped with Supplemental Restraint Systems (SRS), more commonly known as airbags. Always disable the airbag system before working in the vicinity of any airbag system components to avoid the possibility of accidental deployment of the airbags, which could cause personal injury (see Chapter 12).*

1   Certain body components are particularly vulnerable to accident damage and can be unbolted and repaired or replaced. Among these parts are the hood, doors, tailgate, liftgate, bumpers and front fenders.

2   Only general body maintenance practices and body panel repair procedures within the scope of the do-it-yourselfer are included in this Chapter.

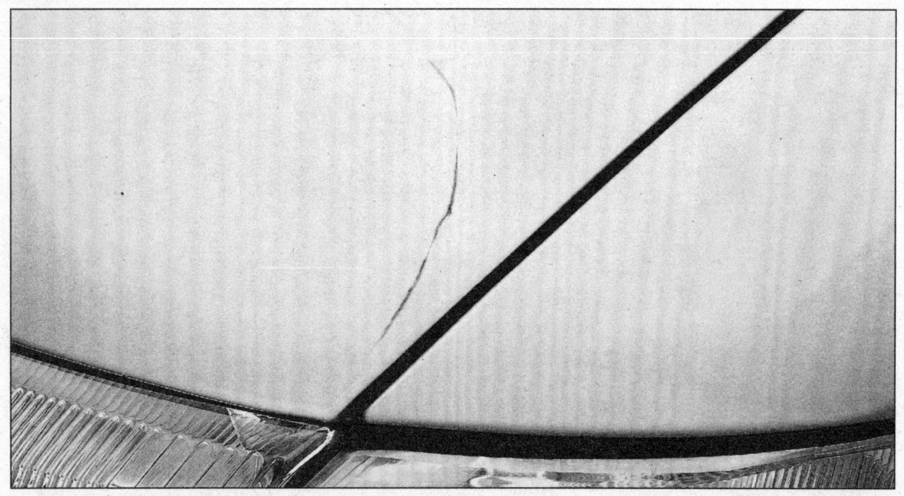

Make sure the damaged area is perfectly clean and rust free. If the touch-up kit has a wire brush, use it to clean the scratch or chip. Or use fine steel wool wrapped around the end of a pencil. Clean the scratched or chipped surface only, not the good paint surrounding it. Rinse the area with water and allow it to dry thoroughly

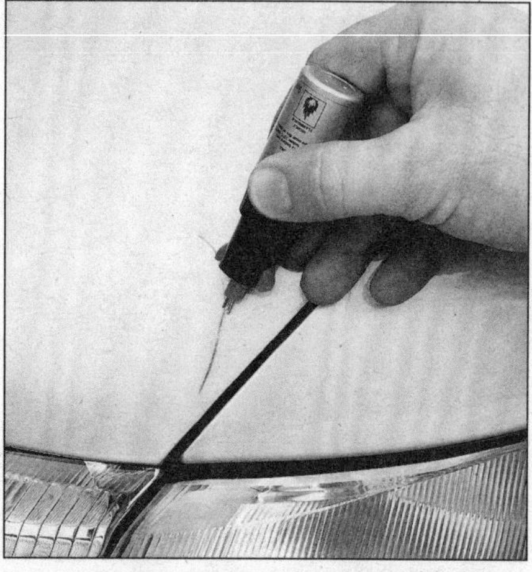

Thoroughly mix the paint, then apply a small amount with the touch-up kit brush or a very fine artist's brush. Brush in one direction as you fill the scratch area. Do not build up the paint higher than the surrounding paint

2   Repairing minor paint scratches

No matter how hard you try to keep your vehicle looking like new, it will inevitably be scratched, chipped or dented at some point. If the metal is actually dented, seek the advice of a professional. But you can fix minor scratches and chips yourself. Buy a touch-up paint kit from a dealer service department or an auto parts store. To ensure that you get the right color, you'll need to have the specific make, model and year of your vehicle and, ideally, the paint code, which is located on a special metal plate under the hood or in the door jamb.

3   Body repair - minor damage

Plastic body panels

1   The following repair procedures are for minor scratches and gouges. Repair of more serious damage should be left to a dealer service department or qualified auto body shop. Below is a list of the equipment and materials necessary to perform the following repair procedures on plastic body panels.

Wax, grease and silicone removing solvent
Cloth-backed body tape
Sanding discs
Drill motor with three-inch disc holder
Hand sanding block
Rubber squeegees
Sandpaper
Non-porous mixing palette
Wood paddle or putty knife
Curved-tooth body file
Flexible parts repair material

Flexible panels (bumper trim)

2   Remove the damaged panel, if necessary or desirable. In most cases, repairs can be carried out with the panel installed.

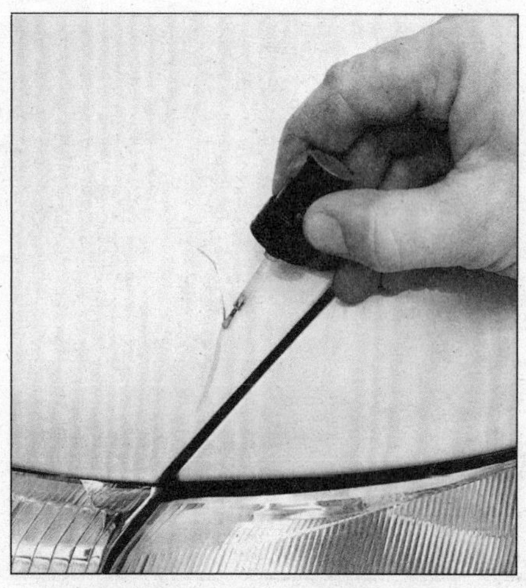

If the vehicle has a two-coat finish, apply the clear coat after the color coat has dried

3   Clean the area(s) to be repaired with a wax, grease and silicone removing solvent applied with a water-dampened cloth.
4   If the damage is structural, that is, if it extends through the panel, clean the backside of the panel area to be repaired as well. Wipe dry.
5   Sand the rear surface about 1-1/2 inches beyond the break.
6   Cut two pieces of fiberglass cloth large enough to overlap the break by about 1-1/2 inches. Cut only to the required length.
7   Mix the adhesive from the repair kit according to the instructions included with the kit, and apply a layer of the mixture approximately 1/8-inch thick on the backside of the panel. Overlap the break by at least 1-1/2 inches.
8   Apply one piece of fiberglass cloth to the adhesive and cover the cloth with additional adhesive. Apply a second piece of fiberglass cloth to the adhesive and immediately cover the cloth with additional adhesive in sufficient

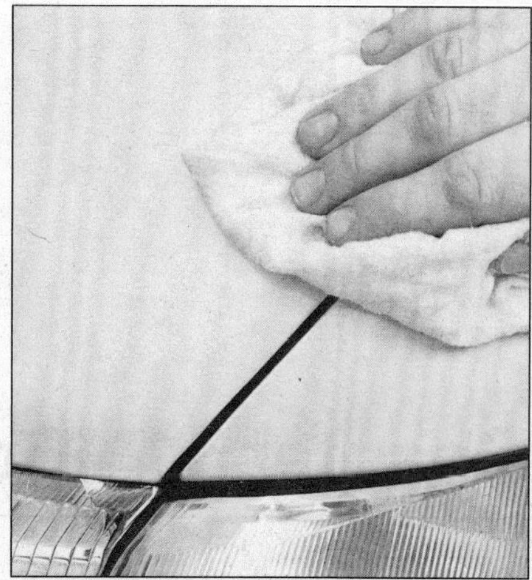

Wait a few days for the paint to dry thoroughly, then rub out the repainted area with a polishing compound to blend the new paint with the surrounding area. When you're happy with your work, wash and polish the area

quantity to fill the weave.
9   Allow the repair to cure for 20 to 30 minutes at 60-degrees to 80-degrees F.
10   If necessary, trim the excess repair material at the edge.
11   Remove all of the paint film over and around the area(s) to be repaired. The repair material should not overlap the painted surface.
12   With a drill motor and a sanding disc (or a rotary file), cut a "V" along the break line approximately 1/2-inch wide. Remove all dust and loose particles from the repair area.
13   Mix and apply the repair material. Apply a light coat first over the damaged area; then continue applying material until it reaches a level slightly higher than the surrounding finish.
14   Cure the mixture for 20 to 30 minutes at

60-degrees to 80-degrees F.

15   Roughly establish the contour of the area being repaired with a body file. If low areas or pits remain, mix and apply additional adhesive.

16   Block sand the damaged area with sandpaper to establish the actual contour of the surrounding surface.

17   If desired, the repaired area can be temporarily protected with several light coats of primer. Because of the special paints and techniques required for flexible body panels, it is recommended that the vehicle be taken to a paint shop for completion of the body repair.

Steel body panels

Repairing simple dents

Note: *These photos illustrate a method of repairing simple dents. They are intended to supplement this Section and should not be used as the sole instructions for body repair on these vehicles.*

18   When repairing dents, the first job is to pull the dent out until the affected area is as close as possible to its original shape. There is no point in trying to restore the original shape completely as the metal in the damaged area will have stretched on impact and cannot be restored to its original contours. It is better to bring the level of the dent up to a point that is about 1/8-inch below the level of the surrounding metal. In cases where the dent is very shallow, it is not worth trying to pull it out at all.

19   If the backside of the dent is accessible, it can be hammered out gently from behind using a soft-face hammer. While doing this, hold a block of wood firmly against the opposite side of the metal to absorb the hammer blows and prevent the metal from being stretched.

20   If the dent is in a section of the body which has double layers, or some other factor makes it inaccessible from behind, a different technique is required. Drill several small holes through the metal inside the damaged area, particularly in the deeper sections. Screw long, self-tapping screws into the holes just enough for them to get a good grip in the metal. Now pulling on the protruding heads of the screws with locking pliers can pull out the dent.

21   The next stage of repair is the removal of paint from the damaged area and from an inch or so of the surrounding metal. This is easily done with a wire brush or sanding disk in a drill motor, although it can be done just as effectively by hand with sandpaper. To complete the preparation for filling, score the surface of the bare metal with a screwdriver or the tang of a file or drill small holes in the affected area. This will provide a good grip for the filler material. To complete the repair, see the subsection on filling and painting.

Repair of rust holes or gashes

22   Remove all paint from the affected area and from an inch or so of the surrounding metal using a sanding disk or wire brush mounted in a drill motor. If these are not available, a few sheets of sandpaper will do the job just as effectively.

23   With the paint removed, you will be able to determine the severity of the corrosion and decide whether to replace the whole panel, if possible, or repair the affected area. New body panels are not as expensive as most people think and it is often quicker to install a new panel than to repair large areas of rust.

24   Remove all trim pieces from the affected area except those which will act as a guide to the original shape of the damaged body, such as headlight shells, etc. Using metal snips or a hacksaw blade, remove all loose metal and any other metal that is badly affected by rust. Hammer the edges of the hole in to create a slight depression for the filler material.

25   Wire-brush the affected area to remove the powdery rust from the surface of the metal. If the back of the rusted area is accessible, treat it with rust inhibiting paint.

26   Before filling is done, block the hole in some way. This can be done with sheet metal riveted or screwed into place, or by stuffing the hole with wire mesh.

27   Once the hole is blocked off, the affected area can be filled and painted. See the following subsection on filling and painting.

Filling and painting

28   Many types of body fillers are available, but generally speaking, body repair kits which contain filler paste and a tube of resin hardener are best for this type of repair work. A wide, flexible plastic or nylon applicator will be necessary for imparting a smooth and contoured finish to the surface of the filler material. Mix up a small amount of filler on a clean piece of wood or cardboard (use the hardener sparingly). Follow the manufacturer's instructions on the package, otherwise the filler will set incorrectly.

29   Using the applicator, apply the filler paste to the prepared area. Draw the applicator across the surface of the filler to achieve the desired contour and to level the filler surface. As soon as a contour that approximates the original one is achieved, stop working the paste. If you continue, the paste will begin to stick to the applicator. Continue to add thin layers of paste at 20-minute intervals until the level of the filler is just above the surrounding metal.

30   Once the filler has hardened, the excess can be removed with a body file. From then on, progressively finer grades of sandpaper should be used, starting with a 180-grit paper and finishing with 600-grit wet-or-dry paper. Always wrap the sandpaper around a flat rubber or wooden block, otherwise the surface of the filler will not be completely flat. During the sanding of the filler surface, the wet-or-dry paper should be periodically rinsed in water. This will ensure that a very smooth finish is produced in the final stage.

31   At this point, the repair area should be surrounded by a ring of bare metal, which in turn should be encircled by the finely feathered edge of good paint. Rinse the repair area with clean water until all of the dust produced by the sanding operation is gone.

32   Spray the entire area with a light coat of primer. This will reveal any imperfections in the surface of the filler. Repair the imperfections with fresh filler paste or glaze filler and once more smooth the surface with sandpaper. Repeat this spray-and-repair procedure until you are satisfied that the surface of the filler and the feathered edge of the paint are perfect. Rinse the area with clean water and allow it to dry completely.

33   The repair area is now ready for painting. Spray painting must be carried out in a warm, dry, windless and dust free atmosphere. These conditions can be created if you have access to a large indoor work area, but if you are forced to work in the open, you will have to pick the day very carefully. If you are working indoors, dousing the floor in the work area with water will help settle the dust that would otherwise be in the air. If the repair area is confined to one body panel, mask off the surrounding panels. This will help minimize the effects of a slight mismatch in paint color. Trim pieces such as chrome strips, door handles, etc., will also need to be masked off or removed. Use masking tape and several thickness of newspaper for the masking operations.

34   Before spraying, shake the paint can thoroughly, then spray a test area until the spray painting technique is mastered. Cover the repair area with a thick coat of primer. The thickness should be built up using several thin layers of primer rather than one thick one. Using 600-grit wet-or-dry sandpaper, rub down the surface of the primer until it is very smooth. While doing this, the work area should be thoroughly rinsed with water and the wet-or-dry sandpaper periodically rinsed as well. Allow the primer to dry before spraying additional coats.

35   Spray on the top coat, again building up the thickness by using several thin layers of paint. Begin spraying in the center of the repair area and then, using a circular motion, work out until the whole repair area and about two inches of the surrounding original paint is covered. Remove all masking material 10 to 15 minutes after spraying on the final coat of paint. Allow the new paint at least two weeks to harden, then use a very fine rubbing compound to blend the edges of the new paint into the existing paint. Finally, apply a coat of wax

---

4   Body repair - major damage

1   Major damage must be repaired by an auto body shop specifically equipped to perform body and frame repairs. These shops have the specialized equipment required to do the job properly.

2   If the damage is extensive, the frame must be checked for proper alignment or the vehicle's handling characteristics may be adversely affected and other components may wear at an accelerated rate.

3   Due to the fact that all of the major body components (hood, fenders, etc.) are separate and replaceable units, any seriously damaged components should be replaced rather than repaired. Sometimes the components can be found in a wrecking yard that specializes in used vehicle components, often at considerable savings over the cost of new parts.

These photos illustrate a method of repairing simple dents. They are intended to supplement *Body repair - minor damage* in this Chapter and should not be used as the sole instructions for body repair on these vehicles.

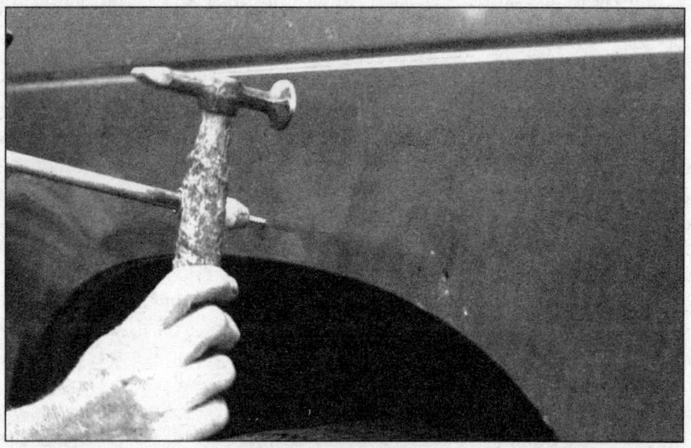

1 If you can't access the backside of the body panel to hammer out the dent, pull it out with a slide-hammer-type dent puller. Tap with a hammer near the edge of the dent to help 'pop' the metal back to its original shape, about 1/8-inch below the surface of the surrounding metal

2 Using coarse-grit sandpaper, remove the paint down to the bare metal. Clean the repair area with wax/silicone remover.

3 Following label instructions, mix up a batch of plastic filler and hardener, then quickly press it into the metal with a plastic applicator. Work the filler until it matches the original contour and is slightly above the surrounding metal

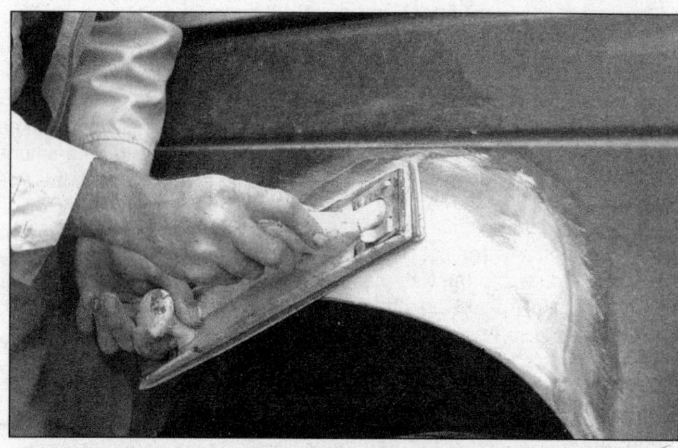

4 Let the filler harden until you can just dent it with your fingernail. File, then sand the filler down until it's smooth and even. Work down to finer grits of sandpaper - always using a board or block - ending up with 360 or 400 grit

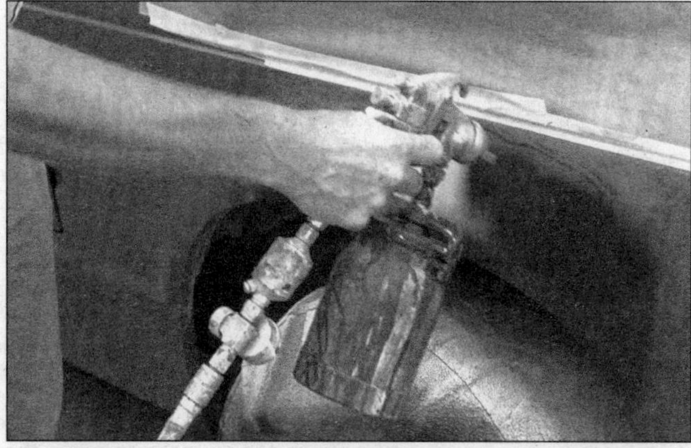

5 When the area is smooth to the touch, clean the area and mask around it. Apply several layers of primer to the area. A professional-type spray gun is being used here, but aerosol spray primer works fine

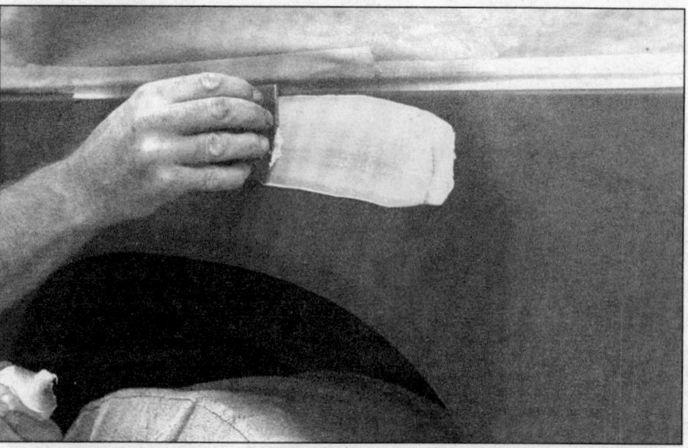

6 Fill imperfections or scratches with glazing compound. Sand with 360 or 400-grit and re-spray. Finish sand the primer with 600 grit, clean thoroughly, then apply the finish coat. Don't attempt to rub out or wax the repair area until the paint has dried completely (at least two weeks)

5 Upholstery, carpets and vinyl trim - maintenance

Upholstery and carpets

1   Every three months remove the floormats and clean the interior of the vehicle (more frequently if necessary). Use a stiff whiskbroom to brush the carpeting and loosen dirt and dust, then vacuum the upholstery and carpets thoroughly, especially along seams and crevices.

2   Dirt and stains can be removed from carpeting with basic household or automotive carpet shampoos available in spray cans. Follow the directions and vacuum again, then use a stiff brush to bring back the nap of the carpet.

3   Most interiors have cloth or vinyl upholstery, either of which can be cleaned and maintained with a number of material-specific cleaners or shampoos available in auto supply stores. Follow the directions on the product for usage, and always spot-test any upholstery cleaner on an inconspicuous area (bottom edge of a backseat cushion) to ensure that it doesn't cause a color shift in the material.

4   After cleaning, vinyl upholstery should be treated with a protectant.

Note: *Make sure the protectant container indicates the product can be used on seats - some products may make a seat too slippery.*

Caution: *Do not use protectant on vinyl-covered steering wheels.*

5   Leather upholstery requires special care. It should be cleaned regularly with saddle-soap or leather cleaner. Never use alcohol, gasoline, nail polish remover or thinner to clean leather upholstery.

6   After cleaning, regularly treat leather upholstery with a leather conditioner, rubbed in with a soft cotton cloth. Never use car wax on leather upholstery.

7   In areas where the interior of the vehicle is subject to bright sunlight, cover leather seating areas of the seats with a sheet if the vehicle is to be left out for any length of time.

Vinyl trim

8   Don't clean vinyl trim with detergents, caustic soap or petroleum-based cleaners. Plain soap and water works just fine, with a soft brush to clean dirt that may be ingrained. Wash the vinyl as frequently as the rest of the vehicle.

9   After cleaning, application of a high-quality rubber and vinyl protectant will help prevent oxidation and cracks. The protectant can also be applied to weather-stripping, vacuum lines and rubber hoses, which often fail as a result of chemical degradation, and to the tires.

6 Fastener and trim removal

1   There is a variety of plastic fasteners used to hold trim panels, splash shields and other parts in place in addition to typical screws, nuts and bolts. Once you are familiar with them, they can usually be removed without too much difficulty.

2   The proper tools and approach can prevent added time and expense to a project by minimizing the number of broken fasteners and/or parts.

3   The chart shows various types of fasteners that are typically used on most vehicles and how to remove and install them. Replacement fasteners are commonly found at most auto parts stores, if necessary.

Fasteners

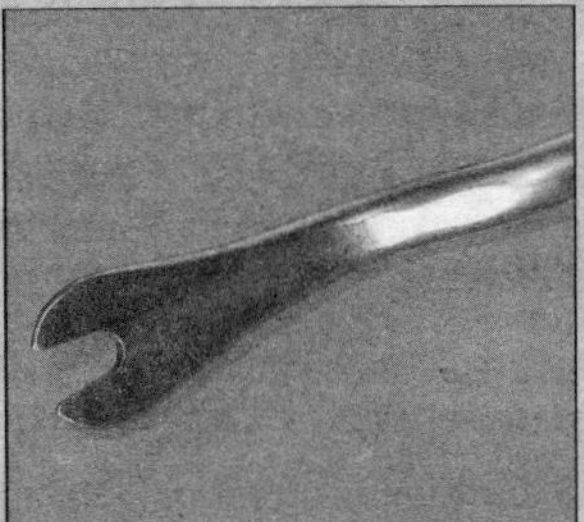

This tool is designed to remove special fasteners. A small pry tool used for removing nails will also work well in place of this tool

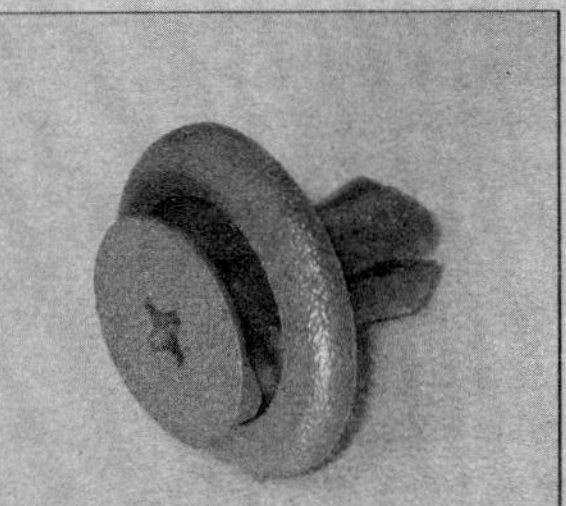

A Phillips head screwdriver can be used to release the center portion, but light pressure must be used because the plastic is easily damaged. Once the center is up, the fastener can easily be pried from its hole

Here is a view with the center portion fully released. Install the fastener as shown, then press the center in to set it

This fastener is used for exterior panels and shields. The center portion must be pried up to release the fastener. Install the fastener with the center up, then press the center in to set it

This type of fastener is used commonly for interior panels. Use a small blunt tool to press the small pin at the center in to release it . . .

. . . the pin will stay with the fastener in the released position

Reset the fastener for installation by moving the pin out. Install the fastener, then press the pin flush with the fastener to set it

This fastener is used for exterior and interior panels. It has no moving parts. Simply pry the fastener from its hole like the claw of a hammer removes a nail. Without a tool that can get under the top of the fastener, it can be very difficult to remove

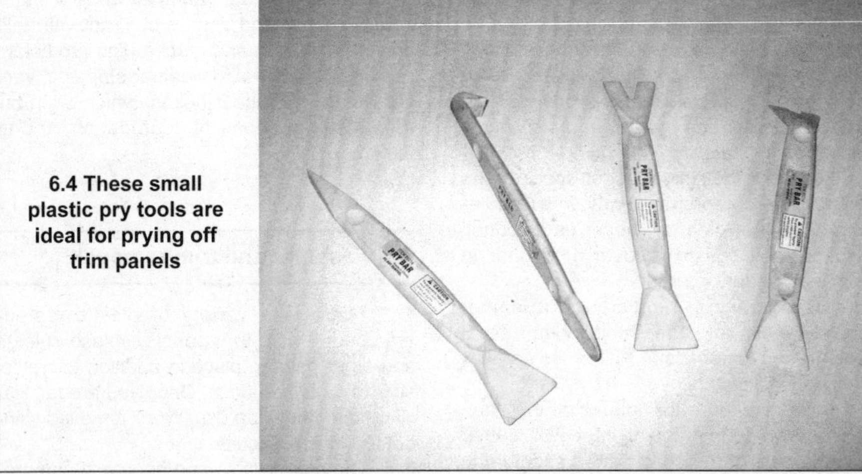

6.4 These small plastic pry tools are ideal for prying off trim panels

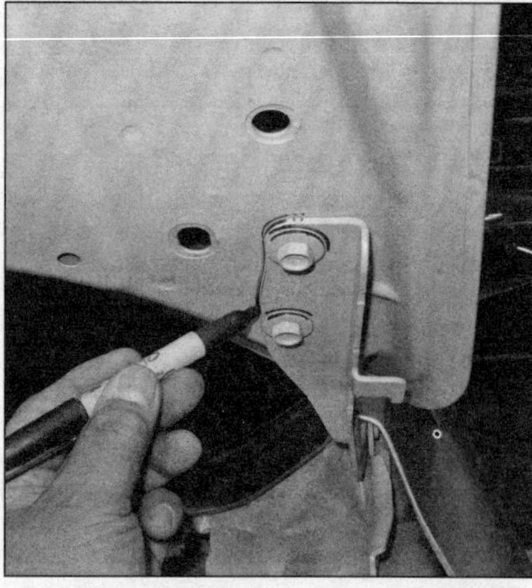

7.2 Draw alignment marks around the hood hinges to ensure proper alignment of the hood when it's reinstalled

4   Trim panels are typically made of plastic and their flexibility can help during removal. The key to their removal is to use a tool to pry the panel near its retainers to release it without damaging surrounding areas or breaking-off any retainers. The retainers will usually snap out of their designated slot or hole after force is applied to them. Stiff plastic tools designed for prying on trim panels are available at most auto parts stores **(see illustration)**. Tools that are tapered and wrapped in protective tape, such as a screwdriver or small pry tool, are also very effective when used with care.

7   Hood - removal, installation and adjustment

Note: *The hood is awkward to remove and install; at least two people should perform this procedure.*

Removal and installation

1   Open the hood, then place blankets or pads over the fenders and cowl area of the body. This will protect the body and paint as the hood is lifted off.

2   Make marks around the hood hinge to ensure proper alignment during installation **(see illustration)**.
3   Have an assistant support one side of the hood. Grasp the lower corner of the hood and use your shoulder to brace the hood **(see illustration)**. Take turns removing the hinge-to-hood bolts and lift off the hood.
4   Installation is the reverse of removal. Align the hinge bolts with the marks made in Step 2.

Adjustment

5   Fore-and-aft and side-to-side adjustment of the hood is done by moving the hinges after loosening the hinge-to-body bolts.
6   Loosen the bolts and move the hood into correct alignment. Move it only a little at a time. Tighten the hinge bolts and carefully lower the hood to check the position.
7   The hood can also be adjusted vertically so that it's flush with the fenders.
8   Turn each cushion clockwise to lower the hood or counterclockwise to raise the hood **(see illustration)**.
9   The hood latch assembly, as well as the hinges, should be periodically lubricated with white, lithium-base grease to prevent binding and wear.

8   Hood latch and release cable - removal and installation

Hood latch

1   Open the hood and scribe a line around the latch to aid alignment when installing, then remove the retaining bolts securing the hood latch to the radiator support **(see illustration)**. Remove the latch.
2   Squeeze the cable retainer to release the cable from the latch assembly, then disengage the cable end plug from the latch **(see illustration)**.
3   Installation is the reverse of removal.

Release cable

4   Working in the engine compartment, remove the hood latch and disconnect the hood release cable from the latch (see Steps 1 and 2).
5   On 2011 and earlier models, remove the radiator grille pin-type fasteners and panel.

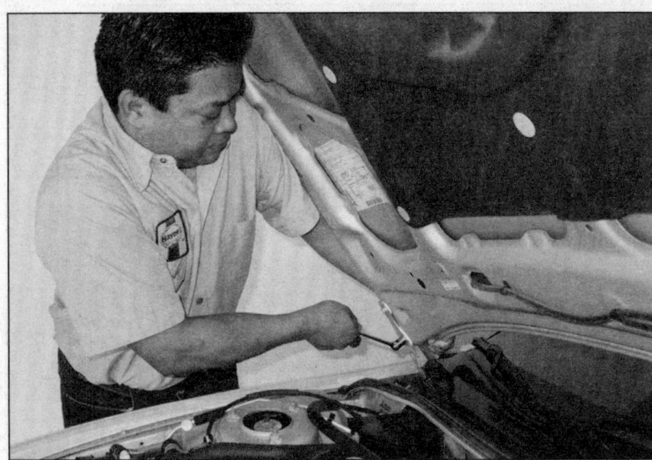

7.3 Support the hood with your shoulder while removing the hood bolts

7.8 There are two vertical height adjustment cushions on the underside of the hood

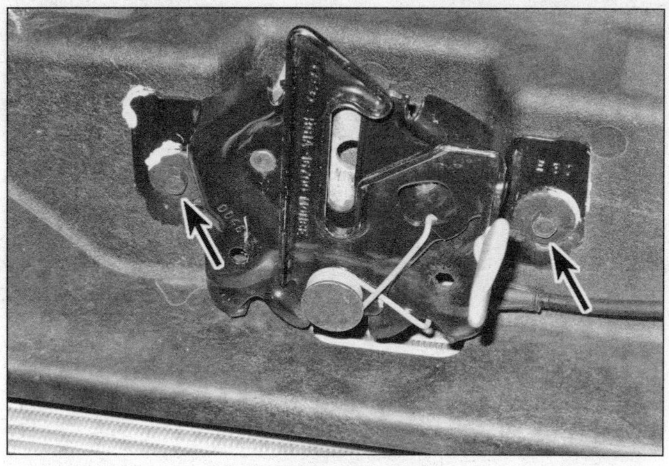

8.1 Hood latch bolts

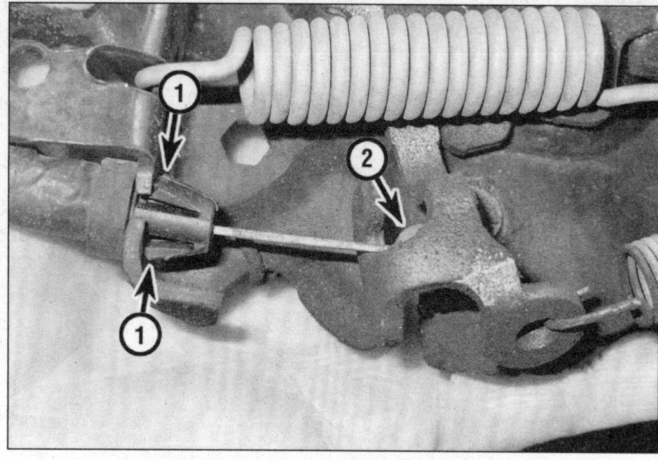

8.2 Hood release cable connection at latch assembly:

1   *Retainer fingers*   2   *Cable end plug*

6   Detach the two release cable clips from the radiator support.

7   On 2012 and later models, remove the battery tray (see Chapter 5) and the air filter housing (see Chapter 4).

8   Loosen the left front wheel lug nuts. Raise the vehicle and place it securely on jackstands. Remove the wheel. Remove the inner fender splash shield (see Section 10).

9   Open the two release cable clips in the upper part of the fender opening and detach the release cable from the clips.

10   On 2012 and later models, remove the Smart Junction Box (SJB) (see Chapter 12).

11   Disengage the release cable clip from the wiring harness.

Note: *It may be necessary to remove the Smart Junction Box on some models.*

12   Remove the two hood release handle mounting bolt(s) **(see illustration)**. Pull out the handle, then disengage the release cable from the release handle and pull the release cable through the firewall.

13   Installation is the reverse of removal.

9   Bumper covers - removal and installation

Note: *Refer to Section 6 for fastener and trim removal.*

Front bumper cover

1   Loosen the front wheel lug nuts, raise the vehicle and support it securely on jackstands.

2   Remove the front wheels. Remove the lower plastic fasteners from under the bumper cover **(see illustration)**.

3   Remove the fasteners that secure the inner fender splash shields to the bumper cover **(see illustration)**.

4   On early models, remove the two lower fender mounting bolts at the rear of the wheel-well opening.

5   Disconnect the electrical connectors from the fog lamps, if equipped (see Chapter 12).

6   Disengage the fastener that secure the upper edges of the bumper cover to the

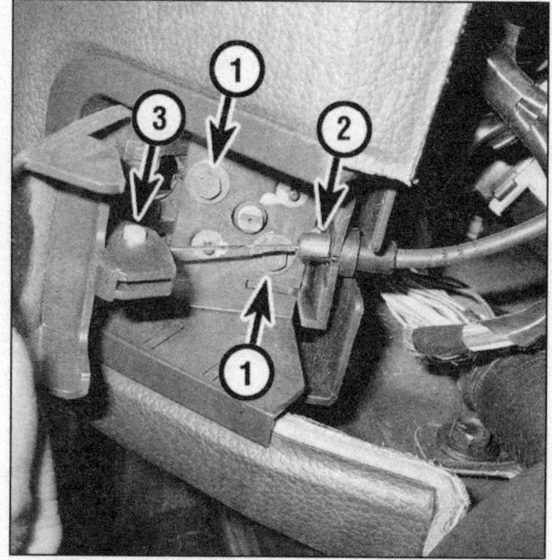

8.12 Hood release cable and release handle details (2011 and earlier models shown, later models similar):

1   *Release handle mounting bolts*
2   *Release cable retainer*
3   *Release cable end plug*

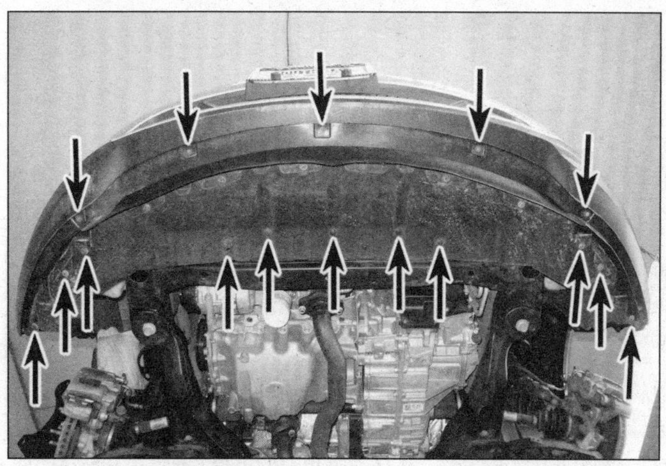

9.2 Bumper cover lower fastener locations

9.3 Inner fender splash shield-to-bumper cover fasteners

9.6 Pull on the bumper cover to disengage the bumper cover-to-fender clips

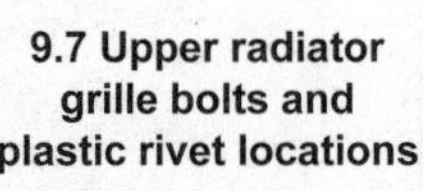

9.7 Upper radiator grille bolts and plastic rivet locations

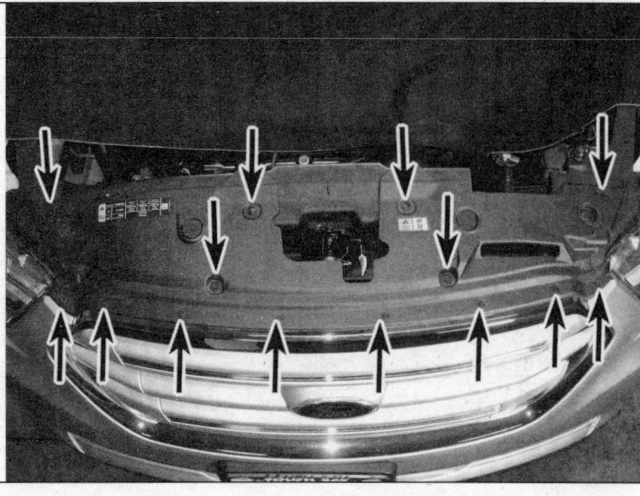

fender **(see illustration)**.

7   Remove the upper radiator grille bolts and plastic rivets **(see illustration)**.

8   Disengage the clips that secure the side

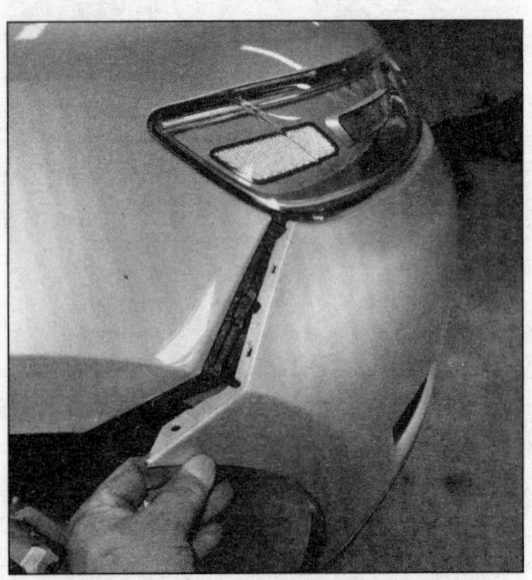

9.8 Pull the bumper cover to disengage the bumper cover-to-fender clips

of the bumper cover to the fender **(see illustration)**.

9   Using a flashlight, do a final inspection and verify that the bumper cover is completely detached, all electrical connectors are disconnected and all wiring harnesses are safely out of the way.

10   With an assistant's help, remove the front bumper cover.

11   Installation is the reverse of removal.

Rear bumper cover

12   Loosen the rear wheel lug nuts, raise the vehicle and support it securely on jackstands. Remove the rear wheels.

13   On 2010 and later models, remove the rear taillight housing (see Chapter 12).

14   Remove the screws from the rear part of the wheel well splash shield **(see illustration)** and push the shields aside.

15   From under the vehicle, remove the rear cover brace-to-body fasteners **(see illustration)**.

16   Disconnect the trailer tow connector and parking aid harness connectors, if equipped.

17   Disengage the corners of the bumper cover from the body panel **(see illustration)**.

18   Using a flashlight, do a final inspection and verify that the bumper cover is completely detached, all electrical connectors are disconnected and all wiring harnesses are safely out of the way.

19   With an assistant's help, remove the rear bumper cover.

20   Installation is the reverse of removal. Again, get help when putting the bumper cover back into position.

10   Front fender - removal and installation

Note: *Refer to Section 6 for fastener and trim removal details.*

1   Loosen the front wheel lug nuts. Raise the vehicle, support it securely on jackstands and remove the front wheel.

2   Remove the rocker panel molding end cap mounting screws, and remove the end cap **(see illustration)**.

3   Remove the fender-to-rocker panel mounting bolts **(see illustration)**.

4   Remove the fasteners that secure the

9.14 Remove the wheel well splash shield fasteners

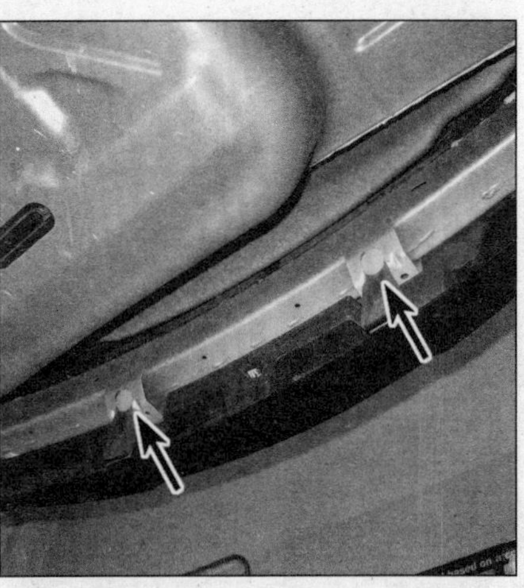

9.15 Rear bumper brace mounting bolt

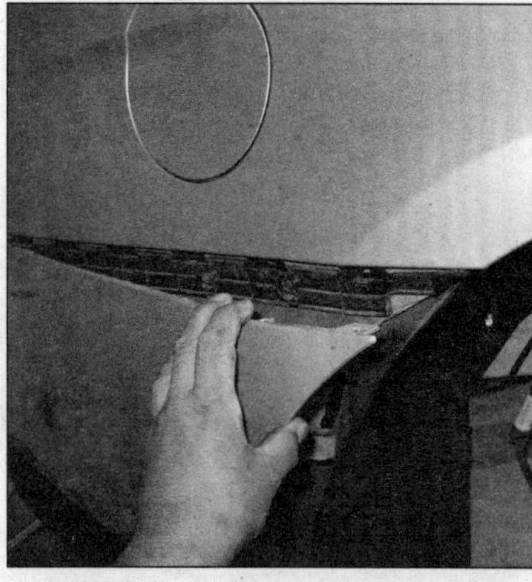

9.17 Pull the bumper cover to disengage the bumper cover-to-body clips

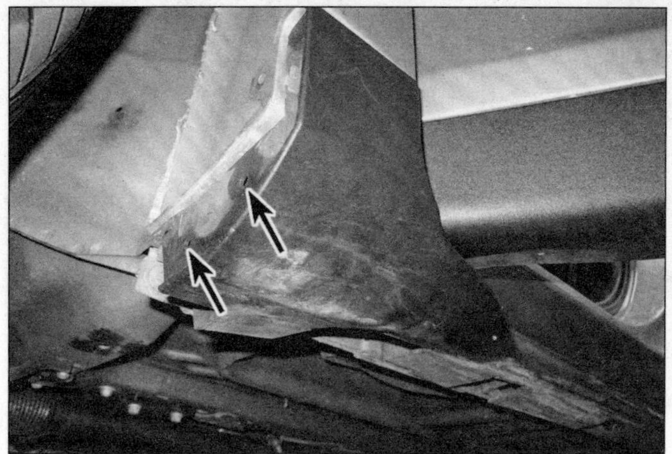

10.2 Remove the rocker panel molding end cap

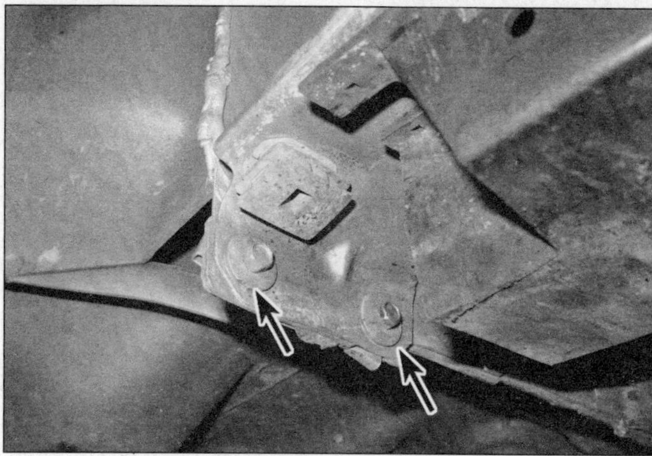

10.3 Fender-to-rocker panel fasteners

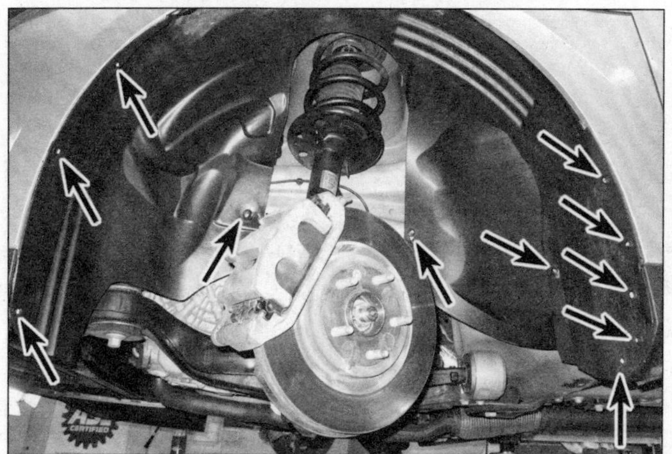

10.4 Inner fender splash shield fastener locations

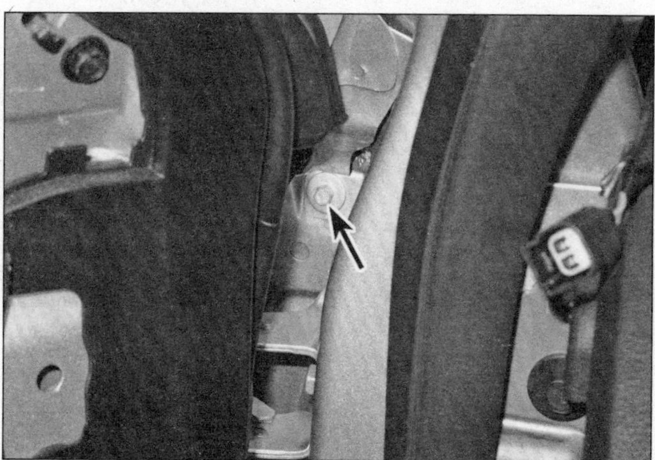

10.5 Fender mounting bolt inside the door opening

10.6 Front fender lower mounting bolt locations

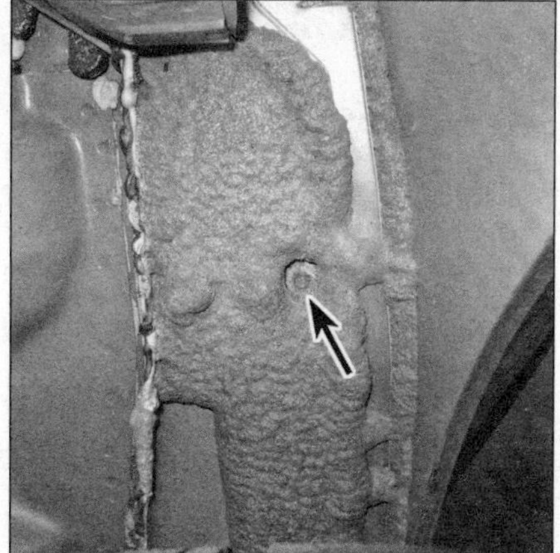

10.7 Front fender inner bolt location

10.8 Upper fender mounting bolts

inner fender splash shield **(see illustration)** and remove the splash shield.

5   Open the door and remove the bolt from the end of the fender **(see illustration)**.

6   Remove the front bumper cover (see Section 9) then remove the front fender mounting bolts **(see illustration)**.

7   Use a putty knife to scrape away the foam sealer to expose the front fender inner bolt inside the fender **(see illustration)**.

8   Remove the upper fender bolts **(see illustration)**, then lift off the fender. It's a good idea to have an assistant support the fender while it's being moved away from the vehicle to prevent damage to the surrounding body panels.

9   Using Flexible Foam repair or equivalent (available from your local dealer or automo-

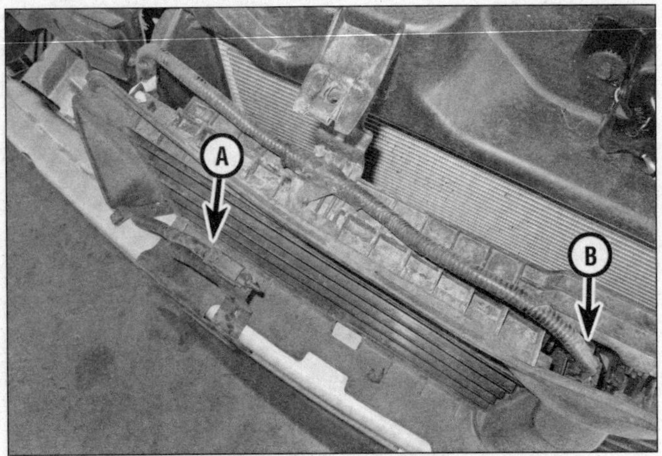

11.6 Impact sensor (A) and shutter actuator (B) electrical connector locations

11.7a Remove the shutter assembly mounting bolts . . .

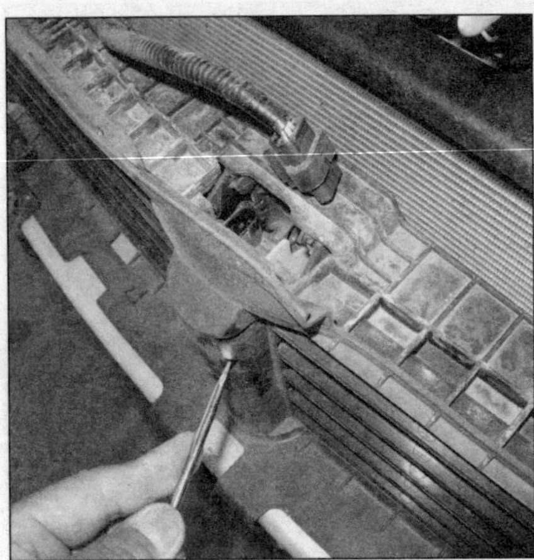

11.7b . . . depress the tab in the center to release the center fastener . . .

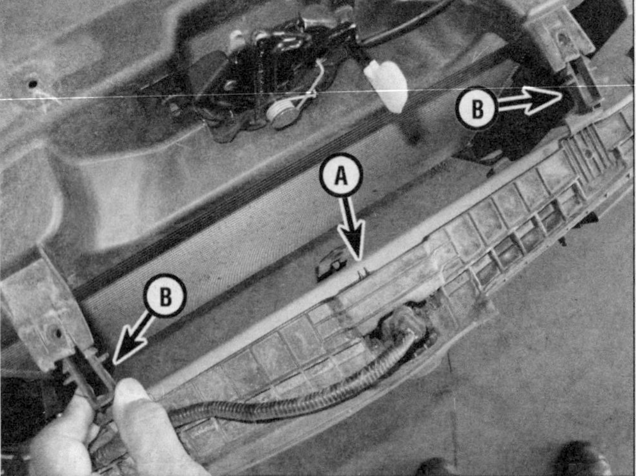

11.7c . . . and squeeze the upper retainers (B) inwards to release them from the radiator support (A)

tive paint store), reseal the area along the seam at the body and around the front fender inner bolt **(see illustration 10.7)**.

10 . Installation is the reverse of removal. Check the alignment of the fender to the hood and front edge of the door before tightening the bolts.

11   Radiator grille and shutter - removal and installation

Radiator grille

Note: *On 2010 and later models, the radiator grille is incorporated into the bumper cover and is not removable from the cover.*

1   Remove the upper radiator panel bolts and plastic rivets, then remove the panel.

2   To remove the manufacturer nameplate, remove the two nuts that secure it to the radiator grille, then pull it off.

3   To remove the grille, tilt the grille forward and remove the lower mounting bolts and grille. On Montego models, the radiator grille is secured with plastic push-pin type rivets at the bottom of the grille instead of bolts.

4   Installation is the reverse of removal.

Grille shutter assembly (2013 and later models)

5   Remove the front bumper cover (see Section 9).

6   Disconnect the electrical connector from the impact sensor and the shutter actuator assembly **(see illustration)**.

7   Remove the grille shutter assembly mounting fasteners from the middle and top of the shutter assembly **(see illustrations)**.

8   Pull the assembly forward until the shutter assembly has cleared the bumper, then remove the shutter assembly.

9   Installation is the reverse of removal.

12   Cowl panel - removal and installation

Note: *Refer to Section 6 for fastener and trim removal techniques.*

1   Remove the wiper arms (see Chapter 12) then disconnect the wiper washer hose.

2   Two small trim pieces fill the gap between the windshield and the front fenders. Carefully pry up the pin-type fasteners **(see illustration)**, and remove the trim panels.

3   Remove the pin-type retainers from the top of the cowl panel **(see illustration)**.

4   Remove the metal clips from each side

12.2 Pry out the gap panel fasteners from each side

12.3 Cowl panel fasteners

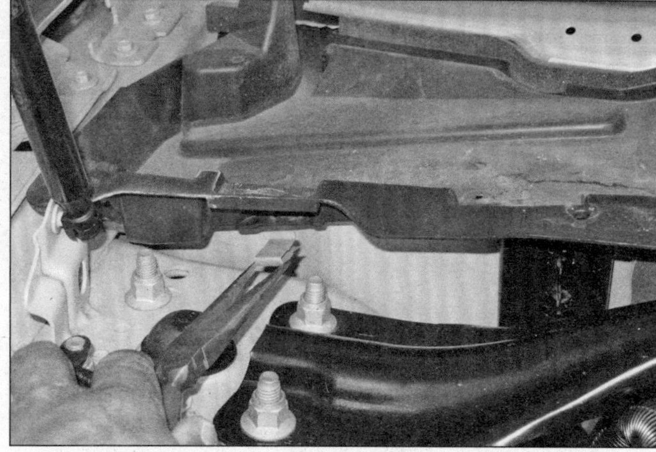

12.4 The clips are slightly hidden below the cowl panel

12.5 Remove the push pin type retainers
and cowl panel

13.9a Remove the trim cover . . .

13.9b . . . then remove the fastener

below the cowl panel **(see illustration)**.

5   Disengage the final push pin type retainers and remove the cowl panel **(see illustration)**.

6   Installation is the reverse of removal.

13   Door trim panel - removal and installation

Caution: *Wear gloves when working inside the door openings to protect against sharp metal edges.*
Note: *Refer to Section 6 for fastener and trim removal.*

Removal

1   Disconnect the cable from the negative battery terminal (see Chapter 5).

Door trim panels

Note: *This procedure applies to both front and rear door trim panels.*

2009 and earlier models

2   Remove the screw head trim cover from the inside door handle bezel and remove the screw from the bezel. Pull out the bezel and disconnect the electrical connector.

3   Remove the two screws inside the door pull handle trim panel on the armrest.

4   Pry the power window switch and door pull handle trim panel from the armrest as an assembly.

5   Remove the mounting screws around the trim panel perimeter.

6   To detach the door trim panel from its mounting clips, work your way around the outside edge of the trim panel, carefully prying loose the clips with a suitable door trim removal tool.

7   Pull the bottom of the panel outwards and lift the panel up and off of the lock rod, disconnecting any electrical connectors.

2010 and later models

8   Pry out the sail panel (see Section 18) and disconnect the electrical connector, if equipped.

9   Remove the trim cover from the inside door handle and remove the bolt **(see illustrations)**.

10   Pry the power window switch panel out of the armrest, starting from the rear end of

the switch, and lift the switch out of the arm rest **(see illustration)**.

11   Carefully pry the door panel applique out of the panel with a trim tool, then remove the two screws below.

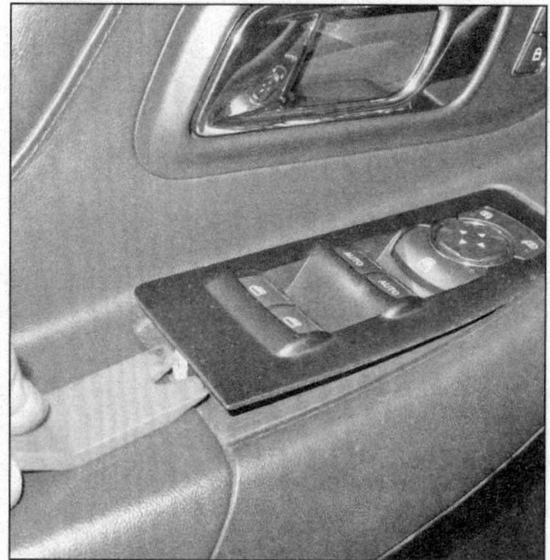

13.10 Pry out the window switch panel
from the armrest and disconnect the
electrical connectors

13.12 Remove the door panel retaining bolt from the armrest

13.13 Bottom edge trim panel screws

13.14a Carefully pry out the trim applique . . .

13.14b . . . then remove the fasteners

12   Remove the door panel fastener from the armrest **(see illustration)**.

13   Remove the trim panel screws from the bottom edge, front edge and rear edge of the door panel **(see illustration)**.

14   Carefully pry out the trim applique, then remove the fasteners **(see illustrations)**.

15   To detach the door trim panel from its mounting clips, work your way around the

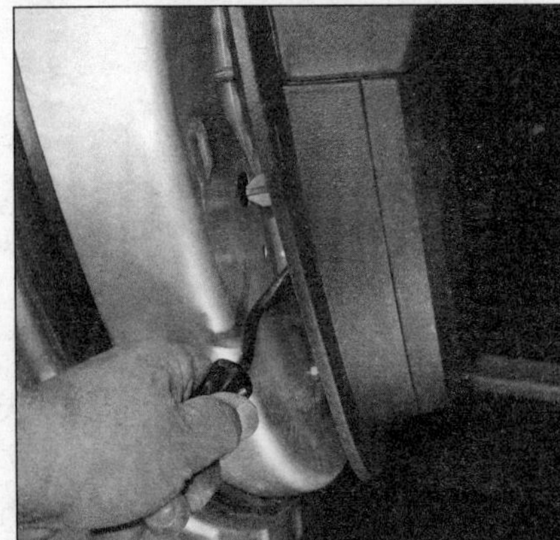

13.15 Carefully pry the door trim panel loose from its mounting clips

outside edge of the trim panel, carefully prying loose the clips with a suitable door trim removal tool **(see illustration)**.

16   Pull the bottom of the panel outwards and lift the panel up and off of the lock rod, disconnecting the inside door handle cable any electrical connectors, and remove the panel.

Installation

17   Prior to installation of the door trim panel(s), reinstall any clips which may have come out the panel was removed.

18   Position the wire harness connectors for the power door lock switch and the power window switch (if equipped) on the back of the panel, then place the panel in position in the door. Press the door panel into place until the clips are seated.

19   The remainder of installation is the reverse of removal.

---

14   Door - removal, installation and adjustment

Warning: *The models covered by this manual are equipped with Supplemental Restraint Systems (SRS), more commonly known as airbags. Always disable the airbag system before working in the vicinity of any airbag system component to avoid the possibility of accidental deployment of the airbag, which could cause personal injury (see Chapter 12).*

Removal and installation

Note: *The door is heavy and somewhat awkward to remove and install - at least two people should perform this procedure.*

Note: *This procedure applies to front and rear doors.*

1   Raise the window completely in the door.

2   Disconnect the cable from the negative battery terminal (see Chapter 5).

3   Open the door all the way and support it with a jack or blocks covered with rags to prevent damaging the outer surface.

4   Pull off the rubber conduit that protects the door's wiring harness, then disconnect the connector.

5   Remove the door stop strut mounting bolt **(see illustration)**.

6   Mark around the door hinges with a pen or a scribe to facilitate realignment during reassembly.

7   With an assistant holding the door to steady it, remove the hinge-to-door fasteners

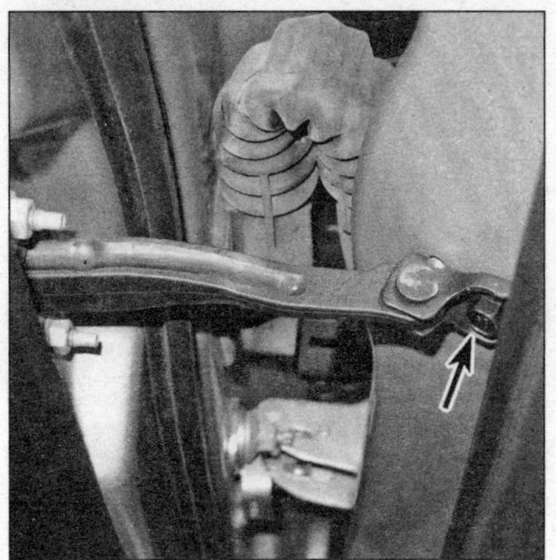

14.5 Door stop strut bolt

14.7a Door upper hinge fasteners . . .

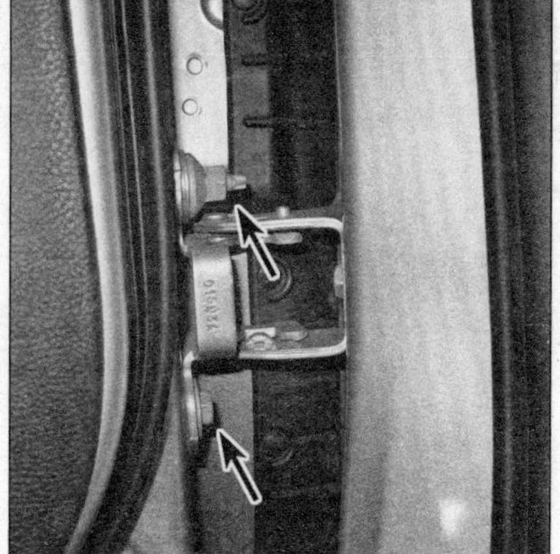

14.7b . . . and lower hinge fasteners

(see illustrations), and lift off the door.

8   Installation is the reverse of removal.

Adjustment

9   Correct door-to-body alignment is a critical part of a well-functioning door assembly. First check the door hinge pins for excessive play. Fully open the door and lift up and down on the door without lifting the body. If a door has 1/16-inch or more excessive play, replace the hinges.

10   If you need to adjust or replace the hinges for a front door, remove the front fender (see Section 10).

11   Make door-to-body alignment adjustments by loosening the hinge-to-body bolts or hinge-to-door bolts and moving the door. When body alignment is correct, the top of each door is parallel with the roof section, the front door is flush with the fender, the rear door is flush with the rear quarter panel and the bottom of each door is aligned with the lower rocker panel. If you're unable to adjust the door correctly, you might be able to obtain body alignment shims that are inserted behind the hinges to correctly align the door.

12   To adjust the door-closed position, scribe a line or mark around the striker plate **(see illustration)** to provide a reference point, then verify that the door latch is contacting the center of the striker. If not, adjust the up and down position first. To move the striker, tap it gently with a small hammer.

13   Once the door latch is contacting the center of the striker, adjust the latch striker sideways position, so that the door panel is flush with the center pillar or rear quarter panel and provides positive engagement with the latch mechanism.

---

15   Door latch, lock cylinder and handles - removal and installation

Outside door handle lever

Note: *This procedure only applies to the outside door handle lever. If you need to replace the outside door handle reinforcement (the actual mechanism for the outside door handle), see Steps 11 through 18.*

1   Remove the trim cap for the outside handle retaining screw **(see illustration)**. Loosen, but don't remove, the screw.

2   Remove the cover from the outside handle **(see illustration)**.

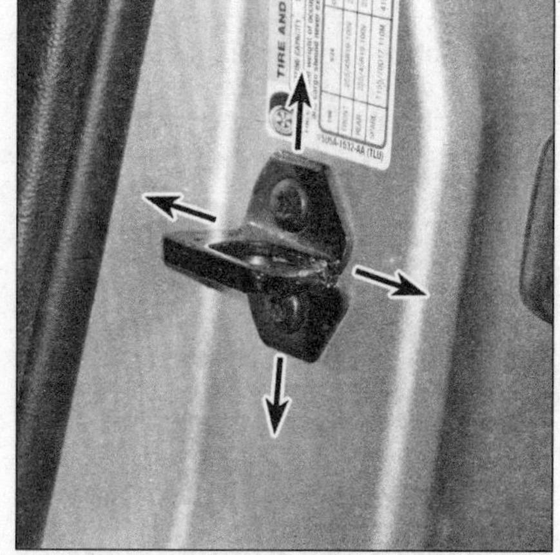

14.12 Adjust the door latch striker by loosening the mounting screws and gently tapping the striker in the desired direction

3   Pull the outside door handle out of the door and to the rear to disengage it from the handle reinforcement inside the door **(see illustration)**.

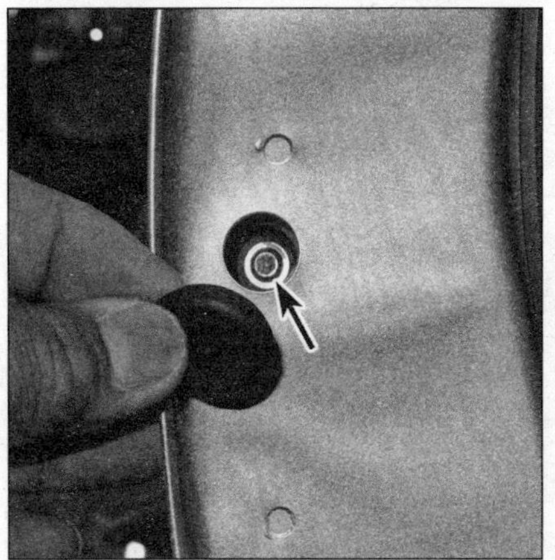

15.1 Outside door handle retaining screw

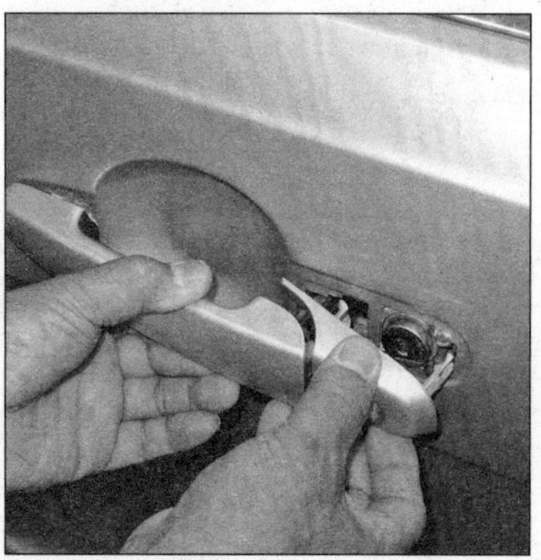

15.2 Remove the outside door handle cover

15.3 To disengage the outside door handle lever from the handle reinforcement inside the door, pull it out of the door and to the rear

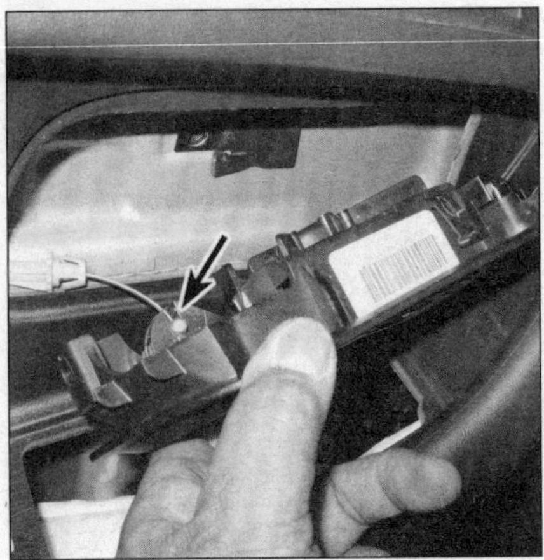

15.8 Align the cable with the slot in the lever then slide the cable out

15.13 Lock rod locations

15.15 Remove the fastener

4   Remove and inspect the outside door handle seals. If the seals are cracked, torn or otherwise deteriorated, replace them.
5   Installation is the reverse of removal.

Inside door handle

6   Remove the door trim panel (see Section 13).
7   Pry the handle out from the door panel.
8   Line up the actuator cable with the slot in the handle lever and pull out the cable end plug **(see illustration)**.
9   Disconnect the actuator by prying out the bushing.
10   Installation is the reverse of removal.

Door latch and outside door handle reinforcement

11   Remove the outside door handle lever (see Steps 1 through 3), then remove the door trim panel (see Section 13).
12   Disengage the upper lock cylinder actuating rod from the handle reinforcement, if equipped.
13   Disengage the lower exterior door handle reinforcement actuating rod **(see illustration)**.
14   Disconnect the keyless entry pad har-

ness retaining clip and move the harness out of the way, if equipped.
15   Remove the reinforcement mounting fastener **(see illustration)** from the outside, pivot the assembly inwards, and remove it from inside the door.
16   Remove the latch mounting fasteners **(see illustration)**.
17   Pull the latch and outside door handle reinforcement from the door as a single assembly, then disconnect the electrical connector from the latch and handle actuator cable.
18   Installation is the reverse of removal.

Door lock cylinder

Note: *Before removing the door lock cylinder on these models, be aware that you cannot simply install a new door lock cylinder. Instead, you must discard the old cylinder and build a new unit with the appropriate lock repair package, which you can obtain from your dealer. The lock repair package includes instructions for how to build the new lock cylinder to the key code of the vehicle.*
19   Remove the outside door handle (see Steps 1 through 4).
20   Disengage the release tab and remove the lock cylinder.

21   When installing the rebuilt lock cylinder, align the D-slot in the lock cylinder with the D-slot in the lock cylinder lever.
22   Installation is otherwise the reverse of removal.

Keyless entry pad

23   Remove the upper trim cap for the outside end of the door.
24   Working through the hole, use a screwdriver to release the clip holding the key pad to the reinforcement handle.
25   Pull the key pad out and disconnect the electrical connector.
26   Installation is the reverse of removal.

---

16   Door window glass - removal and installation

---

1   Remove the door trim panel (see Section 13).
2   Remove the front door speaker (see Chapter 12).
3   Peel down the plastic watershield **(see illustration)**.
4   On 2009 and earlier models, lower the

15.16 Door latch mounting fasteners

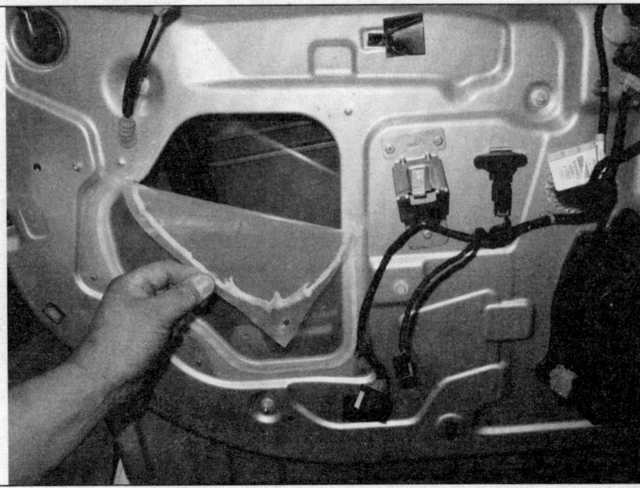

16.3 Slowly peel the watershield downwards, trying not to tear it

16.5 Use a screwdriver to push each glass-to-regulator clamp locking tab inwards

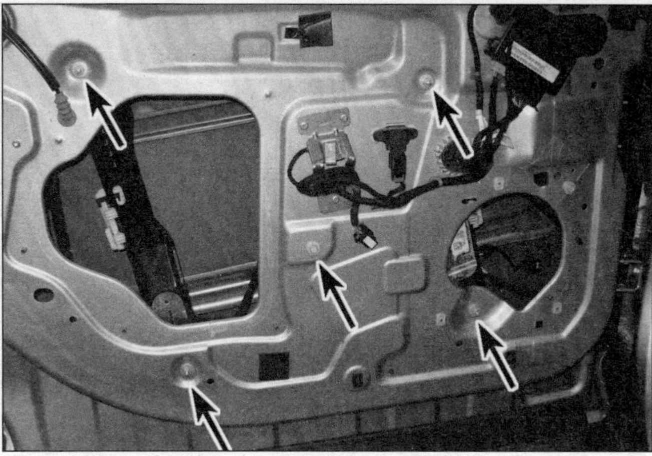

17.14 Regulator fastener locations

window glass until the glass clamp bolts are accessible through the access holes. Loosen (but don't remove) both glass clamp bolts, then secure the window in place with tape so that it won't go down.

5   On 2010 and later models, temporarily reconnect the power window switch and lower the window glass until the glass clamp locking tabs are accessible through the access holes. Using a screwdriver or other tool, push in each glass-to-regulator clamp locking tab **(see illustration)**, then gently lift the glass up and secure the window in place with tape so that it won't go down.

Note: *If the door window regulator motor is broken or disconnected, you'll have to remove it (see Section 17) and move the window glass manually.*

6   Lower the window regulator, then guide the window up and tilt it outward to remove it through the window opening.

7   Installation is the reverse of removal. Perform the de-initialization/initialization procedures in the following order.

De-initialization procedure

8   Turn the ignition key to ON.

9   Activate the power window control switch in the one-touch up-mode and simultaneously remove power from the window motor while the window is moving, using one of the following methods:

- *Disconnect the battery negative cable while the window is moving.*
- *Disconnect the power window motor electrical connector while the window is moving.*
- *Remove the left or right front power window motor fuse while the window is moving.*

10   The power window motor is now de-initialized and the motor is reset to its original factory settings.

11   Reconnect the negative battery cable, power window motor electrical connector or power window motor fuse before proceeding to the initialization procedure.

Initialization procedure

12   Turn the ignition key to ON.

13   Press and hold the window control switch until the window glass stalls for two seconds into the glass top run, then release the switch.

14   Pull and hold the power window control switch until the window glass stalls for two seconds at the bottom of its travel, then release the switch.

15   Test the operation of the power window by activating the power window switch in the one-touch up-mode. If the window doesn't operate correctly, repeat this procedure.

---

17   Door window regulator and motor - removal and installation

---

Door window regulator

1   Remove the door trim panel (see Section 13).

2   Carefully pull the plastic watershield from the door, if equipped **(see illustration 16.3)**.

3   Remove the front door speaker (see Chapter 12).

2009 and earlier models

4   Lower the window glass until the glass clamp bolts are accessible through the access holes. Loosen (but don't remove) both glass clamp bolts, then secure the window in place with tape so that it won't go down.

Note: *If the door window regulator motor is broken or disconnected, you'll have to remove it and move the window glass manually.*

5   Lower the window regulator mechanism until it stops at the bottom of the regulator tracks.

6   Disconnect all electrical wiring harness connectors and harness clips, the power mirror electrical connector (see Section 18), and the harness connection to the A-pillar. Remove the harness grommet retaining bolts.

7   Working through the speaker hole, dis-

engage the retaining clip attaching the harness to the door from the inside. Disengage the clips on the weather strip and feed the harness between the weather strip and the door.

8   Remove the door latch, outside door handle, lock cylinder and keyless entry pad, if equipped (see Section 15).

9   Loosen the exterior door handle reinforcement screw.

10   Remove the regulator module assembly mounting bolts and remove the module from the door.

11   Installation is the reverse of removal. Perform the de-initialization/initialization procedures (see Section 16).

2010 and later models

12   Temporarily reconnect the power window switch and lower the window glass until the glass clamp locking tabs are accessible through the access holes. Using a screwdriver or other tool, push in each glass-to-regulator clamp locking tab, then gently lift the glass up and secure the window in place with tape so that it won't go down **(see illustration 16.5)**.

Note: *If the door window regulator motor is broken, you'll have to remove it and move the window glass manually.*

13   Disconnect the electrical connector from the power window motor.

14   Remove the five window regulator fasteners **(see illustration)**, then remove the window regulator and motor assembly through the large opening in the door.

15   Installation is the reverse of removal. Perform the de-initialization/initialization procedures (see Section 16).

Regulator motor

16   Remove the door trim panel (see Section 13).

17   Carefully pull the plastic watershield from the door.

18   Remove the front door speaker (see Chapter 12).

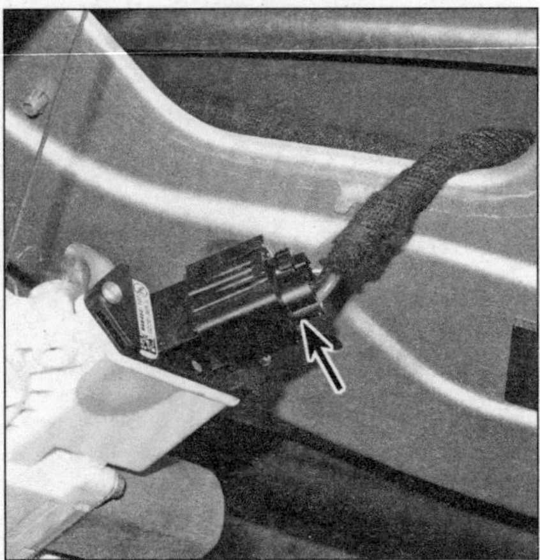

17.19 Window regulator motor electrical connector

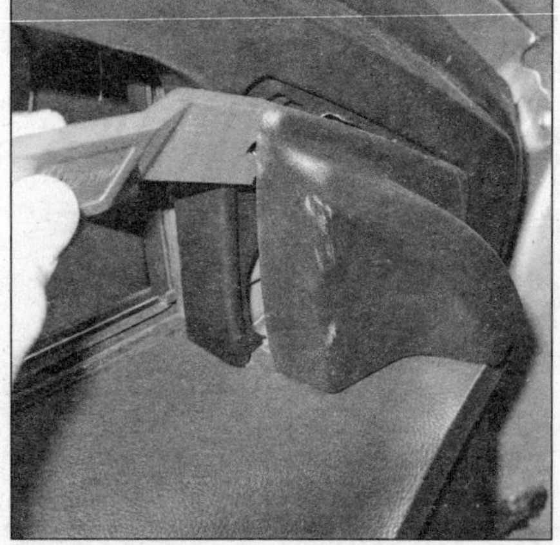

18.1 Pry out the sail panel

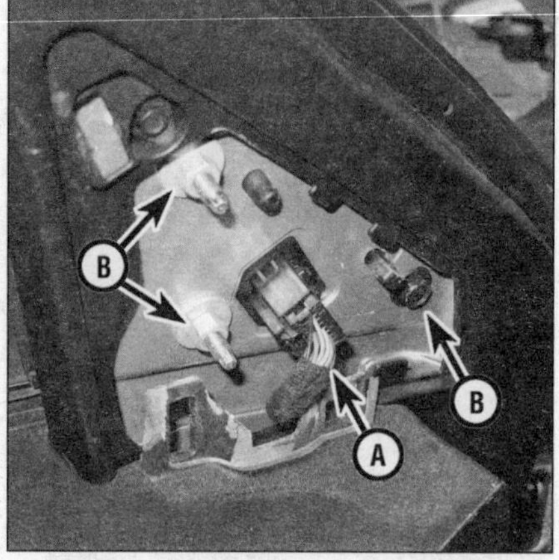

18.2 Mirror electrical connector (A) and mounting nuts (B)

19   Disconnect the electrical connector from the regulator motor **(see illustration)**.
20   Secure the window in place with tape.
21   On 2009 and earlier models, remove the three regulator motor mounting screws, then remove the motor.
22   On 2010 and later models, the regulator and motor must be removed as a unit to access the three mounting screws **(see illustration 17.14)**.
23   Installation is the reverse of removal. Perform the de-initialization/initialization procedures (see Section 16).

18   Mirrors - removal and installation

1   Disengage the sail panel clips and remove the panel **(see illustration)**.
2   Disconnect the electrical connectors from the mirror **(see illustration)** and sail panel, if equipped.
3   Remove the mirror mounting fasteners **(see illustration 18.2)** and remove the mirror.
4   Installation is the reverse of removal.

19   Trunk lid - removal and installation

Note: *The trunk lid is heavy and awkward to remove and install; two people should perform this procedure.*
1   Open the trunk lid.
2   Disconnect the electrical connectors from the trunk lid. Disengage all wiring harness clips and set the harnesses aside.

3   While an assistant supports the trunk lid, detach the support struts **(see illustration)**.
4   Mark or scribe around the hinges, then remove the hinge nuts and detach the trunk lid from the vehicle **(see illustration)**.
5   Installation is the reverse of removal.

20   Trunk lid key lock cylinder and latch - removal and installation

Key lock cylinder
Note: *A special rivet installation tool is required to install new rivets during key lock cylinder installation.*
1   Remove the pull-down strap fasteners and remove the strap, then use a plastic trim tool to remove the pin-type fasteners **(see illustration)**. Remove the trunk lid trim panel.
2   Disconnect the trunk lid actuator cable from the key lock cylinder.
3   Disconnect the electrical connector from the lock cylinder **(see illustration)**.
4   Drill out the two lock cylinder rivets and remove the lock cylinder.
5   Installation is the reverse of removal.

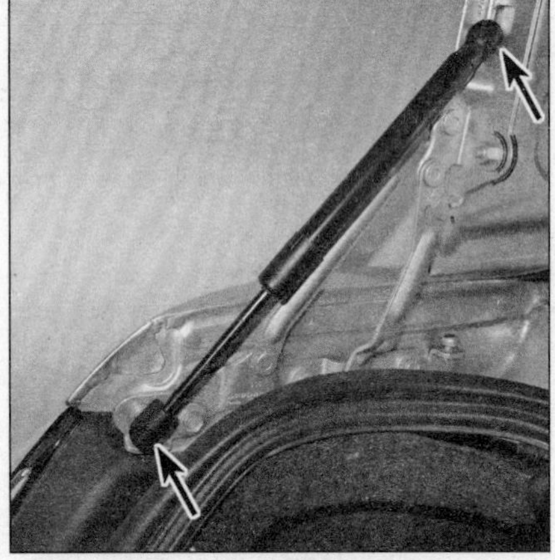

19.3 Detach the trunk lid support strut

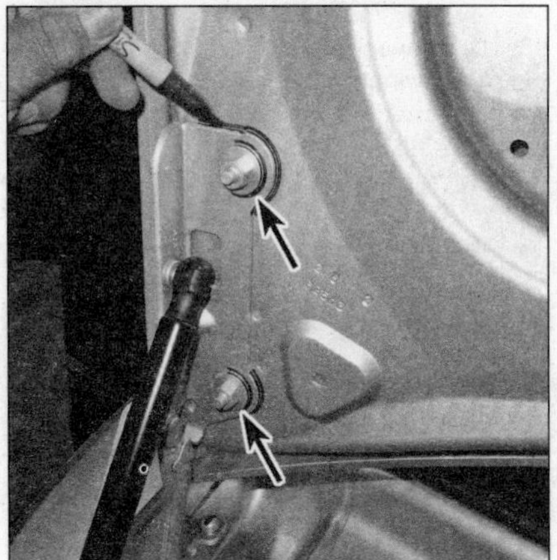

19.4 Trunk lid hinge nut locations

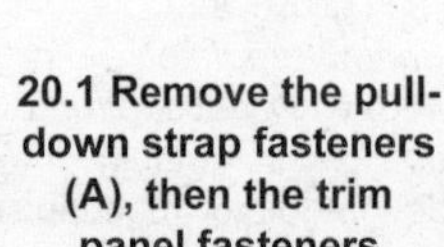

20.1 Remove the pull-down strap fasteners (A), then the trim panel fasteners

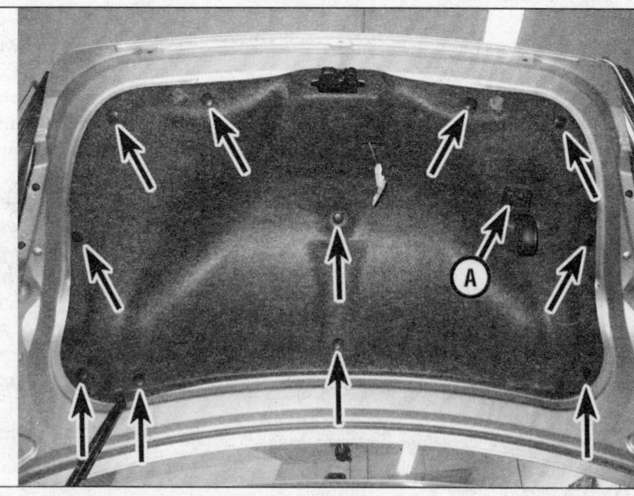

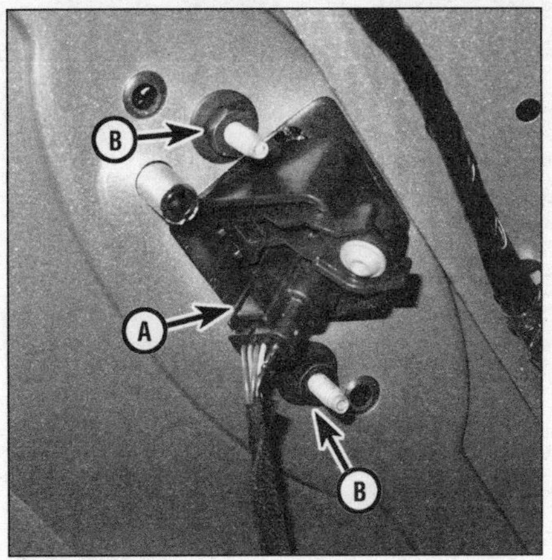

20.3 Trunk lid lock cylinder electrical connector (A) and mounting nuts (B)

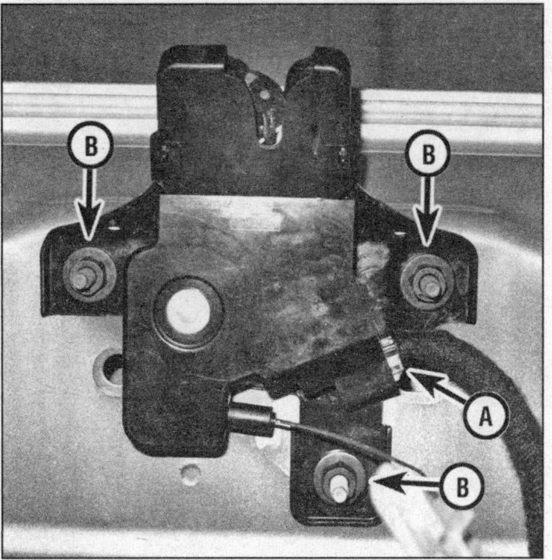

20.7 Trunk lid latch electrical connector (A) and mounting nuts (B)

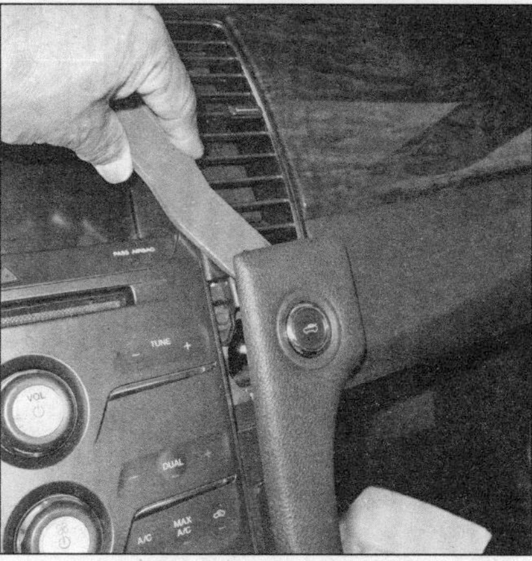

21.13a Starting from the top, pry up the console edge trim from each side . . .

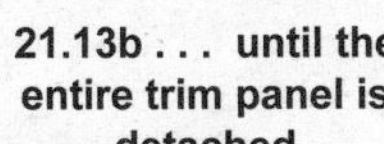

21.13b . . . until the entire trim panel is detached

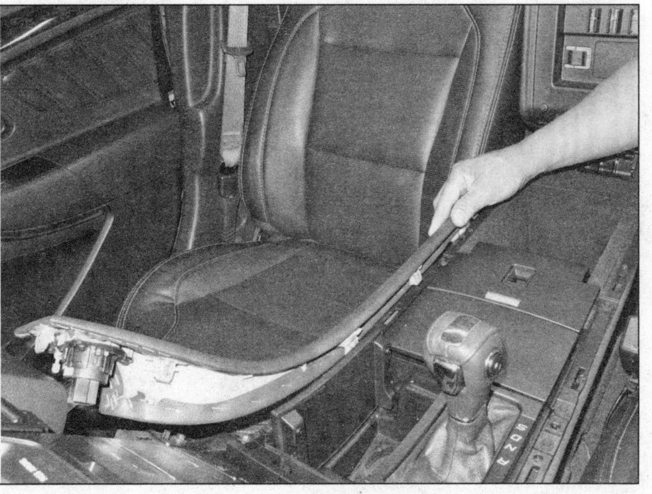

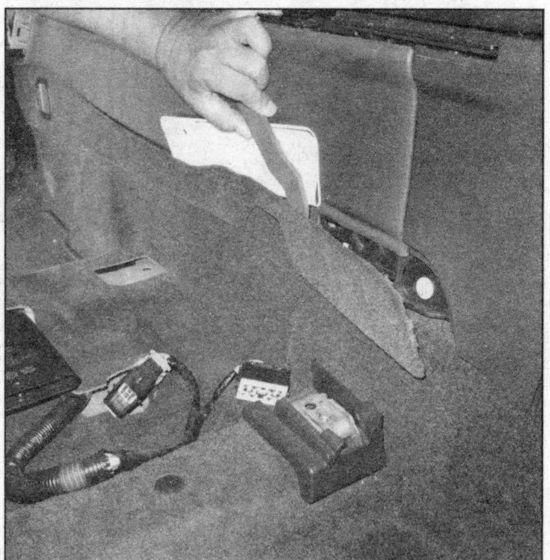

21.14 Place a piece of cardboard against the panel to protect it as you pry the lower panel loose

Latch

6   Remove the trunk lid trim panel **(see illustration 20.1)**.

7   Disconnect the electrical connector from the trunk lid latch **(see illustration)**.

8   Remove the latch mounting nuts **(see illustration 20.7)** and remove the latch.

9   Installation is the reverse of removal.

---

21   Center console - removal and installation

2009 and earlier models

1   Carefully pry off the shifter trim from around the shifter.

2   Carefully pry loose the console finish panel/cup holder and disengage it from the mounting clips.

3   Working around the perimeter of the side panels, use a trim removal tool to carefully pry out the left and right side trim panels from the console.

4   Raise the seats as high as they can go, then slide the front seats all the way forward. Remove the two rear console bolts, then slide the seats all the way rearward, and remove the two forward console bolts.

5   Remove the two front console bolts from each side of the console.

6   Remove the storage bin fasteners and remove the bin.

7   Remove the console-to-instrument panel bolts just below the heater/air conditioner control assembly.

8   Lift up the console and disconnect all electrical connectors from the console.

9   Remove the center console.

10   Installation is the reverse of removal.

2010 and later models

11   Apply the parking brake and place the shift lever in the neutral position.

12   Slide the front seats all the way rearward, then place them in the fully reclined position.

13   Using a trim tool, carefully pry off the console edge trim from both sides of the console **(see illustrations)**. On the passenger's side edge trim, disconnect the electrical connector from the top of the trim.

Note: *The console edge trim starts from the end of the console and ends at the middle of the instrument panel.*

14   To prevent damage to the console, place a piece of cardboard or a rag between the panels **(see illustration)** as they are removed.

15   Push forward on the lower side trim panels until the pin-type retainers are disengaged, and remove the panels **(see illustration)**.

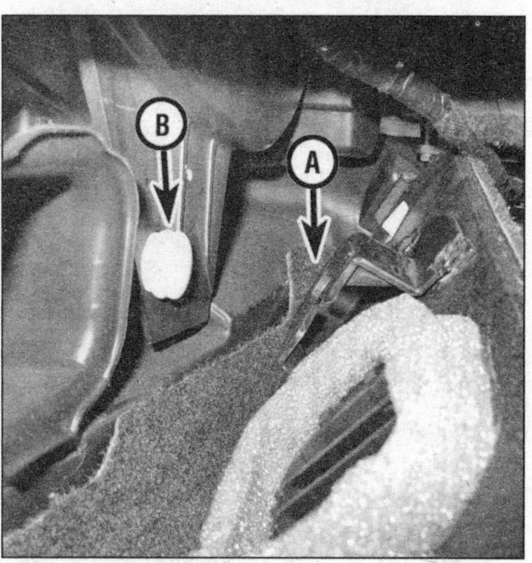

21.15 Disengage the panel (A) from the retaining clip (B)

21.16 Pry out and remove the left and right side trim panels - seat removed for clarity

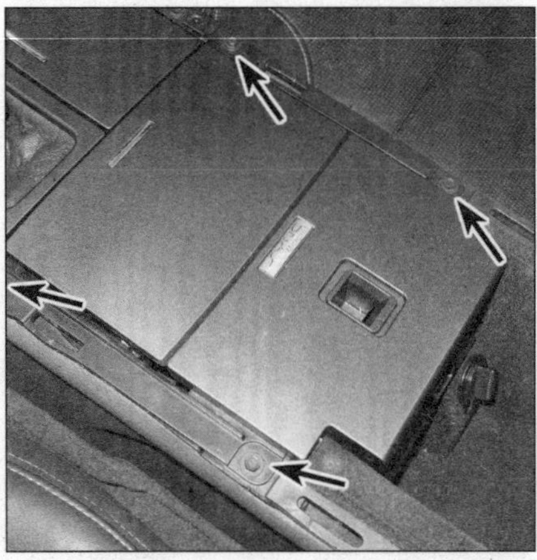

21.18 Cup holder assembly fastener locations

21.19 Disconnect the main harness connector at the base of the cup holder

21.20a Remove the shift lever trim panel screws from the top of the panel . . .

21.20b . . . then disengage the boot tabs

21.21 Media/storage compartment panel fastener locations

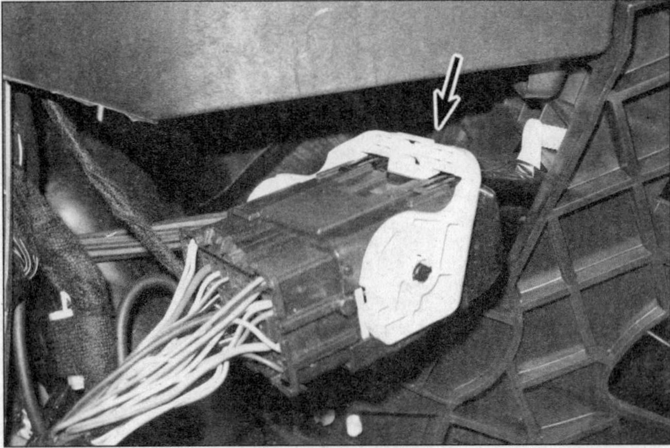

21.24a Rotate the locking lever to the rear to disconnect the main harness connector . . .

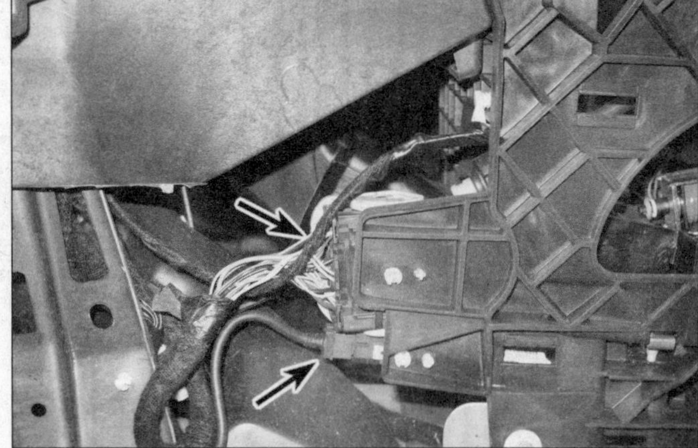

21.24b . . . then disconnect the remaining connectors to the console assembly

16   Working around the perimeter of the panels, use a trim removal tool to carefully pry out and remove the left and right side trim panels from the console **(see illustration)**.

17   Remove the shift lever mounting screws and remove the lever (see Chapter 7A).

18   Remove the four screws and lift the cup holder assembly from the center console **(see illustration)**.

19   Disconnect the main harness connector at the base of the cup holder assembly **(see illustration)**, then remove the assembly.

20   Remove the four mounting screws from the top of the shift lever trim panel, disengage the shift lever boot tabs, and remove the shift lever trim panel **(see illustrations)**.

21   Remove the four screws from the media/storage compartment and remove the unit **(see illustration)**. Disconnect the electrical connector from the light/outlet.

21.26 Console upper mounting bolt locations

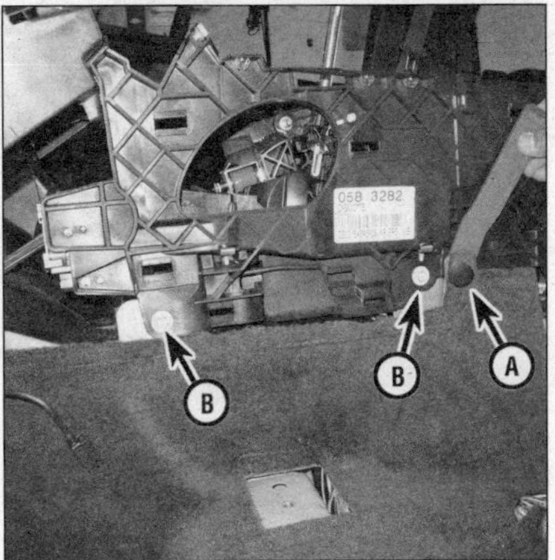

21.27a Carpet-to-console retainers (A) and console mounting bolts (B) (middle and front base of the console; right side shown, left side similar)

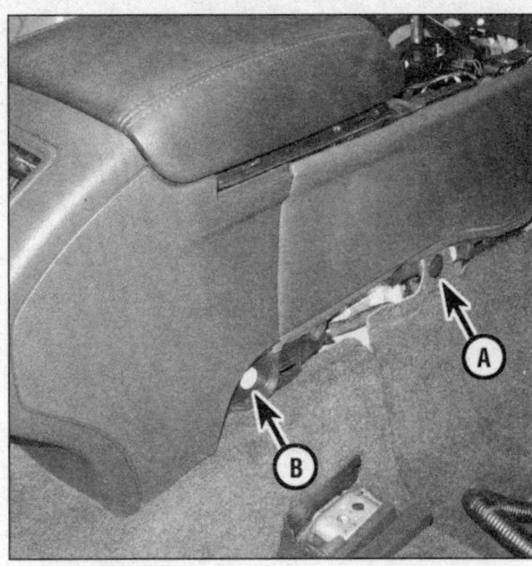

21.27b Carpet-to-console retainers (A) and console mounting bolts (B) (rear; right side shown, left side similar)

21.28 Lift the assembly up from the rear and maneuver it from the vehicle

22.2 Pry off the end trim panel

22   Unclip the ambient light harness from the front finish panel. Rotate the ambient light counterclockwise to remove it. Remove the finish panel.

23   Remove the shift cable from the shift lever and bracket (see Chapter 7A).

24   Disconnect the main harness electrical connector from the firewall and any other remaining electrical connectors from the console **(see illustrations)**.

25   Detach the carpet-to-console fasteners **(see illustration 21.27a and 21.27b)**.

26   Remove the console mounting bolts from the top of the console **(see illustration)**.

27   Remove the console mounting bolts from the base of the console **(see illustrations)**.

28   Lift up the console from the rear and remove the center console **(see illustration)** disconnect any electrical connectors attached at the rear of the console.

29   Installation is the reverse of removal.

22   Dashboard trim panels - removal and installation

Warning: *Models covered by this manual are equipped with a Supplemental Restraint System (SRS), more commonly known as airbags. Always disable the airbag system before working in the vicinity of any airbag system component to avoid the possibility of accidental deployment of the airbag, which could cause personal injury (see Chapter 12).*

Note: *Refer to Section 6 for fastener and trim removal.*

1   Removing various dashboard trim panels provides access to electrical/electronic components such as the instrument cluster, the audio unit, the heater and air conditioning control unit and various instrument panel-mounted switches. If you're going to remove the entire instrument panel, you'll need to remove all of the trim panels to access the instrument panel mounting bolts.

Left or right dashboard end trim panels

2   Carefully pry off the end trim panel **(see illustration)**.

3   Installation is the reverse of removal.

Instrument cluster trim panel

2009 and earlier models

4   Disconnect the cable from the negative battery terminal (see Chapter 5).

5   Remove the knee bolster trim panel (see Steps 22 and 23).

6   Remove the steering column covers (see Section 23), then place the steering column in the lowest position.

7   The cluster trim panel is a thin, narrow trim piece that runs along the lower edge of the instrument cluster. Disengage the locating tabs from the panel gap trim piece and the instrument cluster trim panel.

8   Remove the screws from the instrument cluster trim panel, then carefully pry off the trim panel.

9   Installation is the reverse of removal.

22.11a Location of the left side trim panel mounting screw

22.11b Pry the panel out from the top

22.13 The right side panel is retained by four clips

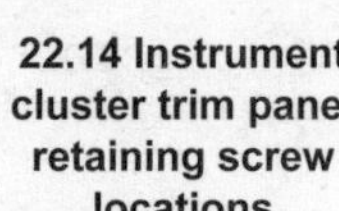

22.14 Instrument cluster trim panel retaining screw locations

22.16 Disengage the retaining clips from the corners

2010 and later models

10   Remove the knee bolster trim panel (see Steps 22 and 23).

11   Remove the left side trim panel fastener, then pry the panel out from the top of the console **(see illustrations)**.

12   Remove the center console, left side trim panel from the console (see Section 21).

13   Using a trim tool, disengage the four retaining clips **(see illustration)** by prying out the corners of the right appliqués below the console and disconnect the electrical connector, if equipped.

14   Disengage the instrument cluster trim boot **(see illustration 23.4)**. Remove the screws from the instrument cluster trim panel, then carefully pry off the trim panel **(see illustration)**.

15   Installation is the reverse of removal.

Instrument panel top (2010 and later models)

16   Carefully pry off the center trim panel, disengaging the retaining clips from the corners **(see illustration)** and center of the panel.

17   Installation is the reverse of removal.

Center instrument panel appliqués - 2009 and earlier models

18   Remove the instrument cluster trim panel (see Steps 4 through 8). Pry out the center instrument panel trim panel.

Note: *The center trim panel runs the entire length of the instrument panel make sure to work evenly along the entire panel before trying to remove it.*

19   Installation is the reverse of removal.

Right side instrument panel appliqués - 2010 and later models

20   Carefully pry off the right side trim appliqué just above the glove box **(see illustration)**.

21   Installation is the reverse of removal.

Knee bolswter trim panel and knee bolster

22   Remove the two knee bolster trim panel screws **(see illustration)**.

23   Carefully pry out the knee bolster, and remove the panel **(see illustration)**.

24   Installation is the reverse of removal.

Glove box

2009 and earlier models

25   Disengage the damper clip from the right end of the glove box.

26   Lower the glove box, pull it from the hinge clips at the bottom and remove the glove box.

27   Installation is the reverse of removal.

2010 and later models

28   Disengage the damper clip from the left end of the glove box **(see illustration)**.

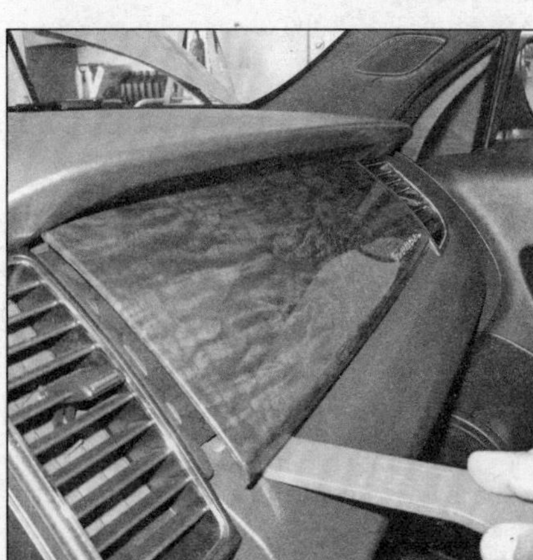

22.20 Pry out the right side trim appliqué evenly from each side

22.22 Knee bolster trim panel retaining screw locations

22.23 Carefully pry the panel out to disengage the retaining clips

22.28 Disengage the damper clip (A) from the left end of the glove box (B)

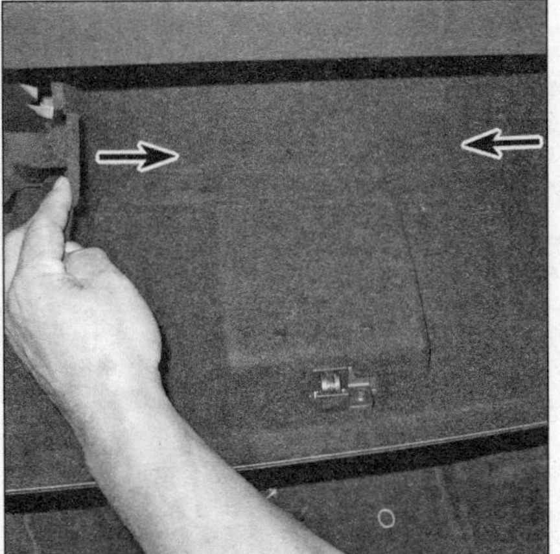

22.29 Push the corners of the glove box inwards until the stops clear, then pull out the glove box

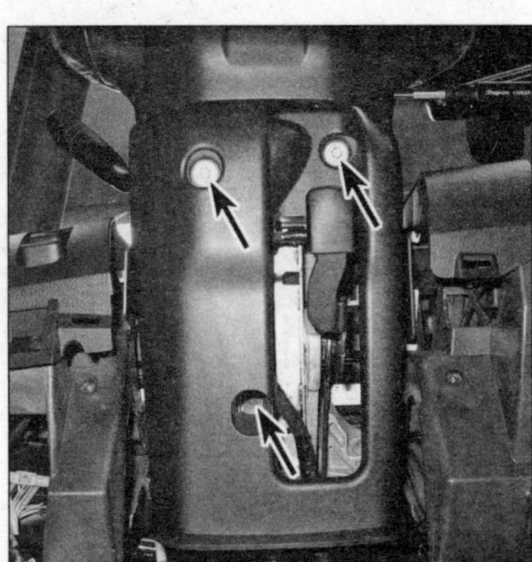

23.3 Lower steering column cover retaining bolts

29   Firmly grasp the corners of the glove box and push them inwards until the stops clear the sides, then remove the glove box **(see illustration)**.
30   Installation is the reverse of removal.

4   On later models, lower the steering column and disengage the column boot from the upper cover **(see illustration)**.
5   To remove the upper column cover, use a trim removal tool to separate it from the instrument cluster trim panel **(see illustration)**.

6   Installation is the reverse of removal.
Note: *On later models, make sure the rubber column boot tabs are pushed into the steering column cover first, or the tabs will be damaged when the shift lever is moved **(see illustration 23.4)**.*

23 Steering column covers - removal and installation

Warning: *Models covered by this manual are equipped with a Supplemental Restraint System (SRS), more commonly known as airbags. Always disable the airbag system before working in the vicinity of any airbag system component to avoid the possibility of accidental deployment of the airbag, which could cause personal injury (see Chapter 12).*
1   Disconnect the cable from the negative terminal of the battery (see Chapter 5).
2   On 2010 and later models, remove the knee bolster (see Section 22).
3   Remove the bolts from the lower steering column cover **(see illustration)**. Press in on the sides of the upper cover and separate the two covers.

23.4 Disengage the boot tabs from the upper column cover

23.5 Separate the column cover from the steering column

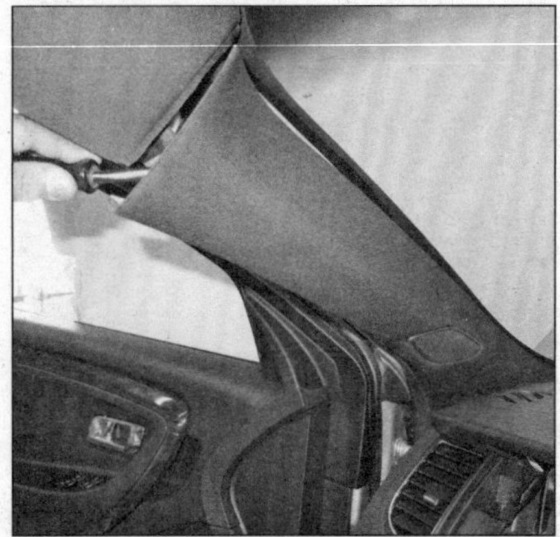

24.2 Carefully remove the A-pillar trim panels by prying them off and disconnecting the tethers

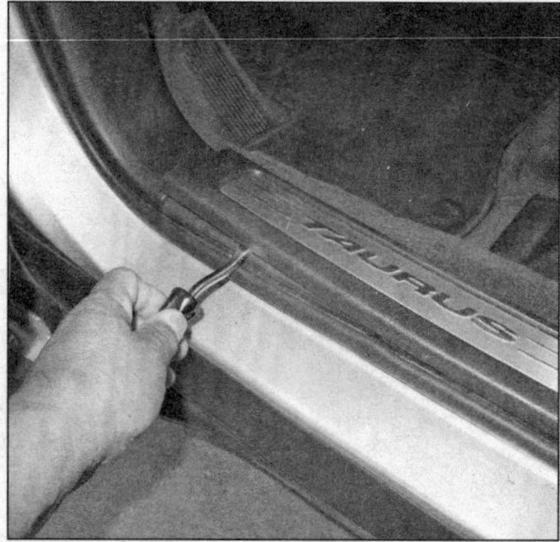

24.3a Carefully pry up the sill panel . . .

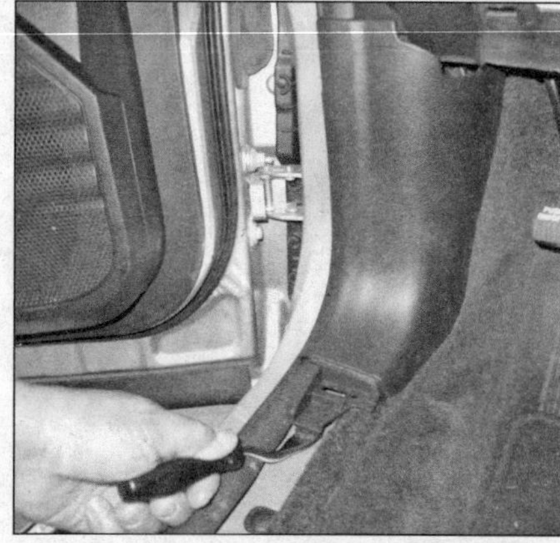

24.3b . . . then the kick panel

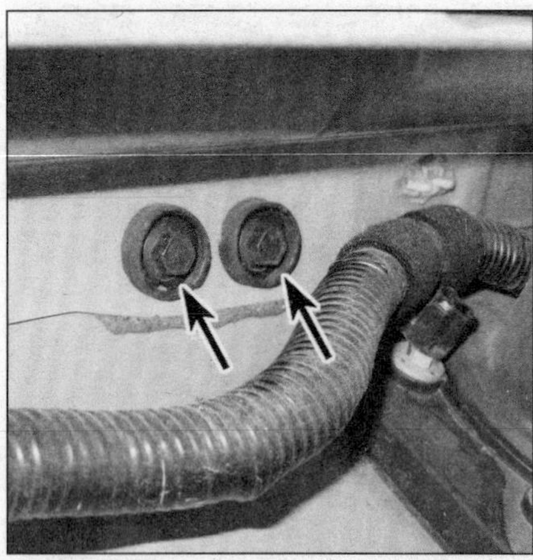

24.5 Remove the firewall-to-instrument panel bolt from the engine compartment side - left side shown, right side identical

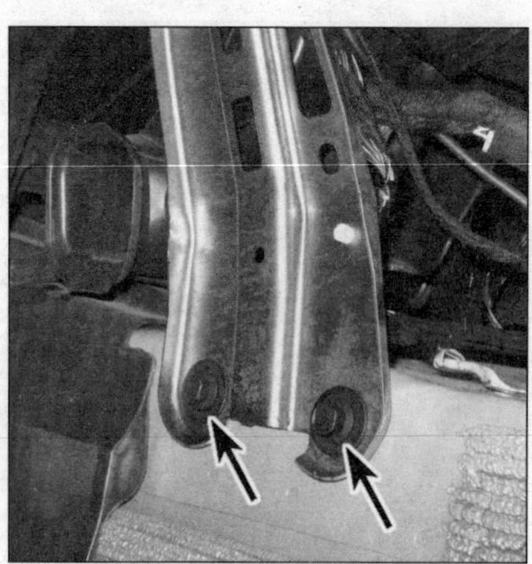

24.19 Instrument panel brace-to-floor bolt locations - left side

24.20 Instrument panel brace-to-floor bolt locations - right side

24 Instrument panel - removal and installation

Warning: *Models covered by this manual are equipped with a Supplemental Restraint System (SRS), more commonly known as airbags. Always disable the airbag system before working in the vicinity of any airbag system component to avoid the possibility of accidental deployment of the airbag, which could cause personal injury (see Chapter 12).*

Note: *This is a difficult procedure for the home mechanic. There are many hidden fasteners, difficult angles to work in and many electrical connectors to tag and disconnect/connect. We recommend that this procedure be done only by an experienced do-it-yourselfer.*

Note: *During removal of the instrument panel, make careful notes of how each piece comes off, where it fits in relation to other pieces and what holds it in place. If you note how each part is installed before removing it, getting the instrument panel back together again will be much easier.*

1   Remove the following parts:
  a) *Steering wheel (see Chapter 10)*
  b) *All dashboard trim panels and the glove box (see Section 22)*
  c) *Air conditioning and heater control assembly (see Chapter 3)*
  d) *Instrument cluster and radio (see Chapter 12)*
  e) *Right lower instrument panel insulator*
  f) *Front seats (though not absolutely necessary, removing both front seats allows more room to work and eliminates the possibility of damage to the seats during the procedure)*
  g) *Center console (see Section 21)*

2   Carefully remove the left and right A-pillar (windshield pillar) trim panel and disconnect the tethers from each of the panels **(see illustration)**.
3   Grasp each front door opening sill panel/ kick panel and pull them off **(see illustrations)**.
4   Disconnect the two electrical connectors in the left kick panel area as well as the bulkhead electrical connector, antenna cable and satellite antenna, if equipped.

5   Remove the cowl panels (see Section 12), then remove the bolts from the engine compartment side **(see illustration)**.
6   Disconnect the electrical connectors to the PCM (see Chapter 6) then remove the PCM and mounting bracket.
7   In the glove box area, disconnect all air conditioning system electrical connectors.
8   Disconnect all electrical connectors and wiring harness clips located on the floor between the two front seats.
9   Disconnect any remaining wiring connectors between the vehicle and the instrument panel.
10   Working in the engine compartment, remove the strut tower cross brace (see Chapter 10).
11   Mark the relationship of the upper steering column shaft to the lower shaft, remove the steering column pinch-bolt and separate the upper column shaft from the lower shaft. Discard the old pinch bolt and install a new one when you reassemble the steering column.
12   Remove the two hood release handle screws and set the handle aside (see Section 8).

24.21 Left side instrument panel bolt locations

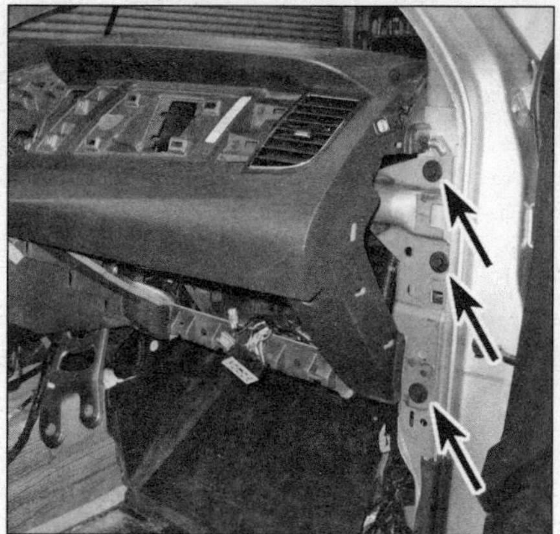

24.22 Right side instrument panel bolt locations (from the passenger's door opening)

24.23 With the help of an assistant pull the panel back carefully and disconnect any electrical connectors that you may have missed

13   If equipped with an in-vehicle temperature sensor aspirator hose, separate the aspirator hose retaining clips from the heater core/evaporator core housing, then pull the hose away from the housing.

14   Disconnect the shift lever cable from the ball stud and remove the cable from the retaining clips (see Chapter 7A).

15   Remove the center console (see Section 21).

16   Disconnect the electrical connectors from the center console, then remove the center console support.

17   Disconnect the Restraints Control Module (RCM) electrical connector.

18   Remove the plastic pushpin-type retainers and pull the carpet back.

19   Remove the two instrument panel brace-to-floor bolts from the left side **(see illustration)**.

20   Remove the instrument panel brace-to-floor bolts from the right side **(see illustration)**.

21   Remove the left side instrument panel mounting bolts from inside the driver's door opening **(see illustration)**.

Note: *Some early models use a Torx head bolt that can't be completely removed; pull the bolt out far enough to allow the instrument panel to clear it.*

22   Remove the right side instrument panel bolts from inside the passenger's door opening **(see illustration)**.

Caution: *To avoid damage to the instrument panel, have an assistant support the instrument panel when removing these bolts.*

23   With an assistant helping you, remove the instrument panel from the vehicle **(see illustration)**.

24   Installation is the reverse of removal. When installing the A-pillar trim panels, attach the tethers.

Note: *The trim panels cannot be installed on the A-pillars without putting the clips back in position.*

25   Seats - removal and installation

Front seats

Warning: *All models covered by this manual are equipped with a Supplemental Restraint System (SRS), more commonly known as* airbags. Always disable the airbag system before working in the vicinity of any airbag system component to avoid the possibility of accidental deployment of the airbag, which could cause personal injury (see Chapter 12).

Warning: *During the removal and installation procedures, if a seat is dropped, or sat in while removed, or if pressure/load is applied to the seat tracks, the Occupant Safety System (OCS) may become damaged and the system may fail in a crash.*

Caution: *The seats are heavy, so have an assistant handy to help you lift the seat from the vehicle.*

Note: *This procedure applies to both front seats.*

1   Remove the covers from the seat mounting bolts and remove the bolts **(see illustrations)**.

2   Tilt the seat forward and disconnect all electrical connectors underneath the seat **(see illustration)**.

3   Using a helper, carefully lift the seat out of the vehicle.

Warning: *The seat is heavy, so trying to remove it by yourself could cause injury.*

4   Installation is the reverse of removal.

25.1a Remove the bolts from the front . . .

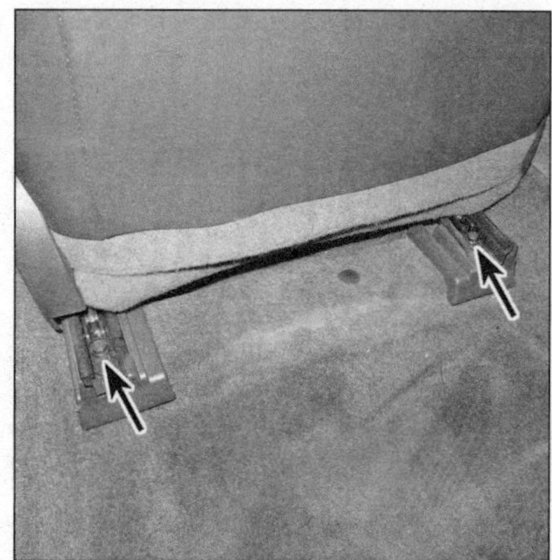

25.1b . . . and the rear of the seat

25.2 Disconnect the electrical connectors by rotating the locking levers away from the harness end

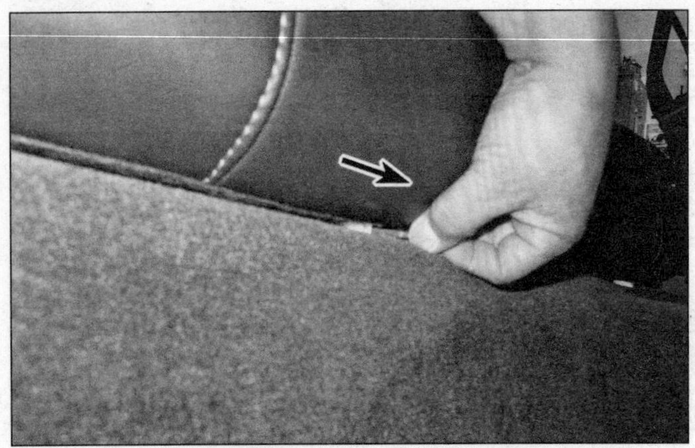

**25.6a Pull the release tab out while lifting up
on the corner of the seat**

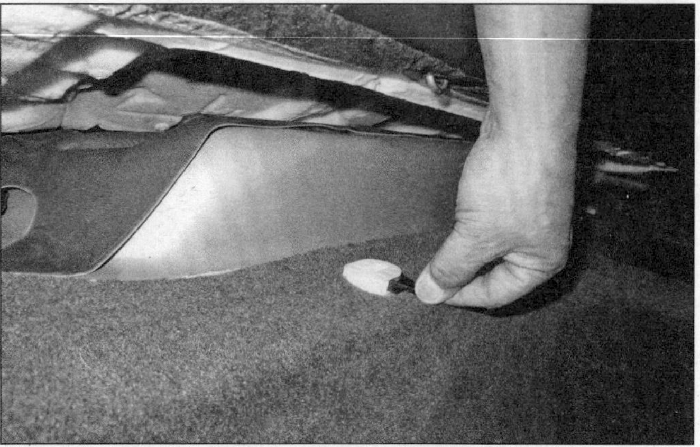

**25.6b Release tab location; seat removed for clarity
(left side shown, right side identical)**

Rear seats

5   Slide the front seat to the forward most position.

6   Working near the corners of the seat cushion, pull the release tabs outwards and lift up the seat cushion **(see illustrations)**.

7   Remove the rear seat back mounting nuts **(see illustration)** then lift the seat back(s) up and out of the vehicle.

8   Installation is the reverse of removal.

26   Parcel shelf – removal and installation

Five Hundred models

1   Remove the rear seat cushion and side bolsters.

2   Remove the C-pillar trim panels.

3   Remove the bezel from the center seat belt, then remove the anchor nut securing the center seat belt.

4   Disconnect the electrical connector from the center high-mounted brake light.

5   Remove the pin-type fasteners and pull the shelf forward to remove it.

6   Installation is the reverse of removal.

**25.7 Rear seat
back mounting
nut locations**

Taurus models

7   Remove the rear seat cushion.

8   Remove the C-pillar and D-pillar trim panels.

9   Remove the lower anchor nut securing the center seat belt.

10   Fold the rear seat backs forward, then remove the bezel from the center seat belt and pull the seat belt outward.

11   Disconnect the electrical connector at the left side D-pillar.

12   Remove the pin-type fasteners and pull the shelf forward to remove it.

13   Installation is the reverse of removal.

Chapter 12
Chassis electrical system

Contents

1 General information

1 The electrical system is a 12-volt, negative ground type. Power for the lights and all electrical accessories is supplied by a lead/acid-type battery that is charged by the alternator.

2 This Chapter covers repair and service procedures for the various electrical components not associated with the engine. Information on the battery, alternator, ignition system and starter motor can be found in Chapter 5.

Note: *It should be noted that when portions of the electrical system are serviced, the negative cable should be disconnected from the battery to prevent electrical shorts and/or fires.*

2 Electrical troubleshooting - general information

1 A typical electrical circuit consists of electrical components, as well as, switches, relays, motors, fuses, fusible links or circuit breakers related to that component and the wiring and connectors that link the component to both the battery and the chassis ground or computer ground circuits. To help you pinpoint an electrical circuit problem, wiring diagrams are provided at the end of this Chapter.

2 Before tackling any troublesome electrical circuit, first study the appropriate wiring diagrams to get a complete understanding of what makes up that individual circuit.

Trouble spots, for instance, can often be narrowed down by noting if other components related to the circuit are operating properly. If several components or circuits fail at one time, chances are the problem is in a fuse or ground connection, because several circuits are often routed through the same fuse and ground connections.

3 Electrical problems usually stem from simple causes, such as loose or corroded connections, a blown fuse, a melted fusible link or a failed relay. Visually inspect the condition of all fuses, wires and connections in a problem circuit before troubleshooting the circuit.

4 If test equipment and instruments are going to be utilized, use the diagrams to plan ahead of time where you will make the nec-

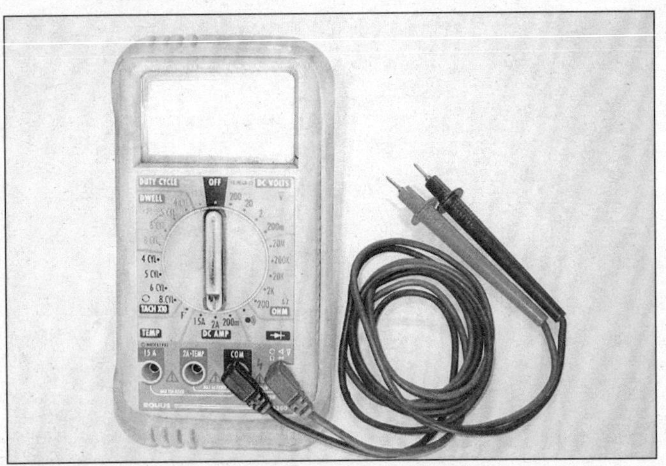

2.5a The most useful tool for electrical troubleshooting is a digital multimeter that can check volts, amps, and test continuity

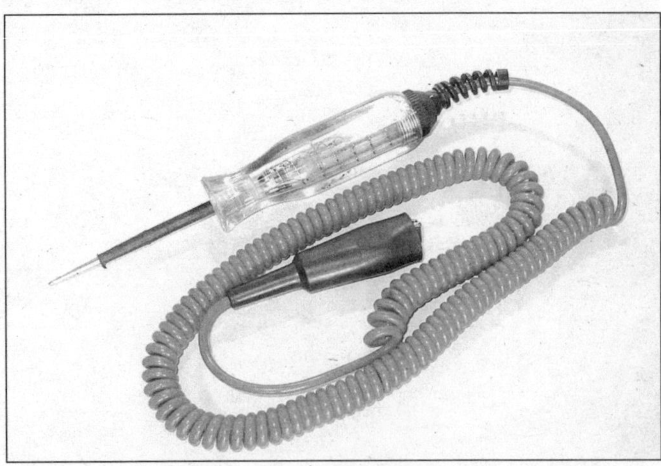

2.5b A test light is a very handy tool for checking voltage

essary connections in order to accurately pinpoint the trouble spot.

5   The basic tools needed for electrical troubleshooting include a circuit tester or voltmeter (a 12-volt bulb with a set of test leads can also be used), a continuity tester, which includes a bulb, battery and set of test leads, and a jumper wire, preferably with a circuit breaker incorporated, which can be used to bypass electrical components **(see illustrations)**. Before attempting to locate a problem with test instruments, use the wiring diagram(s) to decide where to make the connections.

Voltage checks

6   Voltage checks should be performed if a circuit is not functioning properly. Connect one lead of a circuit tester to either the negative battery terminal or a known good ground. Connect the other lead to a connector in the circuit being tested, preferably nearest to the battery or fuse **(see illustration)**. If the bulb of the tester lights, voltage is present, which

means that the part of the circuit between the connector and the battery is problem free. Continue checking the rest of the circuit in the same fashion. When you reach a point at which no voltage is present, the problem lies between that point and the last test point with voltage. Most of the time the problem can be traced to a loose connection.

Note: *Keep in mind that some circuits receive voltage only when the ignition key is in the Accessory or Run position.*

Finding a short

7   One method of finding shorts in a circuit is to remove the fuse and connect a test light or voltmeter in place of the fuse terminals. There should be no voltage present in the circuit. Move the wiring harness from side-to-side while watching the test light. If the bulb goes on, there is a short to ground somewhere in that area, probably where the insulation has rubbed through. The same test can be performed on each component in the circuit, even a switch.

Ground check

8   Perform a ground test to check whether a component is properly grounded. Disconnect the battery and connect one lead of a continuity tester or multimeter (set to the ohms scale), to a known good ground. Connect the other lead to the wire or ground connection being tested. If the resistance is low (less than 5 ohms), the ground is good. If the bulb on a self-powered test light does not go on, the ground is not good.

Continuity check

9   A continuity check is done to determine if there are any breaks in a circuit - if it is passing electricity properly. With the circuit off (no power in the circuit), a self-powered continuity tester or multimeter can be used to check the circuit. Connect the test leads to both ends of the circuit (or to the power end and a good ground), and if the test light comes on the circuit is passing current properly **(see illustration)**. If the resistance is low (less than 5

2.6 In use, a basic test light's lead is clipped to a known good ground, then the pointed probe can test connectors, wires or electrical sockets - if the bulb lights, the part being tested has battery voltage

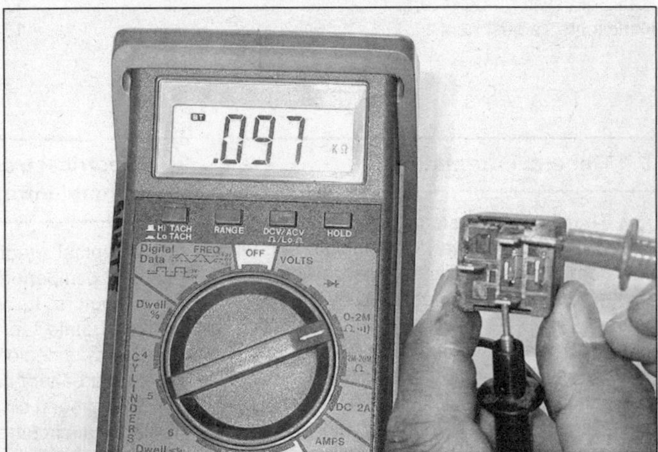

2.9 With a multimeter set to the ohms scale, resistance can be checked across two terminals - when checking for continuity, a low reading indicates continuity, a high reading indicates lack of continuity

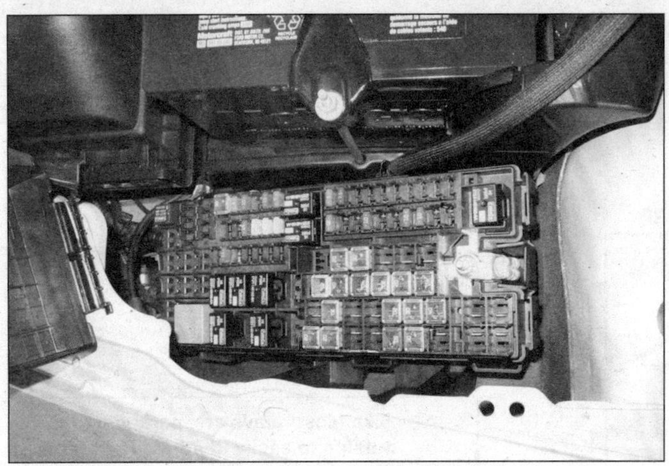

3.1a The engine compartment fuse and relay panel is located at the left side of the engine compartment (2013 Taurus shown, other models similar)

3.1b The passenger compartment fuse box is located under the left end of the instrument panel

ohms), there is continuity; if the reading is 10,000 ohms or higher, there is a break somewhere in the circuit. The same procedure can be used to test a switch, by connecting the continuity tester to the switch terminals. With the switch turned On, the test light should come on (or low resistance should be indicated on a meter).

Finding an open circuit

10 When diagnosing for possible open circuits, it is often difficult to locate them by sight because the connectors hide oxidation or terminal misalignment. Merely wiggling a connector on a sensor or in the wiring harness may correct the open circuit condition. Remember this when an open circuit is indicated when troubleshooting a circuit. Intermittent problems may also be caused by oxidized or loose connections.

11 Electrical troubleshooting is simple if you keep in mind that all electrical circuits are basically electricity running from the battery, through the wires, switches, relays, fuses and fusible links to each electrical component (light bulb, motor, etc.) and to ground, from which it is passed back to the battery. Any electrical problem is an interruption in the flow of electricity to and from the battery.

---

3 Fuses and fusible links - general information

Fuses

1 The electrical circuits of the vehicle are protected by a combination of fuses, circuit breakers and fusible links. The main fuse/ relay panel is in the engine compartment **(see illustration)**, while the interior fuse/ relay panel is located inside the passenger compartment **(see illustrations)**. Each of the

fuses is designed to protect a specific circuit, and the various circuits are identified on the fuse panel itself.

2 Several sizes of fuses may be employed in the fuse blocks. There are small, medium and large sizes of the same design, all with the same blade terminal design. The medium and large fuses can be removed with your fingers, but the small fuses require the use of pliers or the small plastic fuse-puller tool found in most fuse boxes.

3 Fusible links are located in the harness to the right of the underhood fuse box.

4 If an electrical component fails, always check the fuse first. The best way to check the fuses is with a test light. Check for power at the exposed terminal tips of each fuse. If power is present at one side of the fuse but not the other, the fuse is blown. A blown fuse can also be identified by visually inspecting it **(see illustration)**.

5 Be sure to replace blown fuses with the correct type. Fuses (of the same physical size) of different ratings may be physically interchangeable, but only fuses of the proper rating should be used. Replacing a fuse with one of a higher or lower value than specified is not recommended. Each electrical circuit needs a specific amount of protection. The amperage value of each fuse is molded into the top of the fuse body.

6 If the replacement fuse immediately fails, don't replace it again until the cause of the problem is isolated and corrected. In most cases, this will be a short circuit in the wiring caused by a broken or deteriorated wire.

Fusible links

7 Some circuits are protected by fusible links. The links are used in circuits which are not ordinarily fused, or which carry high current, such as the circuit between the alternator and the battery. Fusible links, which are

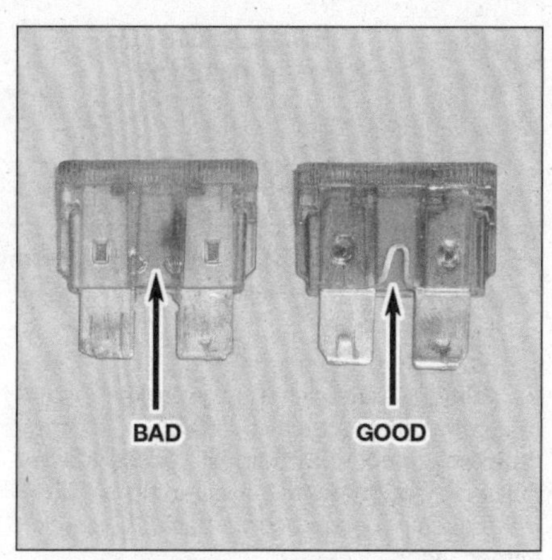

3.4 When a fuse blows, the element between the terminals melts

usually several wire gauges smaller in size than the circuit that they protect, are designed to melt if the circuit is subjected to more current than it was designed to carry. If you have to replace a blown fusible link, make sure that you replace it with one of the same specification. If the replacement fusible link blows in the same circuit, make sure that you troubleshoot the circuit in which the fusible link melted BEFORE installing another fusible link.

---

4 Circuit breakers - general information

1 Circuit breakers protect certain circuits, such as the power windows or heated seats. Depending on the vehicle's accessories, there may be one or two circuit breakers, located in the fuse/relay box in the engine compartment.

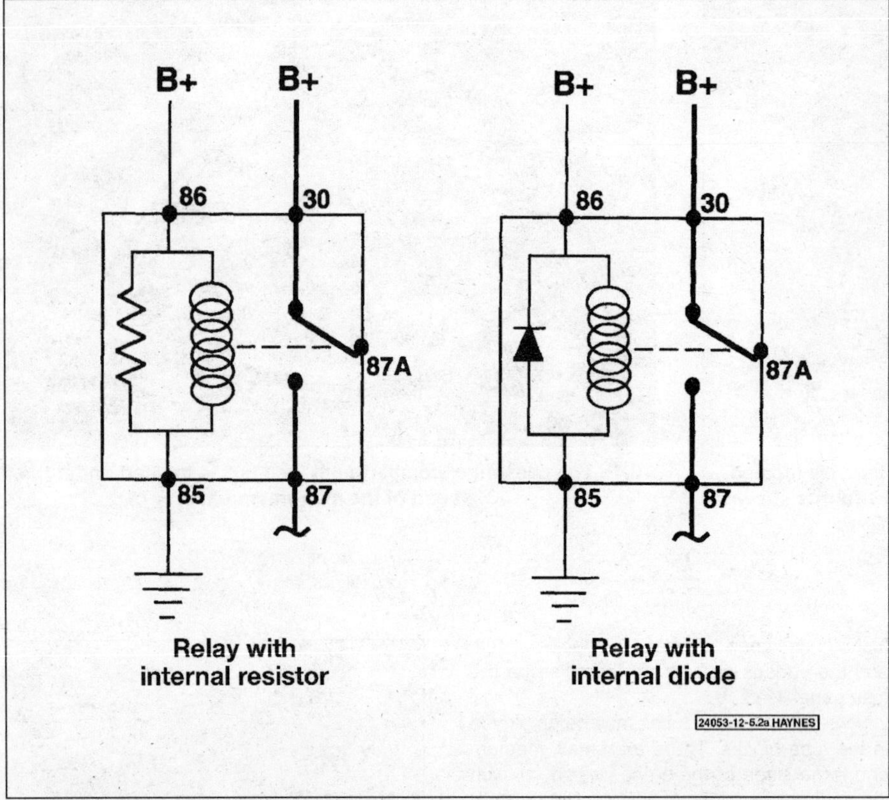

5.2a Typical ISO relay designs, terminal numbering and circuit connections

5.2b Most relays are marked on the outside to easily identify the control circuit and power circuit - this one is of the four-terminal type

2   Because the circuit breakers reset automatically, an electrical overload in a circuit breaker-protected system will cause the circuit to fail momentarily, then come back on. If the circuit does not come back on, check it immediately.

3   For a basic check, pull the circuit breaker up out of its socket on the fuse panel, but just far enough to probe with a voltmeter. The breaker should still contact the sockets. With the voltmeter negative lead on a good chassis ground, touch each end prong of the circuit breaker with the positive meter probe. There should be battery voltage at each end. If there is battery voltage only at one end, the circuit breaker must be replaced.

4   Some circuit breakers must be reset manually.

5   Relays - general information and testing

General information

1   Several electrical accessories in the vehicle, such as the fuel injection system, horns, starter, and fog lamps use relays to transmit the electrical signal to the component. Relays use a low-current circuit (the control circuit) to open and close a high-current circuit (the power circuit). If the relay is defec-tive, that component will not operate properly. Most relays are mounted in the engine compartment and interior fuse/relay boxes. If a faulty relay is suspected, it can be removed and tested using the procedure below or by a dealer service department or a repair shop. Defective relays must be replaced as a unit.

Testing

2   Most of the relays used in these vehicles are of a type often called ISO relays, which refers to the International Standards Organization. The terminals of ISO relays are numbered to indicate their usual circuit connections and functions. There are two basic layouts of terminals on the relays used in these vehicles **(see illustrations)**.

3   Refer to the wiring diagram for the circuit to determine the proper connections for the relay you're testing. If you can't determine the correct connection from the wiring diagrams, however, you may be able to determine the test connections from the information that follows.

4   Two of the terminals are the relay control circuit and connect to the relay coil. The other relay terminals are the power circuit. When the relay is energized, the coil creates a magnetic field that closes the larger contacts of the power circuit to provide power to the circuit loads.

5   Terminals 85 and 86 are normally the control circuit. If the relay contains a diode, terminal 86 must be connected to battery positive (B+) voltage and terminal 85 to ground. If the relay contains a resistor, terminals 85 and 86 can be connected in either direction with respect to B+ and ground.

6   Terminal 30 is normally connected to the battery voltage (B+) source for the circuit loads. Terminal 87 is connected to the ground side of the circuit, either directly or through a load. If the relay has several alternate terminals for load or ground connections, they usually are numbered 87A, 87B, 87C, and so on.

7   Use an ohmmeter to check continuity through the relay control coil.

a)   *Connect the meter according to the polarity shown in the illustration for one check; then reverse the ohmmeter leads and check continuity in the other direction.*

b)   *If the relay contains a resistor, resistance should be indicated on the meter, and should be the same value with the ohmmeter in either direction.*

c)   *If the relay contains a diode, resistance should be higher with the ohmmeter in the forward polarity direction than with the meter leads reversed.*

d)   *If the ohmmeter shows infinite resistance in both directions, replace the relay.*

8   Remove the relay from the vehicle and use the ohmmeter to check for continuity between the relay power circuit terminals. There should be no continuity between terminal 30 and 87 with the relay de-energized.

9   Connect a fused jumper wire to terminal 86 and the positive battery terminal. Connect another jumper wire between terminal 85 and ground. When the connections are made, the relay should click.

10   With the jumper wires connected, check for continuity between the power circuit terminals. Now, there should be continuity between terminals 30 and 87.

11   If the relay fails any of the above tests, replace it.

6 Electrical connectors - general information

1 Most electrical connections on these vehicles are made with multiwire plastic connectors. The mating halves of many connectors are secured with locking clips molded into the plastic connector shells. The mating halves of some large connectors, such as some of those under the instrument panel, are held together by a bolt through the center of the connector.

2 To separate a connector with locking clips, use a small screwdriver to pry the clips apart carefully, then separate the connector

halves. Pull only on the shell, never pull on the wiring harness, as you may damage the individual wires and terminals inside the connectors. Look at the connector closely before trying to separate the halves. Often the locking clips are engaged in a way that is not immediately clear. Additionally, many connectors have more than one set of clips.

3 Each pair of connector terminals has a male half and a female half. When you look at the end view of a connector in a diagram, be sure to understand whether the view shows the harness side or the component side of the connector. Connector halves are mirror images of each other, and a terminal shown on the right side end-view of one half will be

on the left side end-view of the other half.
Note: *It is often necessary to take circuit voltage measurements with a connector connected. Whenever possible, carefully insert a small straight pin (not your meter probe) into the rear of the connector shell to contact the terminal inside, then clip your meter lead to the pin. This kind of connection is called "backprobing." When inserting a test probe into a terminal, be careful not to distort the terminal opening. Doing so can lead to a poor connection and corrosion at that terminal later. Using the small straight pin instead of a meter probe results in less chance of deforming the terminal connector.*

Electrical connectors

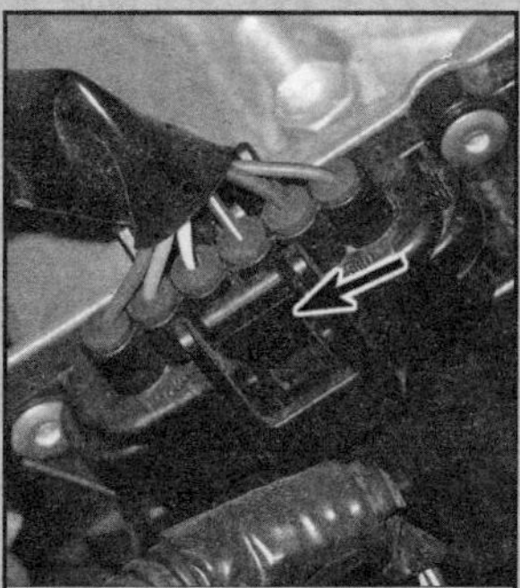

Most electrical connectors have a single release tab that you depress to release the connector

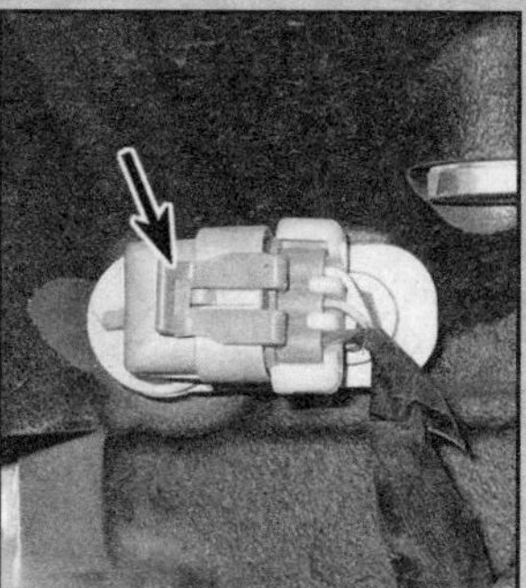

Some electrical connectors have a retaining tab which must be pried up to free the connector

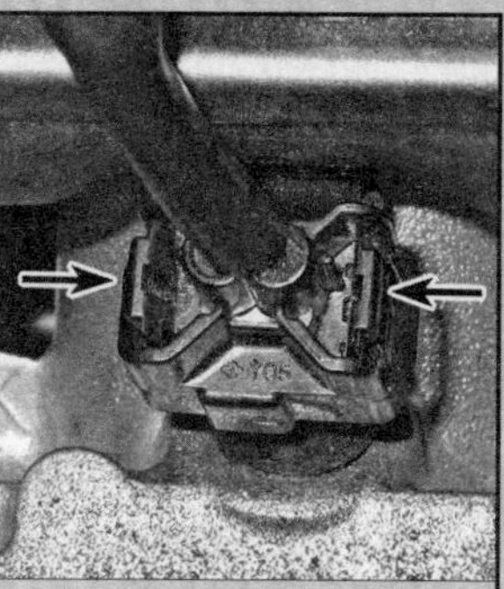

Some connectors have two release tabs that you must squeeze to release the connector

Some connectors use wire retainers that you squeeze to release the connector

Critical connectors often employ a sliding lock (1) that you must pull out before you can depress the release tab (2)

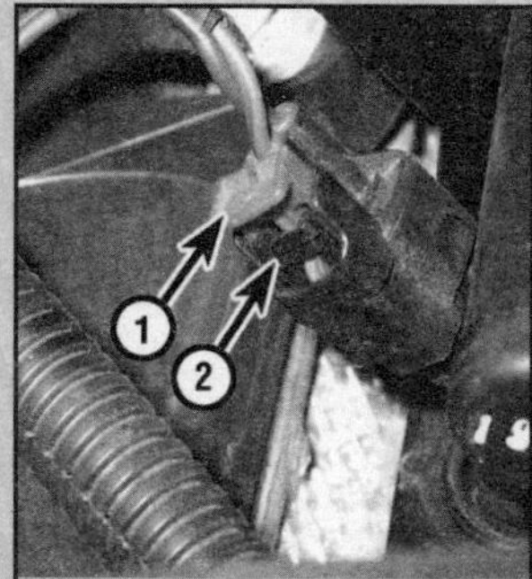

Here's another sliding-lock style connector, with the lock (1) and the release tab (2) on the side of the connector

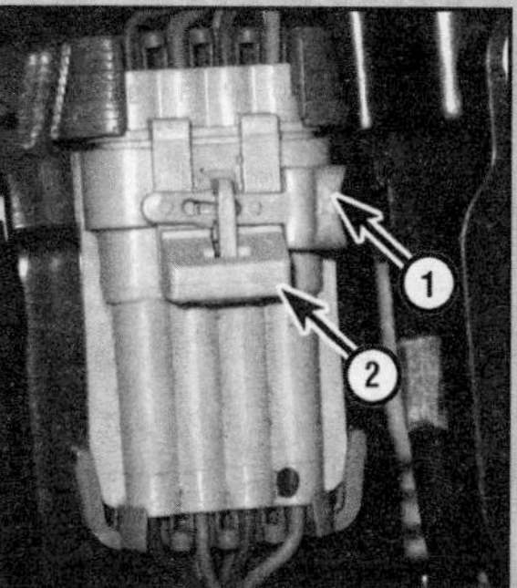

On some connectors the lock (1) must be pulled out to the side and removed before you can lift the release tab (2)

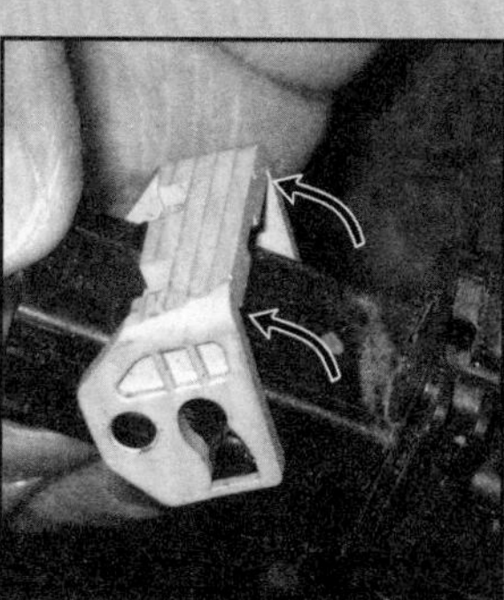

Some critical connectors, like the multi-pin connectors at the Powertrain Control Module employ pivoting locks that must be flipped open

7.12 Remove the two Torx screws

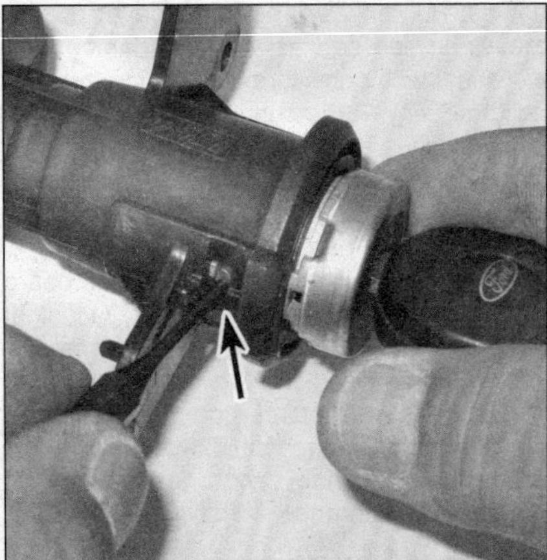

8.4a Use a small round pin to press in the release tab on the lock cylinder housing . . .

8.4b . . . and pull the cylinder from the housing

7   Multi-function switch - replacement

Warning: *The models covered by this manual are equipped with Supplemental Restraint Systems (SRS), more commonly known as airbags. Always disable the airbag system before working in the vicinity of any airbag system components to avoid the possibility of accidental deployment of the airbags, which could cause personal injury (see Section 27).*

2007 and earlier models

1   Disconnect the cable from the negative terminal of the battery (see Chapter 5).
2   Remove the steering wheel (see Chapter 10).
3   Remove the steering column covers (see Chapter 11).
4   Remove the screws and pull the multi-function switch away from the steering column.
5   Installation is the reverse of removal.

2008 and 2009 models

6   Remove the steering column covers (see Chapter 11).
7   Disconnect the multi-function switch electrical connector.
8   Remove the two Torx retaining screws from the multi-function switch and detach the switch.
9   Installation is the reverse of removal.

2010 and later models

10   Remove the steering column covers (see Chapter 11).
11   Turn the steering wheel 90 degrees.
12   Remove the two retaining screws **(see illustration)**.
13   Slide the multi-function switch away from the steering column.
14   Disconnect the electrical connector and remove the switch.
15   Installation is the reverse of removal.

8   Ignition switch and key lock cylinder - replacement

Warning: *The models covered by this manual are equipped with Supplemental Restraint Systems (SRS), more commonly known as airbags. Always disable the airbag system before working in the vicinity of any airbag system components to avoid the possibility of accidental deployment of the airbags, which could cause personal injury (see Section 27).*

Key-type ignition

Lock cylinder

1   Disconnect the cable from the negative terminal of the battery (see Chapter 5).
2   Remove the steering column covers (see Chapter 11).
3   Insert the key and turn it to the ACC position.
4   Use a small round tool and depress the release pin and pull the key lock cylinder out **(see illustrations)**.

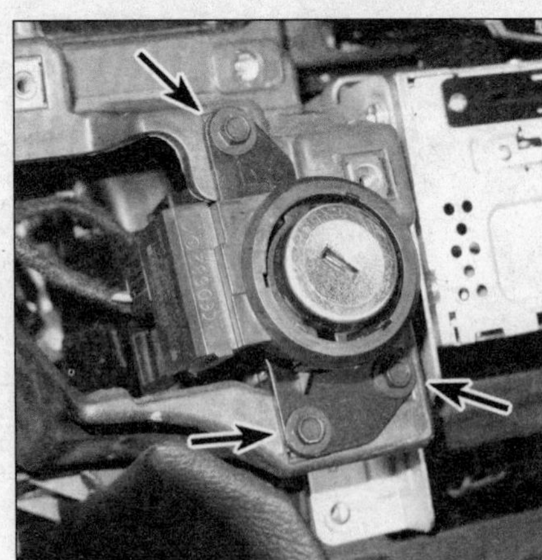

8.11 Key lock cylinder housing mounting fasteners

Ignition switch

2009 and earlier models

5   Disconnect the cable from the negative terminal of the battery (see Chapter 5).
6   Remove the steering column covers (see Chapter 11).
7   Disconnect the electrical connection.
8   Release the two locking tabs and pull the switch away from the steering column.
9   Installation is the reverse of removal.

2010 and later models

10   Remove the center console trim panel (see Chapter 11).
11   Remove the ignition switch housing bolts **(see illustration)**.
12   Pull the housing out of the dash and disconnect the electrical connector.
13   Depress the tabs on the sides of the switch and remove it from the housing **(see illustration)**.
14   Installation is reverse of removal.

Note: *If you are changing the keys or the tumbler you will have to reprogram the new keys and tumbler to the vehicle. Be sure to have a way of programming before attempting to re-*

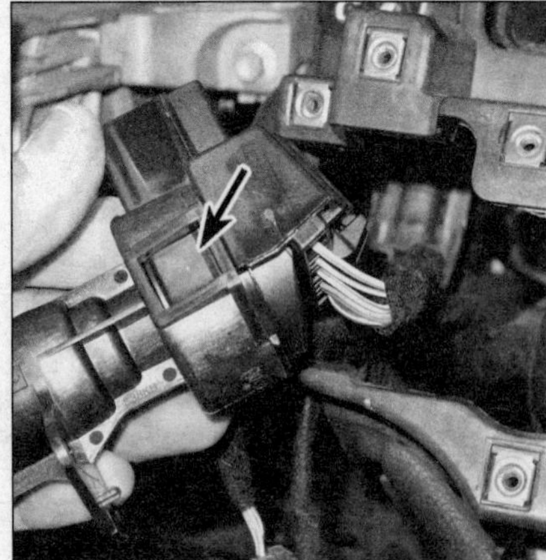

8.13 These tabs (one on either side) need to be pushed inwards to release the ignition switch from the housing

9.5 Instrument cluster mounting screws

9.6 Instrument cluster electrical connector (2013 model shown)

place the tumbler or keys. The vehicle will not start unless this procedure is followed.
Note: *When installing the switch, make sure that it snaps into place. Installation is otherwise the reverse of removal.*

Push Button Start System

15 The push button start system uses electronic modules instead of a lock cylinder and key. The Remote Function Actuator (RFA) uses battery voltage to perform the same function as turning a conventional key. The start/stop button on the dash sends a momentary signal to the module while the module is looking for the Brake Pedal Position (BPP) switch input, transmission gear select, engine parameters, and the wireless Intelligent Access (IA) key fob signal. The RFA module uses the IA key fob signal to authorize the car to start. A lot of the testing and repairs for this type of system is beyond the scope of the typical home garage. Take your vehicle to an appropriate repair facility for testing and service.

9 Instrument cluster - removal and installation

Warning: *The models covered by this manual are equipped with Supplemental Restraint Systems (SRS), more commonly known as airbags. Always disable the airbag system before working in the vicinity of any airbag system components to avoid the possibility of accidental deployment of the airbags, which could cause personal injury (see Section 27).*
Note: *Before replacing the Instrument Panel Cluster (IPC), the IPC information must be uploaded and saved to be reentered into the replacement IPC; this must be performed by a dealer service department or other properly equipped repair shop. If the replacement IPC has a different Passive Anti-Theft System (PATS) or is equipped with Intelligent Access (IA) and it is NOT a match to your vehicle, a no-start condition could result.*

Note: *All keys will be erased when the replacement IPC is programmed. Be sure to have two known good keys in order to reprogram the keys to the vehicle. Verify there are two working keys prior to removing the IPC.*
1 Disconnect the cable from the negative battery terminal (see Chapter 5).
2 Release the tilt wheel lever and lower the steering wheel to its lowest position.
3 Remove the instrument cluster upper and lower trim panels (see Chapter 11).
4 Remove the instrument cluster bezel (see Chapter 11).
5 Remove the instrument cluster mounting screws **(see illustration)**.
6 Carefully pull out the instrument cluster from the instrument panel and disconnect the electrical connectors **(see illustration)**.
Note: *Have the cluster information dowloaded into the replacement instrument cluster by the shop that uploaded it. Program as necessary.*
7 Installation is the reverse of removal.

10 Radio and speakers - removal and installation

Warning: *The models covered by this manual are equipped with Supplemental Restraint Systems (SRS), more commonly known as airbags. Always disable the airbag system before working in the vicinity of any airbag system components to avoid the possibility of accidental deployment of the airbags, which could cause personal injury (see Section 27).*
Note: *The entertainment system consists of the Audio Control Module (ACM), a Front Control Interface Module (FCIM), speakers, steering column controls, and various antennas. The entertainment systems have different levels of performance, from a Base stereo system to a Premium system, as well as a full navigation system. All the systems require some programming when replacing the ACM or the FCIM with another unit. Have the proper information uploaded from the original component before removing it from the vehicle.*

10.3 ACM mounting screws

Audio Control Module (ACM)

Caution: *If you are replacing the unit, see your local dealership or qualified independent repair shop to upload the needed program information before proceeding.*
1 Disconnect the cable from the negative battery terminal (see Chapter 5).
2 Remove the center console side trim moldings (see Chapter 11).
3 Remove the ACM mounting screws **(see illustration)**. Pull out the ACM and disconnect the antenna cable and all electrical connectors.
4 Installation is the reverse of removal. Have the module information downloaded into the replacement module by the original service facility that retrieved the information for you.

Front Control Interface Module (FCIM)

Caution: *If you are replacing the unit, see your local dealership or qualified independent repair shop to upload the needed program information before proceeding.*
5 Remove the center trim panels (see Chapter 11).

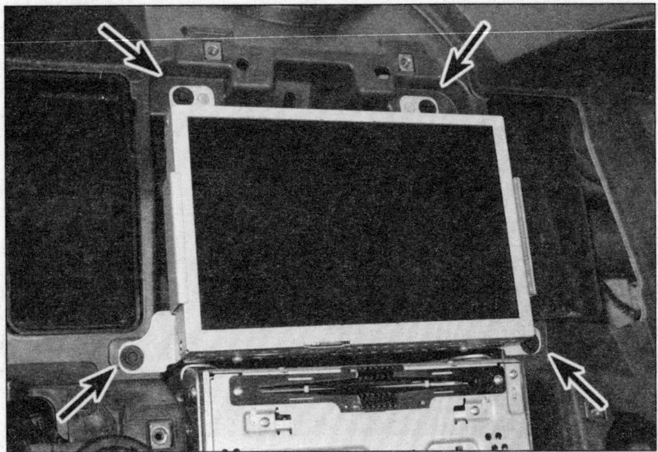

10.6 Remove the four screws retaining the FCIM unit

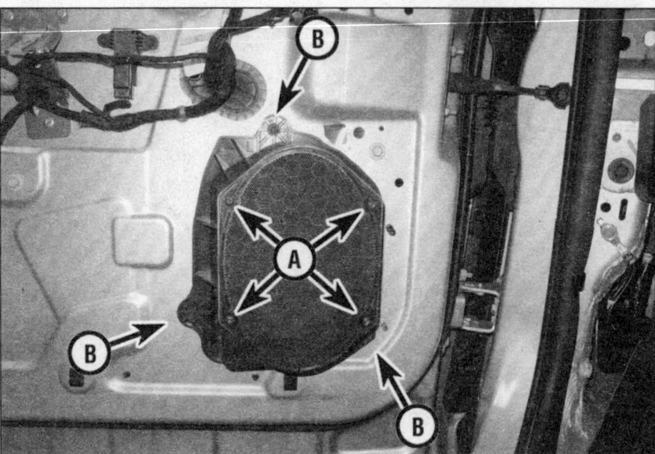

10.10 Speaker mounting screws (A) and speaker enclosure screws (B)

6   Remove the FCIM unit retaining screws **(see illustration)**.
7   Pull out the unit and disconnect the electrical connectors.
8   Installation is the reverse of removal. Have the module information downloaded into the replacement module by the original service facility that retrieved the information for you.

Speakers

Door speakers

Note: *This procedure applies to front and rear door speakers.*
9   Remove the door trim panel (see Chapter 11).
10   Remove the speaker mounting screws **(see illustration)**.
11   Pull the speaker out of its enclosure and disconnect the speaker electrical connector(s).
12   Installation is the reverse of removal.

Parcel shelf speaker

13   Remove the parcel shelf (see Chapter 11).

14   Disconnect the electrical connector.
15   Remove the screws securing the speaker to the parcel shelf and remove the speaker.
16   Installation is the reverse of removal.

---

11   Antenna - removal and installation

Note: *If you do not have a fender mounted antenna, the AM/FM antenna is part of the windshield. It is not serviceable by itself.*

Fender-mounted antenna

Note: *The fender mounted antenna is for AM and FM reception.*
1   Remove the right front inner fender splash shield (see Chapter 11).
2   Remove the antenna mast, boot, and bolt.
3   Disconnect the cable.
4   Remove the antenna.
5   Installation is the reverse of removal.

Satellite antenna

Note: *The antenna cable runs from the radio up through the passenger-side windshield pillar under the headliner.*
6   Lower the headliner.
7   Disconnect the antenna cable.
8   Remove the bolt securing the antenna to the roof.
9   Remove the antenna from the roof.
10   Installation is the reverse of removal.

---

12   Headlight switch - replacement

2007 and earlier models

1   The headlight switch is secured with tabs on the top and bottom of the switch. Remove it by inserting a thin plastic (flat) pry tool and carefully prying it from the panel.
2   Installation is the reverse of removal

2008 and later models

3   Remove the dash side trim with a thin (flat) pry tool **(see illustration)**.
4   Reach behind the dash and depress the

12.3 Pry off the dash side trim

12.4 Reach behind the switch and release the tabs, then push it from the instrument panel

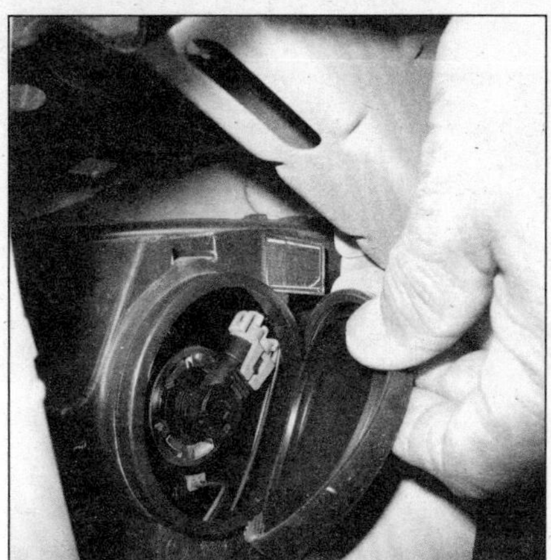

13.2 Remove the access cover from the back of the headlight

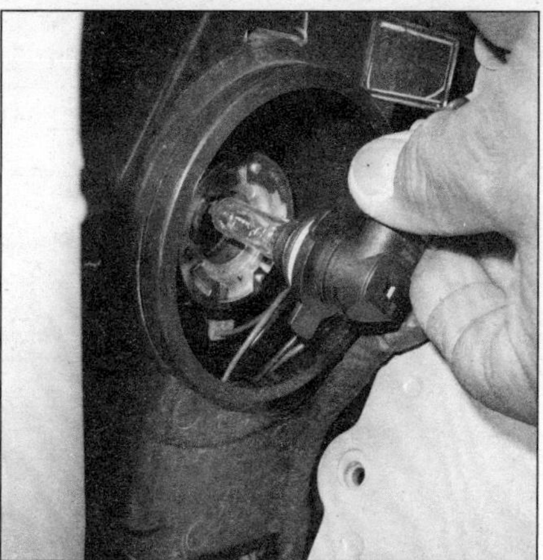

13.3 Rotate the bulb holder counterclockwise to release the tabs and pull it out of the housing

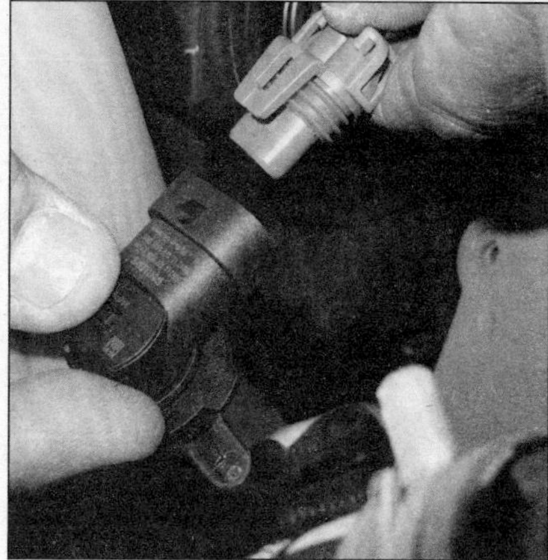

13.4 Disconnect headlamp from the connector by raising the tab on the connector

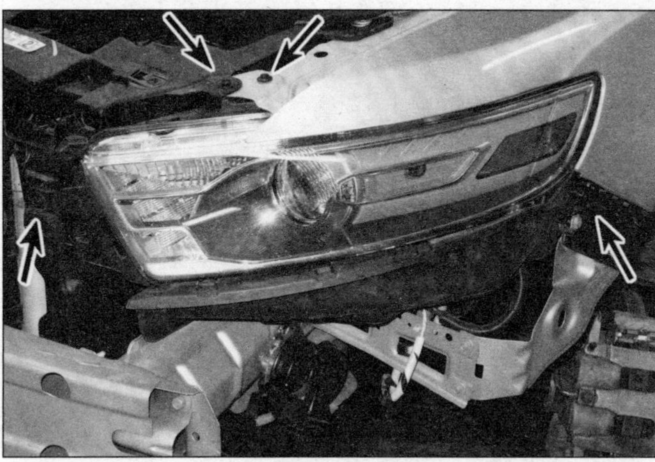

14.2 Headlight housing mounting fasteners (2010 and later models shown)

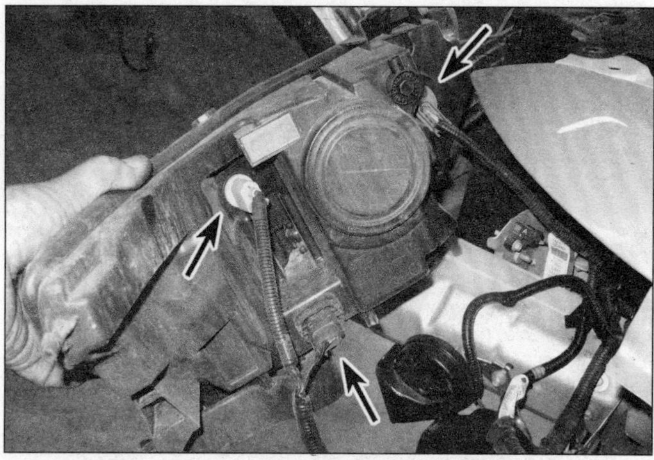

14.3 Pull out the assembly and disconnect the electrical connectors

three tabs while pressing the switch outwards **(see illustration)**.

5   Installation is the reverse of removal.

13   Headlight bulb - replacement

Halogen headlights

Warning: *Halogen bulbs are gas-filled and under pressure and might shatter if the surface is scratched or the bulb is dropped. Wear eye protection and handle the bulbs carefully, grasping only the base whenever possible. Don't touch the surface of the bulb with your fingers because the oil from your skin could cause it to overheat and fail prematurely. If you do touch the bulb surface, clean it with rubbing alcohol.*

All models except Montego

1   Disconnect the cable from the negative battery terminal (see Chapter 5).
2   Remove the bulb access cover **(see illustration)**.
3   Rotate the bulb holder counterclockwise and pull it out of the housing **(see illustration)**.
4   Disconnect the electrical connector **(see illustration)**.
5   Installation is the reverse of removal.

Montego models

6   Remove the headlight housing (see Section 14).
7   Remove the six screws and the headlight access cover.
8   Rotate the bulb holder counterclockwise and remove it from the housing.
9   Disconnect the electrical connector.
10 Installation is the reverse of removal.

High Intensity Discharge (HID) headlights

Warning: *Some models use High Intensity Discharge (HID) bulbs instead of conventional halogen bulbs. According to the manufacturer, the high voltages produced by this system can be fatal in the event of a shock. Also, the voltage can remain in the circuit even after the headlight switch has been turned to OFF and the ignition key has been removed. Therefore, for your safety, we don't recommend that you replace these bulbs yourself. Instead, have this service performed by a dealer service department or other qualified repair shop.*

14   Headlight housing - removal and installation

1   Remove the front bumper cover (see Chapter 11).
2   Remove the headlight housing mounting fasteners **(see illustration)**.
Note: *There are three bolts on the 2008 and 2009 Taurus, four bolts on the Sable, Five Hundred, and Montego. 2010 and later Taurus has three bolts as well as an additional push pin rivet that needs to be removed.*
3   Pull out the headlight housing and disconnect the electrical connectors **(see illustration)**.
4   Installation is the reverse of removal.

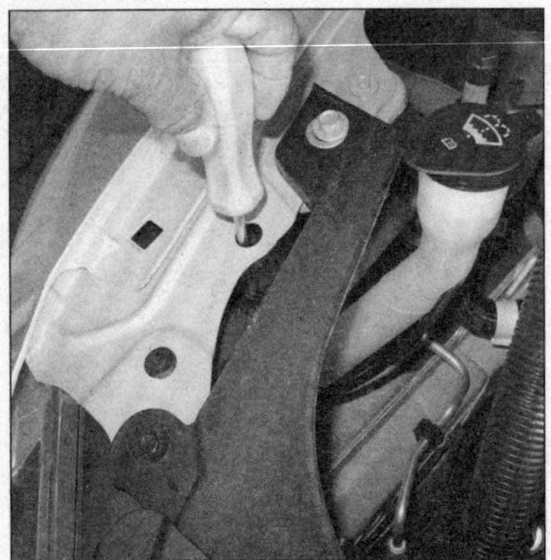

15.1 The headlight adjustment screw is accessed through a hole in the fender (2010 and later models shown)

15   Headlights - adjustment

Warning: *The headlights must be aimed correctly. If adjusted incorrectly, they could temporarily blind the driver of an oncoming vehicle and cause an accident or seriously reduce your ability to see the road. The headlights should be checked for proper aim every 12 months and any time a new headlight is installed or front-end bodywork is performed. The following procedure is only an interim step to provide temporary adjustment until the headlights can be adjusted by a properly equipped shop.*

Note: *The headlight aiming procedure is dependent on which type of headlamp system is in your car. Vehicles may come with Vehicle Optically aligned Left (VOL) or Vehicle Optically aligned Right (VOR). It is marked on the front of the lens as VOL SAE or VOR SAE. If your car is equipped with either system it is suggested that you see a qualified repair facility with the correct type of photometric aiming equipment to adjust them correctly.*

1   The headlight adjustment screw **(see illustration)** controls up-and-down movement.

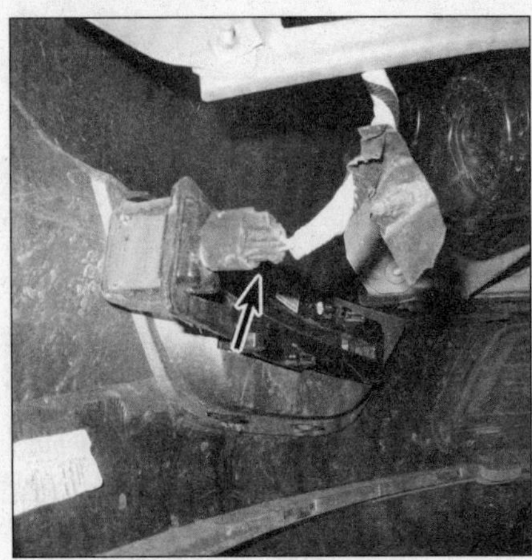

16.2 Electrical connector

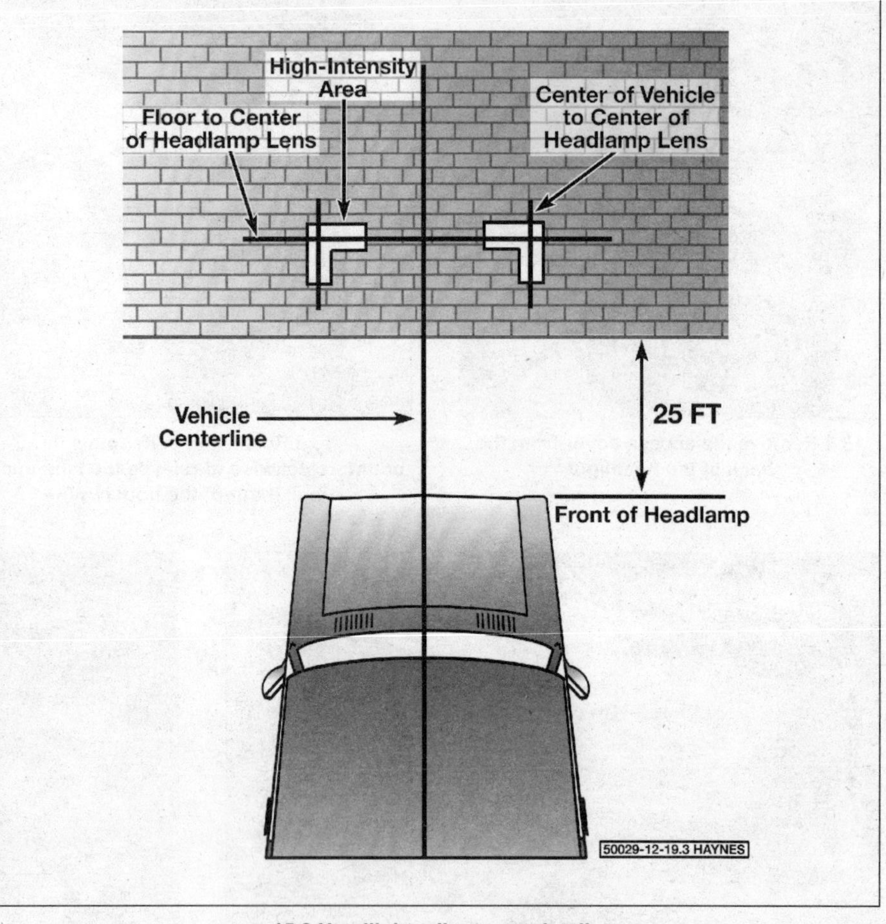

15.2 Headlight adjustment details

Left-and-right movement is not adjustable.

2   There are several methods of adjusting the headlights. The simplest method requires a blank wall 25 feet in front of the vehicle and a level floor **(see illustration)**.

3   Position masking tape on the wall in reference to the vehicle centerline and the centerlines of both headlights.

4   Measure the height of the headlight reference marks (in the centers of the headlight lenses) from the ground. Position a horizontal tape line on the wall at the same height as the headlight reference marks.

Note: *It may be easier to position the tape on the wall with the vehicle parked only a few inches away.*

5   Adjustment should be made with the vehicle sitting level, the gas tank half-full and no unusually heavy load in the vehicle.

6   Turn on the low beams. Turn the adjusting screw to position the high intensity zone so it is two inches below the horizontal line.

7   Have the headlights adjusted by a dealer service department at the earliest opportunity.

Automatic High Beam Sensitivity Adjustment

8   The sensitivity adjustment allows the driver to select either near or far high beam control.

9   The battery should be fully charged before the beginning of this procedure.

10   Vehicle has to be set up before attempting the adjustment:

   a)   *The vehicle must be in Park*
   b)   *The key must be in the Run position*
   c)   *The headlights must be set on low beams*

11   Cycle the headlamp switch from ON to the AUTOLAMP position three times within two seconds ending with the switch in the ON position.

12   Cycle the FLASH-TO-PASS three times.

13   The high beams will cycle ON then OFF to confirm the sensitivity level has changed.

16   Front auxiliary parking light - removal and installation

1   Remove the front lower air deflector (see Chapter 11).

2   Disconnect the electrical connector **(see illustration)**.

3   Carefully pry the lock tabs loose from the lens cover **(see illustration)**.

4   Press the four locking tabs to release the light fixture **(see illustration)**.

5   Installation is the reverse of removal

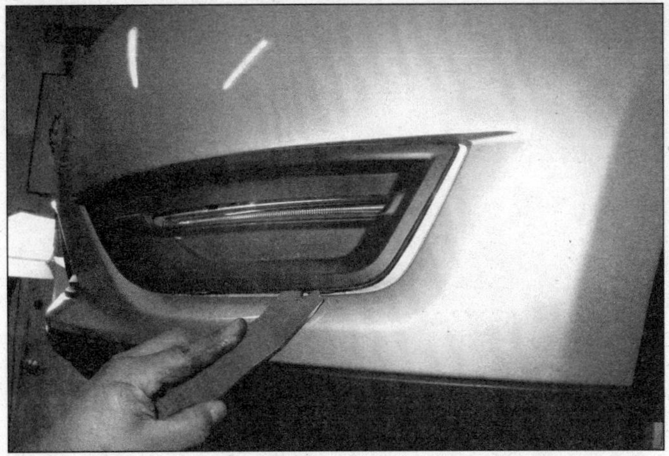

16.3 Use a thin flat plastic pry tool to remove the cover

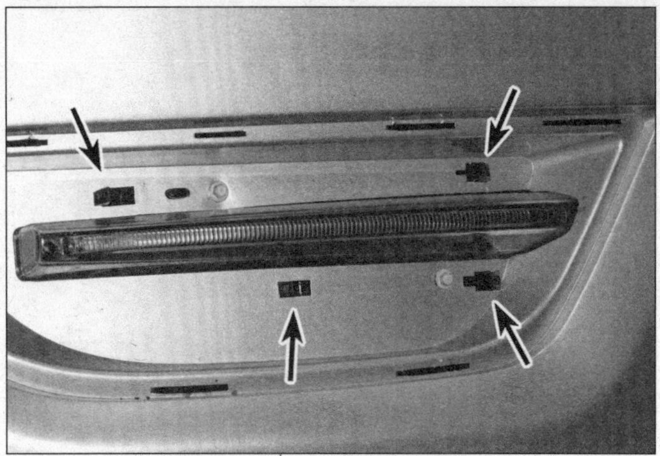

16.4 Push the tabs in to remove the light fixture

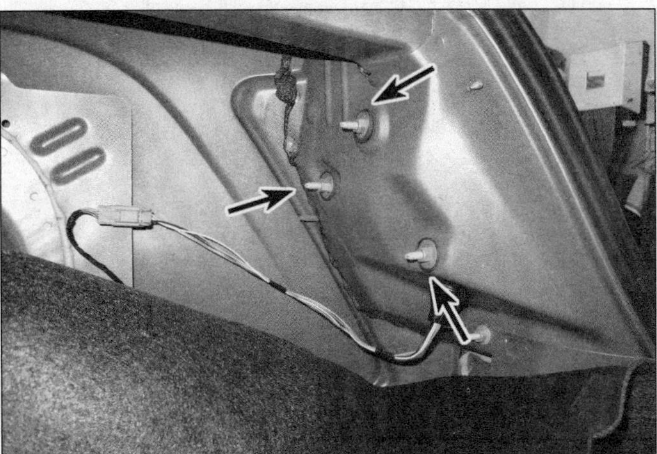

17.3a Remove the mounting fasteners . . .

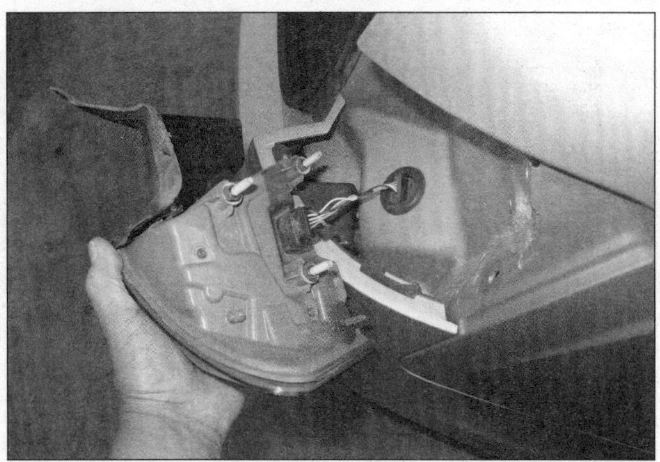

17.3b . . . then pull the housing straight back

17 Taillight housing - removal and installation

1   Open the trunk.
2   Pull the trunk liner out of the way on the side you're working on.
3   Remove the taillight housing mounting fasteners and remove the taillight housing **(see illustrations)**.
4   Disconnect the electrical connector from the taillight housing.
5   Installation is the reverse of removal.

18 Bulb replacement

Exterior light bulbs

Front turn signal/parking light bulbs

1   Turn the bulb holder counterclockwise and remove it from the headlight housing **(see illustrations)**.
2   It's not necessary to disconnect the electrical connector to replace the bulb.
3   Remove the bulb from the holder and install a new one.
4   Installation is the reverse of removal.

High mount (center) brake light

2009 and earlier models

5   Remove the parcel shelf (see Chapter 11).
6   Remove the high mount stop light retaining screws.

7   Disconnect the electrical connector.
8   Installation is the reverse of removal.

2010 and later models

9   Remove the rear seat head rest from the left hand side.
10   Slide your finger between the base and

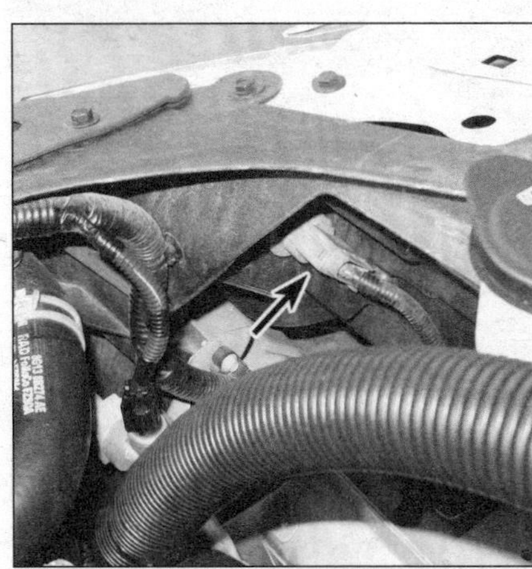

18.1a Location of the front turn signal/ parking light bulb (2010 and later models shown)

18.1b Turn the bulb holder counterclockwise and remove it from the headlight housing

Bulb removal

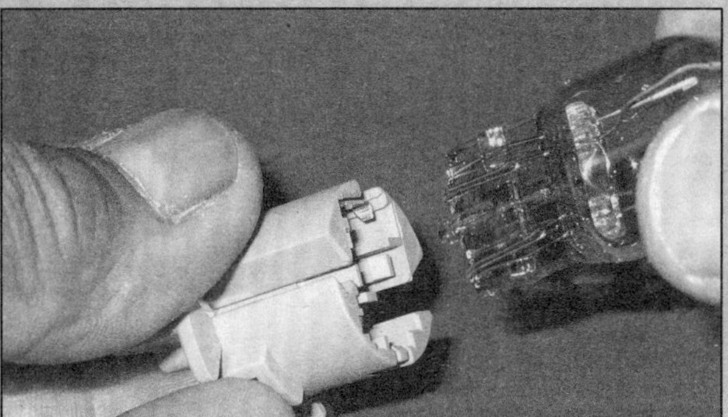

To remove many modern exterior bulbs from their holders, simply pull them out

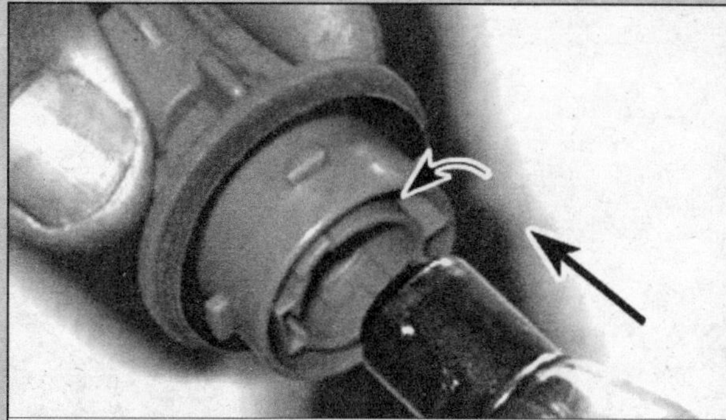

On bulbs with a cylindrical base ("bayonet" bulbs), the socket is spring-loaded; a pair of small posts on the side of the base hold the bulb in place against spring pressure. To remove this type of bulb, push it into the holder, rotate it 1/4-turn counterclockwise, then pull it out

If a bayonet bulb has dual filaments, the posts are staggered, so the bulb can only be installed one way

To remove most overhead interior light bulbs, simply unclip them

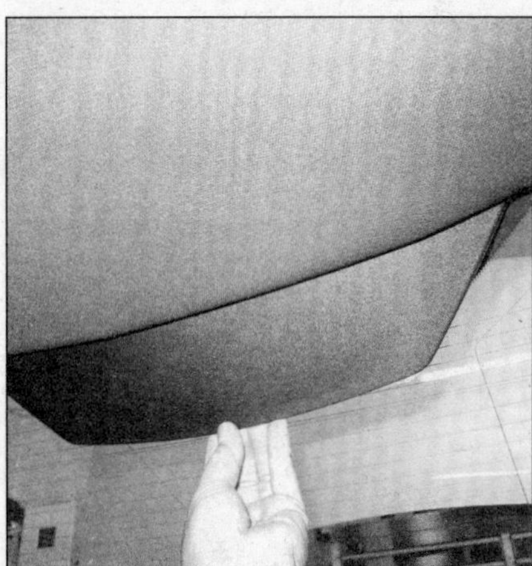

18.10 Pull down on the trim plate to remove it

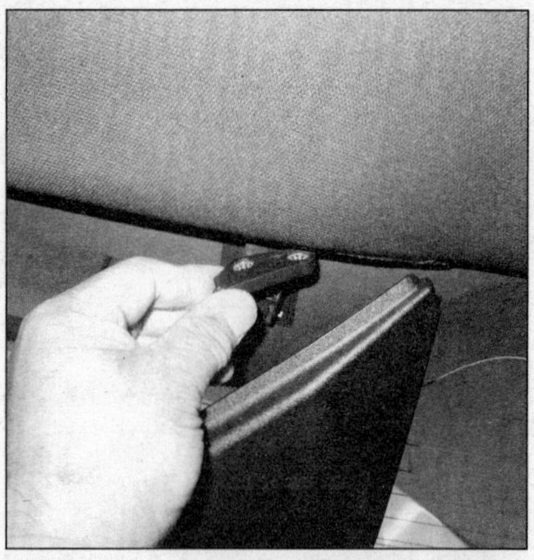

18.11 Disconnect the electrical connector

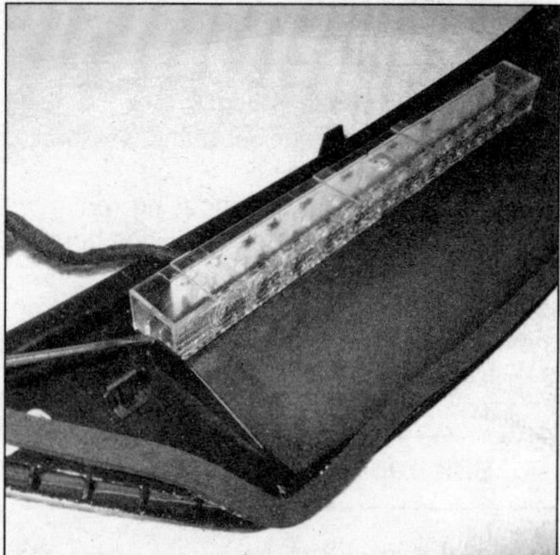

18.12 Pry gently from either end to remove the LED light assembly from the fixture

cover to release the hook and loop strip **(see illustration)**.

11   Disconnect the electrical connector **(see illustration)**.

12   Using a thin flat tool, carefully unsnap the two clips securing the light bar to the cover **(see illustration)**.

13   Installation is the reverse of removal.

Taillight bulbs

14   Remove the taillight housing (see Section 17).

15   Rotate the bulb holder counterclockwise and pull it out of the taillight housing. To remove the bulb from the socket, pull it straight out.

16   Installation is the reverse of removal.

18.17 Pry off the lens cover with a small flat screwdriver or pry tool (2010 and later models shown)

18.24 Turn the socket counterclockwise to remove it (2013 Taurus shown)

Puddle light bulbs

Note: *The puddle lights, which illuminate the ground below the front doors, are located in the outside mirrors.*

17   Release the puddle light housing tab and remove the puddle light housing from the bottom of the mirror housing **(see illustration)**.

18   Remove the puddle light bulb from its socket and install a new bulb in the socket.

Note: *To install the bulb socket in the puddle light housing, insert the socket into the housing. You will hear an audible click when the socket is fully seated and locked into place.*

19   Installation is the reverse of removal.

License plate light bulbs

20   Using a small screwdriver, unclip the tab at the side of the lens that secures the license plate light housing, or remove the screws, depending on design. Remove the housing.

21   Remove the license plate light socket by rotating it counterclockwise and pulling it out of the license plate light housing. To remove the bulb from the socket, pull it straight out.

22   Installation is the reverse of removal.

Back up lights - replacement

23   Open the trunk and remove inside trim to the lid of the trunk.

24   Turn the bulb socket counterclockwise and remove socket and bulb **(see illustration)**.

25   Installation is the reverse of removal.

Interior light bulbs

Interior front overhead light bulb

26   Remove the overhead light lens by prying it off with a thin trim tool or small flat blade screwdriver **(see illustration)**.

27   Replace the bulbs as necessary.

28   Installation is the reverse of removal.

---

19   Wiper motor and washer reservoir/pump - replacement

Wiper motor

1   Disconnect the cable from the negative terminal of the battery (see Chapter 5).

2   Remove the wiper arm nuts and mark the relationship of the wiper arms to the wiper linkage pivot shafts before removing them

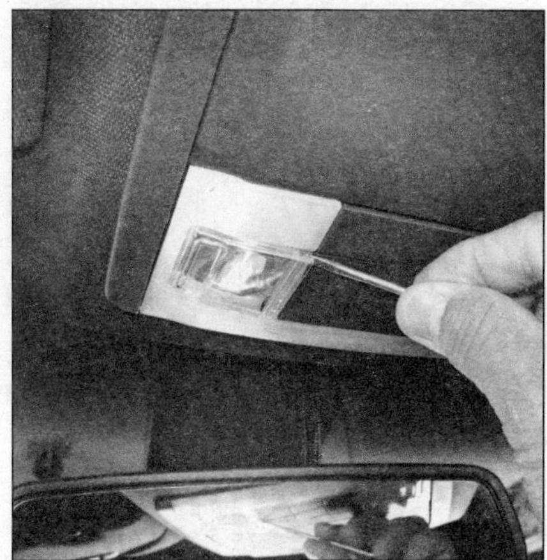

18.26 Pry carefully to avoid damaging the lens

(see illustration).

3   Remove the plastic cowl cover (see Chapter 11).

4   Remove the three linkage arm assembly bolts **(see illustration)**.

19.2 Mark the relationship of the wiper arms to their shafts

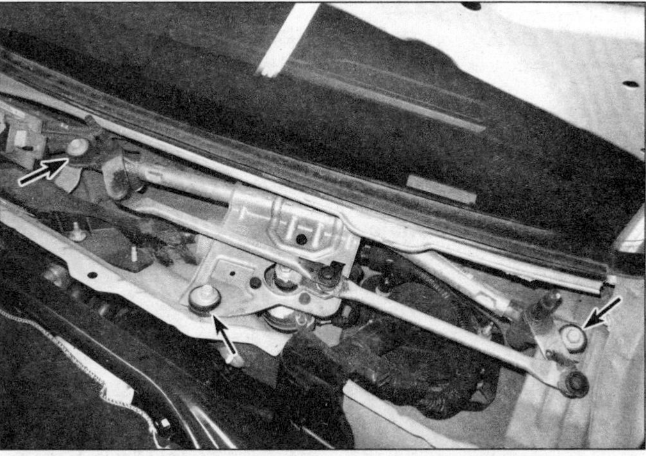

19.4 Remove the three bolts securing the wiper linkage assembly

19.5 Wiper motor electrical connector

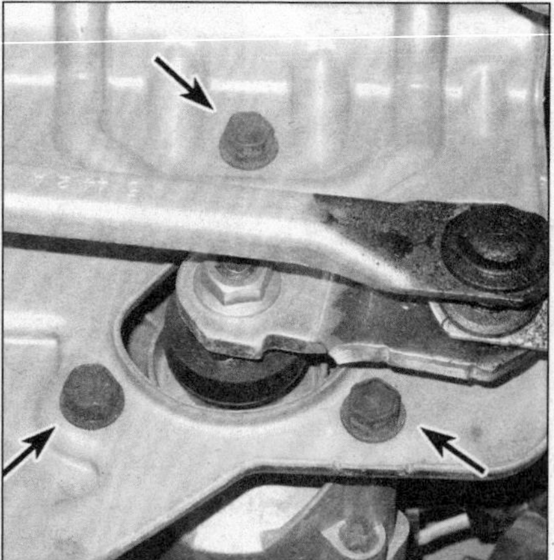

19.6 Remove these three bolts

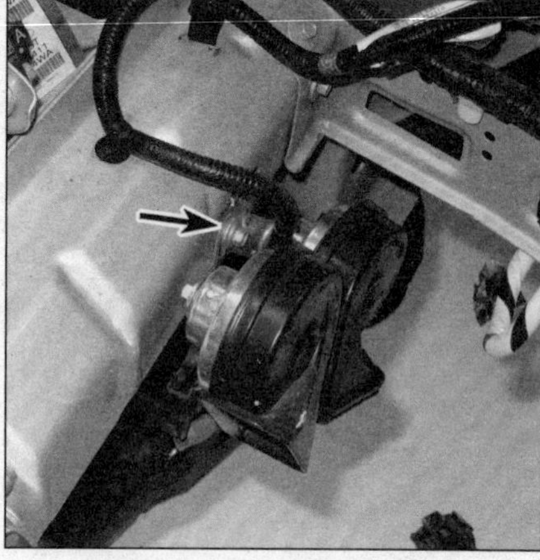

20.6 Remove the horn assembly mounting bolt

5   Tilt the entire linkage arm and motor assembly up slightly and disconnect the electrical connector **(see illustration)**. Remove the wiper motor and linkage assembly as a unit.
6   Remove the three wiper motor bolts **(see illustration)**.
7   Remove the nut securing the linkage arm to the motor shaft.
Note: *The wiper motor should be in the park position before removing the linkage arm. Be sure the linkage arm is in the same orientation as it was on the original wiper motor.*
8   Using a trim removal tool or a screwdriver, carefully separate the linkage from the motor's crank arm.
9   Install the replacement motor back on to the linkage, then reinstall the assembly.
10   Installation is the reverse of removal.
Caution: *Make sure that all the bolts are secured and the electrical connections have been made, and be sure to have all your tools and other loose items out of the linkage arms movement area before proceeding any further.*
11   Turn the ignition on (engine off) and cycle the wiper switch from high to off to be sure the motor is in the park position.
12   Reinstall the cowl cover and wiper arms.
13   The proper adjustment of the wiper arm from the bottom of the windshield is 1-1/2 inches for the passenger blade and 2 inches for the drivers side wiper arm.
14   Cycle the wiper switch again and check alignment. If they need to be adjusted, remove the arms and reset them.

Windshield washer reservoir or washer pump replacement

2007 and earlier models

15   Unbolt the coolant expansion tank and position it aside (see Chapter 3).
Note: *There is no need to disconnect the hoses to the expansion tank. Just carefully place the hoses and the tank out of the way.*
16   Disconnect the washer fluid sensor electrical connector.
17   Unbolt the bracket securing the high-side refrigerant line next to the reservoir.
18   Remove the three washer-type nuts

securing the reservoir.
19   Disconnect the washer lines and drain the reservoir.
20   Disconnect the washer pump electrical connector.
21   If necessary, replace the washer pump. The washer pump is secured to the tank by a rubber grommet. Twist and pull to remove it from the reservoir.
22   Installation is the reverse of removal.

2008 and later models

23   Remove the lower front air deflector shield.
24   Remove the right side inner fender splash shield (see Chapter 11).
25   Disconnect the washer fluid level sensor connector. Disconnect the washer pump connector.
26   Disconnect the washer pump hose and drain the reservoir.
27   Remove the reservoir bolt and the two washer-type reservoir nuts.
28   Remove the reservoir out from the bottom.
29   If necessary, replace the washer pump. The washer pump is secured to the tank by a rubber grommet. Twist and pull to remove it from the reservoir.
30   Installation is the reverse of removal.

20   Horn - replacement

2009 and earlier models
Note: *The horn is located behind the right side of the radiator grille.*
1   Remove the radiator grille (see Chapter 11).
2   Disconnect the electrical connectors and unbolt horn assembly.
3   Remove the horn mounting bolt, then remove the horn from the bracket.
4   Installation is the reverse of removal.

2010 and later models
Note: *The horn assembly is located in the front of the vehicle, on the bottom left side of the radiator support.*

5   Raise front of vehicle and support it securly on jackstands.
6   Remove the horn assembly mounting bolt **(see illustration)**.
7   Disconnect the electrical connectors and remove the horn assembly.
8   Installation is the reverse of removal.

21   Rear window defogger - check and repair

1   The rear window defogger consists of a number of horizontal elements baked onto the glass surface.
2   Small breaks in the element can be repaired without removing the rear window.

Check

3   Turn the ignition switch and defogger system switches to the ON position. Using a voltmeter, place the positive probe against the defogger grid positive terminal and the negative probe against the ground terminal. If battery voltage is not indicated, check the fuse, defogger switch and related wiring. If voltage is indicated, but all or part of the defogger doesn't heat, proceed with the following tests.
4   When measuring voltage during the next two tests, wrap a piece of aluminum foil around the tip of the voltmeter positive probe and press the foil against the heating element with your finger **(see illustration)**. Place the negative probe on the defogger grid ground terminal.
5   Check the voltage at the center of each heating element **(see illustration)**. If the voltage is 5 or 6-volts, the element is okay (there is no break). If the voltage is zero, the element is broken between the center of the element and the positive end. If the voltage is 10 to 12-volts, the element is broken between the center of the element and ground. Check each heating element.
6   Connect the negative lead to a good body ground. The reading should stay the same. If it doesnít, the ground connection is bad.

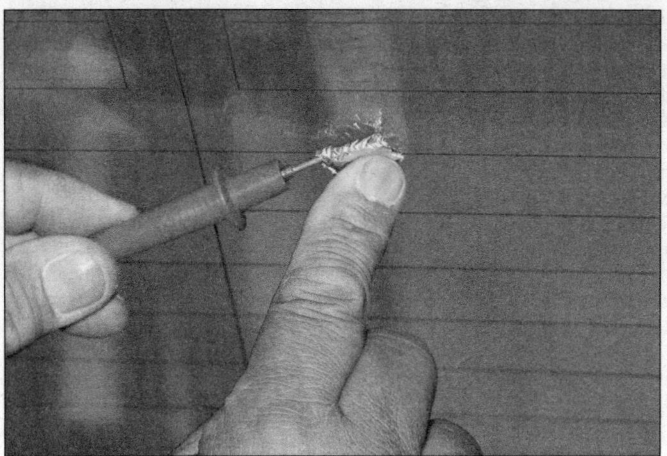

21.4 When measuring the voltage at the rear window defogger grid, wrap a piece of aluminum foil around the positive probe of the voltmeter and press the foil against the wire with your finger

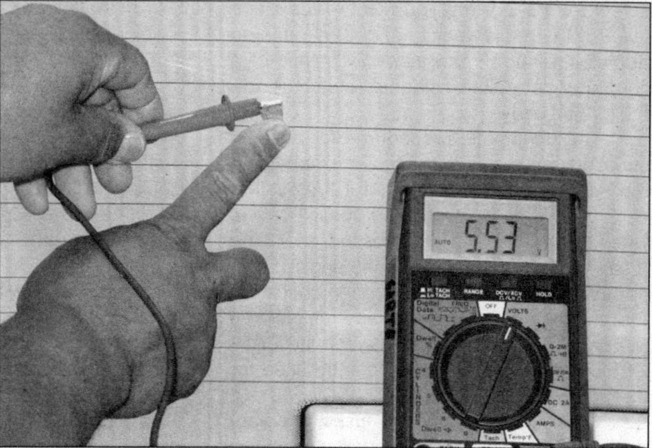

21.5 To determine if a heating element has broken, check the voltage at the center of each element; if the voltage is 5 or 6 volts, the element is unbroken, but if the voltage is 10 or 12 volts, the element is broken between the center and the ground side. If there is no voltage, the element is broken between the center and the positive side

7   To find the break, place the voltmeter negative probe against the defogger ground terminal. Place the voltmeter positive probe with the foil strip against the heating element at the positive terminal end and slide it toward the negative terminal end. The point at which the voltmeter deflects from several volts to zero is the point at which the heating element is broken **(see illustration)**.

Repair

8   Repair the break in the element using a repair kit specifically recommended for this purpose, available at most auto parts stores. Included in this kit is plastic conductive epoxy.
9   Prior to repairing a break, turn off the system and allow it to cool off for a few minutes.
10   Lightly buff the element area with fine steel wool, then clean it thoroughly with rubbing alcohol.
11   Use masking tape to mask off the area being repaired.
12   Thoroughly mix the epoxy, following the instructions provided with the repair kit.
13   Apply the epoxy material to the slit in the masking tape, overlapping the undamaged area about 3/4-inch on either end **(see illustration)**.
Note: *Allow the repair to cure for 24 hours before removing the tape and using the system.*

22   Power mirror control system - description and check

1   Electric rear view mirrors use two motors to move the glass; one for up and down adjustments and one for left-right adjustments.
2   The control switch has a selector portion which sends voltage to the left or right side mirror. With the ignition ON but the engine OFF, roll down the windows and operate the mirror control switch through all functions

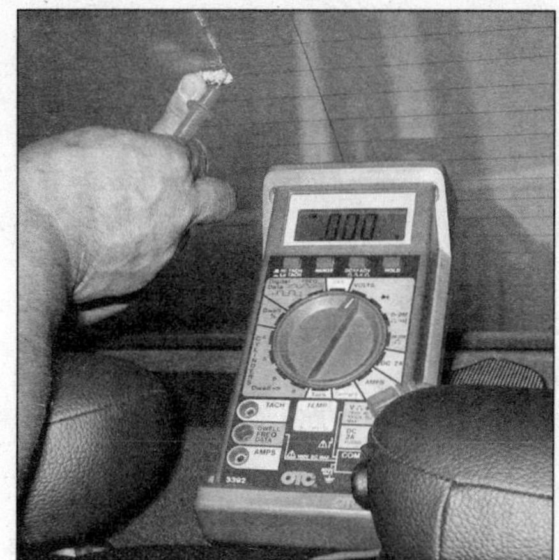

21.7 To find the break, place the voltmeter negative lead against the defogger ground terminal, place the voltmeter positive lead with the foil strip against the heating element at the positive terminal end and slide it toward the negative terminal end. The point at which the voltmeter reading changes abruptly is the point at which the element is broken

(left-right and up-down) for both the left and right side mirrors.
3   Listen carefully for the sound of the electric motors running in the mirrors.
4   If the motors can be heard but the mirror glass doesn't move, there's probably a problem with the drive mechanism inside the mirror. A lot of instances you'll hear a rather loud snapping sound and you might notice the mirror actual try to move. This is usually the gear mechanism inside the mirror housing that has broken. It is not repairable. Replace the mirror assembly.
5   If the mirrors do not operate and no sound comes from the mirrors, check the fuse (see Section 3).

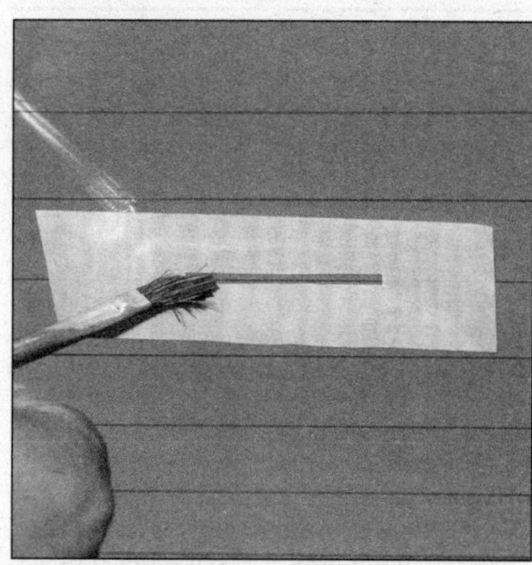

21.13 To use a defogger repair kit, apply masking tape to the inside of the window at the damaged area, then brush on the special conductive coating

6   If the fuse is OK, remove the mirror control switch from its mounting without disconnecting the wires attached to it. Turn the ignition ON and check for voltage at the switch. There should be voltage at one terminal. If there's no voltage at the switch, check for an open or short in the circuit between the fuse panel and the switch.
7   If the mirror motor fails to operate as described, replace the mirror assembly (see Chapter 11).

23   Cruise control system - description and check

1   All models have an electronically-controlled throttle body - there is no accelerator cable (or cruise control cable). When you

select the speed that you want to maintain, the PCM controls vehicle speed by opening and closing the throttle plate by means of a computer-controlled solenoid (motor) inside the throttle body.

2   The diagnostic procedures for troubleshooting the cruise control system are beyond the scope of this manual, but if the system can't be set, or the set speed doesn't cancel when the brake pedal is depressed, check the fuses. Start with the fuses in the engine compartment fuse and relay box, then check the fuses in the under-dash fuse and relay box. If the set speed doesn't cancel when the CANCEL button is depressed, check the fuse for that circuit.

3   Other than checking the fuses, the diagnostic procedures for troubleshooting the cruise control system on these models are beyond the scope of this manual. A dealer service department should handle any further testing.

24   Power window system - description and check

1   The power window system operates electric motors, mounted in each door, which lower and raise the windows. The system consists of the control switches, the motors, regulators, glass mechanisms.

Caution: *Some of the newer models covered in this manual use computer controlled window systems that are beyond the scope of the home mechanic. Each door switch works with the Body Control Module (BCM) for window operation. The BCM can communicate with the proper type of scanning equipment for diagnostic purposes. See your local dealership or qualified independent repair facility for any service work needed.*

2   The power windows can be lowered and raised from the master control switch by the driver or by remote switches located at the individual windows. Each window has a separate motor that is reversible. The position of the control switch determines the polarity and therefore the direction of operation.

3   The circuit is protected by a fuse and a circuit breaker. Each motor is also equipped with an internal circuit breaker; this prevents one stuck window from disabling the whole system.

4   The power window system will only operate when the ignition switch is ON, and for a period of time after the ignition key has been turned Off (unless one of the doors is opened). In addition, many models have a window lockout switch at the master control switch which, when activated, disables the switches at the rear windows and, sometimes, the switch at the passenger's window also. Always check these items before troubleshooting a window problem.

Note: *These procedures are general in nature, so if you can't find the problem using them, take the vehicle to a dealer service department or other properly equipped repair facility.*

5   If the power windows won't operate, always check the fuse and circuit breaker first.

6   If only the rear windows are inoperative, or if the windows only operate from the master control switch, check the rear window lockout switch for continuity in the unlocked position. Replace it if it doesn't have continuity.

7   Check the wiring between the switches and fuse panel for continuity. Repair the wiring, if necessary.

8   If only one window is inoperative from the master control switch, try the other control switch at the window.

Note: *This doesn't apply to the driver's door window.*

9   If the same window works from one switch, but not the other, check the switch for continuity.

10   If the switch tests OK, check for a short or open in the circuit between the affected switch and the window motor.

11   If one window is inoperative from both switches, remove the switch panel from the affected door. Check for voltage at the switch and at the motor (refer to Chapter 11 for door panel removal) while the switch is operated.

Note: *A stuck or binding window motor is a common problem. With the key in the On position and the door open, pay attention to the dome light. As you press the switch to move the window, see if the light dims a bit. This indicates that the proper voltage is at the motor but the motor is not moving. Remove the door panel (see Chapter 11) and check for any binding or a faulty motor.*

Note: *Unusual noises from the door as the window is operated can indicate broken mechanical parts, or that the motor has come loose. Remove the door panel (see Chapter 11) and check for any broken or loose components.*

12   If voltage is reaching the motor, disconnect the glass from the regulator (see Chapter 11). Move the window up and down by hand while checking for binding and damage. Also check for binding and damage to the regulator. If the regulator is not damaged and the window moves up and down smoothly, replace the motor. If there's binding or damage, lubricate, repair or replace parts, as necessary.

13   If voltage isn't reaching the motor, check the wiring in the circuit for continuity between the switches and the body control module, and between the body control module and the motors. You'll need to consult the wiring diagram at the end of this Chapter. If the circuit is equipped with a relay, check that the relay is grounded properly and receiving voltage.

Driver's window initialization

14   Some of the models in this manual are equipped with "Smart Windows." These windows feature express (one touch) down and an automatic reverse if an object is in the way as the window is closing. Any time work is preformed on the window system, a de-initialization procedure must be performed before

the auto feature will work again. Failure to de-initialize the system first will keep the system from operating correctly with the new replacement parts.

De-initialization Procedure

15   Turn the ignition switch to On.

16   Operate the window in the one-touch mode. While the motor is running, remove power from the motor by disconnecting the motor, pulling the fuse, or disconnecting the battery.

17   This will restore the window to the original factory settings and will allow you to set up the initialization procedure to reset the one-touch feature again.

Initialization procedure

18   Turn the ignition key to On.

19   Operate the window to its fully closed position and hold the window switch on for an additional two seconds.

20   Operate the window to its lowest position and keep the window switch depressed for an additional two seconds after the window has stopped.

21   Test the one-touch feature by operating it normally. If it does not work, repeat the process.

25   Power door lock and keyless entry system - description, check and battery replacement

Note: *These models are equipped with a Smart Junction Box (SJB) (manufacturer terminology for fuse box), a Body Control Module (BCM) and a Driver's Door Module (DDM)* **(see illustration).** *Several systems are linked to these control modules, which allows simple and accurate troubleshooting, but only with a professional-grade scan tool.*

Note: *The Driver's Door Module (DDM) operates the driver's door lock only, and the Smart Junction Box (SJB) operates all the other door locks. When a commanded is sent from the keyless entry, door lock switch or the entry pad, a ground signal is sent from the BCM to the SJB and then onto the DDM to operate the driver's door lock. All other lock signals are directly from the SJB to operate the remaining locks at the same time.*

Note: *The BCM governs the door locks, the power windows, the ignition lock and security system, the interior lights, the Daytime Running Lights system, the horn, the windshield wipers, the heating/air conditioning system and the power mirrors. In the event of malfunction with this system, have the vehicle diagnosed by a dealership service department or other qualified automotive repair facility.*

Warning: *The BCM is programmed to the car. Removing the BCM and replacing it with another one may result in the vehicle not starting. Check with your local dealership or qualified independent facility for proper servicing of these units.*

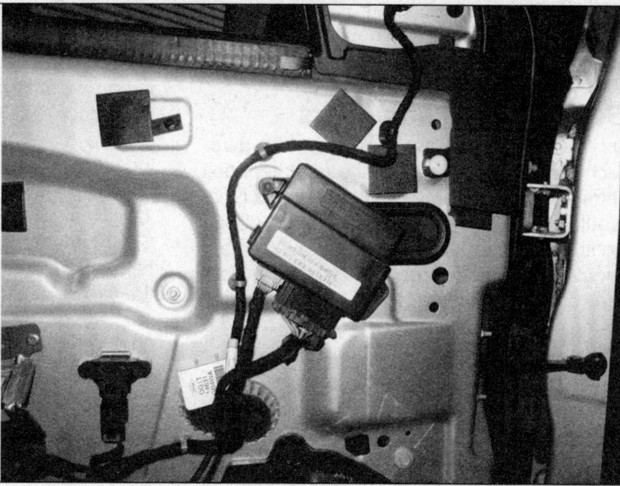

25.0a Typical Driver's Door Module (DDM) location (2013 model shown)

Description and check

Note: *Diagnosis can usually be limited to a few simple checks of the wiring connections and the actuators. If after following these basic steps the door lock system is still not operating see your local dealership or qualified independent repair facility.*

1   Power door lock systems are operated by bi-directional solenoids located in the doors. The lock switches have two operating positions: Lock and Unlock.

2   Always check the circuit protection first. Some vehicles use a combination of circuit breakers and fuses. Refer to the wiring diagrams at the end of this Chapter.

3   If the switch has continuity, check the wiring between the switch and door lock solenoid.

Note: *To check continuity disconnect the switch and use an ohm meter connected to two of the terminals on the switch while depressing the switch in either the lock or unlock position. One terminal of the switch is common to both directions while the remaining two connections are the individual lock or unlock leads. Rock the switch in both direction. Continuity should only be on two leads in one direction at one time.*

4   If all but one lock solenoid operates, remove the trim panel from the affected door (see Chapter 11) and check for the proper signals at the solenoid. While the lock switch is depressed in the lock position one of the wires should have voltage and the other lead should have a ground signal. When the lock switch is depressed in the unlock position the signals should be the opposite polarity.

5   If the inoperative solenoid is receiving the proper signals, replace the solenoid.

Keyless entry system

6   The keyless entry system consists of a remote control transmitter that sends a coded infrared signal to a receiver, which then operates the door lock system.

7   Replace the battery when the transmitter doesn't operate the locks at a distance of ten feet. Normal range should be about 30 feet.

Key remote control battery replacement

8   Use a coin to carefully separate the case halves **(see illustration)**.

9   Replace the battery **(see illustration)**.

10   Snap the case halves together.

Transmitter programming

Note: *Programming replacement transmitters requires the use of a specialized scan tool. Take the vehicle and the transmitter(s) to a dealer service department or other qualified repair shop equipped with the necessary tool to have the transmitter(s) programmed to the vehicle.*

26   Daytime Running Lights (DRL) - general information

1   The Daytime Running Lights (DRL) system used on some models illuminates the headlights whenever the engine is running. The only exception is with the engine running and the parking brake engaged. Once the parking brake is released, the lights will remain on as long as the ignition switch is on, even if the parking brake is later applied.

Note: *The DRL system supplies reduced power to the headlights so they won't be too bright for daytime use, while prolonging headlight life.*

27   Airbags - general information

1   These models are equipped with a Supplemental Restraint System (SRS), more commonly known as airbags. This system is designed to protect the driver and the front seat passenger from serious injury in the event of a head-on or frontal collision. It consists of an airbag module in the center of the steering wheel and another airbag module on the right side of the instrument panel plus, on some and later models, side airbags and curtain shield airbags designed to protect the occupants in a side impact and a sensing/diagnostic module which is mounted in the center of the vehicle below the instrument panel. These models are also equipped with a pair of impact sensors that are located at the front of the vehicle.

2   Some models are equipped with seatbelt pre-tensioners, also part of the airbag system. The pre-tensioners are pyrotechnic (explosive) devices designed to retract the seat belts in the event of a collision.

3   On models equipped with pre-tensioners, do not remove the front seat belt retractor assemblies. Problems with the pre-tensioners will turn on the SRS (airbag) warning light on the dash. If any pre-tensioner problems are suspected, take the vehicle to a dealer service department.

Airbag module

Steering wheel-mounted

4   The airbag inflator module contains a housing incorporating the cushion (airbag) and inflator unit, mounted in the center of the steering wheel. The inflator assembly is mounted on the back of the housing over a hole through which gas is expelled, inflating the bag almost instantaneously when an elec-

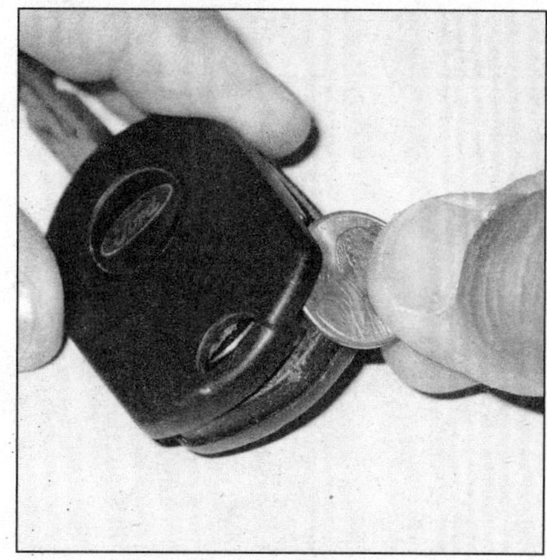

25.8 Using a coin, carefully pry the halves of the transmitter apart

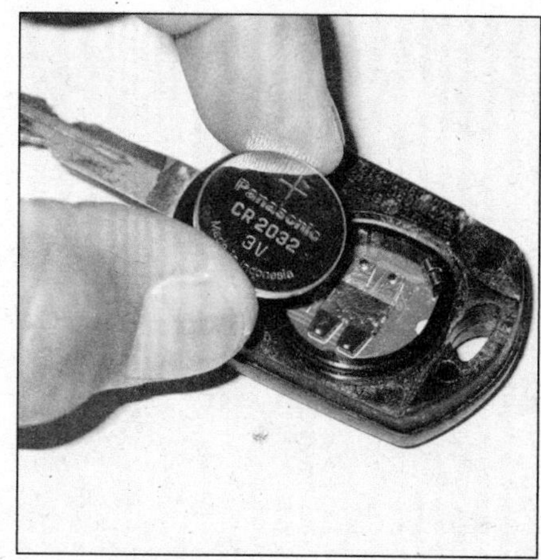

25.9 Remove the battery

trical signal is sent from the system. A spiral cable assembly on the steering column under the module carries this signal to the module. This spiral cable assembly can transmit an electrical signal regardless of steering wheel position.

Instrument panel-mounted

5   The passenger side airbag is mounted above the glove compartment and designated by the letters SRS (Supplemental Restraint System). It consists of an inflator containing an igniter, a bag assembly, a reaction housing and a trim cover.

6   The passenger airbag is considerably larger than the steering wheel-mounted unit and is supported by the steel reaction housing. The trim cover has a molded seam which splits when the bag inflates.

Side and curtain airbags

7   The side airbag and inflator modules are mounted on the sides of the front seats and contain an inflator containing an igniter and bag assembly. The curtain shield airbag assemblies run along the interior of the roof from the front A-pillar to the rear of the passenger compartment. In the event of a side impact, both airbag assemblies are activated by the sensors mounted at the base of the center pillar behind the seats.

Sensing and diagnostic module

8   The sensing and diagnostic module supplies the current to the airbag system in the event of the collision, even if battery power is cut off. It checks this system every time the vehicle is started, causing the "AIR BAG" light to go on then off, if the system is operating properly. If there is a fault in the system, the light will go on and stay on, flash, or the dash will make a beeping sound. If this happens, the vehicle should be taken to your dealer immediately for service.

Seat belt pre-tensioners

9   Some models are equipped with pyrotechnic (explosive) units in the front seat belt retracting mechanisms. During an impact that would trigger the airbag system, the airbag control unit also triggers the seat belt retractors. When the pyrotechnic charges go off, they accelerate the retractors to instantly take up any slack in the seat belt system to more fully prepare the driver and front seat passenger for impact.

Warning: *The airbag system should be disabled any time work is done to or around the seats. Never strike the pillars or floorpan with a hammer or use an impact-driver tool in these areas unless the system is disabled.*

Precautions

Disabling the SRS system

Warning: *Failure to follow these precautions could result in accidental deployment of the airbag and personal injury.*

Warning: *Never install a memory-saver device, used to preserve PCM memory and radio station presets, when working on or around any of the airbag system components.*

10   Whenever working in the vicinity of the steering wheel, instrument panel or any of the other SRS system components, the system must be disarmed. To disarm the system:

a) *Point the wheels straight ahead and turn the ignition key to the LOCK position.*

b) *Disconnect the cable from the negative terminal of the battery.*

c) *Wait at least two minutes for the back-up power supply capacitor to be depleted.*

11   Whenever handling an airbag module, always keep the airbag opening (trim side) pointed away from your body. Never place the airbag module on a bench or other surface with the airbag opening facing the surface. Always place the airbag module in a safe location with the airbag opening (trim side) facing up.

12   Never measure the resistance of any SRS component. An ohmmeter has a built-in battery supply that could accidentally deploy the airbag.

13   Never use electrical welding equipment on a vehicle equipped with an airbag without first disconnecting the negative battery cable.

14   Never dispose of a live airbag module. Return it to your dealer for safe deployment, using special equipment, and disposal.

28   Wiring diagrams - general information

1   Since it isn't possible to include all wiring diagrams for every year and model covered by this manual, the following diagrams are those that are typical and most commonly needed.

2   Prior to troubleshooting any circuits, check the fuses and circuit breakers (if equipped) to make sure they are in good condition. Make sure the battery is properly charged and has clean, tight cable connections (see Chapter 1).

3   When checking the wiring system, make sure that all electrical connectors are clean, with no broken or loose pins. When unplugging an electrical connector, do not pull on the wires, only on the connector housings themselves.

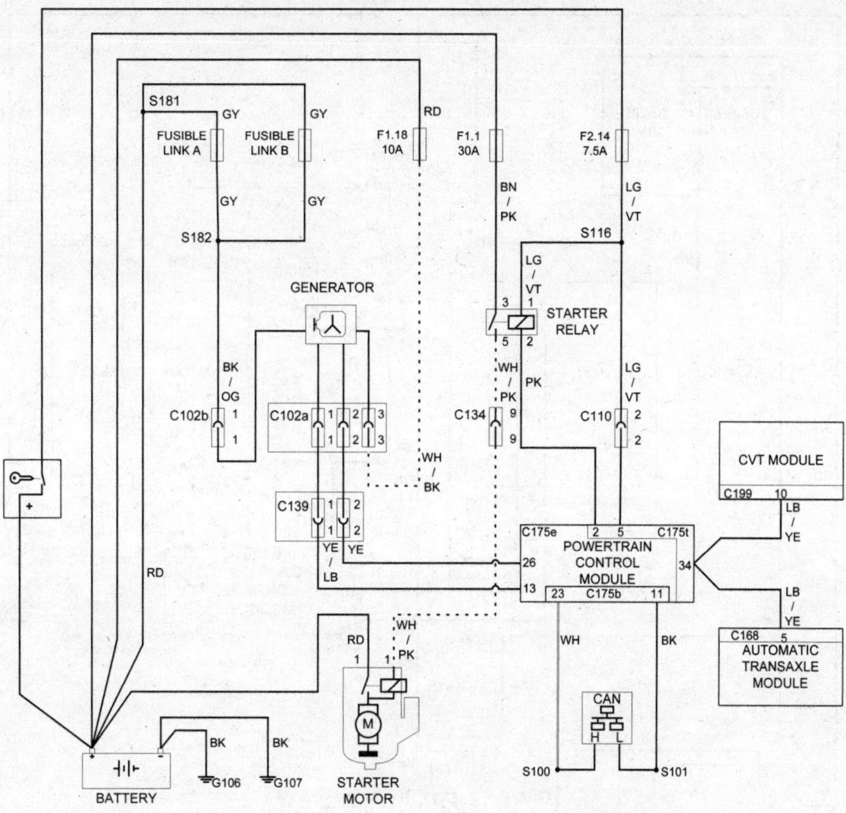

Starting and charging systems - 2005 and 2006 models

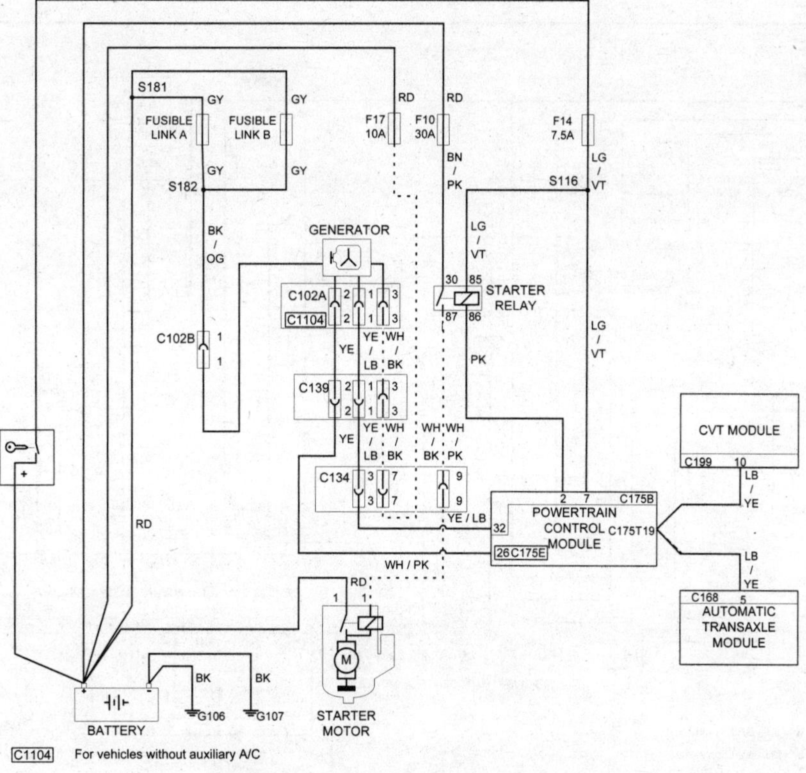

Starting and charging systems - 2007 models

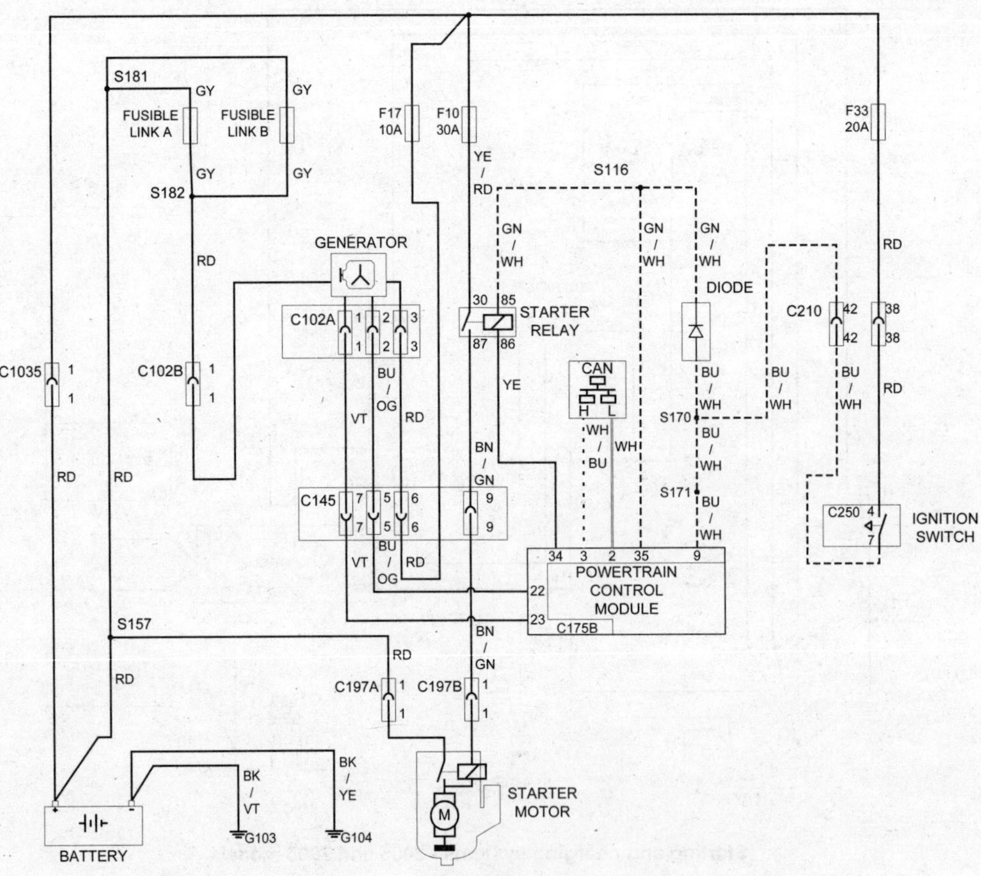

Starting and charging systems - 2008 and 2009 models

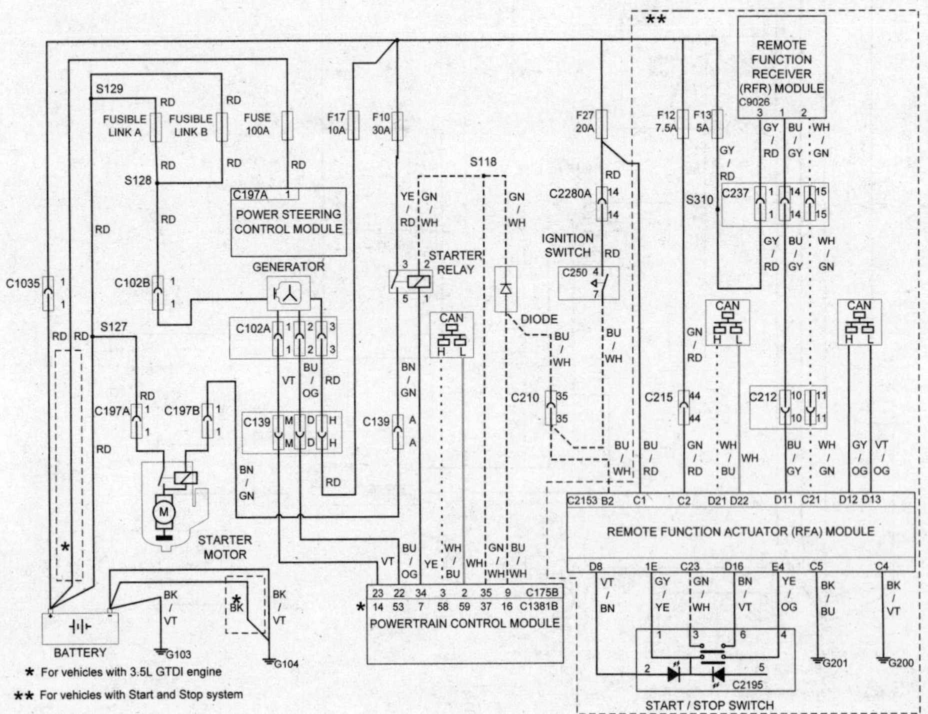

* For vehicles with 3.5L GTDI engine

** For vehicles with Start and Stop system

Starting and charging systems - 2010 through 2012 models

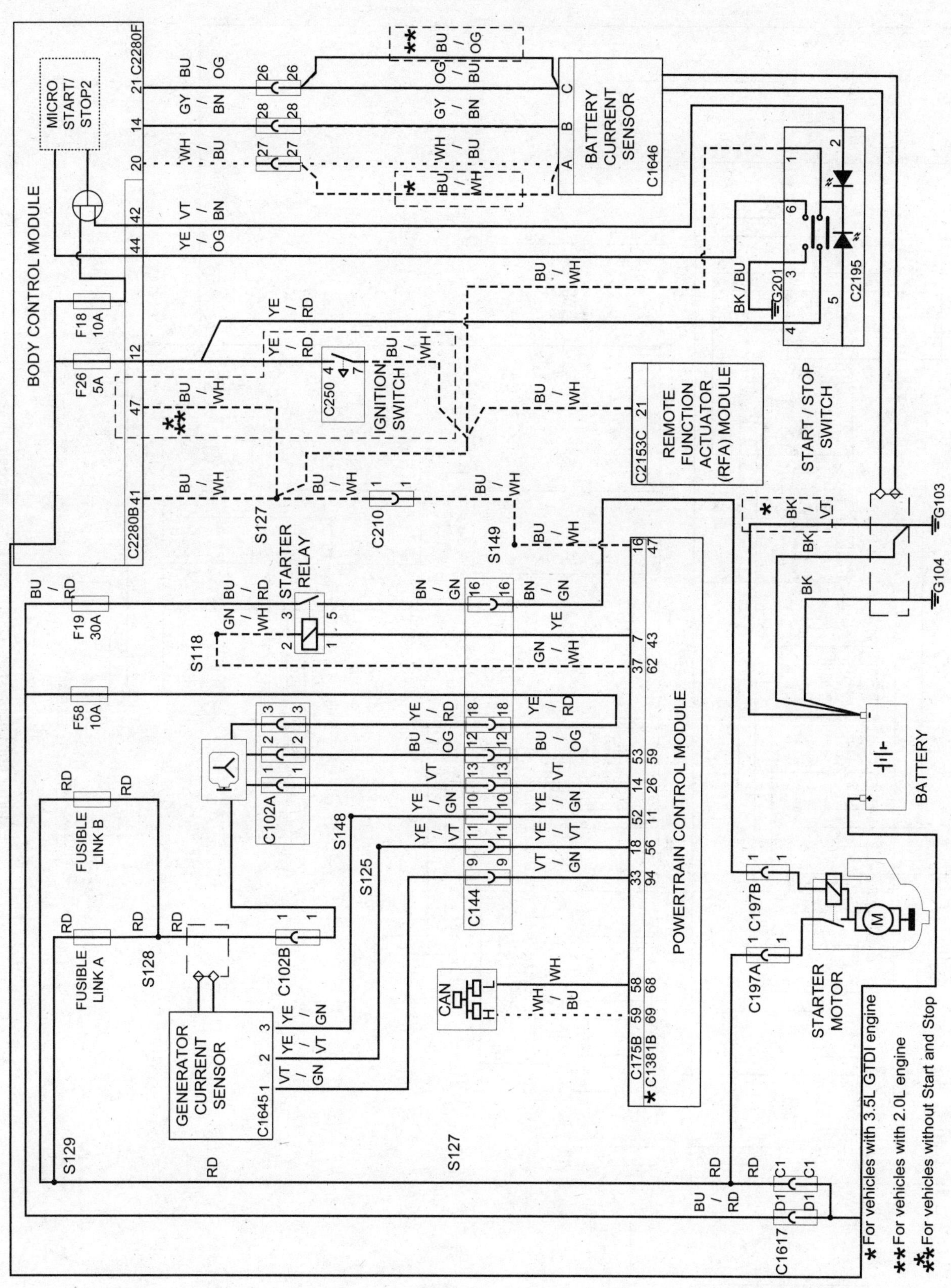

BODY CONTROL MODULE
MICRO START/STOP2
21 C2280F
BU
OG
26 26
GY
BN
14
28 28
WH
BU
20
27 27
VT
BN
42
YE
OG
44
BATTERY CURRENT SENSOR
C1646
A B C
BU
WH
BK / BU
G201
C2195
START / STOP SWITCH
F18 10A
YE
RD
F26 5A
12
IGNITION SWITCH
C250 4 7
BU
WH
47
BU
WH
C2153C 21
REMOTE FUNCTION ACTUATOR (RFA) MODULE
C2280B 41
BU
WH
S127
C210 1 1
BU
WH
S149
BU
WH
16
47
BK
VT
BK
BK
G103
G104
STARTER RELAY
BU / RD
F19 30A
S118
GN
WH
BU
RD
2 3 1 5
BN
GN
16 16
BN
GN
YE
WH
37 7 62 43
F58 10A
C102A
3 3
2 2
1 1
BU
OG
YE
RD
18 18
BU
VT
OG
12 12
YE
RD
13 13
53 59
YE
GN
VT
YE
GN
10 10
14 26
YE
VT
GN
YE
VT
GN
11 11
18 52
VT
GN
9 9
33 94
FUSIBLE LINK B
RD
RD
FUSIBLE LINK A
RD
RD
S128
RD
S125
C144
POWERTRAIN CONTROL MODULE
CAN H L
WH
BU
58 68
C175B 59 69
C1381B
GENERATOR CURRENT SENSOR
C16451 2 3
VT YE
GN VT
C102B 1 1
C1617
BU / RD
RD
D1 C1
D1 C1
C197B 1 1
C197A 1 1
STARTER MOTOR
M
BATTERY
S129
S127
RD
RD
RD

Starting and charging systems - 2013 and later models

* For vehicles with 3.5L GTDI engine
** For vehicles with 2.0L engine
*** For vehicles without Start and Stop

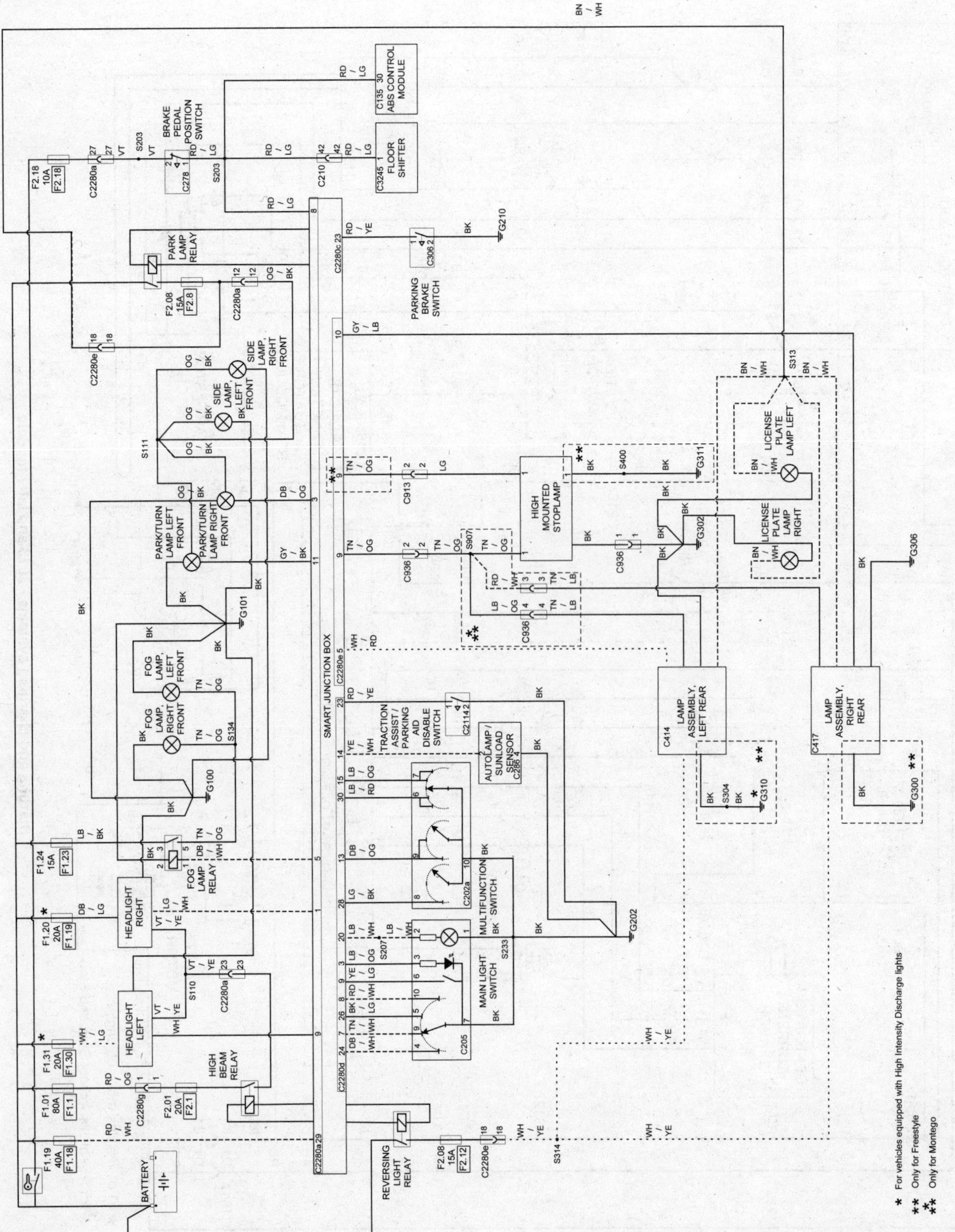

Exterior lighting system - 2007 and earlier models

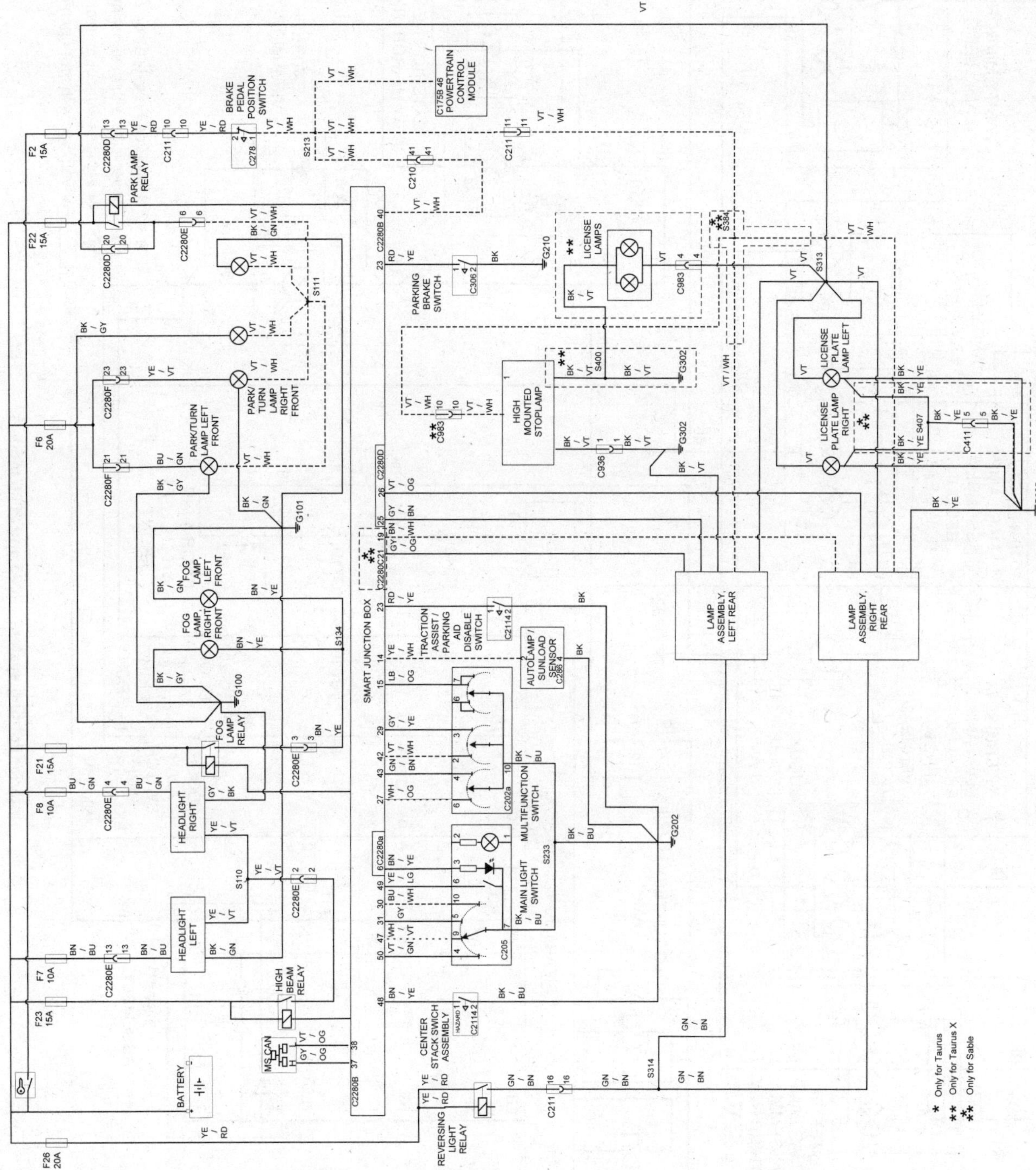

Exterior lighting system - 2008 models (later models similar)

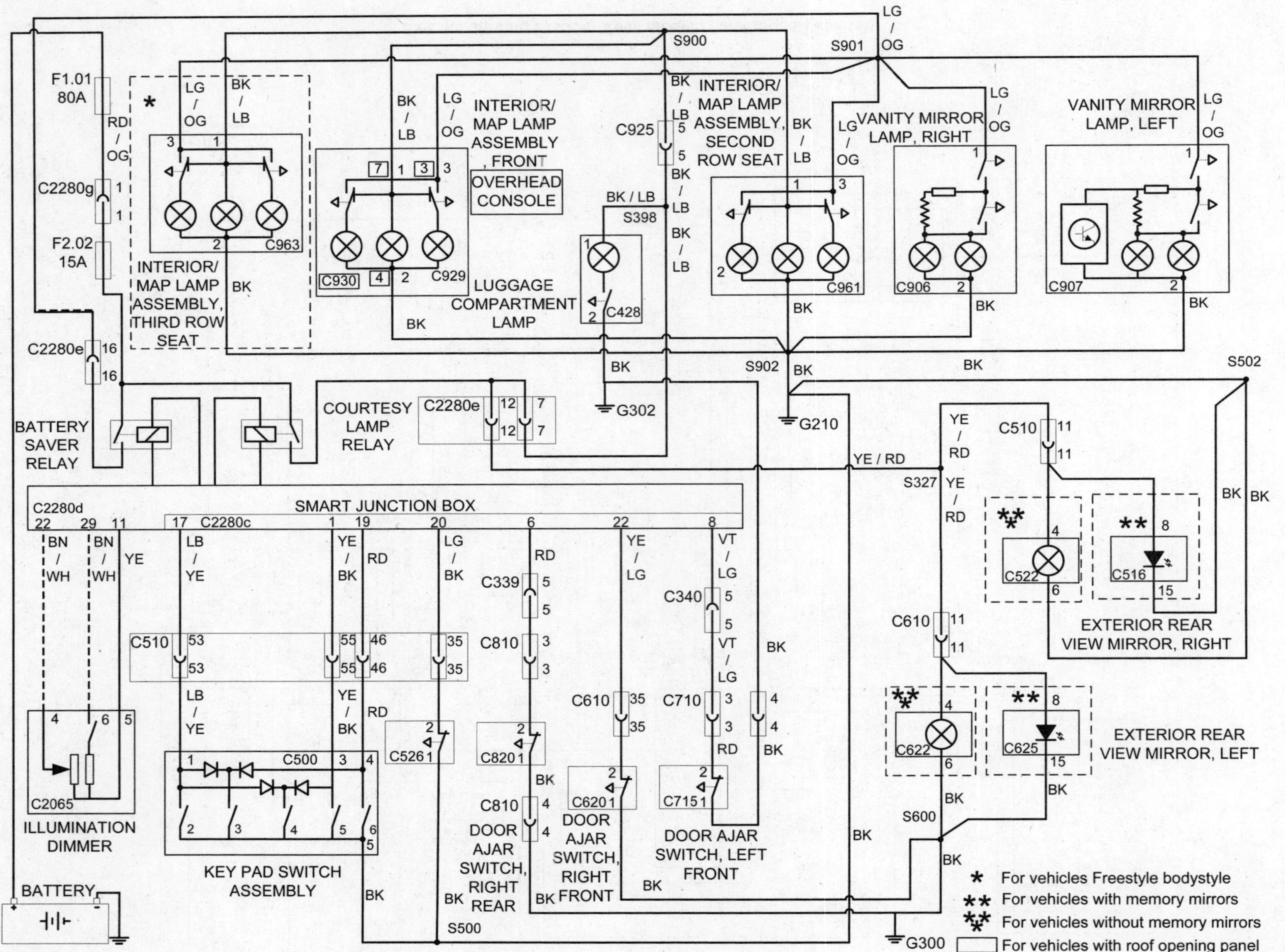
F1.01 80A
C2280g
F2.02 15A
C2280e
INTERIOR/MAP LAMP ASSEMBLY, THIRD ROW SEAT
C963
C930
C929
INTERIOR/MAP LAMP ASSEMBLY, FRONT OVERHEAD CONSOLE
LUGGAGE COMPARTMENT LAMP
C428
S398
C925
INTERIOR/MAP LAMP ASSEMBLY, SECOND ROW SEAT
C961
VANITY MIRROR LAMP, RIGHT
C906
VANITY MIRROR LAMP, LEFT
C907
S900
S901
S902
S502
G302
G210
BATTERY SAVER RELAY
COURTESY LAMP RELAY
C2280e
SMART JUNCTION BOX
C2280d
C2280c
C510
C500
KEY PAD SWITCH ASSEMBLY
C2065
ILLUMINATION DIMMER
BATTERY
C339
C810
C5261
C8201
DOOR AJAR SWITCH, RIGHT REAR
C610
C6201
DOOR AJAR SWITCH, RIGHT FRONT
C340
C710
C7151
DOOR AJAR SWITCH, LEFT FRONT
S500
YE / RD
S327
C510
C522
C516
EXTERIOR REAR VIEW MIRROR, RIGHT
C610
C622
C625
EXTERIOR REAR VIEW MIRROR, LEFT
S600
G300
* For vehicles Freestyle bodystyle
** For vehicles with memory mirrors
*** For vehicles without memory mirrors
For vehicles with roof opening panel
Interior lighting system - 2005 and 2006 models

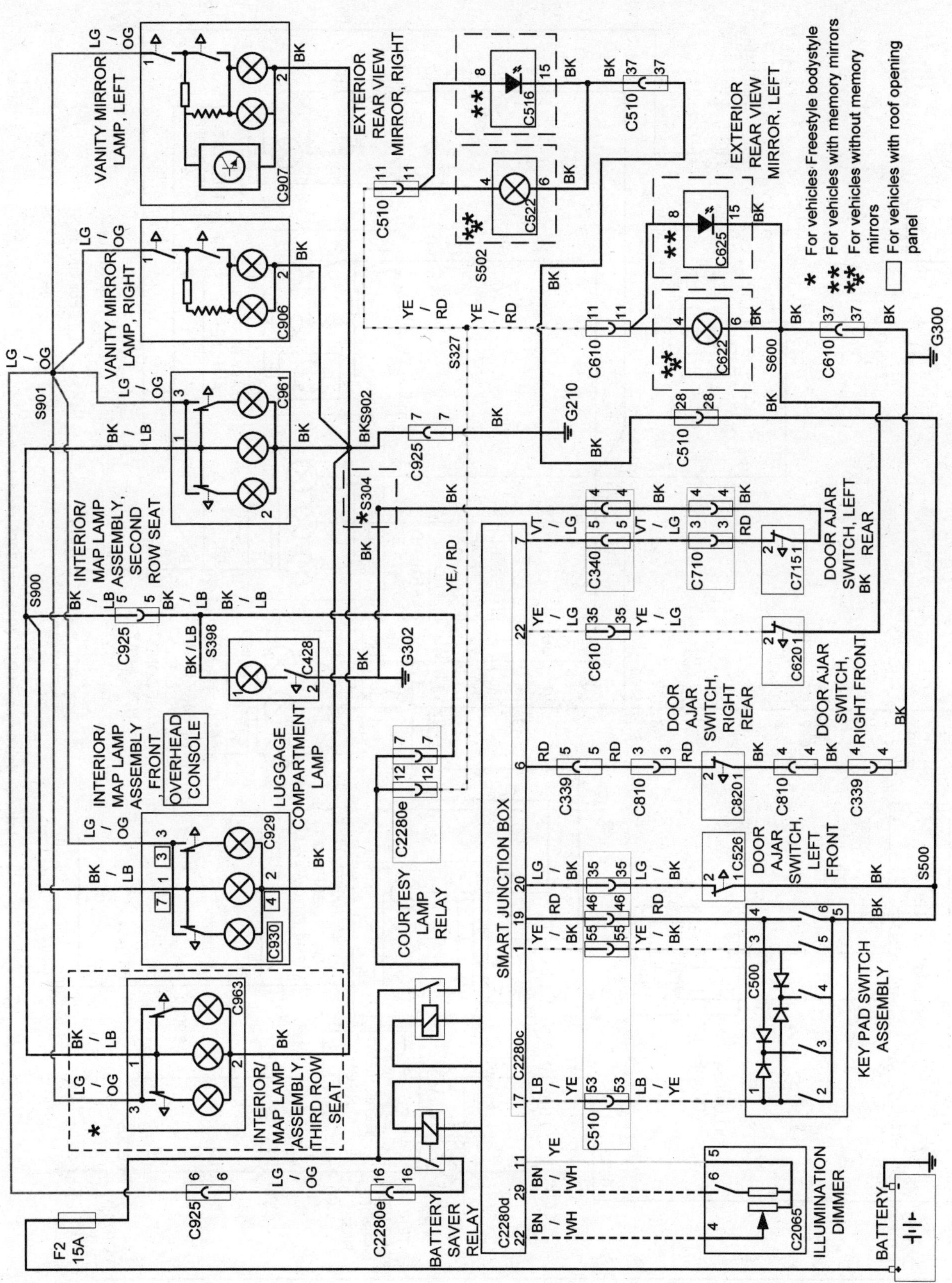

VANITY MIRROR LAMP, LEFT
VANITY MIRROR LAMP, RIGHT
INTERIOR/MAP LAMP ASSEMBLY, SECOND ROW SEAT
INTERIOR/MAP LAMP ASSEMBLY, FRONT
OVERHEAD CONSOLE
LUGGAGE COMPARTMENT LAMP
INTERIOR/MAP LAMP ASSEMBLY, THIRD ROW SEAT
COURTESY LAMP RELAY
BATTERY SAVER RELAY
EXTERIOR REAR VIEW MIRROR, RIGHT
EXTERIOR REAR VIEW MIRROR, LEFT
SMART JUNCTION BOX
DOOR AJAR SWITCH, LEFT REAR
DOOR AJAR SWITCH, RIGHT REAR
DOOR AJAR SWITCH, RIGHT FRONT
DOOR AJAR SWITCH, LEFT FRONT
KEY PAD SWITCH ASSEMBLY
ILLUMINATION DIMMER
BATTERY
For vehicles Freestyle bodystyle
For vehicles with memory mirrors
For vehicles without memory mirrors
For vehicles with roof opening panel
Interior lighting system - 2007 models

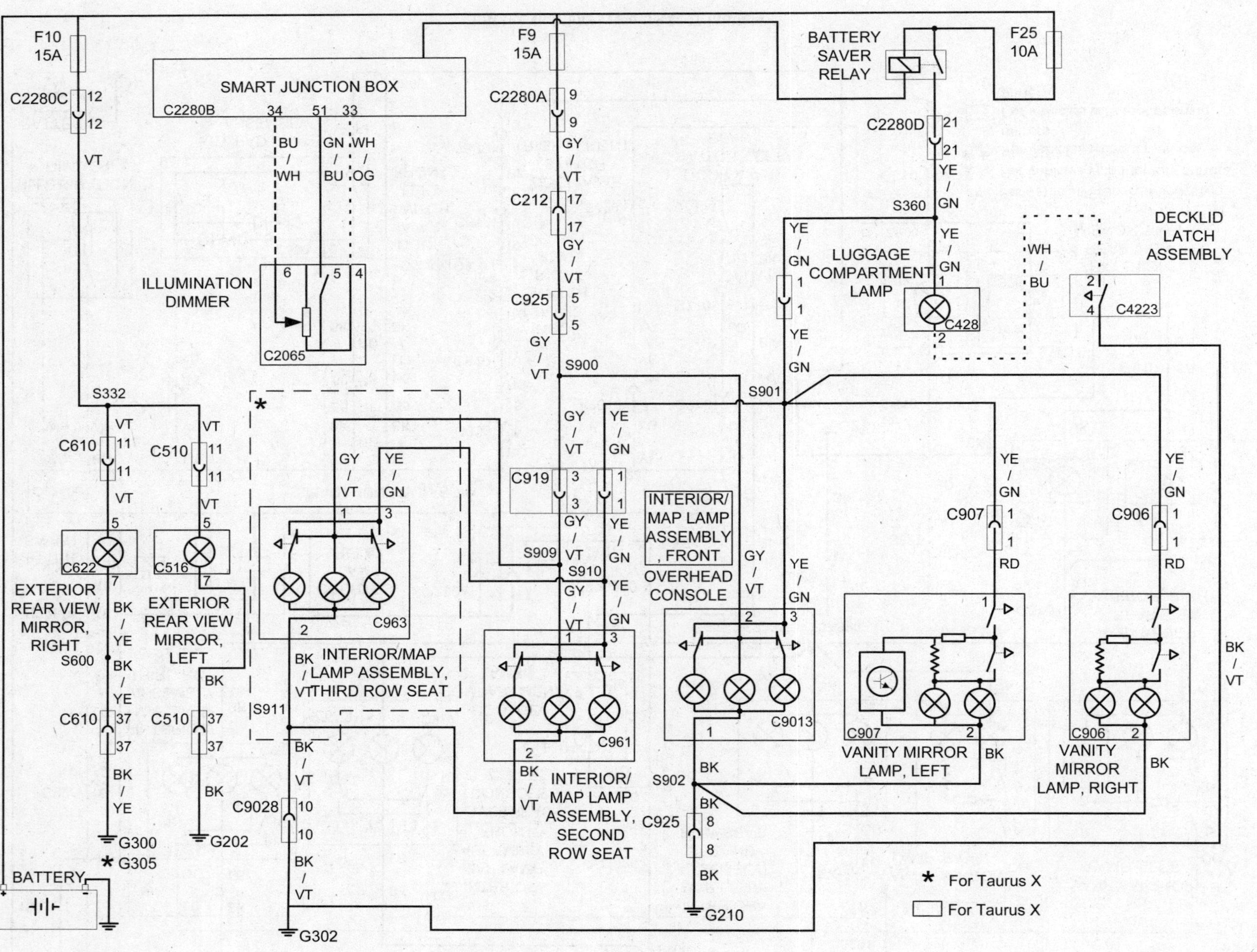

F10 15A
C2280C 12 12
VT
SMART JUNCTION BOX
C2280B 34 51 33
BU/WH
GN/BU
WH/OG
ILLUMINATION DIMMER
C2065
6 5 4
F9 15A
C2280A 9 9
GY/VT
C212 17 17
GY/VT
C925 5 5
GY/VT
S900
S332
C610 11 11
VT
C510 11 11
VT
C622 5 7
EXTERIOR REAR VIEW MIRROR, RIGHT
S600
C516 5 7
EXTERIOR REAR VIEW MIRROR, LEFT
C610 37 37
BK/YE
C510 37 37
BK
G300
G305
BATTERY
BK/YE
G202
C9028 10 10
BK/VT
G302
INTERIOR/MAP LAMP ASSEMBLY, THIRD ROW SEAT
C963
GY/VT
YE/GN
BK/VT
S911
C919 3 3
S909 S910
GY/VT
YE/GN
INTERIOR/MAP LAMP ASSEMBLY, SECOND ROW SEAT
C961
BK/VT
INTERIOR/MAP LAMP ASSEMBLY, FRONT OVERHEAD CONSOLE
C9013
GY/VT
YE/GN
S901
S902
BK
C925 8 8
BK
G210
BATTERY SAVER RELAY
F25 10A
C2280D 21 21
YE/GN
S360
YE/GN
LUGGAGE COMPARTMENT LAMP
C428
YE/GN
WH/BU
DECKLID LATCH ASSEMBLY
C4223
C907 1 1 RD
VANITY MIRROR LAMP, LEFT
C907
YE/GN
C906 1 1 RD
VANITY MIRROR LAMP, RIGHT
C906
YE/GN
BK
BK/VT
For Taurus X
For Taurus X
Interior lighting system - 2008 and 2009 models
Chapter 12 Chassis electrical system

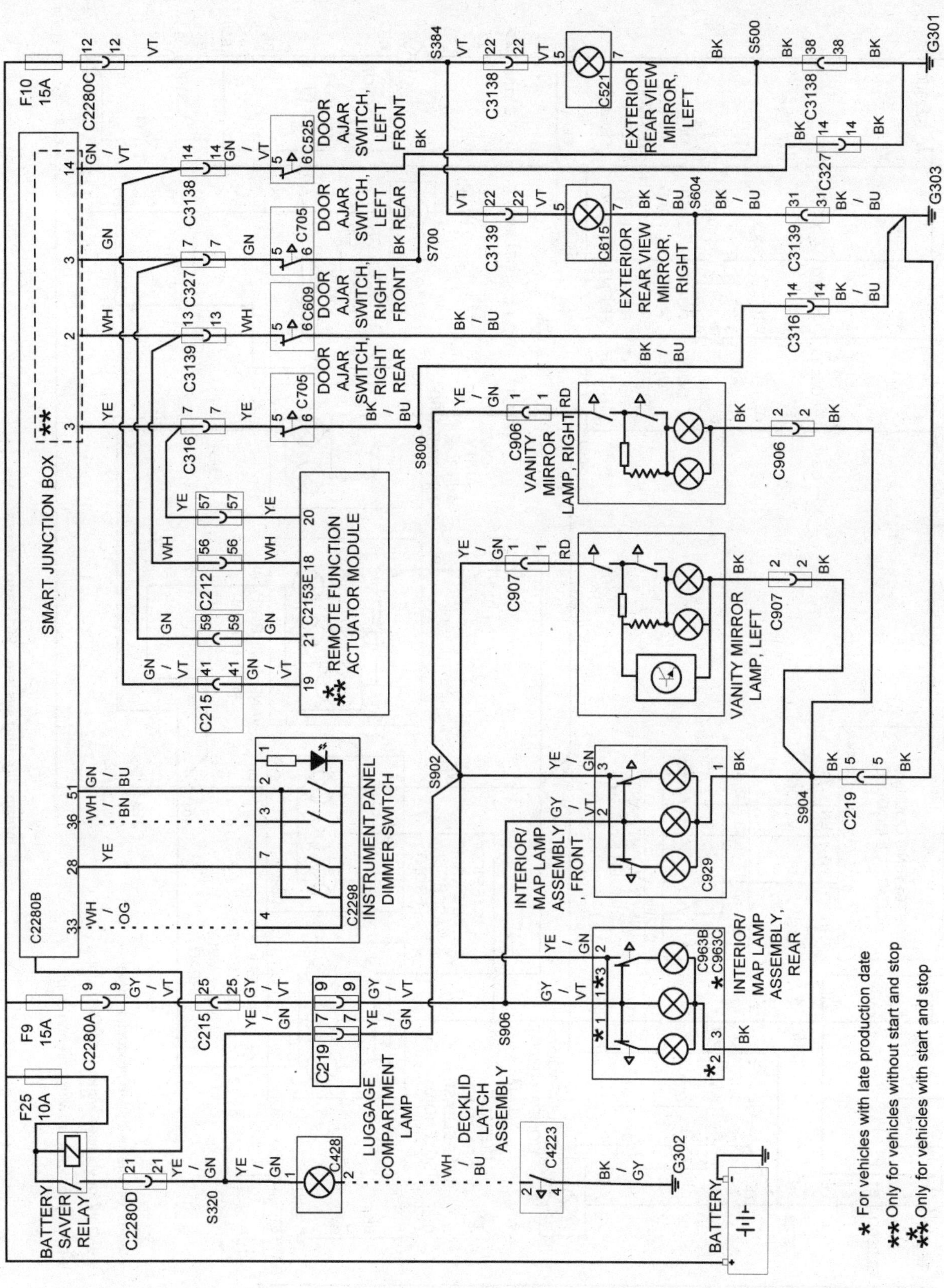
F10 15A
C2280C
SMART JUNCTION BOX
DOOR AJAR SWITCH, LEFT FRONT
DOOR AJAR SWITCH, LEFT REAR
DOOR AJAR SWITCH, RIGHT FRONT
DOOR AJAR SWITCH, RIGHT REAR
EXTERIOR REAR VIEW MIRROR, LEFT
EXTERIOR REAR VIEW MIRROR, RIGHT
REMOTE FUNCTION ACTUATOR MODULE
INSTRUMENT PANEL DIMMER SWITCH
VANITY MIRROR LAMP, RIGHT
VANITY MIRROR LAMP, LEFT
INTERIOR/MAP LAMP ASSEMBLY, FRONT
INTERIOR/MAP LAMP ASSEMBLY, REAR
LUGGAGE COMPARTMENT LAMP
DECKLID LATCH ASSEMBLY
BATTERY SAVER RELAY
BATTERY
* For vehicles with late production date
** Only for vehicles without start and stop
**** Only for vehicles with start and stop
Interior lighting system - 2010 through 2012 models

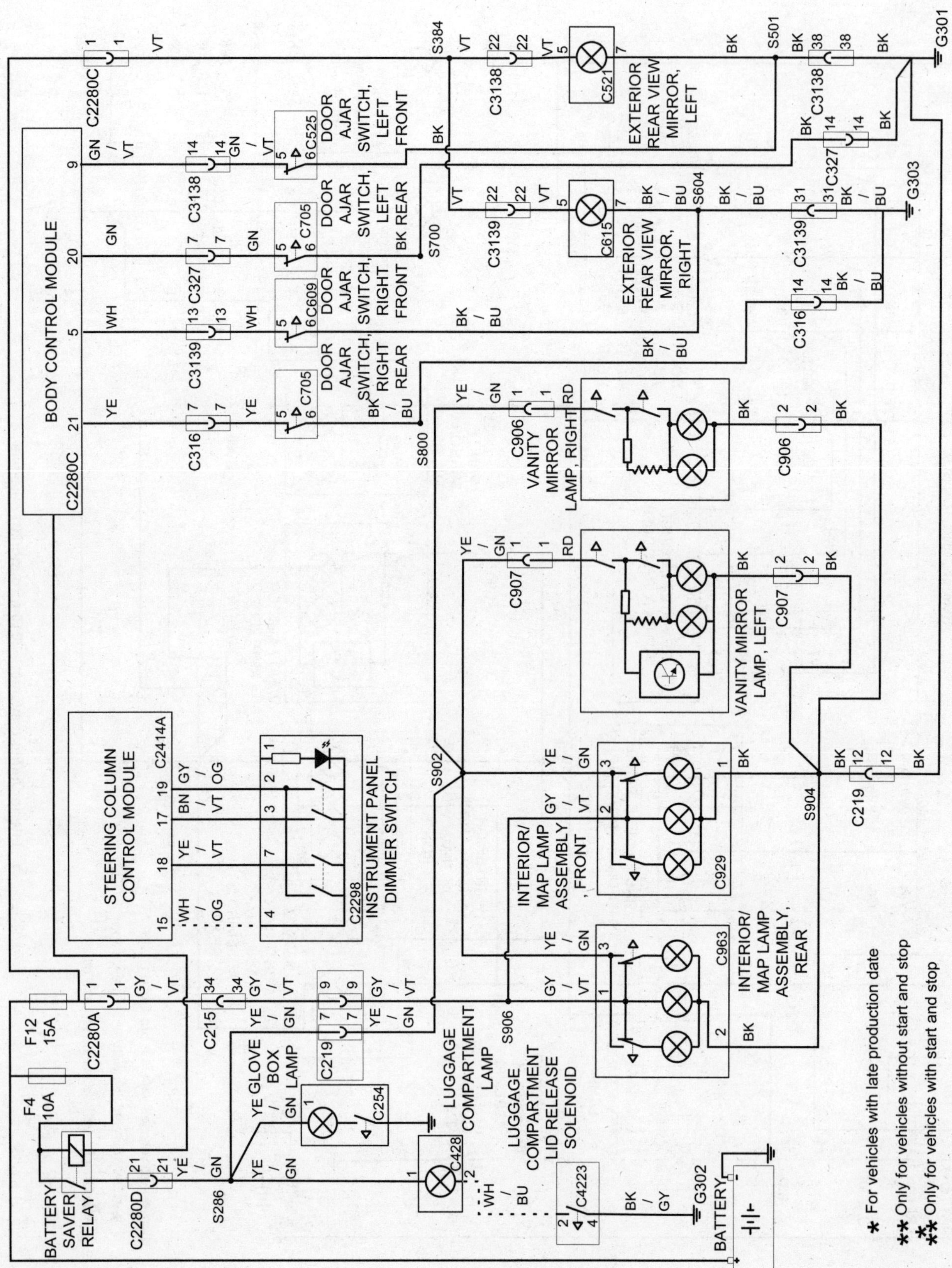

Interior lighting system - 2013 and later models

* For vehicles with late production date
** Only for vehicles without start and stop
*** Only for vehicles with start and stop

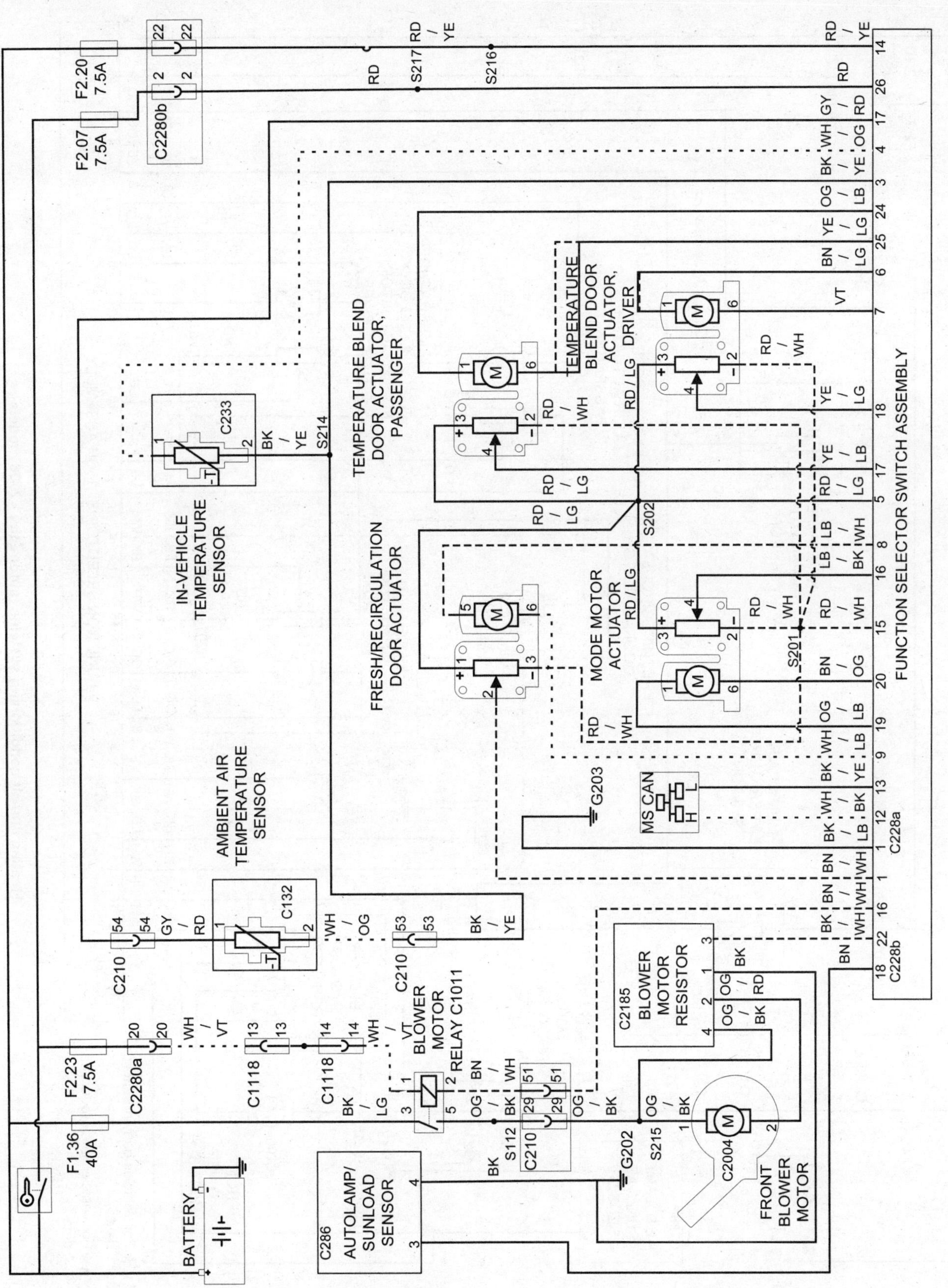

Heating and air conditioning systems (automatic) - 2005 models

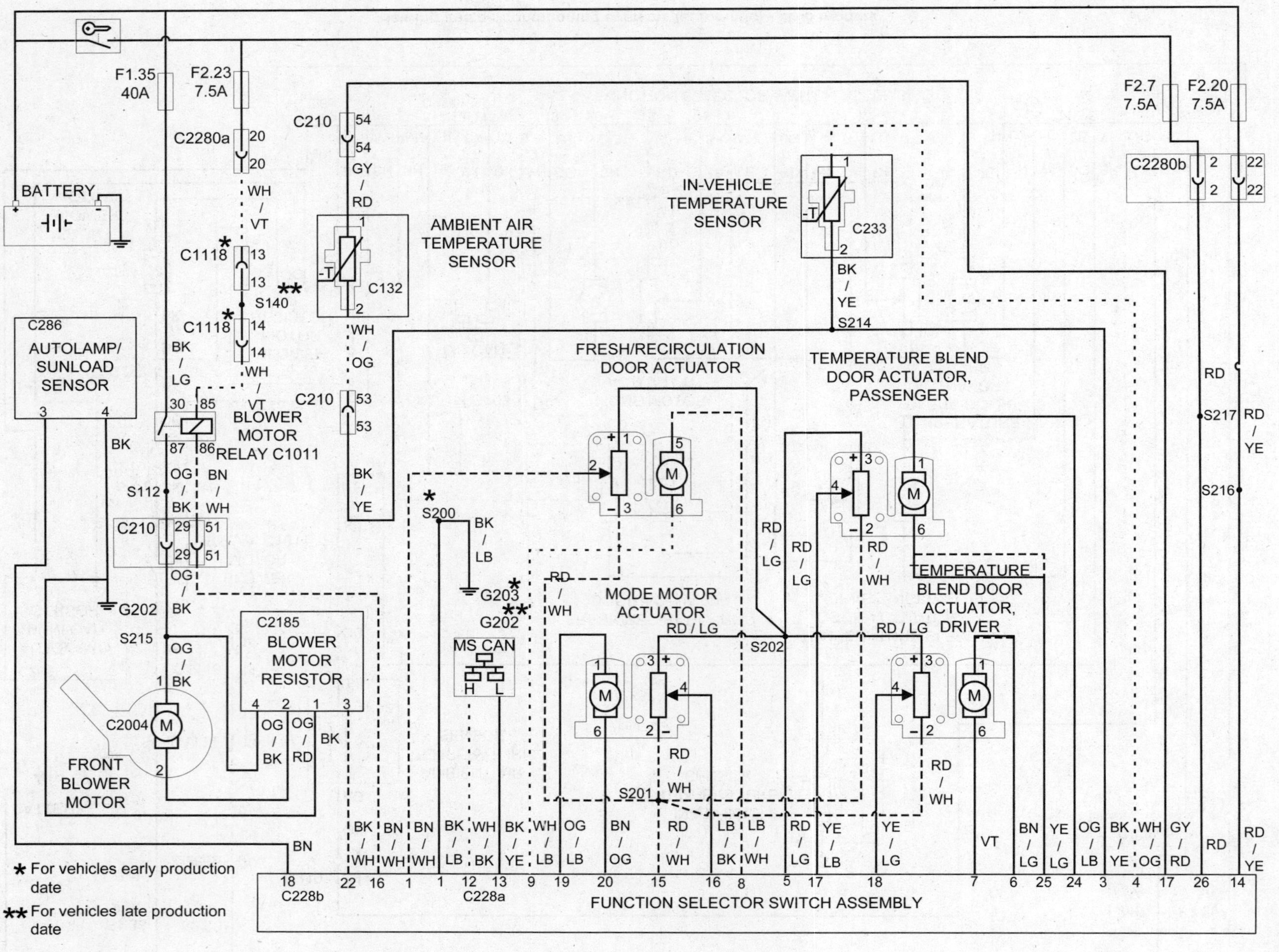

BATTERY
F1.35 40A
F2.23 7.5A
F2.7 7.5A
F2.20 7.5A
C2280a
C2280b
AUTOLAMP/ SUNLOAD SENSOR
C286
C1118
S140
BLOWER MOTOR RELAY C1011
AMBIENT AIR TEMPERATURE SENSOR
C132
C210
IN-VEHICLE TEMPERATURE SENSOR
C233
S214
FRESH/RECIRCULATION DOOR ACTUATOR
TEMPERATURE BLEND DOOR ACTUATOR, PASSENGER
TEMPERATURE BLEND DOOR ACTUATOR, DRIVER
MODE MOTOR ACTUATOR
MS CAN
S200
S201
S202
G203
G202
S112
C210
S215
BLOWER MOTOR RESISTOR
C2185
FRONT BLOWER MOTOR
C2004
S217
S216
FUNCTION SELECTOR SWITCH ASSEMBLY
C228a
C228b
For vehicles early production date
For vehicles late production date
Heating and air conditioning systems (automatic) - 2006 models

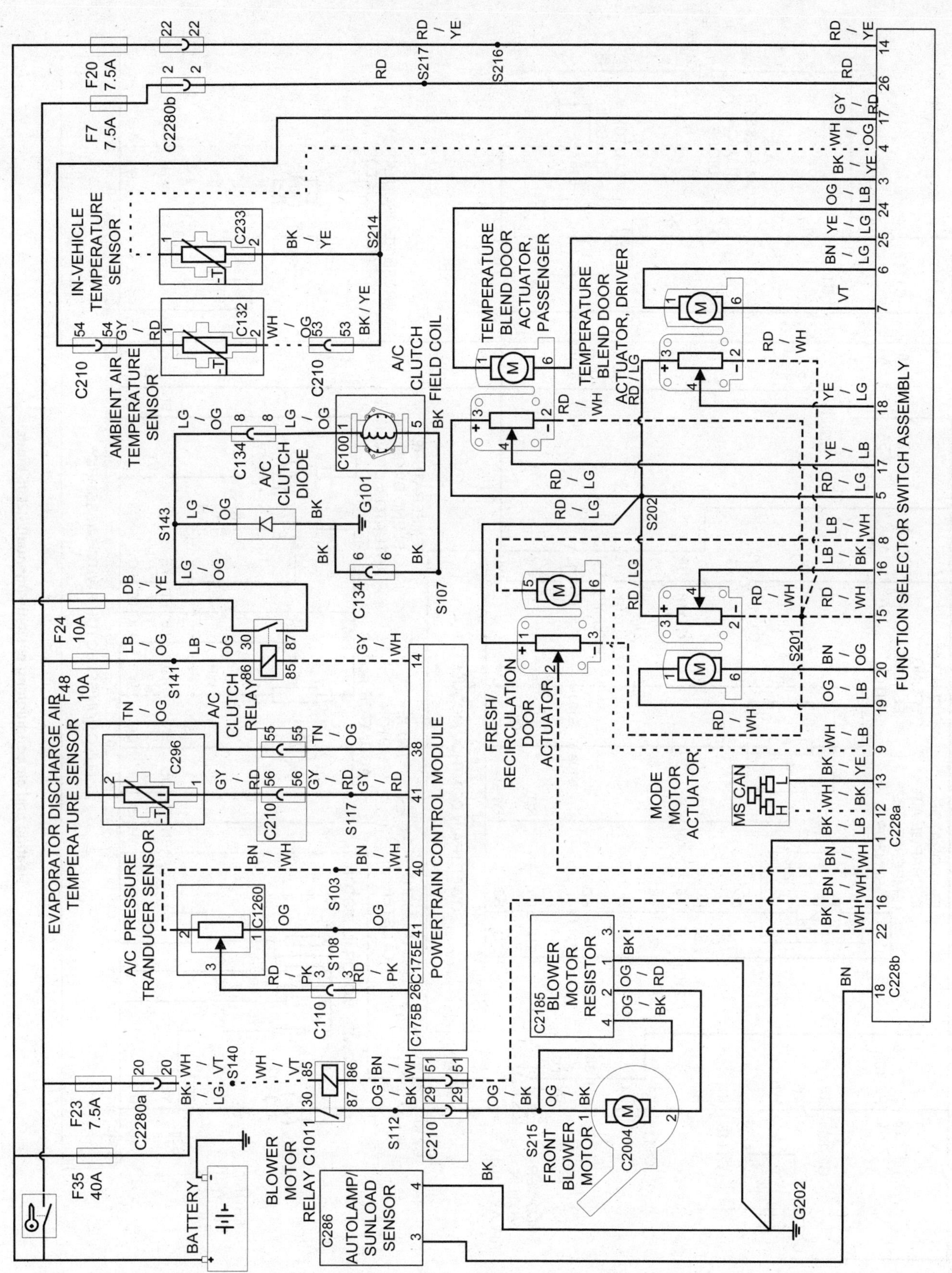

Heating and air conditioning systems (automatic) - 2007 models

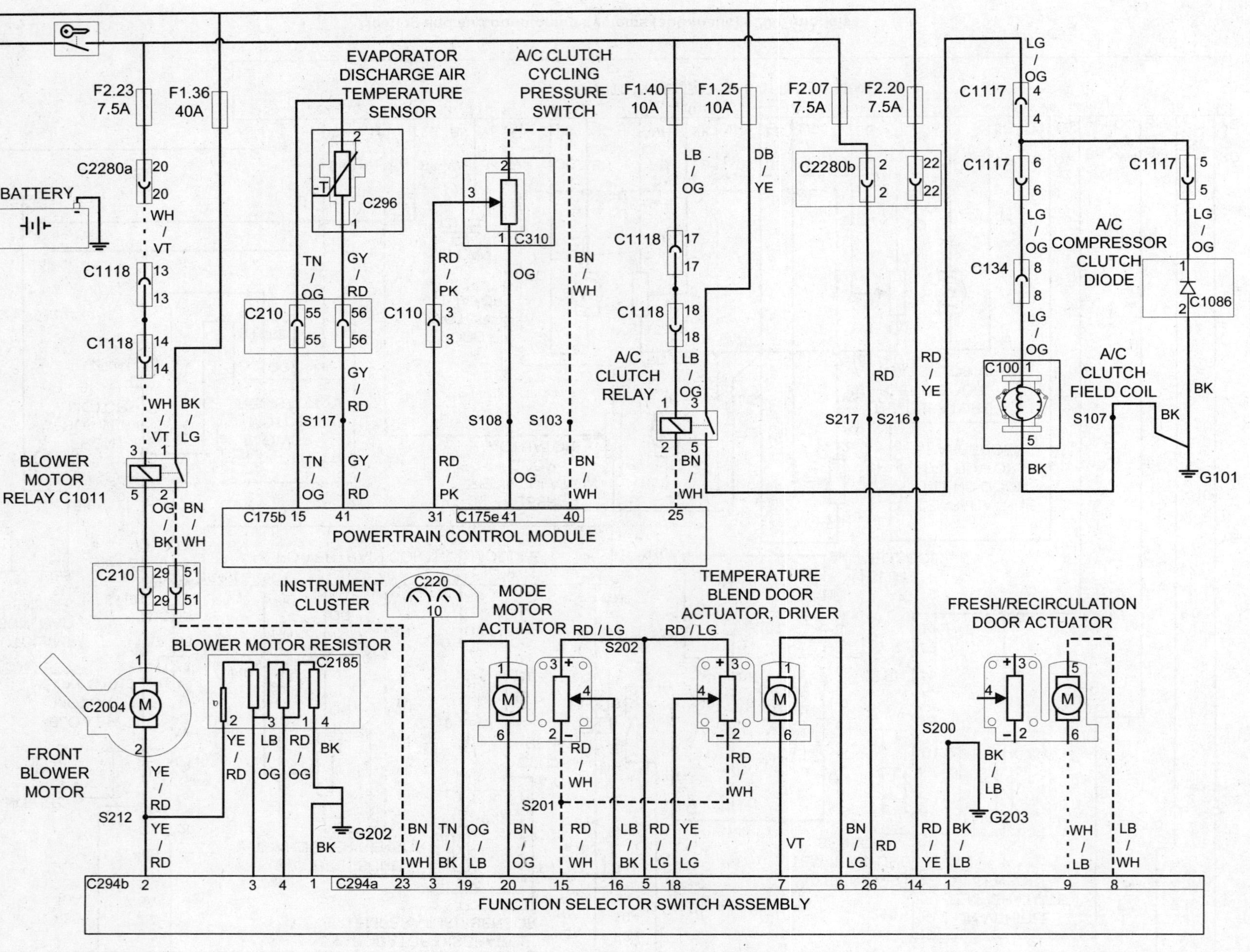

Heating and air conditioning systems (manual) - 2005 models

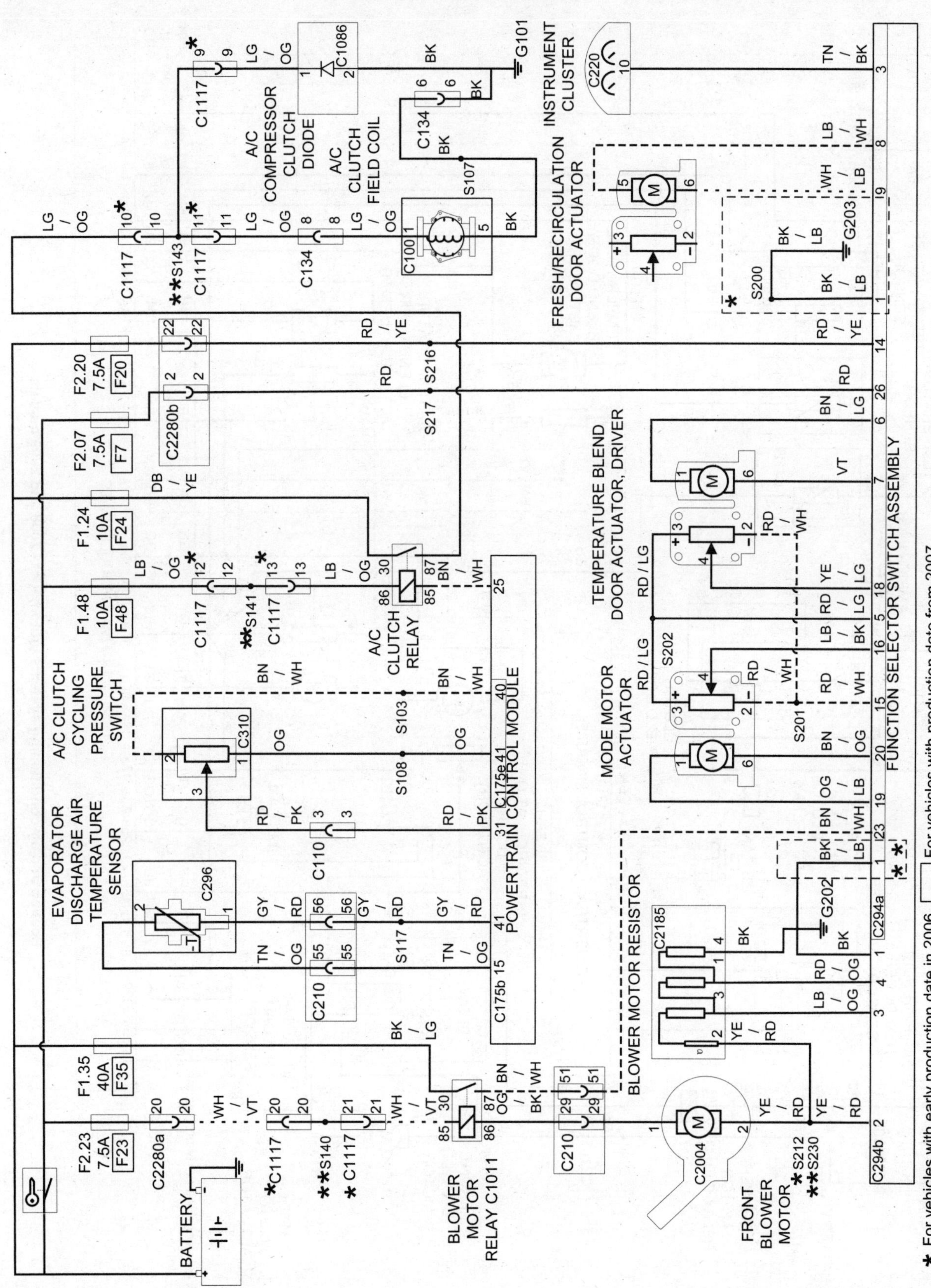

Heating and air conditioning systems (manual) - 2006 and 2007 models

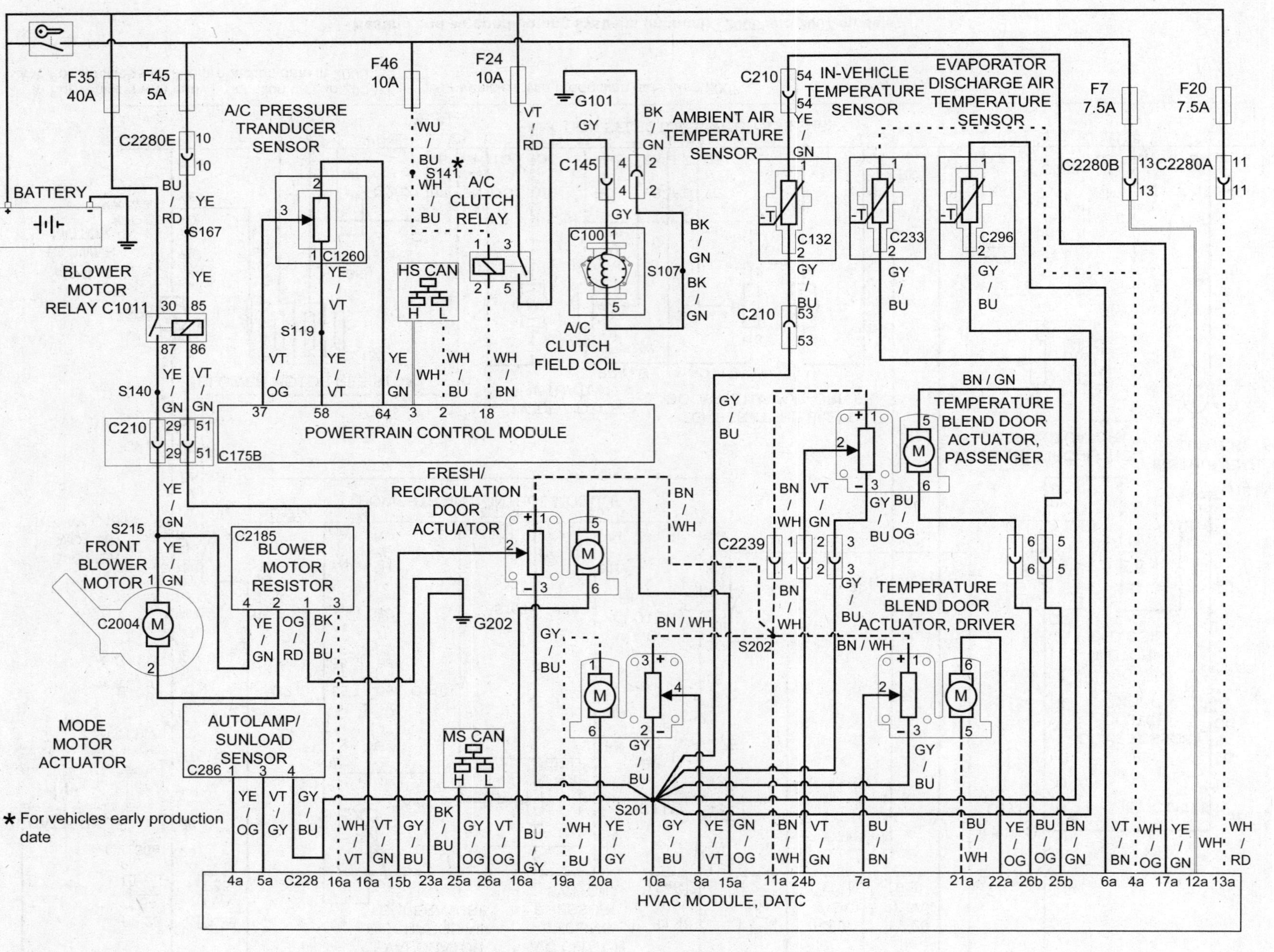

Heating and air conditioning systems (automatic) - 2008 and 2009 models

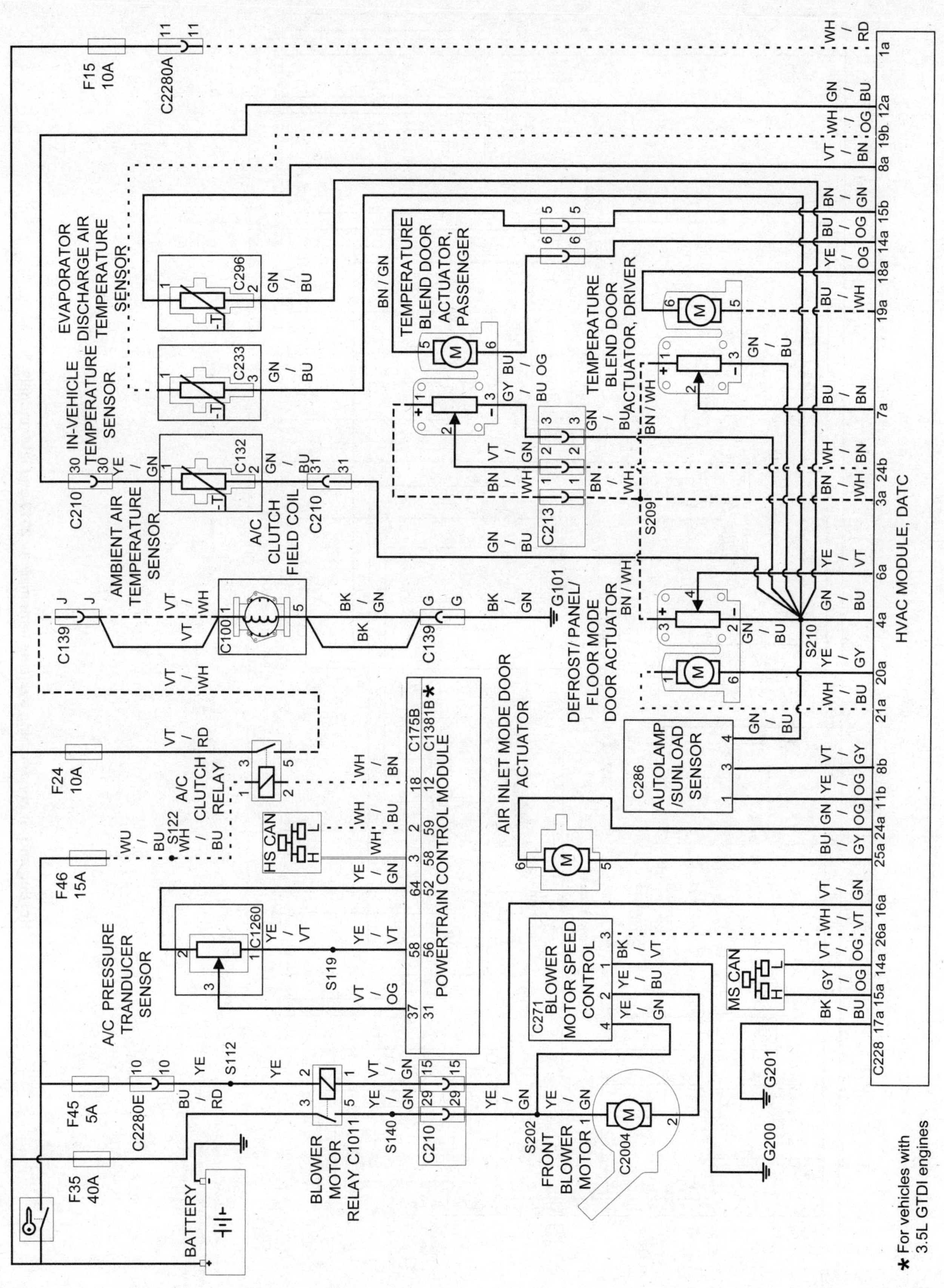
Heating and air conditioning systems (automatic) - 2010 through 2012 models

* For vehicles with
3.5L GTDI engines

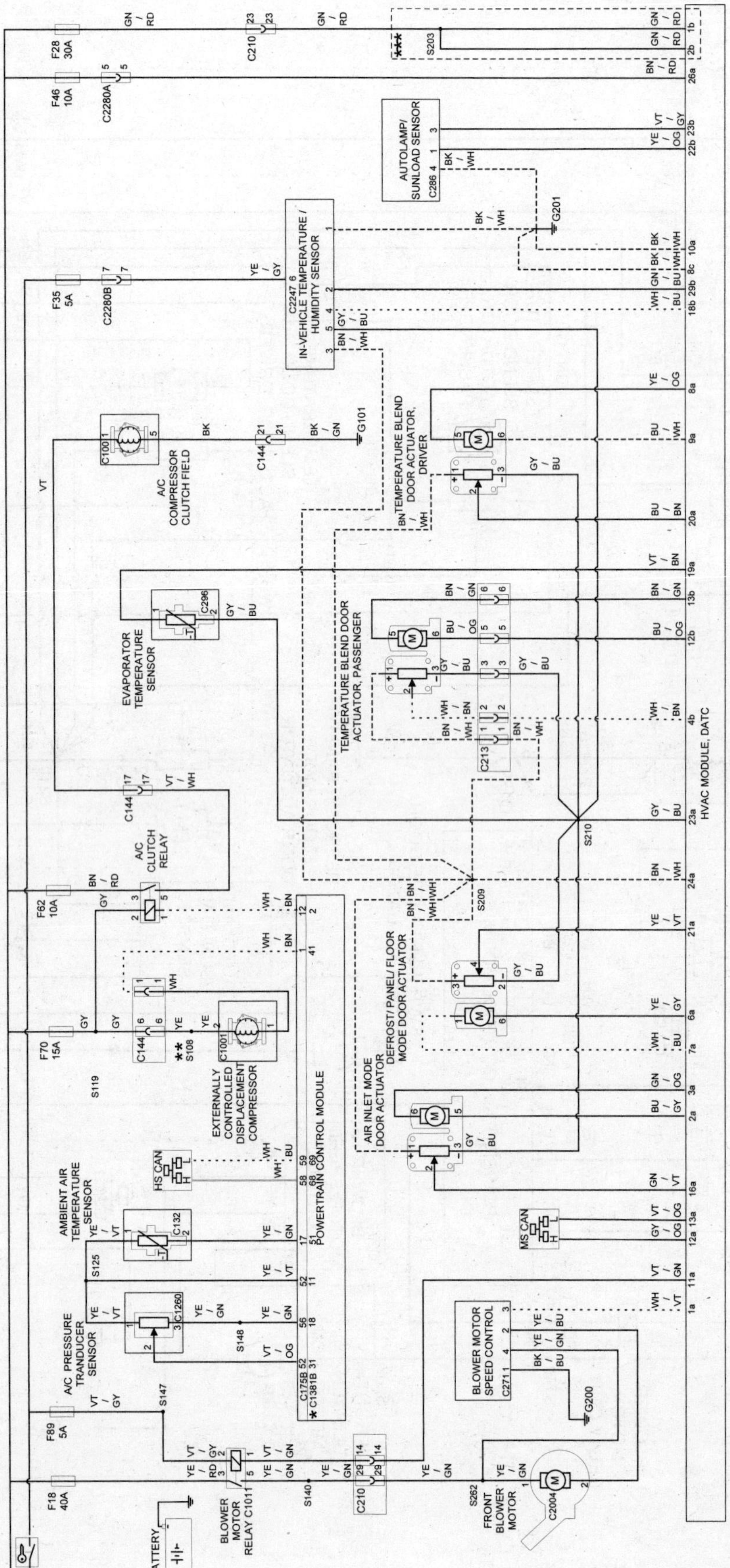

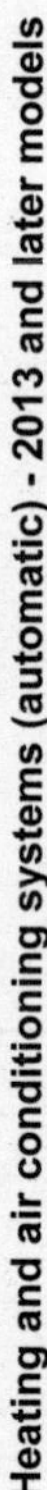

Heating and air conditioning systems (automatic) - 2013 and later models

★ For vehicles with 3.5L GTDI engines
★★ For vehicles with 2.0L engines
★★★ For vehicles with heated seats

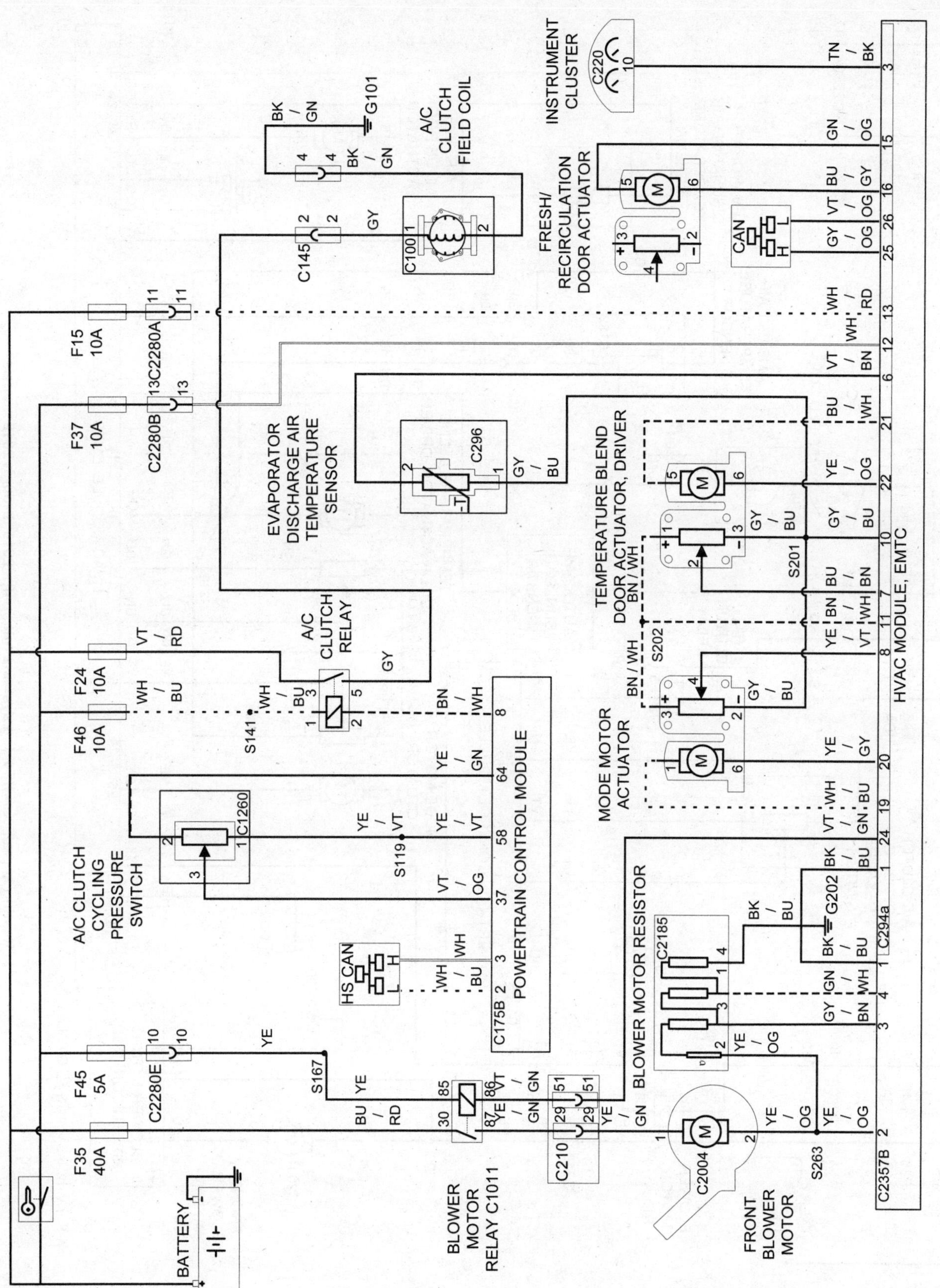

Heating and air conditioning systems (manual) - 2008 and 2009 models

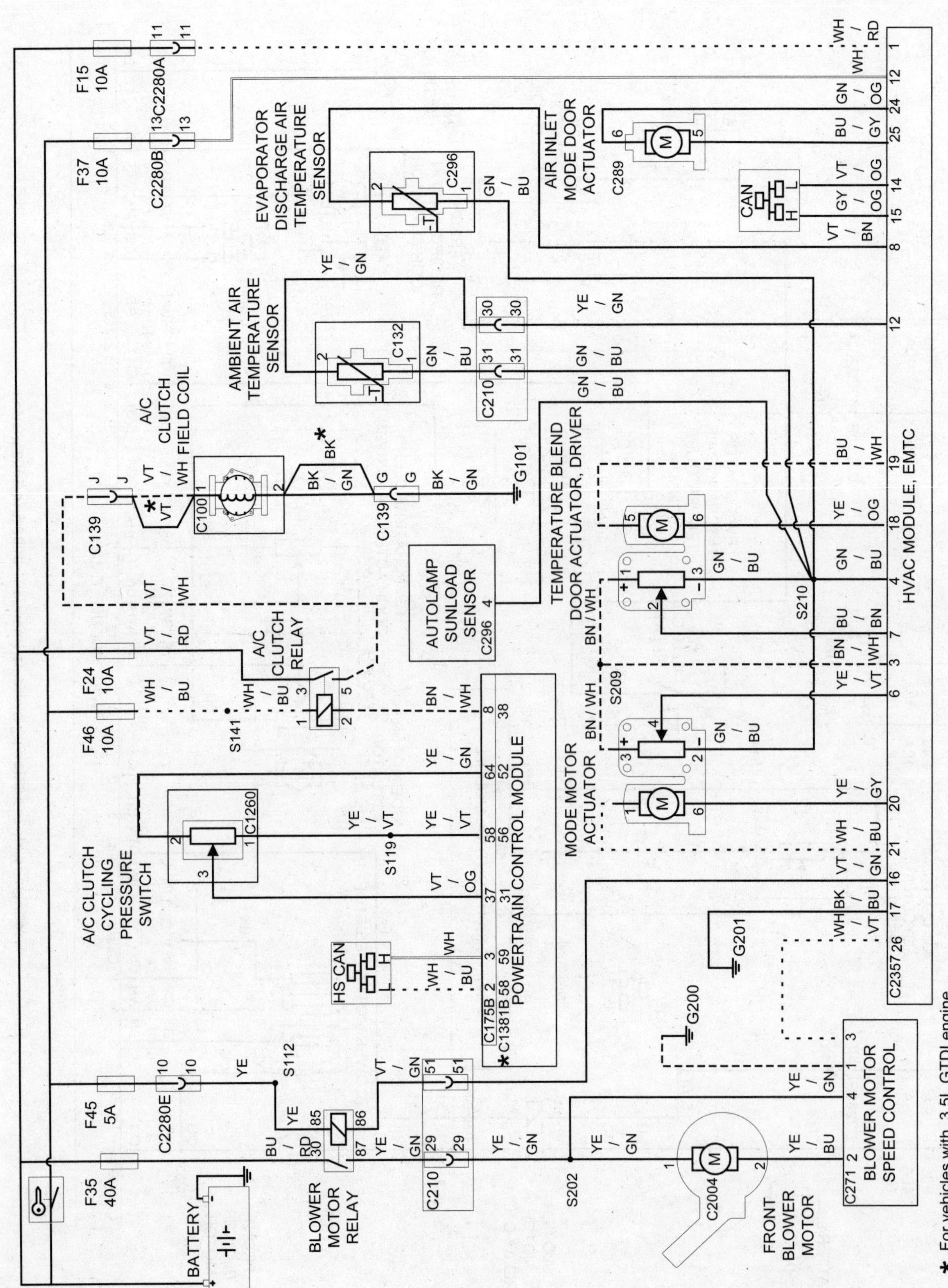

Heating and air conditioning systems (manual) - 2010 through 2012 models

* For vehicles with 3.5L GTDI engine

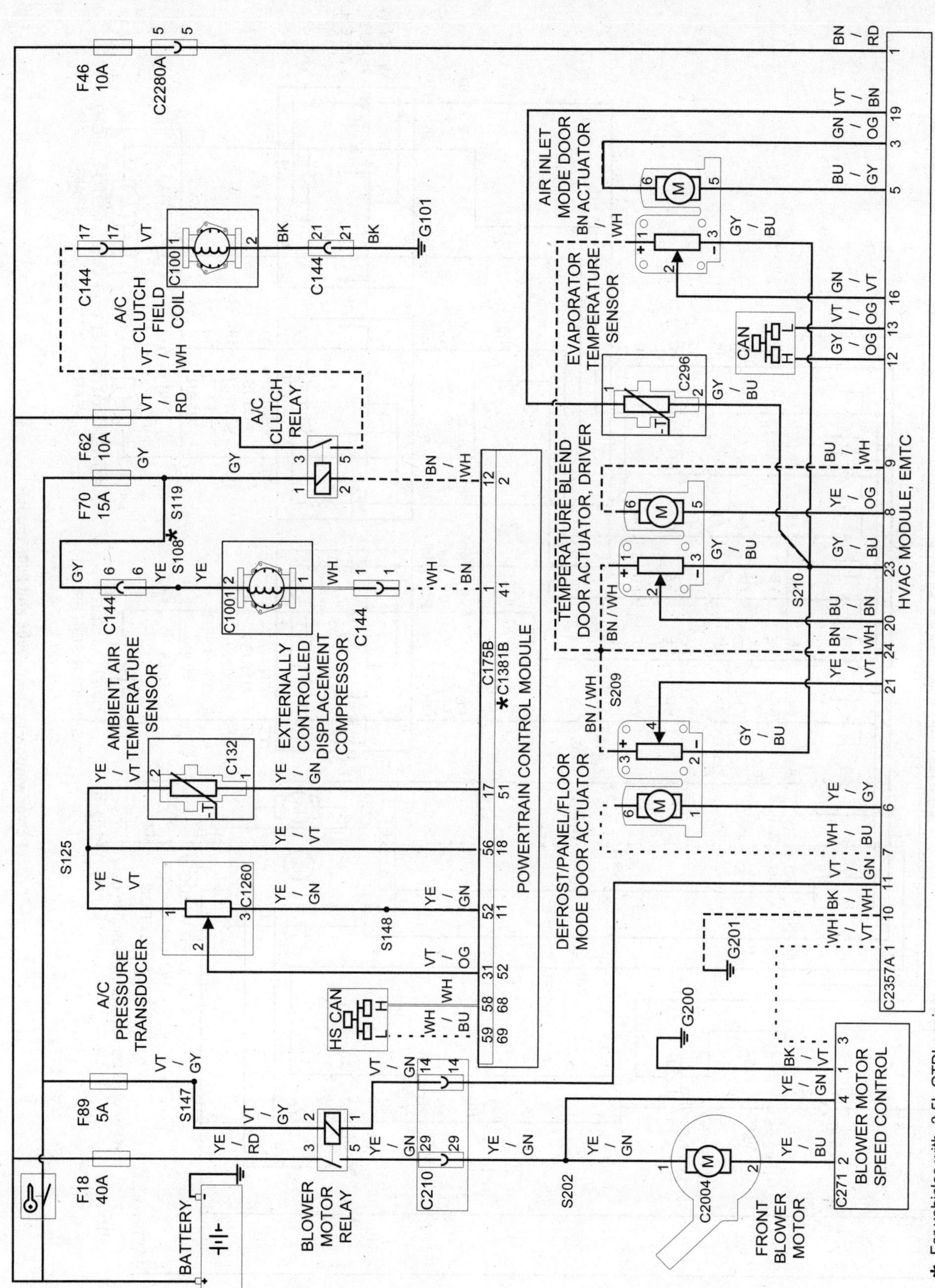

Heating and air conditioning systems (manual) - 2013 and later models

* For vehicles with 3.5L GTDI engine

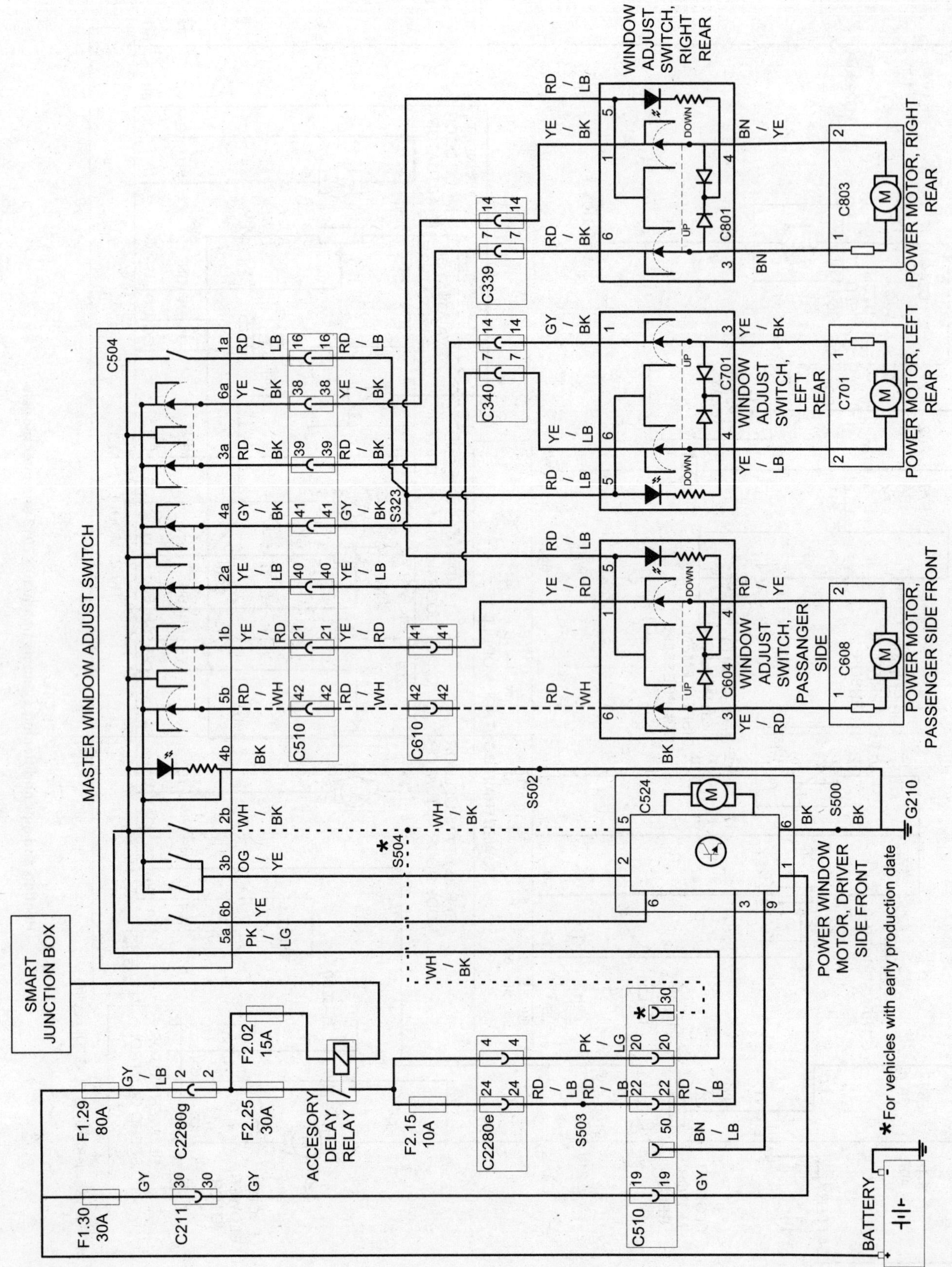

Power window system - 2005 and 2006 models

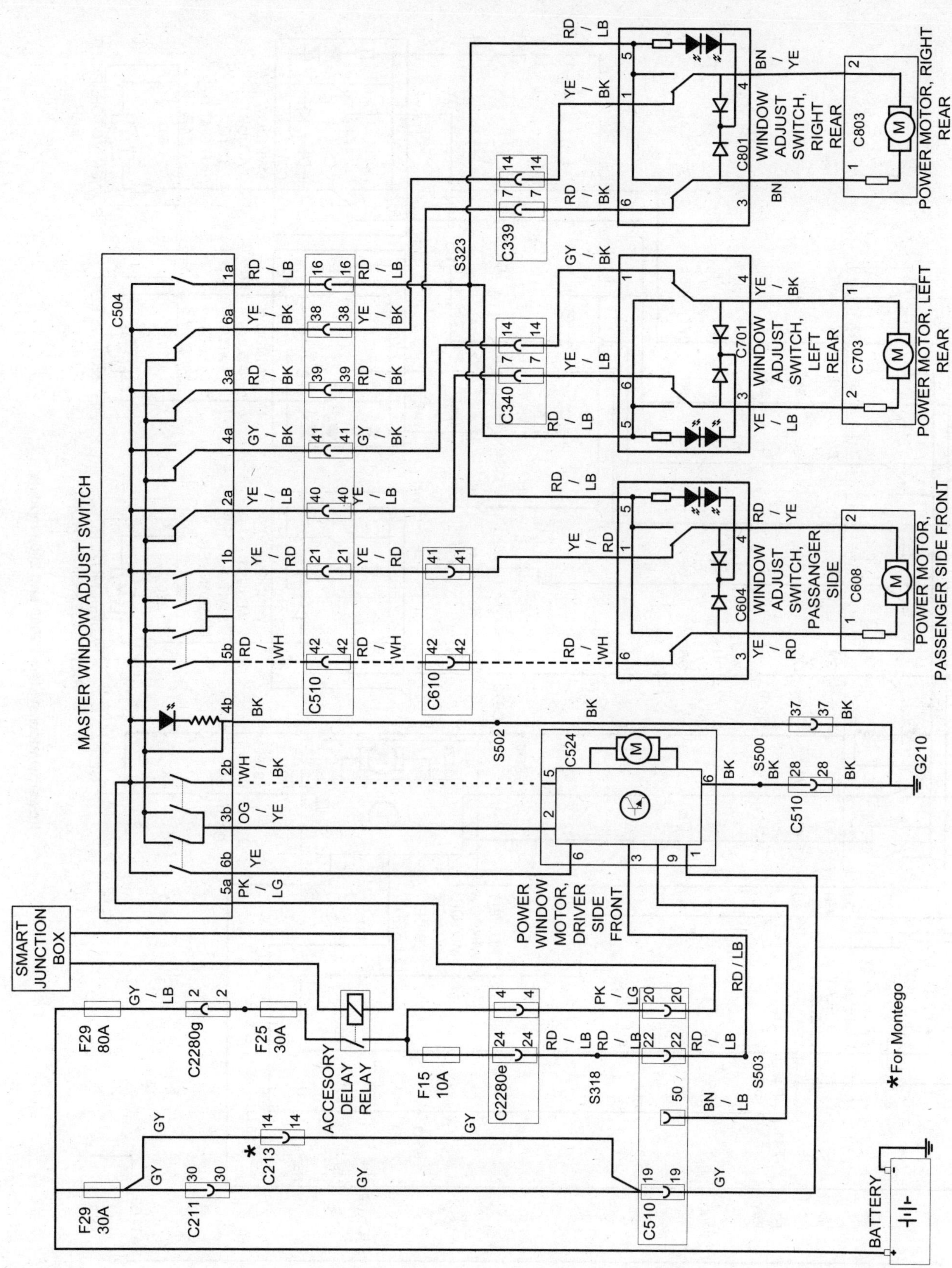
MASTER WINDOW ADJUST SWITCH
POWER MOTOR, RIGHT REAR
WINDOW ADJUST SWITCH, RIGHT REAR
POWER MOTOR, LEFT REAR
WINDOW ADJUST SWITCH, LEFT REAR
POWER MOTOR, PASSANGER SIDE FRONT
WINDOW ADJUST SWITCH, PASSANGER SIDE
POWER WINDOW MOTOR, DRIVER SIDE FRONT
SMART JUNCTION BOX
ACCESORY DELAY RELAY
BATTERY
Power window system - 2007 models
* For Montego

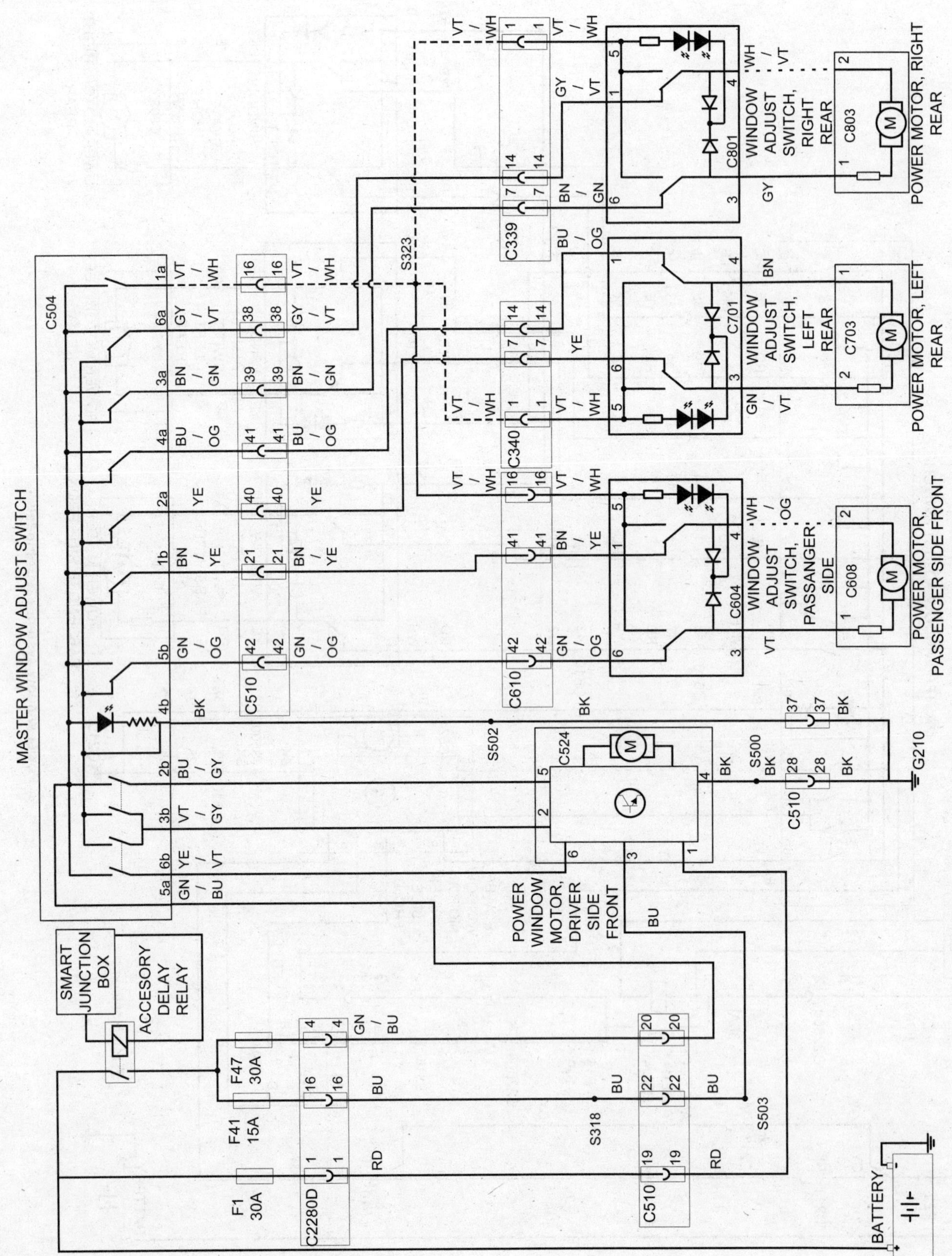
Power window system - 2008 and 2009 models

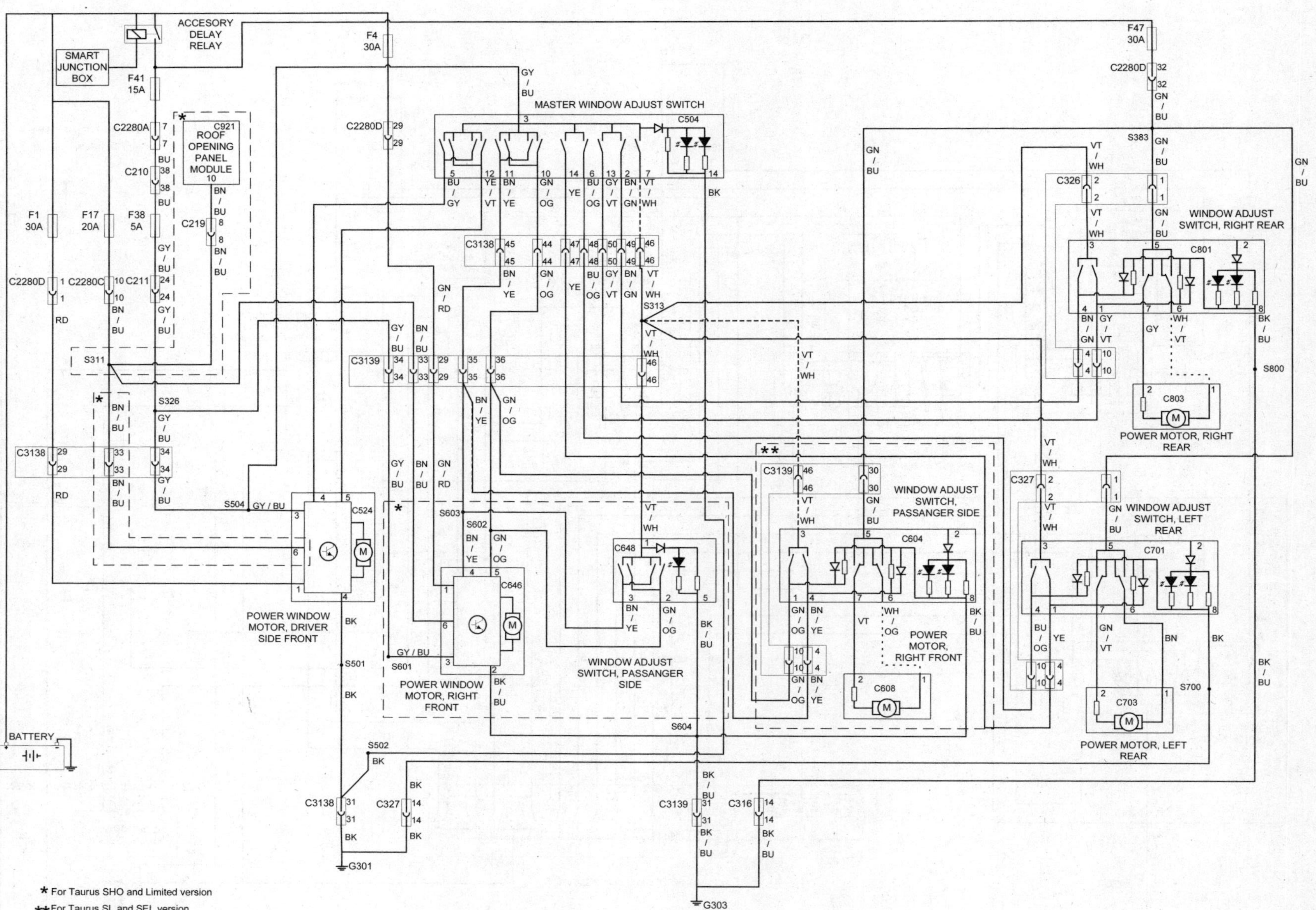

Power window system - 2010 through 2012 models

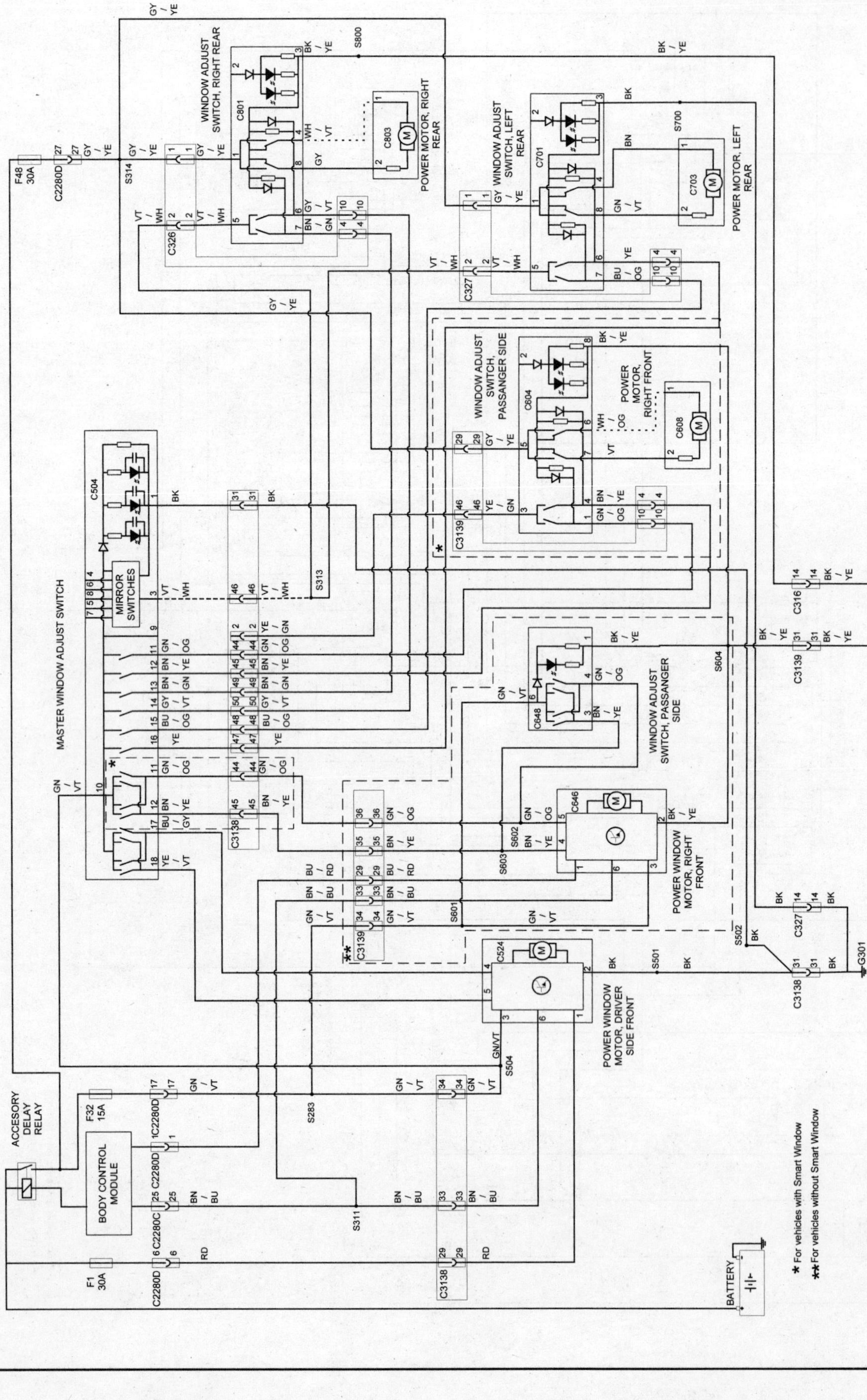

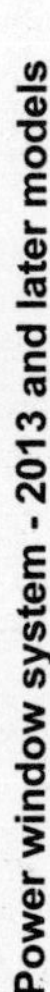

Power window system - 2013 and later models

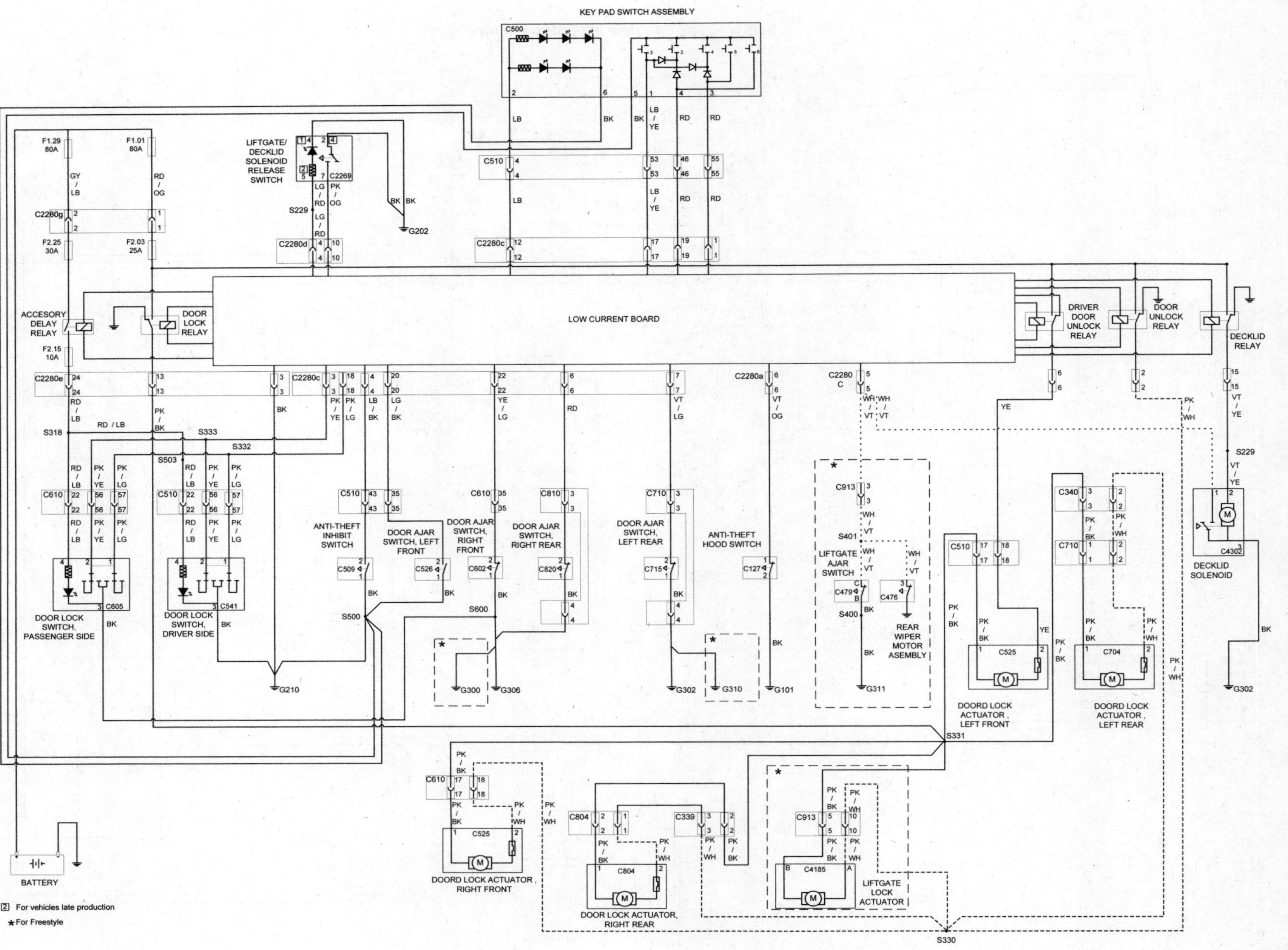
KEY PAD SWITCH ASSEMBLY
LOW CURRENT BOARD
LIFTGATE/ DECKLID SOLENOID RELEASE SWITCH
ACCESORY DELAY RELAY
DOOR LOCK RELAY
DRIVER DOOR UNLOCK RELAY
DOOR UNLOCK RELAY
DECKLID RELAY
DECKLID SOLENOID
DOOR LOCK SWITCH, PASSENGER SIDE
DOOR LOCK SWITCH, DRIVER SIDE
ANTI-THEFT INHIBIT SWITCH
DOOR AJAR SWITCH, LEFT FRONT
DOOR AJAR SWITCH, RIGHT FRONT
DOOR AJAR SWITCH, RIGHT REAR
DOOR AJAR SWITCH, LEFT REAR
ANTI-THEFT HOOD SWITCH
LIFTGATE AJAR SWITCH
REAR WIPER MOTOR ASEMBLY
DOORD LOCK ACTUATOR, LEFT FRONT
DOORD LOCK ACTUATOR, LEFT REAR
DOORD LOCK ACTUATOR, RIGHT FRONT
DOOR LOCK ACTUATOR, RIGHT REAR
LIFTGATE LOCK ACTUATION
BATTERY
Power door lock system - 2005 and 2006 models
[2] For vehicles late production
★ For Freestyle

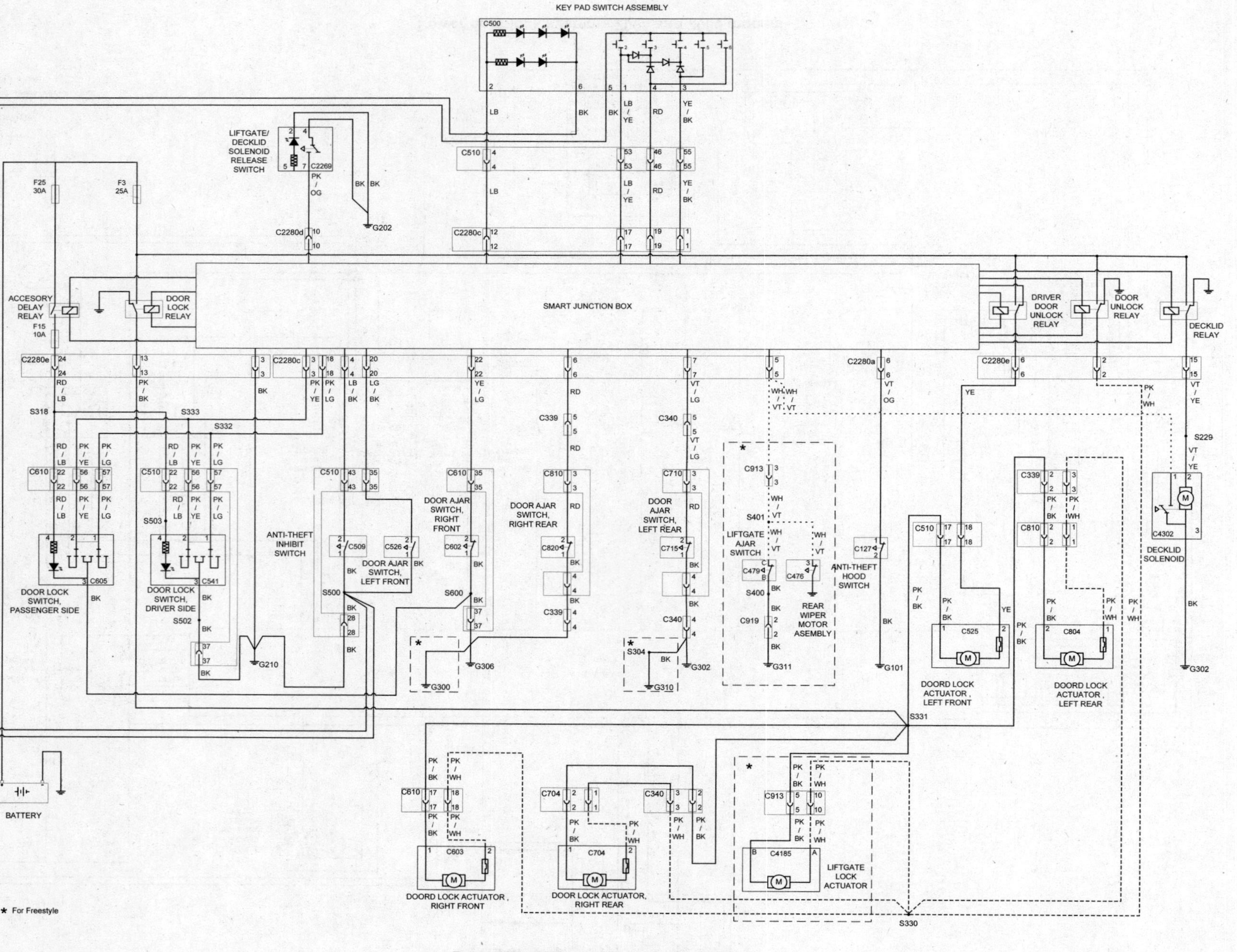

Power door lock system - 2007 models

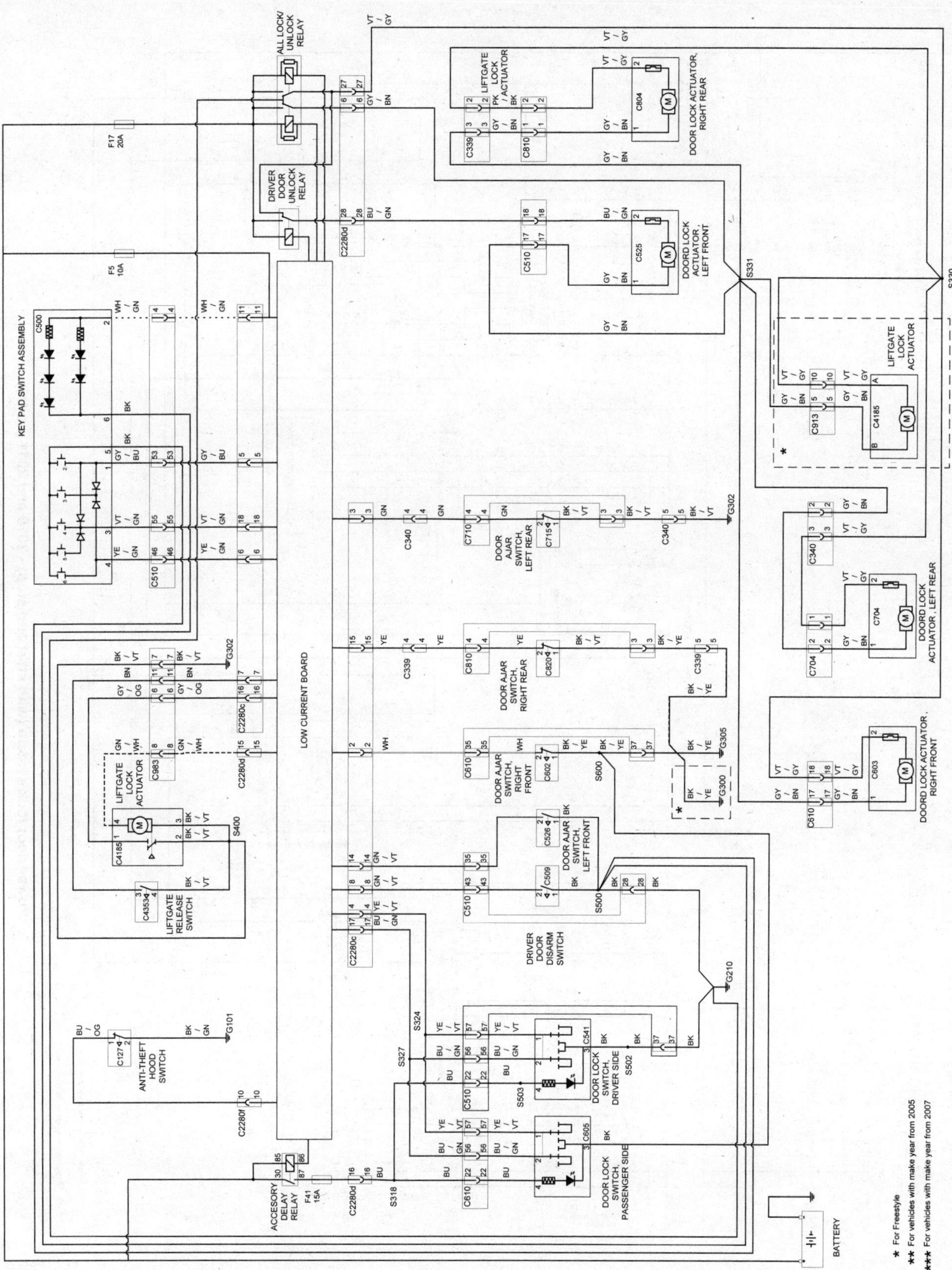

Power door lock system - 2008 and 2009 models

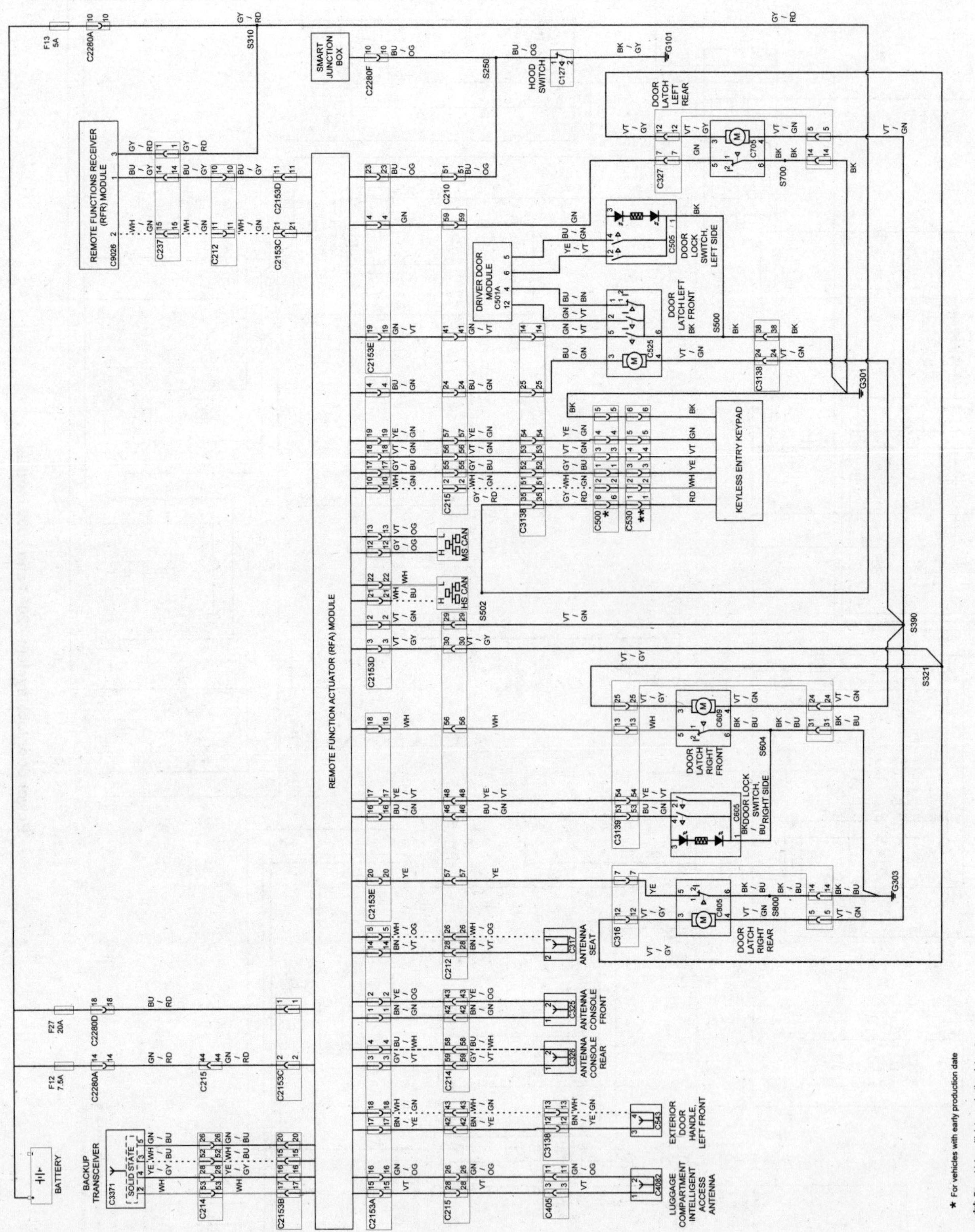

Power door lock system (with start and stop) - 2010 and 2011 models

* For vehicles with early production date

** For vehicles with late production date

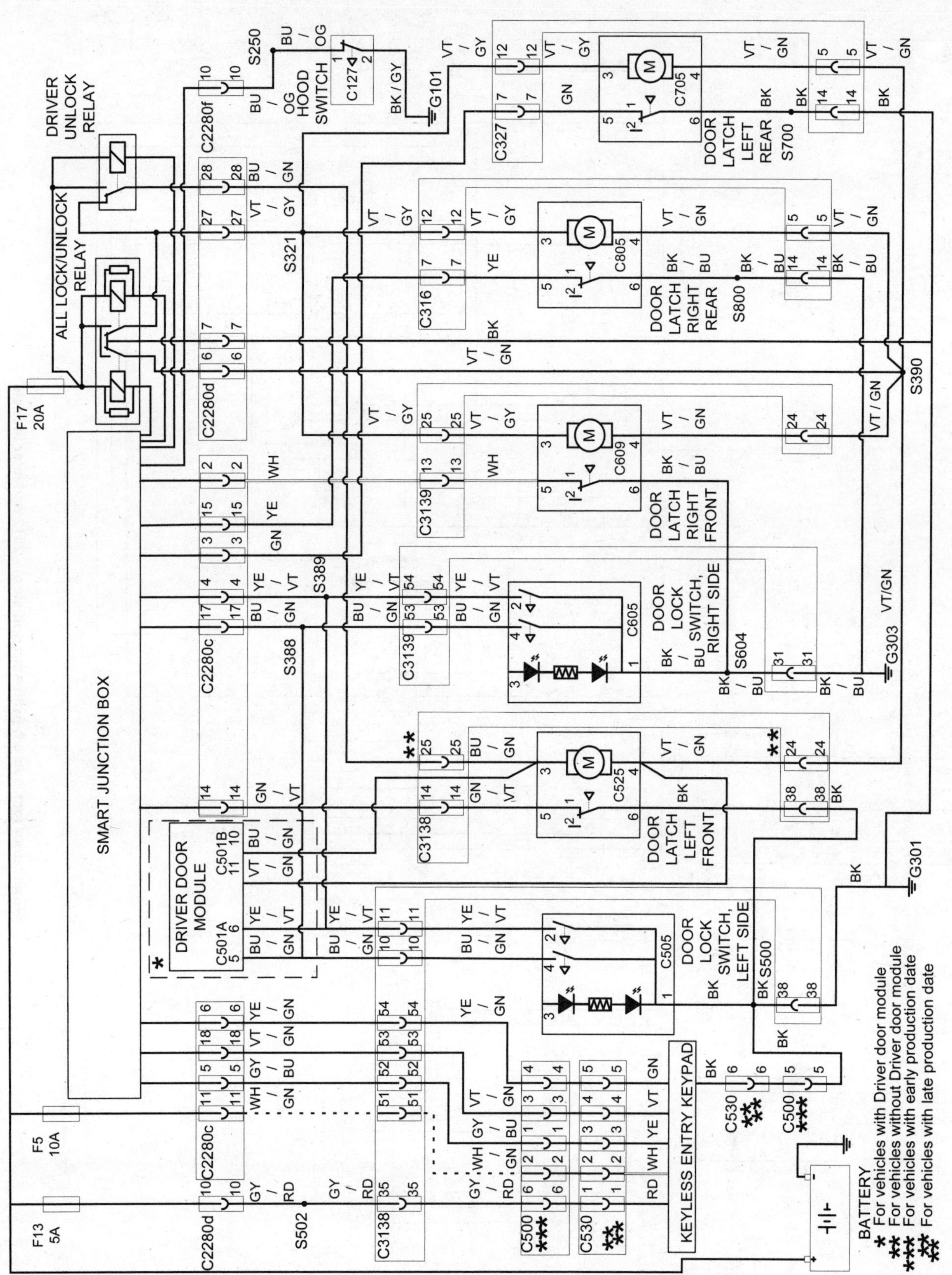

Power door lock system (without start and stop) - 2010 and 2011 models

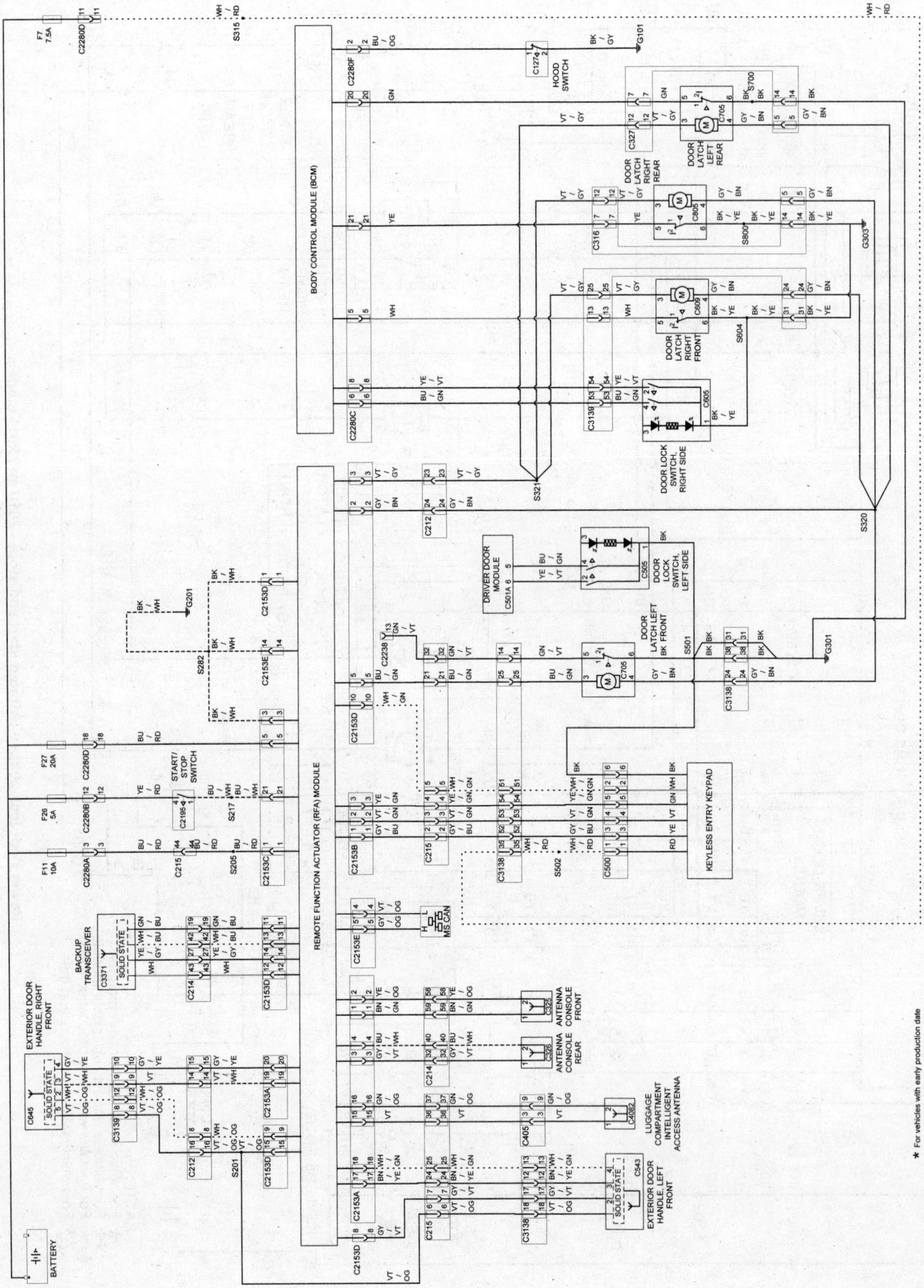

Power door lock system (with start and stop) - 2012 and later models

* For vehicles with early production date

** For vehicles with late production date

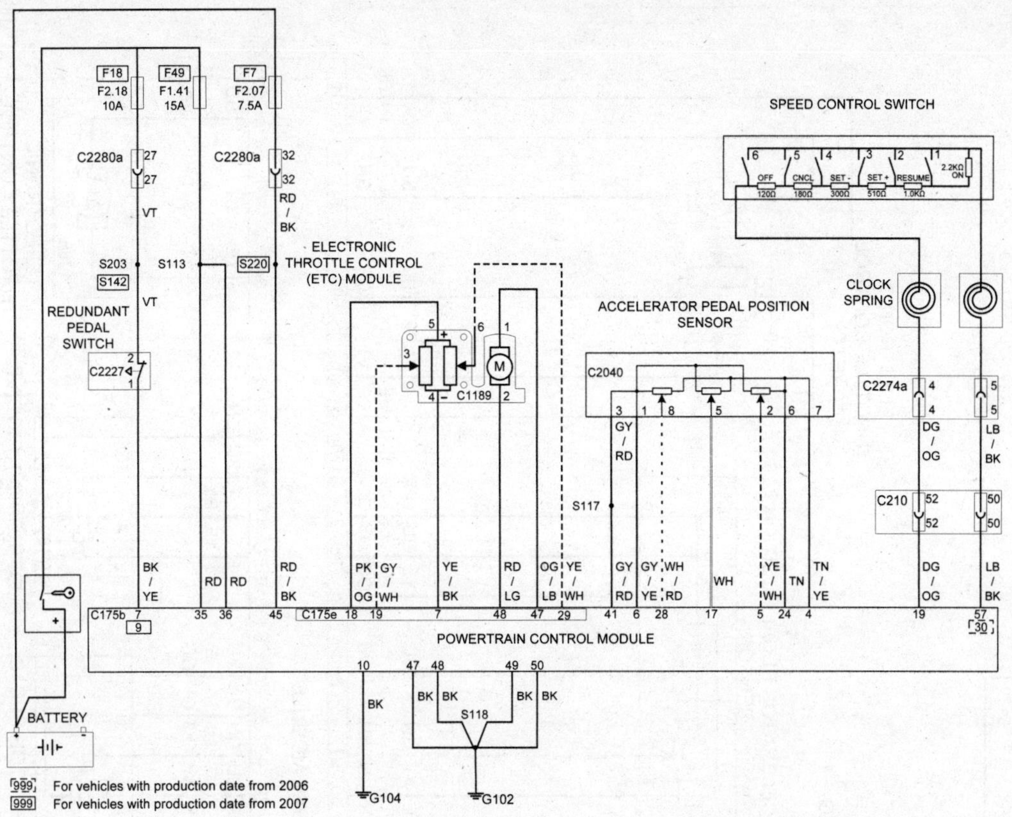

Cruise control system - 2007 and earlier models

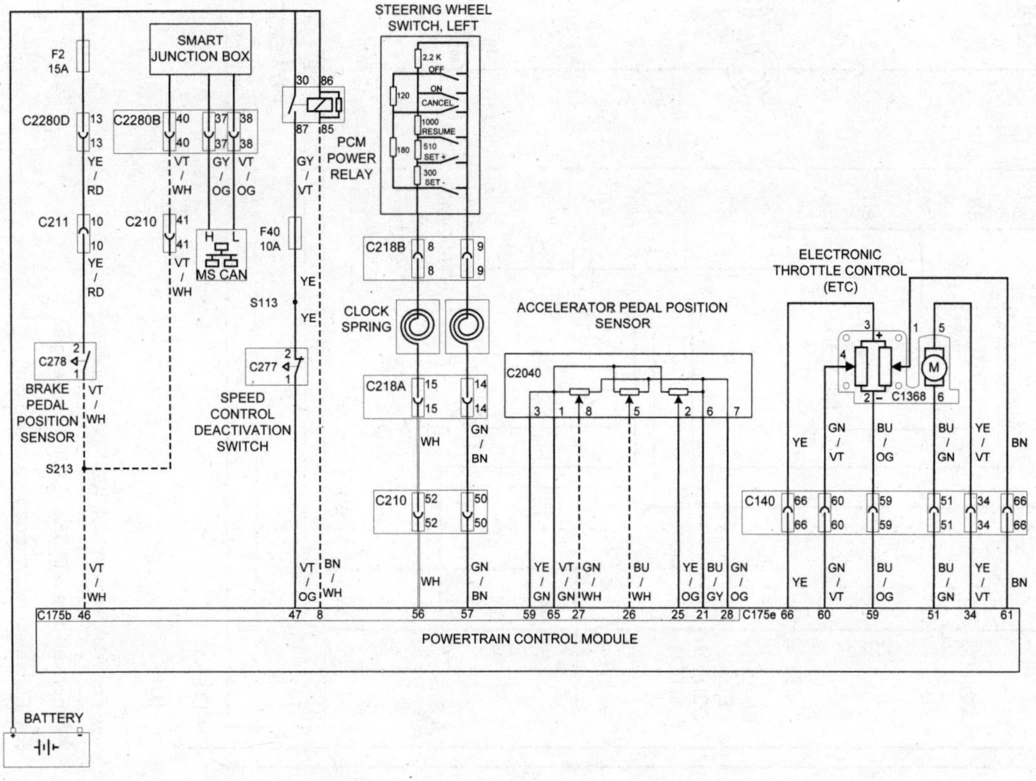

Cruise control system - 2008 and 2009 models

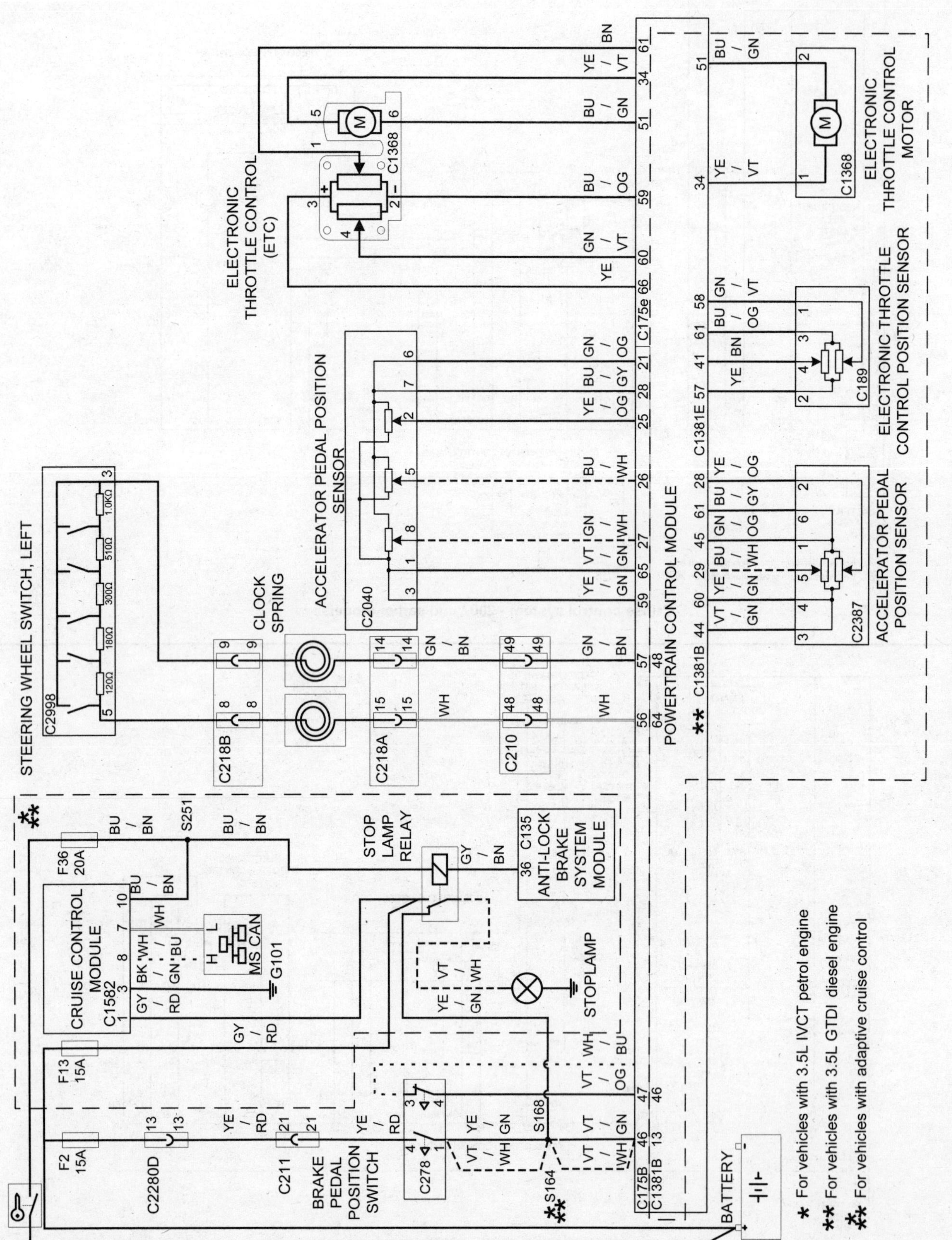

STEERING WHEEL SWITCH, LEFT
C2998
1.0KΩ
510Ω
300Ω
180Ω
120Ω
CLOCK SPRING
ACCELERATOR PEDAL POSITION SENSOR
C2040
ELECTRONIC THROTTLE CONTROL (ETC)
C1368
M
ELECTRONIC THROTTLE CONTROL MOTOR
C1368
M
ELECTRONIC THROTTLE CONTROL POSITION SENSOR
C189
ACCELERATOR PEDAL POSITION SENSOR
C2387
POWERTRAIN CONTROL MODULE
CRUISE CONTROL MODULE
C1582
MS CAN
G101
STOP LAMP RELAY
ANTI-LOCK BRAKE SYSTEM MODULE
C135
STOPLAMP
BRAKE PEDAL POSITION SWITCH
BATTERY
S251
S168
S164
C278
C211
C2280D
F2 15A
F13 15A
F36 20A
C218A
C218B
C210
Cruise control system - 2010 through 2012 models
* For vehicles with 3.5L IVCT petrol engine
** For vehicles with 3.5L GTDI diesel engine
** For vehicles with adaptive cruise control

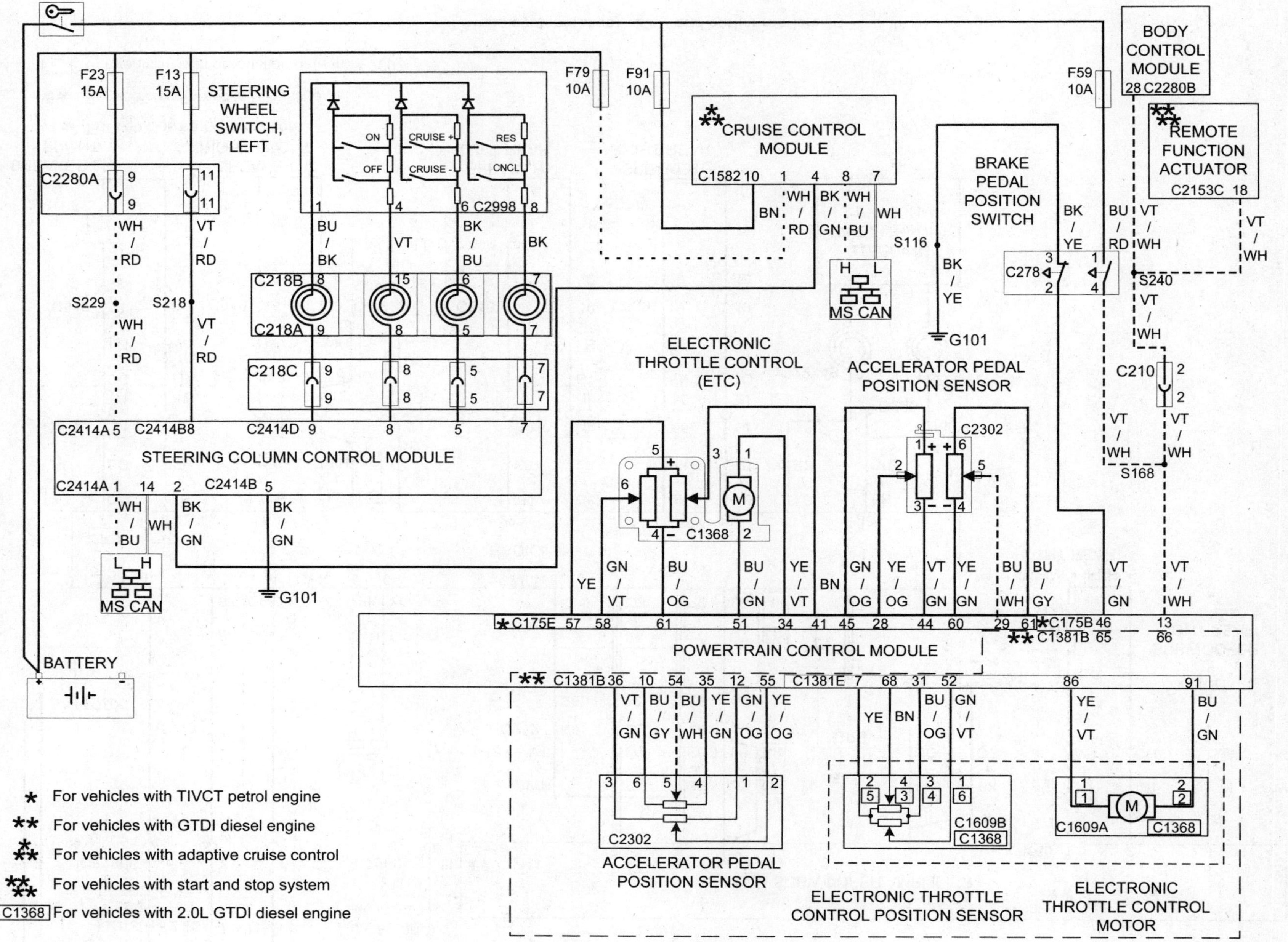

Cruise control system - 2013 and later models

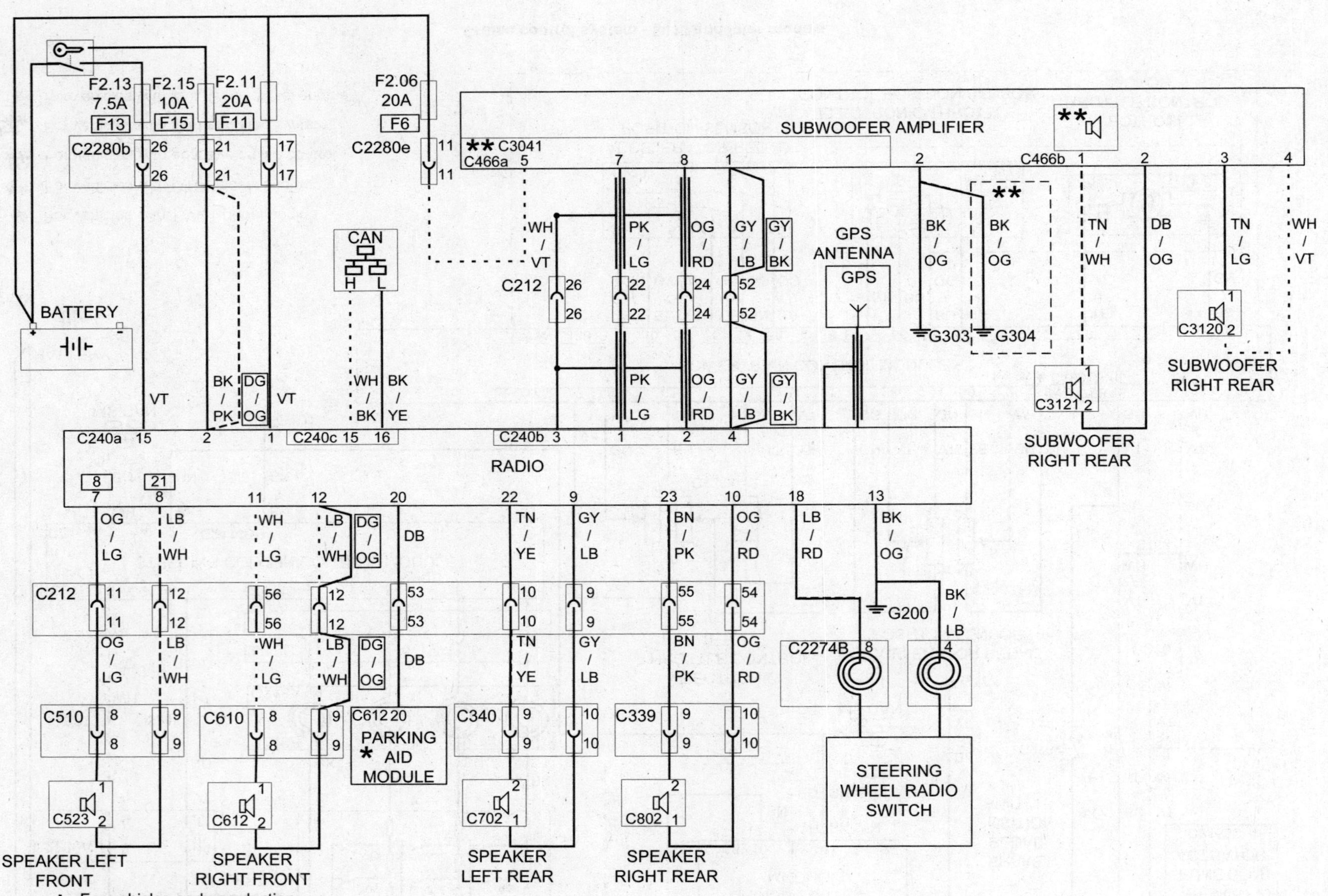

Audio system (base) - 2007 and earlier models

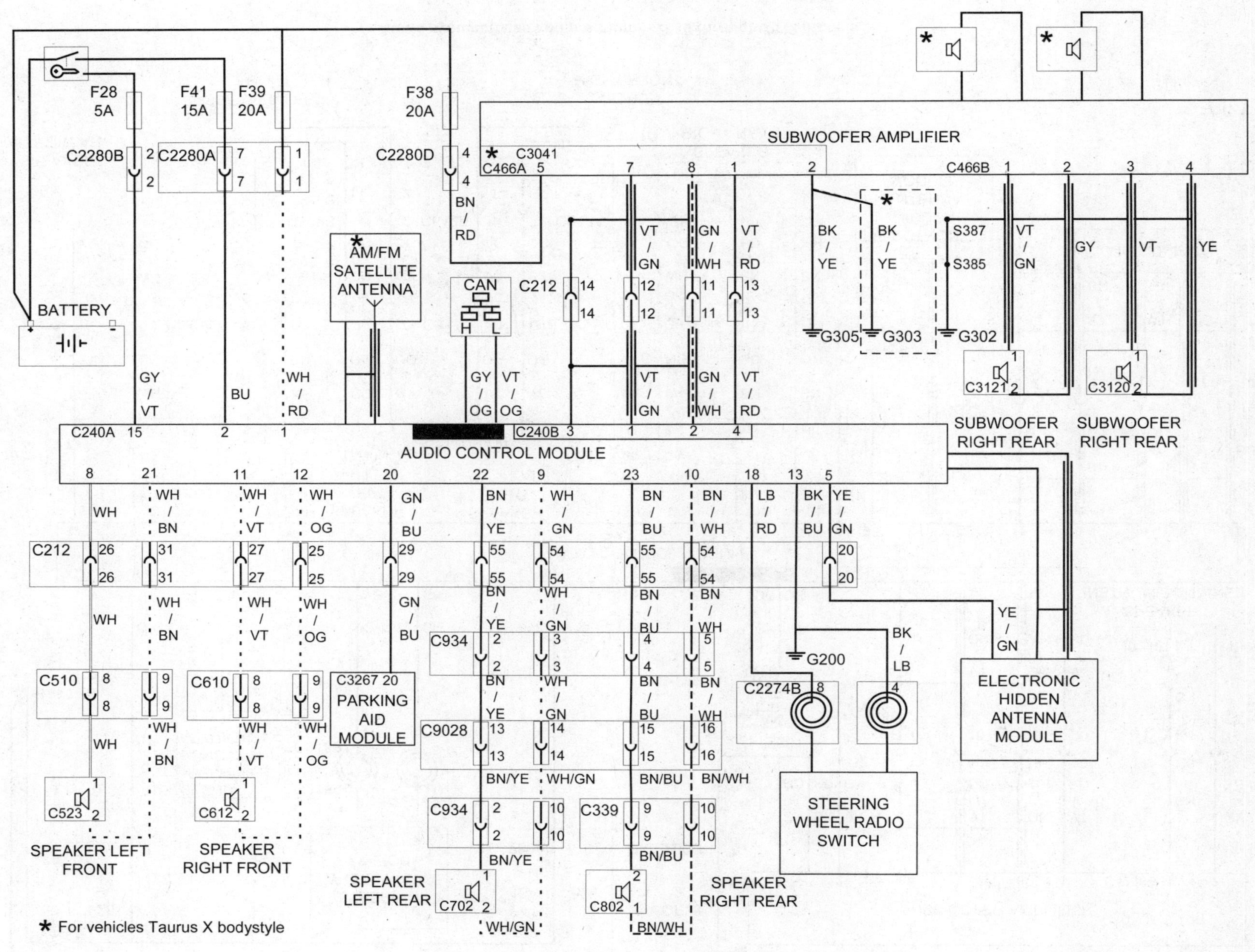

Audio system (base) - 2008 and 2009 models

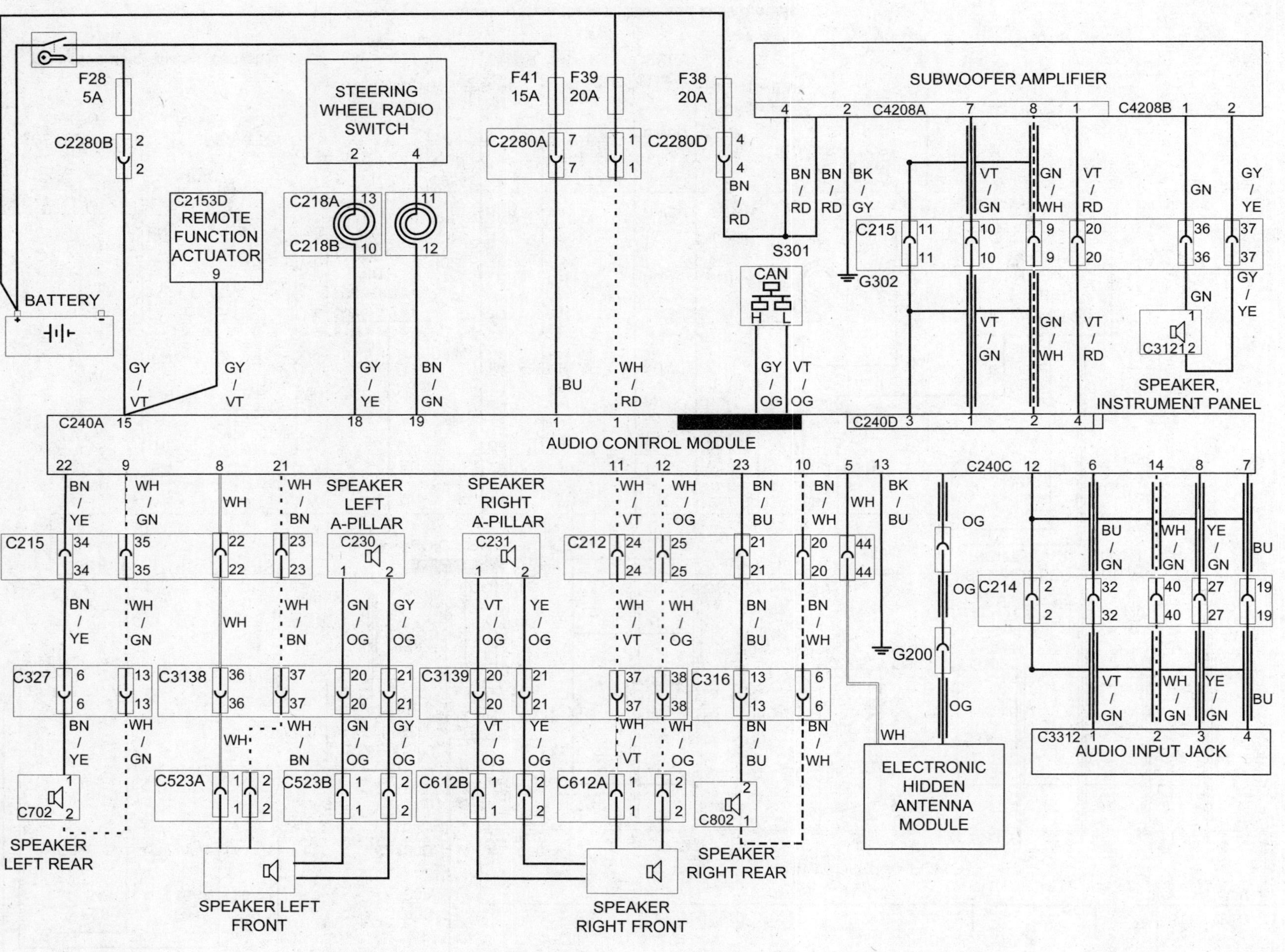
Audio system (base and premium) - 2010 through 2012 models

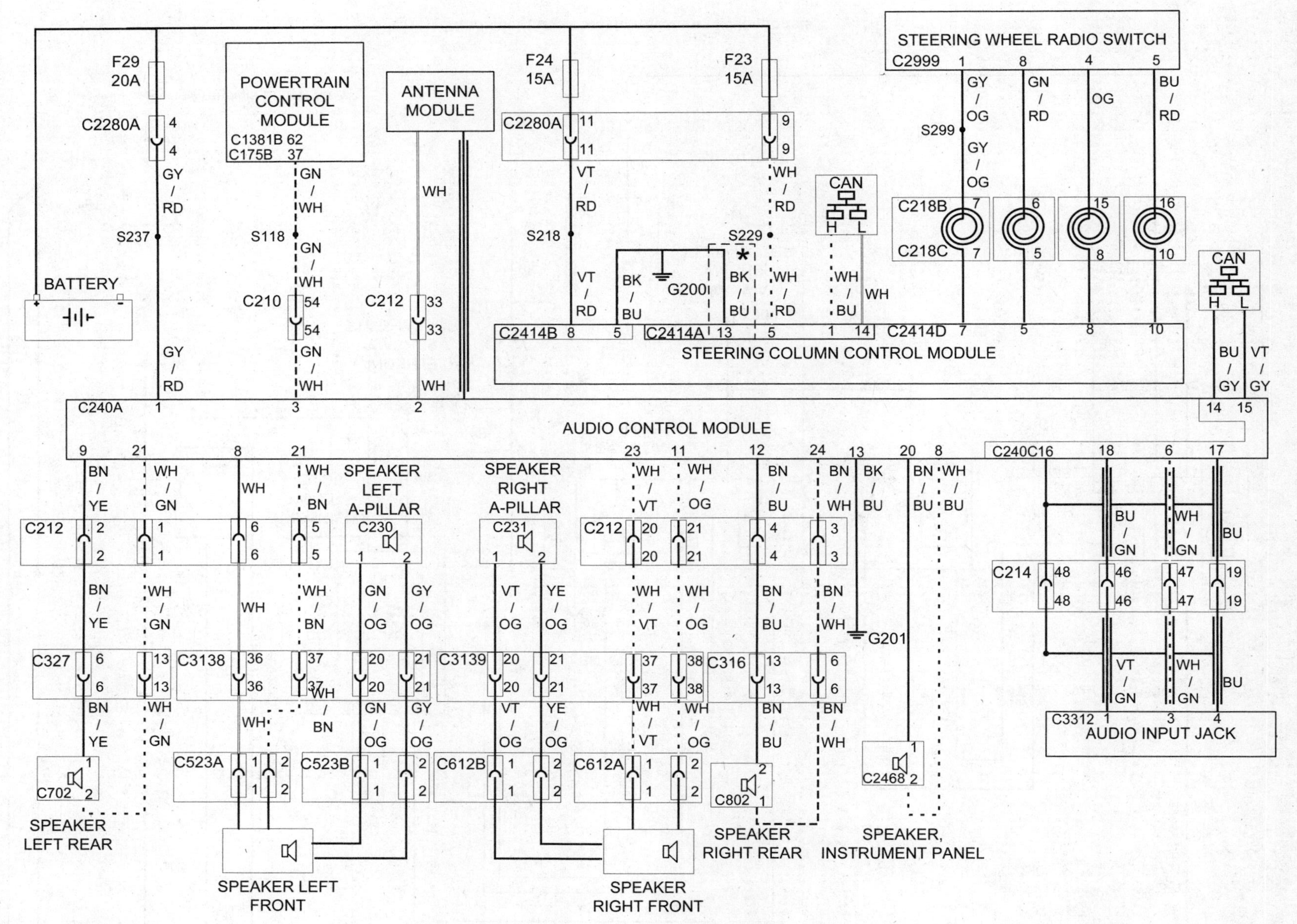

* For vehicles with adjustable steering column

Audio system (base and premium) - 2013 and later models

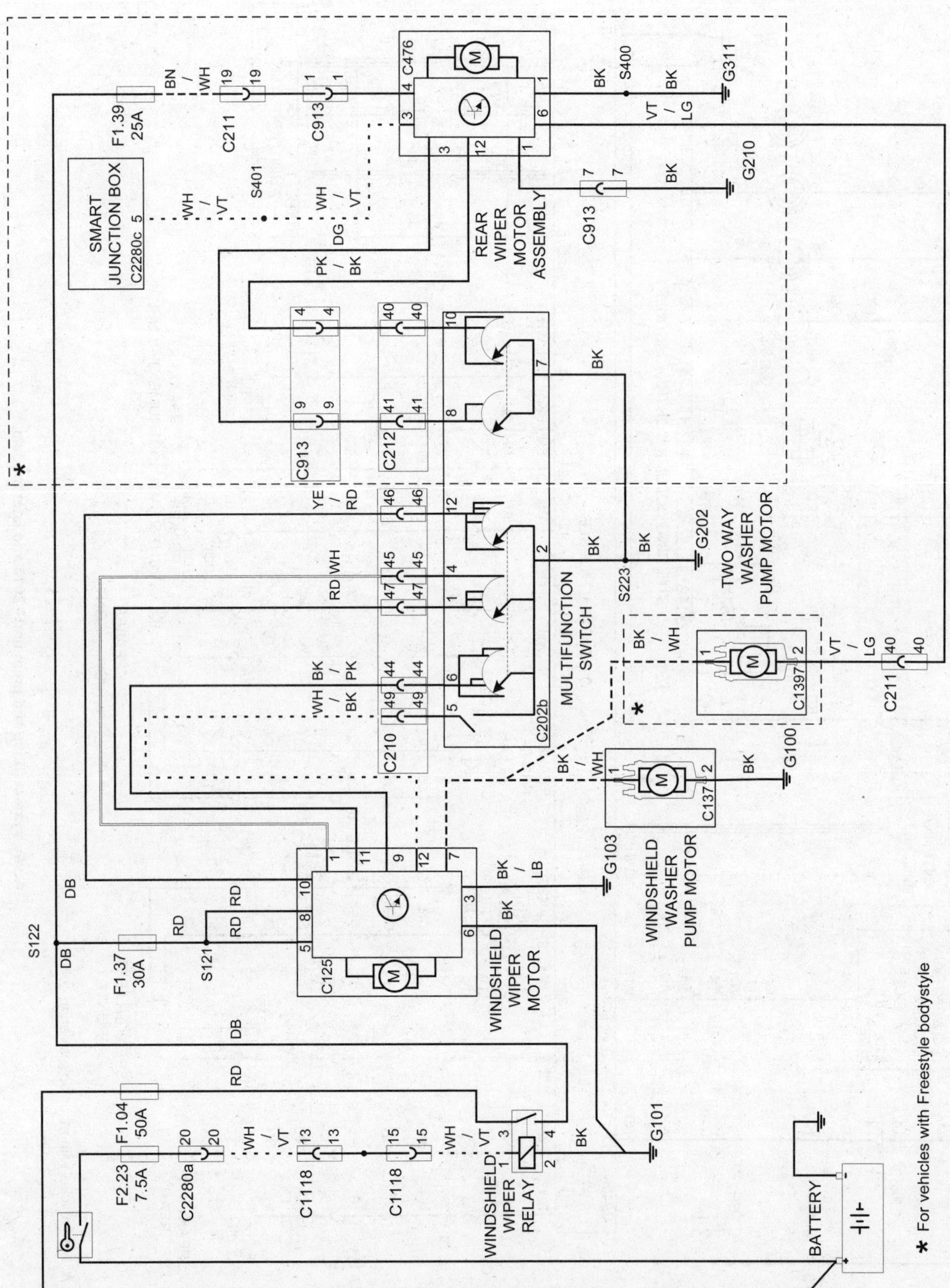

Windshield wiper/washer system - 2005 models

* For vehicles with Freestyle bodystyle

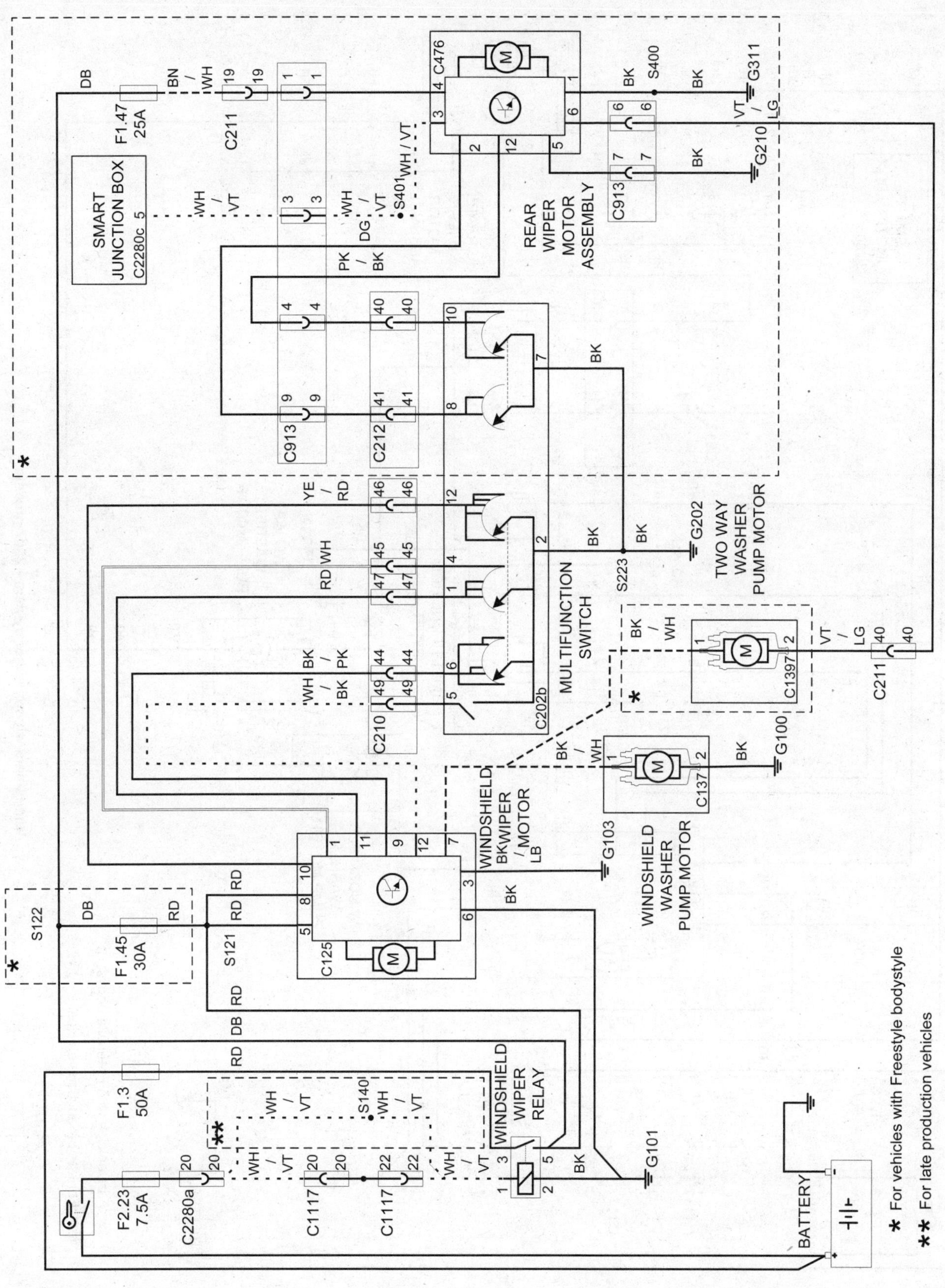

Windshield wiper/washer system - 2006 models

* For vehicles with Freestyle bodystyle

** For late production vehicles

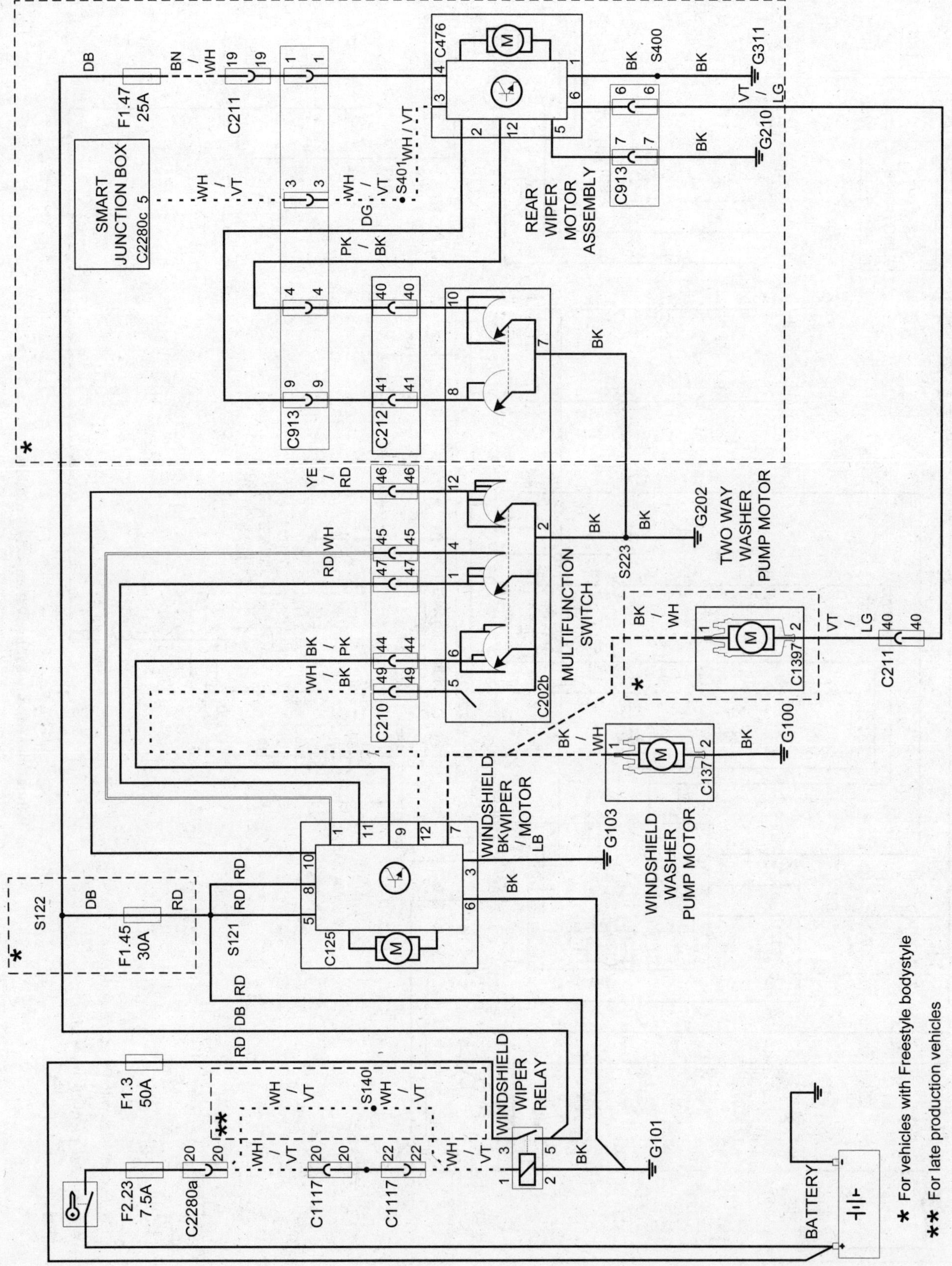

Windshield wiper/washer system - 2007 models
SMART JUNCTION BOX
REAR WIPER MOTOR ASSEMBLY
MULTIFUNCTION SWITCH
TWO WAY WASHER PUMP MOTOR
WINDSHIELD WIPER / MOTOR
WINDSHIELD WASHER PUMP MOTOR
WINDSHIELD WIPER RELAY
BATTERY
* For vehicles with Freestyle bodystyle
** For late production vehicles

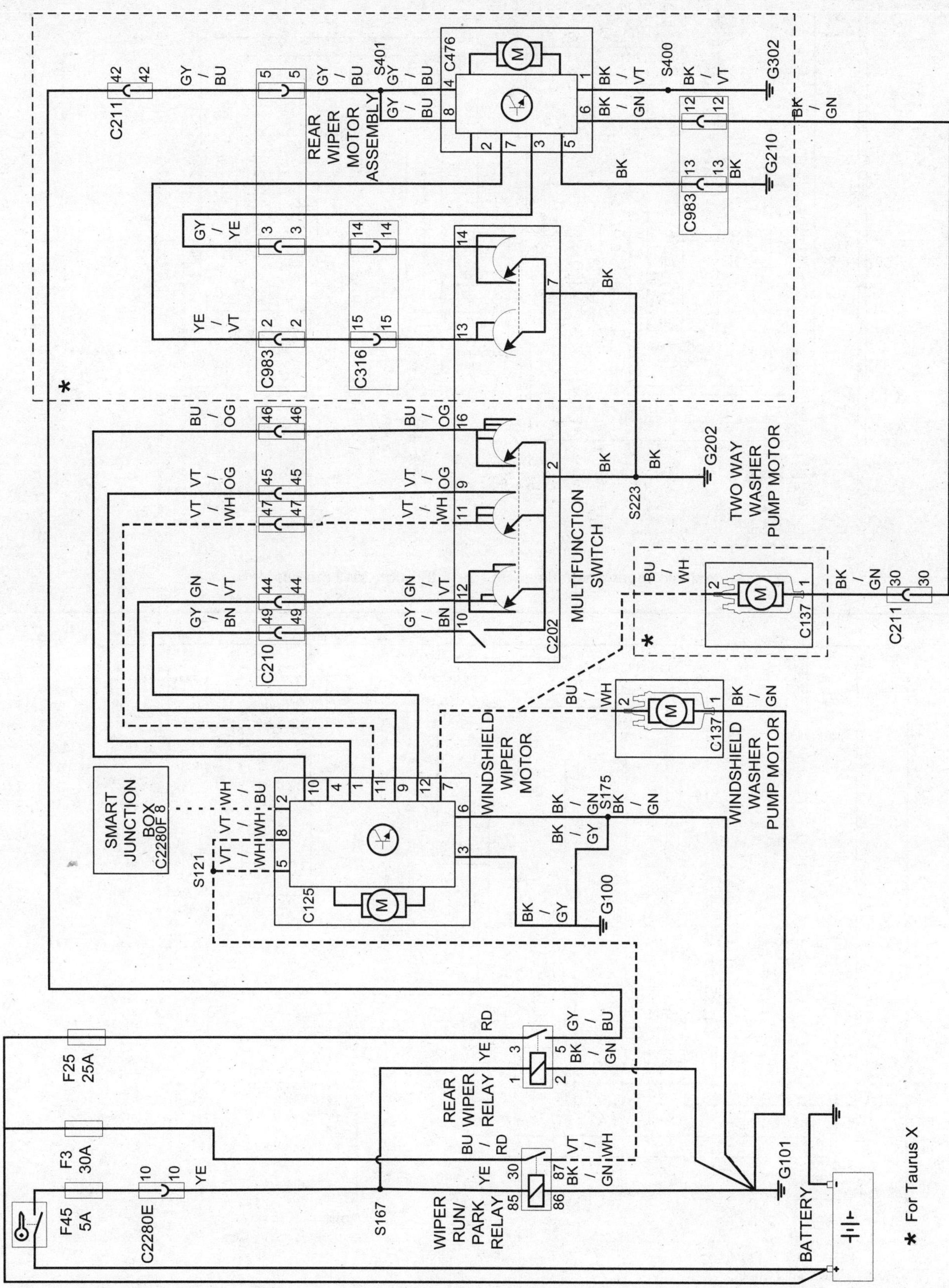

C211
42 42
GY / BU
5 5
REAR WIPER MOTOR ASSEMBLY
GY / BU
S401
GY / BU
8
4 C476
M
GY / BU
2 7 3 5
1
BK / VT
S400
BK / VT
G302
BK / GN
6
12 12
C983
G210
13 13
BK
GY / YE
3 3
14 14
14
7
BK
YE / VT
2 2
C983
15 15
C316
13
G202
TWO WAY WASHER PUMP MOTOR
BU / OGI
46 46
BU / OG
16
BU / WH
2
M
1
C137
BK / GN
30 30
C211
VT / WH OG
45 45
VT / WH OG
9
C210
WINDSHIELD WIPER MOTOR
WINDSHIELD WASHER PUMP MOTOR
Windshield wiper/washer system - 2008 and 2009 models
VT / WH
47 47
VT / WH
11
GY GN / BN VT
44 44
GY GN / BN VT
12
49 49
10
C202
MULTIFUNCTION SWITCH
BK
S223
BK
BU / WH
2
M
1
C137
SMART JUNCTION BOX C2280F 8
VT / VT / WH
2
10 4 1 11 9 12 7
S121
WH WH BU
8
5
6
M
3
C125
BK BK
GY GN
S175
GN
G100
BK / GY
G100
BK / VT
GN WH
F25 25A
YE RD
3
BK GY
2 5
GN BU
1
REAR WIPER RELAY
F3 30A
BU / RD
WIPER RUN/ PARK RELAY
YE
30
85
BK VT
87
86
GN WH
S167
F45 5A
C2280E
10 10
YE
BATTERY
G101
* For Taurus X

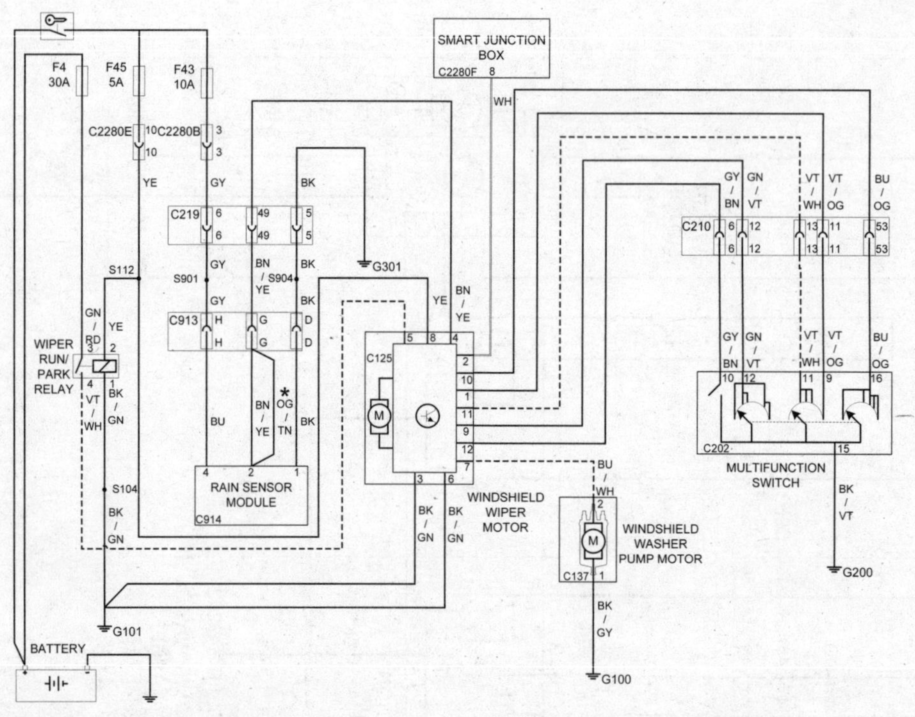

* For vehicles with make year from 2011

Windshield wiper/washer system - 2010 through 2012 models

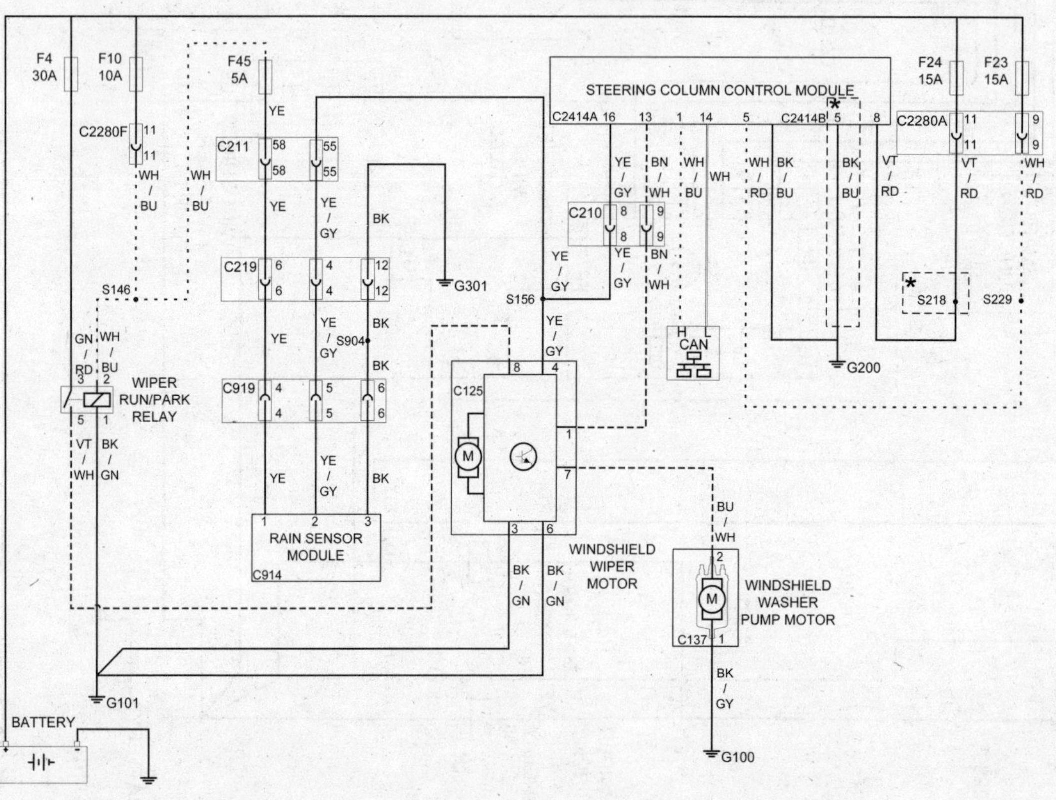

* For vehicles with adjustable steering column

Windshield wiper/washer system - 2013 and later models

Index

Haynes Automotive Manuals

ACURA

- **12020** Integra '86 thru '89 & Legend '86 thru '90
- **12021** Integra '90 thru '93 & Legend '91 thru '95
  Integra '94 thru '00 - *see HONDA Civic (42025)*
  MDX '01 thru '07 - *see HONDA Pilot (42037)*
- **12050** Acura TL all models '99 thru '08

AMC

- **14020** Mid-size models '70 thru '83
- **14025** (Renault) Alliance & Encore '83 thru '87

AUDI

- **15020** 4000 all models '80 thru '87
- **15025** 5000 all models '77 thru '83
- **15026** 5000 all models '84 thru '88
  Audi A4 '96 thru '01 - *see VW Passat (96023)*
- **15030** Audi A4 '02 thru '08

AUSTIN-HEALEY

Sprite - *see MG Midget (66015)*

BMW

- **18020** 3/5 Series '82 thru '92
- **18021** 3-Series incl. Z3 models '92 thru '98
- **18022** 3-Series incl. Z4 models '99 thru '05
- **18023** 3-Series '06 thru '14
- **18025** 320i all 4-cylinder models '75 thru '83
- **18050** 1500 thru 2002 except Turbo '59 thru '77

BUICK

- **19010** Buick Century '97 thru '05
  Century (front-wheel drive) - *see GM (38005)*
- **19020** Buick, Oldsmobile & Pontiac Full-size
  (Front-wheel drive) '85 thru '05
  Buick Electra, LeSabre and Park Avenue;
  Oldsmobile Delta 88 Royale, Ninety Eight
  and Regency; Pontiac Bonneville
- **19025** Buick, Oldsmobile & Pontiac Full-size
  (Rear wheel drive) '70 thru '90
  Buick Estate, Electra, LeSabre, Limited,
  Oldsmobile Custom Cruiser, Delta 88,
  Ninety-eight, Pontiac Bonneville,
  Catalina, Grandville, Parisienne
- **19027** Buick LaCrosse '05 thru '13
  Enclave - *see GENERAL MOTORS (38001)*
  Rainier - *see CHEVROLET (24072)*
  Regal - *see GENERAL MOTORS (38010)*
  Riviera - *see GENERAL MOTORS (38030, 38031)*
  Roadmaster - *see CHEVROLET (24046)*
  Skyhawk - *see GENERAL MOTORS (38015)*
  Skylark - *see GENERAL MOTORS (38020, 38025)*
  Somerset - *see GENERAL MOTORS (38025)*

CADILLAC

- **21015** CTS & CTS-V '03 thru '14
- **21030** Cadillac Rear Wheel Drive '70 thru '93
  Cimarron - *see GENERAL MOTORS (38015)*
  DeVille - *see GENERAL MOTORS (38031 & 38032)*
  Eldorado - *see GENERAL MOTORS (38030)*
  Fleetwood - *see GENERAL MOTORS (38031)*
  Seville - *see GM (38030, 38031 & 38032)*

CHEVROLET

- **10305** Chevrolet Engine Overhaul Manual
- **24010** Astro & GMC Safari Mini-vans '85 thru '05
- **24013** Aveo '04 thru '11
- **24015** Camaro V8 all models '70 thru '81
- **24016** Camaro all models '82 thru '92
- **24017** Camaro & Firebird '93 thru '02
  Cavalier - *see GENERAL MOTORS (38016)*
  Celebrity - *see GENERAL MOTORS (38005)*
- **24018** Camaro '10 thru '15
- **24020** Chevelle, Malibu & El Camino '69 thru '87
  Cobalt - *see GENERAL MOTORS (38017)*
- **24024** Chevette & Pontiac T1000 '76 thru '87
  Citation - *see GENERAL MOTORS (38020)*
- **24027** Colorado & GMC Canyon '04 thru '12
- **24032** Corsica & Beretta all models '87 thru '96
- **24040** Corvette all V8 models '68 thru '82
- **24041** Corvette all models '84 thru '96
- **24042** Corvette all models '97 thru '13
- **24044** Cruze '11 thru '19
- **24045** Full-size Sedans Caprice, Impala, Biscayne,
  Bel Air & Wagons '69 thru '90
- **24046** Impala SS & Caprice and Buick Roadmaster
  '91 thru '96
  Impala '00 thru '05 - *see LUMINA (24048)*
- **24047** Impala & Monte Carlo all models '06 thru '11
  Lumina '90 thru '94 - *see GM (38010)*
- **24048** Lumina & Monte Carlo '95 thru '05
  Lumina APV - *see GM (38035)*
- **24050** Luv Pick-up all 2WD & 4WD '72 thru '82
- **24051** Malibu '13 thru '19
- **24055** Monte Carlo all models '70 thru '88
  Monte Carlo '95 thru '01 - *see LUMINA (24048)*
- **24059** Nova all V8 models '69 thru '79
- **24060** Nova and Geo Prizm '85 thru '92
- **24064** Pick-ups '67 thru '87 - Chevrolet & GMC
- **24065** Pick-ups '88 thru '98 - Chevrolet & GMC
- **24066** Pick-ups '99 thru '06 - Chevrolet & GMC
- **24067** Chevrolet Silverado & GMC Sierra '07 thru '14
- **24068** Chevrolet Silverado & GMC Sierra '14 thru '19
- **24070** S-10 & S-15 Pick-ups '82 thru '93,
  Blazer & Jimmy '83 thru '94,
- **24071** S-10 & Sonoma Pick-ups '94 thru '04,
  including Blazer, Jimmy & Hombre
- **24072** Chevrolet TrailBlazer, GMC Envoy &
  Oldsmobile Bravada '02 thru '09
- **24075** Sprint '85 thru '88 & Geo Metro '89 thru '01
- **24080** Vans - Chevrolet & GMC '68 thru '96
- **24081** Chevrolet Express & GMC Savana
  Full-size Vans '96 thru '19

CHRYSLER

- **10310** Chrysler Engine Overhaul Manual
- **25015** Chrysler Cirrus, Dodge Stratus,
  Plymouth Breeze '95 thru '00
- **25020** Full-size Front-Wheel Drive '88 thru '93
  K-Cars - *see DODGE Aries (30008)*
  Laser - *see DODGE Daytona (30030)*
- **25025** Chrysler LHS, Concorde, New Yorker,
  Dodge Intrepid, Eagle Vision, '93 thru '97
- **25026** Chrysler LHS, Concorde, 300M,
  Dodge Intrepid, '98 thru '04
- **25027** Chrysler 300 '05 thru '18, Dodge Charger
  '06 thru '18, Magnum '05 thru '08 &
  Challenger '08 thru '18
- **25030** Chrysler & Plymouth Mid-size
  front wheel drive '82 thru '95
  Rear-wheel Drive - *see Dodge (30050)*
- **25035** PT Cruiser all models '01 thru '10
- **25040** Chrysler Sebring '95 thru '06, Dodge Stratus
  '01 thru '06 & Dodge Avenger '95 thru '00
- **25041** Chrysler Sebring '07 thru '10, 200 '11 thru '17
  Dodge Avenger '08 thru '14

DATSUN

- **28005** 200SX all models '80 thru '83
- **28012** 240Z, 260Z & 280Z Coupe '70 thru '78
- **28014** 280ZX Coupe & 2+2 '79 thru '83
  300ZX - *see NISSAN (72010)*
- **28018** 510 & PL521 Pick-up '68 thru '73
- **28020** 510 all models '78 thru '81
- **28022** 620 Series Pick-up all models '73 thru '79
  720 Series Pick-up - *see NISSAN (72030)*

DODGE

- **400 & 600** - *see CHRYSLER (25030)*
- **30008** Aries & Plymouth Reliant '81 thru '89
- **30010** Caravan & Plymouth Voyager '84 thru '95
- **30011** Caravan & Plymouth Voyager '96 thru '02
- **30012** Challenger & Plymouth Sapporro '78 thru '83
- **30013** Caravan, Chrysler Voyager &
  Town & Country '03 thru '07
- **30014** Grand Caravan &
  Chrysler Town & Country '08 thru '18
- **30016** Colt & Plymouth Champ '78 thru '87
- **30020** Dakota Pick-ups all models '87 thru '96
- **30021** Durango '98 & '99 & Dakota '97 thru '99
- **30022** Durango '00 thru '03 & Dakota '00 thru '04
- **30023** Durango '04 thru '09 & Dakota '05 thru '11
- **30025** Dart, Demon, Plymouth Barracuda,
  Duster & Valiant 6-cylinder models '67 thru '76
- **30030** Daytona & Chrysler Laser '84 thru '89
  Intrepid - *see CHRYSLER (25025, 25026)*
- **30034** Neon all models '95 thru '99
- **30035** Omni & Plymouth Horizon '78 thru '90
- **30036** Dodge & Plymouth Neon '00 thru '05
- **30040** Pick-ups full-size models '74 thru '93
- **30042** Pick-ups full-size models '94 thru '08
- **30043** Pick-ups full-size models '09 thru '18
- **30045** Ram 50/D50 Pick-ups & Raider and
  Plymouth Arrow Pick-ups '79 thru '93
- **30050** Dodge/Plymouth/Chrysler RWD '71 thru '89
- **30055** Shadow & Plymouth Sundance '87 thru '94
- **30060** Spirit & Plymouth Acclaim '89 thru '95
- **30065** Vans - Dodge & Plymouth '71 thru '03

EAGLE

Talon - *see MITSUBISHI (68030, 68031)*
Vision - *see CHRYSLER (25025)*

FIAT

- **34010** 124 Sport Coupe & Spider '68 thru '78
- **34025** X1/9 all models '74 thru '80

FORD

- **10320** Ford Engine Overhaul Manual
- **10355** Ford Automatic Transmission Overhaul
- **11500** Mustang '64-1/2 thru '70 Restoration Guide
- **36004** Aerostar Mini-vans all models '86 thru '97
- **36006** Contour & Mercury Mystique '95 thru '00
- **36008** Courier Pick-up all models '72 thru '82
- **36012** Crown Victoria &
  Mercury Grand Marquis '88 thru '11
- **36014** Edge '07 thru '19 & Lincoln MKX '07 thru '18
- **36016** Escort & Mercury Lynx all models '81 thru '90
- **36020** Escort & Mercury Tracer '91 thru '02
- **36022** Escape '01 thru '17, Mazda Tribute '01 thru '11,
  & Mercury Mariner '05 thru '11
- **36024** Explorer & Mazda Navajo '91 thru '01
- **36025** Explorer & Mercury Mountaineer '02 thru '10
- **36026** Explorer '11 thru '17
- **36028** Fairmont & Mercury Zephyr '78 thru '83
- **36030** Festiva & Aspire '88 thru '97
- **36032** Fiesta all models '77 thru '80
- **36034** Focus all models '00 thru '11
- **36035** Focus '12 thru '14
- **36045** Fusion '06 thru '14 & Mercury Milan '06 thru '11
- **36048** Mustang V8 all models '64-1/2 thru '73
- **36049** Mustang II 4-cylinder, V6 & V8 models '74 thru '78
- **36050** Mustang & Mercury Capri '79 thru '93
- **36051** Mustang all models '94 thru '04
- **36052** Mustang '05 thru '14
- **36054** Pick-ups & Bronco '73 thru '79
- **36058** Pick-ups & Bronco '80 thru '96
- **36059** F-150 '97 thru '03, Expedition '97 thru '17,
  F-250 '97 thru '99, F-150 Heritage '04
  & Lincoln Navigator '98 thru '17
- **36060** Super Duty Pick-ups & Excursion '99 thru '10
- **36061** F-150 full-size '04 thru '14
- **36062** Pinto & Mercury Bobcat '75 thru '80
- **36063** F-150 full-size '15 thru '17
- **36064** Super Duty Pick-ups '11 thru '16
- **36066** Probe all models '89 thru '92
  Probe '93 thru '97 - *see MAZDA 626 (61042)*
- **36070** Ranger & Bronco II gas models '83 thru '92
- **36071** Ranger '93 thru '11 & Mazda Pick-ups '94 thru '09
- **36074** Taurus & Mercury Sable '86 thru '95
- **36075** Taurus & Mercury Sable '96 thru '07
- **36076** Taurus '08 thru '14, Five Hundred '05 thru '07,
  Mercury Montego '05 thru '07 & Sable '08 thru '09
- **36078** Tempo & Mercury Topaz '84 thru '94
- **36082** Thunderbird & Mercury Cougar '83 thru '88
- **36086** Thunderbird & Mercury Cougar '89 thru '97
- **36090** Vans all V8 Econoline models '69 thru '91
- **36094** Vans full size '92 thru '14
- **36097** Windstar '95 thru '03, Freestar & Mercury
  Monterey Mini-van '04 thru '07

GENERAL MOTORS

- **10360** GM Automatic Transmission Overhaul
- **38001** GMC Acadia '07 thru '16, Buick Enclave
  '08 thru '17, Saturn Outlook '07 thru '10
  & Chevrolet Traverse '09 thru '17
- **38005** Buick Century, Chevrolet Celebrity,
  Oldsmobile Cutlass Ciera & Pontiac 6000
  all models '82 thru '96
- **38010** Buick Regal '88 thru '04, Chevrolet Lumina
  '88 thru '04, Oldsmobile Cutlass Supreme
  '88 thru '97 & Pontiac Grand Prix '88 thru '07
- **38015** Buick Skyhawk, Cadillac Cimarron,
  Chevrolet Cavalier, Oldsmobile Firenza,
  Pontiac J-2000 & Sunbird '82 thru '94
- **38016** Chevrolet Cavalier & Pontiac Sunfire '95 thru '05
- **38017** Chevrolet Cobalt '05 thru '10, HHR '06 thru '11,
  Pontiac G5 '07 thru '09, Pursuit '05 thru '06
  & Saturn ION '03 thru '07
- **38020** Buick Skylark, Chevrolet Citation,
  Oldsmobile Omega, Pontiac Phoenix '80 thru '85
- **38025** Buick Skylark '86 thru '98, Somerset '85 thru '87,
  Oldsmobile Achieva '92 thru '98, Calais '85 thru '91,
  & Pontiac Grand Am all models '85 thru '98
- **38026** Chevrolet Malibu '97 thru '03, Classic '04 thru '05,
  Oldsmobile Alero '99 thru '03, Cutlass '97 thru '00,
  & Pontiac Grand Am '99 thru '03
- **38027** Chevrolet Malibu '04 thru '12, Pontiac G6
  '05 thru '10 & Saturn Aura '07 thru '10
- **38030** Cadillac Eldorado, Seville, Oldsmobile
  Toronado & Buick Riviera '71 thru '85
- **38031** Cadillac Eldorado, Seville, DeVille, Fleetwood,
  Oldsmobile Toronado & Buick Riviera '86 thru '93
- **38032** Cadillac DeVille '94 thru '05, Seville '92 thru '04
  & Cadillac DTS '06 thru '10
- **38035** Chevrolet Lumina APV, Oldsmobile Silhouette
  & Pontiac Trans Sport all models '90 thru '96
- **38036** Chevrolet Venture '97 thru '05, Oldsmobile
  Silhouette '97 thru '04, Pontiac Trans Sport
  '97 thru '98 & Montana '99 thru '05
- **38040** Chevrolet Equinox '05 thru '17, GMC Terrain
  '10 thru '17 & Pontiac Torrent '06 thru '09

GEO

Metro - *see CHEVROLET Sprint (24075)*
Prizm - '85 thru '92 *see CHEVY (24060)*,
'93 thru '02 *see TOYOTA Corolla (92036)*
- **40030** Storm all models '90 thru '93
  Tracker - *see SUZUKI Samurai (90010)*

(Continued on other side)

Haynes Automotive Manuals (continued)

*NOTE: If you do not see a listing for your vehicle, please visit **haynes.com** for the latest product information and check out our **Online Manuals!***

GMC

Acadia - *see GENERAL MOTORS (38001)*
Pick-ups - *see CHEVROLET (24027, 24068)*
Vans - *see CHEVROLET (24081)*

HONDA

42010 **Accord CVCC** all models '76 thru '83
42011 **Accord** all models '84 thru '89
42012 **Accord** all models '90 thru '93
42013 **Accord** all models '94 thru '97
42014 **Accord** all models '98 thru '02
42015 **Accord** '03 thru '12 **& Crosstour** '10 thru '14
42016 **Accord** '13 thru '17
42020 **Civic 1200** all models '73 thru '79
42021 **Civic 1300 & 1500 CVCC** '80 thru '83
42022 **Civic 1500 CVCC** all models '75 thru '79
42023 **Civic** all models '84 thru '91
42024 **Civic & del Sol** '92 thru '95
42025 **Civic** '96 thru '00, **CR-V** '97 thru '01
& **Acura Integra** '94 thru '00
42026 **Civic** '01 thru '11 **& CR-V** '02 thru '11
42027 **Civic** '12 thru '15 **& CR-V** '12 thru '16
42030 **Fit** '07 thru '13
42035 **Odyssey** all models '99 thru '10
Passport - *see ISUZU Rodeo (47017)*
42037 **Honda Pilot** '03 thru '08, **Ridgeline** '06 thru '14
& Acura MDX '01 thru '07
42040 **Prelude CVCC** all models '79 thru '89

HYUNDAI

43010 **Elantra** all models '96 thru '19
43015 **Excel & Accent** all models '86 thru '13
43050 **Santa Fe** all models '01 thru '12
43055 **Sonata** all models '99 thru '14

INFINITI

G35 '03 thru '08 - *see NISSAN 350Z (72011)*

ISUZU

Hombre - *see CHEVROLET S-10 (24071)*
47017 **Rodeo** '91 thru '02, **Amigo** '89 thru '94 & '98 thru '02
& Honda Passport '95 thru '02
47020 **Trooper** '84 thru '91 **& Pick-up** '81 thru '93

JAGUAR

49010 **XJ6** all 6-cylinder models '68 thru '86
49011 **XJ6** all models '88 thru '94
49015 **XJ12 & XJS** all 12-cylinder models '72 thru '85

JEEP

50010 **Cherokee, Comanche & Wagoneer Limited**
all models '84 thru '01
50011 **Cherokee** '14 thru '19
50020 **CJ** all models '49 thru '86
50025 **Grand Cherokee** all models '93 thru '04
50026 **Grand Cherokee** '05 thru '19
& Dodge Durango '11 thru '19
50029 **Grand Wagoneer & Pick-up** '72 thru '91
Grand Wagoneer '84 thru '91, Cherokee &
Wagoneer '72 thru '83, Pick-up '72 thru '88
50030 **Wrangler** all models '87 thru '17
50035 **Liberty** '02 thru '12 **& Dodge Nitro** '07 thru '11
50050 **Patriot & Compass** '07 thru '17

KIA

54050 **Optima** '01 thru '10
54060 **Sedona** '02 thru '14
54070 **Sephia** '94 thru '01, **Spectra** '00 thru '09,
Sportage '05 thru '20
54077 **Sorento** '03 thru '13

LEXUS

ES 300/330 - *see TOYOTA Camry (92007, 92008)*
ES 350 - *see TOYOTA Camry (92009)*
RX 300/330/350 - *see TOYOTA Highlander (92095)*

LINCOLN

MKX - *see FORD (36014)*
Navigator - *see FORD Pick-up (36059)*
59010 **Rear-Wheel Drive Continental** '70 thru '87,
Mark Series '70 thru '92 **& Town Car** '81 thru '10

MAZDA

61010 **GLC (rear-wheel drive)** '77 thru '83
61011 **GLC (front-wheel drive)** '81 thru '85
61012 **Mazda3** '04 thru '11
61015 **323 & Protegé** '90 thru '03
61016 **MX-5 Miata** '90 thru '14
61020 **MPV** all models '89 thru '98
Navajo - *see Ford Explorer (36024)*
61030 **Pick-ups** '72 thru '93
Pick-ups '94 thru '09 - *see Ford Ranger (36071)*
61035 **RX-7** all models '79 thru '85
61036 **RX-7** all models '86 thru '91
61040 **626 (rear-wheel drive)** all models '79 thru '82
61041 **626 & MX-6 (front-wheel drive)** '83 thru '92
61042 **626** '93 thru '01 **& MX-6/Ford Probe** '93 thru '02
61043 **Mazda6** '03 thru '13

MERCEDES-BENZ

63012 **123 Series Diesel** '76 thru '85
63015 **190 Series** 4-cylinder gas models '84 thru '88
63020 **230/250/280** 6-cylinder SOHC models '68 thru '72
63025 **280 123 Series** gas models '77 thru '81
63030 **350 & 450** all models '71 thru '80
63040 **C-Class:** C230/C240/C280/C320/C350 '01 thru '07

MERCURY

64200 **Villager & Nissan Quest** '93 thru '01
All other titles, see FORD Listing.

MG

66010 **MGB** Roadster & GT Coupe '62 thru '80
66015 **MG Midget, Austin Healey Sprite** '58 thru '80

MINI

67020 **Mini** '02 thru '13

MITSUBISHI

68020 **Cordia, Tredia, Galant, Precis & Mirage** '83 thru '93
68030 **Eclipse, Eagle Talon & Plymouth Laser** '90 thru '94
68031 **Eclipse** '95 thru '05 **& Eagle Talon** '95 thru '98
68035 **Galant** '94 thru '12
68040 **Pick-up** '83 thru '96 **& Montero** '83 thru '93

NISSAN

72010 **300ZX** all models including Turbo '84 thru '89
72011 **350Z & Infiniti G35** all models '03 thru '08
72015 **Altima** all models '93 thru '06
72016 **Altima** '07 thru '12
72020 **Maxima** all models '85 thru '92
72021 **Maxima** all models '93 thru '08
72025 **Murano** '03 thru '14
72030 **Pick-ups** '80 thru '97 **& Pathfinder** '87 thru '95
72031 **Frontier** '98 thru '04, **Xterra** '00 thru '04,
& Pathfinder '96 thru '04
72032 **Frontier & Xterra** '05 thru '14
72037 **Pathfinder** '05 thru '14
72040 **Pulsar** all models '83 thru '86
72042 **Roque** all models '08 thru '20
72050 **Sentra** all models '82 thru '94
72051 **Sentra & 200SX** all models '95 thru '06
72060 **Stanza** all models '82 thru '90
72070 **Titan pick-ups** '04 thru '10, **Armada** '05 thru '10
& Pathfinder Armada '04
72080 **Versa** all models '07 thru '19

OLDSMOBILE

73015 **Cutlass V6 & V8 gas models** '74 thru '88
For other OLDSMOBILE titles, see BUICK,
CHEVROLET or GENERAL MOTORS listings.

PLYMOUTH

For PLYMOUTH titles, see DODGE listing.

PONTIAC

79008 **Fiero** all models '84 thru '88
79018 **Firebird** V8 models except Turbo '70 thru '81
79019 **Firebird** all models '82 thru '92
79025 **G6** all models '05 thru '09
79040 **Mid-size Rear-wheel Drive** '70 thru '87
Vibe '03 thru '10 - *see TOYOTA Corolla (92037)*
For other PONTIAC titles, see BUICK,
CHEVROLET or GENERAL MOTORS listings.

PORSCHE

80020 **911** Coupe & Targa models '65 thru '89
80025 **914** all 4-cylinder models '69 thru '76
80030 **924** all models including Turbo '76 thru '82
80035 **944** all models including Turbo '83 thru '89

RENAULT

Alliance & Encore - *see AMC (14025)*

SAAB

84010 **900** all models including Turbo '79 thru '88

SATURN

87010 **Saturn** all S-series models '91 thru '02
Saturn Ion '03 thru '07 - *see GM (38017)*
Saturn Outlook - *see GM (38001)*
87020 **Saturn L-series** all models '00 thru '04
87040 **Saturn VUE** '02 thru '09

SUBARU

89002 **1100, 1300, 1400 & 1600** '71 thru '79
89003 **1600 & 1800** 2WD & 4WD '80 thru '94
89080 **Impreza** '02 thru '11, **WRX** '02 thru '14,
& WRX STI '04 thru '14
89100 **Legacy** all models '90 thru '99
89101 **Legacy & Forester** '00 thru '09
89102 **Legacy** '10 thru '16 **& Forester** '12 thru '16

SUZUKI

90010 **Samurai/Sidekick & Geo Tracker** '86 thru '01

TOYOTA

92005 **Camry** all models '83 thru '91
92006 **Camry** '92 thru '96 **& Avalon** '95 thru '96
92007 **Camry, Avalon, Solara, Lexus ES 300** '97 thru '01

92008 **Camry, Avalon, Lexus ES 300/330** '02 thru '06
& Solara '02 thru '08
92009 **Camry, Avalon & Lexus ES 350** '07 thru '17
92015 **Celica Rear-wheel Drive** '71 thru '85
92020 **Celica Front-wheel Drive** '86 thru '99
92025 **Celica Supra** all models '79 thru '92
92030 **Corolla** all models '75 thru '79
92032 **Corolla** all rear-wheel drive models '80 thru '87
92035 **Corolla** all front-wheel drive models '84 thru '92
92036 **Corolla & Geo/Chevrolet Prizm** '93 thru '02
92037 **Corolla** '03 thru '19, **Matrix** '03 thru '14,
& Pontiac Vibe '03 thru '10
92040 **Corolla Tercel** all models '80 thru '82
92045 **Corona** all models '74 thru '82
92050 **Cressida** all models '78 thru '82
92055 **Land Cruiser** FJ40, 43, 45, 55 '68 thru '82
92056 **Land Cruiser** FJ60, 62, 80, FZJ80 '80 thru '96
92060 **Matrix** '03 thru '11 **& Pontiac Vibe** '03 thru '10
92065 **MR2** all models '85 thru '87
92070 **Pick-up** all models '69 thru '78
92075 **Pick-up** all models '79 thru '95
92076 **Tacoma** '95 thru '04, **4Runner** '96 thru '02
& T100 '93 thru '08
92077 **Tacoma** all models '05 thru '18
92078 **Tundra** '00 thru '06 **& Sequoia** '01 thru '07
92079 **4Runner** all models '03 thru '09
92080 **Previa** all models '91 thru '95
92081 **Prius** all models '01 thru '12
92082 **RAV4** all models '96 thru '12
92085 **Tercel** all models '87 thru '94
92090 **Sienna** all models '98 thru '10
92095 **Highlander** '01 thru '19
& Lexus RX330/330/350 '99 thru '19
92179 **Tundra** '07 thru '19 **& Sequoia** '08 thru '19

TRIUMPH

94007 **Spitfire** all models '62 thru '81
94010 **TR7** all models '75 thru '81

VW

96008 **Beetle & Karmann Ghia** '54 thru '79
96009 **New Beetle** '98 thru '10
96016 **Rabbit, Jetta, Scirocco & Pick-up**
gas models '75 thru '92 & Convertible '80 thru '92
96017 **Golf, GTI & Jetta** '93 thru '98, **Cabrio** '95 thru '02
96018 **Golf, GTI, Jetta** '99 thru '05
96019 **Jetta, Rabbit, GLI, GTI & Golf** '05 thru '11
96020 **Rabbit, Jetta & Pick-up** diesel '77 thru '84
96021 **Jetta** '11 thru '18 **& Golf** '15 thru '19
96023 **Passat** '98 thru '05 **& Audi A4** '96 thru '01
96030 **Transporter 1600** all models '68 thru '79
96035 **Transporter 1700, 1800 & 2000** '72 thru '79
96040 **Type 3 1500 & 1600** all models '63 thru '73
96045 **Vanagon Air-Cooled** all models '80 thru '83

VOLVO

97010 **120, 130 Series & 1800 Sports** '61 thru '73
97015 **140 Series** all models '66 thru '74
97020 **240 Series** all models '76 thru '93
97040 **740 & 760 Series** all models '82 thru '88
97050 **850 Series** all models '93 thru '97

TECHBOOK MANUALS

10205 **Automotive Computer Codes**
10206 **OBD-II & Electronic Engine Management**
10210 **Automotive Emissions Control Manual**
10215 **Fuel Injection Manual** '78 thru '85
10225 **Holley Carburetor Manual**
10230 **Rochester Carburetor Manual**
10305 **Chevrolet Engine Overhaul Manual**
10320 **Ford Engine Overhaul Manual**
10330 **GM and Ford Diesel Engine Repair Manual**
10331 **Duramax Diesel Engines** '01 thru '19
10332 **Cummins Diesel Engine Performance Manual**
10333 **GM, Ford & Chrysler Engine Performance Manual**
10334 **GM Engine Performance Manual**
10340 **Small Engine Repair Manual,** 5 HP & Less
10341 **Small Engine Repair Manual,** 5.5 thru 20 HP
10345 **Suspension, Steering & Driveline Manual**
10355 **Ford Automatic Transmission Overhaul**
10360 **GM Automatic Transmission Overhaul**
10405 **Automotive Body Repair & Painting**
10410 **Automotive Brake Manual**
10411 **Automotive Anti-lock Brake (ABS) Systems**
10420 **Automotive Electrical Manual**
10425 **Automotive Heating & Air Conditioning**
10435 **Automotive Tools Manual**
10445 **Welding Manual**
10450 **ATV Basics**

Over a 100 Haynes
motorcycle manuals
also available

10/22